An American Fraud

One Lawyer's Case against Mormonism

By

Kay Burningham

Dedicated to those who dare question.

"In a time of universal deceit, telling the truth is a revolutionary act."

—GEORGE ORWELL, *1984*

AV

Published by AmicaVeritatis
ISBN#: 978-0615465890
Revised First Edition, September, 2011

Cover photo: *Replica of golden plates displayed in LDS Church North Visitors Center, Salt Lake City Temple Square, December 28, 2010.*
Cover Design: *Daniel B. Grant © 2011*

DISCLAIMER

This book and its conclusions are not intended to be a substitute for legal, psychological, or any other professional advice to any one individual. Most people who are not part of the legal profession have a limited understanding of the law. This is especially true *vis a vis* dealing with corporations. This book discusses currently established and acknowledged (though perhaps not well-known) facts about Mormonism in conjunction with previously decided relevant law from Utah and other jurisdictions within the U.S.A.

Since education is the great equalizer, my hope is that after reading this book, the reader will benefit from an increased general understanding of the relationship between Mormonism's hierarchical organization and Mormon Church members in general, in the context of the Religion. If any reader has a specific, individual claim against the LDS Church, s/he is advised to consult with an attorney. Any specific application of the opinions in this book is at the reader's discretion and is his or her sole responsibility.

TABLE OF CONTENTS

Part I   My Life as a Mormon

Part II   The Case against Mormonism

PREFACE

April, 2010, I had just watched LDS General Conference, now held in the 1.5 million square foot LDS Conference Center. It was the 180th year of biannual conferences since the Mormon Church was established. I heard beautiful music from the hundreds of vocalists in the Mormon Tabernacle Choir. On this Easter Sunday morning the choir sang the *Halleluiah Chorus* from Handel's *Messiah*.

During these weekend sessions Church leaders focused on the atonement and resurrection of Jesus Christ. They told stories of Church acts of charity for recent disasters. Priesthood brethren and female auxiliary leaders counseled young people to avoid making icons of worldly celebrities, beware pornography and to submit to authority. They preached compliance with the Lord's plan of salvation, meaning obedience in keeping LDS covenants, particularly scripture reading and temple attendance. If these things were done, the leaders promised, then Mormon faithful would be ensured salvation and their families would remain together for eternity.

What beautiful promises! Nostalgic for the hymns I had known as a girl, I listened further. On Saturday, after a Church official sustained Church President Thomas S. Monson as the prophet and each of the twelve apostles as seers and revelators, the choir and audience joined together and sang *"We Thank Thee O God for a Prophet."*

We thank thee, O God, for a prophet
To guide us in these latter days.
We thank thee for sending the gospel
To lighten our minds with its rays.
We thank thee for every blessing
Bestowed by thy bounteous hand.
We feel it a pleasure to serve thee
And love to obey thy command.
When dark clouds of trouble hang o'er us
And threaten our peace to destroy,
There is hope smiling brightly before us,
And we know that deliv'rance is nigh.
We doubt not the Lord nor his goodness.
We've proved him in days that are past.
The wicked who fight against Zion
Will surely be smitten at last.

We'll sing of his goodness and mercy.
We'll praise him by day and by night,
Rejoice in his glorious gospel,
And bask in its life-giving light.
Thus on to eternal perfection
The honest and faithful will go,
While they who reject this glad message
Shall never such happiness know.[1]

During the singing of the song, the broadcast camera panned over the Church leaders—'general authorities,' *aka* the Brethren, who were in attendance and who sat in the plush seats behind the pulpit and then stood for the hymns. Body language was telling. As the Mormon faithful audience enthusiastically belted out the words of the hymn, the Brethren manifested various levels of interest, indifference, apparent discomfort and perhaps, outright shame. Many of them looked from side to side; one fumbled with his neck tie; some shifted their weight from foot to foot. Another, third to the end on the back row, hung his head and did not look up during the entire hymn. Was he praying or was he embarrassed?

What is Mormonism? Is it, as claimed by the leaders of the Church of Jesus Christ of Latter-day Saints, God's one and only true Church based upon the restored gospel of Jesus Christ as revealed to its founding prophet, Joseph Smith? Or is it a nineteenth-century pious fraud, promulgated over the decades by powerful, yet generally ignorant men who have taken extreme advantage of the general good nature of those they lead, culminating in a grand delusion?

Most Mormons are good people, but are preoccupied with the many demands of their religion. These legalistic requirements constrict LDS Church members' individuality in favor of an unquestioning obedience to the innumerable rules imposed by the Church of Jesus Christ of Latter-day Saints, the Mormons. The result is a culture of anti-intellectualism unlike any other in the western world.

Although accounts of the oppression and abuse of women and children in the FLDS (Fundamental Latter-day Saint) sect have been publicized, mainstream Mormonism remains for the most part, curiously exempt from public criticism. Over the past century the Mormon Church has worked hard to attain a degree of normalcy and respectability in American Society.

This book is my attempt to add structure to the existing body of historical primary source material which has recently become widely available and, when taken as a whole, exposes the carefully crafted Mormon image offered for public consumption for the highly organized bureaucratic deception that it is.

I've wanted to share feelings about my personal experience in the Mormon Church for years. Concern about a critical thesis was always present. As a child in "the Church," one is warned against any and all exposure to anti-Mormon thinking and literature. Implicit in this edict is that all literature which is non-supportive of LDS Theology is intentionally written to effect its demise.

Belonging to the self-proclaimed one and only true Church of God is always a battle. Them against us, God's chosen, the most righteous, the saved, the only who will attain the Celestial Kingdom, Mormonism's highest level of heavenly exaltation.

How does this church differ from other Abrahamic-based religions? The answer is in this book: Mormonism was founded on deception, and continues to build upon that deception. Contrary to the lyrics of a favorite hymn, *How Firm a Foundation* (appropriated from a 1787 Baptist minister's hymnbook) is not an accurate description of Mormon Theology. Instead, the origins of Mormon Doctrine are easily exposed as man-made.

Scholarly historic consensus is that the scripture upon which the religion is based is a nineteenth century fiction centered on various alter-egos of a disturbed Joseph Smith who, it appears, acted in collaboration with his third cousin, Oliver Cowdery and perhaps others. *The Book of Mormon* addresses theological issues prevalent in the Protestant Evangelical Revival of the early nineteenth century, issues which personally affected Smith's family. It contains plagiarized excerpts from the King James Version of the Bible, with names lifted from the biblical apocrypha. Its story content is similar to popular works promulgated just prior to Joseph Smith's writing, such as Ethan Smith's *View of the Hebrews.*

One need only look at the Mormon Church's own primary sources, access to which has generally been denied even to its own members, to determine the true origins of *the Book of Mormon.* The remaining two works of canonized, claimed scriptural works, the *Doctrine and Covenants* and *Pearl of Great Price,* are also transparent attempts by Mormonism's founders to bolster Joseph Smith's pretended revelations.

Joseph Smith ingratiated himself into the annals of American religions, claiming a new and restored version of the gospel of Jesus Christ through chicanery. Perpetuation of the Religion requires the same deceptive tactics as Smith and his cohorts used in creating the Church. In comparison to most other Abrahamic traditions, it is questionable whether Mormonism's founders ever did make a good faith effort at divining an absolute ecumenical truth. Instead, from the primary sources now readily available, it appears that Mormonism was a collaborative effort, and that its founders were opportunists, driven to create an organization where they could acquire the social status and financial resources that they lacked.

For its mostly unsophisticated members, the repercussions of the devout practice of Mormonism can be psychologically devastating. The State of Utah has suffered politically and environmentally. Utah Mormons have serious psychosocial problems, unique and concentrated in the State of Utah, but prevalent throughout LDS Church membership worldwide. This relatively young church, so brazen in its claims and so convinced of its righteousness, is not the embodiment of the word and work of a beneficent God, but was built on a foundation of plagiarized imposture and as a result, its cumulative, contemporary theology is a hodgepodge of nonsensical rules and regulations, all urged upon LDS Church members through emotional appeals to the Spirit.

Mormonism's unassuming adherents deserve the truth regarding its origins and how the continued misrepresentations of those origins are in fact tortious; the facts proving that deception have been well-documented and are widely available. What I offer is an explanation of the legal framework within which to view this betrayal, including the consequences or damages naturally flowing from the LDS Church leaders' significant wrongdoing over decades of indoctrination.

The format for this message was another issue. I am a trial lawyer. I wanted to say what I had to say, undisguised with metaphor or softened through euphemism. I also wanted to present my personal experience struggling with the truth of this Church. Therefore, this book has a two-part structure and is a combination of writing styles. The first six chapters (approximately one-third of the book) are a memoir, a partial autobiography, illustrating my experiences with Mormonism. The last six chapters (approximately two-thirds of the book) are exposition, an analysis of Mormonism under the law and the damage it has caused many members in particular, and the State of Utah in general.

Certainly others have had different experiences than mine. Some Mormon faithful seem to have lived charmed lives, skating through their existence with no apparent thought in their heads, but plenty of manufactured emotion in their hearts. However, I am not alone in my disaffection. As former Mormon Paul Toscano so eloquently explained in frustration at the denial of a real dialogue between LDS Church membership and its leaders, "My anger and the anger of other loyal Mormons is not motivated by hostility but by grief, sorrow, depression, helplessness."[2]

Most Mormons are born into the religion. It is much easier to inculcate a child with the dogma from birth than to convince an adult, particularly an educated adult, of its value. Growing up Mormon, one can appear to have experienced a safe, happy childhood. But once that child reaches adulthood, the consequences of a life given over to the authoritarian control mandated by Church leaders are devastating.

From my view in the theatre of life, Mormonism destroys the human soul, replacing it with a façade of happiness. Underneath is a mass of turmoil and despair on the verge of eruption. The anger many Mormons naturally feel for all this structured ordering of his or her life quite naturally turns inward, into chronic depression. In other cases it is forced outward, thrust upon any non-believer, voiced with behind-the-back gossip, self-righteous anger, bigotry and biting criticism.

Having thought about documenting my experience for years, I have just recently been compelled to share my thoughts. The time has come. There is enough lying, depression, self-righteousness and suicide. Unless Mormons read, the anti-intellectualism of Mormonism will grow unabated, causing Church members to become even more insular.

At the turn of the last century I was living in the San Francisco Bay Area with my former husband. A female classmate whom I had known in law school wrote me a disconcerting note:

> ...I would need a hypnotherapist to remember my last date (you could freeze ice on these lips) and my body is in the advanced stages of mass entropy. Aaaah! I'm ready for the next life—this one has been a major disappointment. ...As my mother said "I stepped back from the Precipice." Forget the slim pickins on this planet; I'm waiting to audition those resurrected boys.
> ...signing off.....*

Teresa was gorgeous, tall, artistic and outspoken. After graduation she worked in Los Angeles, writing romance novels in her spare time. During law school she was attracted to one student in particular, a young Mormon who had completed an LDS mission. But her affection for him was not returned. She and I planned to meet after a conference I attended in Santa Monica in the spring of 1999. Teresa never showed up. While waiting for a temple-worthy Mormon man, she passed up an adventurous love affair with a handsome Greek who saw in her all the beauty and potential that the average Mormon male missed, or was too intimidated to appreciate.

She had served a Mormon mission as a young woman, but despite her best efforts, Teresa never attained the only role for a woman she had been taught was proper, wife and mother; consequently she felt she had failed in life. Teresa died alone, from an overdose of Vicodin. She was found lying on her single bed in her trash-filled studio apartment in a Los Angeles slum, dressed in her temple garments. Her death in May, 2000 and our friendship renewed the year before inspired my search for the truth about Mormonism.

As I read book after book of primary sources relating to the origins of Mormonism, world theology, philosophy, neuroscience and epistemology, it all came together in one epiphanic moment: Mormonism's teachings had leveled a huge negative effect on my life. I saw its role as the primary cause in my long term depression, my college eating disorder, my protracted naïveté and my failed marriages.

Teresa, this is for you and for all the other women (and men) who feel it is their individual failings which cause them to be at odds with the mandates of Mormonism's mold. It is not. It is simply that the mold Mormonism casts and uses is wrong, terribly wrong and must be discarded in order for an individual to live an authentic life.

Today Mormon leaders, colloquially known as general authorities, number in excess of one hundred. These deceivers continue their deception, maintaining power and control over the deceived, particularly in the Mormon Corridor and especially in my home state, the State of Utah. Mormonism, and indeed all of Christendom, teaches meekness, charity and to "murmur not." But at what point does the philosophy of passivism make clear the path of the despot, toward the unending suffering of the meek?

For almost two centuries, Mormon leaders have, if not knowingly, at least recklessly misrepresented the true origins of the Religion and by perpetuating those misrepresentations, have adversely affected millions of lives, usurping the time, financial resources and most significantly, the sanity of its faithful. *An American Fraud: One Lawyer's Case against Mormonism,* chronicles the deception and control which Mormon leaders have had and continue to have over the minds and lives of LDS Church members.

The intent of this book is not to provide an historical treatment of Mormonism, Utah's political climate, or the LDS Church. This has already been done, and done well by various independent scholars, especially over the past few decades.

As a trial attorney I take relevant, established facts and then base my argument upon those facts. In *An American Fraud,* I have told the story of one woman's life growing up and then living in Mormonism (part one) and then, building upon those facts about Mormon origins and history for which the evidence is overwhelming, I have applied the law to reach my conclusion (part two).

Through its public relations department, the LDS Church has been the primary source of information about Mormonism for far too long. This book provides the other side of the story.

I hope this brief note will serve to lay clear the intent of my book and to quell anticipated arguments that this work is a screed or a polemic— for while it may be both of those, it is the truth. These days most people are hesitant to lay out the truth in a straightforward manner. I leave it to the reader, as juror, to determine the verdict in this case against Mormonism.

Characters and Sources

All the people in my book are real characters. I have left the real names of those individuals who are public figures, including Mormon Church leaders, BYU academic and Church leaders, business executives, a missionary, theatre directors and one great choreographer. In one section of the book, I have combined experiences with two different college roommates into one sequence of scenes. In another, I have changed the gender of a friend and changed the details of some friends' lives. Out of respect for my sister, I have referenced her only as "my sister," or "my little sister." With the exception of the first names of some family members, I have changed, or entirely omitted the names and some facts about those friends and family whose privacy might be invaded through my retelling of our interaction over time; I don't want to harm any of them.

I have attempted to be as accurate as possible with my description and dialogue. Some of this has come from journals I have kept. Some of it cannot be recalled exactly, but the tenor and substance of these conversations is there. As to the fictitious names, any resemblance to living persons with the same name is purely coincidental.

The name of my Civil Procedure law professor was changed. Given the facts of his teaching tenure, my law school classmates could identify him; however, I did not think it necessary to use his real name.

Additionally, I have quoted many primary sources from the early nineteenth century. Whenever there is an asterisk following the quotation, it means that the misspellings and grammatical errors are from the original text and have not been corrected. This has been done in order to preserve the integrity of the original text. Bracketed additions to primary source words or grammar have sometimes been added in order to clarify the original writer's intent. Where used, these bracketed additions have been generally recognized by historians of Mormonism. Finally, "[sic]" is occasionally used where there is a glaring original misuse of a particular word.

The "Table of Authorities," includes cases, statutes, rules of evidence and constitutional provisions I have cited. Where free access to the case, statute or rule is readily available, I have provided a link. Complete copies of these authorities can be accessed through *Westlaw*™ or *Lexis-Nexis*™ legal research (paid) programs.

The Index generally relates to information provided in Part Two of the book. However, occasionally a relevant aspect of Mormonism noted in Part One is referenced as well.

Acknowledgments

Many thanks to my editor, William G. "Bill" Thompson, truly a gentleman and professional of the first order, who firmly but graciously and expertly helped turn an emotionally charged therapeutic piece of writing into my final manuscript and to Anita Melograna, his assistant.

Thank you to Louis "Bud" Shrader, who encouraged me during the early drafts, to Ed Cosnyka, whose keen eye helped edit out stray typos and who has also been encouraging and extremely helpful through his copy editing of the manuscript. To "John," whose candid stories about his employment at LDS Church Headquarters have enriched both my understanding and the content of this book.

Additionally, a big 'thank you' to my son, Danny, who formatted the manuscript into its Kindle Edition over Christmas break, with little complaining and lots of hard work and to my son, Chris, who also spent part of his Christmas break proofreading.

Finally, thank you to Sandra Tanner, a true LDS history expert. She and her husband, Jerald Tanner (deceased) have researched and brought forth innumerable and invaluable Mormon historical primary sources from which myself and other scholars of LDS history have drawn. Without their half-century long, hard work, many contemporary Mormon treatises would not have been. Mrs. Sandra Tanner operates Utah Lighthouse Ministry, a non-profit Christian organization in Salt Lake City, Utah. Many of the primary sources used herein can be ordered from her website: http://www.utlm.org/

Part I: My Life as a Mormon

CHAPTER ONE: Awakening amidst Apartheid

"Every man takes the limits of his own field of vision for the limits of the world."—Arthur Schopenhauer

"You're making a mistake," clipped the man's voice on the other end of the receiver.

I hope not, I thought, spitting out the hangnail I'd gnawed to its root while waiting for the director's response to my decision to pass on his offer.

"Thank you, Mr. Youngreen," I said.

I hung up the BYU Wilkinson Student Center phone, relieved the uncomfortable call was over.

Getting the second lead in the summer musical *Butch and the Kid* at Jackson Hole's Pink Garter Theatre was a *coup*, though I had no idea what second lead meant where Katherine Ross was the only female in the movie. Giving it up was an even bigger deal.   I was nineteen and in the spring of 1974, fifty dollars a show was great pay for a dancer. Instead, the decision made, this summer would be spent performing *gratis* with three other dancers, eight singers, and our band, touring Southern Africa.

Looking toward the rehearsal stage, I caught Harry's eye and nodded my head in his direction. Harry Schultz was our director for the Africa Tour.   Harry planned to cull the best talent at Brigham Young University and merge it with the South African Defense Force (SADF) Military Orchestra into one big variety show extravaganza. He took the four female *Young Ambassador* (*YA*) dancers, including me, along with the *YA* Band and the *Sounds of Freedom* singers and put them into one group, renamed *Sounds* (minus the *Freedom*) for the Tour. We would tour the Republic of South Africa, then under apartheid rule and Rhodesia, performing in all the major cities to raise money for terrorist victims of the guerrilla "Bush Wars," so-called by the White Rhodesians. In 1974, Rhodesia was in the middle of a nasty civil war, something I had never fully realized back then. Together we were *Forces '74.*

The last time this terrorist charity had sponsored a fund-raising event, the celebrity singer they had hired didn't show up—some drug thing —so the organizers were left with sold-out audiences and no entertainer. Sponsored by Rhodesian and Utah businessmen, Reg Nield and John

Kinnear, Brother Kinnear said we'd be a sure thing because we were just as talented as the no-show A-lister, but wholesome and reliable. I felt lucky to be a part of something so altruistic.

Africa—how could I *not* go? Raised in Bountiful, a middle-class suburb just north of Salt Lake City, Utah, I had never traveled outside the States. My best childhood memories were growing up in a small home on the edge of my grandparents' property. The land was covered with cherry, apricot and almond trees just east of Bountiful's main road, Orchard Drive. Originally the front yard had a pond used for baptisms and ice-skating in the winter. Heber C. Kimball, first counselor to Mormon Prophet Brigham Young, built Grandma and Grandpa Thomson's home which was large by mid-nineteenth century pioneer standards. With high ceilings and thick walls, the walnut floors, matching dark wood in the study, and mission style furnishings richly framed the rose-colored carpets throughout the home.

My parents married young, at nineteen and twenty. We could have lived in the big house, but Dad, who had just started his job as Bountiful High's speech and drama teacher, wanted his independence and so both grandfathers and my father remodeled the chicken coop into a little place for our family. Mom, Dad, my little sister and I lived in the new home situated about a two minute skip up the hill on the back part of the property behind the main house. The chicken coop had three rooms, separated by curtains and a little bathroom with a shower. The back yard had a shaded sand pile and led out to the cool woods and Mill Creek. My sister and I had our baths in the kitchen sink.

But most of my childhood memories are from my maternal grandparents' home. Every Saturday morning Grandma Thomson baked her chewy, crusty white bread. The smell wafted up the hill through the windows of our coop, signaling my sister and me down the path to eat our fill.

The big house had a screened-in back porch where Grandpa Thomson sat for hours smoking his *Camels* and rocking. Grandpa, a Jack Mormon (someone who might believe in Mormonism, but breaks the rules just a little and doesn't usually attend church meetings) had cornflower blue eyes, wore striped bib overalls and was retired from the Union Pacific Railroad. As a little girl, I remember sitting on his lap while we flipped through sketches of natives and explorers, strange lands and animals, in *Heroes of the Dark Continent,* a late nineteenth century pen and ink picture book.

"Why are those men so black?" I asked, pointing at a sketch of dancing Africans.

"Well Katy, these people live near the equator, where it's very hot and there is lots of sunshine. God made their skin black so they wouldn't get bad sunburns."

"Oh," I said.

Grandpa always made sense.

If one spoke of 'the Church,' there was never a question of which church. Neither Mom nor Dad seemed to take the Church too seriously, though they were married in the Salt Lake Temple. Unlike his two younger brothers, Dad was a Jack Mormon like Grandpa Thomson, partly because he didn't serve a mission. My father didn't go to church and that was all right with me because that meant we got to buy ice-cream on Sundays. Dad said that when he died he would be satisfied to be the Lord's greens keeper on his heavenly golf course. My father was the most honest man I have ever known.

My sister had been born just eighteen months after me. Dad loved me the most, and Mom loved her more. Mom told me that from the moment I was born I looked "just like [my] Dad," which was a good thing, I thought. Mom always told me how pretty my sister was.

"But you're very smart and talented," she would add.

When I was about five, about the time my little brother Kyle was born, Dad would cast me in the opening scene of his first musical, "Carousel." I walked on stage with my [high school age] 'parents,' holding a balloon in the opening amusement park scene—not a big part, but very exciting for a little girl.

One summer day, Dad's little sister, Aunt Jeen, watched us while Grandpa Burningham and Dad got ready for the pheasant hunt. Grandma Burningham had given birth to Jeen when she was in her mid-forties, almost twenty years after Dad was born. When Aunt Jeen became a teen, she changed her given name, Loa Jean, to just 'Jeen'. That brave move made her the coolest of all my relatives.

My sister was not yet two and I was about three-years-old. We were hiding under the chicken coop-house kitchen table, sitting cross-legged on the linoleum floor, eating Oreos and counting the money in our piggy banks. Nine-year-old Aunt Jeen was talking on the phone.

3

We had each dumped out the entire contents of our banks. My sister went to the bathroom. By the time she returned, I had a plan.

"Listen, I have a deal ..."

"What?" My little sister looked up at me with her big round eyes. She was very sweet.

"See all these big nickels in my pile?'

She nodded.

"You know that big money is worth more than little money, right?"

"Uh-huh..." Her trusting eyes never questioned me for a second.

"Well I'll give you all my big nickels if you give me your little dimes—okay?"

"Um...okay."

I took her stack of eighteen dimes and gave her eighteen nickels in exchange. I had just swindled my baby sister out of ninety cents.

Jeen hung up the phone and told us to clean up our mess because Mom would be home soon.

I did a really bad thing, and even at three I knew it. It was true; I was mean to my little sister. Mom wanted me to take her when I played campfire girls with my best girlfriend Susan in the field next door, but I thought she was a pest. At not quite age two, my baby sister couldn't run very fast and could barely talk and I wanted to do important things, like explore my Grandparents' property, climb trees and play grownup games in our stick-furnished lilac cave by the big house.

I didn't sleep that night.

Early in the morning hours, exhausted from my guilt over the coin con, I sneaked out of bed, stepping quietly onto the cold linoleum so nobody would wake up. I crept into the kitchen area where my father was still sitting and reading by the stove. He put down his evening *Deseret News* and motioned for me to sit by him on the old couch. Hanging my head, with a lock of blonde hair covering my eyes, I slowly scuffled my too-big pajama feet toward him.

He looked at me with his deep brown eyes. I could never hide anything from those eyes. Before he could ask what was wrong, I blurted out everything that happened yesterday about the coins.

"Trading your nickels for her dimes? That's stealing Katy—you know better."

Reluctantly, I let the full weight of what I had done sink in.

"Well?"

4

He looked at me with his kind eyes.   I sat small and still beside him.

"What are you going to do, Muffin?"

I knew what had to be done.

"I'll give her back her dimes," I offered.

He wanted more.

"I'm sorry, Dad."

"Tell your sister, not me."

I nodded.

"That's my girl."

He patted me on the head, and then picked me up and gave me a big hug; the type only fathers can give their children.   Then I went back to bed.

That next morning, as I was apologizing to my little sister and dropping her dimes back into her bank, Mom called—"Time for church!"

She bundled my little sister and me into the old Studebaker and we drove to Church.   We wore identical dresses with lace pinafores or quilted jumpers, handmade by my father's mother, Grandma Burningham.

We walked to the Junior Sunday School where all children twelve and under met together.   Our lesson was on Joseph Smith.   The teacher showed a picture of a handsome red-haired man with kind, blue eyes. They told us how noble he was and that despite his lack of formal education he was chosen by God at age fourteen to restore the one and only true Church, the Church of Jesus Christ of Latter-day Saints.   Joseph Smith, our teacher said, was second only to Jesus Christ in importance for our eternal salvation.   We sang the song we had sung many times:

The golden plates lay hidden deep in the mountainside,
Until God found one faithful, In whom he could confide.
A record made by Nephi, Written in days of old;
Now in the Book of Mormon, The story is retold.[3]

I wondered about those gold plates.   *Where were they?*   But when I asked, the teacher told me it wasn't important.   She said what was important was their message.   The Sunday school teacher went on to show us photos of each of the LDS prophets since Joseph Smith.   We memorized their names and even sang a song about them.

"How was church, Katy?"   Dad asked when we returned home.

5

"Okay," I said.

Mom, Dad, my little sister and I went to Black Sambo's Restaurant for breakfast some weekends. Aside from the mural of the little Indian boy chasing the tigers, who I then thought was a little African boy, Grandpa Thomson's picture book, *Heroes of the Dark Continent* and Sidney Poitier in *To Sir with Love*, I had never seen a Negro in person. But that would change with this trip.

***

On the way over, the BYU performers stopped to see the Andrew Sisters on Broadway and then stayed a couple of days in a hotel on Piccadilly Circus in London. Next, we boarded South African Airways for the sixteen-hour flight to Johannesburg. Our plane was chartered so each of us had plenty of room to move around on the long flight. There would be one stop, to re-fuel at the Canary Islands. The trip was going to be a blast.

Since I would be spending a lot of time in the air, I had taken my standard works on the plane. These core Mormon scriptures, *the Book of Mormon (B of M)*, *Doctrine & Covenants (D&C)* and *Pearl of Great Price (PGP)* were published in a three-in-one combination set for missionaries and other students of Church doctrine.[4] After high school graduation, I bought the newest edition with the post-tithing tips saved from waitressing my senior year. It was a leather zippered set with my name engraved in gold on the front cover.

Lying on my stomach, stretched out on my own row of seats, I flipped through the well worn, filmy pages to a marked-up section of the *D&C*. Although the Church had publicly declared polygamy illegal in 1890, the principle was still preached as a requirement for the afterlife under the euphemism 'celestial marriage.' This doctrine was codified in §132 of the *D&C*, claimed to be a direct revelation from God to Joseph Smith. I re-read the verses:

> 61 And again, as pertaining to the law of the priesthood—if any man espouse a virgin, and desire to espouse another, and the first give her consent, and if he espouse the second, and they are virgins, and have vowed to no other man, then is he justified; he cannot commit adultery for they are given unto him; for he cannot commit adultery with that that belongeth unto him and to no one else.
>
> 62 And if he have ten virgins given unto him by this law, he

cannot commit adultery, for they belong to him, and they are given unto him; therefore is he justified.

63 But if one or either of the ten virgins, after she is espoused, shall be with another man, she has committed adultery, and shall be destroyed; for they are given unto him to multiply and replenish the earth, according to my commandment, and to fulfil the promise which was given by my Father before the foundation of the world, and for their exaltation in the eternal worlds, that they may bear the souls of men; for herein is the work of my Father continued, that he may be glorified.

64 And again, verily, verily, I say unto you, if any man have a wife, who holds the keys of this power, and he teaches unto her the law of my priesthood, as pertaining to these things, then shall she believe and administer unto him, or she shall be destroyed, saith the Lord your God; for I will destroy her; for I will magnify my name upon all those who receive and abide in my law.*

I hated that scripture and couldn't imagine a God who talked like that.

Beginning in ninth grade, Utah public school LDS students are allowed to leave campus for one class period a day and walk across the street or next door to a seminary building, separately owned and operated by the LDS Church. There, they receive religious instruction in Mormon Doctrine. Just like all my Mormon friends, I had taken seminary. The seminary instructor had spent extra class time responding to my questions on polygamy.

"Why can't women have more than one husband?" I asked.

It wasn't fair and didn't make sense to me.

"More boy babies are born than girls," I offered, quoting a statistic I'd found in the library.

"Well, Kay," he responded, in that paternalistic, churchy monotone, typical of many LDS leaders. "We don't know all the reasons for this commandment; it may have been that there weren't enough valiant men to take care of the faithful pioneer women. Certainly if we talk about becoming gods and goddesses, every priesthood-holder would need many wives in order to populate his planet. It would be impossible to accomplish this heavenly task with a single partner."

7

The seminary instructor nodded, seemingly pleased with his own response.

The boys in class sat unfazed; most of the girls looked down at their desks. It seemed I was the only student incensed by his explanation. I was furious. The thought of an eternity sharing my husband with other women, me being pregnant most of the time, was not my idea of heaven. If that was the case, I'd be satisfied to spend my eternity in one of the lower heavenly kingdoms, the terrestrial or even the telestial, where certainly the male to female ratio would be more favorable.

I continued the discussion that evening with my high school boyfriend Mike, who had already suffered through hours of my complaining on the subject.

"Polygamy is a choice," Mike said. "Nobody will have to enter the covenant unless it is of their own free-will and as I told you, I don't want anyone but you…"

Though less than two years older than me, Mike watched me with a look which out-fathered any look I had ever gotten from my Dad.

I started to pound his chest.

"You have no idea how worthless this all makes me feel!"

I threw the scriptures on his parents' floor. Mike calmly picked them up, smoothed the pages and returned the book to the sofa table. He pulled me close and held me tight.

"I don't claim to understand how you feel about this principle; I can only try to empathize."

Yes, Mike really talked like that—even at age seventeen. He had the biggest vocabulary of anyone I had ever met in my young life.

We stood quietly and nervously, worried that his parents would return and interrupt our intimate moment. Ordinarily Mike's words calmed and encouraged me, but not that time, not about polygamy.

I returned from my reverie as I felt our plane changing direction, set down the scriptures and shook my head, trying to forget the stirred up feelings of my past. I looked at my watch; we were almost there. We had traveled to the Southern Hemisphere where in June it was winter.

The plane began its descent, but I was compelled to continue to read the scriptures. From the *D&C*'s section on polygamy, I flipped to *the Book of Mormon* tab marked 'Lamanites.' The Lamanites were the villains in *the Book of Mormon's* main story. In contrast, the Nephites were generally obedient and favored by God. I read silently from Alma chapter three, verse six: "And the skins of the Lamanites were dark, according to the mark which was set upon their fathers, which was a curse, upon them because of their transgression." I opened my cross- references which had been marked and tabbed in seminary for the weekly scripture chase, and continued to read about the dark-skinned people [Lamanites] in First Nephi, chapter twelve, verse twenty-three: "And it came to pass that I beheld, after they had dwindled in unbelief they became a dark, and loathsome, and a filthy people, full of idleness and all manner of abominations."

The description of the Lamanites as dark and loathsome cross-referenced with another scripture in Second Nephi, chapter five, verse twenty-one: "And he had caused the cursing to come upon them, yea, even a sore cursing, because of their iniquity ...wherefore, as they were white, [referring to the Nephites] and exceeding fair and delightsome, that they might not be enticing unto my people the Lord God did cause a skin of blackness to come upon them."

Grandpa Thomson's first name was Nephi—he was very white.

I read from the *Pearl of Great Price*, also Mormon scripture, Book of Moses, chapter seven, verse eight: "For behold the Lord shall curse the land with much heat... and there was a blackness came upon all the children of Canaan, that they were despised among all people."

This time God was talking about Negroes. I recalled the time I had read through parts of the *Journal of Discourses*, which I had been told were copies of nineteenth century sermons from LDS general authorities. My grandparents had an old copy in the barrister's bookcase in their study. Brigham Young and John Taylor, the second and third presidents of the Church, preached sermons to the Mormons which had been transcribed. They said:

You see some classes of the human family that are black, uncouth, uncomely, disagreeable, sad, low in their habits, wild, and seemingly without the blessings of the intelligence that is generally bestowed upon mankind. The first man that committed the odious crime of killing one of his Brethren will be cursed the longest of any one of the children of Adam. Cain slew his brother. Cain might have been killed, and that would have put termination to that line of human beings. This was not to be and the Lord put a mark on him, which is the flat nose and black skin. Trace mankind down to after

9

the flood, and the[n] [an]other curse is pronounced upon the same race - that they would be the "servant of servants;" and they will be, until that curse is removed; and the Abolitionists cannot help it, nor in the least alter that decree.*[5]

After the flood we are told that the curse that had been pronounced upon Cain was continued through Ham's wife, as he had married a wife of that seed. And why did it pass through the flood? Because it was necessary that the devil should have a representation upon the earth as well as God;*[6]

"Kay!" Sherri, the Young Ambassador cellist, sitting across the aisle-way, startled me.

"We're landing—put on your seat-belt," she whispered to me.

Sitting up, I closed my scriptures and opened the plane's window shade. We descended rapidly through the clouds in twilight. Suddenly the lights of a city spread low and wide appeared out the window. From the air Johannesburg was nothing like the Manhattan skyline, forced close by the island's geography; neither did it have London's historic structures artfully placed along the meandering Thames. It looked ordinary and unexpectedly still.

"Welcome to Johannesburg," the flight attendant announced in her not quite British, Afrikaner accent. "Please secure your seat-belts for landing."

The plane's landing gear clunked down from its undercarriage in a loud two-beat jolt. Soon the *Suid Afrikaanse Lugdiens* 747 executed a flawless landing.

I looked around. The others were collecting their carry-ons and coats. I stuffed my scriptures into my bag and reached down the row of seats for my tan overcoat with the "Sounds" emblem on the lapel and then joined the other performers standing in the aisle, waiting to deplane.

Would I finally see what the Church had taught? What was it about these black people—could they really be the devil's representatives?

The jet-way locked on the plane and we moved toward the exit. Looking out at dusk from the plane's doorway, I saw a vast countryside with rolling hills. The sprawling lights of Johannesburg twinkled in the distance.

Chapter 1: Awakening amidst Apartheid

Whisked away in private vehicles, our group was denied any preview of the City until after we had completed our rehearsals with the SADF in Pretoria, outside Johannesburg, situated on the high grassy *veldt*. Expecting jungle, I wouldn't see my idea of Africa until we visited Victoria Falls, weeks later.

***

Forces '74 was in rehearsal. It was just three days before opening night at the Johannesburg Coliseum. The SADF Orchestra had been working on the score for weeks while the student performers practiced at BYU. Now it was time to put it all together.

Our opening number, the Doobie Brothers' *Long Train Running*, went smoothly. I loved the dancers' long sleeved, cuffed, orange satin blouses and sequined bright yellow jumpsuits. Over the two hour show we had at least a dozen costume changes.

Half-way through our first dress rehearsal, the dancers' number was up—no singers, just the four *YA* girl dancers. This instrumental number was our turn to steal the show.

I pulled my red knickers over my white tights and turtle neck, and quickly fastened the suspenders. The body suit made me too warm to be comfortable while dancing, but as performers we wore whatever the BYU Costume Department made for us. There were no sleeveless or above-knee costumes in our show. This was not unusual for Mormon girls.

I remembered the proms at Bountiful High. I don't recall seeing spaghetti straps or strapless gowns on any of the girls, although there might have been some worn. Instead, I remember making a velvet gown: long, full-sleeved and turtle-necked for my junior prom from yards of red velvet. My slim, sixteen year-old body had been draped head to toe.

The music's cue startled me out of my daydream. The words pounded through my body: "Get it on in the morning now." Perfectly synchronized trumpets blared the interlude. "I'm gonna tell you what I'm gonna do"—trumpets again. "I'm going to make love to you."

Those trumpets—I was never happier than when dancing. I isolated my hips, ribcage and arms—jazz movements—very Fosse. Choreographed by Lori Regas Marsh, daughter of Jack Regas, a Hollywood musical choreographer from the forties, our dance numbers were great. Lori had moves that I had never learned in any class offered through the BYU Dance Department. At least at BYU, ballroom dance styles in the seventies were much too stilted. I began college as a dance

11

major and with my fill of ballet and modern dance, learning and then dancing to Lori's choreography was a dream.

"In the number by Chase, the dancer stage left needs to tone it down a bit," Brother Kinnear shouted from the back of the auditorium, zeroing in on me.

I blushed, but smiled and immediately stopped dancing.

The band quit playing. Nobody laughed. I looked around for friendly support, but had no close friends on the Tour. It seemed that the other student performers were all so serious and very religious.

Jill would've understood. If she was here, she would've broken the tension with that laugh of hers. With strawberry blonde hair and sea green eyes, Jill was the prettiest and most popular girl in school. Her father was a local church leader, and so even though the boys flirted with her, they knew she wouldn't mess around.

My family had moved further west into a subdivision of tract homes by the time I started junior high. Jill lived above Orchard Drive on the East Bench, in one of the big houses on the hill.

Jill and I became friends in math class. When cheer-leading tryouts were announced, she and I made the squad. Despite my braces and scrawny frame, I was on the cusp of becoming cool.

The cheerleaders hung out with the basketball team's first string. We trolled the neighborhoods around Millcreek Junior and Bountiful High, looking for something to do. Since we were all too young to drive, unless another friend had planned a basement make-out party, we walked.

One afternoon after school at Jill's house, she and I had just downed a bag of chips and a plate of cookies with milk. Since there was nothing else to eat, we went into the living room so we could talk without her mom hearing our conversation.

"Hey Burningham, I saw you and Bobby frenching at Deb's party," Jill taunted, sticking out her tongue and throwing a pillow at my head. I rolled my eyes and blushed. Jill had a way of reading my mind. I looked at her sprawled on the living room floor in her tight violet jeans and white sweater. I hadn't said a word about Bobby and me at the party, and she and Greg had disappeared into one of the bedrooms, not that they ever did anything below the neck, I was sure about that, but somehow she knew about Bobby and me.

Suddenly, Jill jumped up off the floor. Steppenwolf's *Born to be Wild* blared from her transistor radio.

"Yeah baby, wild…"

Jill started dancing around the living room, hips undulating. Her mom was in the kitchen just through the doorway. I was mortified.

"Shut-up Jill," I hissed.

She just laughed and danced harder.

"Kay and Bobby sitting in a tree, k-i-s-s-i-n-g," she teased.

I leapt from the chair and started chasing her—she screamed, and then I screamed. We ran down the stairs to her lower level recreation room which opened out onto a big grassy backyard, and then back up into the entryway of her house, just as the front door opened.

It was Jill's dad.

"Jill, what's going on?"

Bishop Watson seemed seven feet tall. He scowled down at us along his thin nose.

Jill abruptly stopped dancing and straightened the hem of her sweater.

"Oh nothing, Dad—Kay and I were just goofing around."

Jill flipped her hair and turned, leading the way down the hall to her bedroom. I smiled nervously at Bishop Watson, lowered my eyes and quietly followed her. Once we were safely behind the door to her bedroom, we looked at each other and burst out laughing.

"My dad has no idea. If he knew about Greg he would kill me…" she smiled.

I was still shaken up from her dad's stare. His presence had changed our mood. We sat silent for a moment. Finally, Jill spoke.

"I almost let Greg feel my boobs," she added, looking for my reaction.

Jill leaned back on her bed, arms stretched out in support of her torso, grinning.

In junior high most of my friends were flat. I was stick thin, had only grown to maybe five three by that time and weighed about eighty-five pounds. With big brown eyes, braces, waifish shoulder length hair and a few freckles across my nose, I looked like the velveteen paintings of waifs which were popular in the sixties.

At thirteen I certainly didn't need a bra. My sister needed one before I did. Mom must have thought I would feel badly if she gave my little sister a bra before me, so she bought me one too; it was one of those bras with no cups, just stretchy material like a band-aid. Jill's figure was

13

different—curvy. She had full breasts and round hips. I remember feeling like a little girl next to her.

***

When I had just started junior high school, Mom was in a bad car crash. She was thirty-seven years old and driving Grandpa Thomson's old Studebaker south on 5th west, about to go under the overpass when a drunken man crossed over the double yellow line into her lane and hit her, head-on. He was killed instantly and Mom was in the hospital with serious injuries for more than two months. She was never the same after that deadly collision, and in hindsight, it was certain that she suffered at least a mild brain injury.

One day soon after the crash, Mom and Dad sat all three of us kids down at the kitchen table and told us they were getting a divorce. But first we were going on a family vacation to Pacific Grove, where Dad had been stationed in the Army when Mom got pregnant with me, and then to Disneyland. My sister, little brother Kyle and I looked at one another, not knowing whether to laugh or cry.

After the divorce I worked for my clothes, lunch and spending money. Dad paid child support, but Mom still had to work hard everyday as a secretary. She always got up early with us kids and cooked us big breakfasts of homemade pancakes and bacon. After work she went dancing. That was okay with me. I was never home and after the divorce, Mom and I always fought.

In ninth grade, after teaching the neighborhood kids dance lessons in Mom's basement for a couple of years, I turned fifteen and got a real job at Pace's Dairy Ann. That job paid 95 cents an hour. Pace's was just a few blocks from my mom's house and so it was an easy walk, but my work there wasn't easy. I stood for eight hour shifts slicing raw onions for homemade onion rings. With a piece of hamburger bun hanging from my mouth to absorb the acrid fumes, I listened to the lyrics "Cheese and Rice, Cheese and Rice," sung to the tune of *Jesus Christ Superstar* by the Pace Twins, the pretty brunette granddaughters of the owners who worked with me. I didn't have the heart to tell them that their lyrics were wrong. The twins bopped around the grill and soda machine. A couple of years older than me, they were cute, naïve and sweet, all the time. This was the first hint I had of the unspoken credo of Mormonism—ignorance is bliss.

With my money from Paces I bought cloth to sew my own clothes and pay for school supplies. By the time I was sixteen I had saved three-hundred dollars for an old Rambler. Finally, I could drive to and from my waitressing jobs and take my sister and me to school.

      ***

"Let's take the dancers' number one more time from the top," Brother Kinnear yelled, staring directly at me.

I quickly moved to my mark on the stage. The band replayed the seventies instrumental version of Chase's *Get it On*. I tried hard not to think of the music's title, and toned down my dancing, but the beat of the music made me remember Mike.

Mike was the senior class president and a wrestler. He was the smartest guy I had ever known. He was a devout Mormon, serious about serving a two year, full-time mission for the Church.

Growing up with a Jack Mormon father and grandfather, I had been raised on the periphery of the Mormon Church, more involved in the culture than the doctrine; but after I started dating Mike, I was sucked into the vortex. We met at the fall stomp, the students' name for an informal dance to rock n' roll music where nobody had a date, but everyone came with friends and danced with whoever they wanted. I cut my finger on something. Mike came to the rescue. He always carried a band-aid in his wallet because after his mission he was going to be a doctor and drive a Jaguar.

By age sixteen I had grown a few inches taller. My hair was seventies long, parted in the middle with bangs. Once the braces came off, my teeth seemed perfect, big and white. I had a reason to smile.

I had been flirting with Trent, a cute dark-haired boy with incredible green eyes. Trent was a renegade; part of what the Mormon kids called the 'parking lot gang,' the smokers and drinkers—the wild ones. Trent usually came to early morning art class after drinking a bunch of beer. That made him really funny. He would joke with me and make me blush.

But Mike and I could talk about anything and although it wasn't immediate chemistry on my part, the relationship grew very serious over the months. We dated all through my sophomore and his senior year, then continued our relationship after he graduated high school while he was a freshman at the University of Utah until he left for his mission. His parents worried I'd get pregnant. They didn't need to worry.

Mike and I spent hours talking and kissing in his '52 Ford, which he jokingly called the 'Jag.' Our usual parking spot was high up on the mountain, just below the 'B,' which had been painted on the mountainside above Bountiful High. Back then there were no houses by the 'B,' just scrub oak and a spectacular view of the Great Salt Lake at sunset.

"Kay—we can't…"

Mike could barely get the words out as I lay on top of him, fully dressed.

I went limp. Our innocent kisses led to making out, which led to both of us crawling over the bench-type seat back of the Jag to get more comfortable, and then to me crawling on top of him.

"We've got to stop this," Mike said.

"Okay."

I looked at him, serious, my brown eyes trying to warm his cool blue ones.

Mike took my hands. Facing me, he kneeled and bowed his head. I mirrored him.

"Our Father in Heaven," he prayed.

"Please forgive us of our sins," he continued. "Help us to remain chaste so that I may be worthy to serve a mission. We ask Thee to give us strength, in the name of thy Son, Jesus Christ, Amen."

"Amen," I whispered.

I looked up at him. He looked through me. Our intimate bond had been pre-empted by something I could not see. We drove down the mountain, past my friends' homes on the East Side, past Bountiful High School and Main Street and finally into the small neighborhood of tract homes where my family had moved from Grandma and Grandpa Thomson's property on the east side of Orchard Drive.

Mike walked me to the door. Mom had left the front porch light on. Mom didn't like Mike. She thought he was conceited.

At the front porch he held me for a few moments.

"You know I love you?" He said solemnly.

"Yes, it's just that—"

He put his fingers to my lips. I knew he loved me. The kindness was back in his eyes.

It would be okay, I thought.

I turned and walked through the front door of my house, where three years ago Mom had announced that she and Dad were divorcing. I walked down the stairs into my bedroom which Dad had built for me in the basement. I took two of my stuffed animals from the window seat and

16

hugged them tight. I crawled into my soft bed and pulled the blanket over my animals, making sure their heads were out so they could breathe.

The next day was MIA (Mutual Improvement Association) Maids, the Church name for a class of young women who were instructed by older LDS women in all aspects of virtuous living. Our class was about to get another of the many lessons on chastity. The teacher wore a sparkling diamond wedding ring on her left hand. She passed a plate of freshly-baked sugar cookies, frosted pink, around to each girl.

"Go ahead, take a bite," she told us.

Each of us eagerly started eating.

"Just one?" One girl asked.

"Yes, well... (teacher was thinking)...you can take two," she said pointing to a particular young woman.

"And you three, and there, you eat half the cookie."

"And you..." teacher pointed to a shy girl in the class, "eat almost all of it, but leave a little bit."

"Okay," the shy girl said, and then quietly finished off her cookie except for a couple of crumbs.

"Now," the teacher said, "place what remains of your cookies on the plate."

She walked in a half circle with her silver dessert plate extended in front of the teenage girls, collecting the cookie remnants. The partially eaten cookies encircled the single, pristine cookie, which remained untouched by anyone in the class.

The teacher sat down and placed the tray on the table directly in front of the group of girls.

"Now," she began, "if you were a returned missionary, a priesthood-holder about to be married in the temple of God, which cookie would you want?"

The girls sat silent for a few seconds, looking at one another. When the meaning of the metaphor finally sunk in, they all more or less said, "the uneaten cookie, Sister Marshall."

I didn't join in the response. Instead, I wondered about boys' cookies.

If I was a boy, would it matter if I ate a lot of half-eaten cookies? I'd still get to eat a lot of cookies. *Was it so important to have just one completely uneaten cookie? And what about different cookies?* I liked chocolate chip cookies better than these sugar cookies and spicy oatmeal-

17

raisin cookies too. *If you chose one uneaten sugar cookie, did that mean you couldn't taste the other kinds? Why were girls the cookies, and not the eaters of the cookies?*

I didn't ask any of these questions, I'd worried I would be laughed at. I had guessed that germs were the problem with finishing lots of different, partly-eaten cookies.

After Mike and I started dating, I went to Church almost every Sunday, sometimes with Mike at his ward or at the University and sometimes at my home ward, and a few times with friends. At age seventeen I was the ward drama director and wrote (along with my talented friend Laurie, who wrote the music) choreographed and directed a road show. These amateur musicals are something which is no longer done in the LDS Church. Back then, the ward would create their musical around a theme issued by the higher-ups, usually a moral or Church theme was involved. The activity was mostly rounding up young, primary-age children and trying to teach them to act in predictable ways.

I read Mormon scriptures daily, prayed morning and night and paid tithing on my paychecks and tips from waitressing at the Carriage House Restaurant, Pepperoni Pizza and Denny's on North Temple in Salt Lake, where I served tired truck drivers coffee and breakfast. I tried to convert a Greek Orthodox guy I knew. I preached LDS scriptures to my family and anyone who would listen. I was a true zealot.

I gave talks in Church and received my patriarchal blessing, something that each Mormon gets just once in a lifetime from the stake patriarch who is sort of a Mormon fortune teller. The blessing is transcribed and usually received when young Mormons are in their teens; it tells your future, predicated on your worthiness to the gospel. Mine said I would get married in the temple, be a mother in Zion, that I shouldn't cause a burden on my family in seeking education and that I had the power of discernment (later I would realize that meant I had a good B.S. detector —not sure if that ended up being true). If I lived the Mormon Gospel my entire life, I was promised to come forth in the first resurrection. Nothing great, all pretty standard, as far as I could tell from comparing with Jill and my other Mormon friends, especially the "mother in Zion," and "coming forth in the first resurrection," part.

When it came time to apply for college I received academic scholarships to both BYU and the U of U, and although my class standing out of more than 500 students would've allowed me to attend an Ivy

League school, I never even considered one. At least one of our graduates went to Yale or Harvard and one friend I know was accepted to MIT, but chose BYU instead. However, back then most Mormon girls never aspired to attend an Ivy League University. If BHS counselors discussed out-of-state colleges at all, it was with the boys. I finally picked BYU, thinking that I'd be able to have a real college experience, living away from home, new friends, new ideas, parties—all the fun college things you hear about in high school.

***

On rare days when no shows were scheduled, we toured Southern Africa's most interesting sites. At that time, South Africa had no television and Rhodesia had just one station. Seldom did a world class entertainer perform in White Africa, so we were treated like celebrities by the white ruling classes. We toured the game preserves, exotic elephant and zebra skin tanneries and Victoria Falls where the thundering Zambezi River made mist for miles. We were a hit—"Las Vegas with the Clothes on and the Smut Removed," one reviewer claimed. Newsreels of *Forces '74* meeting with Rhodesian Prime Minister Ian Smith and other dignitaries aired in South African movie theaters before each film.

We visited Lesotho, a tiny independent nation of native Bantu, which was completely surrounded by White South Africa. The grassy countryside was dry. Bantustans were formed as a piece of South Africa set aside for it indigenous tribes by the conquering Dutch. However, throughout Southern Africa's tumultuous history, Lesotho remained an independent nation.

As we toured South Africa's major cities, I was struck by the one thing I saw in each town, the words *Blanke* and *Nie-Blanke*. I saw these signs everywhere, from buses with the word *Kaffir* added to the older, more dilapidated buses, to post office entrances, restaurants and Indian Ocean beaches in the coastal resort town of Durban. *Blankes* were the Afrikaner and English-speaking Caucasians, the two segments of society that controlled the apartheid government. *Nie-Blanke* had a hierarchy, ranging from Indian, or other Asian, all the way down to the Bantu, the native Africans. In-between the Indian and native Bantu were coloreds or mulattos, who seemed to be socio-politically one step ahead of South Africa's indigenous tribes.

Becky, one of the other female dancers, and I stayed with an Afrikaner family in Pretoria. Theirs was a middle-class home with a well-landscaped garden. Mango and papaya fruit grew on the trees. Dinner was always a major affair with a late night snack of waffles with mangoes and chocolate ice-cream or milktert, an Afrikaner custard pie. The Voorhees had four Bantu servants: a cook, a housekeeper, a laundress, and a gardener —no nanny.

For years I had become accustomed to doing my own laundry.

"May I use your washing machine?" I asked Mrs. Voorhees, showing her my muddied raincoat.

"Don't bother, dear. My girl will do it." She smiled warmly at me.

"Here." She reached out for the soiled coat and called in a high shrill voice, "Dora—come quickly."

A young black woman appeared and immediately took the raincoat. Smiling and bowing, she backed out of the entryway. A modern washer or dryer was an expensive purchase. Instead, the cheap native labor provided the luxurious lifestyle common among the middle-class Afrikaners.

One afternoon, Becky and I ventured into Johannesburg. The noise of downtown was at a level and sound unlike any I had ever heard. The deep clicking tongues of the native *Xhosa* dialect punctuated the low rumble of the moving, mixed population. *Nie-Blanke* and *Blanke* walked —the Blacks in the streets and Whites on the sidewalks.

Amazing black women strode with perfect posture carrying packages as large as a small refrigerator on their heads, hands free. The women were dressed in fresh, colorfully-printed, low-slung skirts wrapped snugly around their graceful hips and long, lean legs. Athletic, young, black men strode the streets with confidence.

Seeing us with cameras, young Bantu children ran in front of the lens. Arms around each other they posed, smiling wide-eyed for unsolicited photographs. The Bantu skin was shockingly darker than any black person I'd seen in photographs, on television or in the movies. The pearly whiteness of the children's smiles reflected against their gleaming black faces.

My mind raced back to the scriptures, *"a filthy and loathsome people?"* *Surely that was a mistake; God was talking about Native Americans—Lamanites here anyway, not native Africans, but...*

In Salisbury, Rhodesia, Reg Nield was at the performances. A native Rhodesian, robust and tanned, together Reg and his wife had a gratuitous role as a dancing cow in one of the Carpenters' numbers. Reg was the back part of the cow. He seemed to take a particular interest in me and we had spoken several times.

Since the beginning of Mormonism and as of 1974, Blacks were denied the Mormon priesthood, something every other male could receive as early as age twelve. At rehearsal that day I pulled Reg aside.

"What do you think about Blacks and the priesthood?" I asked.

"Will they ever get it?"

He stood up straight from his bent over position as the rear half of the cow. He spoke quietly with a sort of scowl on his ordinarily pleasant face.

"Kay, Black people aren't like us. They are intellectually and spiritually not equipped to handle this great gift and responsibility from God. Personally, I doubt we'll ever see the day when the priesthood is given to them." With that pronouncement, Reg leaned back against a stage prop. He folded his arms and as he did, the cow costume fell, crumpling around his ankles.

I walked away, pensive. *These beautiful people didn't seem innately inferior; any inferiority seemed due to the oppression of those who governed them.* Besides, women couldn't hold the priesthood in the Mormon Church. I paused and wondered, *was I spiritually and intellectually inferior too?*

***

The student members of *Forces '74* were set to speak at a Mormon fireside. Firesides, Sunday evening meetings directed toward the youth of the Church, were social gatherings with refreshments held to encourage the young people to remain steadfast in the Gospel. Tonight, besides young Mormons, the Church building was filled with parents and single adults. I looked over the sea of white Africans, stuffed side by side in the chapel pews, with the overflow, slouching and straight, mostly middle-class and wealthy, standing along the back wall. Others lingered at the doorways on either side of the chapel. There was not a black, or even a brown face among them.

Most of the students in our group had already borne their testimonies; the meeting was emotionally charged. The mission president was just finishing his speech.

...because of these talented young students' performances throughout our beloved country we have raised hundreds of

21

thousands of rand. Forces '74 has done more than help fight terrorism—it has successfully proclaimed the message that members of the LDS Church, especially these young people, are wholesome, charitable, and willing to help when needed.

The mission president turned his head back to the student performers seated on the stand and addressed us directly. "Just halfway through your Tour, you have yet to perform in Rhodesia, but already the show has greatly enhanced the missionary effort in our country. For that, we are eternally grateful."

The leader sat down. One last boy singer stepped up to speak.

Worn out from back to back performances, I had almost dozed off by the time he wound up his speech. "…as a returned missionary, I know that this Church is the one and only true Church and that Joseph Smith was a prophet sent of the Lord to restore the gospel in this, the last dispensation. I bear this testimony in the name of Jesus Christ, Amen."

It was my turn. Slowly, I walked up to the pulpit and looked at the audience again. I don't know what I was expecting, but had hoped they wouldn't look as eager as they did. They seemed to be waiting for me to confirm their beliefs, beliefs that as Mormons they were special, part of something bigger than themselves or their families, or even their strife-torn country.

"I am thankful for the experience to visit your beautiful country," I started, and then stopped and stared back at the sea of white faces.

I continued, "I have truly felt the Spirit of God in these performances."

I hadn't yet repeated the crux of the typical Mormon testimony: "I know that Joseph Smith was a prophet and that this is the one and only true Church."

I waited, trying to force the words—but somehow I just couldn't say that part.

"Thank you," I said instead.

At once the organist pounded out the stalwart Mormon hymn, "The Spirit of God like a Fire is Burning." Everyone, on the stand and seated in the pews, stood and sang, filling the chapel with heartfelt words of hope. I felt a warm sensation and tried to relax. I felt the Spirit too. *What we were doing had to be good and right, didn't it?*

***

Chapter 1: Awakening amidst Apartheid

Capetown was my favorite place. The beautiful coast, covered in poinsettia during the African winter months, reminded me of Northern California. We visited Table Mountain and the rocky beaches at Africa's tip during our days off.

That night was our first performance in Capetown. There were more English speaking *Blanke* here, fewer Afrikaners. The feeling was different than it had been in Pretoria and Johannesburg, where Afrikaners were the majority of the Whites.

We had just finished a Loggins and Messina number. The dancers dressed in white polyester jumpsuits with silver, fanned-sleeved blouses ran off stage followed by the singers. The packed audience was mid-applause when we were interrupted.

Brother Kinnear's voice boomed authoritatively over the loudspeaker:

"Ladies and gentlemen, we need to take a brief intermission. There is no cause for alarm; please use the exits, the *uitgangs*, on either side of the auditorium. Those in the balcony please make your way down in an orderly fashion."

Backstage the performers wondered about the problem. We figured it had to be some technical difficulty, lighting or sound. After a few minutes we joined the audience outside the theater and signed autographs while everyone waited for instructions to return to their seats.

A tall, ruddy-skinned young man in standard missionary attire approached me.

"Hi, I'm Elder Russ Blood. I just wanted to tell you how much I like your dancing." Elder Blood stuck out his hand and shook mine vigorously.

"You guys are great; it's really a help to the missionary effort." He grinned.

I smiled politely. This missionary was just one of dozens who told the girl performers more or less the same thing after each performance. I looked at his scuffed black shoes and beat-up raincoat. It was obvious that he really believed in his work, but was happy to have the diversion of live theatre. I signed the press release photograph of the group under my particular picture and handed it back to him.

He smiled at reading "Russ," instead of "Elder Blood." It wasn't proper protocol to call missionaries by their first names, but "Russ" was quicker to write and sounded better than "Elder Blood."

"So, how are things in the mission field?" I asked. "Do you teach many natives?"

"Oh that—well, I guess most of the investigators are Afrikaners, but we do have some Bantu who are interested." I looked around at the audience mingling in the cool coastal night air—not one *Nie-Blanke* anywhere.

Almost half an hour later, Brother Kinnear came back on the loud speaker and told us it was all right to return to the auditorium—no mention of what had happened. Later we learned that someone who identified himself as from the African National Congress had called with a bomb threat. During the break some of the local Afrikaner police force came and checked out the auditorium, making sure there was no danger. The BYU performers, SADF orchestra and the entire audience filed back inside and resumed the rest of the show without incident.

***

Having seen Capetown, it was time for a trip to the famed Kimberly Diamond Mines.

"Careful ye all, don't fall down," the mine manager warned in his native accent. The old manager was as wrinkled as a raisin.

We looked over the railing into a large open pit where dozens of Bantu workers continued digging, uninterrupted by our touristy remarks and stares.

"These boys," he said, indicating the mine workers, "come from all over Southern Africa. They stay months at a time and send their rand back to their families. The single ones spend it all in Sun City."

The whistle blew; the workers lined up. Exiting the mine, we walked straight through to the outside while another boss man was leading the native workers into a back room.

"Where're they going?" someone asked.

"Oh don't mind that, we do it with all the Kaffir—got to keep 'em honest. Yeah, some been smuggling in any part they got, not just teeth," the manager grinned.

The boys in our group bought uncut diamonds at the Kimberley store for their future wives. If uncut, the customs taxes were lower. Some got great deals. I didn't buy one. I wasn't in the market for a wife and didn't have any extra money anyway.

While I was still at home, Mike had written me long letters from the mission field. I cried many nights missing him. But two years was too

24

long.

In my senior year of high school I started dating Ryan with my mom's approval; she thought he was so handsome. Ryan and I dated more as friends than anything, but the fun we had made me forget about Mike. I finally broke up with Mike while he was still on his mission. I wrote him the classic 'Dear John' letter. Later he told me he had a ceremonial fire on the beach, where he burned all my letters along with his copy of my senior class photograph. Eventually Ryan also left for a foreign mission.

The day for Ryan's missionary farewell was also the day of Mike's homecoming and despite the long distance break-up, I was there to welcome Mike back. In Mike's parents' car on the way back from the airport he asked me to marry him. He might as well have been ordering fast food at a drive-in restaurant. I couldn't believe he asked me there, in front of his parents. The discussion was very impersonal and out of place, not at all like the Mike I remembered.

I had started college by then, and for months after his return Mike made the trip to BYU trying to persuade me to marry him. I was not convinced. I was nineteen and Mike didn't seem as intelligent as I remembered. He was different in many ways. As far as I was concerned, the old feeling we had between us was gone.

"I don't want to get married," I said flatly.

"What about all our plans?" he asked.

I was crushing him. I had shoe-boxes full of love letters he had written me over the years.

"I don't love you," I said.

I did love him—the old Mike; but this new person was someone else, more intent on getting married than really getting to know me again. I didn't think I loved this person. After months of trying to persuade me, he gave up. Right then that was all right with me; marriage was the last thing on my mind. I was about to leave for South Africa and my head was full with dreams of dancing around the world.

***

During the course of the Tour we stayed in Church members' homes or in five star hotels where the food was plentiful and delicious. We flew from city to city in Southern Africa and South African Airways had the best airplane food I have ever eaten to this day. For breakfast, it wasn't just bacon or ham and eggs, but bacon, ham, steak, bratwurst, eggs, fresh mangoes or papaya, fresh orange juice and croissants. The local Church members and restaurants filled the green room with pastries, snacks and fruity drinks to sustain us between numbers at each performance. By the end of the Tour, all of the performers had gained a few pounds. My white polyester and silver-sequined jumpsuit used during the opening and closing numbers had become very tight.

In Rhodesia, everywhere we flew our chartered plane was escorted on either side by Rhodesian military jets. The sponsors of our Tour didn't want any more bomb scares. So far no *Nie-Blanke* had attended any of our performances. But at this particular show, held on the outskirts of Chiredzi, Rhodesia, just a few miles from the border with Mozambique, our show was in the open air. Since it was the only truly outdoor performance on the Tour, the *Forces '74* sound technicians were having difficulty adjusting the acoustics.

White Rhodesians packed tightly together, seated on the folding chairs, in the cordoned-off audience area. Finally, the show began. As the show progressed, local Bantu wandered in and out of the audience perimeter. By the time we were into the second act, a substantial part of the audience included indigenous natives, seated on the grass at a respectful distance from the stage and beyond the rows of Whites.

"Sing a Song," by the Carpenters was up next. I had changed into a blue and white polka-dotted dress and was skipping through the audience, down the grassy makeshift aisles. Midway through the song it was planned for me to run up on stage and get Jim, the singer who had changed into a life-like gorilla costume and who was waiting offstage. This was done all the time in the other shows, and it was not a big deal—I think Harry thought it was sort of a tribute to the African venue.

I grabbed Jim's hand and pulled him onto the stage, then down into the audience. Holding hands, the little girl in the polka-dot dress and the life-like gorilla skipped through the aisles, me smiling and Jim grunting. What happened next was straight out of an American cartoon. Upon seeing the gorilla, the natives in the audience jumped, shrieked and ran back into the baobab trees bordering the stage. The performers and the Whites in the audience couldn't help stifle a laugh.

For the last few shows we returned to Johannesburg. Our final performance was at the same theatre where we had debuted, the Johannesburg Coliseum. The theatre had a large main floor and four balcony levels. Brother Kinnear told me that the top row had been reserved for the Bantu. I looked to see the faces of the audience, but the footlights made it impossible to see beyond the first couple of rows in the orchestra section.

After the finale, the audience stood, bombarding us with giant pink proteas, the country's national flower. The student performers dodged dozens of them bursting past us onto the stage floor. Pushing aside the heavy blooms, we re-assembled, grouped on our knees and encored with a favorite LDS children's song:

> *I am a child of God, and he has sent me here*
> *Has given me an earthly home, with parents kind and dear*
> *Lead me, guide me, walk beside me, help me find the way*
> *Teach me all that I must do, to live with him someday...* [7]

Here comes that feeling again. I was crying like a baby by the end of the hymn. I looked sideways at the rest of the cast, most of the girls and a few of the boys were crying too. I felt just like I did at the fireside, after all of the testimonies and the speech by the mission president and really, like the feeling I had after each and every show on this Tour. *We must be doing the right thing,* I thought, *the Spirit is so strong.*

The house lights came up to reveal the audience still standing, clapping furiously, many of them weeping as well. After the protracted applause had ended, the audience began to leave the theater. I looked toward the highest level balcony for the *Nie-Blanke*, but all I saw were the backsides of the *Blanke* making their way toward the exits.

***

Rio de Janeiro! Flying low over the legendary Latin City of love, our plane descended to a place where the calm aquamarine waters of the bay-broken Pacific met the jagged shores of beach-trimmed jungle. Aluminum and cardboard shanties jammed the steep mountainside. Lean skyscraper hotels cluttered the shoreline. From the air, I could see the giant Christus with arms spread, and Sugarloaf Mountain, which to this Utah girl was more of a mound than a mountain. Jungle all around, with the exception of Victoria Falls, Brazil looked more like Africa than Africa had to me.

Since we hadn't been paid, Harry promised us three days of R & R as a reward for our summer of rehearsal and intense schedule of performances. The plane landed and we were hurried off to a nice hotel on Copacabana Beach. Traffic was crazy. Our taxi driver paid no attention to the sparse traffic signs or lines on the pavement. He crossed medians and honked his way through the crowds of other taxis. As we drove up to our hotel, the building's interior lights flickered like specks of fire caught in the sleek waterfront structure. I jumped out of the car, forgetting to wait for my bags, and ran, legs stretching, toward the white sandy shore.

Tearing through the hundreds of Brazilians and tourists, I took in the beaches at dusk. The salty moist air, so thick, so unlike the arid Utah climate, made me feel alive. In just seconds I made a path through the sprinkling of mini-cabanas and lounging, partying, drinking, hugging, dancing groups of people. Rhythmic beats from the scattered musicians changed with each sandy step I took toward the water.

The red sun had almost vanished behind Sugarloaf, but the hum of the beach-goers didn't seem to notice. Half the women were topless and the men wore those tiny Speedos™, even the men with distended tummies and hairy backs. I wondered about the girl from Ipanema; it seemed there were dozens of them, tall, and tan and young and lovely. I thought about my one-piece bathing suit stuffed in the pocket of my suitcase, just in case we were allowed to go to the beach.

"Careful now," Harry yelled. "No going to the beaches after dark. There's lots of crime here."

I stopped short, just a few yards from the tide. Looking back, it seemed I was the only one of our group who had headed down to the water. The rest were lugging their bags, heading toward the hotel entrance.

"Come on, Kay," Sherri yelled, "we can come back tomorrow."

I wanted to pretend I didn't hear them. But then, as I looked around at the unfamiliar brown and tanned faces and the vast expanse of sea, I remembered the discussion we'd had just last year in high school seminary on water-skiing. Some of the kids in our senior class had planned a water-skiing trip to East Canyon Reservoir. The discussion focused on whether man-made reservoirs were included in the bodies of water which are a part of Satan's realm. Every seminary student knew that particular *Doctrine & Covenants* scripture well: "Behold I, the Lord, in the beginning blessed the waters; but in the last days, by the mouth of my servant John, I cursed the waters. Wherefore, the days will come that no flesh shall be safe upon the waters." (*D&C* 61:14-15).

Dad had been stationed at the old Fort Ord Army base in Pacific Grove, California when Mom got pregnant with me. As I grew inside her, she lounged on the beach most everyday. They returned to Utah that fall and I was finally born on a cold November day, but my fetal development was accompanied by the crashing sounds of the California Pacific and I am convinced that is why I love the ocean.

I turned and trudged back to the bus, picked up my bags and headed for the hotel lobby. Inside the door was a bar restricting those under age eighteen. The Brazilian music was loud and the bar was packed. I was old enough to go dancing at this bar, but that was not allowed.

The next day everyone was excited to go shopping. They bought lots of plates with dead butterfly wings arranged in hideous designs under glass, and more gems—here it was emeralds. I wished I was at the beach.

CHAPTER TWO: Cognitive Dissonance

"This place needs a laxative."—Frankie Geldof, Irish rock singer, re: the EEC bureaucracy.

It was a beautiful September morning; aspen and scrub oak covered the jagged Wasatch Mountains towering east of the campus.   A huge whitewashed 'Y,' projecting from the mountainside behind campus declared Brigham Young University the principal presence in this valley just south and around the point of the mountain from Salt Lake.

Daily dancing and celebrity adoration were now in the past as I headed back to the real world college campus in the fall of nineteen seventy-four.   My sophomoric lens, dimmed and dustier than the rose-tinted view from which I had seen the campus as a freshman was new and uncomfortable to wear, but impossible to remove.

I slowly made my way toward the Wilkinson Student Center auditorium where Sunday services were held, joining the swarm of socializing students dressed in their best.   The opening hymn had just finished and a student was at the pulpit in prayer:

…and Father in Heaven, we thank Thee for being able to attend Thy university where all knowledge is given to us through not only study, but worship, obedience and prayer. We ask only that Thou keep us prepared and worthy to continue our studies, so that upon graduation, we may serve Thee as fathers and mothers in Zion. We say these things humbly in the name of Thy Son, Jesus Christ, Amen.

"Amen." The clear voices of the students sounded as one.

The prayer-giver sat down and another man, indistinguishable from the first except for a slightly more worn appearance, stepped up to the pulpit. He straightened his tie and the reading glasses poised on his nose.

"Last Sunday we discussed the decision of the valiant in the pre-existence and the third of the host of heaven who chose the Savior's plan to come to Earth."

He cleared his throat of non-existent phlegm. "Additionally, as we know, a third of the pre-mortal spirits followed Satan."

31

Heads nodded. Those in attendance had heard the same story since the age of three in primary, Sunday school, sacrament meeting, the weekly MIA nights for young people, in priesthood and relief society—all those meetings—hours of meetings.

"And then there was the indecisive third," the teacher continued, "the spirits who sat on the fence so to speak. Though these spirits eventually followed Christ, they were less valiant. Those brothers and sisters have been cursed in this life. The *Book of Abraham* teaches us that these descendants of Ham shall not have the Priesthood."

The Sunday school teacher read from the tenth president of the Church, Joseph Fielding Smith's *Doctrines of Salvation*, Volume One, pages 66-67:

> ...there is a reason why one man is born black and with other disadvantages, while another is born white with great advantage. The reason is that we once had an estate before we came here, and were obedient, more or less, to the laws that were given us there. Those who were faithful in all things there received greater blessings here, and those who were not faithful received less.... There were no neutrals in the war in heaven. All took sides either with Christ or with Satan. Every man had his agency there, and men receive rewards here based upon their actions there, just as they will receive rewards hereafter for deeds done in the body. The Negro, evidently, is receiving the reward he merits.'*[8]

"So what did the prophet teach us about choice in the pre-existence?" the teacher asked, straining his neck from a collar which was obviously too tight.

"There is a reason for the Negro Race; it's a mark from God because those souls were less valiant in the preexistence," one student offered.

"Yeah, not for Christ," another added.

"Elder Mark E. Peterson says righteous Negroes will be our servants in the celestial kingdom."[9]

The BYU students continued to discuss the reasons for the existence of the Black Race. I looked around the room at their sanguine faces—not a thing out of place—no scuffed shoes or facial hair. I had attended BYU my entire freshman year, yet the bland fungibility of the students had never struck me as it did on that particular morning.

It hadn't occurred to me at the time, but just before we left for the South African Tour, the World Council of Churches came out publicly in support of the terrorist activities as a legitimate weapon in the fight against apartheid in South Africa. Sending a group of university entertainers to team with the Republic of South Africa's all-white military orchestra meant that the Mormon Church had acted in direct opposition to the Council's mandate. Just weeks before we left, while we were still in rehearsal in Provo, our visas were delayed. It looked as if the Tour would be canceled. It all made sense now.

I sat awhile longer, through the closing song and another prayer not much different from the opening one. Surveying the amphitheatre, I saw boys with pasty white faces, too soft to be the masculine young men they should have been in their early twenties. After two years of missionary service, after having woken and retired according to schedule, after the daily repetition of a canned set of discussions and countless doors slammed shut in their faces, these young men seemed to have lost their edge.

Unlike the young men, during the entire lesson the young women in the class remained silent. Demure and fresh, these girls had no apparent reaction to what, in any other university, would raise at least a modicum of controversy. Their senses had been dulled and their thinking stunted or assumed by their male counterparts. All young Mormon women were taught to honor the priesthood. Young women in the Church don't challenge men and certainly never offer dissenting opinions on scriptural principles.

The ending bell buzzed. Temporarily spared from the inane, I made my way through the crowd. The usual post-meeting chatter among the students became a deafening chirping sound, blocking my thoughts like the buzz of so many grasshoppers. I strode through the noise into the clear mountain air. I walked past written rules, speeches, and reminders posted throughout campus. The students continued their socializing.

"How many converts did he get on his mission?" One young man asked another.

"Is this too short?" One girl asked, as she spun around in a full dress skirting her knees.

"I heard they're getting married in the Hawaii Temple!"

"What shall we serve at family home evening?" another girl

33

asked.

Even though everyone's families were in truth miles away, pseudo-families were created within the student wards, compelling both genders of randomly selected roommates to mingle in Monday night socials, known as family home evenings.

I returned to my empty dorm room. My newly formed paradigm, altered in a way that only international travel can accomplish, showed me that despite its claims, Utah Mormonism was not the center of the world, or even the United States. In my mind, at that moment, I saw the Church as just another example of the oppression manifest by the South African Government over its indigenous people.

Thinking back to the first weeks of fall, nineteen seventy-three, my freshman year at BYU, I recalled that female students weren't allowed to wear jeans, no hemlines above the knee and no sleeveless tops. The dress code for the boys banned mustaches, beards and long hair, though the beard ban has since been amended to allow clean beards.[10]

Besides the dress code and grooming restrictions, upon admission to BYU, each student, whether Mormon or not, had to sign an oath swearing to no sexual intimacy outside marriage and to no street drug or alcohol use. At age eighteen, I didn't have a problem with the moral code, but hated the restrictions against women wearing jeans. Living in an on-campus dormitory was required of all freshmen so as to soften exposure of their innocence to the real world of Provo, Utah. That meant there were serious restrictions on my basic supplies: no tampons in the campus ladies' restroom and no *Coca-Cola™* or TaB™ in the soda machines, only caffeine-free drinks.

My freshman roommate Jan, was a French major who I had known in high school and like me, wanted only to concentrate on her studies. Dinner for me was usually a quart of chocolate milk; Jan would eat a much healthier cottage cheese and canned pineapple. Whatever we did it was more comfortable than shared tuna casserole eaten with forced participation in superficial conversation with our other roommates, who were four nice Mormon girls we didn't know.

One afternoon, Jan's boyfriend Eddie, rode his bike the fifty miles from Bountiful to visit her for the weekend. That evening, he sneaked into our room and crashed asleep on a bag on the floor between our beds. I looked down at Eddie as he slept, thinking how much he must love Jan to make that long trip. It was no big deal to me to have him stay overnight with us, but one of our other dorm mates found out that we had a boy in our room and called the Norwegian dorm-mother who screamed and chased him out at 3:00 a. m. in the freezing fall to bike all the way back to Bountiful.

Academically, undergraduate courses at BYU were rather easy—not much harder than high school really, so I wasn't motivated to study. I prayed and attended my meetings but didn't do the daily scripture study. I was busy enough with dancing and my regular classes. Besides, I had read the entire standard works, including the Bible, at least twice each. After all the years growing up a Mormon girl, and especially after my years in high school with my devoutly Mormon boyfriend and popular Mormon classmates, I felt spiritually unworthy.

I wanted to do better and tried hard to open up to what the BYU leaders were saying. Trying my best to wrap myself in the claimed spirituality of the school, I wrote in my journal:

Sunday, September 16, 1973

Sacrament meeting was the highlight of my whole day. I almost didn't go, but I'm so thankful I did. The theme of the meeting was Relief Society. Our branch presidency spoke and a high councilman added his remarks. The talk that especially touched me was given by the Relief Society President. She was very pretty and not fat and has seven children. Her boys have all gone on missions and all of her children have been married in the temple. She says she finds joy in doing simple things like laundry for her family. She challenged us to be the perfect woman, to strive for excellence in housekeeping, household financial management, scripture reading and in serving others. She gave me an incentive to make the most of every moment and to be my true self in attaining perfection. She emphasized that our only true happiness would be when we found our eternal partner and became married for time and all eternity in the temple. Our true calling was motherhood, but until we attained that privilege we should work hard and strive to keep the commandments. She gave me an incentive to make the most of every moment and to be my true self in attaining perfection, all the while following the counsel of the Brethren.

As soon as I made the journal entry I realized that I was conflicted. I had never liked housecleaning and rarely did it. My bedroom was a disaster after my parents' divorce; clothes covered the floor and I had to clear a path from my door to my bed. And I didn't like children; at this point in my young life I was certain I wouldn't have any. "Attaining perfection," seemed impossible to me.

When I was about twelve, before I had the idea to teach the neighborhood kids dance lessons in my basement, I babysat for some neighbors down the street—I forget their names. They had two boys ages seven and eight and they paid me twenty-five cents an hour. Mr. Neighbor was in the ward bishopric, so one would expect his children would have been well-behaved, but I had seen those boys at sacrament meeting and knew they were wild. I had no other way to earn money and so I took the job.

When their parents left, the boys started running and screaming around the whole house. They had bunk beds. Both crawled onto their beds and lay on their backs, the oldest on the top bunk and the younger underneath. The older boy let his head hang over the side of the bed and the youngest positioned himself in line with his similarly situated brother lying face up on the lower bunk. I got the feeling this was a trick they had played before. The boy on top started to work up a mouthful of spit then let it drip out of the corner of his mouth down his face into a long, slimy thread and onto the closed eyelids of his little brother below. I stood in their bedroom doorway, aghast. Both boys laughed so hard they cried tears and ran to their bathroom to pee. That was the end of my babysitting.

I stirred from my reminiscences of freshman life and babysitting kids in my neighborhood, to another Monday at school my sophomore year. The chimes from BYU's bell tower rang out across campus. It was time for the weekly devotional. Streams of students filed into the Marriott Center. Another Church general authority whose name I didn't know was poised at the pulpit. The message was always the same: work hard, obey the commandments and you'll reap your reward which was also always the same: a temple marriage, large family and eternal exaltation. "Be ye therefore perfect, even as your Father in Heaven is perfect," was a typical theme.[11]

My experience in South Africa had upset my thinking. I didn't believe that less-valiant, pre-mortal spirit heaven story and wondered how any God could sentence a whole race of people to inferior status. My

Chapter 2: Cognitive Dissonance

Church-taught beliefs were at odds with my innate sense of justice.

But race relations and other social issues of the day didn't seem to intrude upon any of the BYU students' thoughts or actions. Instead, a superficial level of happiness and contentment abounded at the 'Y.' The students would congregate, not just Sundays, but whenever in their young lives they felt afraid or uncertain—it helped them cope. They avoided having to examine themselves while surrounded with similar people. Like the infinity mirrors, mirrors mirroring mirrors in all the sealing rooms of the LDS temples, at BYU the students' likenesses were reflected back to them wherever they looked.

There was no need to look deeper and acknowledge, let alone examine, the troubling issues of the seventies. As of fall, nineteen seventy-four, the Vietnam War would last another six months. But, there were no protests at God's university, no thought-provoking independent films at the student center, just family movies. On BYU's campus back then, one wouldn't even have known we were in a war.

The slogan displayed at the southwest entrance proclaimed "The World is our Campus." It was more nearly the truth that the campus was our world. Hunger, war and inequality are, after-all, unpleasant topics. There were so many agreeable people and so many Church activities that BYU students had an easy time keeping their minds preoccupied with Church obligations. Mormon doctrine, from its nineteenth century beginnings, through the mouths of the many, modern apostles and local leaders, contains a morass of material—it was easy to get lost in the minutiae while ignoring the world's real issues.

Was it me? Was I the problem? According to LDS principles and teachings, I was selfish and impatient. I certainly didn't love everyone; I liked some people more than others, cats more than dogs and fresh bread more than steak. Unfortunately, I didn't like many of the people whom I had met at BYU.

Was it wrong to be so discerning? What was the essence of a person if s/he was not defined by her tastes?

I wondered about those of us who maybe just wanted to drive a fast sports car and travel the world awhile and then rest on some comfy heavenly real estate. It seemed that neither the Church requirements nor the rewards for meeting those requirements could possibly be tailored to fit individual taste or talent. These thoughts never seemed to occur to any of the other BYU students—if they did, they weren't spoken, at least not in the circle of students with whom I was acquainted.

The BYU monolith, not the physical structure of the buildings but the student body, administration and faculty, seemed to conspire to convince me of my worthlessness. It wasn't that I couldn't live the gospel, I didn't want to.

Obedience, obedience they all clamored—to what—to the words of dead prophets and living relics? Don't curse, no matter how angry, don't demonstrate regardless of the political climate and don't ask real questions, those deep, root questions which occur to the brightest students in any college class, because they will never be answered; you will feel like a fool for asking.

Looking back, I would realize that when I studied the social sciences and, as required, *the Book of Mormon* and Mormon History, I had never been taught the real story on these subjects. Entirely omitted was any accurate history of the Mountain Meadows Massacre, or unfortunate fourteen-year-old girls induced to marry narcissists under threat of God's disapproval. Instead, BYU taught only a history of obedient happiness, lessons about the stalwart, but maligned Mormon founders and the gallant pioneers. And despite a complete lack of interest in the subject, I would learn the skills of organizational behavior—ten habits for successfully coping with collectivism.

According to graduated Harvard students, undergraduates wish they could have more exposure to an "evidence-based way of thinking," which helps them "choose among alternatives, from a core philosophy and transcend opinions they arrived with, even strongly held opinions."[12] On the other hand, the 'Harvard of the West,' incredibly so-called by some students at BYU, was not a sanctuary of learning and independent thought, but a place for reinforcement of Mormon principles through Mormon professors who interpreted all but the most objective of disciplines with a Mormon subtext. Psychology, history and sociology courses were steeped in Mormon overlay; the subject matter would have been virtually unrecognizable at true universities. It was more difficult to spin accounting, mathematics and engineering, but at BYU even the hard sciences were vulnerable to Mormonization.

My sophomore year passed in hazy chunks of time. Between stints living at home in my mom's basement and returning to school, I conformed temporarily in order to win the Miss Bountiful and second runner-up to Miss Utah scholarship money.

Chapter 2: Cognitive Dissonance

The glamor of the beauty pageants contrasted with the tedium of my real life. I craved a way out and thought I could find it through continued external stimulation, the performing, the applause, the satisfaction of a concrete sign of importance. But these things weren't real and didn't last.

In the spring of seventy-five, at the end of my sophomore year, I was picked for one of the eight places on the BYU varsity cheer-leading squad. Our team consisted of eight girls and four guys, or yell-leaders. By the time of cheer-leading tryouts, I had lost the South African Tour weight and had slimmed down to my prime dancing weight.

The cheerleaders practiced all summer. During this time I lived off campus with Cheryl, an English major from Arizona. We rebelliously wore bikinis and brought our cans of TaB with us to sunbathe at the Campus Plaza Pool. If we ate too much that day, we ran at night. It worked at first, but then I started bringing home pies.

Marie Callender's Restaurant is known for its homemade pies. I worked at Marie's to pay for expenses. If you worked the late shift you could take home as many as four or five leftover pies.

"Pies!" the night manager would call at midnight after we had closed and cleaned up. The waitresses and staff ran to the front counter where that day's dozens of partially-eaten pies had been collected: cream cheese, fresh strawberry, coconut cream, lemon meringue, German chocolate. Every closing worker took home three or four of them. The restaurant never sold day-old pies; they were baked fresh each morning.

I started living off those pies: lemon meringue, black bottom and pecan were my favorites. Rich vanilla ice cream piled on a warm piece of boysenberry was another regular treat. Soon, I had gained five pounds, then ten, then fifteen.

By the end of the summer, even before the first football game of the season, the weight gain had become apparent. With a figure just like Grandma Burningham's, my excess weight turned into surprisingly large breasts and a tummy that couldn't be sucked in.

Cheryl and I had just shared a pizza from Heaps O' Pizza and then drove to get *Baskin-Robbins* ™ ice cream. We wolfed down a pint each of our favorite, happily stuffing ourselves behind the closed door of our bedroom.

There was a knock at our door. I almost choked on the brownie piece in my ice-cream.

"Are you sure you won't join us for dinner?" our perfect roommate asked.

"No thanks," we shouted back in unison. Cheryl and I looked at each other guiltily.

Our roommates thought we were just antisocial, not addicted to junk food. I would jam the boxes full of left-over pies in the fridge at night, but by morning it was clear that only Cheryl and I had eaten them.

One of our other roommates had some once, but it was a proper slice. She ate it as dessert, after dinner, on a real separate china plate with a fork. She didn't grab a spoon and dig into the whole pie while it was still in the tin, like I did.

1975-76 was BYU's Centennial Year. By the start of football season I had gained so much weight—twenty pounds—that I could barely fit into my cheer uniform, which had been custom-made for me in the spring just after try-outs. I had to get my weight under control. But knowing I had to lose weight and that I had no choice in the matter only made me more obsessed with food and increased my compulsive eating. I was up for anything.

"Hold still, this is a mess," my roommate yelled.

Cheryl carefully cracked the egg on the edge of the bathroom counter and held it over my open baby-bird mouth. I could see her reaction in the mirror as first the yolk and then the gelatinous egg white, complete with umbilical cord, slimed into my mouth. I gagged before the raw egg could go any further down my throat.

"This is gross," I said, spitting the egg into the sink.

The feel of the quivering, mucous-like white and thick egg yolk made me want to vomit, but I couldn't do it. Standing over the bathroom sink with raw egg dripping down my chin, I wiped the mess from my face.

My roommate and I looked at each other and cracked up laughing. It was impossible. I could never throw up. Back then I'd never heard of bulimia or anorexia; later I'd become certain that I wasn't the only BYU coed with an eating disorder.

The next day was a home game—I was petrified. The football stadium teemed with blue and white clad student fans. It was near the end of football season and I was still twenty pounds overweight. Halfway through the BYU cougar fight song, the button on my royal blue and white cheer vest popped.

The school song ended and I ran relieved and breathless to the sidelines. Certainly the crowd was paying no particular attention to me, but I felt as though all eyes were staring at the imposter who had become so fat she couldn't cheer. It was no use looking for my button; it was lost somewhere in the stadium's turf. I hung my head, red-faced.

Grotesque, with large breasts and the protruding abdomen of a woman in her sixth month of pregnancy, I hid during all the crisp days of fall behind a navy knee-length coat while I surreptitiously drove my beat-up Rambler to the bakeries for éclairs and glazed doughnuts. These trips were made alone. I had completely passed Cheryl's threshold in the binge eating game. In secret I ate the junk food so fast I barely tasted it. Then, sitting amid empty cartons of ice cream and crumpled pastry bags, I lay on my back crying, tears streaming down my red puffy face.

A dancer—a beauty queen? Who was I kidding?

I skipped class often and called in sick at work. Finally, on a grey November day, before I could be further humiliated on the Marriott Center basketball court, I quit the BYU varsity cheer-leading squad.

"Can I take your coat?" the student athletic director asked.

"No thanks," I said, pulling the protective wool tight across my tummy.

"You can't quit. We've spent thousands of dollars on you." He reprimanded me.

I nervously eyed the director's office door, which he had left ajar. Athletic department employees passed by and occasionally peeked in the doorway as I shifted in my seat and wished the director would lower his voice and close the door.

"Well I just—I can't do this—I don't know…"

I really didn't have a legitimate reason to give him. How could I tell this guy I felt embarrassed because I was too fat to cheer? He'd just tell me I wasn't all that fat and to buck up and live up to my obligation. After all, I was picked from hundreds of wanna-be cheerleaders—Jay Osmond had even been one of the judges. Tears welled up in my eyes; I was never very good at hiding emotion.

"Your uniforms were custom tailored, and the school spent hundreds of dollars sending you to the cheer camp at UC Santa Barbara and …," he went on and on.

I sat there looking down at my tummy, safely hidden under my coat.

"We'll have to bring in the alternate for basketball season, I don't even know who that is," the director said, walking over to a filing cabinet in the corner of his office.

***

Quitting the BYU varsity cheer-leading squad was just another sin to add to my growing pile of guilt. I left BYU that December disgraced, and moved back home with my mom.

I needed time to think about things, to decide what I really wanted to do with my life. I was sure that everyone I saw was staring at my overweight body. Whenever I left the house I wore that same navy blue coat I had bought during football season. I didn't take it off until June.

At Mom's I spent hours in introspection, hiding out in my basement bedroom, the one Dad had built for me after we moved into the new house. The gold plush carpet and dark wood paneling were still there, but when I looked at my window seat, my stuffed animals were gone. The lion Dad won for me at Lagoon Amusement Park and the walrus-pajama bag, a gift from a girlfriend, had disappeared. The only thing left was the sad-eyed dog Mike had given me for Valentines Day. Mom told me she gave my stuffed animals away; there were too many of them and they were cluttering her house.

The sun couldn't get through the tiny basement window above my barren window seat, the glass dirty from years of neglect. But that was all right. I didn't want any sun; darkness was in my soul and it seemed appropriate that I should remain in the dark basement bedroom. I stayed in my room for days, crying, praying, and only coming up to buy something to eat or go to the bathroom.

Mom pretty much left me alone. I'm sure she was concerned, but she didn't know what to do about me. I didn't want to see Dad; I didn't want him to see me like this.

One day it was snowing, but I didn't care. Standing in front of the bedroom mirror in my underwear, I scrutinized my body. I hated it. I thought my body was the ugliest thing I had ever seen—certainly far from perfect. Over a matter of months my hair, which had been long, thick and dark in high school, had become a thin ash blonde.

The snow was falling slowly, lighting on the crusty stuff that had settled in during last week's snowstorm. Without bothering to dress, I walked outside into the backyard. There, I fell to the ground, my body crumpled into the cold snow, laughing until I cried.

Mom looked out the sliding glass doors. I don't remember

whether she tried to talk or reason with me first, she probably did. But eventually she called the psychiatric hospital and had the proverbial men in white coats come and take me away.

My life up to that point passed before me. I was a failure. It was all ending at barely age twenty-one, in the psycho ward. Mom had sent me off to the loony bin and I hated her for that.

     ***

That first night I awoke from my sleep in the sterile hospital bed, the tightly tucked covers pulled from their snug position during my sleepless thrashing. I could never stand tucked-in bed sheets; I like to wrap the blankets and sheets around my legs, hug them and have them move with me.

It was completely dark in the room, except for a shard of light from the hallway coming through my partially closed door. I sensed a presence, very close. At first I couldn't see, but I could feel someone staring at me.

Slowly I focused on the face of a confused young man no more than four inches from mine. Stringy pale hair framed his gaunt face and huge sunken eyes. I screamed.

"What are you doing?" I shrieked.

He jumped back.

"Have you seen my bike? I'm looking for my bike," the lanky teen stuttered, backing away from my bed.

I stared at him, trying to understand what was happening.

He paced slowly in circles around my room. It was clear he meant me no harm.

"Get out," I shouted.

He looked at me, as if for the first time, and then darted out the doorway.

I grabbed my robe and walked out to the nurse's station. Nobody was there. I heard a clanging sound coming from the lockers and looked around the corner. Another patient dressed in nightclothes was banging his knuckles against the staff lockers. His blood dripped down the rusty, tan metal. The orderlies and staff pulled at him but he clung to an open locker door. Muttering nonsense, he occasionally wailed like a beast. I tried to get the attention of the staff, but they were all occupied with the knuckle-banger.

43

More depressed than ever, I returned to my room. I closed the unlock-able door and pushed a chair against it, hoping to keep out any more stray patients. Convinced I was the sanest patient there, I crawled into my narrow bed and tried to sleep.

The next morning I sat at lunch between two women with serious eating disorders. One appeared to be more than three-hundred pounds, the other stick thin. Both had special diets. My lunch was the same as all the rest of the patients. I watched the obese woman look longingly at the thin woman's apple pie, meatloaf and gravy, then back to her salad, steamed vegetables and chicken breast. The thin young woman sat staring at all the food on her own plate, overwhelmed.

I met with the hospital psychiatrist that afternoon.

"So am I crazy, doctor?"

Desperately, I looked at the well-dressed man seated across from me. He had reviewed my records and had told me that he had seen many young LDS women like me over his career, but at that time I thought I was horribly unique.

He had those kind eyes, just like Mike's. I had a feeling he wasn't a member of the Church—Holy Cross was a Catholic Hospital after all.

No Kay, you're not crazy. Your problems stem from your understandable reluctance to submit to your religion's authoritarianism—and from sexual repression. You have recently begun to confuse hunger with your emotions. Stop it. Don't worry about the weight; you're not really anything other than average weight. Eat right and exercise. Give it time; your weight problem will work itself out.
One more thing—transferring to the University of Utah sounds like a good idea, but get out of that basement.

His assessment seemed confident and I was temporarily relieved. His was the sanest advice I had ever heard. But knowing the cause of my problems on an intellectual level and implementing changes in my life to reconcile those issues would be another matter, particularly where almost everyone in my social and familial circles were active participants in Mormonism.

After a three day stay as an inpatient I was released. Despite my mother's conviction that I was crazy, the official diagnosis was situational depression.

I moved out of my mother's house the next week and into a little place by the University of Utah. Transferring from BYU it seemed, would help my problems. I moved in with another girl I had known slightly in high school, two nursing students and a Canadian girl.

Despite my psychiatrist's advice to lose weight slowly, patience was never one of my virtues. Miserable, I vowed to lose the weight any way I could so I tried every crash diet I could find. I couldn't stand being even ten pounds overweight, let alone twenty.

Although it had been several months, I still wasn't used to being overweight and as a dancer, was not used to having anything but full control over my body. Unaccustomed to my size, I grazed against pieces of furniture. My blouses had to be pinned closed across my chest.

I tried fasting for days. I tried the chalky protein powder mixed with tap water made into a shake—the farthest thing from an ice cream milkshake ever. I starved for three days and then ate everything in sight on the fourth: graham crackers and peanut butter, boxes of cookies, and bags of sprinkle-covered frosted animal cookies—the kind I used to share with Mike, when each of us would eat from one end until our lips met and we laughed and kissed. Obsessed as I was, neither my cupboards nor the fridge had any fresh food, just a boxed assortment of packaged products made mostly from white flour and corn syrup with chocolate something or other in it.

I rarely returned to Bountiful, but did meet up with Jill. At nineteen Jill had married Craig, a returned missionary a few years older than us. I asked her why she did it. She said because she was doing "God's will." She believed it was her time to marry and have children. This news was very sad because I knew Jill really loved a handsome athlete who was our age and was still on his mission. It seemed Jill was marrying not for love, but out of a sense of timing and duty.

During this same time my little sister was married in the Salt Lake Temple. I couldn't attend because I had not yet been through the temple to take out my endowment, the initial induction ritual into the Mormon Temple. At that time, young Mormon women were not allowed to go through a dedicated temple until just before their wedding, or unless they had been called on a mission.

My sister was nineteen; her husband, three or four years older, was from a small Southern Utah town. He clearly loved her. Although Mom's house was modest, the landscaping by Dad was beautiful and so my sister and her husband decided to hold their reception in our back yard.

Flowers bloomed everywhere. The pagoda in the rock garden that Dad had built in our back yard had been strung with tiny lights. I remember floating lilies in the rock waterfall pond.

By August of 1976, I was still at my fattest and looked even worse dressed in a polyester empire-waisted, floral print bridesmaid gown. My sister was gorgeous. I was happy for her, but too embarrassed by my weight to actively join in the celebration, so I backed off from the crowd.

An elderly neighbor woman approached me while I stood on the edge of the gathering.

"Don't worry dear, your turn will come."

She smiled and patted my hand, then looked at my sister.

I had no response to her comment, but she didn't want one. It was a pronouncement.

The old woman slowly walked away in her flat shoes, holding tight to her plate of crudités. She sat on one of the folding chairs placed in a circle on the patio around the waterfall. Balancing her plate on the skirt covering her thin knees, she glanced back at me and whispered loudly to the woman beside her. The other woman looked at me, and then they both smiled and nodded their heads.

Their pity was palatable. I wished they'd quit judging me and assessing my future. At just twenty-one, I felt like an old maid.

A few months later I had my chance to marry my own returned missionary. Brent, a boy I dated when we were both freshmen at BYU before the South African Tour, had returned from his mission to Finland and wanted to marry me. I rolled my eyes at the prospect. A nice boy from Idaho, Brent had been a singer in *The Sounds of Freedom*, but couldn't go with us to Africa because he had been called on his mission. We were both now twenty-one. As a good young Mormon male, it was time for him to marry. Brent kept trying to help me. He thought if I married him I wouldn't be depressed; I told him it would just get worse.

One night, Brent was supposed to pick me up at seven. We were going out to dinner. I paced in my room. I had just eaten a box of brownie batter with a quart of milk.

A dinner date—how could I?

"Your boyfriend's here," T.J. told me with a scowl.

My Canadian roommate turned and almost hit Brent in the face with the screen door as she walked back into the house. T.J. was from Quebec, pronounced 'ka beck,' she constantly reminded the other roommates. She rarely bathed and appeared sexually androgynous. She spoke with lots of '*merde*' and '*sacrama*' fillers. I thought she was the most interesting person in the house. T.J. always wanted me to play basketball with her, but I felt too fat.

***

I was working at the University of Utah library stacks at the time, re-shelving books. Mahmood, an Iranian graduate student who also worked at the library, didn't think I was fat. He was an expert in the Middle Eastern Collection. He was very dark and hairy; his intense physical presence creeped me out.

"Hey, you know, we should go out sometime," he said, his eyebrows rising repeatedly while he stared me down.

"No thanks, I'm not interested," I said, walking away from him.

"You have no boyfriend, no?" he whispered at me loudly as I disappeared in the library stacks.

***

"Come on, my brother's in the car." Brent said, with his nervous, sweet smile.

He was wearing a popular seventies returned missionary outfit, tight sweater vest, tucked in tie and long sleeved button-down shirt. He had perfectly combed thick, brown hair with a deep side part. His tenor voice was the same range as Karen Carpenter's and all the other singers in *The Sounds of Freedom* teased him about it.

We went to dinner with his brother. I ate nothing but half of a roll. Afterward, Brent told me he thought I had a problem with food.

"You never eat in public anymore," he said.

He was right. I did all my eating in private. I was too embarrassed to be seen eating when I was so fat.

I broke up with Brent that night. He would never understand my problems and he was pushing too hard for marriage. I wasn't ready.

The next couple of years passed in a daze. I decided to return to BYU because the University of Utah wouldn't accept many of my credits, such as *the Book of Mormon* and other LDS scripture-based classes. It took me a total of five years, between switching from a dance major to a history major and all the back and forth, but in December of 1978 I finally graduated with a B.A. in History from BYU.

Six months earlier, in June of 1978, then LDS Prophet Spencer W. Kimball received a shocking revelation: worthy Black men could now hold the priesthood. It seemed that this new rule was generally accepted by the Church membership without question. It didn't occur to them that an omniscient God would not be changing his rules. The explanation offered by Apostle Bruce R. McConkie was that:

> ...it is time disbelieving people repented and got in line and believed in a living, modern prophet. Forget everything that I have said, or what President Brigham Young or President George Q. Cannon or whomsoever has said in days past that is contrary to the present revelation. We spoke with a limited understanding and without the light and knowledge that now has come into the world.... We have now added a new flood of intelligence and light on this particular subject, and it erases all the darkness....It doesn't make a particle of difference what anybody ever said about the Negro matter before the first day of June of this year [1978].[13]

The fall of 1978 was my last semester at BYU. A class on the history of Africa was offered by a Professor Moore, who was not only a professor of history, but of law as well. We began a friendship when it became apparent that there would be just two students in the history of Africa course: me and Russ Blood, the missionary I had met in Capetown. The three of us often took the scheduled time outside the classroom, walking around the BYU campus grounds, talking more of religion and philosophy than African history.

Professor Moore had a round face and dough-boy frame, usually stuffed into an unfashionable three-piece polyester suit. His oily dark hair, short around the ears in compliance with BYU standards, was combed together into a long bang curling in the middle of his forehead. His watery blue eyes bulged with intellectual curiosity; his lips were unnaturally full. He was thirty-four to my twenty-three, with a penchant for metaphysics that kept me engrossed in conversation. I felt as if he was my own private guru.

Professor Moore had an office in the law school building across the street from the University's main campus. He convinced me I should apply to law school.[14] Although dance was my first love, I thought my days as a dancer were over—my body being the stumbling block. I had

48

done well in debate in high school; my uncle was my coach, and my father the debate coach at Viewmont High, Bountiful High's cross-town rival. So the idea of a career in law was not totally foreign to me. Besides, unless I moved to New York City or Los Angeles, the opportunities to dance professionally would be limited.

I had been to Professor Moore's office twice, once to discuss my senior paper for the African history class and another time to pick up his letter of recommendation for my law school application. Educated in an Ivy League school, with a graduate degree from Cambridge, Professor Moore was a convert to the Church. My connection with him was that of a young student starved for an academic experience with true intellectuals, the type of people I rarely encountered while living in Utah.

This afternoon I noticed Professor Moore had closed the blinds of his windows. I was seated in a chair. He sat behind his desk. After we discussed my future in the legal profession, the conversation turned to controversial aspects of Mormon doctrine. We had occasionally spoken of Church issues, but...

"Polygamy," he said, "is misunderstood. Taken in the right spirit it is a beautiful principle. But the common Church members never were ready for the truth; it takes someone really special to be able to appreciate the principle."

I sat stunned at this statement, especially coming from someone I respected.

Professor Moore moved his chair around to the front of the desk, by mine. The dark office closed around me. He put his hand on my knee, over the fabric of my slacks.

His plump face started to sweat. Clearing his throat, he continued.

"I've been praying about this, Kay..."

I couldn't believe what I was hearing.

"I'm certain you were meant to be my second wife," he blurted.

I jumped up from my chair. Professor Moore stood as I jumped. He was just inches from me. He grabbed me by the shoulders, pulled me to his chest and kissed me hard.

The sudden feel of his unwanted, fleshy mouth on mine, made me sick to my stomach. I stepped back, shocked, terrified. He was married. I had no interest in, or physical attraction to this man. Until that moment he had been my academic mentor, and I thought, a friend.

"I don't think this is a good idea."

49

My words shot out at him. My words were a shield, defending myself in that moment from harm—a threat I had never expected—a sort of casualty of friendly fire.

He just stared at me. I didn't know what he expected.

"I have to go…" I stammered.

Professor Moore began to tremble. His crazed blue eyes had turned green. Despite his shaking, the swirl of pomaded black hair in the middle of his forehead stayed perfectly still.

I turned and bolted from his office, running down the back law school stairs. Confused, I wondered how he could have misinterpreted the relationship. The encounter haunted me for months, even past December graduation, when I had moved back to Salt Lake.

I worked at the Utah State Historical Society from the time I finished my undergraduate degree until law school began. I took photographs and wrote histories of old Victorian homes in Salt Lake's Avenues District for nomination on the National Register of Historic Sites. Jared, a co-worker and returned missionary, and I became friends. Sitting on the lawn outside the Salt Lake City & County Building under a large oak tree, eating our lunches on a warm summer day, I confessed the kissing incident to him.

"Well, I don't know, I just want to forget about it," I said.

"You really can't go forward until you confess and repent." Jared looked at me, concerned.

"But what I am supposed to confess?   It would seem more like telling on this guy, who I think just got carried away." (I didn't tell Jared about the second wife part, it was too embarrassing.) "He really is a good person," I protested.

"Well, I think it's clear that even though he kissed you, he was a married man and you need to tell your bishop. Then the bishop can advise you. Confession to the proper authorities is the last step in repentance."

Jared had summed up the problem and given me the solution, only it wasn't the answer I wanted. I wanted to forget about the whole thing. Law school would start next month. The thought of attending law school anywhere besides BYU, didn't seriously occur to me—the J. Reuben Clark Law School was new and was supposed to be a good one. Professor Moore was the one who urged me to go to law school, praising my intelligence, telling me that the degree would open lots of doors.

Chapter 2: Cognitive Dissonance

On July 23, 1979, more than six months after the incident and just a month before beginning my first year at Brigham Young University's J. Reuben Clark Law School, I wrote in my journal:

I think I have found the root of my problems. I haven't fully repented of my involvement with Professor Moore. I need to confess to Bishop Burton. Perhaps when I have been cleared of the sin by the right authority I will no longer be stifled in my progression (spiritually as well as in all other areas). I am going to make an appointment with him as soon as possible. Then soon, maybe I will stop this self-destructive behavior once and for all and will be able to achieve my goals and continue on in my path toward perfection. Jared (intern at work and returned missionary) helped me realize just how wrong I've been. He did this largely through his good example, but we also had a good talk today.

I didn't want any awkward feelings between me and one of my professors. I was going to be a first year student. I'd seen movies about law school and knew it would be a tough time. So, I followed Jared's advice and set up a meeting with the leader of my student ward, Bishop Burton.

Burton was a thin man with just a fringe of dark hair along his receding hairline. He never stood when I entered his office, but sat straighter, shuffling the stack of papers on his desk. He looked up at me from behind the large, heavy-grained oak desk, his chin raised just a bit too high in the air. His tone was very serious.

"So what did you want to talk about?" he asked.

I told him about Professor Moore.

Burton leaned forward over the pile of papers, elbows on his desk, hands clasped.

"Well, now are you sure there was only kissing involved?"

"Yes," I said, instinctively pushing my chair away from the front edge of his desk.

He seemed to want to hear some lurid details, but there were none. I didn't want to tell him I was a virgin. That was none of his business. I sat silent.

He seemed to be thinking for a moment and then he commented in a loud voice.

51

"The Church of Jesus Christ of Latter-day Saints is not a smorgasbord," he boomed. "It is a full course meal. You cannot merely pick and choose which laws of the gospel you will obey and which ones you will ignore. You have to partake of the whole thing."

Burton pounded his scrawny fist on the old oak desk.

I didn't respond, but sat there, inwardly shaking my head. This man was angry. Where were the caring, elderly, Church general authorities I had watched speaking from the tabernacle at General Conferences for so many years?

I glanced at the clock on his wall. Almost a full minute had passed. It seemed like forever.

"Well..." he said finally.

I shrugged and looked down at the handbag on my lap.

"This is a serious matter," Burton continued. "I believe you need to go to your stake president with this," he said nodding.

"But, it's over, it was a one time thing, he just kissed me on the spur of the moment and I don't want to make him feel awkward. I might have him as a teacher this fall at the law school."

Burton shook his head and scribbled something in the file. Slamming it shut, he stood and walked around his desk to show me out, but I was quicker than he; I had left.

Leaving the bishop's office I felt exposed. *Who was this man anyway that he should be privy to my private thoughts and interpersonal relationships, however messed up they were?*

Something was terribly wrong here. I was upset more by the coerced confession and the prospect of re-telling the incident to yet another, higher, Church authority, than with the incident itself. I couldn't let this interfere with graduate school and so I resolved to forget about it.

***

The first week of law school was like nothing I had ever experienced. I had always been one of the top students in my classes. "A" grades came easily to me without consistent studying; I would cram for tests and do well. This was different.

Although it had been in the planning stages for over a decade, in 1979 the law school had been in existence for only a few years. It started out with lots of press and donations, hiring the best and brightest practitioners and scholars from all over the United States, regardless of their personal religion. Rex E. Lee, the founding Dean, was a renowned constitutional lawyer and would become the Solicitor General for the United States under President Reagan.

Most of my classes were in the big amphitheater classroom, with close to the entire class of one-hundred and fifty in attendance. I looked around. Our class had fewer than twenty women, several of whom would eventually drop out before graduation.

Almost all of the students in the class of one-hundred and fifty were men who were returned missionaries, very earnest and diligent. Most were married. Their wives brought them lunch and even dinner as they arrived at 6:00 a.m., and then stayed until midnight. As I skipped dinner and munched my M & Ms at my study carrel in the law school basement, I wished I had a wife.

During the first few weeks of law school I read more than I had ever read in my life. My eyes were tired and my butt was sore from all the sitting. Chocolate and TaB (later Diet Coke), the Mormon version of amphetamines, got me through the long hours of the night until I was finished with my reading for class the next day. Study groups were chosen and there was constant talk of 'law review,' the significance of which was never discussed openly among the students, but secretly in hushed tones and with competitive glances.

I raised my hand often in class. My comments were not stupid, nor were they brilliant. In law school there were a few brilliant students and a few students who seemed to have been admitted because large donations had been made to BYU by their families. Most of us fell into one category: former straight 'A' students who, when thrown together in an intense graduate school situation and compared to one another, were absolutely average.

Each student had a mailbox where they would receive notices from their professors along with other academic announcements. These were actual physical mailboxes, the seventies/eighties version of e-mail.

One morning I headed to my mail box to pick up any new information before going to my Civil Procedure class. It was the third week of classes and it seemed that the Professor Moore incident had resolved. Professor Moore was in fact my Civil Procedure Professor. In his class I sat way back in the amphitheatre and listened, but did not make eye contact with him. I figured it would go all right. His class, the big section of Civil Procedure, was actually quite interesting. He was a good teacher. We were talking about adding parties under the federal rules.

"Interpleader, is when the 'ins' want out; impleader, when the 'outs' want in," he gestured, describing one case with parties fighting over property and another, regarding the necessary joinder of certain indispensable parties to litigation. Clearly, he enjoyed his role teaching young minds.

I grabbed the paper from my box. Among the mimeographed and typed notices was an envelope with "Sister Burningham," handwritten in tiny letters. I momentarily froze, then ducked into the nearest ladies room and ripped open the envelope. In the same cramped handwriting I read: "You must speak to the stake president. You have not fully repented of your sin. Please contact me immediately to set up an interview." It was signed in a tiny, inky-smeared scrawl, "Bishop Robert (can't recall his middle initial—but you can be sure it was there) Burton."

I immediately thought of something I had recently read in a Church Magazine, "When the Prophet speaks the debate is over." [15] This statement was generally construed to apply to all Church priesthood leaders, even the lower members of the hierarchy.

The tears poured out. *Dammit! Why couldn't he leave me alone?* This thing was being blown all out of proportion.

I waited until my tears were gone and the sniffles wiped away. While looking in the mirror, I splashed cold water on my face and then ran to Civil Procedure, sliding into my seat just before the tardy bell rang.

It was hard to concentrate in class that day, but I made it through. Afterward, I couldn't focus enough to read my cases and so decided to go for a run. Since I wasn't dancing any longer, I needed some form of exercise. As Professor Moore would say, law school study was the equivalent of mental gymnastics. My mind was being exercised and stretched to the limits of its analytical ability. My body needed equal time.

I pulled on my sweats and running shoes and brushed my hair back into a pony tail. The sun was still high enough in the sky to give me a good hour. I had never been much of a runner, maybe a mile or so, but I took off, at a walk/run pace with no particular destination. I walked up the hills, north of campus to the Provo Temple, a spaceship looking structure identical to the one in Ogden, about eighty miles north. I walked around the grounds but felt no spirituality or inspiration. I expected something from this place. Although I had never been inside a holy temple I thought at least the grounds would be peaceful, but peace was not to be found.

Chapter 2: Cognitive Dissonance

I sat on the curb and cried some more. Now was not the time to have emotional issues. This was first year law school and as competitive as it came. Just yesterday one of the wives of the men in my class asked me how I could, in good conscience, take one of the one hundred and fifty places in the class of 1982. After all, I was just a woman and that meant that there would be "...one less priesthood-holder who would not get a fine legal education and the opportunity to support his wife and children." Those were her exact words.

What was I thinking?

The next morning I woke up determined not to let this Bishop Burton ruin my day. I called him at 8:00 a.m. and left a message. I told him I considered the matter resolved and to please not bother me anymore.

That afternoon I was called out of my class into the law school administrative office for a private phone call. It was Burton. He told me that I must meet with a stake president, either my own or Dean Lee, because the Dean of the law school was also a stake president who would have jurisdiction over the matter. He told me if I didn't meet with a higher priesthood authority he would go directly to Professor Moore to confront him and get the truth about the matter. That was the last thing I wanted.

I agreed to meet with Dean Lee on the condition that our conversation would remain confidential. I had just learned about the priest-penitent evidentiary privilege in criminal law. To ensure confidentiality and the continued functioning of the relationship, a priest was forbidden to testify about anything told to him by one of his parishioners during confessional. Dean Lee assured me it would all be kept between us, and so I agreed to a meeting the next week.

Those next several days were torture. I had Civil Procedure twice over that time and could not bear to look at Professor Moore. I was even more distracted than usual and couldn't concentrate on my reading. We had picked study groups by now, and I was late with my assignment. This did not endear me to the group.

On an overcast late October afternoon I arrived at Dean Lee's office. We had never spoken face to face before. I knocked, tentatively.

His deep voice yelled, "Come in."

I walked in and looked at him for some sign of kindness. His face showed no sign of emotion. After directing me to the chair in front of him, he walked back to his desk chair and casually stretched his long thin legs out onto his desk.

The Dean's office was large with long narrow windows and great views of the mountains behind the law school. I looked at all the diplomas and awards on his wall.

"So Kay, tell me about Professor Moore."

I was surprised at his direct approach.

"Well, it's really nothing. I don't want anything to happen to him. Will you promise me that?"

"I will," he said, his dark eyes piercing, yet appearing sincere.

I explained the situation in Professor Moore's office, the kiss and the fact that we had had no contact since that time, almost a year earlier. He had written my letter of recommendation to law school before any of this happened and even though I was now in his Civil Procedure class, he had never called on me or otherwise spoken to me directly. Of course, I had never raised my hand in his class either.

"This thing is being blown all out of proportion and I just want to concentrate on my studies. It seems like nobody takes me seriously, first Professor Moore and now Bishop Burton."

I started to cry, then broke down into sobs, pleading with him for something, I didn't know what.

Dean Lee leaned back in his executive desk chair. He crossed one of his legs, clad in slick, navy blue, over his other knee, and then scratched his chin. His eyes narrowed, focusing even more intently on me.

Dean Lee stood and walked back to the set of panoramic windows behind his desk. This time of the year the mountains were topped by snow and this particular afternoon was cold and dreary. Suddenly he turned on his heel and spoke as if he had an audience of more than a single first-year student.

"Now Kay, don't worry, even if you never practice law a day in your life, law school will have been worth it!"

I stared at him, waiting for what would surely be some words of encouragement.

"With a law degree you should consider yourself a *twenty cow* wife, why a wife with a law degree could be very valuable to a young man!"[16]

He made a fist and shook it at the air.

A twenty cow wife—was he kidding?

Dean Lee folded his arms across his narrow chest, looked at his watch and hurriedly began escorting me out.

"Well now, don't you worry, we'll take care of this. Everything will be all right. You did the right thing coming here to tell me. This is the last stop in repentance, and now you have been forgiven and you can go on with your life."

By now my sobs had stopped.

"But this is confidential, right? Nothing will happen to Professor Moore?"

He guided me to the door. "Yes, yes of course," he said.

The whole thing seemed resolved and somehow I made it through my first semester.

That first semester I made friends with Sharon, also a first year student. She asked me to go home with her for Christmas to visit her family. Mom didn't care and Dad had a new girlfriend by then, so I thought it would be more fun than staying home.

Sharon's parents lived in Connecticut. They were very welcoming and her little brother, who was the same age as my brother Kyle, was home from college. We saw *Hansel and Gretel* at New York's Metropolitan Opera House. Even though the opera was in English, it was hard for me to appreciate; I wanted the singers to move. I had my first taste of lox and bagels with cream cheese. Sharon's brother and I went skiing in the Poconos. It was a fun holiday vacation.

After the Christmas break we returned to find our grades posted on the wall by our mailboxes. Mine were not even close to law review, but my grades weren't the only problem. Whenever I walked down the hall the other students looked at me curiously. I had always felt a bit out of sync with the students in my class, and since speaking with Dean Lee I felt more dissociated than ever. After the holiday break I returned to overhear what they had been talking about.

"Did you hear about Professor Moore?"

"He was fired," a second year student said.

I couldn't believe it, but it was true. I looked at the second semester schedule; there was a new Civil Procedure teacher. Professor Moore was gone. *Had I ruined this man's career?*

CHAPTER THREE: Into a World I'd Never Known

"Life does not accommodate you, it shatters you. It is meant to, and it couldn't do it better. Every seed destroys its container or else there would be no fruition."—Florida Scott-Maxwell

After the Professor Moore mess, I laid low and finished my first year of law school. A Salt Lake City firm hired me as a law clerk that summer. Relegated to document review on the defense of a huge accounting malpractice case, this was no stimulating summer stint. With dour faces, the firm's attorneys worked hunched over desks covered in dozens of files. All my assignments were tedious. Contrary to what I had seen on television and in the movies, real law firm life seemed a boring road to nowhere.

Discouraged with law, and with no money for second year tuition, I stayed home and worked full-time the first semester of my second year, but then returned in January, 1981. My Constitutional Law class was taught by Dean Lee. I tried to ignore his breach of confidentiality over the Professor Moore incident and instead, concentrate on the subject matter.

Just a year before, Sonia Johnson had been ex-communicated from the Mormon Church due to her outspoken advocacy on behalf of the Equal Rights Amendment. Though it had passed both houses of congress in 1972, supporters were three states short for the necessary two-thirds ratification required to amend the Constitution. Dean Lee had written a book arguing against the adoption of the amendment.

"Women shouldn't be forced to fight on the battlefield's front lines," he posited.

"Who will be home with our children if men and women are forced into combat?" he queried our class during a discussion over the merits of the ERA.

The law students debated the pros and cons of the proposed amendment, consensus being that our current laws were sufficient. Nobody wanted women in battle or otherwise forced to do manly tasks.

The amendment was defeated about the time I graduated law school, in part due to organized Mormon opposition, including thousands of Mormon women acting under priesthood direction. Had I been able

59

then, to step back and view the situation with Professor Moore (years later I learned that I wasn't the only female law student he had harassed) and the LDS system of coerced confessions objectively, I would have seen it as a good example of the gender oppression proponents of the ERA were fighting and would've helped support the cause. But at age twenty-four, I lacked the perspective needed to participate in such a fight.

At the end of the semester, I was hugely disappointed with my 'C' grade in Constitutional Law. Dean Lee's words, 'twenty cow wife,' flashed across my mind.

***

Strapped by mounting student debt, I searched for a way to pay down my loans. A comparably stressed classmate told me about a new program with the Army Reserves. The Army promised to pay back all student loans for just six years of reserve service. Reserve duty was only one weekend a month and a few weeks in the summer, something which sounded easy enough. But anyone who accepted this offer had to complete nine weeks of basic training, as an enlisted soldier. I signed up.

How difficult could it be?

A few weeks later, halfway through law school, I received my orders. I would spend that next summer in Fort Jackson, South Carolina.

***

Summer in Ft. Jackson is a steam bath. When it isn't pouring rain, the high humidity holds constant. Moist air stuck the long-sleeved, heavy green cloth to the length of the enlisted soldiers' bodies. These battle dress uniforms, or BDUs, were worn daily. With camouflage fatigues, stiff, shin-high army boots, and steel-pot helmets held tight to our heads with who-knows-who had worn them before grimy grosgrain chinstraps, an outsider might not realize the entire platoon was all female.

"Sound off Bravo Company," Sergeant Santiago shouted as he stood straight and tall behind the platoon of girls running the verdant South Carolina foothills.

The handsome six foot plus Puerto Rican Viet Nam Vet surveyed the first ever female group to undergo infantry training in the Army. The mocha colored skin of his forearms glistened in the moist air. Peering out from beneath his Smokey-the-Bear hat, he appeared unflappable as he squinted from the sun and ordered us through our physical training (P.T.). Down to his impeccably pressed slacks and starched shirt, every bit of him appeared perfect.

Chapter 3: Into a World I'd Never Known

Top down orders to all the drill instructors for Bravo Company were to treat us no differently than the men. And so it was *Reveille* wake-up at 4:00 A.M., unless assigned K.P. duty and then it was up at 3:00 a.m. to prepare the powdered scrambled eggs and link sausages for breakfast. Lights went out promptly at nine. If a soldier drew C.Q. duty, it meant that she was in charge of quarters and that at midnight she would dress in full uniform, load her rifle and stand guard in front of some random building on the base.

There was no room in this man's army for menstrual cramps or other medical conditions unique to the female gender and the Holy Bible was the only reading material allowed. Sound sleep was not part of the regime, maybe that's why they called our uniforms fatigues. It seemed obvious that the military's intent, at least for the enlisted soldier, was to push each soldier to her limits, not just physically but emotionally as well. Stripped of our individuality, the group would make a more easily directable killing machine—an unquestioning, collective consciousness, ready to fight.

Trained from the first day to be ready for the unexpected, my mind could never really relax and fall into that deep REM sleep. To add to the insomnia, there were the erratic nighttime noises in the barracks. Compared to barracks living, sharing an apartment with five other girls at BYU campus housing was easy.

"Are you awake?" one soldier whispered to the girl a few beds down from me.

"Yeah, come on."

The two female soldiers squeezed under the same tight military-made bed sheets and lay together for several minutes. When all was quiet I could hear a rhythmic sound from that bed, and then some low moans. I didn't want to think about what was happening then.

As of summer 1981, homosexuality had never crossed my mind, especially the existence of lesbian dalliances. But here it was, and it went on, in one bed or another for the entire course of basic training.

I asked my boyfriend back home to send me some earplugs.

Girls in bed together weren't the only noises that kept me awake. Private Grunewald was the platoon driver. She was a tall girl with dark eyebrows and a lanky frame, shoulder length straight hair and a sort of sarcastic look about her. She sneaked cigarettes and though she couldn't have been more than twenty-five, she always looked tired. As the

61

designated platoon driver, she was excused from regular duties to drive Sergeant Santiago around whenever and wherever he commanded. Sometimes at night I would hear her locker open and close and knew she was taking Sgt. Santiago out, to do what, I didn't know. But there she was the next morning, always first, at role call.

"Kill, Kill, Kill. Take that hill. All the way Bravo Company—all the way!"

Each morning we shouted and repeated the brutal bromides taught to us by the various drill instructors, all of whom seemed to enjoy giving orders to the young women.

"You girls will not be pussies!" the red-haired Master Sergeant Kofoed proclaimed.

"You will be tough, you will work hard and at the end of basic training, you will be soldiers!"

Master Sgt. Kofoed was a Green Beret from the Deep South. It took me a full week before I could make sense of his thick, Southern dialect. Not quite my height, his booming voice belied his stature.

"Anybody caught with any contraband, anybody caught disobeying orders and especially anybody caught fraternizing with Charlie Company (the boy soldiers on the other side of the base) will be disciplined."

The female soldiers of Bravo Company stood straight at attention. Sgt. Kofoed walked around the periphery of the platoon formation, back to front; then, swiveling on his heel like our high school drill team, he abruptly faced the group of girls.

"When the enemy attacks there is no Private Nelson or PFC Burningham. There is only Bravo Company, armed and ready to defend the United States of America."

He raised his hands, signaling for the platoon to break attention and cheer. On cue we all whistled and whooped and then segued into those rhythmic grunting noises taught the first day of Basic.

Master Sergeant Kofoed started down the line of soldiers for that morning's role call. I was up. The Sergeant walked straight to me and turned with that heel spin. Nose to nose, he stared at me while his face was no more than three inches from mine.

"PFC Burningham, where is Private Sanchez?"

"I believe she left for the infirmary; she became symptomatic with —"

"PFC Burningham! Don't use those f***ing big ass words with me."

Kofoed spit the words from his mouth.

What big words? I searched my immediate memory for something. I honestly didn't know what he was talking about. I stood still, but felt sick inside.

"Drop and give me twenty," he screamed, eyes burrowing into mine.

I dropped to the barracks floor. Grimacing, I barely made my quota. This was getting old. Besides pushups as punishment, the more mail a soldier received, the more push-ups she did. The young guy I had dated before I left for Basic was consistent about writing, which made for more pushups.

Sgt. Kofoed pointed a sharp finger at random soldiers and yelled: "I want you and you and you, you, you to scrub the latrine."

The Sergeant shoved an army-issue toothbrush each, to five unsuspecting girls.

"You will scrub the sinks, the toilets, the floors and walls and they will sparkle. And then you will scrub the trashcans around the latrine until they sparkle," he pronounced.

There was just one latrine for all sixty girls in our platoon. I cowered, hoping he wouldn't add my name to the duty. The latrine had six toilets, six sinks and six open shower stalls. After *Reveille* we had just thirty minutes to get ready for the day, with beds made to military standards and rifles polished. There was no time for make-up, hair or primping. Each morning, right after showering, I braided my wet hair and splashed cold water on my face. Concern for my appearance was a far second to survival.

A few weeks into Basic, my new buddy and I were practicing shooting from foxholes. By then there had been lots of target practice. I touched the marksmanship medal I'd earned just a few days ago that was pinned to my uniform, remembering that I really could hit my targets.

"All right y'all keep in mind to keep that weapon down range. Last week a soldier had her head blown off 'cause her buddy didn't keep her weapon down range," warned the drill instructor in charge of the training exercise.

I looked at my new buddy, who I didn't know at all, a heavy-set southern black girl with a thick accent in the 3' X 4' waist-deep foxhole standing next to me. My life depended on her following the safety rules with her weapon. I failed to consider that she also depended on me.

We fired at our targets located downrange about fifty yards. Between the foxhole and the target was the barbed wire. Laid horizontally, it covered the entire fifty yards, and appeared to be just about eighteen inches above the muddy southern soil.

On command, we lifted ourselves up out of our foxhole. Using our elbows and forearms, we began to drag our bodies under the spiky canopy toward the other end of the barbed wire spread, making sure that our butts were tucked down. If they stuck up, our pants would be ripped by the wire. Despite her size, my buddy was fast.

Suddenly my butt stuck to the overhead barbed-wire.

"Buddy, help!" I yelled at her.

She was now a full body length ahead of me.

Without a second delay, she turned and low-crawled back to me, took out a knife that none of us had been issued and in one motion, freed my BDU pants seat from the wire. She turned again and was on her way. It was all very graceful and professional.

"Thanks buddy!" I yelled. *She really was a buddy,* I thought. *I would have to get to know her name.*

Soldiers from another platoon, on the far end of the barbed wire, fired directly at us, just above waist level. I wasn't sure if the ammo was live, but I wasn't going to risk it. The steel pot protected (at least I thought it did) our heads. The barbed wire was there to protect us as well, to train us to keep low, under the "enemy" fire. We both made it through in record time. And I had a new friend, Private Jefferson.

Low-crawling under barbed wire was the most frightening thing I had ever done, until that next week when our platoon hiked down a mountain gorge to see a single strand rope strung across a deep crevasse, maybe fifty yards across, above a narrow creek below. The rope was taut and at that moment it seemed like miles from one side to the other.

"You have two choices," Sergeant Santiago instructed.

"You can crawl over the rope. To do that you must pull hard, using all that upper body strength developed over the past weeks to keep on moving across, or you will fall."

Master Sergeant Kofoed demonstrated this method, as if it was no big deal.

"Or you can do it the pussy way and hang underneath, using your legs to propel you forward."

Sgt. Kofoed demonstrated this alternative method, as the soldiers hissed and booed at him. Clearly, we all wanted to do it the first way—but that's not what happened.

I had no choice; my legs were still my strength. My upper body had become stronger, but not enough to bet my life.

I can do this, I thought.

I grabbed the rope with my legs and hands and let my body hang down below the taut cord. Being second in the lineup, after Private Grunewald, who happened to have the record on pushups and so easily pulled herself over the top of the rope across the crevasse, I thought I would be ridiculed. But to my surprise, the platoon cheered me on.

"Go, go, go…" the other soldiers in my platoon chanted.

The rope swung wildly. I had to maintain an even, rhythmic stretch, reach and scoot type of maneuver, with no stopping. A little over half way across the ravine I made the mistake of looking down. The crevasse seemed to spin; the tiny creek of water seemed miles below.

The soldiers gasped as I stopped; the taut rope slackened and swayed from side to side. I hung upside down like a possum and waited for what seemed an eternity until it finally stilled. Gathering my courage, I began once again the process of reaching and pulling, until at last I made it to the other side. The whole platoon, including Private Jefferson and Sergeant Santiago, cheered.

All but two of the remaining girls did it the same under-hanging way and nobody made fun of anybody. When we had all finished, there were smiles and back slaps and a great collective sigh of relief.

I felt the same type of camaraderie I had felt in South Africa, when the producers of *Forces '74* had announced to us that we had raised hundreds of thousands of South African Rand for the victims of terrorism. Today our platoon of young women had succeeded at something very difficult. It was a good feeling which transcended each individual soldier and settled over the entire platoon. But there was no moral component in crossing the crevasse. The goal of this exercise was to build courage and confidence in a group which needed to develop these attributes in order to survive in the face of danger.

***

"Did you hear about Sergeant Santiago and Private Grunewald?" a solider whispered at lunch.

"No, what's the deal?" the solider seated next to her asked.

My ears pricked up. I had always suspected there was something more than driving going on between those two, but I didn't get the details. Instead, one by one each soldier in Bravo Company was questioned by the General. Although the charges were brought against Sgt. Santiago, the questioning became a fishing expedition for any kind of Army rule violation.

Frightened, the female soldiers spilled their guts. The girls were having relationships with the boys in Charlie Company, there was more than one sergeant-private affair, one girl had run off AWOL and another had, unknown to most of the soldiers, jumped from the second floor barracks. Two more cut their wrists in attempts at discharge.

With my lawyer-in-embryo reaching out from within, I counseled the female soldiers to just answer the question and/or to take the fifth—trying to ease their fear. But the Article Fifteen investigation was a case of extreme male authority over a group of frightened, mostly teenage girls. And though I had several years of life experience on most of the soldiers, I don't think I helped much. In the end, the hearing was based upon some evidence of marijuana in the barracks, including a couple of ounces found in Sergeant Santiago's office—"Jeez Louise," as Dad would say.

This U.S. Military was a foreign organization to me. I couldn't believe it was part of these United States, the government I had studied in my history and political science classes, the country I had been brought up to love and was now being trained to defend.

I saw similarities in my military training to the LDS Church's training of Mormon youth, from childhood indoctrination, through the rote teachings and hymns extolling the prophets and pioneers, to safeguarding the young women for motherhood and the rigorous control of mind and body in the mission field. The tightly fit puzzle pieces of my safe Mormon-girl life had cracked during the South Africa Tour and now they were coming apart.

***

After nine weeks of constant physical exhaustion, I made it through Basic and returned to law school with a stronger upper body and an appreciation for the freedom of ordinary daily choices in life. Peaking at a good clip for five miles about three times a week, I kept up my running and forgot about losing weight, but tried to eat healthily, indulging in an occasional sweet. My weight stabilized at a comfortable level; I no longer felt fat and eventually disassociated my emotions from food.

I was set to graduate law school in December of 1982, one semester behind my class. That fall I had interviews with several law firms from Seattle to Portland, all the way down the coast to San Diego.

Without a spare tire or checking the oil, I took off alone in my '74 Karmann Ghia in the fall of 1982 to interview. I had just turned twenty-eight years old and was excited for the road trip of a life. I had never been to the Pacific Northwest and was awed by the beauty of the tall pines and lush greenery. Even the cool rain was a refreshing change from the arid Utah climate.

My next interview down the Pacific coast was with a firm in the east San Francisco Bay. I wanted to continue the interviews down to Southern California, especially the one in San Diego.

Dad and I (and sometimes Grandma Burningham) always had a great time when we visited San Diego to see BYU play in the WAC whenever they faced-off against San Diego State University. We'd stay at the Mission Bay Hilton.

But before I had made it to Sausalito, my car blew a cylinder. I slowly drove over the Golden Gate and then, the Bay Bridge, to the east Bay firm. I made it, barely. Knowing this was the end of the road for my faithful vehicle, I accepted an offer from the firm on the spot, drove my car to the nearest junkyard and with the money from my vehicle's salvage, flew back home to finish the final weeks of law school before moving to California.

***

Walnut Creek in 1983 was green, lush with honeysuckle and with alternating pink or white flowering bushes blooming in the freeway medians. 1983 was before the full effect of Proposition Thirteen's tax cuts had become apparent in the withdrawal of the financial support which maintained California as an artificial tropical paradise. My apartment complex, a twelve-unit building surrounding a swimming pool, had eucalyptus trees and was located just a few blocks from the firm. It was an easy walk to work.

It was a fresh beginning with the move and starting work as a law clerk for the firm in January, then the bar review course that summer, followed by the three day July Bar Exam. The work was new and interesting. I had a lot to learn.

Working at the firm was a male associate attorney, just a few years older than me. His name was Frankie and he was not only smart and nice, but very handsome. He flirted with me at work and we got together a few times for my first taste of alcohol, a rum and coke, and for St. Patrick's Day at a local Irish pub. I wished this cute Irish-Catholic boy had been more serious about me. The few times we met were brief and I was giddy. I had absolutely no idea how to behave around a successful, eligible bachelor who was not beholden to God to the exclusion of having a good time.

Soon after I moved in, I met Marla who lived in the neighboring apartment in the same complex. Maybe twenty years old, Marla had long white-blonde hair and was a couple of inches taller than me. Despite my breasts, I was slim-hipped and boyish while Marla was voluptuous. She followed me around, ran with me and hung out at the pool while I studied for the bar exam that summer. Marla was a struggling model; I thought of her as a little sister.

One night she invited me to a party in the complex. I dropped in after dark, drawn by the provocative beats blaring out of Marla's open apartment window. It was Duran Duran's *Hungry like a Wolf.* I ran to her door, which was partly open and couldn't believe what I saw. The apartment was packed with young people, snorting artfully drawn lines of white powder from mirrored plates of glass with rolled up twenty dollar bills. Dozens of razor blades lay abandoned on the glass after every bit of the powder had been inhaled.

These Bay Area kids laughed, danced and made-out up against the tiny apartment walls. There must have been sixty or seventy people packed into Marla's tiny one-bedroom apartment. I took one look at what I presumed was cocaine, and fearful of the whole scene and not fitting in at all, I retreated across the complex pool into my own little one-bedroom apartment.

In the dark I sat alone. These twenty-somethings had knowingly lost all control. I'd never experienced a scene like that. It was too wild— too much. Yet Mormon Utah was so staid. I wanted someplace in between, someplace where people were normal, but not boring, fun but not too crazy. I wondered if I would ever find that place.

***

As soon as I began work in January of 1983, I assisted on a lengthy federal court case. Our firm had been retained to conduct the defense of a Bay Area city in a civil rights case brought by the mothers of two young men who had been shot and killed by the City's renegade police officers. This was one of the first of many excessive force cases against municipal police departments that would follow in California and eventually, nationwide. My job was to assist the senior partner with client interviews and to take notes during trial.

The case was assigned to a liberal San Francisco federal court judge. Experienced *amicus* counsel from the NAACP represented the plaintiffs.

After almost four months of trial our client lost. The trial ended with the jury finding that the City's Police Department was responsible for violating the civil rights of the victims and awarding a three million dollar verdict, one and one half million dollars each—at that time huge amounts —to the families of the two young black men who had been killed.

The day after the verdict I sat at my desk, staring at all the work that had piled up while I had accompanied the senior partner every day to the trial in San Francisco.

The intercom line in my office buzzed.

"Have your bags packed and be ready to leave this afternoon. We have a 4:00 p.m. flight to my condo to discuss the appeal."

The gruff voice on the other end of the line was familiar by now; it was the senior partner, in his mid-forties and all business. He was also single.

Dutifully and naively I packed a weekend bag for what I thought would be a couple of days with the defense team to figure out how we were going to handle the appeal. I grabbed an extra legal pad and made sure my good pen was in my purse.

I drove to the San Jose Airport, and parked. Meeting up with my boss in the ticketing area, I looked around for the associates who had worked on the case. When I saw my boss alone at the counter, I became nervous.

He motioned me over and told me to show the ticketing agent my identification. He paid for the tickets and then, in the style typical of his interaction with me each day of the trial, hurried me down through the gate to the small plane bound for Southern California. I kept looking over my shoulder, hoping to see Mr. Cutler or Mr. Ford, the bookish associates who had worked so hard on the case. Neither one of them was in the airport.

The plane was small, maybe twenty or so seats. I sat uncomfortably close to my boss the whole way to the desert. He talked only business.

"Where is Mr. Cutler?" I asked.

My boss ignored my question and kept talking about the verdict. I thought that maybe he didn't hear me, but I was too intimidated to repeat the question. I didn't want to sound stupid.

I wanted to call Frankie and tell him what was up, but we didn't have that kind of relationship. Although I was twenty-eight years old, I felt like a school girl around the cute associate. I was afraid he'd think I was a Utah hick and he would be right.

We arrived in Palm Desert, or was it Palm Springs? I frankly don't remember now. I do remember walking down a palm-lined street of shops and into a women's clothing store. There, my boss told me to pick out an outfit. Embarrassed and confused, I bowed my head and grabbed the first thing I thought would fit me, a pair of cuffed shorts and a cap-sleeved shirt. My boss paid and we left.

We arrived at his condominium, on some celebrity-named golf course. Without a word to me, he went into the master bedroom. I absent-mindedly dropped my overnight bag in the entryway and then wandered down the hall and put the shopping bag with the new outfit in another bedroom. I sat on the bed, bewildered. I hadn't been seated for more than a minute when I heard his command.

"Come in here. I need a neck rub," my boss yelled down the corridor.

Instinctively, I jumped and walked down the hallway into the master bedroom where he sat on the bed, expressionless, apparently waiting for me to massage his neck. I walked around the huge bed slowly, taking my time while I tried to figure out what to do. I cautiously crawled on top of the bed, kneeled behind my boss's back and placed my quivering hands above his hunched-over shoulders.

And then I froze. I couldn't touch him. The thought of it made me ill.

"I can't do this—why did you take me here?" I mumbled.

I was truly bewildered. I had never shown any personal interest in this man. I had been attentive and accommodating during the long trial but I was just doing a good job, so I thought. It was not until that moment that I fully realized this trip was not about an appeal.

My boss's face turned a purple-red. He fumed.

"You know how many women I could've asked to come down here for the weekend?" he yelled.

I had no response. I was still trying to process what was happening.

"Don't play stupid with me," he growled.

Without a word, running as fast as I could, I dashed into the kitchen area where I grabbed the rental car keys off the counter and then snatched my bag from the entryway floor.

Shaking and crying so hard I could barely see, I drove to my high school friend Laurie's parents' home in Alta Loma, near the Ontario, California Airport. I told her the whole sordid story. She was a Mormon girl, just like me and couldn't believe it either. Then, after I calmed down, I booked a flight back to San Francisco.

I cleaned out my desk on a Sunday and left a short resignation note. I couldn't face anyone. Returning to my apartment was depressing.

What was I doing here? I thought.

I wanted to call Frankie and tell him the whole story, but was much too embarrassed. My naïveté had been exposed, and at the expense of my career. I was humiliated and so I never spoke to him about the incident. It seemed that sexual harassment, a cause of action that had not yet been widely recognized in the courts, wasn't limited to the Mormons.

The immediate course of my career had changed, but I was already registered for the California Bar Exam and was going to pass regardless of my employment status at the firm. I threw myself into studying and running. The review course was eight weeks, and I had saved just enough to get through the course and take the exam before I would need to make other plans. The next two months were spent taking the Bay Area Rapid Transit (BART) train into the City for the multi-state review course and then driving to U.C. Berkeley for the California portion of the review.

I left the public transport at Castro Station. It was 1983 and AIDS had yet to become a household word. Twice a week for those eight weeks, I walked the length of Castro, up the hill to the multi-state bar review building. Dozens of good looking young men loitered on Castro Street. Some of them were dressed in leather chaps. Many went shirtless in the balmy summer bay weather. I walked directly in front of them, but I didn't get the response I expected. Instead, heads turned away and dialogue grew louder between the young men, as if to pointedly ignore my presence. This happened on every trip. I was convinced I had lost my sex appeal.

A young man who lived in my apartment complex and I became friendly and he set me straight. We had gone out to dinner a couple of times.

"I think Marla is jealous," he said to me one night.

"What do you mean?" I asked. "I didn't think she had any interest in you."

"She doesn't."

He looked at me, waiting for his comment to sink in.

I thought back to the time when I took bar review study breaks. Marla came over to my apartment and we would watch *The Young and the Restless*. She always seemed to languish. I would sit on my couch and she would lay her pretty head in my lap and I would brush her hair. She had seemed so lost. We developed an emotional bond my real sister and I never had.

"Marla is a lesbian," he said.

Once I understood what he meant, I thought about the men on Castro Street. Suddenly it all made sense: San Francisco—homosexuals, 'gay,' as I realized they had come to be known.

"What about Castro Street?" I asked, light bulb finally switched on.

"What about it? It's a place for gay pickups," he said casually.

Social savviness—I had none. Maturity wise, I seemed to be years behind my biological age. Just one of the prices for growing up a Mormon girl, I supposed.

My experiences in San Francisco made me question life in the outside world. Maybe Utah wasn't so bad after all. I wished I'd learned how to needlepoint from Grandma Burningham about then. Something, anything to take my mind off the unfamiliar, threatening world of reality and back to those feelings of security and comfort, when I was a child living safely in Bountiful, Utah.

***

There must have been almost a thousand wanna-be lawyers sitting for the July, 1983, California Bar at the San Francisco Civic Center. I'd taken BART into the City and prepared with sharp pencils, my calculator and some raw almonds for energy. I sat quietly as the proctor passed out the first day's test booklets. At the signal, we all ripped open our packets and laid the questions and blue books out in our little testing spaces.

Nobody said a word. Everyone here was at least as intelligent as the average person and most, much smarter, if not more ambitious.

I had just completed three of the six essay questions, when suddenly a sharp pain in my left side interrupted my concentration. At first I thought this was nothing more than bowel cramps, but it felt different. It couldn't be appendicitis—wrong side. I breathed deeply, willing the pain to disappear. Instead, the pain came again, sharper and more piercing. I looked around. Everyone had their heads down, writing as fast as possible. I stood up and walked toward one of the several individuals who were monitoring the test.

"Can you direct me to the ladies restroom?" I asked hurriedly.

"Sure." The proctor pointed the way.

I walked fast, at almost a run.

When I was safely and anonymously secured in the toilet stall, I let out a wail. This thing, whatever it was, was no joke.

Could it be stress? I wondered. I sat waiting for my body to function and get rid of the menacing pain—but nothing happened, nothing, no blood, no waste, nothing. After about five minutes I decided I couldn't spare anymore time away from the exam. The pain had dulled, so I washed my hands and left the restroom. Head bowed, I walked quickly back to my test spot. Somehow I finished the essays.

When I returned to my apartment after that first day, the friend who had clued me in on Marla's sexual preference came over and we talked while I lay on my back amidst the dozens of legal pads filled with notes, bar review books, and empty cans of *Diet Coke*. Finally, he convinced me to go to the hospital.

The E.R. doctor palpated my abdomen and told me that it must be stress, nothing more. Low grade pain continued after the first day and through the next two days of the examination.

After I had completed the bar exam, I packed my car and drove home to Bountiful where I took a job with the Salt Lake County Attorney's Office. After weeks of continued and increased incidents of abdominal pain, my mother put me in the hospital. This time I didn't fight her.

Mom was right, there was something very wrong. A gynecologist diagnosed my problem as severe endometriosis. He told me immediate surgery was the only thing that could relieve those stabbing pains, which had recurred several times since the bar exam. I consented to exploratory, diagnostic surgery. I also consented to whatever procedure the doctor deemed necessary once he had opened my abdominal cavity, a clause very common in surgical consent forms, never anticipating that a complete hysterectomy would ever be considered.

Waking from the anesthesia, I focused in on my gynecologist, looking kindly down at me.

"You have the worst case of endometriosis I've ever seen," he said, shaking his head.

"Because you're so young, I didn't perform a hysterectomy. But the endometrium had grown outside your uterus. I removed your left and most of your right ovary. You may never be able to have children, but there is still a possibility if you have them soon."

I had never wanted kids until I was told that I might not be able to have any.

"How much is left of my right ovary?" I asked.

"Well. I can't really say—only that I had to scrape a lot of endometrial growth off. The pain you felt during the exam was a cyst rupturing. The left ovary was totally destroyed."

Part of *one ovary* I thought, trying to picture just how that would look. It didn't sound like much from which to produce any baby-making eggs.

***

While recovering and waiting for the California Bar results, I thought seriously about having children. I wasn't married and wasn't even in a relationship. These maternal thoughts, along with my Mormon background, prompted me to attend the Church's Sunday worship service for young, single Mormons.

On a snowy February Sunday in 1984, I made the drive from Mom's place in Bountiful up Victory Road to attend the Salt Lake singles ward. There was certain to be more eligible young men in the city congregation than would attend in suburbia.

Wrapped in my old navy fat coat, I was more confident than when I had been overweight, but was now saddled with a new burden, that of a twenty-nine year old single woman looking for a husband in Mormon, Utah. By Mormon standards, I was way past my expiration date.

There, on that first Sunday, as I looked around at the single young Mormon adults, I spotted Trent, the cute rebel from high school art class. It was him. He looked better than ever, jet black hair, perfect skin and those devilish green eyes. I glanced in his direction.

74

Did he see me? I wondered.

After the service was finished, Trent walked confidently toward me.

"So, Kay Burningham, what brings you here?" He asked with a smirk.

"Hi, Trent."

I was a shy sixteen-year-old girl all over again.

"I just moved back from California where I've been working for awhile," I said, not wanting to be too intimidating, knowing that Trent was not an academic of any sort.

"Really? What do you do?" He asked.

"I went to law school. I think I'm a lawyer, but I'm not sure—I just took the Utah Bar and my California results came in an envelope last December, but I'm afraid to open them."

Trent studied me for a moment. A definite physical attraction had always been there between us, at least on my part. He cracked silly jokes and we kidded around as if we were still in high school.

***

With the words of my gynecologist in mind, I agreed to marry Trent just six weeks after we had become reacquainted. Temple marriage was the only choice. After all, according to Mormon doctrine, it was the only way one could guarantee that one's entire family would be together in the afterlife, in the highly touted and coveted Celestial Kingdom, that is, if worthy lives were lived by all.

I passed the Utah Bar in February. I realized that even if I had flunked California, which always has the lowest pass rate of any state in the nation, I could at least work in Utah. So I was surprised when I finally opened the envelope to find out I'd passed the California Bar last July as well. This news required serious consideration and possibly a change in plans.

Trent had spent a few years living on the beach in Malibu and liked it, so we both agreed to return to the West Coast. After a short search, I landed my first job as an associate attorney with an Orange County law firm. Trent, who had an accounting degree, was offered a job with a California computer software company. We leased an apartment in Tustin, just outside Santa Ana.

I was about to jump into a whole new life, become a married woman, and then, God willing, become a mother. As a Mormon woman, I had been taught that marriage and children would be my ultimate fulfillment. God knows that by then I wanted a complete family, a stable family. I wanted one of those 1950s families where mother and children felt safe with a strong, competent, father, a protector and provider. I hoped that my dream would come true.

CHAPTER FOUR: Commitment—Bound by Bizarre Rituals

Now for my proposition; it is more particularly for my sisters, as it is frequently happening that women say they are unhappy. Men will say, 'My wife, though a most excellent woman, has not seen a happy day since I took my second wife,' 'no, not a happy day for a year,' says one; and another has not seen a happy day for five years. It is said that women are tied down and abused: that they are misused and have not the liberty they ought to have; that many of them are wading through a perfect flood of tears... "I wish my own women to understand that what I am going to say is for them as well as others, and I want those who are here to tell their sisters, yes, all the women of this community...I am going to give you from this time to the 6th day of October next, for reflection, that you may determine whether you wish to stay with your husbands or not, and then I am going to set every woman at liberty and say to them, Now go your way, my women with the rest, go your way. And my wives have got to do one of two things; either round up their shoulders to endure the afflictions of this world, and live their religion, or they may leave, for I will not have them about me. I will go into heaven alone, rather than have scratching and fighting around me. I will set all at liberty. 'What, first wife too?' yes, i will liberate you all.

I know what my women will say; they will say, 'You can have as many women as you please, Brigham.' But I want to go somewhere and do something to get rid of the whiners; I do not want them to receive a part of the truth and spurn the rest out of doors. I wish my women, and brother Kimball's and brother Grant's to leave, and every woman in this Territory, or else say in their hearts that they will embrace the Gospel —the whole of it. Tell the Gentiles that I will free every woman in this Territory at our next Conference. 'What, the first wife too?' Yes, there shall not be one held in bondage, all shall be set free. And then let the father be the head of the family, the master of his own household; and let him treat them as an angel would treat them; and let the wives and the children say amen to what he says, and be subject to his dictates, instead of their dictating the man, instead of their trying to govern him.

...say to your wives, 'Take all that I have and be set at liberty; but if you stay with me you shall comply with the law of God, and that too without any murmuring and whining. You must fulfil the law of God in every respect, and round up your shoulders to walk up to the mark without any grunting."..." But the first wife will say, 'It is hard, for I have lived with my husband twenty years, or thirty, and have raised a family of children for him, and it is a great trial to me for him to have more women;' then I say it is time that you gave him up to other women who will bear children. If my wife had borne me all the children that she ever would bare, the celestial law would teach me to take young women that would have children...

This is the reason why the doctrine of plurality of wives was revealed, that the noble spirits which are waiting for tabernacles might be brought forth... "Sisters, i am not joking, I do not throw out my proposition to banter your feelings, to see whether you will leave your husbands, all or any of you. But i know that there is no cessation to the everlasting whining of many of the women in this territory; I am satisfied that this is the case. And if the women will turn from the commandments of God and continue to despise the order of heaven, I will pray that the curse of the Almighty may be close to their heals, and that it may be following them all the day long.... there is a curse upon the woman that is not upon the man, namely, that 'her whole affections shall be towards her husband,' and what is the next? 'He shall rule over you.'

But how is it now? Your desire is to your husband, but you strive to rule over him, whereas the man should rule over you... "Prepare yourselves for two weeks from to morrow; and I will tell you now, that if you will tarry with your husbands, after i have set you free, you must bow down to it, and submit yourselves to the celestial law. You may go where you please, after two weeks from to-morrow; but, remember, that i will not hear any more of this whining.*[17] –Brigham Young to his polygamous wives, 1856.

When I announced that Trent and I planned to be married in April, just two months after we had become reacquainted, my parents were skeptical, but knew they couldn't change my mind. Nobody really tried to change our opinion to go ahead with the wedding, no one except Trent's father, Dr. Jones.

Trent was living in his adopted father's sprawling condominium in an upscale section of Salt Lake's East Bench. By this time, Dr. Jones had given up delivering babies and was semi-retired. His office was on the top and Trent lived in the lower level with a refrigerator, full set of weights, television and all the comforts of the nice home he had grown up in. We met with him on a day in March.

Dr. Jones seemed old even then; he must have been in his late sixties. Trent told me that his abusive adopted mother, pressured from the demands of her children, both natural and adopted, and with an absentee obstetrician as a husband, had suffered from a nervous breakdown years earlier, and so Trent's adopted parents divorced. Dr. Jones remarried a woman who had several children of her own. While the second Mrs. Dr. Jones was effusive and gushing, running up to kiss and hug me at our first meeting, my initial encounter with Dr. Jones was much different. He sat solemnly at his office desk directing Trent and me to sit in front of him like two patients about to be given bad test results. Wearing his physician coat of authority, he spoke directly.

"Why do you want to marry him?" he asked, eyes burrowing a hole in my soul. Before I could even think of an answer to his unexpectedly blunt question, he blurted out another comment.

"He's not good enough for you."

Stunned, I couldn't imagine a father, even an adoptive one, making such a comment, especially in his son's presence. I looked at Trent, certain he had heard the harsh words, but he remained stoic.

"Well, you're wrong about that. We love each other and it will be fine," I protested.

Trent and several other children had been adopted after Dr. Jones already had six children of his own. The arrogance exhibited in Dr. Jones' sequential adoptions pales only slightly in comparison to the stark selfishness of Trent's birth mother. She had given him up despite being married at the time and having an older and then eventually, a younger child. Trent didn't fit into her family planning schedule.

We ignored Dr. Jones' warning and instead went ahead with the plans for our wedding. Trent and I never talked about not getting married in the temple. As young Mormons, neither of us questioned where we would marry. Trent had served a two year mission and Dr. Jones always made his children attend church.

With a wedding date in April, and our temple recommends in hand, I anxiously anticipated taking out my endowment. The process (taking out of one's endowment) was not really clear to me and when questioned about, only led to obfuscation by the older, temple-going Mormons. In the mid-eighties it was still Church policy that single women were allowed to take out their endowments only if they were about to be married or had been called to serve a mission.

Nothing you learn as a young Mormon prepares you for the temple. Thinking that it would be a very spiritual event, I was excited. When I finally went through the endowment ceremony, I did get a feeling of sorts, but not the kind I'd anticipated. Instead, I found the whole experience bizarre. Only later did I discover that the ceremony had been modeled by Joseph Smith after nineteenth century Masonic Temple Rites, and that many first time temple-goers, or patrons as the Church calls them, have similar feelings about the temple's strange rituals.

The Salt Lake Temple seemed beautiful from the outside back then. The landscaping of temple square is always perfect, no matter the season. Over the Christmas holidays tens of thousands of tiny lights are strung on the bare winter trees, making it seem like a magical place.

It was April, 1984 and as usual, tulips, brightly-colored perennials and blossoming hardwood trees covered the temple grounds. I picked out a white wedding dress with long sleeves, and a high neckline, certain to comply with Mormon modesty standards. The day before our wedding I was scheduled to take out my endowment. But before the ceremony I had to purchase the sacred temple garments.

These garments are issued to all temple initiates, and are supposed to be worn continuously and forever. Mormon legends say that some garment wearers even bathe with them on, taking an arm or a leg out one limb at a time so as not to ever be completely uncovered by the holy garments. Other Mormon myths involve fires which burned the victim everywhere but the garment-covered parts of his or her body. Some even claim that no Mormons had been harmed in the 9-11 World Trade Center attacks.

Initially these garments were a shin to wrist, wooly one-piece jumper with openings in the crotch. Perversely, this enabled furtive sexual relations while clothed. Children conceived while their parents were wearing the holy garments were deemed to be 'born under the covenant.' Those I bought, an updated version, were a two-piece polyester outfit, crotch included thank goodness.

But the design was so tawdry, just the thought of wearing the clothing next to my skin made me sweat. I pulled the garments on my naked body and immediately felt suffocated, like Satan incarnate had wrapped himself around me.[18] I had always had a bit of claustrophobia, the type where you don't want too many other people in the elevator, or rarely feel like going to packed spectator sports stadiums. But this was a more intimate, personal, invasion of my space. I clenched my teeth and told myself I would get used to them.

The time to go through the endowment ceremony had arrived. I was dressed in my garments and then covered with a long white temple gown, white slippers on my feet. My wedding dress was for the separate wedding or sealing ceremony to be held the next day.

Inside the temple, the patrons assembled. The men sat on one side of the spacious room and the women on the other. I looked over at my soon-to-be husband and Dr. Jones, dressed identically with all the other men in what looked like white baker hats, and green leaf-shaped satin aprons (the women wore the same type aprons) sitting straight and serious, listening to the live theatre depicting Lucifer tempting Eve.

Then I looked at my sister. Our eyes met and we both had to stifle a laugh. Me, from the absurdity of it all; my sister, since she had first gone through the temple almost a decade earlier, most probably from the fact that she and I had a history of laughing at inopportune moments, not consciously, but due to some genetic predisposition, a weakness neither one of us could control.

"Raise your hand to the square," the ceremony officiator commanded

"Pay-Lay-Ale, Pay-Lay-Ale." [19]

I repeated the absurdities and obeyed the commands, which included making "the sure sign of the nail," all the time wondering what these words had to do with anything.

As I looked around, I noticed that the chanting and commands didn't seem to bother anyone else. All the patrons' eyes focused straight ahead.

The temple ceremony officiator continued:

"We will begin by making the sign of the first token of the Aaronic Priesthood; the sign is made by raising the right hand to the square, the palm forward, the fingers close together, and the thumb extended. This is the sign."

The officiator demonstrated what the patrons were to mimic.

"The execution of the penalty is represented by placing the right thumb under the left ear, drawing the thumb quickly across the throat to the right ear, and dropping the hand to the side."

These actions, repeated several times in different contexts, were parroted pantomimes of slitting our throats, and self-disembowelment. In effect, the temple patrons promised to endure a grisly death if any of us were to reveal the secret temple ceremony to outsiders.

The Church claims the temple ceremony has never changed. A 2001 Church magazine quoted Joseph Smith who taught: 'Ordinances instituted in the heavens before the foundation of the world, in the priesthood, for the salvation of men, *are not to be altered or changed.*'[20]

Earlier, a more equivocal statement had been issued: "As temple work progresses, some members wonder if the ordinances can be changed or adjusted. These ordinances have been provided by revelation, and are in the hands of the First Presidency. Thus, the temple is protected from tampering."[21]

However, the undisputed historical record of the temple ceremony, since its introduction to the Church by Joseph Smith in 1842 to the present time, reveals that there have been several modifications to the wording and forced pantomimes over the decades. For example, in 1984, the year Trent and I married, women were commanded to obey the law of their husbands. I remember it well.

"We will put the sisters under covenant to obey the law of their husbands."

I stood with the other female patrons as instructed.

"Each of you bring your right arm to the square. You and each of you solemnly covenant and promise before God, angels, and these witnesses at this altar that you will each observe and keep the law of your husbands, and abide by his counsel in righteousness. Each of you bow your head and say 'Yes.'"

All the women responded affirmatively.

"That will do," the officiator said.

We all sat back down in our seats.[22]

In the nineteenth century, the language accompanying the endowment ceremony pantomimes was more gruesome. [23]

***

I lay in bed the night after receiving my endowment, the eve of my wedding day, trying to get comfortable in my new skin. The polyester was hot and stuck to me. I took a deep breath and tried to think of the good things, of starting a new life, and having someone I cared for at my side. But deep down, I felt that something was terribly wrong. Waking periodically to look at my alarm clock, and then trying to dismiss the negative thoughts, sleep was impossible.

Morning finally arrived. My anxiety and second thoughts remained, but by then I had convinced myself they were normal pre-wedding jitters. The problem was that the temple endowment ceremony had thrown one more wrench into my view of Mormonism. Suddenly, I wasn't sure about any of my feelings, about the Church, about Trent—nothing.

When I think now of the way young adults are set up to keep from finding out Mormonism's true requirements and cultish rituals until they have committed to something grand—usually young women to their weddings, and young men, a mission—I am infuriated. Mormonism and indeed any religion, intrudes and assures its presence at all important life events: births, marriages, deaths. When religion is tied so directly to these heralded milestones, it's high-level of importance is ingrained into the human psyche.

Certainly with either a wedding or a mission at stake, complete with announcements to friends and family and with reputations on the line, a young Mormon is reluctant to question the validity of the endowment ceremony, a conveniently timed prerequisite to the big event. Feelings of unworthiness will flood the young adult when he or she needs it least. To question one's birth religion at such an inopportune time would be unthinkable. Psychologically, it is much easier to think that it is oneself who needs to change, to become more spiritual, more worthy, to fit in and accept what had always been described to young LDS children and adolescents as the 'wonderful blessings of the temple.'

***

I woke up early and dressed in my wedding gown. It looked nice but I didn't feel special—not especially pretty, nor happy or any of the things a new bride should feel on her wedding day.

The doorbell rang. I opened the door to see my father, still dressed in his golf shirt and slacks. I could see his tuxedo on a hanger inside the cab of his truck. Dad stood at the threshold of the door, tentative. I had never known him to be tentative before.

"Come in, Dad," I said.

I took his hand and led him to the couch where we sat, side by side. Again, something I had never done before. I turned to face him, but before I could speak, he choked out the words—

"I just wish I could walk my little girl down the aisle..."

I didn't know what to say to him.

Mom's kitchen wall clock ticked every time the second hand moved. It reminded me that it was time to leave for the temple again.

"I know, Dad."

My eyes filled with tears. On what should have been the happiest day of my life, I couldn't have my wonderful father by my side. He wasn't considered temple worthy. He didn't attend Church meetings, it had been ages since he had paid tithing and he drank an occasional beer while golfing. Yet he was the kindest, most honest man I knew.

"I'll see you after—at Jeen's," I said, faking cheerfulness.

"All right, Muffin."

He stood, not quite resolved and gave me one of those big bear hugs. I tried hard not to cry as Dad opened the screen door to leave.

I wanted to run to him—to ask him why he didn't go to Church, if he thought I was right to marry Trent, and lots of other questions—but I didn't do any of those things and I don't know why.

***

Kneeling at the white sateen-covered altar in the temple sealing room, I tried to screen out the strange feelings I had and focus on Trent, who was across from me dressed in white. So handsome, today he looked like an angel. Although I had seen glints of devilishness from those green eyes as well, I always told myself it was playfulness, nothing more. Even though I certainly didn't know him well, in the two short months since we had become reacquainted, I thought he would be a good father. The fact that we had gone to high school together also gave me a nostalgic feeling, a connection with my past which I had longed for over the tumultuous years in my twenties.

Chapter 4: Commitment—Bound by Bizarre Rituals

On the walls of either side of the altar were the eternity mirrors. Our reflections went on for what looked like forever in the mirrors reflecting mirrors. I looked around the room at my sister, Jill, Dr. Jones, Trent's stepmother and many members of Trent's immediate adopted family. But neither of my parents was able to attend.

The officiator, a man I had never met, and who looked like all the other elderly Mormon males I had seen in my brief temple experience, stood at one end of the altar and spoke.

This is it, I thought.

The officiator asked Trent,

...do you take Sister Burningham and receive her unto yourself to be your lawful wedded wife for time and all eternity, with a covenant and promise that you will observe and keep all the laws, rites and ordinances pertaining to this Holy Order of Matrimony, the New and Everlasting Covenant, and this you do in the presence of God, angels and these witnesses of your own free will and choice?

"Yes," Trent said.

The officiator then looked towards me.

"...do you take Brother Jones by the right hand and give yourself to him?"

"Yes."

By virtue of the Holy Priesthood and the authority vested in me, I pronounce you legally and lawfully husband and wife for time and all eternity, and I seal upon you the blessings of the holy resurrection with power to come forth in the morning of the first resurrection clothed in glory, immortality and eternal lives, and I seal upon you the blessings of kingdoms, thrones, principalities, powers, dominions and exaltations, with all the blessings of Abraham, Isaac and Jacob and say unto you: be fruitful and multiply and replenish the earth that you may have joy and rejoicing in the day of our Lord Jesus Christ. All these blessings, together with all the blessings appertaining unto the New and Everlasting Covenant, I seal upon you by virtue of the Holy Priesthood, through your faithfulness, in the name of the Father, and of the Son, and of the Holy Ghost, Amen.

That was it. There were no promises to love each other or stick by each other through good and bad, or any of the vows I had expected. The entire ceremony was disappointing.

That afternoon our reception was held at Aunt Jeen's. She and her husband had graciously volunteered their beautiful home on the East Bench of the Bountiful Wasatch foothills for the occasion. All we had to do was show up. We formed a greeting line, Trent and I, his parents, Trent's sisters and mine. Friends from high school and from BYU came through the line.

We had a cake and there were gifts. The one thing missing was dancing. You always see dancing at weddings in the movies. But dancing wasn't customary then for Mormon wedding receptions, though it isn't forbidden, and some surely do have dancing; for the most part, I think that the occasion of a Mormon wedding is so solemn that those at the reception rarely think to dance. Ironically, nineteenth century Mormons danced a lot. The pioneers danced Saturday nights on the way to Salt Lake and once settled in the valley with Brigham Young.

It didn't matter, because in my case, I don't know that I was happy enough to dance. The experience in the Mormon Temple and the solemn and strange promises I had made had shaken me to the core. Suddenly, the religion of my childhood, to which I had promised lifelong allegiance, had become a foreign system. This occupied my thoughts to the exclusion of everything else, even being with Trent for the first time, and that would happen soon because our honeymoon would start after the reception.

***

"So we're going to stay tonight at the Little America Hotel," Trent announced after all the guests had left and we were driving away in his car.

It was early evening when we pulled up to the Little America, a landmark hotel and one of the best in Salt Lake back then. We had changed into traveling clothes. We hoisted our bags from the trunk and began the walk to our hotel room which was on the bottom floor, with a garden view.

There was serious remodeling going on just a few yards away. As soon as Trent had parked the car, we heard construction sounds. It was after five o'clock, not yet dark. As we got closer to our room, the vague noise became identifiable. I looked over my shoulder and saw a man working with a jackhammer just a few yards from the door of our room.

"Oh great," I complained, looking desperately at Trent for a solution.

But Trent only looked back at me, with the same stoic face he displayed when Dr. Jones had pronounced our marriage doomed. I wanted him to respond with indignation, at least ask the worker how much longer he would be.

Trent shrugged.

I swallowed the feeling of disappointment in my throat, but didn't say anything else. I couldn't believe my husband was not on his way to the office to demand a better room. This was our honeymoon after all. Hanging my head, I avoided any eye contact with Trent.

As soon as we had our bags in the room, Trent locked the door and set up our suitcases. When all of our things were organized, we both sat on the foot of the bed, silent for a long time.

In order to qualify for temple marriage, our pre-marital relationship had been limited to a few make-out sessions. That evening, the first time we became intimate, was very awkward. With the sound of the jackhammer in the background, we performed the marital union ceremony. Much like the temple ceremony, it was methodical and rote, devoid of emotion. Immediately afterward, Trent dressed in his garments and then pajamas; I did the same.

Devastated, I had expected romantic whisperings and tender lovemaking, but our intimacy was nothing close to my expectations. Trent turned on the television. He found a sports channel, sat on the bed and watched a basketball game while I pulled out my scriptures.

I fought back the tears. If he could be emotionless, then so could I. I bit my lower lip and read silently from Matthew.

"Be ye therefore perfect even as your father in heaven is perfect."

I tried to remain optimistic.

Look at the bright side, I told myself. We were on our way to Mexico, we both spoke Spanish and it was sure to be an adventure. After the honeymoon I would be starting a new job with an Orange County law firm.

Maybe it would get better in time.

Finally it was dark. I wished Trent would hold me, but after the game he only said good night, turned his back to me and instantly fell asleep.

I lay in that hotel room, black with the heavy curtains drawn, crying silently, afraid of what would happen if Trent heard me. I tossed and turned, but luckily didn't wake my husband. I felt trapped in an absurd religion and in a marriage with someone I barely knew.

Later that night, drenched in sweat, I ran to the bathroom and stared at myself; I was sopping wet with white polyester stuck to my skin. My body had rebelled. Furiously, I ripped off the garments, and for the first time noticed that the markings over each breast were in the shape of a compass and a square, more signs appropriated from the Masons.

I peeled the now translucent cloth from my body. Luckily, I found a pair of regular panties and a cotton T-shirt stuffed in the pocket-part of my suitcase from when I worked in San Francisco.

The next morning I woke up early and dressed in my street clothes, hoping to avoid Trent's detection that I wasn't wearing the garments. He had been up awhile and was already dressed. We ate a quick breakfast in the dining room. Trent didn't say a word as we sped out of town and began the long drive to Enseñada.

Enseñada, Baja California—in 1984 our hotel was a true bargain. The beaches were beautiful but the food was awful. I got sick on some Mexican cheese from an omelet and we left within days. Trent and I returned from our Mexican honeymoon to an apartment we had rented in Tustin, near my office in Santa Ana. I was excited to begin my new career.

After a few weeks on the job, I received my first paycheck. Ecstatic at finally making some real money after years of school, I showed my earnings to my husband. Up until that point, although he never showed much emotion, Trent had never been anything but kind to me.

Trent looked carefully at my paycheck, then pulled out the checkbook to our joint account and wrote a check for ten percent of the gross amount.

"What's this?" I asked, looking at the check he had written to the 'Church of LDS.'

"Tithing," he said flatly. Again, with the stoicism.

"You can't write tithing on my paycheck."

We hadn't ever discussed how we would handle tithing.

"Why not? We promised to pay it."

He seemed to revel in his pronouncement.

"Yes, but it's my money; I'll decide what to do with it."

"You are not living up to your commitments," Trent warned.

I looked at him and tried to really see what was in there, behind those green eyes; I couldn't see past the veneer.

"I don't even know if I believe in this Church. The whole temple thing, it's so strange—"

"What do you mean you don't believe in the Church?"

He was shouting now.

"There are lots of people more intelligent than you and they don't question the Church!"

Oh boy, how could I argue with that?

I grabbed the check he had written. I had no problem depositing my paycheck into our joint account, but when Trent tried to tell me how to handle the tithing on what I'd earned, I became angry.

Defiantly, I ripped up the tithing check and threw it in the air. The little pieces of paper drifted like big snowflakes to the kitchen floor.

No longer stoic, Trent glared at me and cursed, using words I hadn't heard since basic training, and certainly never before from him. I ran from the apartment kitchen into our bedroom and locked the door. Almost immediately Trent was on the other side, swearing loudly and pounding. Luckily, the lock held until he calmed down.

***

As I settled into my work, things between Trent and me only became worse. The weeks passed and our relationship remained rocky. Our marriage was not a stable one; the communication was poor.

Naively and desperately I thought having a child might help. And contrary to the concerns of my gynecologist, I easily became pregnant. The pregnancy was going well; I was through with the first trimester morning sickness and was feeling pretty good. But when I was about six months pregnant, Trent and I had a terrible fight. I was sitting on our bed, reading from a book I had recently purchased, a compilation of writings by one of my favorite philosophers, Ralph Waldo Emerson. His essay on *Self-Reliance* had been one of my favorites and kept me inspired after my parents' divorce and through the awkward, prepubescent phase of junior high.

"Trent," I said, "Listen to this..."

I was excited to share part of Emerson's thoughts with him. I started to read:

"Whoso would be a man must be a nonconformist. He who would gather immortal palms must not be hindered by the name of goodness, but must explore if it be goodness."[24]

89

"What are you doing?" he asked.

"What do you mean?"

I had no idea what he meant with that question, 'what are you doing?' It seemed obvious to me: I was trying to share something I loved with him.

"Showing off again, miss smarty pants?" he said in a mimicking tone. Trent turned and left the room in disgust.

Shocked at his unexpected reaction, I stifled the tears and went on silently with my reading, thinking back to the times Mike and I had talked late into the morning hours about ethics, religion and philosophy. I had to face the fact that Trent just wasn't interested in these types of conversations. He was put off by my attempt to share anything philosophical with him.

His presence at the door a few seconds later startled me.

"You f***ing bitch!" he yelled, hurling a heavy cooking pot in my direction.

Instinctively, I leaned to one side, barely dodging the pot which would have hit me directly in the abdomen. It grazed my hip and clanked to the ground near the bedpost.

Stunned, I slowly realized just how close Trent had come to hurting our unborn child. This incident was different from his previous outbursts. Before I was disappointed by Trent's behavior; now I was extremely frightened for my safety and that of my child.

I didn't know where to turn. After that, the fights were frequent and bad. Though Trent lifted weights and so had about fifty pounds of pure muscle on me, that fact didn't keep me quiet. During our arguments I tried to reason with him, and that would only make him angrier.

How foolish to eternally commit to a man I had known only superficially. But that is what can happen when chastity and obedience are revered to the exclusion of honesty and authenticity. Combine this with a strong desire and urging from the Brethren to marry, and it's the quintessential recipe for disaster.

Mormon leaders tell young people that a marriage will work between any man and woman as long as they both obey the principles of the gospel. *Not true, Mormon gerontocracy.* Not true because young men and women, usually boys and girls emotionally, if not physically, come to marriage with wounded pasts, false preconceptions and unrealistic expectations.

Chapter 4: Commitment—Bound by Bizarre Rituals

Not even a Saint should have to endure physical abuse. And a young man who never had a mother's love is one who is most likely to inflict abuse on his wife. Trent was the victim of dual horrors. Tragically, it seemed that he hadn't been loved by either his adopted or biological mother, or arguably his adopted father—not the way parents should love their children. Over the course of our short marriage, it was clear that Trent's latent misogyny was focused on me.

In Mormondom, families are forever. This promise is binding only if the couple is married in the temple for time and all eternity and becomes quite complicated if there is divorce or death and remarriage. I didn't think I could spend forever with Trent, but I was glad I would soon give birth to our son.

Chris was two weeks overdue. I was in labor for almost three days with a Pitocin drip before he finally decided to come into the world. I perceived the birth as an out-of-body experience. I remember looking down, with my back stuck to the ceiling, toward an O.R. table. Lots of technicians and at least one M.D. in blue surgical garb walked quickly and worked diligently, hovering around some poor woman. The obstetric staff finally pulled the tiny newborn free and at that moment I realized the woman I had been watching was me.

My consciousness merged with my body and reality hit me like lightning. The baby had long blonde hair and an inability to focus both his blue eyes straight ahead; he was our little hippie, born in 1985 but right out of the seventies. He was beautiful. After the nurse cleaned him up, Trent gently took our son and holding him so carefully, as if he were the most precious thing in the world, walked over to me and gently laid him in my arms. That was the beginning of an improved stage in our relationship. Trent and I got along quite well when Chris was an infant. I'm sure it was because he viewed me as fulfilling my God-given role as a woman.

Brigham Young and subsequent LDS leaders have proclaimed that spirit children are waiting in heaven, in their pre-mortal existence, for their turn to be born. In a popular Mormon musical from the seventies, these pre-mortal spirits ride a carousel waiting for their turn to dismount and come to Earth. Like the biblical blessings given to the Old Testament prophet Abraham, Mormon leaders have preached that the greater a man's progeny, the more blessed he is—hence, the reason for the Church-sanctioned and practiced polygamy. The principle implies that the more children a couple are able to raise in their loving Mormon families, the

91

more valiant and more deserving of eternal blessings they are. A look at most of the one hundred and fifteen male leaders of the current Mormon Church reveals that they average four to five children each. Dr. Jones, with six children of his own and several more adopted ones, was certainly paving his way to the Celestial Kingdom by providing a heavenly home for these numerous spirits.

*****

The peace didn't last.

I had always loved cats, and so did Trent, at least that's what he said. I thought it would be good for Chris to have a pet, so we bought a cat, a Persian tabby with copper eyes and beautiful gray striped fur. We named him Rambo because he was such a rambunctious kitten. The next week we saw the trailer for the movie *Rambo: First Blood Part II,* starring Sylvester Stallone. After we saw the film, our kitten's name made us both laugh whenever we called him.

Rambo was great and loved by the whole family, especially Chris. We had moved when I received an offer from a downtown San Diego law firm and had just purchased our first home in San Diego County, a townhouse located on the edge of the canyon in Poway. The new neighbor noticed our toddler and the kitten and warned us against the canyon coyotes.

"Keep them inside," she said. "They especially love to eat cats."

Trent heard the warning as well as I did.

One night I had to stay late to prepare for a series of depositions in a complicated case. I left work past nine o' clock and arrived home long after dark. Chris was in bed. After checking on him, seeing that he was sleeping sweetly in his crib, I asked about the cat.

"Where's Rambo?"

"I don't know," Trent answered, annoyed.

I could see that he was upset with me for working so late.

"Sorry I'm so late, but these depos—"

"Yea, yea, I know, big lawyer stuff," he scowled at me.

I searched the house—no Rambo.

"Maybe Chris let him out," Trent said shrugging.

Translation: I don't give a damn about that cat.

Chris could barely walk and at his age, would never have been able to open the heavy sliding glass door to the patio outside. I looked at Trent helplessly, but he only scowled at me.

I cursed under my breath, changed into my running shoes, grabbed a flashlight and ran down into the canyon. Breathing in the ragweed dander, I walked up and down the prickly slopes, calling out our beloved pet's name. I began my search before midnight and by three in the morning, I had given up. Sadly, I went to bed, aware of an early morning appointment.

I couldn't sleep. A little more than a half hour after retiring, I heard the most horrible sounds—wailing, screaming and growling sounds of coyotes—but no cat sounds. The raucous noise lasted less than a couple of minutes, but I knew what had happened. Rambo had met a horrible death, all because my husband was so furious at me for my late hours at the office that he couldn't bother with our pet.

Some psychologists say that testosterone gives men two urges: to fuck or to kill. Trent wanted to kill me, but he was doing it slowly, through indifference, disrespect and ultimately, violence. Next morning at breakfast I made my feelings known to him.

"So Rambo is gone—dead and you blamed it on Chris—what really happened?" I hung my head over my breakfast and focused on my cereal. I knew it was coming. I knew what his reaction would be; only I needed an explanation for his indifference to the whole incident.

In just seconds Trent was standing right next to me. I could see his blue-jean covered leg in my peripheral vision to the left, I sensed his body tensing. Finally I looked up, afraid of what I would see.

"Why don't you just take these and end it right here?" he shouted, handing me a pair of orange-handled scissors, blades pointed toward him.

"What are you talking about?" I asked, again in disbelief.

Trent seemed to go from a discussion in which I asked him a question he couldn't answer directly to physical violence. There was no reasoning with him. His whole body tensed up. I'd sensed this change in him too many times.

Chris was already with his caretaker. I took my dishes to the sink, and then went upstairs to comb my hair. Trent followed. The stomping of his footsteps on the townhouse stairway terrified me. I kept combing, furiously, getting ready to leave for work.

"You f***ing bitch," he yelled.

Trent stood at the doorway between our bedroom and the master bath. Without hesitating he came right at me. He grabbed me by the shoulders and threw me against the far wall. I crumpled to the floor. He grabbed me again, this time by my forearms and stood me up, then, pulling my earlobe, he dragged me over to the mirrored closet doors in our bedroom and slammed me into the glass.

"You have to open your mouth and provoke me again?" He screamed in my ear.

I recalled the words from *Carousel*, "It's possible for someone to hit you, hit you hard and not hurt you at all."

It wasn't true.

Bewildered, I slumped to the floor again, a sobbing mess. This was not going to change—I knew it. Trent's problems with women were deep-rooted and I only brought out the worst in him. He wanted a wife who would submit to him unquestionably. I couldn't do it. Trent and I separated and I filed for divorce. I had to leave him, but the process was gut-wrenching nevertheless.

A few months later, on a night when the doors in the townhouse were locked, Trent appeared. I was about to close the vertical patio door blinds and take Chris up to his bedroom, when I saw him through the glass sliding doors. He was standing with his fists clenched by his sides, arms tense and face dark.

Trent forced the door open. Screaming, I pushed at him, trying to keep him out of the house. Chris had just finished putting his toys in his toy box which we kept under the open staircase in the living area. I was worried for him and hoped he had already gone upstairs and didn't see what was happening. Still struggling, Trent and I yelled at each other. And then, I heard another voice.

"Don't hurt my mom or I'll shoot you!" the small voice shouted from behind me.

I turned around to see our two-year-old son holding his toy gun, pointed at his dad. The diversion was enough to distract Trent for a moment. I quickly shut and then locked the glass door and ran to hold my little boy. Chris and I both cried, and although from my position under the staircase I couldn't see out into the night onto the patio, so, I'm sure, did Trent.

CHAPTER FIVE: Sexual Awakening and Self Doubt

"Grant me some wild expressions, Heavens, or I shall burst."—
George Farquhar

We stipulated to the terms of the divorce. With few assets, just the townhouse really, it was easy paperwork although very difficult emotionally. I felt guilty for breaking my temple vows, but the thought of living with Trent's misdirected anger for time and all eternity was too much.

Separated from Trent, with my two-year-old son, I was not looking for a new relationship when Wade swaggered into an ordinary witness deposition. My heart stopped. He was six feet plus of pure muscle, a triathlete and the hired gun of trial lawyers.

"This seat taken?" he asked with a half smile, half smirk. He pulled up the chair next to me.

Since neither of us represented key parties in the litigation, our questioning finished quickly. After the short deposition, I grabbed my legal pad, smiled cordially, and started walking to my car, all the while my heart pounding.

"Kay?" Wade's voice stopped me.

"Are you single?" he asked.

Trent and I had been legally separated for months. Though the divorce was yet to be final; it was just a matter of waiting out the required time period.

"Separated," I stuttered, surprised by his directness.

"Can I have your number?" He asked, just like that.

Wade and I started an intense relationship. He loved to dance almost as much as I did, which back then, at least in my experience, was something rare for an athletic guy. We danced at the Mission Bay Hilton, where Dad and I had often stayed. We ate at fine restaurants and took romantic three day weekends. It was a fairy tale.

Wade told me I was beautiful and sexy. Unlike the Mormon men with whom I had been involved, he was not afraid of me or his sexuality, or of committing some irrevocable sin. He was, after all, Catholic. Initially, I was surprised when he told me he regularly attended church, but weekly confession suited his lifestyle. Truthfully, he was a more genuine person than any Mormon man I had known.

Our love affair began where my high school boyfriend and I left off. After a few weeks I was through with the high school stuff and let Wade get to the serious love-making. My relationship with Wade was my sexual awakening and my passion for him was unquenchable. We made love often and furiously as if to relieve the built up stressors of our highly competitive careers.

    ***

Wade had souvenirs from every triathlon and marathon he had raced over the years. He dismissed the accomplishments as if they were nothing. But when he found out I was interested, I became his cheerleader for several triathlons.

Leaving on a Thursday evening became *de rigueur.* At the airport, Wade would fold up his lightweight bicycle for the bike part of the triathlon and have it checked as his only luggage. Everything else he needed was in his carry-on. We would arrive late Thursday night, crash and spend the next day touring the locale. He would check out the route and we would shop and have a good time.

The morning of the race, he was up before 5:00 a.m. I got up to have coffee with him. Wade was okay with cowboy coffee, ground beans in boiled water. Once I started to drink it each morning, I had to have Kona, percolated, with half and half.

We had driven to San Felipe, at that time a remote fishing village on the east coast of Baja California. Instead of searching Mexico for something fit to eat so early in the morning, Wade popped open the trunk of the car and *sans* fork, wolfed down the pasta with clam sauce from Stefanos, the restaurant where we had eaten the night before.

On those triathlon trips, I waved goodbye at the starter's gun, after Wade had inked his race number on his arms and swim cap and wherever else they made you write them. His energy was incredible. After the athletes took off, I'd go back to the hotel and read or sleep, setting my alarm for a time when I expected the first of them to finish. Waiting expectantly, I'd see him biking down the end of the route and speeding over the finish line. Cheered, he showered, we'd eat and then we'd dance and make love. We returned to San Diego refreshed for another intense work week.

    ***

96

This was the first time I had been in Wade's Pacific Beach condominium. We sat on the ocean front deck at sunset.

"Hey baby, I've got a trial in the morning, wanna listen to my opening?"

"Sure," I said.

It was a perfect San Diego night. We had walked along the beach. I went into the water up to my knees and Wade went for a short swim.

We had returned to his condo to change and warm up. Wade cast off his swim shorts. I towel-dried in the air, while watching my naked lover rehearse his opening statement to me, as the sole, mock juror.

My concentration on his words began to drift.

"No eyes below the neck," he warned with a laugh.

I tried to keep focus on his words, his face, and the facts of the case. He was good and never needed a note, but then my eyes would drift, down his muscled shoulders, toward his sculpted abdominals. His silhouette showcased a perfectly toned athlete's form, ending incongruously with twisted toes, some without nails, hammered by running too many miles.

"Hey, baby!"

He caught me.

"Sorry," I said.

But I wasn't sorry.

We both laughed, knowing it was an impossible task, the chemistry was too strong. He took me inside and we lay by the smoldering log-burning fire. The bad Catholic boy and the good Mormon girl, it was an improbable and ultimately, unworkable love affair.

***

Wade had invited me and Chris to his place for dinner. His only child, Chloe, a high school junior, would be there. I was nervous. Wade was cooking salmon. Long before the media pumped it as the anti-aging protein, he made annual trips to Alaska to catch the wild fish.

We had a makeshift highchair for Chris. Chloe sat at one end of the table and Wade at the other. I was proud of Chris' table manners—no spills, no fussing—good boy.

"So Kay, how is work at the firm?" Chloe asked politely.

"Great, you know billable hours…"

"How are your classes this year?" I asked back.

"A challenge, but I enjoy them," she responded.

This seventeen-year-old young woman spoke with adult confidence.

Wade smiled at this exchange, clearly proud of his daughter whose maturity belied her youth. Chris was happily playing in his rice, mixing it up with pieces of fish.

"Chris did his first cartwheel yesterday; he's in gymnastics and loves it, his—"

"Sorry Dad, I've got to run," Chloe interrupted. She pushed her chair abruptly from the table.

I felt bad, and so it seemed, did Wade, but he brushed it off.

Chloe left the table and then, the house. She hadn't once acknowledged Chris' presence during the entire meal.

"You know, Chloe's got a full-ride to Berkeley?"

I didn't know it, but it didn't surprise me. Chloe was an incredible child.

Wade and I finished the meal and cleaned up. Chris was happy as usual, now working on the apple pie. Nicknamed the "California Kid," by my dad after he had visited us many times in San Diego, Chris was at home near the beach and in the sun, his blonde hair and his tanned, lithe, little body running and playing in the sand. After dinner we went to the beach and "Ade" as Chris called him, threw the beach ball. We all played, almost like a happy little family.

Merging families in a relationship after divorce is a major obstacle to rebuilding a life, especially if children are involved. Not only does each person in the couple need to bond with the other's child, but those children must have a degree of amicability toward one another. There is almost always jealousy between the partners' children from another marriage. Sometimes these feelings, or perceived feelings, are insurmountable, ultimately dead-ending the relationship.

***

Dancing at the Mission Bay Hilton was a weekly date for Wade and me. The view of the Coronado Bridge at night, the lights of the City and the sunset over San Diego Bay couldn't be beat. We walked into the restaurant, sat at our usual table and ate our typical fresh fish fare. After dinner I ordered chocolate cake for desert, a-la-mode. Wade had none. He laughed when he saw the waiter bringing out the cake and pointed to my side of the table as if the cake were contaminated.

"Go ahead, have a bite," I offered.

I put a small piece of cake, no ice cream on my fork and extended it to him. He backed away like it was poison.

"Hey baby, you know I don't eat that stuff."

I looked at his empty salad plate with the squeezed lemon on its edge and not a hint of dressing; same thing with his potato. He had the most disciplined diet of anyone I knew.

After dinner we walked into the bar where our favorite band played on Thursday nights. The female lead sang Whitney Houston songs with great dance beats. Wade and I danced for hours. Often, a circle of bar patrons would form around us and watch us as we danced. Anita Baker's *Sweet Love* and *No One in the World* were favorite slow dances and became our songs, at least in my mind.

    ***

We were driving to Utah for some holiday; Wade was reading to Chris in the passenger seat. We stayed overnight in Vegas. In the car the next morning, Wade asked.

"Do you want another child?"

I wasn't sure how to take his question. He probably meant it seriously, but the response I gave (so he says—I still don't remember) was "I couldn't conceive of it." I guess that ended our discussion of a future together as parents. Frankly, I was just so happy that I was with a masculine, decisive man, that I felt unworthy of his attention. The confidence I had developed in my youth, nurtured carefully by my father, had been stripped away by the awful marriage to Trent and the bizarre Mormon rituals which had imprinted the second-class status of my gender on my psyche.

    ***

Dana was a beautiful attorney, a few years younger than me, just out of law school, with olive skin and dark hair and eyes, who joined the firm about a year after I had. Dana dressed impeccably in designer suits and shoes. Her hair was styled differently every day. We became fast friends at work.

Our firm had annual client cocktail parties at the San Diego Yacht Club, major affairs with ice sculptures, chilled shrimp, drinks and hors'dourves. The young associates were expected to chat up the clients, being simultaneously witty and intelligent. A young lawyer could never anticipate the random legal question on the heels of a joke.

These client-firm parties were worse than work. They say some people are energized when socializing in large groups; others have their energy drained—I'm in the latter group. I'd rather spend my evening doing legal research than interacting with the usually much older, droll clients. But it was part of the job.

One evening, after Dana and I had charmed the old male claims adjuster clients for a couple of hours, we sneaked out of the firm party to a local bar. B Street Café was just a few blocks from the firm's downtown San Diego office. Back then, it had wonderful live jazz. Many young San Diego professionals frequented the café regularly, after long hours at the office.

Dana and I arrived just as the crowd was starting to fill into the bar. Weary from the long day, we removed out suit coats. She began telling me about her latest romantic encounter. I listened wide-eyed, taking in another of her juicy stories. Compared to her, I was straight off the farm.

Three young guys came up and sat next to us on the bar stools, forming a semi-circle around a high table next to the west window at B Street.

"So…what do you girls do?" one of them asked.

Dana discreetly nudged my knee under the table.

"Oh we're stewardesses."

I raised my eyebrow, but played along.

"Yeah, we're beat; just got in from Paris," I added

Clearly impressed, the guys eagerly pulled their bar-stools up a little closer.

"Sounds like you girls have an exciting life!"

"Yeah," said Dana, "we're always flying somewhere new, TWA you know; nothing boring—like lawyers or something."

"I hate lawyers," one of the guys said. "They're the worst."

"Yeah, did you hear the one about…?"

One of the other three young men told a lawyer joke, which was followed by another and then we all agreed that lawyers were just about the worst types of people on the face of the Earth.

After the guys had a few drinks, Dana winked at me.

"So Kay, we better get back to the firm; they might be missing us by now."

With that, Dana put on her jacket which still had her name-tag from the yacht club party, including the position 'Associate Attorney,' after the firm's name. Then I pulled on my jacket with my name-tag. The guys read the white tags on our dark jackets and looked up at us in surprise. Two of them almost spilled their drinks.

"Yeah, that's right we're lawyers," Dana said. She nearly spat in their faces, and then turned to leave the bar.

Above the cacophony of the crowd, she turned and shouted "Bye guys, have a great night," as we walked toward the café door. Sheepishly, I followed her out. I looked back in at the men who sat speechless, staring after us and then looking down into their beer.

***

"Hey baby, how about coming to San Francisco this weekend? We need some down time."

"Sure," I said, excited. I hadn't been there since my clerking job.

"Pack light," he laughed.

Taking the day off work Friday would be fine. I worked late Wednesday night. We both skipped our weekly Thursday night at the Hilton to get ahead on our workload so that missing a Friday wouldn't be so bad the following Monday.

The flight from San Diego to San Francisco is a short one. We took a cab to one of the best hotels in the City. The San Francisco Bay was beautiful that Friday morning, sunny and warm. Strolling Fisherman's Wharf, we temporarily forgot the piles of files awaiting our return at our respective offices.

That night we ordered in and stayed in bed into the next day too. We found a place to dance Saturday evening and then had a leisurely brunch on Sunday where I stocked up on croissants and fruit while Wade ate smoked fish. We hopped a small plane back to San Diego that evening.

***

My friendship with Dana continued. She often dropped by my office almost daily to chat. This day Dana popped her head in and asked, "So how's it going with Wade?"

I motioned her in and she quietly closed the office door. The lawyers at the firm visited each other's offices often, just like on television, but Dana and I never worked on any files together. Instead, each young associate worked with a partner at the firm. I was assigned to the senior partner, a lovely man who truly mentored me and who later became a Superior Court Judge.

Lately, whenever Dana and I talked, it was about Wade.

101

"He's so great. He raced last weekend and he did really well and then we danced and…" I eagerly repeated every detail of last weekend's trip. Dana sat still, taking in every word. I forget whether she was then single, or between marriages. So beautiful, she attracted men like a flower does bees, but her relationships, like mine it seemed, were always tumultuous.

    ***

In the eighties the Blackstone Ball was the biggest event of the year for the San Diego Bar. I wore a puff-sleeved, black beaded gown; Wade looked perfect in his tux. After a night of great food and lots of dancing, he told me he loved me. He said the words in the throes of passion, but I counted it nonetheless.

I thought we had been getting closer, but after that night, Wade began pulling away. I would never call him—having grown up in an era and culture where the men did all the wooing, to openly play the aggressor was unthinkable.

Over the weeks and then months, from fall into winter, things changed. Days and then weeks passed with no contact. Our Thursday night dancing dates became sporadic and then the week we did go dancing together, we ate in silence. Nobody watched us dance—the energy just wasn't there. He didn't call me for Christmas or New Years; it was as if the holidays never happened.

In early January he called asking how my holidays had been and then came over to my place.

I knew it was over between us.

"I can't do this anymore," I told him.

"What do you mean?"

He had to know what I meant, but Wade was ever the charming gentleman, at least superficially. Deep down he was always in control and things were always done his way or else he didn't participate.

"You've told me you never want to marry again (he did warn me about that when we first met, but of course I thought I could change his mind), has that changed?"

"No," he said evenly.

"Well…" My eyes teared up—*damn it – I wished I had an ounce of that Trent Jones stoicism about then.*

"Chris needs a father, some stability. I can't go on being a part of your life whenever it's convenient for you."

"I know, I just thought..."

He looked away.

"I can't keep up this relationship knowing there is no future."

"I understand," he said a little too quickly.

He'd been ready for this discussion, for how long who knew? Maybe ever since we'd met.

"I'll miss you," Wade said. He was sincere.

He left my house that night while the tears streamed down my face. I knew I had done the right thing, but it was the most difficult thing I had ever done.

***

This would be fun I thought, as I walked from my car to the downtown hotel where the San Diego County Bar was hosting a spring fashion show. Both Wade and I, along with several other attorneys and a judge or two, had been asked to model to raise money for the Bar Association charity. As I walked, worried about my scraggly hair and pale skin, Wade pulled into the parking lot, slammed the door of his car and ran up to join me.

"*Oh great*," I thought.

I was nervous. It had been at least three months since we ended our relationship in January.

"How have you been?" His tone was sincere.

I knew he truly cared about me, but I also knew that he couldn't care only about me. We walked in silence at a brisk pace the few blocks to the hotel. Arriving in the hotel lobby, we were directed to our separate dressing rooms. I looked back at him.

"Break a leg," he waved at me then disappeared behind the male models' door.

In the women's dressing room, I looked over the clothes with my name on them—three sets. I dressed in the first outfit, checked my hair and make-up and waited offstage in the wings for my cue. I watched as the audience applauded the model before me. I began my walk and had barely entered the runway when, in my peripheral vision to the left, I saw them.

Dana, hair piled high on her head with dark ringlets hanging down her back in a couture luncheon dress which out-styled any of the clothing being modeled that day, ran up to Wade and flung her arms around him. They embraced in the center of the round luncheon tables which had been set up for the Bar member audience. Although I was the only model on

103

stage, all the attention was directed to the scene between Dana and Wade.

Horrified at their open display of affection, at that moment, the jigsaw puzzle pieces of the last year fell into place: Dana's questions about Wade and me, Wade's emotional distance. It seemed to me that Dana must have used the information I'd told her in confidence, to her advantage with Wade. And though for all I knew, Wade and I had ended our relationship by the time they started dating, in hindsight I realized that Dana and Wade had probably connected many months ago.

All's fair in love and war, but it didn't seem fair to this Mormon girl. Dana was the other, certainly worldlier woman who had caught his eye, and the little Mormon girl from Utah had been played the fool. My heart was broken. The height of my happiness with Wade directly correlated to the depth of my wound.

The fashion show incident had destroyed my self-esteem which had been incrementally rebuilt, though still shaky, since I had left Trent.

After my emotions calmed, I sat looking at myself in the mirror, analyzing every flaw. I was thirty-four. Objectively, and in hindsight, I was pretty and young, but that's not the face that reflected back to me. According to Mormon standards, I was at least a decade past my prime.

Be ye therefore perfect...

A cartoon was once forwarded to me by a friend. A man and a woman were looking in mirrors, side by side. The woman, pretty and voluptuous, saw her reflection as ugly and overweight. The man, paunchy and balding, saw himself as a handsome body-builder. Such is the difference in the perceived self-worth of each gender.

This self-loathing, sometimes to the point of body dysmorphia, is particularly true of many Mormon women, who are taught that any number of women—ten virgins according to §132—could be given to our husbands if not here, in the afterlife and that we should accept the divided love with humility or be cast into hell. No wonder then, that many Mormon women are especially harsh critics of their appearance. Per capita, Utah residents have recently been documented as having the most plastic surgery of any state.[25]

There are exceptions, of course. Some Mormon women age gracefully and have developed such a personality of submission and service that their pure motives and selflessness form a light that emanates from their faces, making them beautiful even at eighty. They have maintained their figures and they dress nicely. Two of these women are my uncles' wives. Both bore their husbands children and have lived frugally on a high school teacher's income, especially the middle brother's wife, whose dedication to her Cary Grant-handsome husband appears unwavering. Though not a natural beauty, over the years she has only grown lovelier.

I suppose this is the goal of all Mormon women; however, it is the rare such woman who is able to achieve that peaceful, serene, matronly contentment at her life's end. Most of these women have had to endure unspeakable insults, are treated like household servants and never asked for their opinions, only to spend their lives at household chores, and bearing and forever rearing children and grandchildren.

Both my aunts by marriage have clearly had supporting roles in their husbands' lives. However, my Aunt Jeen and her husband had, from all appearances, a truly egalitarian relationship. Jeen built a successful crafts business and is the consummate hostess and gourmet cook.

Likewise, Jeen's mother, my Grandmother Margie Burningham, was the star matriarch of the Burningham family. She wore form-fitting sweaters and dresses over her voluptuous figure, and always spoke her mind. Although I believe she attended church, at least occasionally, I have no doubt that the Church was there for her use and not *vice versa*. In a tribute written shortly after her death in 1995, her youngest son called her one of the first local feminists.

Margie Burningham was born in 1904, the youngest of about a dozen children in the Jed Stringham family of Bountiful, Utah. Stringham was a local leader in the Mormon Church. Margie married Rulon Burningham who smoked and played baseball for the Salt Lake Bees. Surely this was a renegade match, and the union no doubt lacked enthusiastic endorsement from father Jed.

There was no question that the Rulon and Margie Burningham family, which eventually included three boys and a little girl, was a matriarchal organization. Margie Burningham was the outgoing, creative, baking, cooking, and crafting horticulturist who spread her vivacious love of life to her immediate and extended family. Rulon was handsome and quiet, somber in a dignified way. But it was Grandma Margie with her scrumptious cooked pheasant, lemon meringue pie, award winning roses, and hand-quilted jumpers that made the memories this grandchild recalls.

Margie and Rulon lived in Bountiful in a small Main Street home on an impeccably landscaped half-acre covered with award-winning rosebushes. An old English style hedge and archway formed the entry to their property. I was the oldest of what would ultimately be fourteen Burningham grandchildren.

We had memorable Christmases around their two-sided rock fireplace which connected the small living area with the kitchen and made a great room long before great rooms became popular. For holiday meals Grandma made roast turkey and orange rind rolls. Pudding filled éclairs could always be found in the fridge. On Christmas Day after all the gifts had been unwrapped, all twenty-five or so of us, stuffed with Christmas sausages and waffles, lounged around a bonfire of wrapping paper in that little fireplace. Dad was the jolliest; he had gained a lot of weight by age forty and so looked most like Santa. Uncle Gary to my cousins, he was the grand-kids' favorite.

A Mormon heritage is difficult to integrate into contemporary society. As a corollary to the Church doctrinal reinforcement of female inferiority, doubt about the propriety of living a life focused on something other than family remains. Any woman's attempt to successfully manage family and career can be easily derailed by the gender bias so prevalent in this Church. I had lived in the LDS Church and I had lived out. Perhaps I could integrate the good in both worlds. Now in my mid-thirties, I had to decide where my future would lie.

    ***

After my relationship with Wade ended, I smoked pot for the first time, drank piña coladas with real rum and hung out with my friend Marissa. I worked and worked, through red-faced tears, sleepless nights and days of funk. I had a year-long fling with another attorney, an irreverent atheist and gourmet cook with a wry sense of humor. We both knew that the relationship was not a long-term type, and we ended it the afternoon I refused to watch golf on television with him.

Resigned to hard work and glad to have more time for Chris, I licked my wounds. Wade had left a hole in my heart. Trent had remarried and moved out of state. Chris needed a dad.

Though my personal life was a mess, I was secure at work, having just won my first jury trial, a difficult case where my client's van rear-ended the plaintiff's car on the freeway. I was young and healthy and my first defense verdict made me excited to continue in my career.

Enter into my life Brian. Five years my junior, he was an engineer with an MBA. Though classically handsome, I didn't feel that chemistry I had with Wade. But he was a great cook and listened compassionately to my story of unrequited love. I made it clear to Brian that at that time I no longer considered myself a Mormon, but a Christian. Born and raised in the Church, Brian had served a foreign mission, but told me that these days he never attended church and that the whole subject of religion was not an issue. He also had a darling little girl from a prior relationship who was not quite a year older than Chris.

Brian had a dog; a rather cute medium-sized Australian Shepherd with one blue and one brown eye. Dog fur was everywhere in his house: on the sofa, on the carpet. Paw prints covered the glass patio doors. I almost ended the relationship when I first saw his place, but then I thought about my car which was usually littered with empty water bottles and pens, and after every road trip the passenger side was ankle-deep in pistachio shells.

I remembered *Luke* 6:41, "And why beholdest thou the mote that is in thy brother's eye, but perceivest not the beam that is in thine own eye?" *Hmm...perhaps the dog thing was just a phase.*

Keeping my offended sensibilities in check, I dismissed the squalor as bachelor pad fallout and told myself that Brian was a good compromise between my uncommitted lover and misogynistic first husband. I had experienced the best physical relationship I then thought possible with Wade, but he didn't seem to have a fraction of the emotional bond toward me that I had for him. With Brian, I'd reached the other end of the proverbial spectrum. My refuge in a relationship with a man who showed few signs of testosterone excess seemed safe. I couldn't have known the real Brian in what turned out to be a six-week courtship. In retrospect, I'm certain that he wanted to marry, and to marry a Mormon girl. I fit the requirements. The fact that I was several years older was probably offset by my seemingly solid career and demonstrated ability to produce children.

Our physical relationship was tepid at best. Never did we have that heat-seeking passion, which at the time was all right with me. I'd had enough passion for awhile and wanted stability. Brian and I talked like best girlfriends. I told him the whole sad tale of my relationship with Wade, right up through the fashion show bomb.

"Those kinds of guys will never stick by you," he said.

We talked constantly, in person and on the phone for hours, everyday. There were occasional drives to the beach where he never removed his shirt. The garment thing never occurred to me because Brian had said he wasn't a practicing Mormon; he wasn't active in the LDS Church. So I ignored any concern for a view of his naked body; our relationship wasn't about that type of thing, he was more of a friend.

It went on like this daily, for a couple of weeks. And then, out of nowhere—

"Well, you should just pray about it," Brian said. "I think it's the right thing."

I looked at him like he was crazy.

"Marry you? We only met a few weeks ago. I'd never marry again without dating for at least a year." I was truly stunned.

"Just pray about it," he insisted.

The next day was spent together and the day after. Each day he asked me whether I had prayed about it. I was confused. Here was a guy who was, as they say, good on paper: smart, objectively good-looking and there were no apparent barriers with our respective children. But there was absolutely no sexual chemistry between us—he never made a move on me. Considering that he was just thirty years old, this was something that should have raised a red flag at the time.

Brian's daily pressure wore me down until eventually I did pray about it. I didn't get any sort of response. Some Mormons say that's okay, no response means go ahead and God will let you know if you are on the wrong track. My connection to God didn't seem to be working these days. Looking for answers, I recalled the words I had often heard from LDS leaders to the young women in the Church:

> Follow the priesthood; they have a direct line to our Father in Heaven. On matters of importance only priesthood-holders should make the decision. You should prepare yourself to follow your husband in righteousness. If there is a disagreement about a big decision, the priesthood-holder is the tie breaker, and always carries more weight, because of this wonderful blessing and power which God has given him.

Later I would learn that the LDS priesthood-holder as tie-breaker argument is used by some Mormon men when couples disagree about something as simple as which movie to see or where to eat. Mormon men will tell their wives that they'd pray about the answer to a question. Then, instead of praying, they'd conference with their buddies or just hang in another room for awhile and come back with, surprise, confirmation of their decision. The women were left powerless, almost always accepting the men's decisions.

In reality, most Mormon men are special only by virtue of their Church-proclaimed divine potential. There are exceptions of course, but many Mormon men remain Mormon because they are average in intelligence, talent, socio-economic status and appearance. It is only their belief in their own potential divinity, with posterity "as innumerable as the stars," which makes them special, in their own minds and in the eyes of the women who love them.

On January 11, 1991, less than six weeks after our first meeting in late November, Brian and I married in the courtroom of the Superior Court Judge who had been my mentor at the law firm. I must have known it wouldn't last because I didn't even tell my parents, let alone my siblings about the marriage until it was a *fait accompli*. I invited a couple of the attorneys from the firm and Marissa who took beautiful photographs. At ages five and six, Chris and Brian's daughter were darling additions to what seemed like a perfect union. Brian looked, as he always does, like a male fashion model in his tux. My demure knee-length ivory-colored dress was appropriate for a second wedding.

Due to our work schedules, we had delayed our honeymoon to Maui until the first part of February. It didn't occur to me at the time that I was making another impulsive, yet life-altering decision. History repeats itself; smart women, foolish choices and a myriad of other phrases now seem *apropos* descriptions of the situation that I found I had placed myself in during the early months of 1991.

CHAPTER SIX: Escape from the Lies

"He jests at scars who never felt a wound."—William Shakespeare,
Romeo & Juliet

On January 30, 1991 I was driving southbound on I-15 to meet with the managing partner of the firm. Traveling several car lengths ahead of me was a vehicle driven by a young, off-duty police officer who was racing another vehicle in the adjacent lane. The cop pulled directly in front of the other guy and slammed on his brakes. Since I was traveling north of this game, in heavy sixty mile-per-hour traffic, I didn't know what had happened until the deposition of an eye witness, months later.

The first clue that there might be a problem was when I noticed a van spin out sideways directly in front of me. I had just seconds to react. Although I swerved to the left and braced myself, I couldn't avoid the T-bone impact of my car into the side of the van. In that split second before I hit the van, I knew the impending crash was God's retribution for my success in arguing to juries that plaintiffs were money-grubbing fakers. All my defense arguments flashed before me in exquisite self-condemnation. At impact, my head felt like a golf ball driven off its tee; my neck screamed in pain. To this day that injury remains, having created more compassion in me than I would ever have had otherwise.

Just a week after the collision, Brian and I were on our way to Maui for our belated honeymoon. Most everyone had canceled their reservations at the Hotel Hana due to the outbreak of Desert Storm and so we had the island almost to ourselves. We spent a couple of days in Kapalua Bay and then made the famous drive to the Hana Hotel on the other side of the island, when news of the war broke. Treated royally on Maui's sequestered east shore, what should have been a romantic retreat was a disaster.

Brian had scheduled a helicopter ride over the Haleakalā Volcano. The vertical swings of the helicopter mixed with my pain medication upset my stomach. Any hope for romance was forestalled when I became sick in the copter's paper bags. Brian understood about my pain, but even later, when I felt better and we had days left on our honeymoon, the intimacy just wasn't there and it couldn't be manufactured to fit the occasion.

The next two years passed without incident. We were like roommates, sharing financial responsibilities and stories of the day's work. Occasionally we would see a movie together but there was little social life. We had no friends in common. Mine drank, cursed and talked shop; his, mostly Mormon, talked about the Church and their children.

We continued on in our marriage in that way until the spring of 1993, when the San Diego Temple was dedicated. Brian convinced me to walk through the open house and thus he began his five year attempt to convert me back to the faith. As with all Mormon Temples built in the recent past, the tour of the San Diego Temple was open to the public before its dedication. After the dedication, only recommend-holding (tithe paying, coffee abstaining and apostate avoiding) Mormons can enter a temple. Perched on a knoll on the east side of the heavily traveled coastal interstate, this bright white, anomalous edifice cannot be missed by traffic in either direction.

While standing in line at the open house, I had that strange *déjà vu* feeling, recalling my family's trip to Disneyland more than two decades ago. Sleeping Beauty's Castle had nothing on this building. White marble chips in white stucco, with white on white etched window glass, it was beautiful in that stark, colorless way of many Mormon Temples.

The visit to the San Diego Temple signaled a new era in our relationship, one in which Brian increasingly reverted toward his Mormon Faith, while I became increasingly skeptical, growing further away. The fact he never removed his temple garments, even while sleeping, should have been my first clue that Brian hadn't really given up the Church. After the San Diego Temple dedication, Brian kept after me about having a child.

In May of 1994, Danny was born while my jury was out in a two week trial in Northern San Diego County. Since I was in labor, my second chair colleague returned to the courthouse for the verdict and assured the jury I was doing well. I credit the good result, at least in part, to Danny's presence growing inside me. He was a sweet little boy from birth. Wise and solemn beyond his years, even as a toddler Danny was truly an old soul.

    ***

"Ted Gardner, nice to meet you." The rotund man extended his hand to me.

Shortly after we were married, Brian and I had moved from our respective homes into a new development of Mediterranean style houses

112

on the rim of the Rancho Peñasquitos Canyon. Ted was the ward's bishop, ecclesiastical head of the neighborhood Mormons.

"Hi, I'm Janet."

His similarly looking wife smiled at me. These were nice, good-hearted people. Janet took to Danny at once.

After we became acquainted with the Gardners, Brian began a regular schedule of Church attendance. We argued over taking the kids. Chris didn't like the regimen and Danny was much too young to have to sit through long hours of service. But at the Church nursery he seemed to enjoy the interaction with the other children, so I agreed. By then, Brian's daughter had moved out of state with her mother so her involvement was never an issue.

It was a typically beautiful San Diego Saturday afternoon. Thick ocean air wafted through the upper room and the setting sun glinted off the mirrored walls onto the shining maple floors in the room we had made into a workout studio. I was helping Chris dress for his baptism into the Mormon Church.

"Why can't you do it, Mom?" he asked.

Chris' silky hair shone. He looked up at me while I was fixing the white collar of his baptismal outfit.

"Because only men have the priesthood," I told him matter-of-factly.

"That's stupid, Mom," he said, straight from the heart. Eight-year-old Chris spoke directly, with observations that cut to the core of any nonsense.

I hugged him tight. "Its okay, Spud," I said.

Brian took Chris to cub scouts and tried to keep him in the Junior Sunday School. But Chris, who we called Chrisser, due to his energy and curiosity, would rather be on his bike, skating or doing flips on the backyard trampoline. He could barely sit still long enough to eat, let alone sit for hours on hard church pews.

To demonstrate my good faith effort at reintegrating into the Mormon lifestyle, I tried attending Relief Society meetings on Sunday mornings. These meetings were held for the women while the men attended priesthood in a separate area of the chapel. The Relief Society organization was the counterpart to the male priesthood. Although led by a trio of females on both the local and Church headquarters levels, the women's group had no authority to make major decisions absent

113

priesthood approval.

I sat in the pastel pink-colored room on an upholstered folding chair and looked toward the tablecloth-covered folding card table upon which the instructor was presenting her lesson. An artificial flower arrangement in the table's center was surrounded by several cloth napkins.

"And this is how we make a swan napkin."

The instructor, who I knew to be a born-in-the-Church stalwart, held out a white cloth square which she laboriously tried to fold into the form of a bird. The origami attempt was not working; the cloth was too thick. Despite the obvious failure, there were 'oohs' and 'aahs' from the women in the audience who, with unfolded napkins in their laps, tried to mimic the instructor.

I was bored to death. In Relief Society meetings, there were four types of lessons given, one for each week of the month: cultural refinement, spiritual living, social relations and homemaking. The lessons were always the same, recycled from year to year, a sort of Mormon female sociology, passed down from each generation of women to the next. With no outside sources from which to draw (these were initially discouraged and later, strictly prohibited), the Mormon scriptures and whatever instruction manual was approved by the Church Correlation Committee, an organization which carefully edited everything to be taught to Church members, the substance of each Relief Society lesson was pure pablum.

My law school friend Sharon and I had taught the gospel doctrine class at BYU while we were first year law students. Each Sunday the students packed our classroom because we quoted from Christian writers such as G.K. Chesterton and C.S. Lewis, long before Mormon General Authority Neal Maxwell quoted Lewis, making him an acceptable source of inspiration among Mormons. In the 1990s, Lewis' writings were so often quoted by LDS Church authorities that he seemed to be accepted by the Brethren as a saint *in absentia.*

Eventually the local Church leaders sat in on our lessons and decided that despite the attendance numbers, our venturing out into non-Mormon Christian writings was not approved. Sharon and I were released from our callings as teachers in the BYU campus ward Sunday school.

***

As Brian grew more involved with the Church, I focused on work and my boys. Occasionally my father would visit us. Having been the landscaper, miniature rose and day-lily hybridizer that he was, Dad usually made annual trips to a nursery in Northern San Diego County to buy new plants. Since I had moved to San Diego and he had retired from teaching, my father made the Southern California trips biannually.

"Katy, my flight arrives tomorrow afternoon," Dad's warm voice announced over the phone.

"Great, Dad. What brings you out?"

What a surprise!

Dad usually planned his trips a couple of weeks in advance to take advantage of the lower rates on flights. It was late August and he had just visited in the spring. I had never known him to travel spontaneously.

"Just wanted to see my girl," he said.

That night my dad played with Chris and baby Danny. Brian cooked a nice dinner.

The next day I took off work. My father and I drove to Torrey Pines Beach where we set up our folding chairs and laid out our towels. Dad settled into one of the chairs, pulled his hat over his eyes, folded his arms across his belly and was about to 'take a snooze,' as he often called it.

I started to read, but wanted to talk with him.

"So Dad, what's on your mind?" I asked.

"What?"

He startled from his quick onset nap, sat up and looked around for a moment as if he had forgotten that he was sitting on the beach in California. When he got his bearings he spoke.

"Oh nothing, Katy…"

He paused, leaning forward, elbow on his knee. Chin in his hand, he gazed out toward the sunset.

"Your grandmother, I…" His eyes watered.

Grandma Burningham had passed away in January of 1995, just eight months earlier. Her passing was very difficult for my father. She and her oldest son had been especially close. At ninety-two to his sixty-five, he still took her grocery shopping and she still did his laundry. They attended theater at the University of Utah and varsity games at Viewmont High School. Everyone could sense their bond.

My father couldn't finish his sentence. Instead he smiled at me and squeezed my hand.

The sun was about twenty minutes from setting over the Pacific. With rolled up jeans, Dad walked slowly out into the water, well past his ankles. There he stood, hands in jeans pants pockets, silently looking at the sun until the last glimmer of light had disappeared over the horizon. I had never seen him so pensive.

He stayed the night and then the next day I took him to the airport. He had been complaining of heartburn that morning but shrugged it off as nothing. I suggested he check in with his doctor when he returned to Utah, but I wasn't too worried.

I returned to the office to prepare for a long deposition the next day. Later that afternoon, I had a passing feeling that I should call my father to check on him, but I dismissed it as nothing and continued to work late that night.

The next morning, early, Brian yelled.

"Kay, telephone!"

I immediately knew it wasn't good news. With trepidation, I picked up the receiver.

"Kay, this is your Uncle Dee."

I was sick inside.

Uncle Dee spoke slowly and solemnly.

"Your father has passed away. I found him sitting in his chair; it looked as if he had been opening the mail in the living room of his apartment."

I deeply regretted not taking the time to have one last conversation with my father, but was thankful for his spontaneous visit, however brief. He must have known he was going.

The funeral was at a Bountiful Mormon chapel, not because my father ever reactivated in the Church, but because it was convenient. The pews were filled with his debate and history students and admirers of his landscaping and the flowers he had perfected over the years.

Danny could walk, but couldn't understand. Chris tentatively touched the casket and solemnly tried to comprehend where his grandfather had gone.

We stayed at Jeen's during this time.

One night it seemed as if I felt Dad's spirit, just as certainly as if he had been in the room. It felt as if he hugged me one final bear hug good-bye.

   ***

Brian was increasingly involved with the Church and increasingly, I wanted to be out. In the fall he accepted an offer from Hewlett-Packard to head up a project management team in their Boulder County, Colorado Office. I had left the San Diego insurance defense firm several months after my collision, not being physically able to handle the heavy caseload and trial schedule. After months of dictating while lying on my back, tons of physical therapy and cortisone injections, all the conservative treatment I ordinarily argued as proper for neck injuries had failed. Ironically, the only treatments which provided any relief were the chiropractic adjustments that cured my headaches.

Since I left the firm in the fall of 1991, I had been in private practice representing the injured. Because Danny was so young, we had a full-time nanny and housekeeper. When Brian told me about the offer to move to Colorado, I agreed. I was missing the seasons and thought perhaps leaving the close proximity of the San Diego Temple would help to distance Brian from Mormonism. Wrong.

***

Boulder County is spectacular in the autumn. Our yard had a beautiful maple tree which had been pruned to perfection and was in high color when we moved into the new development of homes at Blue Heron Estates. The season was truer fall than I remembered along Utah's Wasatch Front. The planners of this peaceful mountain community had impeccable foresight. Boulder Creek runs down from the Rocky Mountains just west of Boulder, eastward. It's a healthy creek, almost a river it seemed to me.

There was more green on this side of the Rockies. The seasons were more colorful; the snowflakes in winter were larger and more dramatic, and the flowers in the spring bigger and more aromatic. The city and county planners had wisely limited building on the mountains and a six foot wide bike path paralleled Boulder Creek from the base of the mountains eastward, throughout the county. Any child was safe on those paths and could ride over the entire county without crossing a road. There were overpasses and underpasses, through Colorado University at the base of the Front Range in the west end, past the open expanse of the prairie in the east.

Sunrise is early; I was pleasantly surprised to have the sun up before I had to get up with the kids for school. Along Utah's Wasatch Front, the towering Rockies to the east block the sunrise every morning. Familiar with sunsets over the Great Salt Lake and long Indian summer evenings into September, the early evening darkness of Northern Colorado took some getting used to.

With stunning views, Mission Bay in San Diego had been the perfect spot to skate. It is surrounded with a wide concrete path which was not too crowded if you knew when to go. Now I needed a replacement route. I was pleasantly surprised to find that the Boulder path was just as picturesque, and covered an even longer distance than the Mission Bay path. I could skate for fifteen to twenty miles round trip, and did it often, with Danny in his stroller.

After Dad died, Brian and I didn't spend much time together. He integrated himself into the local Mormon ward, and persuaded me to attend at times. In turn, he went with me and the children to the local Christian church. The kids liked the contemporary music. The trained ministers had good things, new things to say. But Brian said he never felt comfortable there.

From the day the San Diego Temple appeared and continuing on after we'd moved to Colorado, Brian relentlessly preached Mormonism to me. Since I had never formally left, a reactivation into the Church was ecclesiastically simple, but emotionally difficult. Finally, worn down and tired of arguing, in an attempt to save our marriage and avoid the disruption of another move, I got worthy. I bought new garments, re-read *the Book of Mormon*, and agreed to accompany Brian through the Colorado Temple. From outside appearances, which seemed to be all that Brian cared about, I was ready. But inside, my uncomfortable feelings, which for years had questioned the truthfulness of Mormonism, had not changed.

Brian and I had never spoken of a temple marriage because although Trent and I had been divorced in a court of law, we were still technically sealed for eternity under the ecclesiastical laws of the Church, that is, if both parties lived up to their covenants. Heavenly living arrangements become confused when there is a divorce, when one party to the marriage becomes inactive or when one decides to leave the Mormon Faith.

The date for our trip to the Denver, Colorado Temple was set. That morning I was sick to my stomach. I couldn't have been more anxious if I'd been forced to eat the prairie dog road-kill I'd seen on Arapahoe Road on the way into the town of Boulder proper.

The Colorado Temple was in the south part of Denver, farther than the ten minutes to the temple from our San Diego home. I dreaded donning the ill-fitting temple clothes. The veil, required for all women, was scratchy and claustrophobic. Reluctantly dressed in the awkward clothing, I left the women's dressing area to join Brian in the main room where the ceremony was to begin. Young and old dressed alike, the placid expressions on their individual faces were indistinguishable, one from the other. It was BYU and the Salt Lake Temple all over again—only worse.

"Raise your hand to the square," the officiator commanded.

Memories of the troubling handshakes and pantomimes flooded my mind. I had never before experienced anything resembling a panic attack, but less than halfway through the initial ceremony, I bolted from the stifling room. Running past the hundreds of dedicated temple Mormons, dressed in all white, gliding along white marble floors, whispering while seated on white sofas and chairs, in rooms lit by clear glass chandeliers, I raced for the temple's main doorway.

Finally, I burst from the doors of the claustrophobic, colorless morgue into the open air. The rich fall colors of Colorado rescued me and assured me I was still on Earth, not in some horrible, tepid hell. My spirit revived, I fell against a tree, relieved.

Later, the Colorado Temple president called and spoke to Brian. Their consensus was that I wasn't spiritual enough to appreciate the sacred Colorado Temple experience.

Brian urged me to meet with an LDS counselor, who referred me to an LDS physician who prescribed Prozac. I took it for a few weeks and turned into a zombie. I had no feelings whatsoever; my soul had been chemically killed.

On the other hand, Brian loved me on the medication. I didn't complain, I didn't question, I merely obeyed. I was a perfect Mormon housewife. But then I threw the pills in the toilet and my personality came back with full force and our relationship continued to deteriorate. At our core, Brian and I were fundamentally different. He is a middle child and will do anything to keep the peace, including omitting facts and tweaking the truth, a trait many Mormons acquire after years of living the religion. Even if I occasionally lacked tact, I valued honesty.

Chris was having problems with his schoolwork. I set up an appointment with a therapist for him. Brian turned the session into marriage counseling for him and me. Thereafter, Chris' problems were not addressed and the nine-year-old stayed home with little Danny while Brian and I met with the counselor. After just a couple of sessions, the therapist told Brian (not me—just Brian) that due to our disparate personalities and world-views, our relationship was doomed.

***

While I was finishing up my San Diego practice and trying to find a job in this new jurisdiction, Brian became involved with a woman in the Church. He volunteered for various ward projects and was called to be a home teacher.[26] One of the women Brian taught was recently divorced with three children all under age eight. Colette, with her thin frame and huge, round eyes, signaled a neediness Brian apparently couldn't resist.

At first I ignored her longing glances across the chapel during sacrament meetings, but soon it became humiliating. When I asked him about those looks, Brian told me I was imagining them. I tried to believe him and endured the situation. Then, one day while I was paying the bills, I found a Boulder hotel receipt for a date Brian had said he was out of state on business. When confronted with the evidence, he admitted Colette had been there, but said nothing had happened. A few nights later, while we were entertaining a couple from the neighborhood, the telephone rang. I picked up the receiver.

"Is Brian there?" a woman's voice asked.

"Who's calling?" I asked, sick inside.

"Brian, Colette's boyfriend, is he there?" The voice on the other end insisted.

I held the phone out for him.

"They want Colette's boyfriend," I announced to Brian, ignoring the uncomfortable guests and trying not to rage. Our guests excused themselves; Brian grabbed the phone and ducked into his office.

I moved myself and the kids out of the house. Colette immediately swooped in to do Brian's laundry and handle the housekeeping bills. She canceled my credit cards and called the Colorado State Bar membership and told them I had moved.

Within a couple of weeks of our moving out, my Boulder housekeeper called to tell me that she had arrived at the Blue Heron House for the weekly cleaning to find the family room covered in chunks of white-blonde hair. It turned out that Colette was living with a homosexual black woman (according to Brian) who came over one day while Colette was in our house and 'beat the crap out of her.' Shelly, our housekeeper, filed a police report.

Brian came to the house where the boys and me were staying and asked me to come back home. I questioned him not only about his past relationship with Colette but about what had happened while we had been apart.

"Nothing happened," he said.

"Really?"

"Colette is a lesbian. She was sexually abused by a male relative. Come back," he said.

Brian showed no sign of emotion during this entire exchange.

After he left, I thought long and hard about reuniting. Danny was a little boy and Chris had been disrupted plenty through the moves. I returned to the Boulder house to try it again.

As soon as I had moved back in to the house, I received a dozen red roses. "Hope all is well with you and Brian, love Colette," the card read.

     ***

Brian told me he was going to get a blessing from the bishop. He had quit his stable job with Hewlett-Packard because they hadn't listened to his ideas. He was then working as a consultant for an obscure telecom company. The work required lots of travel and he was at odds about his future.

One afternoon, Brian came home very excited. He told me that he had just received a blessing from the ward bishop and that, coincidentally, he had a new employment offer.

"The Lord told me I would make millions and millions of dollars and be able to support lots of people," he said.

I raised my left eyebrow.

Here we go, I thought.

"Right after I got my blessing, a guy named Morris called. He cashed out big with the MCI /WorldCom deal. He and his MCI buddies have a start-up—high speed DSL. I told you this would be the big thing. They want me to head program management."

He was talking faster than ever.

"Wow," I said. "That sounds great."

"One catch, we'd have to move to San Francisco. That's NorthPoint's headquarters."

Oh no, not another move, I thought.

I had to meet with that ward bishop.

121

***

I sat in the bishop's office intending to ask him about this blessing. Before I had said a word, or even before we had properly introduced ourselves to one another, he blurted out.

"You know, I was going to go to law school, but I was called to the bishopric."

I nodded my head, and could see where this was going.

The bishop leaned back in his chair and looked around his office at smiling photographs of LDS ward members, apparently posted on his wall over his years as bishop.

"I am so pleased I am able to guide people and direct them. There is nothing better."

I didn't know what to say. I didn't disagree. My father had been a high school teacher, so were my uncles. Teaching and counseling could be very rewarding.

What did he think an attorney did?

We ended our conversation, which was really just me listening to the bishop talk about the pleasure he received from his position as leader of the ward. When I finally asked what prompted him to say those things to Brian, he looked at me incredulously.

"That was the Lord speaking. I have never been so inspired to pronounce such wonderful blessings upon anyone. Your husband will be incredibly successful."

"What about Colette?" I asked, hoping for what response, I didn't know.

"Oh that was nothing." He pooh-poohed the matter. "Just a lonely young woman."

Okay, I thought, not really convinced of anything. I thanked him for his time and left his office.

Since the Bishop and I didn't have the best rapport, I asked for a blessing by the stake president, the priesthood-holder in the LDS Church organization who is the bishop's immediate supervisor. Maybe this man would be more reasonable. Though I hadn't done it for years, I fasted and prayed that the blessing would give me direction in my life and in my relationship with my husband.

"Listen to your husband and abide his counsel," was all that the stake president told me. Later I learned that before each woman's blessing, the bestower of blessings has a private meeting with her husband or father

122

to see what it is she really needs.

    ***

I had mixed feelings about a move back to California; the kids had been relocated less than three years ago from their home in San Diego. They both liked living in Colorado.

Brian persisted.

"This is a great deal, I'll get stock options and they are paying me more than HP did. Besides, the options will be worth millions. The company is planning on going public in just a year or two, once the cable is laid and we have our customers."

It all sounded perfect for Brian. He had an intuitive brilliance working with any electronics engineering issues, including communications technology.

"The internet will change the world," he had told me when Danny was born in 1994 and I was hesitant to learn some new computer thing. He was right about that.

"But you need to get all this in writing, Brian," I countered. "The salary, the stock options, when they vest, all these things."

"Don't worry. Morris is a great guy, we don't need a contract."

I was dumbfounded. Brian had worked for a federal government defense contractor for years in San Diego. He knew the value of the written agreement.

"But, if the worst happened, we could sell the house, relocate the kids and then they could fire you within a year," I said. "You have no guarantee. California employment is at-will. (I had successfully represented Trent in a wrongful termination case after our divorce and so I knew something of California employment law). Unless you have a contract—"

"Don't be so negative," he interrupted.

He was high on this new prospect, making the money the bishop had promised him.

NorthPoint flew us out to their headquarters in San Francisco's Financial District. At lunch Morris explained the vesting schedule for the stock options. Brian was to get 132,500 options at a strike price of one dollar and fifty cents, which meant that after the IPO, when the stock had an acknowledged value on the open market, he could buy that number of shares at what would be a very low price and would make a killing on the difference.

I had some questions.

"When do the options vest?" I asked. "Does Brian get them for moving and accepting the job?" Stock options were new to me.

"No, there is a four-year vesting schedule. The first quarter of the stock vests after the first year of employment; the second after two years of employment, and so on," Morris explained.

Brian didn't seem to be listening. He had Danny on his lap and was staring out the window at the cable car on the street.

I was uncomfortable without a contract. How many cases had I seen where there had been verbal agreements, 'Don't worry, the boss says we can't change the contract, but I'll make sure...' In an ideal world everyone's word would be good and an agent wouldn't promise anything his principal couldn't deliver, but in real life we have to have lawyers so the weaker party doesn't get screwed. Despite lack of written confirmation, and again, against my better judgment, that inner voice which whispers to us all in times of indecision, our family made the move.

NorthPoint paid our moving costs and financed a house hunting trip. We looked north in Marin County—too expensive. Downtown San Francisco was out of the question for the same reason. I already knew I didn't want to live in the East Bay, too far from the ocean. On the last day of our trip we drove south along the coast and discovered Half Moon Bay, just a half hour south of the City along the picturesque Pacific Coast Highway. Compared to other California beach cities like La Jolla, in 1998 Half Moon Bay was an undeveloped little town populated by artistic types, where property values were reasonable by Bay Area standards.

We found a delightful new neighborhood in Miramar, where you could indeed see the sea. The house was one of about a dozen being built in the woodsy neighborhood by the sons of Irish emigrants who had purchased these coastal residential lots years before, from a judge who had originally bought them for a steal. Mavericks Surf was right out our window. In order to get financing on our new home, I leveraged our stock options and negotiated directly with the builder. We made a good deal.

We settled in. Brian commuted up the Pacific Coast Highway to the NorthPoint Office in the financial district, a quick half-hour drive on perhaps the most scenic part of the Northern California coast. Chris took to the ocean, learning to surf. Danny loved walking through the eucalyptus trees to kindergarten and playing with a new friend on a wooden playhouse that Brian built. We had moved the old trampoline originally bought in San

124

Diego, from Colorado. We built a redwood patio-deck and bought a hot tub, placing it at the perfect position to take full advantage of our view of the sunsets over the Pacific. Our house was finished with new paint and furniture. The kitchen with the windows out to the west and glass doors onto the redwood deck let in plenty of sunshine.

***

When Brian was cooking he almost flew around the kitchen in a perfectly choreographed sequence of moves, cleaning up as he worked. By the time he was done, we had a wonderful meal and the dishes were only those left from the dinner table, no pots or pans. After just a couple of months in San Francisco, Brian seemed to forget all about the Church.

This particular April Sunday afternoon, Brian made barbeque sauce with onions, garlic and liquid smoke, then carved up a couple of chickens, breasts for me and the boys and the dark meat for himself. The chicken pieces returned crispy from the outdoor grill and were served dripping in homemade sauce. Brian rarely used a recipe; the talent was in his head, learned from his mother.

We sat down to eat.

The boys smacked their lips. Brian gnawed on the last bit of cartilage from a leg.

"This is so good, Dad, I love this chicken," Danny said.

Danny stopped for a moment.

"Mom," he asked.

"Where does chicken come from?"

I gulped. A couple of years ago, when Danny was just a toddler and had been eating his first steak I told him that steak, as all meat, beef, pork, and so on was from the meat tree, which grew to provide meat just like the berries in the woods and apples on the trees. As a two-year-old who had not yet begun to read, he readily accepted that explanation.

But he was older now.

"Mom!" Danny's intelligent hazel eyes bore into mine.

At that moment I knew he had put it all together.

Danny had seen chickens on cartoons and in farm animal books and now he was eating something with the same name.

Oh boy.

"*This* is a chicken," he said, pointing to the piece of meat he had suddenly dropped onto his plate.

Chris and Brian looked at me. No one spoke for a moment.

"Yes dear, it's true."

I felt like such a traitor.

Danny sat stunned for a moment.

"What about the Easter Bunny?" he asked.

"Mom," I said, pointing to myself.

"And the Tooth Fairy?"

I raised my hand.

Danny stopped, sober and dour-faced. He raised his little voice in a disbelievingly high-pitched moan.

"And Santa Claus, Mom?"

"Mom and Dad," I shrugged sheepishly.

The next day after kindergarten I received phone calls from irate parents whose five-year-old children had been told the truth about Santa Claus by my precocious son. They were not happy.

***

In May we bought two Himalayan kittens, brothers who had been raised under foot and so were very friendly. Each boy was allowed to choose one kitten. Chris chose the only seal point, a beautiful, silky, chocolate and champagne colored kitten. Danny's cat, a stocky sweet-faced, blue-point, picked him, running out to him as soon as the cage was opened. The kittens ran and frisked about, chest butting and chasing one another through the house and into the yard. In the foggy evenings they would join us on the redwood deck while we soaked in the hot tub.

Those first few months were peaceful. NorthPoint had two pre-IPO stock splits which almost quadrupled the number of options Brian had originally been promised. At the IPO in May 1999, the value of the stock debuted at $24.00 and rose to more than $43.00 that first trading day. NorthPoint's young officers and employees were ecstatic. NorthPoint had become the darling of the dotcoms.

***

On a rare sunny coastal day, just a couple of months after NorthPoint's successful IPO, Brian returned from San Francisco with disturbing news.

"I think I'm going to be fired," he said.

"What?" I asked.

All my warnings about Brian's failure to get the terms of his employment in writing came back to me. It hadn't yet been a year since we'd moved and so technically none of his stock options had vested. His one year anniversary with NorthPoint was still a couple of months away. Although I was furious, I forced myself to keep quiet. A caustic 'I told you so,' was the last thing he needed.

"Liz Fetter is getting rid of me and my team."

At first I wondered why, but then I realized what the problem was. Brian had a hard time dealing with women as superiors. I had listened to his past comments about Liz Fetter and knew that they didn't get along well. With her established reputation as a successful executive, Ms. Fetter had been brought in late to the NorthPoint game. But from the time she arrived at the company, Brian and she were philosophically at odds over program management's role in NorthPoint's operations.

"Really? Fired?"

I couldn't believe it in a way.

Lately, Brian had begun attending the local Mormon ward. After this bit of news he didn't miss a Sunday meeting. And he was right about getting fired. In October of 1999, less than two weeks before his one year anniversary, and the vesting of 25% of his stock options, he came home with the bad news.

"I was fired today," he said.

He started walking upstairs and then turned and threw his cell phone down. It hit the hardwood floor and broke into pieces. Before I could respond he walked upstairs to the master bedroom and slammed the door shut. We had never had much physical intimacy, but his termination from NorthPoint ended forever what little there had been.

NorthPoint offered Brian a termination agreement which 'gave' him 25% of his options (which he would have earned in a couple of weeks anyway) in exchange for a covenant not to sue the company for his dismissal. I thought he should sign it and be done. The stock still had a value of about $25.00 a share, making our gain on just a fourth of Brian's options almost a million dollars. I told him we should sell the stock, pay off our debt and put money away for the kids' college. Instead, Brian wanted to sue NorthPoint for wrongful termination, breach of contract, and recovery of all of the stock options. And he wanted me to represent him.

Masseuses massage their spouses, physicians write prescriptions for their children and dentists give free exams to their extended families. My husband expected I would be his lawyer.

Besides what I'd heard on the stock options, I didn't know what had been said in negotiations on the other employment issues. I did happen to get confirmation of the stock options in a fax sent from Morris to our mortgage lender before we closed on the house. It read as though Brian received the stock in one lump-sum. This was some evidence that what Brian claimed was true: that he received the stock options for his initial relocation and that they were not subject to a four-year vesting schedule.

I was uncomfortable in this dual role as witness and advocate, but I agreed to go ahead because maybe I had not heard Morris correctly at lunch that day. I was beginning to doubt my judgment and my memory. Brian's insistence made me do that a lot. *What did I know?* He had consistent dealings with Morris and the other officers and I was just a woman. So, trying to trust my husband, who, it seemed hadn't proven all that trustworthy in the past, I filed the complaint on his behalf.
        ***

The case was intense. NorthPoint hired one of the biggest firms in the City as defense counsel. I sat at Brian's side during his two-part deposition, objecting where appropriate and trying to be supportive. But the stress of representing my husband was killing me. Brian didn't seem to care, so intent was he on getting back his elusive millions. The lawsuit dragged on.

We justifiably claimed that the release and covenant not to sue in exchange for one fourth of the promised stock options was void since it was executed under duress. However, I foresaw that NorthPoint would certainly depose me as a potential witness. With conflicting roles as an officer of the court vs. an advocate/dutiful Mormon wife, I was trapped in lawsuit hell.

Protesting this continued, coerced labor, I searched hard to find a law firm to take over the case. Finally, an Orange County colleague agreed to do it for an hourly fee. I ultimately claimed the marital privilege which allowed me to refrain from testifying and possibly being asked anything which could be used against Brian. In the end NorthPoint settled. After paying attorney's fees, costs, and especially considering the toll the entire NorthPoint matter had on our marriage, it was not worth the fight.

Consoling himself with the options he did have, Brian was convinced that the stock price would go back up, increase, even double or triple in value and then we would sell.

"I always pay my tithing," he said.

I remembered the faith promoting stories I had read in Church magazines over the years, stories of struggling, sometimes destitute Church members who always paid their tithing first, even in the face of enormous debt. "The windows of Heaven," were promised to be opened to those faithful tithe-payers.[27]   A recent article in a Church magazine entitled "Tithing—a Commandment Even for the Destitute," reads: "One of the first things a bishop *must* do to help the needy is ask them to pay their tithing. Like the widow, if a destitute family is faced with the decision of paying their tithing or eating, they should pay their tithing…"[28]

But the stock didn't go up. NorthPoint's earnings statements had been revised and reduced. The lower stated profits caused the Company to lose a pending merger deal with Verizon. After the Verizon deal failed, even our broker at Morgan Stanley advised us to sell, but with the words of the Colorado bishop in mind, Brian refused to sell the stock he did have. Over the next year NorthPoint's stock spiraled downward until it was valued at $.50 cents per share, a dollar less than our strike price. Ultimately, NorthPoint went bankrupt.

   ***

The year 2000 made its grand debut. The computers didn't blitz and the new millennium came without a sign of the Lord. Brian's retreat into Mormonism after the failed promises of the Colorado bishop had me seriously questioning the interplay between faith and life events. Although I was probably never as deeply committed to the doctrine as many members of the LDS Church, it seemed that even my tangential relationship with the Church had an enormous negative effect on my life. Maybe, I thought fleetingly, it was because I was lukewarm, as the scriptures say, and in danger of being "spit out of [God's] mouth." [29]

My nephews both served missions during our time in Half Moon Bay. The younger one bore his testimony in a handwritten letter asking me to read the scriptures and pray: "I challenge you to do it individually and personally, you will become so strong in your testimony and your life will be so much easier…say your prayers and read your scriptures and then write me back and tell me if you didn't gain a testimony of the truthfulness of these things."

His challenge motivated me. I decided once and for all that I would find out whether Mormonism was true or false, not just by feelings, which by then I had realized were unpredictable and could be easily manipulated, but by objective, evidence-based study, the type of analysis a lawyer did.

I studied all the Mormon scriptures and every other Church history primary source that I could obtain. I re-read the historic sermons by Brigham Young and other early Mormon leaders in the *Journal of Discourses,* early twentieth century Church leader B.H. Roberts' questions about *the Book of Mormon* and everything I could find on world religion. It wasn't until the move to the Bay Area that I accessed and read Fawn Brodie's groundbreaking biography of Joseph Smith, *No Man Knows My History.* I read Attorney Thomas Ferguson's documentation of his trips to Central America and his reluctant conclusion that archeological evidence to support *the Book of Mormon* was non-existent.

I drove to the Bay Area university libraries and read books on every subject even tangentially related to theology: *The Tao of Physics, God and Religion in the Postmodern World,* the *Denial of Death, Existentialism from Kierkegaard to Sartre, Irrational Man,* multiple works on metaphysics and non-duality, consciousness and the subconscious, neurology and thought processes.

I wrote to LDS Apostle Neal Maxwell about the issues I had with the Mormon Temple ceremony. He sent me back one of his books, *Men and Women in Christ,* along with a letter which told me that he "knew and liked" my uncle, and then, without any response to my questions about the temple, told me that I lacked humility.

Charges from Amazon.com soon appeared as the biggest expense on my monthly credit card statement. Throughout this entire process Brian ignored my quest. He absolutely refused to listen with an open mind to anything I had read.

***

On a foggy day in May, 2000, Dale Aldridge called me. Dale and I had met in the fifth grade at Bountiful Elementary. He lived just down the street from our house on Bountiful's west side. In sixth grade we were both teased as teacher's pets, sharing the shame of the smarty-pants outcasts. During depressing stints in my early twenties, while I lived in Mom's basement, Dale and I would commiserate in his. One lazy summer afternoon, we talked at his parents' house.

"There was just so much suffering. The Church and its teachings seemed irrelevant," he told me, referring to his two year LDS mission to a poor Asian country.

"Do you have anything to eat?" I asked.

Dale could have kept on talking for hours, but I was hungry.

"Sure." He leaped up the stairs two at a time.

Soon he was back with an open can of cranberry jelly, the kind you eat with turkey at Thanksgiving if the cook is lazy and doesn't make the real cranberries, and a spoon. He stuck the spoon in the can and handed it to me. I looked inside at the quivering, purplish gelatin.

"No thanks," I said, thinking that I wasn't so hungry after all.

"Sorry, that's all there is."

He started digging into the can, matter-of-factly eating spoonfuls of jelly. After two years in Asia, Dale would eat anything. Years later, he would work in China and eat all sorts of strange and delicious things.

Now, in 2000, I was pleasantly surprised to hear from Dale. The cranberry jelly incident had been over twenty years ago. When Dale worked in Silicon Valley we met at the Stanford campus and walked and talked about the usual, Mormonism. He gave me a list of his favorite books, many of which I would read while trying to determine the truth of my childhood religion. Except for that, we hadn't kept in touch much.

"Hi Kay, this is Dale Aldridge." His voice was shaky.

"I've got some bad news," he said. "Teresa Armandson has passed away."

An image of Teresa flashed across my mind. In law school Teresa ran and biked and had an athletic physique. Even in her forties, she was sure to have been physically healthy.

"How?" I asked Dale.

"The family said she was ill, had a bad flu virus. The funeral is in Salt Lake. I think there was an autopsy," he added.

I looked out my window to the Pacific Ocean. It was a sunny, beautiful day. Nothing had changed except that my friend Teresa was no longer in this world.

I hung up the phone and sat for a minute. Then I picked it up again.

"Los Angles County Coroner's Office please," I asked directory assistance.

The autopsy report listed cause of death as Vicodin overdose —'accidental.' A history of alcohol and prescription medication abuse was noted in the report. Those who found her described the scene:

Location: A five story low income housing development in ...
Los Angeles, California...the scene is a small studio

131

apartment. The room is very small and cramped with furniture and personal items. There is debris strewn through the room on the floor, there is an absence of trashcans in the unit and the floor appears to be the main collector of the rubbish and debris. The decedent is lying supine in the bed which is next to the front door. [She is] dressed in white and red shorts, a green shirt and a white undershirt. There are no visible signs of trauma noted to her person. ..*

I re-read the card Teresa had sent to me just last year. Her dream of attaining the perfect Mormon family was never realized. Instead, she died soon after our planned meeting. Had I known the depth of her depression, I would have tried harder to reconnect with her, to help her see the positive. Maybe I wouldn't have been much help, but I had experienced similar feelings.

Teresa's death spurred me on in my reading and research. I had to decide. I read *the Book of Mormon* one more time. The words rang false and repetitive. I could see that part of it was a clear plagiarization of the Bible. I compared exact quotations to Isaiah, found similarities to the Sermon on the Mount and numerous parallels between the conversion stories of Paul and *the Book of Mormon* prophet, Alma.

Why hadn't I seen these things before? It seemed so clear to me now. *Book of Mormon* stories were childish plagiarizations from both the Old and New Testament, and though supposed to have been written before 600 A.D., read in the style of the King James Version of the Bible.

After long hours of prayer and meditation I came to the conclusion that Mormonism was false. I remember the event vividly. It was a foggy evening in January of 2001. The boys were both in bed; everyone had been asleep for hours. I had been holed up in my office, door closed, secretly praying. Leaving my study, I skipped my nightly hygiene routine and trudged up the stairs to the guest bed on the third floor. The slanted attic window toward the west gave a clear view of a navy ocean against a grey foggy sky. Moonlight pierced through a break in the heavy fog and glinted off Mavericks' Surf that early morning when I finally hit the bed, emotionally exhausted and physically drained.

The next morning I woke up early for a Sunday and felt completely different. I looked out the attic window. The fog had dissipated; the sky was clear. The sluggishness was gone from my body. I awoke knowing that Mormonism was a fraud. I couldn't claim I had seen a vision, but I knew it was a lie as well as I knew my own name or the faces of my sons.

Everyone in the house was still sleeping. I tiptoed quietly into the master bedroom, past Brian into the master bathroom. Instinctively I stepped on the scales. My weight read five pounds less than yesterday—a heavy burden had left me. After years of fighting through an irresolute funk, I was no longer depressed.

I wrote my letter of resignation and mailed it to LDS Church Headquarters, attention: Membership Records Department. That was it. After forty-six years, I was no longer a Mormon girl.

***

Disturbed by the utter indifference of the NorthPoint management, who had seemingly turned on one of their own, in a moment of sentimental reflection I yearned for refuge in the Utah Mountains. Thinking I would discover it in the comfort of family and childhood friends, we flew to Utah and found a house in Park City, away from the crazy tech boom/bust. Utah would be safe from the wolves, with a more reasonable cost of living, less crime and better schools—that was my thinking.

Park City seemed to be the only centrally situated town with some cultural diversity, so lacking in the communities along Salt Lake's Wasatch Front. Park City would be conservative, but not Mormon. As a billboard eastbound on Interstate 80 then advertised, *Escape Utah, Come to Park City.*

We sold our California house, exiting at the top of the Bay Area real estate market, the downturn of which quickly and predictably followed the tech bust. Brian was consulting in the telecom industry and could work from any city situated near an airport. Park City schools were the best in the State. I thought it was a good move.

There had been no intimacy between us since Brian was fired from NorthPoint, almost two years now. Brian didn't talk about it. Whenever he was home he spent hours on his computer, past midnight; but he had always been that way.

I'm sure he felt my lack of respect for him had grown since the NorthPoint debacle. It was true, but not for the reason he imagined. I didn't fault him for being fired, but for his ready eagerness to accept and commit to his Colorado bishop's inspired pronouncement of his future, to the exclusion of any practical legal advice from me. This vision of wealth remained paramount in his mind, overshadowing all rational attempts to initially ensure his compensation in writing, and then later, to minimize our losses from his termination and the declining stock value.

When I tried talking with Brian, his eyes would glaze over and he wouldn't let me in. Whatever troubled him was pushed even deeper now. Although I never felt as if I knew the real Brian, the wall between us became thicker and his real self shrank further inside. The barrier between us had grown insurmountable.

    ***

September 11, 2001: we had been in the Park City house a little over two months. I was cleaning the kitchen and smelled gas coming from the family room. The fireplace pilot light seemed to have a leak. I asked Brian to check it. Irritated, he looked at the fireplace and then adjusted the key in the adjacent wall.

"Its fine, don't worry," he said.

But I did worry. I could hear the slow leak and there was a gas smell.

"I can call the gas company, there's no charge."

"No, I told you there is no leak!"

He screamed at me and then, walking in long strides, slammed out the front door.

His uncharacteristic overreaction to my concern upset me. I stood and mindlessly stared at the fireplace.

After some unknown amount of time, something in my peripheral vision caught my attention. I turned toward the television screen. CNN was reporting that the World Trade Center had just been hit by a jet aircraft. I watched as the first and then the second tower collapsed. The buildings appeared to implode.

My God, what is happening?

I didn't know where Brian had gone.

Later, I called the gas company. They sent a repairman who confirmed and then repaired the leak.

Brian didn't return home until that next day. Frightened as we all were after news of the disaster, I wanted to reach out and talk with him, feel safe with him. But I didn't and he didn't and we never did. Instead, the day after 9-11, he told me he was going to Bangkok. He had accepted a six month consulting contract to set up cell phones for a company in Thailand and left almost immediately.

134

Chapter 6: Escape from the Lies

Danny and I flew to Bangkok and visited Brian that November. Although he went with us to a crocodile farm and some Buddhist temples, it was a quick trip because Brian didn't feel well. I guessed that he'd been working too hard.

Descendants of Utah Mormon pioneer immigrants,
English and Danish, 1956: Grandma Margie Stringham
Burningham, Grandma Delpha Reynolds Thomson, my baby sister,
Grandpa Nephi C. Thomson, Grandpa Rulon Burningham, my
mother, Barbara Burningham, my father, Gary R. Burningham and
me.

My childhood photo, one girl in about 1.4 million Mormons, 1956

My senior photo, one teen of about 3.3 million Mormons, 1973

Photo of me with a Forces'74 singer dressed as an ape, Rhodesia, 1974

Looking out the window at our jet escort after Capetown bomb scare, 1974

Feeling fat while standing next to BYU Mascot Cosmo the cougar, 1975

Dad, after my LDS Temple wedding ceremony he couldn't attend, 1984

Chris, age 8, and me, two of about 9 million Mormons, 1993

Danny, age 13 and me, 2007. *I am one of an estimated 1-1.5 million Mormons who have resigned from the LDS Church since 1995. (See Chapter Eleven for resignation figures from which the above number was extrapolated). Danny is formally still a member of the Church (his father refused to allow him to resign), but he does not attend and considers himself an atheist.*

PART II: The Case against Mormonism

CHAPTER SEVEN: The Utah Theocracy

"We used to have a difference between Church and State, but it is all one now. Thank God."—Third LDS President, John Taylor, September 20, 1857[30]

Upon our return from Bangkok, I focused my attention on Utah. What had been happening in my home state in the almost twenty years since I had left to work in California? With the population growth and the upcoming 2002 Winter Olympics, I had hoped we would find a welcoming place where our family would fit in. Instead, what I found was an entirely new, polarized Utah, rich with a history of violence and power struggles between Mormon and gentile which continue in one form or another in the State even to this day.

Utah Public Schools Teach a Partisan History of Utah

The study of Utah history is mandatory for Utah's public elementary and middle/junior high school students. But the history I learned, and even that which is taught today, is a superficial accounting of Utah's strife-torn origins. As a student in Utah public schools in the sixties and seventies, I never learned of gentile attempts to wrest control of the Utah Territory from the Mormons. Federal jurist complaints, the Mountain Meadows Massacre, the Utah War and the various federal laws criminalizing polygamy and dis-empowering Church control of the Territory were never mentioned or were at most, footnotes in my textbooks.

This history taught to Utah children is never objective, but told with a favorable bent toward Mormon immigration and settlement. The texts used are those approved by the Utah State Board of Education, which is usually made up of a quorum of Mormons. Despite Utah's 1896 Constitution, which explicitly requires that: "Neither the Legislature nor the State Board of Education shall have power to prescribe textbooks to be used in the common schools,"[31] the State Board makes available to each school district a list of materials for every subject, marking the preferred text to be used as "highly recommended."

In 2010, the Social Studies Chairman told me that each school district may use any book on the "approved list," but it is a very short list. In 2010 *only one text is listed* for each grade's course in Utah history, and that same text is 'recommended.'[32]   The text then recommended for seventh grade students, *Utah, a Journey of Discovery*, devotes about one-half page (of 336 pages) to the cumulative federal efforts to control Mormon polygamy and Mormon challenges to federal sovereignty, with just a few lines each to the Morrill Act, Poland Bill, Edmunds and Edmunds-Tucker Acts.[33]   The text then makes light of Utah's criminal polygamists by comparing them to roosters in a hen house.[34]

Frederick Buchanan, a retired University of Utah professor and scholar on the history of Utah education, said in 2007 that: "The [Utah] public school system reinforces the LDS values at every turn.   That's one reason there are so few Mormon parochial schools.   When the federal government pushed Utah to establish public schools to replace the Mormon church-controlled system, Mormon leaders decided, 'We'll make them our schools.'" [35]

The LDS pioneering plan was to raise the Kingdom of God on Earth and "Zion will become a terror to all nations."[36]   Thus, from a very young age, Utah public school students, regardless of their familial religion, receive a partisan history of Utah Mormon colonization.

Most of the early Church struggles over power and leadership, doctrine and tradition, remain unknown to the majority of contemporary Mormons, and are certainly never taught to their children by either the public schools or the Church.   However, raw emotions are replete in the *Journal of Discourses*, a multi-volume compilation of mostly sermons by early Church leaders.   These speeches were published in LDS newspapers from 1854-1886. With Church leaders' endorsement, stenographer George D. Watts led the effort to publish the entire series.   In these twenty-six volumes, uncensored, true Mormon history can be found.

Mormonism claims a doctrine of continuing revelation by living seers.   When the multi-volume *Journal of Discourses* was first published as a set, Church leaders endorsed it as scripture.[37]   Today, however, the Church has officially recanted its former position: "The Journal of Discourses is not an authoritative source of Church doctrine," is now the official statement.[38]

Chapter 7: The Utah Theocracy

The Kingdom of God on Earth—Establishing Mormon Zion

Mormonism was a magnet for the poor and the uneducated—those people who were at the same time highly determined, driven by a religious fervor which remains among the Saints even today. If Joseph Smith was the founder, the mystic and revelator for Mormonism, then Brigham Young was the director and coordinator of the whole adventure. Young was the ultimate pragmatist, a harbinger of popular Covey-esque organizational behavior. Without Young's hard-driving leadership, Mormon pioneer prominence in settling the American Mountain West would most likely not have been.

Establishing and maintaining a theocracy in a young United States, founded upon freedom of religion, but also from religious interference, was a grand goal. An *a priori* requirement to an effective theocracy is to unite the prospective governed, at least philosophically if not politically; even better, to acquire such a degree of power over the governed that those who carry out their heavenly appointments, the governors, are never questioned. One way the Brethren attempted to accomplish this goal was to effect control of the Saints' assets and income. Early in Mormon history Joseph Smith attempted such an economy with the United Order, a business enterprise organized around principles of communism, but it failed. With some exceptions, even good Mormons were hesitant to donate all they had to the Church.

According to the LDS law of consecration, all property was to be held in common by the Church and apportioned to each Saint according to his need. "...and behold, thou shalt consecrate all thy properties, that which thou hast unto me, with a covenant and a deed which can not be broken..." [39] One commentator during the early years of the Church wrote that this method of ownership was merely a way to avoid the "vexatious lawsuits," that always seemed to follow Joseph Smith [whether for unfound money, unpaid debts, or other men's wives]. If Smith's and the other Church leaders' assets were not held personally or in any form as a recognized business entity, then, so the reasoning went, the satisfaction of any judgment obtained against either the Prophet or his Church would be difficult, if not impossible.

Smith's successor Brigham Young tried again once the Saints arrived in Utah. Initially he took a more palatable part: ten percent of all

145

the convert had acquired and from then onward, ten percent of his increase. In the late nineteenth century Smith's United Order was resurrected and economic cooperatives, such as Zion's Mercantile Cooperative Institution (Z.C.M.I.), "more than 150 local general stores... miles of railroad, woolen and cotton mills and...at least 500 local cooperative manufacturing and service enterprises," were created.[40] Mormons were expected to patronize these establishments to the exclusion of gentile businesses. Remnants of these enterprises have all but died. Z.C.M.I. remained a viable department store throughout the twentieth century, but today no longer exists. Now, the LDS conglomerate invests in agribusiness, real estate, stocks and bonds, utilities, and communications. As for tithing, for the majority of LDS history, the ten percent model has been in place, and remains.[41]

Since Mormonism was more than a religious belief—it was to be the Kingdom of God on Earth—its leaders' attempts to govern all that the Saints individually possessed or occupied necessarily came into conflict with those who already resided in Zion. At every attempt, from Kirtland, Ohio, through Nauvoo, Illinois and Mormon settlements in between, Smith's success at establishing Zion was temporary. Not until after his death, when Brigham Young took leadership, did they permanently settle. The remote Great Basin allowed Young and his pioneers to settle in the Salt Lake Valley and outlying areas which would be governed solely, if only temporarily, according to Mormon priesthood rule.

Reasons given for continued Mormon moves westward varied. Church history claims that the Saints were subject to continual persecution —that they had been peaceful, law abiding citizens who were unjustly treated because of their beliefs. And although there is at least one seemingly unjustified incident of killing eighteen Saints at Haun's Mill, Missouri in 1838, many of the crimes committed against the Mormons by the gentiles (including many who were former members of the Church) were done in retribution for the initial thieving and criminal activity by their new Mormon neighbors. Indeed, what the Saints have labeled persecution and eviction from their peacefully-formed communities, are called the 'Mormon Wars,' (Missouri, 1838; Illinois, 1844 and Utah, 1857) in the rest of the nation's history books.

Thus, though each new community was initially called Zion and thought to be the Saints' final resting place, post-colonization disagreements and disputes with the original residents of the Saints' new communities made Smith dig in his heels. The disagreements almost always turned criminal, if not murderous, until finally the Mormons had to move further west, always prompted by a new revelation, in an attempt to escape the jurisdiction of any government but their own.

For years now, Mormons have claimed they have been discriminated against, unfairly treated and the objects of crimes and bigotry. University of Utah historian and former Mormon (who was excommunicated in 1993 as one of the September six—a half dozen Mormon intellectuals who had published controversial ideas about LDS doctrine), author D. Michael Quinn explains, "I don't think the Church will ever break out of its persecution complex. The headquarters of the Church is only two steps away from a siege mentality. It's imbedded within the psyche of the culture."[42]

Even today Church leaders claim religious persecution. For example, after the public backslash in response to LDS support of California's Proposition 8 banning gay marriage, LDS Apostle Dallin Oaks compared prejudice against the LDS Church to the intimidation of southern African Americans at voting polls during the 1960s civil rights movement. [43]

However, others have viewed Mormon migration history differently. Nineteenth century Mormon stalwart, Bishop John D. Lee, who witnessed and would later participate in many crimes including murder and a practice (especially in Missouri) of Saints thieving gentile property, wrote: "...much of the trouble that came upon the Church was brought on through the folly and fanaticism of the Saints."[44] Some who witnessed the disputes argue that first generation Latter-day Saints "... committed the crimes that produced disaster and disgrace among the people of Missouri, and finally resulted in their own expulsion from that state." [45]

Despite Church pretensions at Christianity, its founding prophet was not a fan of turning the other cheek; rather, he encouraged his followers in their criminal actions. According to one eye-witness, Joseph Smith supported these crimes. "Go Ahead! Do all you can to harass the enemy. I never felt more of the spirit of God at any time than since we commenced this stealing and house burning." [46]

An affidavit by G.B. Frost, signed in 1842 before a justice of the peace in Suffolk County, attests to the founding prophet's drunkenness and criminal intent:

147

On or about the middle of June, 1837, I rode with Joseph Smith, Jr., from Fairport, Ohio to Kirtland. When we left Fairport, we had been drinking pretty freely; I drank brandy, he brandy and cider, both together; and when we arrived at Painesville, we drank again; and when we arrived at Kirtland we were very drunk.

In July, William Smith, one of the twelve Apostles, arrived at Kirtland, from Chicago, drunk, with his face pretty well bunged up; he had black eyes and bunged nose, and told John Johnson that he had been MILKING THE GENTILES to his satisfaction, for that time.

About the last of August, 1837, Joseph Smith, Brigham Young, and others were drunk at Joseph Smith, Jr.'s house, all together; and a man, by the name of Vinson Knight, supplied them with rum, brandy, gin, and a port wine, from the cash store; and I worked in the loft, over head. He, Joseph, told Knight not to sell any of the rum, brandy, gin or port wine, for he wanted it for his own use. They were drunk and drinking, for more than a week.

Joseph Smith said that the Bank was got up on his having a revelation from God, and said it was to go into circulation to MILK THE GENTILES. I asked Joseph about the money. He said he could not be paid for it, —so he told me, —and they must do the best they could about it.

October 13—Hyrum Smith's wife was sick, and Brigham Young prayed with her, and laid on hands, and said she would get well; but she died at six o'clock at night.

Joseph Smith, Jr. and others went to Canada, in September. Said he, Joseph, had as good a right to go out and get money, as any of the brethren. He took money, in Canada, from a man by the name of Lawrence, and promised him a farm, when he arrived in Kirtland; but when he arrived, Joseph was among the missing and no farm for him (He took nine hundred dollars from Lawrence). William Smith [Joseph's younger brother] told Joseph if he did not give him some money he would tell where the Book of Mormon came from; and Joseph accordingly gave him what he wanted.*[47]

Joseph Smith's lack of integrity continued in Brigham Young's blatant disregard for the average Mormon, especially toward the women.

A more despotic governance of Mormonism's dedicated adherents would be hard to imagine.

The Bottom Line at All Costs: the Mormon Handcart Pioneer Debacle

Since its 1830 creation, missionaries from the Church had been preaching in Northern Europe and had achieved incredible success with the poor. Once Brigham Young assumed leadership, he continued to expand Church efforts into Europe, growing the Church's tithing base. The Perpetual Emigration Fund (PEF) was established in 1849 to help bring European converts to Utah. Rather than continue the costly immigration to Salt Lake by ox-driven wagons, once the first Saints were settled, Young concocted a scheme whereby additional European emigrants could walk and pull their necessities in handcarts.

The Martin and Willie Companies traveled from Northern Europe by ship to New York and then to Iowa, where they were outfitted with rickety handcarts, limited to seventeen pounds of baggage and a daily ration of a pound (in the end much less) of flour each, and little else to eat. They struggled along the Mormon Trail, approximately thirteen hundred miles from Iowa City to the Salt Lake Valley. Through a series of faulty communications and the failure of appropriate oversight, these handcart companies were allowed to leave Iowa late in the summer. Thus, even with good time, the handcart pioneers would not have made it to the Salt Lake Valley before the first mountain snow.

Though he was certainly aware of the late departures, it was rumored that Young was preoccupied with local industry and couldn't be bothered with the immigrants' well-being. More than two hundred, or as many as 25% of the handcart pioneers met their death through starvation and exposure; many others suffered severe frostbite requiring not just fingers or toes, but full limb amputation.[48] According to historian David Roberts, the Church has never kept an accurate record of those devoted handcart pioneers who died enroute to Utah's Zion, but "the Mormon catastrophe of 1856 remains far and away the most deadly in the history of westward migration in the United States."[49]

Although Young ordered rescue parties to assist on the last leg of the journeys, an October effort was far too late for many of the handcart pioneers. Once they finally arrived in the Valley, starved and gaunt, the reaction of the settled Saints was mixed. They made room for the new Saints as boarders in their established residences, but the newly arrived pioneers had to struggle to fully integrate. This outrageous indifference to new immigrants, along with the historical criminal actions of the Church leaders, led to questioning of the Religion and its policies by many long-time leaders of the Church. When issue was taken with the actions of Mormon leaders, those who dared speak against them were labeled apostates and preemptively excommunicated.

One-time Church Apostle Lyman Wight, along with several of Joseph's original twelve, was excommunicated from the Church.[50] Wight had witnessed the handcart pioneer suffering. He reported seeing:

> ...one hundred and ninety women and children driven thirty miles across the prairie...with three decrepit men only in their company; the ground was thinly crusted with sleet, and I could easily follow on their trail by the blood that followed from their lacerated feet on the stubble of the burnt prairie.*[51]

There are at least two versions of "Handcart Days," as it was called for years in Utah: the Church's "All is well," a phrase from the hymn "Come, Come Ye Saints" version, and the true horrors of the trek, as could only be told and documented by those who lived through it. At nineteenth century Church conferences the treks were spinned as a success by Young and his colleagues. The failure, if any, was placed on Young's administrative subordinates.

Most of the handcart pioneers refused to talk of their experience until decades later. A few might have idealized it, even then. Those who criticized the effort seemed to wait until Brigham Young died to voice their criticism, though one Danish emigrant who returned to his homeland wrote a contemporaneous critique of the journey.[52]

The "Handcart Days," celebration when I was a girl is now more commonly known as the "Days of Forty-Seven," or "Pioneer Day," when Brigham Young and the first Mormon pioneers arrived. It is a Utah State Holiday, celebrated with parades in major cites and fireworks on the 24th of July. Historically, this celebration, rather than the July 4th celebration of the United States' Independence Day, has been the grander for Utah residents. Some Mormon children and their families participate in short reenactments of the handcart pioneers' journey with a several day trip, driving to Wyoming, then walking for miles (with plenty of food and while wearing good athletic shoes) to show respect for their ancestors.

The Mormon Reformation: Forced Compliance with Despotism

Young, who had wrested control of the Church from Smith's son, Joseph III and others vying for the title of second president, nicknamed the "Lion of the Lord," or "Bloody Brigham," depending on who was doing the talking, was anything but meek. His actions and admonitions to his people were generally not Christian. Instead, he is an acknowledged despot by most scholarly historians of the period.

One of his former wives was Ann Eliza [Webb] Young, who divorced him after just a few years of marriage. She chronicled her experience with Mormonism and in particular, with her prophet-husband, in her memoir, *Wife No. 19*, published in 1876. She wrote about Brigham Young: "He has no natural religious nature; indeed, he is at times a positive sceptic. He has made the church a stepping-stone to temporal prosperity, and the Mormon people have been the pliant tools with which he has carved out his fortune."*[53]

Only in the last few decades have Mormon leaders, perhaps embarrassed by Mormonism's true history, attempted to recast portions of Church doctrine in order to conform its teachings more nearly to the rest of Christendom. While many of *the Book of Mormon* teachings can be argued as Christian (because much of the book is a plagiarization of the King James Bible), *Journal* excerpts from Young's sermons and those preached by other leaders support the curious and non-Christian doctrines of polygamy, blood atonement, pagan temple rites and polytheism; some early Church leaders even openly deprecated Christianity. Young claimed:

When the light came to me I saw that all the so-called Christian world was groveling in darkness...With a regard to true theology, a more ignorant people never lived than the present so-called Christian world. The Christian world...are heathens as to the knowledge of the salvation of God.*[54]

Young's first counselor, Heber C. Kimball, preached:

Christians—those poor, miserable priests brother Brigham was speaking about—some of them are the biggest whoremasters there are on the earth, and at the same time preaching righteousness to the children of men. The poor devils, they could not get up here and preach an oral discourse, to save themselves from hell; they are preaching their fathers' sermons —preaching sermons that were written a hundred years before they were born. ...*[55]

Once the Saints were settled, somewhat comfortable and accustomed to their daily lives in the Utah desert, signs of apostasy and a general failure to strictly adhere to Mormonism appeared throughout Zion. Naturally, when not pressed for food or shelter, the Saints began to slack off in their perfect dedication to their prophet and church, which, during Brigham Young's reign, seemed to be one and the same.

In a reactionary series of speeches, Young instituted what has become known as the Mormon Reformation. Preaching dire eternities to those who weren't strict about living their religion, he rebuked his people for their lackadaisical living of Mormon laws, especially the developing cavalier attitude toward tithing.

During this interim period, throughout the handcart emigration and after the onset of Young's reformation, there was indeed an unsettling among the Saints. Various historians have chronicled the savage attacks on those who happened to pass through the Utah Territory uninvited, or who were appointed by federal authority in an attempt to govern the Territory. These atrocities were committed by a group of Mormon thugs called the Danites, originally organized under the auspices of Joseph Smith. They carried out all sorts of crimes before the Saints immigrated to Utah. 'Destroying Angels,' were their leaders, the key executors for the Danites.

While some Danites stayed behind or left the Church after Joseph and Hyrum Smiths' assassination in 1844, some followed Brigham Young to Utah, including three key members of the group: John D. Lee, Bill Hickman and the notorious Orrin Porter Rockwell.

William Law, a member of the LDS First Presidency under Joseph Smith, is quoted as admitting that Joseph Smith sent Danite Porter Rockwell to kill Missouri Governor Boggs, "I sent [Orrin] Rockwell [leader of the Danites] to kill Boggs, but he missed him, it was a failure; he wounded him instead of sending him to Hell."*[56]

The existence and express purpose of the Danites is verified by both the Prophet Joseph, and David Whitmer, an early Mormon convert and one of the original three witnesses to the golden plates. Smith admitted:

> We have a company of Danites in these times, to put to right physically that which is not right, and to cleanse the Church of every great evil[s] which hitherto existed among us inasmuch as they cannot be put to right by teachings & persuasyions ...*[57]

Book of Mormon witness David Whitmer wrote:

> In the spring of 1838, the heads of the Church and many of the members had gone deep into error and blindness...In June, 1838, at Far West, Mo., a secret organization was formed, Doctor Avard being put in as the leader of the band; a certain oath was to be administered to all the Brethren to bind them to support the heads of the Church in everything they should teach. All who refused to take this oath were considered dissenters from the Church, and certain things were to be done concerning these dissenters, by Dr. Avard's secret band...my persecutions, for trying to show them their errors, became of such a nature that I had to leave the Latter Day Saints...*[58]

A hearing was held in U.S. District Court in 1903, just prior to the beginning of the U.S. congressional hearings to determine whether elected Mormon Reed Smoot, Senator from Utah, could be seated. In the Utah matter, many witnesses, both Mormon and former Mormons, were subpoenaed. This particular case involved a determination of whether an immigrant to Utah could be both a good U.S. Citizen and a Mormon if in the LDS endowment house he had sworn allegiance to the LDS oaths of vengeance against those who killed the Smith Brothers.[59]

Generally those who testified in support of the petitioner [most of whom were members of the LDS Church], "...is [was] characterized throughout by unwillingness of the witnesses to testify to any facts, by evasion, by feigned ignorance, by defective memory, by subterfuge, and by downright contradictions in their statements in the direct and cross-examination."*[60] Charles W. Penrose, editor of the *Deseret News*, was held in contempt for his refusal to answer the question of how many wives he had. [61]

Danite murders committed by Destroying Angel, Bill Hickman, were testified to under oath in this U.S. District Court matter in 1903. For instance, Bishop Andrew Cahoon was sworn. He came to Utah in 1848 and had been a member of the LDS Church for forty years, having joined in Kirtland, Ohio. He testified in pertinent part:

"It was considered no crime to take from those who opposed the Church, because they were the enemies of the Kingdom of God."

Q. "Did you ever hear that doctrine taught?"

A. "Oh yes, oh yes. All of those that pretended to lead and guide and govern the Church taught that it was lawful to take anything from our foes, from those that were enemies to the Kingdom."

Q. "Well, just tell us an instance, the time, the place, and who were present?"

A. "Well, those that pretended to have authority in the priesthood led the way and others followed along;—in Missouri, for one place, —at Adam-ondi-Ahman it was the president of the branch, Lyman Wight."

Q. "Can you name any instance in this country where that doctrine was taught or practiced?"

A. "Well it wasn't supposed to be taught publicly—secretly."

Q. "How did you find it out?"

[*Non-sequitur* follows in the original].

A. "O, lots of them. I haven't been familiar with that it. I was instructed that it would do no harm to put that man out of the way—a certain individual, — I can't name him now, — I didn't put nobody out of the way, —I didn't consent to it."

Q. "What man said it?"

A. "Orson Hyde.

Q. "Did you ever know of any man being put out of the way for that?"

A. "O lots of them. I haven't been familiar with that because, as I say, I wasn't trustworthy in that dirty work."

Q.   "Well, tell who they were, tell some one man who was put out of the way—you can name somebody?"
A.   "Well, I will tell one, that is Almon Babbitt for one, —the Secretary of State."
Q.   "Where was he put out of the way?"
A.   "Out on the road east."
Q.   "Well, who did it?"
A.   "Why, I don't know, I am sure, I wasn't there."
Q.   "Do you know who ordered it done?"
A.   "Such things as that are kept very secret and private. It was reported that he was killed by the Indians."
Q.   "Do you know who killed him?"
A.   "I can't say whether there was a white man by the name of Bill Hickman there."
Q.   "Do you know he was?"
A.   "I say he might have been there and done the job, he might have had some Indians to help him. I can't say." *[62]

The journal entry admitting the existence of the Danites made by Joseph Smith was originally concealed. In the official *History of the Church*, also ostensibly authored by Smith, the existence of the Danite groups was expressly denied.[63] However, over the past two decades, true copies of Smith's journals found by diligent historians of Mormon history have been made available to the public.

These disclosures have forced the Church to at last publish their own multi-volume set of Smith's papers, an expensive facsimile version: *The Joseph Smith Papers*. To date, two of the planned volumes have been released, one with Smith's journals and another with his revelations and translations.

More evidence of Danite deeds comes from one of the Church's own: according to BYU professor William G. Hartley, "There is no question that Latter-day Saint rangers [Danites] burned buildings at Millport and Gallatin... It is certain that some Danites played the thief, and it is possible, although unproven, that one or two were murderers."[64]

While the Danites enforced Mormon laws, the 'Council of 50,' organized in 1844, was formed as an *ad hoc* legislature to conform local laws with the ever-changing rules of Mormonism, and, according to Smith, to "eventually rule over the political Kingdom of God on Earth."[65] Once the Church was stabilized in the Great Basin and Brigham Young was Governor of the Territory, it was easy to transfer the essence, if not the individuals which comprised the *de facto* legislative Council of 50, to a recognized state legislature *de jure*. With regard to the Council, Brigham Young proclaimed: "'It is the right of the Twelve (apostles) to nominate the officers and of the people [to] receive them'...The council passed laws, levied taxes, conducted negotiations in the name of the community and sat as jurors and judges in all disputes."*[66] Even today, a substantial majority of Utah's legislature and judiciary is Mormon. As of the year 2000, all five justices sitting on Utah's Supreme Court were (at least at that time) Mormon. [67]

The Mormon Reformation also breathed new life into the controversial doctrine of 'blood atonement,' only mentioned in passing by Joseph Smith. The principle as taught by Brigham Young was that some sins, such as apostasy, shedding innocent blood and women committing adultery, are so egregious that only the shedding of the sinner's blood (impliedly nullifying the Christian atonement) would provide redemption. Found in discourses by Brigham Young and Apostle Jedediah M. Grant, the doctrine was particularly enforced against gentiles and apostates: "In regard to those who have persecuted this people ... if any miserable scoundrels come here, cut their throats. (All the people said, Amen.)"*[68]

Leaders' speeches in the *Journal of Discourses* illustrate that the doctrine was prophet-approved:

> There are sins that men commit for which they cannot receive forgiveness in this world, or in that which is to come, and if they had their eyes open to see their true condition, they would be perfectly willing to have their blood spilt upon the ground, that the smoke thereof might ascend to heaven as an offering for their sins; and the smoking incense would atone for their sins, whereas, if such is not the case, they will stick to them and remain upon them in the spirit world...I know, when you hear my Brethren telling about cutting people off from the earth, that you consider it is strong doctrine; but it is to save them, not to destroy them... there are transgressors, who, if they knew themselves, and the only condition upon which they can obtain forgiveness, would beg of their Brethren to shed their blood...There are sins... [that] must be

156

atoned for by the blood of the man.*[69]

Will you love your brothers or sisters likewise, when they have committed a sin that cannot be atoned for without the shedding of their blood? Will you love that man or woman well enough to shed their blood? That is what Jesus Christ meant.*[70] We have those amongst us that are full of all manner of abominations, those who need to have their blood shed, for water will not do, their sins are of too deep a dye... if they are covenant breakers we need a place designated, where we can shed their blood...*[71]

Though current official commentary disavows the doctrine, ratification of the practice continued into the twentieth century through the exhortations of the Brethren. Tenth LDS President (1970-72), Joseph Fielding Smith (son of Joseph F. Smith, who was a nephew of Church founder, Joseph Smith, Jr.), while he was serving as President of the Quorum of the Twelve Apostles, wrote in his book, *Doctrines of Salvation*, published in 1954, that "...And men for certain crimes have had to atone as far as they could for their sins wherein they have placed themselves beyond the redeeming power of the blood of Christ."[72] President Smith continued:

...the founders of Utah incorporated in the laws of the Territory provisions for the capital punishment of those who willfully shed the blood of their fellow men. This law, which is now the law of the State, granted unto the condemned murderer the privilege of choosing for himself whether he die by hanging, or whether he be shot and thus have his blood shed in harmony with the law of God; and thus atone, so far as it is in his power to atone, for the death of his victim. Almost without exception the condemned party chooses the latter death.[73]

The next decade, Apostle Bruce R. McConkie continued to emphasize the doctrine when he wrote: "...there are some serious sins for which the cleansing blood of Christ does not operate, and the law of God is that men must have their own blood shed to atone for their sins."[74]

An original part of the temple oath was to avenge Joseph and Hyrum's perceived martyrdom by seeking vengeance against the United States and to teach this oath to LDS children. The Saints were to obey the oath under penalty of disembowelment. Heber C. Kimball acknowledged that some Church leaders were charged with treason for covenanting (as did he) that "[I] never will rest nor my posterity after me until those men who killed Joseph & Hyrum had been wiped out of the earth."*[75]

The former words and pantomimes of the LDS Temple endowment ceremony certainly support the concept that apostates or those who divulge the nature of the secret temple ceremonies were to personally atone for their sin by slitting their own throats or by self-disembowelment. Even in the early twentieth century this remained the temple endowment language. Though the language was changed years ago, the throat slitting and bowel removal pantomimes remained until the 1990 changes. I had performed them when I took out my endowment, the day before I married Trent in 1984.

These important and substantial changes were made only after publication of a controversial article questioning the appeal of the temple endowment ceremony in a 1987 issue of *Dialogue,* a scholarly LDS Journal.[76] Subsequently, the Church conducted a survey, with at least seventy-seven questions, including sub-parts, sampling some (3,400) Church members' attitudes regarding the temple ceremony[77] Though neither the fact of the survey, nor its results were made known to the general LDS membership, presumably based upon the results of the survey, the gruesome pantomimes were finally removed from the endowment ceremony. And then, as with nearly all changes in LDS doctrine, there was no formal notice given to the lay membership; the changes were quietly made and put into effect and for most of the Saints, no questions were asked.[78]

Though certainly the practice of blood atonement by mainstream Mormons has not been documented for many years, those involved in break-off or fundamentalist sects of the Religion have more recently used the principle. For example, blood atonement, along with a citation to the God-sanctioned killing of Laban in *the Book of Mormon,* was used by the defense to justify the fundamentalist Mormon Lafferty Brothers' murder of their sister-in-law and her infant daughter in 1984, on July 24th Pioneer Day, in Utah.[79]

***

Mid-nineteenth century Mormon lawlessness was frankly inapposite to accepted laws and even common decency, as practiced in what was then, the United States. In an attempt to rid Deseret from outside governance, a Mormon militia drove Justice William W. Drummond, Chief Justice of the Utah Territory, who had only recently been appointed by the U.S. in 1854, from the bench. In 1856, Justice Drummond and two other federal officials working in Utah fled Zion. The following are the reasons he gave for his resignation:

1. The Mormons look to Brigham Young alone as the ultimate legal authority over them. Thus, no law of the federal government is considered binding on the LDS;
2. Members of the 'Holy Priesthood' swear an oath to acknowledge no law except that which comes through Brigham Young;
3. There is a set of men specifically set apart to take the lives and property of persons who question the authority of the church;
4. The records of the Supreme Court have been destroyed by order of the church and with approval of Young, and federal officers have been insulted for raising issue with this treasonable act;
5. Federal officers are constantly insulted harassed and annoyed by the Mormons without redress;
6. The American government, including the president, is constantly slandered by the Mormons and Mormon leaders;
7. I have witnessed specific instances of convicted murderers being pardoned and conversely non-Mormon young men convicted without due process and serve time in the state penitentiary of Utah;* [80]

Ann Eliza Webb's compelling eye-witness account of Mormon history experienced when she was a young girl in the company of Mormonism's founders and then, traveling westward through the various way stations in Missouri and Illinois (her father was a wagon maker), settling in Utah and eventually marrying the Prophet Brigham Young when she was twenty-five, describes the practical application of the doctrine of blood atonement in the revenge effected by Young on unbelievers.

It is a significant fact that most of the persons who thus perished were Gentiles, apostates, or people who, for some reason or other, were suspected by, or disagreeable to, Brigham Young; and it came presently to be noticed that if anyone became tired of Mormonism, or impatient of the increasing despotism of the leader, and returned to the East, or started to do so, he invariably was met by the Indians and killed before he had gone very far.*[81]

Mountain Meadows Massacre—
Mormon Fundamentalism at Its Worst

During that frenzied and paranoid period of the Mormon Reformation, on September 11, 1857, Mormons, who initially claimed the dastardly deeds were perpetrated solely by Paiutes, killed one hundred and twenty Arkansas pioneers (the Fancher Party *aka* the Baker Company) enroute to California at Mountain Meadows, a location about 35 miles west of Cedar City (southern), Utah. Though he was certainly one of the participants, Danite John D. Lee was fingered by Brigham Young as the sole scapegoat for the savage attack and was finally executed by federal authorities in 1877.

Some scholars and historians suggest that the culture of unquestioned obedience to Church leaders and perhaps even the blood atonement doctrine were foremost in some Utah Saints' minds, precipitating the Mountain Meadows Massacre and other nineteenth century top-down encouraged, if not ordered, gentile and apostate atrocities. Avenging their founding prophet's death, and more recently, the death of Apostle Parley P. Pratt, who had been killed by the spurned husband of a woman he took as the last in a line of several wives, created a continued culture of revenge. This theory was proposed in 1875 by Mormon Fanny Stenhouse, an eyewitness to the culture of the time. She explains in her autobiography *Tell it All*:

As, from President Young down to the most illiterate "Elder," everyone is supposed to be specially inspired, and to be immediately guided by the spirit of the Holy ghost, education is utterly unnecessary to the members of the Mormon Priesthood; in fact it has always been looked upon as an impediment to its possessor. *Obedience* is consider the highest qualification, and it was the strict enforcement of obedience on the part of the ordinary people and the lower grades of the Priesthood towards the higher that alone could have made possible that state of affairs which existed during the "Reformation." Hence also it is that Brigham Young and the leaders are rightly held responsible for the deeds of violence and fanaticism which their followers may perpetrate; for it is well known that *no* Mormon, in a matter of grave importance, would dare to act upon his own responsibility and without he felt sure that what he did would meet with the approbation of those in authority.* [82]

Writer Will Bagley concurs with Mrs. Stenhouse's assessment in his book, *Blood of the Prophets*:

Brigham Young's relentless commitment to the Kingdom of God forged a culture of violence from Joseph Smith's theology that bequeathed a vexatious heritage to his successors. Early Mormonism's peculiar obsession with blood and vengeance created the society that made the massacre possible if not inevitable. These obsessions had devastating consequences for Young's own family. In New York in 1902, William Hooper Young, the prophet's grandson, slit the abdomen of an alleged prostitute and wrote the words "Blood Atonement" in his father's apartment. [83]

There is no clear evidence that Brigham Young ordered the murders, or failed to stop them, knowing they were imminent, but on August 5, 1857, a little more than a month before the Massacre, in anticipation of federal troops invading Utah, he declared martial law throughout the Territory. Just two days after the massacre a local church leader received a note from Young calling the whole thing off. But it was too late. Only Bishop John D. Lee (who had at one time been adopted by Brigham Young as his son) was ultimately prosecuted and convicted of the crimes.

When justice for the dead was attempted, the Prophet contradicted himself in affidavits, revised discovery responses and as quoted in the press of the times. He admitted that "Isaac Haight had alerted him [prior to the slaughter] 'concerning a company of emigrants called the Arkansas Company.'" Another time he asserted that despite his position as Indian superintendent, he learned nothing of the attack "...until some time after it occurred—then only by floating rumor." [84]

Abundant circumstantial evidence supports Mormon involvement in the Massacre. The spoils were collected by the Cedar City tithing office after the Paiute Indians received their cut. [85] John D. Lee claimed that "$4,000 in gold that the Fanchers were taking to California to buy land was taken by an LDS priesthood-holder to Salt Lake City and [given] to Brigham Young."* [86]

The *Harper's Weekly* August 13, 1859 cover illustrated the killing field described by federal officer Brevet Major Carleton at Mountain Meadows [as]:

> ... too horrible and sickening for language to describe. Human skeletons, disjointed bones, ghastly skulls and the hair of women were scattered in frightful profusion over a distance of two miles... the remains were not buried at all until after they had been dismembered by the wolves and the flesh stripped from the bones...[87]

In the mid-twentieth century, when historian Juanita Brooks was researching her treatise on the atrocity, she became aware of the existence of several affidavits of eyewitness accounts to the Massacre which were then in the possession of LDS Church leaders. Brooks made concerted attempts to obtain the affidavits. Then Apostle (and next in the line for president) David O. McKay and President J. Reuben Clark, counselor in the first presidency and after whom BYU's law school is named, had reviewed the affidavits and Clark "had decided not to give them to her." Though she had traveled 300 miles and waited hours for the evidence, the assistant laid the sealed affidavits on the table before her as he was explaining the Brethren's decision to deny her access to that evidence. [88] Despite the taunting tactics used to bait Brooks, her book became a seminal work. Unless they have been destroyed, it is likely that these important affidavits, eyewitness testimony to the slaughter, remain in the Church's vault.

Suppression of important primary source documents seems to be routine with Mormons in leadership positions. According to Will Bagley, Kate B. Carter, President of the Daughters of the Utah Pioneers:

> ...told BYU faculty members that she purged documents of controversial passages [in pioneer diaries] before publication. "I

never allow anything into print that I think will be injurious to my church," Carter insisted, "or that will in any way reflect discredit upon our pioneers."...Legend has it that Carter excised and destroyed all references to Mountain Meadows in documents that came into her possession. Brooks may have heard that Carter boasted of burning the critical minutes of the September 6, 1857, Stake High Council Meeting in Cedar City, which voted to destroy the Fancher Party.[89]

Mountain Meadows was not the first indignity perpetrated against innocent pioneers who, by necessity had to cross through Utah on their way west to the Pacific. In 1857, several other federal officials and disaffected Mormons were also believed to have been killed by order of council: Capt. John W. Gunnison, for writing a book which offended Brigham Young and the Aiken Party, six men who were traveling through Kaysville with $25,000.00 who had been accused of being spies. Mrs. Alvira L. Parrish testified that her son and husband and a Mr. Potter were killed by Danites. Testimony was also received that the Danites involved were glad to be rid of the gentiles and apostates. "There had been public preaching at Springville, to the effect that no apostates would be allowed to leave, if they did, hogholes would be stopped up with them." *[90]

In August 1857, just before the Mountain Meadows Massacre, S. B. Hosea and George B. Davis, members of the Duke's Train, passed through Salt Lake and noted preparations for war. They paid Mormons almost $2,000 dollars for guides and interpreters, but then were robbed of 326-375 head of cattle by "Indians...with light blue eyes and painted hair." [91] The Aiken Party murders occurred during this same period.[92]

Judge John Cradlebaugh, the federal authority who attempted to prosecute the Mormon officials responsible for the murders wrote to President Buchanan in frustration after the local authorities failed to serve warrants on any of the dozens of defendants charged with the crimes. These LDS government officials wouldn't serve warrants on members of their own church.

As the Judge explained, "...in regard to all the murders for which writs have been issued, that the perpetrators are men holding high civil and church offices; and the evidence shows that the crimes were committed by "order of council".*[93]

Local marshal, P. K. Dotson had other unserved warrants: "...I also have in my possession warrants against Aaron V. Johnston, a bishop; Snow, of Provo City, a President of the Church, [Brigham Young] and certain others, for the murder of the Parrishes; also a warrant against bishop Hancock, and others, for the murder of Jones and mother."*[94] According to Will Bagley, "Dotson had arrest warrants he could not serve for almost one hundred murders, "including the participators in the horrific butcheries at Mountain Meadows."*[95]

In 1860 Judge Cradlebaugh attested to this continued ecclesiastical abuse of power: "I assert...

1st That the Mormon people are subject to a theocratic government, and recognizes no law as binding which does not coincide with their pretended revelations...

4th That they teach the doctrine of "The shedding of human blood for the remission of sin," as defined by their own ecclesiastical code, and these teachings are carried into practice...

5th That they teach the doctrine that it is right and godly that Mormons should rob Gentiles whenever they can do so with facility and escape public exposure...

6th That they teach the doctrine and practice it, of castrating men, and have declared from their pulpit, with public acquiescence, that the day was near when their valleys would resound with the voice of eunuchs. I am prepared here and now with proofs to sustain these charges...*[96]

Brigham Young made an after-the-fact admission that Mormons were indeed perpetrators of the crimes. Apostle Wilford Woodruff accompanied him to the Mountain Meadows Massacre site in May, 1861 and wrote:

We visited the Mt. Meadows Monument put up at the burial place of 120 persons killed by Indians in 1857. The pile of stone was about twelve feet high but beginning to tumble down. A wooden cross is placed on top with the following words, Vengeance is mine and I will repay saith the Lord. *Pres. Young said it should be Vengeance is mine and I have taken a little.*[97]

164

Another Mormon described Young's desecration of the rock cairn monument:

> He [Young] didn't say another word. He didn't give an order. He just lifted his right arm to the square, and in five minutes there wasn't one stone left upon another. He didn't have to tell us what he wanted done. We understood. *[98]

More than a century later, remains of twenty-nine of the slaughtered were discovered during the ground preparation for the erection of an LDS Church memorial on the site. In 1999, LDS-hired archeologists found thousands of bones and remnants of scalps in the area of Mountain Meadows. In order to ward off a public relations crisis, LDS President Gordon B. Hinckley made a public statement, which included a declaration that his words should not be construed as an admission of responsibility for the killings.[99]

Utah State law in existence at the time required reporting of human remains found on private property and a scientific analysis made to determine the cause of death. However, in part due to an e-mail sent September 6, from then, Utah Governor Mike Leavitt, and then an immediate change to the law requiring death analysis, the bones of these dead were hurriedly reburied in a mass grave vault, without permission or approval of the decedents' descendants. [100]

The LDS memorial makes no reference to Mormon involvement in the killings.

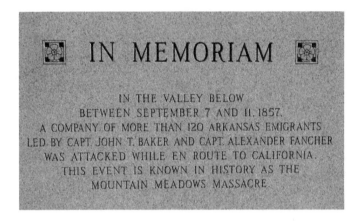

*Mountain Meadows Massacre Memorial erected by
LDS Church in 1999*

It was only after publication of Will Bagley's book, *Blood of the Prophets* in 2002, that one of the LDS Church apostles, Henry B. Eyring, on September 11, 2007, the 150th anniversary of the Mountain Meadows Massacre, publicly declared an apology.

Although the federal government spent $10,000.00 to ensure the safe return to Arkansas of the seventeen very young children saved from the Massacre, no reparations for the victims or their descendants have ever been paid by the Mormon Church. During the nineteenth century, some of the victims' young children who had been spared, claimed to have seen their families' possessions: buggies, dresses and jewelry, used or worn by the Mormons. But not even the personal property, including animals or wagons taken by those responsible for the Massacre, was ever returned to these young survivors. [101]

Mormon leaders didn't stop with the savage treatment of non-Mormons, apostates and the subjugation of their females. These nineteenth century leaders even subjected young men, members of their own faith, to unspeakable atrocities. The most chilling account is relayed by Danite John D. Lee, whose confession was written while he was in prison, awaiting his execution for his part in the Mt. Meadows Massacre:

Warren Snow was Bishop of the Church at Manti, San Pete County, Utah. He had several wives, but there was a fair, buxom

166

young woman in the town that Snow wanted for a wife. She told him she was then engaged to a young man, a member of the Church, and consequently could not marry the old priest...He told her it was the will of God that she should marry him...

The girl continued obstinate. The "teachers" of the town visited her and advised her to marry Bishop Snow....Then the authorities called on the young man and directed him to give up the young woman. This he steadfastly refused to do. He was promised Church preferment, celestial rewards, and everything that could be thought of—all to no purpose. He remained true to his intended, and said he would die before he would surrender his intended wife to the embraces of another.

The young man was ordered to go on a mission to some distant locality, so that the authorities would have no trouble in effecting their purpose of forcing the girl to marry as they desired. But the mission was refused...

His fate was left to Bishop Snow for his decision. He decided that the young man should be castrated, Snow saying, "When that is done he will not be liable to want the girl badly, and she will listen to reason when she knows that her lover is no longer a man."

It was then decided to call a meeting of the people who live true to counsel,...in Manti,...The young man was there, and was again requested, ordered and threatened, to get him to surrender the young woman to Snow, but true to his plighted troth, he refused to consent to give up the girl. The lights were then put out. An attack was made on the young man. He was severely beaten, and then tied with his back down on a bench, when Bishop Snow took a bowie-knife, and performed the operation in a most brutal manner...

The party then left the young man weltering in his blood,...The young man regained his health, but has been an idiot or quiet lunatic ever since,...To make a long story short, I will say, the young woman was soon after forced into being sealed to Bishop Snow.

Brigham Young, when he heard of this treatment of the young man, was very mad, but did nothing against Snow. He left him in Charge as Bishop at Manti, and ordered the matter to be hushed up. This is only one instance of many that I might give to show the danger of refusing to obey counsel in Utah.*[102]

This was not the only account of calculated Mormon castration. Mormon Judge Hosea Stout (himself, a member of the Danites) and one who held various Utah government positions recorded that on Feb. 27, 1858, "several persons disguised as Indians entered Henry Jones' house and dragged him out of bed with a whore and castrated him by a square & close amputation."*[103]

J. H. Beadle, attorney for Bill Hickman, the Chief Danite of Utah, and editor of Hickman's autobiography *Brigham's Destroying Angel*, claimed, "The eunuch is the natural result of a polygamous society, and already several such cases have occurred in Utah." [104]   Benjamin Winchester, a young Mormon convert in the days of Joseph Smith, claims Joseph's brother Hyrum told him:

> ...when I spoke to him about the numerical equality of the male and the female sexes he explained that that difficulty could in time be surmounted BY MAKING EUNUCHS of surplus men who should be "hewers of wood and drawers of water," and that the church dignitaries and the more worthy brethren would be left the choice of plenty of women. *[105]

Perhaps the uncertainty of Brigham Young's continued control over his gathered Saints led to these reactionary events chronicled by the first federally appointed judicial officers, Danites and former Mormons. Given the pervasive control of the Territory by the Mormon Zionist Theocracy, these gentile jurists were doomed to fail in their attempts at enforcing the laws conducive to a civilized society.

Deseret v. the U.S. Government

The execution of the treaty of Guadalupe-Hidalgo on February 2, 1848, less than a year after Brigham Young's entry into the Salt Lake Valley, ended the Mexican-American War. Through the Organic Act of 1850, Congress established the Utah Territory, leaving the creation and specifics of the local judiciary up to the territorial government. In 1851, just a few months later, Utah Mormon leaders defiantly claimed the same area as the Deseret Territory. Thus, sovereignty over this vast expanse of newly annexed land, which then included almost all of Nevada, most of Arizona, the western half of Colorado, and the southernmost part of California, including today's San Bernardino all the way to the Pacific at San Diego, populated with Mormon and gentile, was placed at issue.

The Utah Territory was located on the well-worn route to the Pacific Territories. Great Basin communities had been charging extreme prices for goods and services needed by émigrés along the way. From the very beginning of the Saints' settlement, through their ostensible claim to sovereignty with no demonstrable ability to follow federal law, or even the moral imperatives of a civilized society, the United States had its eye on the Mormon problem.

Once news of the Mountain Meadows Massacre and the other questionable deaths of Pacific coast bound pioneers reached the East, the federal government stepped up its initial effort, the first of many—military, legislative and judicial—to rid the West of the Mormons. Relations between the federal government and the Mormons had become openly hostile.

In May of 1857, U.S. President James Buchanan sent a military force of about 1,500 troops to Salt Lake to quell the blatant disregard of federal authority. These actions culminated in the Utah War (1857-58) with skirmishes in what is now southwestern Wyoming where a Mormon militia blocked access to Salt Lake Valley and a Mormon cavalry burned Army supply trains. By then, per their Prophet's order, the Saints had left their communities in Northern Utah for the southern part of the Territory. Nick-named 'Buchanan's Blunder,' in the States, on June 26, 1858, the U.S. Army marched through a deserted Salt Lake City.

The Utah War didn't change much in the State. Mormon Utah continued in their polygamy practice and flaunting of federal law. And due to the nation's ongoing civil war, Congress took ten years from the date of the Church's public acknowledgment that polygamy was indeed part of official LDS doctrine (1952) for it to pass the Morrill Anti-Bigamy Act. Abraham Lincoln signed it into law in 1862. It banned polygamy, revoked the 1855 Deseret Territory's law incorporating the LDS Church, and mandated that no religious organization could own real estate valued at more than \$50,000.[106] In support of this law, congressional and judicial testimony emphasized Mormonites' failure to peacefully integrate with society in the settlements they had made on their way west, that Heber C. Kimball, first counselor to Young, referred to his women as 'cows,' and the 'blasphemous nonsense,' contained in the Mormon bible. [107] However due to the Morrill Act's stringent evidentiary requirements and Mormon control of the probate courts, few polygamists were convicted under this law. The Act was impossible to enforce.

The Organic Act's forfeiture of federal control in favor of Utah territorial rights would eventually be realized as a huge mistake by the federal government. As a result of the Act's provisions, probate courts (ordinarily limited to estate litigation) in Utah had usurped jurisdiction over all civil matters, including domestic litigation and prosecution under federal anti-bigamy laws. The probate courts were staffed by Mormons and Mormon jurors were seated, with few if any gentiles or those who had left Mormonism serving. Convictions for any kind of crime were rare if the defendant was a member of the LDS Church. It would take decades of federal legislation and United States Supreme Court decisions to eventually resolve the struggle between the Deseret Territory and the U.S. Government.[108]

One unique example of the jurisdictional wrangling between the federal government and the Mormon Theocracy is documented in the original edition of the *Journal of Discourses*. The application of early Utah homicide law is found in the closing statement and jury instruction regarding the choice of law in a case involving a manslaughter charge brought against Howard Egan for killing the man caught sleeping with his wife.

Defendant's attorney, LDS apostle and cousin to founding Prophet Joseph Smith, George A. Smith, argued that the "law of the mountain," should be: "The man who seduces his neighbor's wife must die, and her nearest relative must kill him." In advocating that the Court adopt this particular rule of law, attorney Smith condemned other jurisdictions, for example Great Britain, where civil suits are brought and "...a few pence is all the scoundrel pays." Attorney Smith then goes on to argue for Egan's acquittal.[109]

Mormon Justice Zerubbabel "Z" Snow followed Egan's suggestion and instructed the jury that if the crime was found to be committed:

>...within that extent of country between this and the Missouri River, over which the United States have the *sole* and *exclusive jurisdiction*, your verdict must be guilty. If you do not find the

170

crime to have been committed there, but in the territory of Utah, the defendant, for that reason, is entitled to a verdict of not guilty.*
110

The Mormon jury acquitted Egan. When U.S. President Millard Fillmore heard about this case, he removed Judge Snow from office.

For years, the Church published and sold a sanitized version of the *Journal of Discourses*, deleting certain unfavorable, or perhaps in the Brethren's collective thought, irrelevant entries such as the choice of law jury instruction in the Egan trial. Recently, in an apparent but belated attempt at full disclosure, the Church-owned Desert Bookstore has begun offering a complete set of the *Journal* with facsimiles of the original text. "There have been no alterations, deletions, or additions to the text," the Bookstore claims.[111]

Freedom of the press, with a balanced view of current events and reporting, has historically been absent in the State of Utah. In the later part of 1858 through May 17, 1859, the *Valley Tan*, a newspaper edited by Kirk Anderson, was published in Salt Lake. The editor heroically reported, detailing Mormon leaders' attempts to keep Mormons ignorant by instituting the ridiculous Deseret Alphabet, a phonetically-based language concocted by Brigham Young. The newspaper also documented the commission, and on most occasions, futile prosecution, of multiple crimes under Brigham Young's rule.

On February 22, 1859, Anderson announced in his paper that thousands of disaffected Mormons were leaving Utah. "MORMON EXODUS, —From the best information we can gather, there will be between four and five thousand persons leave this territory for the States and California, apostates from the Church."* Finally in his last article of May 17, 1859, the brave editor gives up, noting that "[We] had scarcely commenced publication before the Utah legislature declared the *Valley Tan* a 'libelous and scurrilous sheet.'" With "no apologies to offer, no retractions to make," the editor ceased his publication.

Wife no. 19 was a huge success outside Zion, but certainly never received favorable press or even an acknowledged distribution, among faithful Mormons. However, the author's first-hand account of the horrors of polygamy likely helped lead to the passage of the 1882 Edmunds Act, which included unlawful cohabitation and polygamy as federal crimes punishable by a fine of $300.00 and/or imprisonment up to six months.

171

The Edmunds Act also denied polygamists the right to hold public office, vote, or serve on a jury in any U. S. territory. As a result of these new federal penalties for polygamy, Mormon leaders began to push their polygamous activities underground and refer to those relationships as spiritual, instead of legal unions. Nevertheless, the practice of polygamy continued.

Subsequently, the more stringent Edmunds-Tucker Act was passed just five years later, in 1887. This Act contained stronger language. It expressly recognized the Mormon Church as a subversive organization, dissolved the LDS Church Corporation by *fiat* and directed the federal government to confiscate all Church properties valued over $50,000. Shortly after its passage, the U.S. Marshall's Office began enforcing the Edmunds-Tucker Act by confiscating Church property. In response, the Mormon Church sued the United States, claiming that it had illegally taken its property.

The Church lost the case. *[The] Late Corporation of the Church of Jesus Christ of Latter-day Saints v. United States, Romney, et. al.*, 1890, 136 U.S. 1, upheld the Edmunds-Tucker Act. The U.S. Supreme Court reasoned that, "The power to make acquisitions of territory by conquest, by treaty, and by cession, is an incident of national sovereignty."[112] Despite Brigham Young's attempt to create a State of Deseret, Mormon leaders lacked sovereignty over the territory they had settled. Thus, the Brethren's proclamation of a formal State of Deseret and their attendant, ostensible acquisition of property were declared a nullity *ab initio*. The High Court found that when the territory west of the Rocky Mountains was acquired from Mexico it became the property of the federal government. Since the Church never had legal title to the properties it originally claimed in the Utah area, the taking of that property under federal eminent domain law was found to be constitutional.

Referencing the barbarous practice of polygamy, the Court explained:

Notwithstanding the stringent laws which have been passed by congress, notwithstanding all the efforts made to suppress this barbarous practice,—the sect or community composing the Church of Jesus Christ of Latter-day Saints perseveres, in defiance of law, in preaching, upholding, promoting, and defending it. It is a matter of public notoriety that its emissaries are engaged in many

172

countries in propagating this nefarious doctrine, and urging its converts to join the community in Utah. The existence of such a propaganda is a blot on our civilization... It is unnecessary here to refer to the past history of the sect; to their defiance of the government authorities; to their attempt to establish an independent community; to their efforts to drive from the territory all who were not connected with them in communion and sympathy. The tale is one of patience on the part of the American government and people, and of contempt of authority and resistance to law on the part of the Mormons.[113]

The Supreme Court's ruling led to the official abandonment of polygamy by the Church. Soon after the ruling, the U.S. Attorney seized several hundred thousand dollars of LDS negotiable instruments. The Church quickly issued the 1890 Manifesto, denying that its members had recently practiced polygamy and simultaneously promising to abandon the practice. Those already established polygamous relationships became illegal *nunc pro tunc.*

In a good faith response to the Manifesto, a congressional resolution released the Church's assets. However, by 1898, according to then President, Wilford Woodruff, the Church was in debt for "...nearly two millions of dollars for business enterprises." [114] After the *Reynolds* polygamy conviction was upheld by the U.S. Supreme Court in 1878 (See Appendix A: *Reynolds v. U.S.*) hundreds of Utah Mormon polygamists were prosecuted. Despite the 1890 Manifesto, by 1893 there had been a total of 1035 convictions in Utah for unlawful cohabitation and polygamy.[115]

In order to attain statehood, Deseret had made repeated proclamations to the rest of the United States that it was not beholden to Mormonism. After years of Brigham Young and his successors (Young died in 1877 from cholera) alternatively lobbying for statehood and threatening succession from the Union, in 1896 Utah obtained statehood. However, despite LDS Manifesto language which pledged to cease polygamy, the Brethren continued to perform polygamous marriages well into the twentieth century.

Church and State: the Blurred Line Continues

After fourth LDS President and signatory to the 1890 Manifesto, Wilford Woodruff died in 1898, Lorenzo Snow was president of the Church for a brief period until his death in 1901, when Joseph F. Smith, was placed in the position and remained president/prophet until his death in 1918. This Smith was the son of the founding prophet's brother, Hyrum.

In 1895, Mormon B.H. Roberts, endorsed by the Church, lost his race for the position of Utah congressman in the U.S. House of Representatives. However, in 1898 he was elected to the 56th Congress, but the House refused to seat him because he was, and continued to be, a well-known polygamist. Later, after statehood, LDS Apostle Reed Smoot was endorsed by Church hierarchy for U.S. Senator. Opponents of his candidacy claimed the seating of such a high-ranking Mormon was the equivalent of allowing a Catholic cardinal the position. A lengthy inquiry into Smoot's fitness for office ensued.

During the Reed Smoot Congressional confirmation hearings (1904-07) Mormon leaders admitted under oath that they had breached the 1890 Manifesto. Others, including Apostles, fled the State and even the Country, in order to avoid being served with subpoenas to testify at the hearing. LDS President Joseph F. Smith admitted that he had eleven children born of various wives, years after 1890. This, in direct violation of the pledges contained within the Manifesto, which pledges had been the very condition upon which Utah was granted amnesty from further prosecution for polygamy, from disenfranchisement and which made possible Utah's admission into the Union. Mormon testimony also included admissions that more than a dozen new polygamous marriages had been performed after 1890 and that several of these involved LDS Apostles.

Mormon Frank J. Cannon, son of LDS Apostle George Q. Cannon, and one-term young senator from Utah, described President Joseph F. Smith's practice of continuing to perform polygamous marriages and the Church's continued interference in both state and federal government. All this was done in direct contravention to the Church's promises in its various manifestos. Church leaders failed in their promise to stay out of politics. After the turn of the 20th century, there were behind the scenes agreements with the Republican Party and guarantees of *en bloc* support of Mormon solidarity in Utah and the western states in exchange for financial consideration toward Church businesses. In his book, *Under the Prophet in Utah*, Senator Cannon writes:

> ...here was a beginning of policy and treachery which the present Church leaders, under Joseph F. Smith, have since consistently practiced, in defiance of the laws of the state and the "revelation of God" with lies and evasion, with perjury and its subornation in violation of the most solemn pledges to the country, and through the agency of a political tyranny that makes serious prosecution impossible and immunity a public boast.
>
> ...testimony was given [in the Reed Smoot hearings] that in 1896 the Church authorities had appointed a committee of six elders to examine all the bills introduced into the Utah legislature and decide which were "proper" to be passed...
>
> All this [Church interference with federal government elections by prescribing candidates] had been done not for the protection of the people, who were threatened with no proscription-and not for the advancement of the faith, which has been free to work out its own future. It has been done as a part of the an alliance between the "financial" prophets of the Church and the "financial" interests of the country-which have been exploiting the people of Utah as they have exploited the whole nation with the aid of the ecclesiastical authorities in Utah. [116]

In about 1905, when it was clear that despite the majority report from Congress being against him, a possibility remained that Smoot would be seated, a group of about a dozen prominent gentile Utahns met and formulated a statement about the true nature of things in the State. This written statement included the fact that Utah remained a theocracy, that executive and legislative branches of Utah State government were dominated by the Church, that:

> ...By means of its immense collection of tithes and its large investment in commercial and financial enterprise, it dominates every line of business in Utah except mines and railroads; and these latter it influences its control over Mormon labor and by its control of legislation and franchises. It holds nearly every Gentile merchant and professional man at its vengeance, by its influence

175

over the patronage which he must have in order to be successful. It corrupts every Gentile who is affected by either fear or venality, and asks of him a part of its power to play the autocrat in Utah and to deceive the country as to its purposes and its operations... (Cannon, *Under the Prophet in Utah,* p. 159).

This quorum of gentiles all agreed upon the facts and intended to present their combined statement to the U. S. Congress to assist in the Reed Smoot decision. Nevertheless, when the time came to "throw down the gauntlet," according to Cannon, these initially brave men were derailed by their collective fear of business ruination from any outright opposition to the Utah Church.

After Smoot had been successfully seated and once polygamy was no longer openly practiced (President Smith had issued another manifesto in 1904, again swearing off polygamy and promising to excommunicate any who continued in the practice), the Brethren had to find another way of ensuring control over its membership and the Utah population in general. In 1919 Utah ratified the Eighteenth Amendment, joining the other states in adopting the prohibition against liquor. This Amendment was superseded and nullified in 1933 when the Utah congressional delegation directly opposed then, LDS Church President Grant's wish to keep the ban on alcohol in place.

Nevertheless, for almost seventy-five years after the abandonment of prohibition, the Utah State Legislature found a way to effectively deter liquor sales. Exercising complete control over the sales of alcohol, it instituted a required club membership fee to be purchased prior to buying just one drink in Utah, and even then only certain 'private clubs' were authorized to sell the memberships. It was impossible to purchase a glass of wine with your meal without belonging to one of these clubs, even if only for an evening.

This restriction on the sale of alcohol led to Utah's reputation as a dry state, which repelled many would-be tourists and residents. With the advent of the 2002 Winter Olympics, enforcement of Utah liquor laws was slackened if not abandoned. Finally in 2009, liquor by the drink came to Utah, but even now the liquor stores are controlled by the State.

Evidence of the intricately linked relationship between Utah's government and the Mormon Church continues. Although impossible to procure exact statistics, a substantial majority of Utah State government decision-makers are members of the Mormon Church. In 2002, James E. Shelledy, editor of the *Salt Lake Tribune*, told a reporter: "The fact is that we live in a quasi-theocracy. Eighty percent of officeholders are of a single party, ninety percent of a single religion, ninety-nine percent of a single race and eighty-five percent of one gender."[117]

Shelledy left in 2003 after twelve years with the paper. The *Desert News* and the *Tribune* had operated under a joint operating agreement (JOA) since 1952 through the Newspaper Agency Corporation, in which the LDS Church owned half the stock. Though some claim this didn't influence the *Tribune's* reporting about the Church, Shelledy told me in a 2010 interview that for decades after the agreement, the *Tribune* reported on nothing about the Church except General Conference.

During Shelledy's employment, the *Tribune* began covering more controversial events. Years of litigation over the JOA and ownership issues ensued. LDS public relations would call and complain about something the *Tribune* had reported on, such as the Mountain Meadows Massacre excavation revealing the buried remains of victims in 1999, or the *Arizona Republic* financial disclosure article, reprinted in'92.

Shelledy was not aware of any peremptory attempts by the Brethren to censor the *Tribune*—no prior-restraint. However, he stressed that though he was editor-in-chief, he wasn't privy to any conversations held between *Tribune* publisher Jack Gallivan and the Brethren.[118] Early on, this media monopoly was recognized and Utah's Attorney General, Robert B. Hansen (1977-1981) contemplated bringing an anti-trust suit against the papers. However, his four year term ended before he could effectively prosecute the claim.

Though the Church denies the continued *de facto* theocracy, the incestuous relationship between the LDS Church and the Utah State Government continues. A reporter for the Associated Press wrote in 1993 that "...house and senate leaders on both sides of the aisle routinely meet before the Utah State legislative general session with the Church's Public Affairs Committee, composed of four members of the Council of the Twelve Apostles, the tier of leadership below the governing First Presidency."[119] The 2006 LDS Church Handbook of Instructions reads, "Church members are encouraged to appeal to legislators, judges, and other government officials [to promote various Mormon Church policies]."[120]

Growing up in Bountiful, Utah, I hadn't noticed a theocracy, but after living out of state for decades, upon my return I was struck with the degree of entanglement between Mormonism and Utah State and local government. I had believed that during those two decades the Utah culture would have necessarily become more diverse. Instead, what I found was a state which is more polarized than ever along religious and political lines.

I had never experienced gender discrimination in any form, while practicing as a young attorney in Southern California. However, as an experienced female trial attorney, the situation in Utah was much different. For example, I have heard male attorneys called 'brother,' by male trial court judges during sidebar conferences. Another trial judge badgered a young woman, who was part of the venire panel during our jury selection with very personal questions. She said she wasn't married. "Not even engaged?" he exclaimed incredulously. "No," she said. She was a dancer with Ballet West.

This chauvinism sometimes turns into downright misogyny when Mormon (and other like-minded) males are faced with female peers. Myself and another female trial attorney have both been assaulted, she in the parking lot by a male LDS attorney, me in my Salt Lake City office during a deposition, by the partner of a medical malpractice defendant. Fortunately my client, a former BYU football player, stepped directly in front of the enraged physician to intercede on my behalf.

Upon my return, I realized that most all the successful Utah businesses, including law firms, were Mormon-owned and operated and catered to Mormon culture. State legislators were also business owners and routinely made new laws advancing their private interests. These legislators didn't seem to recognize the widespread conflicts of interest; if they did they had come to accept them. In the nineteenth century Utah was an admitted theocracy. This original failure to separate government from private interests, whether religious or business, continues and continues to be overlooked.

I researched some of the cases decided during my absence: some had made it into the local press; news of other cases had been circumspectly limited to court documents. In the mid-1980s, Mormon Mark Hoffman killed two persons and accidentally injured himself with homemade pipe bombs. LDS leaders were implicated in purchasing forged historical documents from Hoffman and in financing at least one of Hoffman's faked documents. Hoffman was charged with the murders and with various counts of forgery.

178

True reporting of the whole messy Hoffman affair in *The Mormon Murders*, written by two Harvard Law graduates, reveals how local prosecutors, and owners of the local media, most of whom were either Mormons or beholden to the Church, were loathe to report Hoffman's crimes accurately and fully.[121] Neither the U.S. Attorney, nor the local prosecutors pushed to take Hoffman to trial for his crimes. They failed to prosecute what ultimately became a clear case. Finally, Hoffman pleaded guilty to manslaughter in a case that would have further cracked the foundation of Mormonism had it been tried and Church leaders like Gordon B. Hinckley and Hugh Pinnock been subpoenaed to testify. If a good job had been done by a prosecutorial staff unaffiliated with the LDS Church, subpoenas would have been issued for the entire contents of the Church records vault, and who knows what would have been discovered among the historical documents hidden away in the secret chambers of the Church. (The Hoffman case is discussed in more depth in the next chapter).

Contemporary Examples of Mormon Influence in Utah Government

In addition to the suppression of the publicity surrounding the Hoffman case, the following are samples of cases, much of it brought or at least assisted by the Utah Chapter of the ACLU, over the past couple of decades, which illustrate the continued influence of Mormonism in Utah. This ecclesiastical influence directly and negatively affects civil rights in the State. "[T]he national ACLU 'has designated the entire state of Utah a 'crisis area: in terms of civil rights infringement.'"[122]

1991—Utah Legislature Unconstitutionally Bans Abortion

The Utah Legislature disavowed *Roe v. Wade*, the 1973 U.S. Supreme Court decision allowing abortion, by enacting a state anti-abortion law in 1991. Jane L. Bangerter sued the State, arguing that the law violated her federally guaranteed constitutional right of privacy. The Tenth Circuit Court of Appeals ruled the Utah law unconstitutional; the State appealed. The U.S. Supreme Court denied Utah certiorari, upholding the lower court's ruling that the Utah State law was unconstitutional.[123]

1994—County Acts in Loco Parentis, Violating Records Disclosure Law

Mormons are instructed to avoid media that contains graphic violence or strong sexual content. In Davis County, just north of Salt Lake, there are mostly suburban communities and with the exception of Utah County, it contains the highest percentage of Mormon residents in the State.

In 1994, the Davis County Sheriff's Office refused to release to the press a 911 audio tape or sheriff's reports involving a double murder-suicide. The 911 calls had been made by the female victim as she was being shot by her estranged husband. The Sheriff's Office claimed that the tape was "too graphic" for the public. The local Fox television affiliate filed suit for an order requiring disclosure of the records. More than a year later, a district court judge ruled that the 911 tape and Sheriff's reports were public records under Utah law and ordered Davis County to release them.[124]

1995—Censorship and Discrimination at the Utah State Fair

Kurt and Cindy Van Gorden were Baptists who for years had been denied a permit to vend their literature at the Utah State Fair. The basis of the denial was that fair patrons complained about their booth's content. In 1996, the Van Gordens were offered a contract to display their materials; however, unknown to the plaintiffs, their particular contract contained restrictions which were not part of other booth rental contracts. After more complaints by patrons, Utah State Fair officials and the Salt Lake Police Department forcibly evicted the Van Gordens during the September, 1998, State Fair.

The ACLU filed suit against the State Fair officials and the Salt Lake Police Department. A settlement was reached in 2001 for lost compensation to the Van Gordens and an agreement that should they wish to return to the Fair, they would be able to rent a booth on the same terms as all other vendors.[125]

Chapter 7: The Utah Theocracy

1996—Meetings re: Gay Rights Held in Secret by Utah Legislators

In 1996, the Utah Senate held a secret meeting to discuss the issue of gay student clubs in public schools. The Senate issued no public notice or agenda for the meeting, nor did it take a vote to convene in closed session for any of the purposes authorized under the Utah Open and Public Meetings Act (Utah Code § 52-4-102, 1996).

The ACLU filed suit in district court; the State moved to dismiss. The Court found that the Senate's action "ignores and overlooks the textual limits of the Utah Constitution, and the Open and Public Meetings Act on the issue of public meetings." [126] A stipulated judgment was eventually reached by the parties, with an admission that the Utah Senate had violated the State's open court's provision of the law. [127]

During the course of the litigation it was noted that one small-town Utah legislator admitted that in recent years "outsiders," who "were not of the faith," had moved into his town. This legislator was reluctant to require town officials to post notices of government meetings. Before the person 'not of the faith' had moved into town, notice of the meetings had only been given at LDS chapels, after Sunday meetings.

1997—Religious and Racial Discrimination by State Employees

Plaintiff husband and wife, William and Nancy Silverman, worked as custodial employees at the Utah State Capital. Over a period of several years, the Jewish couple was harassed and they were the victims of racial and religious slurs and graffiti. The ACLU eventually negotiated a settlement on their behalf. [128]

1998—Lesbian Teacher Terminated from her Position
For Talking about her Sexuality

A Utah federal judge ruled in favor of a high school teacher who claimed she was fired as a volleyball coach because she is a lesbian. Plaintiff Wendy Weaver said Defendant, Spanish Fork High School, violated her rights with a gag order which prevented her from talking with students or staff about her sexual orientation, even outside of school. U.S. District Judge Bruce Jenkins agreed that her rights of free speech, equal protection and due process had been violated.

181

An American Fraud: One Lawyer's Case against Mormonism

1998—Utah County Confiscates Names of "Pornographic" Video Renters

Utah County officials obtained a warrant to enter and search the Movie Buffs stores in the Utah County cities of Lehi and American Fork. During the searches, the Sheriff's Department confiscated hundreds of 'pornographic' videos and lists of those who had rented them. Movie Buffs filed a Title 42 USC §1983 civil rights action against Utah County alleging First and Fourth Amendment violations.

The ACLU of Utah intervened in the lawsuit on behalf of three individuals who believed their names appeared on the confiscated lists. The complaint-in-intervention alleged that release of the renters' names violated their privacy rights. The District Court had yet to rule on the motion to intervene, when the Tenth Circuit Court of Appeals dismissed Movie Buffs' action on the grounds that the federal courts should abstain from such litigation until the resolution of the then, pending criminal proceedings against Movie Buffs.

In March 1999, the jury in the criminal trial acquitted the Movie Buffs owner of all criminal charges. Subsequently, the ACLU obtained an order from the federal court for destruction of the seized lists in order to protect the video renters' rights to privacy.[129]

1999—Author Exposing Smith's Egyptian Papyri Fraud Fired from Position as High School Teacher

Charles Larson was a public school teacher and religious scholar. Shortly after publishing a critique of the claimed origins of the Book of Abraham (see the excellent exegesis, "...by *his own hand upon papyrus*, cited in this bibliography) considered by LDS faithful to be ancient scripture, Larson was terminated from his teaching position in the Provo School District. His termination was ostensibly part of a reduction in force. Later, Larson became aware that his termination was in fact based on religious discrimination.

Upon investigation of his employment discrimination complaint, the Federal Equal Employment Opportunity Commission (EEOC) concurred. Nevertheless, the local school district refused to reconsider its position. In January 1999, the ACLU and cooperating attorneys filed a complaint for violation of Title VII and the United States Constitution. A settlement was ultimately reached.[130]

2000—Salt Lake City School Board Denies Students' Rights to Free Speech and Association

In 1995, an East High School student wanted to form a student club to be called the Gay/Straight Alliance (GSA) to provide a safe forum for gay and lesbian students. The Federal Equal Access Act of 1984 mandated that any school which received federal funding must give all non-curricular clubs equal access to a school's resources. The student's request was denied by both East High School and the Salt Lake City School Board. After years of litigation brought by the ACLU and other non-profit local and national organizations, Utah school districts were forced to change their laws to comply with federal non-discrimination laws for non-curricular clubs.[131]

2003—City Councilman Requests that Prayer to Mother in Heaven is Allowed before Council Meetings

It has long been the custom in Utah, as with the U.S. Congress, to have prayer before state and local government meetings. However, one non-Mormon city councilman became fed up with the degree to which Mormonism was entangled in city council meetings and did something quite memorable about it. Prior to one particular meeting he began to offer up an unusual prayer, one sure to have incited the rancor of the devout LDS council members.

The text of Mr. Snyder's proposed opening prayer was as follows:

OUR MOTHER, who art in heaven (if, indeed there is a heaven and if there is a God that takes a woman's form) hallowed be thy name, we ask for thy blessing for and guidance of those that will participate in this meeting and for those mortals that govern the state of Utah;

We fervently ask that you guide the leaders of this city, Salt Lake County and the state of Utah so that they may see the wisdom of separating church and state and so that they will never again perform demeaning religious ceremonies as part of official government functions;

183

We pray that you prevent self-righteous politicians from mis-using the name of God in conducting government meetings; and, that you lead them away from the hypocritical and blasphemous deception of the public, attempting to make the people believe that bureaucrats' decisions and actions have thy stamp of approval if prayers are offered at the beginning of government meetings;

We ask that you grant Utah's leaders and politicians enough courage and discernment to understand that religion is a private matter between every individual and his or her deity; We beseech thee to educate government leaders that religious beliefs should not be broadcast and revealed for the purpose of impressing others; we pray that you strike down those that mis-use your name and those that cheapen the institution of prayer by using it for their own selfish political gains;

We ask that the people of the state of Utah will some day learn the wisdom of the separation of church and state; we ask that you will teach the people of Utah that government should not participate in religion; we pray that you smite those government officials that would attempt to censor or control prayers made by anyone to you or to any other of our gods;

We ask that you deliver us from the evil of forced religious worship now sought to be imposed upon the people of the state of Utah by the actions of mis-guided, weak and stupid politicians, who abuse power in their own self-righteousness;

All of this we ask in thy name and in the name of thy son (if in fact you had a son that visited Earth) for the eternal betterment of all of us who populate the great state of Utah. Amen.[132]

In 2003, the Utah Supreme Court wisely held that Tom Snyder's recitation was in fact a prayer and therefore was entitled to as much indulgence as any LDS or any other religions' (or any non-sectarian) pleas. "If Murray City chooses to continue to open its city council meeting with prayer, it must strictly adhere to the neutrality requirements set forth in prior case law."[133]

Chapter 7: The Utah Theocracy

2005—LDS Church Prevails in Protracted Effort to Own a Portion of Historically Public Main Street

In April 1999, the Salt Lake City Council voted 5-2 to sell the downtown block of Main Street between North and South Temple to the LDS Church, effectively transforming the historic Eagle Gate section of Main Street from a public thoroughfare to a private passageway or plaza. However, in the real estate transaction, the City retained a pedestrian easement (right-of-way). Nevertheless, since the Church acquired ownership of the plaza, first amendment rights were heavily censored.

In November, 1999, the ACLU filed suit on behalf of the First Unitarian Church, Utahns for Fairness and the Utah National Organization for Women. The ACLU of Utah argued that due to Main Street's role in Salt Lake City's history, it should continue to be a public forum. In 2001, U.S. District Judge Ted Stewart dismissed the claims. The ACLU appealed to the Tenth Circuit Court of Appeals arguing separation of church and state and first amendment rights. On October 9, 2002, the Tenth Circuit issued a ruling reversing the district court decision and declaring the Main Street Plaza sidewalks a public forum. In response to an order to the lower court from the Tenth Circuit Court of Appeals, on January 29, 2003, the District Court issued a judgment and permanent injunction in favor of the plaintiffs:

> ...It is further ORDERED, ADJUDGED AND DECLARED that the pedestrian easement reserved to Salt Lake City Corporation pursuant to the April 27, 1999 Special Warranty Deed is a public forum to which the First Amendment applies; that the restrictions on expressive conduct on the pedestrian easement contained in sections 2.2, 2.3, and 3 of the April 27, 1999 Special Warranty Deed violate the First Amendment of the United States Constitution; and said restrictions are therefore invalid.

In June 2003, the Salt Lake City Council voted 6-0 to exchange the plaza's public easement for land owned by the Church on the west side of Salt Lake and funds for a new community center.[134] In August 2003, the ACLU filed a lawsuit again asking the Tenth Circuit to intervene; however the suit was dismissed because no part of the plaza remained public property—the easement had been exchanged for adequate consideration in

185

a *bona fide* real estate transaction.[135]

Since the final ruling in this case, the Church has posted signs advising that it is private property. In 2009, LDS security guards were videotaped accosting a man on the plaza who had just kissed his male partner on the cheek.

Photograph looking south on the west side of Main Street Plaza from the north end, May, 2010.

2008—Utah Legislators Exhibit Bigotry and Ignorance during Debate

In contrast to the Utah Supreme Court's usually sound, if at times conservative, interpretation of the law, the Utah State Legislature is notorious for allowing its members' personal prejudice and beliefs, particularly religious beliefs, to overshadow reason.

Regarding SB48, a bill which proposed equalizing school construction funds among the various school districts in the state, West Jordan City Republican State Senator Chris Buttars commented in the February 2008 debate. West Jordan Republican Howard Stephenson had called it "the ugly baby bill." Then, as Senator Buttars stood to vote, he added a comment that revealed his innate racial bigotry: "This baby is black; I'll tell ya, it's a dark ugly thing."[136] Despite widespread negative press over the racial slur, the Utah State Senate refused to sanction their colleague, Senator Buttars, for his remark.

Another example of the degree of control the Mormon Church has over the Utah State Government can be found in the Utah State Senate's denial of Utah District Court Judge Robert Hilder's approval for appointment to the Utah Court of Appeals on November 19, 2008. The Senate refused his confirmation despite the fact that the majority of litigators as well as other judges in the state rated him as the best of trial court judges. The dissenting congressmen pointed out that Judge Hilder didn't appear to have the proper demeanor for an appellate court judge.

One comment in particular by a Utah state senator is indicative of the provincial rationale used to legislate in Utah. Senator Lyle Hillyard initially moved to recommend Judge Hilder, and then quite disingenuously discussed Hilder's first marriage and divorce, told the group that Judge Hilder relayed his story about his conversion to Mormonism as a young man in Australia, but noted that the Judge had said nothing about his activities as of late (the implication being that they couldn't be certain he was still an active member of the LDS Church). Senator Hillyard also noted that he had heard that Judge Hilder was going through a sort of "male menopause," as a preface to his inappropriate remarks concerning Judge Hilder's personal life.[137]

2009—Discriminatory Tax Upheld in Violation of the First Amendment Freedom of Expression

Though lobbied against by the ACLU and other organizations as an illegal and selective taxation violative of both the First Amendment and the equal protection guarantees of the 14th Amendment, the Utah Legislature passed H.B. 239, "Sexually Explicit Business and Escort Service Tax," during its 2004 general session. The law imposed a substantial tax on businesses that provide escort services or feature "any nude or partially denuded individual."

Suit was filed in 2004 on behalf of several of Utah's escort and nude dancing establishments. The ACLU filed an amicus brief. The case was heard by the Utah Supreme Court. *Bushco v. Utah State Tax Commission,* 2009 UT 73, 225 P.3d 153 (Utah 2009), claimed that the State's interest in targeting sex crimes was sufficient to justify the law. This decision was made, though no evidence was provided linking nude dancing or escort services with sex crimes. Chief Justice Durham dissented.

2010—Execution by Firing Squad—Blood Atonement in Practice

Utah's death by firing squad, necessarily shedding the convict's blood, remained an option for capital punishment until it was changed in 2004. According to sponsoring Representative Sheryl Allen, Republican from Bountiful, the rationale for the change was not because it could be considered cruel and unusual punishment; rather, the State legislators sought to avoid negative press concerning Utah's historic method of execution.[138]

On June 18, 2010, convicted killer Ronnie Lee Gardner was executed by firing squad. Gardner's choice of execution is indicative of the residual beliefs in blood atonement held by some Utahns. Even today, in order to ensure an impartial jury in first-degree murder and other capital cases, good criminal defense attorneys question prospective jurors about their views on blood atonement.[139]

2010—Utah Legislative and Executive Branches Attempt to Rid the State of Respected Female Chief Justice

The Utah Constitution mandates separation of church and state—even more emphatically than the U.S. Constitution. Although Utah promotes the advancement of females in state government (there are many Utah state court female judges and for a brief period an appointed governor, Olene Walker, who filled a gubernatorial vacancy) some State officials seem to be uncomfortable with Utah's female Chief Justice.

In the January 2010 Utah State Legislative Session SB 109S01 (amended as to the term of the Chief Justice) was introduced and passed, despite opposition by the entire Utah Bar. This bill changed the process of appointment for the Chief Justice of the Utah Supreme Court from an election by the entire five justice court, to an appointment by the Utah Governor.

In his speech on the Senate floor, sponsoring Utah Senator Scott Jenkins consistently referred to [the] Supreme Court 'chief justices' [sic] in the plural, making one wonder if he knew that there was only one chief justice. He initially stated that the bill was necessary because the supreme court justices has [sic] too much power which leads the senator to claim [these justices] they "are very domineering people." At the same time he claimed that "other states are jealous of Utah's judiciary," and that with regard to the Utah Supreme Court [there are] "... too few checks from the executive." [140]

This bill appeared to be a transparent attack on the decisions of Chief Justice Christine M. Durham, recipient of the William H. Rehnquist Award for Judicial Excellence, who has a record of superior and tireless service as a justice on the Utah Supreme Court for almost two decades and as Chief Justice since 2002.

2010—Citizen's Initiative for Ethics Reform in Utah State Legislature

In a report published in June of 1996, Utah was ranked 47th out of 50 and given an "F" grade on its state legislators' ethics by the Washington Center for Public Integrity. The survey considered personal financial disclosures of state lawmakers in order to determine whether and to what degree they were able to influence legislation for companies in which they had a business or personal interest. The bottom three states had absolutely no disclosure requirements; Utah was next lowest with a single, effectively meaningless requirement. [141] Utah was one of only ten states without an independent ethics commission and one of only five with no limits on campaign contributions.[142]

Continuing the long-standing tradition of combining state and religious titles, the Utah legislators had no ban on or prohibition against a Utah congressman serving in the state legislature while simultaneously serving on the board of directors of a corporation and then participating in legislation which affected that business interest. Historically, there have been many instances in which Utah legislators have acted as private business lobbyists while seated in congress.

Tiring of this patent lack of ethics, Utahns for Ethical Government (UEG) was formed with the support of former State legislators, Republican and Democratic, Mormon and non-Mormon. UEG successfully mounted a several year campaign, and ultimately gathered sufficient signatures to allow its initiative on the November, 2010 ballot in the form of a constitutional amendment prohibiting certain conflicts of interest and establishing an ethics commission to investigate violations by state congress people.

In a preemptive attempt to detract from UEG's goals, the then current State legislature adopted their own limited ethics reform. However, the UEG initiative was successful and passed with 67% of all voters in the 2010 election voting in favor of the constitutional amendment. State Senator Chris 'black baby,' Buttars was quoted in the voter information pamphlet as opposing the amendment. No doubt his opposition caused some Utahns to vote in favor of the amendment.

***

In the days of Brigham Young, the streets of Salt Lake City were originally constructed and laid out in all directions from Temple Square, a downtown city block which contains the historic Salt Lake Temple and tabernacle housing the giant organ pipes which serve as background for the Mormon Tabernacle Choir. But now with the City's complete relinquishment of Main Street Plaza to the Church, together with the Church's incremental purchase of several entire downtown city blocks, Salt Lake City is slowly becoming Vaticanized.

Prior to the year 2000, two competing shopping malls had occupied this downtown area: the Z.C.M.I. Center, owned by the LDS Church and Crossroads Plaza, also situated on mostly Church land, but the land was leased and the complex was owned by a Maryland-based mall operator. In 2003 the Church purchased the more successful Crossroads Plaza Mall. Now City Creek Center, a downtown combined shopping mall and residential development, is being built by the Church in Salt Lake City and is expected to cost more than three billion dollars.

Before its demolition several years ago, Crossroads Plaza had usurped the Z.C.M.I. Center's original position as *the* downtown shopping mall While Crossroads became ever more popular, with busy department stores like Nordstrom and Mervyns, the Z.C.M.I. Center was slowly dying with tenants such as Deseret Book.

Chapter 7: The Utah Theocracy

A turn of the twenty-first century comparison of the food courts in both malls was indicative of the mood in each. While Crossroads Plaza served coffee and was upbeat, the Z.C.M.I. Center was full of mostly overweight Mormon office employees, employees from Mormon law firms or retail outlets, or even from the Church Office Building, who sat somber-faced and ate their fast food lunches. Never a sleeveless arm or a bare thigh was seen at the Z.C.M.I. food court, even in the absolute 100 degree heat of Salt Lake's arid Augusts. The misery of these Mormon devotees was palpable. The Z.C.M.I. Shopping Center eventually became a dead zone, especially with the construction of the Gateway, an outdoor retail mall covering several blocks on Salt Lake City's west side.

***

I believed my letter to LDS Church Headquarters mailed out in 2001 from Half Moon Bay requesting that my name be removed from the membership of the Church had reached its destination. I had no reason to think otherwise until a day in 2008 when I received a letter addressed to "Sister Burningham," from the Park City East Canyon Creek Ward. Then I realized that the proper recipient had not been reached all those years ago, so I contacted the bishop for the Park City Ward, a very nice professional gentleman, who returned my call personally. He apologized for the oversight and asked me to write another letter and he'd make sure it was received by the proper authorities.

On March 30, 2008, I received an initial letter from the Church which read in part:

> As discussed on the phone, the effect of having your name removed is to effectively cancel your baptism and confirmation as well as any temple blessings and ordinances you may have received (including any temple sealing to your former spouse). Should you ever want to rejoin the Church, you would need to be re-baptized and re-confirmed following appropriate interview with priesthood leaders...Your request can be rescinded within 30 days by sending a written request to the Stake President...

It was signed by the bishop, with a copy to the stake president. I sighed, folded the letter and put it away in my desk drawer. In May I received a second letter from the manager of the Church membership

191

records. It read:

> This letter is to notify you that in accordance with your request, you are no longer a member of The Church of Jesus Christ of Latter-day Saints. Should you desire to become a member of the Church in the future, the local bishop or branch president in your area will be happy to help you.

I had no second thoughts; I was done.

CHAPTER EIGHT: Mormon Theology— a Foundation in Fraud

"Each of us has to face the matter—either the Church is true, or it is a fraud. There is no middle ground. It is the Church and kingdom of God, or it is nothing."—LDS President Gordon B. Hinckley, April Conference and "Loyalty," *Ensign*, May, 2003.

"Our whole strength rests on the validity of that [first] vision. It either occurred or it did not occur. If it did not, then this work is a fraud." *— Gordon B. Hinckley, 2002 & 2005. [143]

"Either The Book of Mormon is what the Prophet Joseph said it is, or this Church and its founders are false, a deception from the first instance onward...[Smith] must be accepted either as a prophet of God or else as a charlatan of the first order." *—LDS Church Apostle Jeffrey Holland, 1997. [144]

For more than thirty years, from the time I had become heavily engaged in Mormonism at sixteen, through LDS Seminary, Young Women's meetings, long talks with my high school boyfriend, teaching Relief Society and Sunday School at BYU and then marrying two Mormon men, until 2001 when I was forty-six years old, I had struggled with my belief in Mormonism. I thought I could do it, be a Mormon and be what I wanted to be—live an authentic life like Grandma Burningham—but it was impossible. I was married to men whose world-view was based upon a fabled construct, ingrained since birth. It seemed goodness was anything that supported the fables believed by Mormons; evil was anything that questioned those fables and reality was quite irrelevant.

There is overwhelming evidence that the Church has misrepresented the true source of Joseph Smith's writing, collectively the *standard works* by claiming that these LDS scriptures are of divine origin. All extant evidence proves that Smith dictated *the Book of Mormon* with his head in a hat containing a seer stone—no plates were used; at times he and his scribe (then Martin Harris) were separated by a hanging curtain to divide the room. Furthermore, most of the translation occurred after Smith's third cousin, school teacher Oliver Cowdery, appeared to write for him, and only then was the book completed.[145]

Over time, the evidence to prove most facts disappears—it is destroyed, lost, or altered. In proving the truth or falsity of the facts upon which most religions are based, the loss of evidence is problematic. The origins of Judaism, Christianity and Islam are obscured by the centuries. However, Mormonism, founded in 1830, is a relatively new religion and evidence of its true origins remains. As demonstrated in the following chapters, the evidence reveals that for decades Mormon leaders, either knowing the true origins of their standard works, or knowing that they have insufficient knowledge upon which to base their claims of divinity, have either intentionally or at least recklessly continued to make misrepresentations about the Religion's origins.

Fraud in the Inducement

In 2009 I argued a case before the Utah Supreme Court. One of the issues I briefed concerned fraud. As I researched this issue for my brief, I realized that not only was *the Book of Mormon* a fraud and the Mormon Religion based upon fraudulent origins (something alleged by Mormonism's critics since it all began), but the continued representation of the Joseph Smith story—that quintessential Mormon fable, complete with heavenly visitations, golden plates, priesthood restoration and temple covenants and ordinances as the God-given truth, for almost two centuries —*that* was the real fraud. Fraud in the inducement had been committed by each collective group of Mormon leaders against every rising generation of born-in-the-church Mormons and innumerable unsuspecting investigators of the Religion who ultimately became converts to the Church. These victims were especially vulnerable before information regarding the facts surrounding the true origins of the Church became readily available through internet portals to the truth. Thus, it is mature Mormons, those who came of age before the information revolution, who had no real opportunity to ascertain the truth. Though still at risk, today's LDS youth and those who are investigating whether to join the Church are not so easily duped.

In 2001 the Utah Supreme Court set forth the elements required to establish fraud in a case brought by the parents of an LDS girl who was sexually molested when she was seven by a teenage boy in her LDS ward. Franco's memory of the abuse was suppressed until she was fourteen.

Upon recollection of the abuse and then reporting it to her bishop and stake president, she was advised to forgive the perpetrator and forget the incident and then was referred to an unlicensed counselor who also advised her to forgive and forget the incident. A secular therapist subsequently met with Franco and her parents. Afterward, he reported the crime to the police. Once the crime was reported, Franco was ostracized by LDS ward members, including local leaders.

In upholding the trial court's dismissal of claims of fraud and infliction of emotional distress, the Supreme Court of Utah declined to rule on the propriety of the clergy-advisor's actions or inactions due to constitutional prohibitions. Importantly, however, in its opinion the Court set forth the necessary elements of fraud: "...a party must prove by clear and convincing evidence each of the following:

> (1) That a representation was made; (2) concerning a presently existing material fact; [distinguishing those statements which involve promises or predictions] (3) which was false; (4) which the representor either (a) knew to be false, or (b) made recklessly, knowing that he had insufficient knowledge upon which to base such representation; (5) for the purpose of inducing the other party to act upon it; (6) that the other party, acting reasonably and in ignorance of its falsity; (7) did in fact rely upon it; (8) and was thereby induced to act; (9) to his injury and damage.[146]

Franco v. The Church of Jesus Christ of Latter-day Saints, 2001 UT 25
¶ 33, 21 P.3d 198, 207-08 (Utah 2001).

From April 6, 1830, the date Joseph Smith formed the Church, until this day, Mormon leaders have represented that *the Book of Mormon* was translated from golden plates and that it contains the restored gospel of Jesus Christ, the original and pure gospel having been lost and distorted or corrupted following the great schism and centuries of fractionalization and apostasy since Jesus Christ's death. Yet the evidence proves that none of this is true.

After Years of Searching, Joseph Smith Finally Finds His Treasure

It all began, so the story goes, in 1820 when in answer to his prayerful petitions asking which of the many religions were correct, young Joseph was visited in a grove by *God the Father and His Son, Jesus Christ.* God said to Smith: *"This is My Beloved Son. Hear Him!"* The Lord told Smith all their creeds were an abomination in his sight; that those professors were all corrupt. He said that: "they draw near to me with their lips but their hearts are far from me, they teach for doctrines the commandments of men, having a form of godliness, but they deny the power thereof." He [one of the personages] forbade Smith to join any denomination and "many other things did he say unto me, which I cannot write at this time.*" ("Joseph Smith," *PGP* 2:17-20, 1974 Ed.)

Next, in 1823, an angel appeared to the adolescent Smith and told him about golden plates hidden in a hill near his home. During this interim period, Smith claimed he had been persecuted by those to whom he relayed his story of the first vision. The angel visited Smith three more times over the next several years and Smith eventually learned the location of the buried plates. Once he attempted to obtain the plates, but was prevented. Here is the official version of Smith's initial discovery of a box containing the plates:

51....under a stone of considerable size, lay the plates, deposited in a stone box. This stone was thick and rounding in the middle on the upper side, and thinner towards the edges, so that the middle part of it was visible above the ground, but the edge all around was covered with earth.
52. Having removed the earth, I obtained a lever, which I got fixed under the edge of the stone, and with a little exertion raised it up. I looked in, and there indeed did I behold the plates, the Urim and Thummim, and the breastplate, as stated by the messenger...
53. I made an attempt to take them out, but was forbidden by the messenger, and was again informed that the time for bringing them forth had not yet arrived, neither would it, until four years from that time; but he told me that I should come to that place precisely in one year from that time, and that he would there meet with me,

and that I should continue to do so until the time should come for obtaining the plates.

54. Accordingly, as I had been commanded, I went at the end of each year, and at each time I found the same messenger there, and received instruction and intelligence from him at each of our interviews, respecting what the Lord was going to do, and how and in what manner his kingdom was to be conducted in the last days. (*PGP*, 2:51-54).

After admittedly digging in vain for buried silver on Josiah Stowell's property, and after eloping with Emma Hale, Smith was finally allowed to retrieve the golden plates in 1827. He is represented as having written:

59. At length the time arrived for obtaining the plates, the Urim and Thummim, and the breastplate. On the twenty-second day of September, one thousand eight hundred and twenty-seven, having gone as usual at the end of another year to the place where they were deposited, the same heavenly messenger delivered them up to me with this charge: that I should be responsible for them; that if I should let them go carelessly, or through any neglect of mine, I should be cut off; but that if I would use all my endeavors to preserve them, until he, the messenger, should call for them, they would be protected.

60. I soon found out the reason why I had received such strict charges to keep them safe, and why it was that the messenger had said that when I had done what was required at my hand, he would call for them. For no sooner was it known that I had them, than the most strenuous exertions were used to get them from me. Every stratagem that could be invented was resorted to for that purpose. The persecution became more bitter and severe than before, and multitudes were on the alert continually to get them from me if possible. But by the wisdom of God, they remained safe in my hands, until I had accomplished by them what was required at my hand. When, according to arrangements, the messenger called for them, I delivered them up to him; and he had them in his charge until this day, being the second day of May, one thousand eight hundred and thirty eight. (*PGP*, 2:59-60).

197

These golden plates are represented by the LDS Church to have contained the histories of several ancient American civilizations, authored by several different American prophets. One tribe, the Jaredites, dated from the fall of the Tower of Babel and two others, the Nephites and the Lamanites, were descendants of a Hebrew family which left Jerusalem in about 600 B.C. to come to the American Continent. All of these *Book of Mormon* tribes were exterminated through tribal warfare by about 472 A.D. Their record includes an appearance of the resurrected Christ on the American Continent. The Church claims: "The Book of Mormon is named after Mormon, a fourth-century prophet-historian who compiled and abridged many records of his ancestors into The Book of Mormon."[147]

This story is taught to young children and investigators in the Church today. The story is also portrayed in a musical pageant-like production by the LDS Church, each summer in Palmyra, New York. The production's venue is located at or near the place where Smith claimed to have retrieved the gold plates: http://www.hillcumorah.org/.

Mural depicting Moroni burying golden plates at Salt Lake Temple Visitors Center, 2010.

A replica of the golden plates is displayed at the North Salt Lake Visitor's Center located on Temple Square.[148] After Smith translated the plates, using at times the Israelites' tool[s] of divination, the Urim and Thummim (rough Hebrew translation is "light and truth"), also claimed to have been found with the plates, they were returned to the angel; nobody has seen them since.

The *Doctrine & Covenants* (*D&C*) and *Pearl of Great Price* (*PGP*) (the other two canonized Mormon scriptures) were said to have been direct revelations from God to Smith such as in the (*D&C*) and parts of the *PGP* (*Book of Moses*) and/or translated by Smith's claimed prophetic powers from ancient Egyptian papyri, as claimed with the *Book of Abraham*, a major part of the *PGP*. The representations, continued to this day, are that these scriptures are based upon either divine translation or divine revelation. These divine scriptures serve as the keystone, the very basis for the Mormon Religion.

Given the fantastical claimed origins of Mormonism's most sacred texts, a short review of how Joseph Smith occupied his time during the period he was preparing to receive the golden plates and then, during their translation into *the Book of Mormon*, is helpful to the question of whether the story of the golden plates is fact or fiction.

Joseph Smith's Early Occupation—Scrying For a Living

Joseph's elder brother Alvin, more than seven years his senior, paved the way for the activity of the prophet to be. From a Rochester, New York newspaper:

If we remember aright, it was in the year 1815, that a family of Smiths moved into these parts, and took up their abode in a miserable hut on the east bank of the river, now near the late David K. Carter's tavern. They had a wonderful son, of about 18 years of age, who, on a certain day, as they said, while in the road, discovered a round stone of the size of a man's fist, the which when he first saw it, presented to him on the one side, all the dazzling splendor of the sun in full blaze — and on the other, the clearness of the moon. He fell down insensible at the sight, and while in the trance produced by the sudden and awful discovery, it was communicated to him that he was to become an oracle — and the keys of mystery were put into his hands, and he saw the unsealing of the book of fate... He told his tale for money. Numbers flocked to him to test his skill, and the first question among a certain class was, if there was any of Kidd's money hid in these parts in the earth. The oracle, after adjusting the stone in his hat, and looking in upon it sometime, pronounced that there was. The result was the Smiths were missing — the enemy did not land — the money-diggers joined in the general execration, and declared that they had their labor for their pains — and all turned out to be a hoax! Now in reference to the two stories [Joseph's gold plates and Alvin's pretensions to treasure] "put that to that, and they are a noble pair of brothers."*[149]

Alvin died at the young age of 25 by an improper use of calomel given for indigestion or possibly food poisoning in 1823, the same year the teenage Joseph claimed to have been first visited by the angel who told him of the buried gold plates .[150]   At Alvin's funeral the Reverend Benjamin Stockton implied that Alvin was going to hell because he hadn't been baptized.[151]   Some suspect this was the impetus for the Mormon doctrine of baptism for the dead. After Alvin's death, Joseph Smith joined the Methodist Church. His mother, Lucy, along with several of her children (Joseph's siblings) joined the Presbyterian Church.[152] The income Alvin had made was a big part of the support for the Smith household. His death placed them in financial jeopardy.

Young Joseph carried on the enterprise begun by Alvin. He represented himself throughout his home and neighboring towns as one who was able to locate hidden treasure, charging a fee for his service. He used various devices in this business: a divining rod, a stick and several seer stones. The young Smith looked for ore, money, water and a chest of watches. While drunk, his father would pretend to enchant guns at a turkey shoot. [153]   Later in his life, Joseph Smith Jr., constantly wore a Jupiter talisman around his neck and both Joseph and his father, Joseph Smith Sr., believed in witches. [154]

There are many instances documenting Joseph Jr.'s drunkenness: "JO got drunk while we were haying for my uncle, Wm. Stafford; also at a husking at our house, and stayed overnight. I have often seen him drunk."* [155]

Levi Lewis, son of Nathaniel Lewis whose wife, Sophia was present at the death of Smith's first-born, testified in court that he "saw him [Smith] intoxicated at three different times while he was composing The Book of Mormon."*[156]

According to Author Dan Vogel, "Martin Harris corroborated [Lewis' statement] then changed his statement under threat of Church discipline to: "Joseph drank too much liquor...previous to the translating of The Book [of Mormon]."*[157]

In Bainbridge, New York, 1826 (the same time period that Smith claims to have been visited several times by the angel), he was living and working for Josiah Stowell who believed there was a Spanish silver mine on his property. Stowell, Joseph and other men entered into a written joint venture agreement for this particular dig, which proved to be futile. Later, upon hearing Joseph discovered gold plates, some of these men would demand a part of the value of the plates based upon this prior contractual agreement.[158]

In 1826, the case "Joseph Smith the Glass-looker," was filed in the Chenango County, Bainbridge, New York Circuit Court before Justice of the Peace Albert Neely. Joseph Smith was the named defendant. The young Prophet was charged with disorderly conduct, a misdemeanor. The charge was based on information provided by Peter G. Bridgman, Josiah Stowell's nephew, who believed that Smith was taking advantage of his uncle. Smith was examined by the Justice of the Peace and testimony was taken from several witnesses in what appears to have been a preliminary or probable cause hearing after which Smith seems to have left the jurisdiction before any actual trial was completed.

According to William D. Purple, "I was an intimate friend of the Justice, and was invited to take notes of the trial, [sic] which I did. There was a large collection of persons in attendance, and the proceedings attracted much attention."* Mr. Purple goes on to state that Smith was called as a witness and asked to show his seer stone. "On the request of the Court, he exhibited the stone. It was about the size of a small hen's egg, in the shape of a high-instepped shoe. It was composed of layers of different colors passing diagonally through it. It was very hard and smooth, perhaps by being carried in the pocket."*[159]

According to the witnesses at the hearing, the young defendant admitted under oath that he could not actually see where any treasure was hidden, but had engaged in the occupation solely to make a living: "To Be

201

candid, between you and me, I cannot, any more than you or any body else; but any way to get a living... Jo was asked by witness [A. S. Austin] if he could see or tel[l] more than others [.] Jo, said he could not and says 'any thing for a living. I now and then Get a sh[i]lling.'"* [160]

A letter by another justice of the peace in the area describes Smith's general reputation:

Jo Smith (Mormon) came here when about 17-18 y. of age in the capacity of Glass Looker or fortune teller...Jo. Engaged the attention of a few indiv [iduals] Given to the marvelous. Dug for money, Salt, Iron Oar, Gold oar, silver Oar, and almost any thing, every thing, until civil authority brought up JO. Standing (as the boys say) under the Vagrant act. Jo., "off, off'—took leg Bail...Jo was not seen in our town for 2 years or more (except in Dark Corners).* [161]

A few years later, in July of 1830, Smith was again charged with being "a disorderly person," in the same court, South Bainbridge, Chenango County, New York, but this time in front of Justice of the Peace, Joseph Chamberlain. However, since the evidence showed Smith had not used glass-looking for more than two years, his case was ultimately dismissed as having been brought beyond the two year statute of limitations. In the trial record, the Judge acknowledged the prior Bainbridge matter, wherein "he [Smith] escaped from the officer and went to Palmyra."* [162]

Soon after this hearing, Smith was charged again in the neighboring Broome County. The nature of the charges and any dispositive resolution are unclear. Though Smith's attorney John Reed is adamant that "nothing was proved," there remains no extant court transcript. However, Smith was again brought before Judge Noble who wrote: "JO was no sooner set on terra firma [referring to the dismissal in the 1830 South Bainbridge case] than [he was] arrested again [and] brought before me in an adjoining County."* [163] According to Judge Noble, the trial lasted "23 hours," and:

Proof [was] manifested by I think 43 witnesses. Proof [that] Jo. [was] a vagrant idler, lazy ([but] not [a] drunkard) but now and then drunk. [Also a] liar [and] deceiver. Jo. [was] a nuisance to good society... [and] any thing but a good man.*[164]

According to the Judge, who once had a record of the matter, Smith testified that:

JO. And others were digging for a chest of money in [the] night. [But they] could not obtain it. They procured one thing and another, together with [a] *black bitch*. The bitch was offered [as] a sacrifice [and its] [blo]od sprinkled. Prayer [was] made at the time ([but] no money obtained).*[165]

Smith's testimony that "...now and then I get a schilling...," is cited in another source and might have been repeated by Joseph Smith in the Broome County matter. [166]

Some of the best evidence of the true origins of Mormonism is recorded by Smith's contemporaries. Ordinarily studied only by historians of Mormon history until made available to the public through internet exposure, these court records, affidavits and other primary source documents have been virtually buried and have certainly never been taught as part of the Church-approved lessons to Mormons.

Though married to Joseph and living with him throughout his period of translation, even working as his scribe for a period of time, Emma never saw the golden plates. According to Emma's accounts and that of Smith's mother, Lucy Mack Smith, these women, along with other members of the Smith family, were allowed to feel the golden plates while they were covered with a cloth. However, none but the three and then the eight witnesses, whose testimony is discussed in the next chapter, ever claim to have seen the plates, and even that witnessing was made with "spiritual eyes," or "eyes of faith," as in a vision.[167] In 1838, Martin Harris admitted at Kirtland Ohio, that [he] "never saw the plates with his natural eyes," and that "the eight witnesses [also] never saw them [with their natural eyes] and hesitated to sign that instrument for that reason, but were persuaded to do it."*[168]

Joseph Smith's father-in-law, Isaac Hale, never liked Joseph. He refused to approve of the marriage, so the couple had to sneak out of her father's house and travel to another state to be married. Emma's father had always maintained that Smith was a fraud.

I first became acquainted with Joseph Smith, Jr. in November, 1825. He was at that time in the employ of... men who were called "money diggers;" and his occupation was that of seeing, or pretending to see by means of a stone placed in his hat, and his hat closed over his face. In this way he pretended to discover minerals and hidden treasure. His appearance at this time, was that of a careless young man — not very well educated, and very saucy and insolent to his father. Smith, and his father, with several other "money-diggers" boarded at my house while they were employed in digging for a mine that they supposed had been opened and worked by the Spaniards, many years since. Young Smith gave the "money-diggers" great encouragement, at first, but when they had arrived in digging, to near the place where he had stated an immense treasure would be found — he said the enchantment was so powerful that he could not see. They then became discouraged, and soon after dispersed...After these occurrences, young Smith made several visits at my house, and at length asked my consent to his marrying my daughter Emma. This I refused, and gave my reasons for so doing; some of which were, that he was a stranger, and followed a business that I could not approve; he then left the place. Not long after this, he returned, and while I was absent from home, carried off my daughter, into the state of New York, where they were married without my approbation or consent... [I] was informed that [smith and his family] had brought a wonderful book of Plates down with them. I was shown a box in which it is said they were contained, which had to all appearances, been used as a glass box of the common window glass. I was allowed to feel the weight of the box, and they gave me to understand, that the book of plates was then in the box -- into which, however, I was not allowed to look...The manner in which he pretended to read and interpret [these plates] was the same as when he looked for the money-diggers, with the stone in his hat, and his hat over his face, while The Book of Plates were at the same time hid in the woods!...After this, Martin Harris went away, and Oliver Cowdery came and wrote for Smith, while he interpreted as above described...Joseph Smith Jr. resided near me for some time after this, and I had a good opportunity of becoming acquainted with him, and somewhat acquainted with his associates, and I conscientiously believe from the facts I have detailed, and from many other circumstances, which I do not deem it necessary to relate, that the whole "Book of Mormon" (so called) is a silly fabrication of falsehood and wickedness, got up for speculation, and with a design to dupe the credulous and unwary — and in order that its fabricators may live upon the spoils of those who swallow the deception.*[169]

The Book of Mormon: **Dubious Beginnings**

Considered holy scripture by true-believing Mormons, others have offered a much different description of the Mormon Bible (as it was called back then). When initially published, one New York newspaper called it blasphemous: "The Book of Mormon has been placed in our hands. A viler imposition was never practiced. It is an evidence of fraud, blasphemy, and credulity, shocking both to Christians and moralists..." [170]

Writer Mark Twain characterized the *Book of Mormon* this way:

The book is a curiosity to me, it is such a pretentious affair, and yet so "slow," so sleepy; such an insipid mess of inspiration. It is chloroform in print... [It] seems to be merely a prosy detail of imaginary history, with the Old Testament for a model; followed by a tedious plagiarism of the New Testament. The author labored to give his words and phrases the quaint, old-fashioned sound and structure of our King James translation of the Scriptures, and the result is a mongrel—half modern glibness, and half ancient simplicity and gravity.*[171]

In 1995, the most difficult part about writing my first novel was to determine names for the characters and locations. The plot, character arcs and theme of the book were easy; I knew what I wanted to say, but finding names was difficult. I turned to the telephone directories. Perhaps Joseph Smith had the same problem. *Book of Mormon* geography contains names similar to locations proximate to Smith's family home in upstate New York, near the border of Canada. These names could have easily been found on nineteenth century maps of the nearby areas. The list below provides some examples:[172]

BOOK OF MORMON	**MODERN NAME**
Lehi (Nephi 1, *passim*)	Lehigh Valley, Pennsylvania
Onidah (Alma 47:5)	Oneida, New York
Angola (Mormon 2:4)	Angola, New York
Morianton (Alma 50:25)	Morgantown, Pennsylvania
Jacobugath (3 Nephi 9:9)	Jacobsburg, Ohio
Alma (Alma, *passim*)	Alma, West Virginia or Alma, Quebec
Shilom (Mosiah 7, 9 *passim*)	Shiloh, Ohio
Kishkumen (Helaman 1, 2)	Kiskiminitas River, Ohio
Moron (Ether 7)	Morin, Quebec
Shurr (Ether 14:28)	Sherbrooke, Quebec
Teancum (Mormon 4)	Tecumseh, Ontario
Ripliancum (Ether 15:8)	Ripley, Maine or Ripley, New York

Initially called "Mormon Hill," (photographs of which were exhibited at the World's Fair in 1893) by residents of the area, even the name of the hill which is claimed to be the depository for the golden plates is suspect. There is evidence that Joseph Smith came up with the name 'Cumorah,' through his familiarity with the stories of Captain William, *aka* Robert Kidd.

Philastus B. Spear, resident of Palmyra and contemporary of the Prophet, said that [Joseph] "had for a library a copy of the *Arabian Nights*, stories of Captain Kidd, and a few novels."*[173] Captain Kidd was said to have buried treasure in 'Camora,' located off the eastern coast of Madagascar on a map, circa 1808. Smith used an early nineteenth century spelling of the islands and seems to have applied it to the hill where he found his buried treasure. Moroni (the name of the angel who first told Smith of the gold plates) is the name of the capital city of the Comoros Islands. The Moroni of the Comoros Islands is a community located at the base of a large, active volcano.

The word Moroni means "place of fire." 'Comoro' has its origins in Swahili and also means 'place of fire.' When the original *Book of Mormon* was published, the spelling of the Hill Cumorah was 'Camorah:' "And I, Mormon, wrote an epistle unto the King of the Lamanites, and desired of him that he would grant unto us that we might gather together... unto the land of Camorah, by the hill which was called Camorah, and there we would give them battle."[174]

In Chapter Nine, I cite evidence that the LDS Church changed not only Smith's account of the first vision, but changed the name of the angel who first told him of the golden plates, from Moroni to Nephi and then back to Moroni again.[175] Author Pomeroy Tucker, another contemporary of Smith, also provides evidence of the Prophet's familiarity with the adventures of Captain Kidd.[176] Since Captain Kidd's stories included the proper name Moroni (Mroni), Tucker hypothesizes that perhaps the messenger-angel's name change from Moroni to Nephi was made in an attempt to distance the main character in Smith's angelic visitation account from Moroni, the place in Captain Kidd's tales.[177]

Noah Webster's 1828 dictionary, the most popular dictionary of the time when Smith was translating from the golden plates, defines "mormo," with the *'n'* following the word indicating it was used as a noun. It reads: **"mormo *n.*** bugbear, false terror." Originally a Greek mythological-type character, the word 'mormo' could have been appropriated by Smith by adding on the *'n'* to create the title of *the Book of Mormon,* the name of its lead prophet, and the eventual nickname for the Church. [178]

Smith claimed the plates were inscribed with a language he labeled "reformed Egyptian." An early effort to confirm the inscripted marks as a legitimate language failed. Smith had initially copied some of the characters from the plates as an exemplar for purposes of translation by linguistic experts. Smith's colleague, Martin Harris, showed the exemplar to Charles Anthon, Columbia classics professor, expert in Greek and Latin. Thereafter, in a letter dated Feb. 17, 1834, Anthon refers to 'Mormonites' as 'wretched fanatics.' "The whole story about my having pronounced the Mormonite inscription to be 'reformed Egyptian hieroglyphics' is perfectly false...I soon came to the conclusion that it was all a trick, perhaps a hoax... [Harris] requested an opinion from me in writing, which of course I declined giving."*[179]

Anthon then details what he saw:

> This paper was in fact a singular scrawl. It consisted of all kinds of crooked characters disposed in columns, and had evidently been prepared by some person who had before him at the time a book containing various alphabets. Greek and Hebrew letters, crosses and flourishes, Roman letters inverted or placed sideways, were arranged in perpendicular columns, and the whole ended in a rude delineation of a circle divided into various compartments, decked with various strange marks, and evidently copied after the Mexican Calender given by Humboldt, but copied in such a way as not to betray the source whence it was derived.*[180]

Besides the claimed writing on the elusive golden plates, there is no evidence of reformed Egyptian used as a language anywhere in recorded world history. The original of Smith's exemplar, shown on the following page, is in the possession of the Community of Christ (RLDS) Church.

Book of Mormon Characters, circa. Dec., 1827-Feb., 1828, *aka The Anthon Transcript* (Note: It is not clear that this fragment is that which was shown to Professor Anthon by Martin Harris)

An analysis of the characters on the Anthon Transcript suggest symbols similar to the signs of the zodiac, those found in the *Farmers' Almanac* and even, when viewed upside down, third line on the right end, spelling "Jo," all of which, according to psychologist, I. Riley Woodbridge, support that the source of the characters was Smith's subconscious. [181] The weight of the historical evidence is that Smith acted as a scryer, a seer who effects a self-induced trance while looking into a crystal or stone and then, through free association, proceeds to access thoughts from his subconscious. This was the kind of work Joseph Smith had been known for in his teens and early twenties, used by his elder brother Alvin and his father, Joseph Smith Sr., the same method he used in his attempts to discover lost money or buried treasure.

Indeed, some psychiatrists reasonably opine that Smith's apparent automatic dictation with his head in a hat, while staring at a seer stone, was his stream of consciousness first novel, with his alter-ego playing out the critical roles that had occurred in his life, with key characters disguised as relatives and friends.[182] One critic even speculates that the Angel Moroni, who appears several times to inform Smith of the golden plates, was Sidney Rigdon, an itinerant preacher and eventually Smith's colleague.[183]

Some critics have argued that the creation of *the Book of Mormon* was a collaborative effort. According to the chief assistant to the printer,

Egbert B. Grandin, when it came time to publish the first edition, "Joseph Smith, Jr., had nothing to do whatever with the printing or furnishing copy for the printers, being but once in the office during the printing of the Bible [Book of Mormon] and then not over fifteen or twenty minutes."[184] The printer's assistant acknowledged that, "Martin Harris, Hyrum Smith and Oliver Cowdery, were very frequent visitors to the office during the printing of the Mormon Bible..."[185]

Eber D. Howe, publisher of the Ohio *Painesville Telegraph* and *Mormonism Unvailed*, an 1834 polemic critical of Mormonism, was certain *the Book of Mormon* was a conspiratorial collaboration.

> That there has been, from the beginning of the imposture, **a more talented knave** behind the curtain, is evident to our mind, at least; but whether he will ever be clearly, fully and positively unvailed and brought into open day-light, may of course be doubted. For no person of common prudence and understanding, it may well be presumed, would ever undertake such a speculation upon human credulity, without closing and well securing every door and avenue to a discovery, step by step, as he proceeded.*[186]

Although it has never been located, early nineteenth century writer and reverend, Solomon Spalding is rumored to have created a work of fiction called *Manuscript Found.* According to Smith's contemporary, Pomeroy Tucker, this unpublished manuscript came into the hands of a printer named Patterson where Smith's colleague, Sidney Rigdon, worked as a journeyman. [187] Tucker theorizes that the original *Manuscript Found* was never published, but was in fact found and it (or a copy) was used by Rigdon in collusion with Joseph Smith and Oliver Cowdery as a story base to which was added the plagiarized Sermon on the Mount, portions of the biblical Isaiah, and various other popular Protestant beliefs as heretofore preached by Reverend Rigdon, culminating in a "grand literary imposture."

According to Tucker, witnesses attest to the appearance of a stranger at Joseph Smith's house during the years preceding the claimed retrieval of the golden plates. It was Rigdon who had made the trip *incognito* from time to time. The story of an initial angelic visitation when Smith was fourteen, and then his annual return trips to the neighborhood hill, until years later when the young prophet was allowed to retrieve the plates, was an after-the-fact addition to the tale.

It was during this time period of several years that the actual creation of the grand imposture came about, through Rigdon's (the mysterious stranger) collaboration with Smith (and perhaps Cowdery). The direct testimony of several other witnesses, as well as circumstantial evidence such as post office addresses, information from contemporaneous area newspapers and real estate records, places Rigdon in the area where Smith was living during the mid 1820s, years before Smith claimed he met Rigdon.[188]

It should be noted that a short fiction by Reverend Spalding entitled *Conneaut Creek* was located, but at least publicly, never the *Manuscript Found*. Mormon apologists have attempted to discredit any theory that *the Book of Mormon* was based in part upon Spalding's writings, since the substance or story of the Conneaut Creek (*aka* the Oberlin manuscript—it ultimately came into the possession of Oberlin College) Manuscript bore little resemblance to the stories of *the Book of Mormon*. However, similarities in the context and phrasing of *the Book of Mormon's* Book of Alma have been highlighted as identical to parts of the Spalding-Oberlin or *Conneaut Creek* manuscript. One analyst identifies similar words and phrases in the Book of Alma, and labels them Spaldingish[189]   Another finds similarities in the discovery of the record/plates, the description of ancient Americans, the sea voyages, racial distinctions, culture, theology, and warlike extermination of the two main tribes: the Nephites and Lamanites.[190]

Mormonism Unvailed contains numerous statements by those who had read the Spalding work and had also read the "golden bible." According to these statements, in all comparisons, the historical part of *the Book of Mormon*, without the religious overtures, was a verbatim plagiarism of Spalding's work of fiction, *Manuscript Found*, down to the names Nephi, Lehi, Moroni and Zarahemla.[191]   Howe theorizes Rigdon's complicity in using *Manuscript Found* along with portions of religious writings to compile the original *Book of Mormon*.[192] Among the statements in Howe's publication, *Mormonism Unvailed*, are the affidavits of Spalding's wife and brother who both emphatically declare the existence of *Manuscript Found* and its similarity to the Mormon book, including the identification of the exact names of key players, Nephi and Lehi.

A Palmyra news article published within three years after the first edition of *the Book of Mormon* suggests Rigdon's collusion.[193] Rigdon maintained *the Book of Mormon* as the word of God until his death; however, just before death he also instructed his wife to burn all of his personal papers.[194]

Stanford-affiliated statistician, Craig Criddle, finds Rigdon's influence in specific word patterns especially in the books of Moroni and 2nd Nephi in *the Book of Mormon*. He explains that these patterns are consistent with the time frame when the Book was written and especially, during the time of Martin Harris' loss of the initially translated 116 pages.[195] Criddle argues that Rigdon had the "motive, means and opportunity" to adapt the Spalding manuscript to the original edition of *the Book of Mormon*. And while Criddle, a professional research scientist, acknowledges his own confirmation bias (he is a former Mormon), his argument is interesting.

However, the Spalding manuscript theory is problematic because the *Manuscript Found*, that supposed additional novel written by Reverend Spalding, referenced by his former wife and his brother, has never been found. Indeed most experts in Mormon history, including biographer Fawn Brodie, reject a *Book of Mormon* authorship based in part upon Solomon Spalding's writings.

Sandra Tanner, an expert on LDS history, agrees with Fawn Brodie's rejection of the Spalding theory. Tanner believes that *the Book of Mormon* is Smith's work alone. "Had Spalding, Rigdon or Cowdery been involved to the degree suggested, they would've written a better book."[196]

Ben Winchester, a former Mormon who had many opportunities to interact with the founding men, said in his 1889 interview with the *Salt Lake Tribune*:

Joseph Smith had a fair degree of dramatic talent by nature and he was cut out by nature for a writer of fiction. Although not an educated man he had a wonderful capacity for weaving and unraveling plots. *I believe that the Book of Mormon was mainly the production of the brains of himself and Cowdery, and by chain of events and reasoning, I say most emphatically that I do not believe that the Spaulding manuscript was utilized in any way in making up that book.* Joseph was away behind Brigham Young in executive ability; he could not hold his adherents together as did

Brigham and he was almost constantly in trouble over dissensions and frequent schisms in the Church.*[197]

Rejection of a Spalding manuscript theory does not necessarily include rejection of any involvement by Sidney Rigdon in *Book of Mormon* authorship. However, based upon the quality and the weight of the available evidence, it appears more probable that Smith read Ethan Smith's (no relation) *View of the Hebrews* (see discussion regarding B.H. Roberts' discovery of the similarities, below) and drew in part upon that premise and other popular early nineteenth century news, books and anecdotes, distilling their story lines, themes and whole verses from the Bible, in readiness for his dictation of *the Book of Mormon.*

According to journalist Steve Benson, evidence presented by his wife, Mary Ann, in a meeting with LDS Elders Dallin Oaks and Neal Maxwell that Solomon Spalding's writing influenced the creator of *the Book of Mormon* compelled Oaks to admit to the Bensons that a small part of *the Book of Mormon* may have been ripped off from other sources—but that even if that was the case, it was "not important."[198]

Here Elder Oaks seems to pragmatically equate the maintenance of belief in a fable with good. If the construct, i.e. Mormonism, works and allows those who are deceived to have faith in something and those who are the deceivers to have the power and control they desire, how can it possibly be bad? To equate a fiction or fable with good, and reality with bad, is the subject of another book, but it is an intriguing idea, given all the currently popular positivity preaching, admonitions for looking on the bright side, avoiding negativity and turning a blind eye to that which is unpleasant.

Doctrine & Covenants: Rewritten Orders from a Zealous Egoist

The LDS Church claims that the *Doctrine & Covenants* (*D&C*), originally entitled *the Book of Commandments*, is a set of revelations received by Smith and some of his colleagues. Many of the revelations contained in the scripture were originally in t*he Book of Commandments*, first published in 1833, but then heavily revised and re-published as the *D&C* after a Missouri mob destroyed the press for *the Book of*

Commandments.

In 1961 Jerald and Sandra Tanner copied the first 41 (of 160 total) pages of the original *Book of Commandments* from BYU. Once the LDS Church historian's office realized that the Tanners had copied the first part of the book, they instructed BYU to deny them access to the remainder of *the Book of Commandments.* The Tanners ultimately obtained a complete copy from Yale University, published it and offered it for sale.

Shortly thereafter, *Joseph Begins his Work*, Volumes 1 and 2, which contain photographic reprints of the original *Book of Commandments* and the first edition of the *Doctrine and Covenants,* was published by Wilford Wood and originally sold by Deseret Bookstore. Wood failed to identify changes between the two original sets of scriptures; the book was merely a verbatim reprint with no comparison between the two.

In October 13, 1963, Presbyterian Reverend Wesley P. Walters tried to obtain a copy of *Joseph Begins his Work* from Deseret Book, but was told it was unavailable. Since that time, according to the Tanners, *Joseph Begins his Work* has been not only out of print, but the publication of Wood's reprint has been suppressed by the Church. [199]

Most of the *D&C* purports to be the "word of God as revealed through his Prophet Joseph Smith." It conveniently consists of revelations received during the same time frame that *the Book of Mormon* was in translation, and shortly thereafter, during Smith's attempts at publication, the formation of the Church and the evolution of its hierarchical organization.

Many of the initial sections in the *D&C* date between 1828 and 1830, the two years when *the Book of Mormon* was being translated and then first published. These scriptures are actually self-serving admonitions to Joseph's father, brothers, friends and wife, Emma. The pronouncements, claimed to be revelations, are in fact transparent attempts by Smith to quell his family's curiosity and impatience at being unable to see the plates and/or engage in anything other than the task of scribe for Joseph. In many of the *D&C* verses, the Smith family's cynicism was quashed by the apparent mouth of God. The curious family and friends were told that "a marvelous work and a wonder," was about to be brought forth by Joseph, that none but Joseph had authority to translate and that if they were patient, maybe they would be allowed, in time, to see the golden plates.

For example, Smith's associate Martin Harris had mortgaged his farm for $3,000 to publish the first edition of *the Book of Mormon.* Harris took 116 pages of the original translation to show his skeptical wife to persuade her that the work was credible. History is unclear as to whether the initial 116 pages were lost or perhaps destroyed by Mrs. Harris. Nevertheless, when Martin Harris returned empty-handed, Joseph received another revelation.

Section Ten of the *D&C* is a rebuke to Smith for allowing Martin Harris to take possession of the initial part of the translation. The Lord wisely told Smith that the 116 pages would fall into the hands of the unscrupulous, who were intent on exposing the Church and would use the original manuscript (the only copy of what had been translated at that time) to compare with any subsequent translation in order to prove Smith a fraud. So as not to enable this *faux pas*, the Lord revealed to Smith, through Smith, that he shouldn't re-translate the 116 pages, but abandon that task and continue with his translation of the rest of the plates. Fortuitously, the Lord also instructed Smith that the substance of that initial 116 page translation would appear elsewhere in the plates, although from a different ancient prophet.

10. And behold, Satan hath put it into their hearts to alter the words which you have caused to be written, or which you have translated, which have gone out of your hands.
11. And behold, I say unto you, that because they have altered the words, they read contrary from that which you translated, and caused to be written;
12. And, on this wise, the devil has sought to lay a cunning plan, that he may destroy this work;
13. For he had put into their hearts to do this, that by lying they may say they have caught you in the words which you have pretended to translate.[200]

Suspecting the deception by Smith, Martin Harris was reluctant to follow through with his financing for the project. However, conveniently and just in time, another revelation was given, rebuking Harris and telling him to sell his property for the sake of the Church: "Impart a portion of thy property, yea, even part of thy lands, and all save the support of thy family. Pay the debt thou has contracted with the printer. Release thyself from bondage."[201]

The financial and familial stress caused by Harris's foolish investment in Mormonism's founding cost him his family and his farm. On January 28, 1832, less than two years after *the Book of Mormon's* initial publication in 1830, he gave his wife an 80 acre tract where she thereafter lived separately and Harris was forced to sell his remaining 150+ acres to pay his debt to the publisher.

Though possibly unsuspected by Smith's brethren in the Church, Smith's adversaries recognized that the Prophet's revelations served as consistently convenient vehicles for financial manipulation.

> The spiritual eye of the prophet ever kept in view the finances of his devoted followers, and to filch from their pockets he had only to issue a revelation. In the foregoing manifesto, Martin is called upon, in propria persona, to lay his money before the Bishop, merely as an example to all others. In this, the prophet judged correctly; he well knew the manner in which Martin was associated with him, and the case with which, through his agency, others could be deceived.[202]

Howe characterizes Smith's hubris most succinctly when he writes, "Never was there a despot more jealous of his prerogative than Smith."[203] Howe explains the power Smith had over his followers:

> Here is a mystery, for aught I know, peculiar to Mormonism; and none but Mormonites, I presume, will attempt to unravel it. But it finds its parallel in the following: Smith assures his followers, that what he speaks by the spirit, and is written, is infallible in operation but if it is not written, he may sometimes be mistaken. — He tells them that the right to deliver written revelations, belongs exclusively to himself, and no other person shall interfere in the business; and if he transgresses he will graciously condescend to appoint another in his stead, and the only proof produced for the support of such assertions, is barely his word, upon which they implicitly rely, and because entirely resigned to place their person and property under his control, and even risk the salvation of their souls upon his say-so. Such glaring duplicity on the one hand, and unaccountable credulity on the other, seldom has

a parallel in the annals of men. [204]

Additional *D&C* sections of the purported revelations from the Lord document the problems Smith had in bringing *the Book of Mormon* to life. This scripture, which is really primary source history, is replete with the Lord's intervention whenever challenges to Smith's authority were raised. Sidney Rigdon and Oliver Cowdery vied for the leader/prophet position ultimately claimed by Smith. Conveniently, through the mouth of the Lord, Smith quelled their aspirations of serving as anything other than his assistants. In a revelation Cowdery was specifically instructed to act as Smith's scribe and not to aspire to translation, Smith's exclusive task.[205]

Smith didn't want to be bothered with menial labor during this intense time of translation and thus he received revelations to that effect. "In temporal labor thou shall not have strength, for this is not thy calling." [206] Instead, it was revealed that various Church members were to build a house, which Smith would make his personal residence and which would also be used to house Mormon travelers and for baptisms for the dead. The revelation limited Smith's investment and directed other Mormons to invest as well.[207] Those who served Smith in this effort were not to question his revelations or methods. Another section was addressed to Emma. It advises her to "murmur not," and to "Let thy soul delight in thy husband."[208]

An example of the evolved import of a particular passage of the *D&C* into something which is generally applicable to all Mormon faithful is found in the section about water. Contrary to what I had been taught in LDS seminary as a girl, that Satan had control over the waters, when put in the context of what Joseph Smith was experiencing at the time the revelation was received, it is clear that the section of the *D&C* about water was not a general revelation by God, but a transparent excuse for Smith's fear of crossing the Missouri River. The scripture reads: "Behold, I, the Lord, in the beginning blessed the waters; but in the last days, by the mouth of my servant John, I cursed the waters. Wherefore, the days will come that no flesh shall be safe upon the waters. "[209] This scripture can be explained in its proper historical context:

The next morning Joseph manifested an aversion to risk his person any more upon the rough and angry current of the Missouri, and, in fact, upon any other river; and he again had recourse to his usual method, of freeing himself from the embarrassments of a former commandment, by obtaining another in opposition to it. A new commandment was issued, in which a great curse was pronounced against the waters: navigating them was to be attended with extreme danger; and all the saints, in general, were prohibited in journeying upon them, to the Promised Land. From this circumstance, the Missouri river was named the river of Destruction.[210]

The Pearl of Great Price—**False Conclusions Drawn from Egyptian Papyri**

After the first edition of *the Book of Mormon* was published in 1830, and the Church of Christ formally organized soon thereafter, the expected sales of the Mormon book and growth of the newly formed Church did not happen immediately. After Sidney Rigdon joined the Church, scores of Campbellites (Baptist followers of Alexander Campbell) were baptized in Kirtland, Ohio. These converts already believed in communalism. After Smith preached a revelation to the General Conference of Saints in Fayette, New York, instructing them to move to Ohio and John Whitmer relocated to Kirtland to act as branch president, the Church began to grow. As early as 1831, the Kirtland-based Church had more than 1,000 members. [211]

However, beginning in 1831 and certainly by the mid-1830s, the married Prophet began to secretly approach and seduce other women. When his brethren realized their Prophet's licentious behavior, they became disenchanted. This was the first five years, the crucial period for any business. Smith needed a method whereby he could prove to his following that despite his individual weaknesses, he was indeed a seer and revelator.

In 1835, traveling exhibitionist Michael Chandler happened through Kirtland and showed Smith his collection of Egyptian mummies. Perhaps in an effort to bolster Smith's faltering reputation as a translator and prophet of God, several of the mummies were purchased by the

Church for about $2,400.00.

As was customary in the late Egyptian period, mummified bodies of wealthy Egyptians were individually wrapped in burial papyrus. Smith claimed to translate from the hieratics inscribed on the papyrus enclosed with each mummified corpse he had purchased. The result was the *Book of Abraham*, claimed to have been written by the Old Testament Prophet Abraham, which included an account of his early life and an explanation of the Cosmos. The *Book of Abraham*, which accounts for almost a fourth of the text (and which depicts these facsimiles from the Egyptian papyri) in the *Pearl of Great Price* (*PGP*) was published in 1842 and canonized as scripture in 1880.

At the time of Smith's translation, linguistic familiarity with the Egyptian language was in its infancy. Though Parisian Jean-François Champollion recognized the existence of Egyptian texts on the Rosetta stone in 1822, it took decades to develop the expertise to read the ancient hieroglyphs which did in fact improve over the nineteenth century.

By the early twentieth century, translation of ancient Egyptian characters had evolved into a reliable linguistic skill. These learned Egyptologists viewed Smith's interpretation of his purchased papyri as pure nonsense. Smith was "absolutely ignorant of the simplest facts of Egyptian writing and civilization."[212] The characters in Smith's notes claimed to have been translated from similar ancient papyri showed absolutely no relationship to the hieroglyphs' true and accurate meaning. Smith's translation was exposed as fraudulent on the front page of the *New York Times,* Magazine Section, published on December 29, 1912.

http://query.nytimes.com/mem/archive-free/pdf?
res=F70914F83A5D13738DDDA00A94DA415B828DF1D3

At that time, the Reverend for the Salt Lake Episcopal Church, Franklin Spencer Spalding, sent a letter to the LDS Brethren in Salt Lake City, informing them of the several opinions of the renowned Egyptologists who had read Smith's interpretation of similar papyri. These experts all concluded that Smith's interpretation of the figures set forth in the facsimiles from the Egyptian papyri as had been published in the *Book of Abraham* for decades was false. Mormonism's founder was pronounced "self-delusional." The notice included the following expert opinions: "It is difficult to deal seriously with Joseph Smith's impudent fraud," wrote Dr. A. H. Sayce of Oxford University. The assistant curator of the New York Metropolitan Museum, Dr. Arthur Mace, called the Mormon translations "...a Figaro of nonsense."[213]

No known response was received by the Reverend. The *Desert News'* only response, authored by Church leader and scholar, B. H. Roberts, contained pleas to the young people of the Church to hold off judgment since the Church had yet to analyze the Egyptian scholars' claims. In a 1913 Church magazine article, a Mormon writer—not one of the Brethren—argued that in order to fairly test Joseph's ability to translate Egyptian "they would have to examine the **original** papyrus, or a copy of it, from which the *Book of Abraham* was translated." [214] Besides Roberts' pleas, it seemed no further official response was published about the issue until more than half a century later.

For more than two decades after Fawn Brodie's 1945 biography of Joseph Smith, research into the origins of the Church, or at least publications about that research, was scant. Then, in 1967, some of the original Egyptian papyri purchased by Smith and upon which he claimed to have based the *Book of Abraham*, were repossessed by the Church. The original papyri were believed to have been sold in 1856 and then burned in the Chicago fire of 1871. However, the New York Metropolitan Museum of Art acquired the actual Joseph Smith papyri in 1918 (no doubt at least in part, as a result of the news of the fraud published in 1912) along with a letter tracing the ownership back to Smith. There they remained, among the numerous carefully preserved stacks and folders of the museum's ancient Egyptian documents section. It was not until almost half a century later that these original Smith papyri were accidentally re-discovered by a non-Mormon University of Utah professor of ancient history, Dr. Aziz S. Atiya:

> [It was in the latter part of] May, 1966, when Professor Atiya was doing research for his new book, *History of Eastern Christianity,* that he made the discovery. A member of the Coptic Church (Egyptian Christian Church) and a careful student of its ancient history, he was checking through files of papyrus manuscripts at the New York Metropolitan Museum of Art in search of Coptic material. He came upon eleven papyrus sheets which instantly held his attention. The writing was hieroglyphic and hieratic, dating back to the era 500 B.C. to 1000 B.C. and obviously having

221

no bearing on his research, but nevertheless, something caught his eye. The first of the eleven sheets, somewhat fragmented and with portions missing, contained a vignette showing three figures: a man on a couch, a standing man nearby, and a bird in mid-air. Dr. Atiya immediately recognized the original of Facsimile No. 1 in the Pearl of Great Price. [215]

Following Dr. Atiya's discovery, Dr. Henry G. Fischer, curator of the Metropolitan Museum of Art's Egyptian documents, was interviewed by Lynn Travers, a member of *Dialogue's* (*a Journal of Mormon Thought*) board of editors. The interview was also attended by three other LDS men from the New York Area.

Mr. Travers asked Dr. Fischer:
"You were aware at that time, in fact, even in 1918, that it [the papyrus] was relevant to the Church; however, you did not at that time contact anyone who was associated with the Mormon Church?"
 Dr. Fischer responded:
"Frankly, we didn't know what the Mormon Church's wishes were [with regard to the disposition of the papyri]."[216]

Thus, the original papyri had lain dormant at the Museum until 1966 when they were actually seen by Professor Atiya. "A few days later, [the Professor] and a friend met with LDS Church President N. Eldon Tanner, and the photographs [of the papyri] were displayed. Later, the photographs were sent to Brigham Young University for inspection by Professor Hugh Nibley, who confirmed that the papyri were from the Mormon Collection."[217]
 These newly discovered papyri were part of the original source for Smith's translation of the *Book of Abraham*, and unlike the golden plates, were now available to compare with the Church's printed and bound scripture to determine whether the translation was accurate. The preface to the *Book of Abraham* in the *PGP* claims that it is: "A Translation of some ancient Records, that have fallen into our hands from the catacombs of Egypt. –The writings of Abraham while he was in Egypt, called The Book of Abraham, *written by his own hand, upon papyrus.*"* [Emphasis added].

However, a contemporary analysis of the discovered fragments of the Joseph Smith papyri provides irrefutable evidence that Abraham was not the author of the papyri inscriptions. Once these papyri were translated by trained Egyptologists, whose expertise and ability to read the ancient hieroglyphs had improved dramatically since the early nineteenth century, it was clear that the papyri had nothing to do with Smith's *Book of Abraham.* The ancient scrolls depicted a common Egyptian embalming ceremony. None of the figures or hieroglyphs mentions anything about a Christian God or Hebrew Old Testament prophet. Instead, the entire contents of the papyri purchased by Smith from the traveling salesman Chandler depict and reference Egyptian deities, both male and female.

According to the official *History of the Church,* Smith makes several diary entries documenting his days spent translating from the Egyptian papyri.[218] Besides the obvious inaccuracy of Smith's translation, dating of the original papyri proved that they are not old enough to have been written by Abraham (who purportedly lived in the earlier part of the second millennium, BCE). [219]

To further add to the humiliating nature of the charade, some of the missing segments of the discovered papyri had been inaccurately drawn in (by Smith or his scribe at his direction) and transposed to Facsimile No. 1 in the *Pearl of Great Price.* Smith erroneously claimed that this facsimile depicts the sacrifice of the Old Testament prophet, Abraham. According to Egyptologists, this particular papyrus originally belonged to specific Egyptians and depicts scenes from their familial books of breathings, an abridgment of The Book of the Dead.[220] The reclining figure claimed by Smith to be Abraham about to be sacrificed, is the Egyptian God *Osiris.* The figure with the sword raised, claimed by Smith to be an idolatrous priest and incorrectly drawn with a human head is correctly identified as the jackal-headed Egyptian God *Anubis.* Smith also incorrectly adds a bird head to the winged soul of *Osiris.*[221]

Facsimile No. 1, on the following page, is located in The Book of Abraham, contained within the LDS scripture, *the Pearl of Great Price.* This particular copy is taken from Ludlow, Daniel, H., ed., *Encyclopedia of Mormonism: the History, Scripture, Doctrine, and Procedure of the Church of Jesus Christ of Latter-day Saints* 5 Vols. (New York: Macmillan, 1992) 468.

An American Fraud: One Lawyer's Case against Mormonism

A FACSIMILE FROM THE BOOK OF ABRAHAM

No. 1

EXPLANATION

Fig. 1. The Angel of the Lord.

Fig. 2. Abraham fastened upon an altar.

Fig. 3. The idolatrous priest of Elkenah attempting to offer up Abraham as a sacrifice.

Fig. 4. The altar for sacrifice by the idolatrous priests, standing before the gods of Elkenah, Libnah, Mahmackrah, Korash, and Pharaoh.

Fig. 5. The idolatrous god of Elkenah.

Fig. 6. The idolatrous god of Libnah.

Fig. 7. The idolatrous god of Mahmackrah.

Fig. 8. The idolatrous god of Korash.

Fig. 9. The idolatrous god of Pharaoh.

Fig. 10. Abraham in Egypt.

Fig. 11. Designed to represent the pillars of heaven, as understood by the Egyptians.

Fig. 12. Raukeeyang, signifying expanse, or the firmament over our heads; but in this case, in relation to this subject, the Egyptians meant it to signify Shaumau, to be high, or the heavens, answering to the Hebrew word, Shaumahyeem.

Photo of Facsimile No.1 from the recovered Joseph Smith Papyri

Correct Ithyphallic drawing based on similar Egyptian papyri [222]

Compare the above papyrus with that published in my 1974 Edition of the *PGP's Book of Abraham* depicted on the previous page. The facsimile version was obviously altered by Smith, or someone at his direction. Note the inconsistencies when compared with the original papyrus: the jackal-headed figure has a human head, the bird like figure's

226

head is much different, the standing figure has a weapon in his hand, is behind the funeral bed (altar) as opposed to in front of it and there is no erect phallus depicted on the reclining figure.

Book of Abraham Facsimile No. 2, depicted on the following page, refers to Kolob as "…the residence next to God."[223] This facsimile is also from the *Encyclopedia of Mormonism,* p. 472. However, 'Kolob,' meaning God's residence, bears no relation to any accepted Egyptian translations.

A FACSIMILE FROM THE BOOK OF ABRAHAM

No. 2

EXPLANATION

Fig. 1. Kolob, signifying the first creation, nearest to the celestial, or the residence of God. First in government, the last pertaining to the measurement of time. The measurement according to celestial time, which celestial time signifies one day to a cubit. One day in Kolob is equal to a thousand years according to the measurement of this earth, which is called by the Egyptians Jah-oh-eh.

Fig. 2. Stands next to Kolob, called by the Egyptians Oliblish, which is the next grand governing creation near to the celestial or the place where God resides; holding the key of power also, pertaining to other planets; as revealed from God to Abraham, as he offered sacrifice upon an altar, which he had built unto the Lord.

Fig. 3. Is made to represent God, sitting upon his throne, clothed with power and authority; with a crown of eternal light upon his head; representing also the grand Key-words of the Holy Priesthood, as revealed to Adam in the Garden of Eden, as also to Seth, Noah, Melchizedek, Abraham, and all to whom the Priesthood was revealed.

Fig. 4. Answers to the Hebrew word Raukeeyang, signifying expanse, or the firmament of the heavens; also a numerical figure, in Egyptian signifying one thousand; answering to the measuring of the time of Oliblish, which is equal with Kolob in its revolution and in its measuring of time.

Fig. 5. Is called in Egyptian Enish-go-on-dosh; this is one of the governing planets also, and is said by the Egyptians to be the Sun, and to borrow its light from Kolob through the medium of Kae-e-vanrash, which is the grand Key, or, in other words, the governing power, which governs fifteen other fixed planets or stars, as also Floeese or the Moon, the Earth and the Sun in their annual revolutions. This planet receives its power through the medium of Kli-flos-is-es, or Hah-ko-kau-beam, the stars represented by numbers 22 and 23, receiving light from the revolutions of Kolob.

Fig. 6. Represents this earth in its four quarters.

Fig. 7. Represents God sitting upon his throne, revealing through the heavens the grand Key-words of the Priesthood; as, also, the sign of the Holy Ghost unto Abraham, in the form of a dove.

Fig. 8. Contains writings that cannot be revealed unto the world; but is to be had in the Holy Temple of God.

Fig. 9. Ought not to be revealed at the present time.

Fig. 10. Also.

Fig. 11. Also. If the world can find out these numbers, so let it be. Amen.

Figures 12, 13, 14, 15, 16, 17, 18, 19, 20, and 21 will be given in the own due time of the Lord.

The above translation is given as far as we have any right to give at the present time.

228

Above, is a section of Facsimile No. 2 (printed in the *Book of Abraham*, part of the *Pearl of Great Price,* in the bottom right-hand section of the complete copy of Smith's rendering of the Egyptian hypocephalus. Note: in order to clearly see this portion of the hypocephalus, it should be viewed upside down). This quarter portion depicts figure number 7, which according to Smith, is "God sitting on His throne, revealing through the heavens the grand Key-words of the Priesthood..." But the figure is actually the Egyptian ithyphallic God of fertility, '*Min.*'

In my 1974 Edition of the *Book of Abraham*, the figure's erect phallus has been omitted. It was apparently restored in the 1981 editions and thereafter. According to one writer, the correct rendering likely caused embarrassment to LDS officials and was considered so explicit that it was falsified in some printings of the *Pearl of Great Price.* [224]

Facsimile No. 3, depicted next, is labeled by Joseph Smith as: "Abraham is reasoning upon the principles of Astronomy in the king's court." *Book of Abraham,* Facsimile # 3 from Ludlow, Daniel, H., ed., *Encyclopedia of Mormonism,* p. 475.

A FACSIMILE FROM THE BOOK OF ABRAHAM

No. 3

ENG-BY R'HEDLOCK

EXPLANATION

Fig. 1. Abraham sitting upon Pharaoh's throne, by the politeness of the king, with a crown upon his head, representing the Priesthood, as emblematical of the grand Presidency in Heaven; with the scepter of justice and judgment in his hand.

Fig. 2. King Pharaoh, whose name is given in the characters above his head.

Fig. 3. Signifies Abraham in Egypt as given also in Figure 10 of Facsimile No. 1.

Fig. 4. Prince of Pharaoh, King of Egypt, as written above the hand.

Fig. 5. Shulem, one of the king's principal waiters, as represented by the characters above his hand.

Fig. 6. Olimlah, a slave belonging to the prince.

Abraham is reasoning upon the principles of Astronomy, in the king's court.

Smith's Interpretation	Accurate Translation
1 Abraham, sitting upon Pharaoh's throne...with a crown upon his head, representing the Priesthood...	1 Represents Osiris, foremost of the westerners.
2 King Pharaoh, whose name is given in the characters above his head.	2 The Egyptian Goddess, *Isis,* the great, the God's mother.
3 Signifies Abraham in Egypt— referring to Abraham...	3 An *Altar* with the offering of the deceased, surrounded with lotus flowers, signifying the defunct.
4 Prince of Pharaoh, King of Egypt, as written above the hand.	4 Figure of *Maat,* Mistress of the gods.
5 Shulem, one of the king's principal waiters, as represented by the characters above his hand.	5 Symbol of *Hor,* the deceased; the *Osiris Hor* justified forever.
6 Olimlah, a slave belonging to the prince.	6 Representative of *Anubis* who makes protection foremost of the embalming booth.

Two females in facsimile No. 3 (whose bodies appear quite feminine) are assigned male gender in Smith's interpretation set forth in the *Book of Abraham*. Smith incorrectly identifies the Egyptian Goddess *Isis*, who some claim was the remnant of the Neolithic great goddess religion and not just one of many goddesses, as King Pharaoh (figure #2). He also mistakes *Maat*, mistress to the gods, as [the] "Prince of Pharaoh," (figure #4).

LDS Church reaction has been typical. Instead of admitting the hoax, the author of a Church magazine article testifies that one cannot know the truths taught in the *Book of Abraham* based upon evidence, but only from the Spirit.[225] Although Mormon leaders tried to make an excuse for the extensive discrepancies, there was really no way to get around the fact that Smith's *Book of Abraham* was a falsified translation from the original papyri.

Questionable Financial Practices, the Kirtland Bank & 'Bogus Money'

Soon after his translation of the Egyptian papyri, Smith attempted to create an independent financial institution whereby he would profit from the deposits of his faithful followers. Here is where the Prophet's outright swindling of the Saints caused the first in a long series of disaffections and apostasies.

Fleecing the Flock: Kirtland Mormon Bank Note of 1837[226]

The fallout from this ill-planned scheme was described by faithful Church member Warren Parrish, who had been an officer in the "bank," created by Smith and colleagues:

232

...I have listened to him [Joseph Smith] with feelings of no ordinary kind, when he declared that the audible voice of God, instructed him to establish a Banking-Anti Banking institution, which like Aaron's rod should swallow up all other Banks (the Bank of Monroe excepted,) and grow and flourish and spread from the rivers to the ends of the earth, and survive when all others should be laid in ruins. I have been astonished to hear him declare that we had 60,000 Dollars in specie in our vaults, and $600,000 at our command, when we had not to exceed $6,000 and could not command any more; also that we had but about ten thousand Dollars of our bills in circulation, when he, as Cashier of the institution, knew that there was at least $150,000. Knowing their extreme poverty when they commenced this speculation, I have been not a little surprised to hear them assert that they were worth from three to four hundred thousand Dollars Cash, and in less than ninety days after, became insolvent without any change in their business affairs. But such has been the audacity of these boasting blasphemers, that they have assumed the authority to curse, or to bless, to damn, or to save, not only this Church but this entire generation, and that they hold their destinies in this world and that which is to come. And such has been their influence over this Church in this place, that they have filched the monies from their pockets and obtained their earthly substance for the purpose of establishing a Bank and various wild speculations, in order that they might aggrandize themselves and families, until they have reduced their followers to wretchedness and want. For the year past their lives have been one continued scene of lying, deception, and fraud, and that too, in the name of God. But this I can account for in my own mind, having a knowledge of their private characters and sentiments, I believe them to be confirmed Infidels, who have not the fear of God before their eyes, notwithstanding their high pretensions to holiness, and frequent correspondence with the Angels of Heaven, and the revelations of Jesus Christ by the power of the Holy Ghost.*[227]

Although the Kirtland Banking Society was an attempted legitimate bank, the Brethren failed to procure a charter with the Ohio State legislature. And though the printed money was worthless in trade outside the circle of Saints, even Church members were admonished not to take in those very notes that had been printed and distributed, but only to accept specie in their trade with the gentiles. When the Kirtland Notes were offered for redemption by either Saints or gentiles, they were rejected.

Cyrus Smalling, a former Mormon, said that the vault with the Safety Society's start-up capital had in it only boxes of lead shot. Instead of silver and gold, just the top layer of each box was covered in coin. Thus, even upon inspection, it appeared that the 'Bank' had more initial capital than it truly had. No doubt this was done to satisfy investors. [228]

Benjamin Winchester, a young Mormon at the time, described the financial institution years later in his interview published in the *Salt Lake Tribune*:

> Joseph was president, and Rigdon was cashier of the concern. This went on until the bank had absorbed a large proportion of the money in that section of the country, and a considerable number of people began to find out that they had some need of some of their deposits. When the demand for redemption began to accumulate the deposits were paid in the paper of an almost defunct bank at Monroe, Michigan, which the schemers had bought. Of course the depositors soon became uneasy after finding that their checks were paid in worthless bank notes of the bank of Monroe, and when the prospect of mob violence became apparent, Smith, Rigdon, and a man named Boyd of New York, connected with the first two in the swindle, decamped between sunset and sunrise. The trio had the money and the people had their experience. Soon afterwards came the collapse of Kirtland. [229]

Smith and Rigdon withdrew from the enterprise and left Warren Parrish and others who were ultimately blamed for the Bank's failure in official Church history. Smith and Rigdon fled west on horseback to avoid creditors. According to Winchester:

> After the collapse at Kirtland, to which I have referred, all of the so-called witnesses to The Book of Mormon, with the exception of the members of the Smith family, left the fold and were never afterwards identified with it at Nauvoo under Joseph Smith, or in

Utah under Brigham Young, and two-thirds of the best talent of the Church then left, and never after had any connection with the concern at either place above named. [230]

Smith and his colleagues continued on in their westward journey, with their habit of defrauding the residents of each new town in which the Saints and their leaders settled, only to eventually flee under threat of legal action brought by local authorities. The Mormon leaders' reputations had preceded them and they were initially refused room and board in Missouri towns. Many Mormons ultimately turned on their leaders. In 1838, eighty-four Mormons accused two of the three *Book of Mormon* Witnesses, Oliver Cowdery and David Whitmer, and another LDS Apostle, Lyman E. Johnson, with counterfeiting. [231]

Smith's financial fraud continued with his successor, Brigham Young. He and other Mormons made counterfeit coins, specie with substantially less than the required 100% silver metal content. This was openly done by the Federal Reserve in 1965 when they reduced the 90% silver content of quarter dollars. In contrast, this 'bogus money' had been passed off to gentiles by many Mormons for years.

In 1845, Young was charged with counterfeiting by the U.S. Circuit Court, District of Illinois, but the case was never prosecuted because the federal government failed to obtain personal jurisdiction over him.[232] Young joked that he avoided arrest on the warrant by having another man impersonate him while he was hiding out in the Kirtland Temple. The federal authorities ended up arresting (in the Prophet's own words) a "bogus Brigham." [233] Eventually, the federal indictments for counterfeiting were dismissed, most likely for the failure to prosecute.

After the dedication of the Kirtland Mormon Temple in March of 1836, and perhaps with the thought that the translation from the purchased Egyptian papyri might not give Smith and his Church the increased following and support needed, Smith made a trip to Salem, Massachusetts in July, 1836, "in search of much treasure."[234] Burgess, a brother in the Church, claimed that that he knew of a house there belonging to a widow. The house was supposed to have had a large treasure in its cellar. On August 6, the day after Smith and his companions arrived in Salem, Smith had a revelation which is found in *D&C* §111, that [the house in Salem's] "...wealth pertaining to gold and silver shall be yours."[235]

There is no evidence that any treasure was ever located. Smith kept no diary during this latter half of 1836 and throughout 1837. Only after the Kirtland Bank failure was a *fait accompli*, by March, 1838, does his journal begin again, recorded by his scribe, George W. Robinson.

Mormon Gullibility and Suppression

In 1980, Mark Hoffman, a Utah resident, former Mormon missionary and collector of rare books exchanged a document he claimed to be the original document that Martin Harris had presented to Charles Anthon for about $20,000 worth of ancient documents from the LDS Church. Hoffman said he had found the document in an old bible. The document was verified by the Church's recognized authority on the handwriting of the Prophet, to be characters copied from the golden plates which Harris had shown to Charles Anthon. According to the senior associate at the LDS Historical Department, Dean C. Jessee, "...it is impossible to conclude that others than Joseph Smith wrote this."[236] As reported in the *Provo Herald*, BYU professors Richard L. Anderson and Hugh Nibley commented:

> "Joseph Smith's story is really vindicated by the finding of the document because he mentioned that he sent Harris to the East to show the characters on the gold plates to 'the learned.' We have Anthon's story in letters explaining exactly what Harris showed to him. What Anthon describes is quite remarkably like what is on the new transcript." Richard L. Anderson also commented: "This new discovery is sort of a Dead Sea School [sic] Equivalent of The Book of Mormon.". . . Mormon scholar Hugh Nibley was quoted as saying: 'This offers as good a test as we'll ever get as to the authenticity of The Book of Mormon...'"*[237]

LDS scholars appeared convinced that the document was authentic, but it was eventually determined by experts to have been forged. In the interim, it and other Hoffman forgeries were included in the first edition of Dean Jesse's book, *Personal Writings of Joseph Smith*, published by Church-owned Deseret Book.

Hoffman had found a market for his forgeries. According to the Tanners (who were personally acquainted with Hoffman) he realized that over time the Mormon Brethren had suppressed publication of early Church historical documents because of the potential damage to its public image.[238] Hoffman had planned to capitalize on their collective fear of exposure of any theretofore unknown historic document that could be interpreted as averse to the Church and its doctrines.

Then, in 1984, when the first document sold to the Church had yet to be proven forged, Hoffman convinced Church leadership to purchase another document he claimed to be a letter authored by Smith's backer, Martin Harris. This forgery referenced a white salamander in Smith's encounter with the golden plates. The fake became known as the Salamander Letter. Once Church leaders realized the *L.A. Times* was about to break the news of Church purchase of the letter, it publicly acknowledged receipt of the document. The Church had paid thousands of dollars for the forgery, initially believing it to be authentic. [239]

Ultimately both documents were proven to be fakes. But during the intrigue, Hoffman's pipe bombs killed two people. The bombs were intended for two Mormon bishops: Steven Christensen and J. Gary Sheets. Christensen suffered a gruesome death at his office in the Judge Building, located in Salt Lake City. Later that morning, it was Kathleen Sheets, instead of her husband Gary, who was also murdered.[240]

Hoffman was charged with two counts of first degree murder and multiple counts of forgery. After a protracted preliminary hearing, he pled guilty to second degree murder and theft by deception, saving Church leaders from having to testify in what surely would have been an embarrassing public exposure of their cumulative gullibility. Hoffman continues to serve his life sentence in the Utah State Prison.

Shortly after the Hoffman crimes, a descendant of LDS historian B. H. Roberts (1857-1933) allowed publication of Roberts' heretofore unpublished manuscripts questioning the origins of *the Book of Mormon*. Though publicly Roberts defended the Church, apparently the 1912 *New York Times* publicity regarding the Egyptian papyri translation had prompted his questioning. In the early 1920s, Roberts repeatedly petitioned for an audience with the Brethren to discuss his research and issues regarding the divine authenticity of the *the Book of Mormon*.

...from 10:00 a.m. until 6:00 p.m. on January 4, 1922, Brigham H. Roberts present[ed a] detailed summary of textual and historical problems in *Book of Mormon* to [a] combined meeting of the First

Presidency, [a]postles and Seventy's presidents. He recommends that these problems should be researched and publicly discussed.*[241]

In his introduction to the first (1985) edition of Roberts' *Studies of the Book of Mormon,* University of Utah history professor, Brigham D. Madsen confirms that Roberts spent most of *two* days with the LDS General Authorities in 1922.[242] In response to Roberts' detailed presentation of problems with the origins of *the Book of Mormon* and plea to the Brethren to come clean with its probable historical source, "...they merely one by one stood up and bore testimony to the truthfulness of *The Book of Mormon.*" Afterward, Apostle Richard R. Lyman asked Roberts "...if there were things that would help our prestige and when Bro. Roberts answered no, he said then why discuss them."*[243]

Roberts' *Studies of the Book of Mormon* raised issues such as Smith's plagiarization of the King James Version of the Bible, the lack of archeological support for the minerals, animals and vegetation referenced in *the Book of Mormon*, and the Book's curious parallel to Ethan Smith's *A View of the Hebrews*. Like many early nineteenth century writings, *A View of the Hebrews* speculates about Hebraic roots in American civilizations.

In support of *Book of Mormon* collaboration, Roberts theorizes:

There is a certain lack of perspective in the things the book relates as history that points quite clearly to an undeveloped mind as their origin. The narrative proceeds in characteristic disregard of conditions necessary to its reasonableness, as if it were a tale told by a child, with utter disregard for consistency...Clearly The Book of Mormon shows evidence of two different minds at work — one imaginative, intelligent and unquestionably learned; the other immature and inconsistent. It is possible, however, to reconcile these seeming contradictions if one presumes that Joseph Smith did not actually write The Book of Mormon, but rather created it by making a clumsy and inconsistent revision, or perhaps even a paraphrase, of someone else's text. *[244]

Copies of *A View of the Hebrews* were widely available during Joseph Smith's alleged ignorant period. Roberts logically argued that Church leaders should "...frankly state events as they occurred, in full consideration of all related circumstances, [and] allow the line of condemnation or justification to fall where it may... "*[245]

B.H. Roberts, with his frank and disquieting queries, was then sent away to serve as LDS mission president for the Eastern United States. There, he continued to push the missionary program and publicly aver his testimony of Mormonism, while privately reading voraciously about the issues which troubled him. It was while he was serving as mission president that Roberts discovered the *A View of the Hebrews* by Ethan Smith, a minister who preached in Poultney, Vermont in the early 1820s, during which time Oliver Cowdery's immediate family were members of the congregation. *A View of the Hebrews* was published in 1823 and 1825 and readily available to Joseph Smith due to Palmyra's heavy commerce from the newly-opened Erie Canal.

Roberts specifically itemized and compared storylines and themes between Ethan Smith's Book and *the Book of Mormon* in a document he had written circa 1827, entitled *A Parallel*. Upon his return from the East, Roberts approached then president of the LDS Church, Heber J. Grant, with his concerns about *Book of Mormon* origins, but was again ignored. Most likely, it was not until 1946, when Roberts' son, Ben E. Roberts, lectured on the subject and gave copies of *A Parallel* to men at the Timpanagos Club (the oldest club for men in Utah), that anyone besides the Brethren and persons in Roberts' immediate family and circle of friends, had access to his written analysis.[246]

Despite authoring three scholarly exposés on *the Book of Mormon* as scripture and exposing Mormonism's claim for the book's divine origins as false, Roberts continued to publicly defend the Church until his death in 1933. For example, at the semi-annual LDS General Conference in April 1928, he was reported to have "Defended *The Book of Mormon* as the word of God... [and] closed his address by bearing an impressive testimony to the divinity of the church." *[247]

Reverend Wesley P. Walters, late minister of the Presbyterian Church, Marissa, Illinois, commented on Roberts' manuscript in a 1979 article, calling all Roberts' work (including the *Parallel* written sometime between 1922 and Roberts' death in 1933) "...undoubtedly the most objective look at the origins of The Book of Mormon ever made by a general authority of the Church of Jesus Christ of Latter-day Saints."[248] While writing his article, Reverend Walters had apparently communicated with an individual who had been affiliated with Brigham Young University in 1925 and who requested to remain anonymous. This person told Reverend Walters in a 1978 letter that: "A few of us at BYU got a few fragments of that [Roberts'] manuscript back in 1925, but were ordered to destroy them and to 'keep your mouths shut.'"[249] It was over fifty years before the comprehensive edition of Roberts' queries (all three manuscripts) was published by the University of Illinois, with the consent of the University of Utah Research Foundation.[250]

The fact that these indictments of *the Book of Mormon's* authenticity had arisen in the early part of the twentieth century and were given excellent documentation by one of the Church's own, yet ignored or even suppressed by LDS leadership, is certainly evidence that Mormon leaders have for decades now, continued their [mis]representations that *the Book of Mormon* was revealed by God if not intentionally, [at least] "... recklessly, knowing that [t]he[y] had insufficient knowledge upon which to base such representations." *Franco v. Church of LDS*, 2001 UT 25 ¶ 33.

Facts v. Feelings: the Witness of the Spirit

One excellent example of Smith's borrowing from other sources and incorporating already existing doctrines, writings and in this case, rituals, can be found in an examination of the roots of the Mormon Temple Ceremony. It is a matter of record that Joseph Smith was inducted into the Masonic Lodge of Nauvoo in spring of 1842. According to the *History of the Church*, first published serially in various LDS newspapers and eventually compiled into a several volume treatise and published in 1846 and offered by the LDS Church to members as authored by Joseph Smith, Smith states: "I was with the Masonic Lodge and rose to the sublime degree."* [251]

Smith established a Nauvoo Masonic Lodge, hoping that this would help grow his religion. When this plan failed and less than two months after he first became a Mason, the temple endowment ceremony was revealed as a part of Mormonism.

This revised version of the Masonic handshakes and oaths was passed off as required oaths and promises promulgated by the Lord. It is obvious that Smith had tweaked the Freemasons' ceremony, adding in the part about women obeying their husbands. In the original Freemasonry organization women were forbidden as initiates; it was a strictly fraternal organization.[252]

In the 1980s, in response to the then, recently published and damning evidence contained in B. H. Roberts' scholarly analysis, and Mark Hoffman's initially successful forgeries, the LDS Church increased its emphasis on faith over historical fact, deriding the importance of the latter. Elder Dallin H. Oaks expressed such sentiments during the height of the Hoffman Salamander Letter scandal, before Church authorities finally discovered the Hoffman document to have been forged. Speaking to a BYU audience, Oaks said: "Our individual, personal testimonies are based on the witness of the spirit, not on any combination or accumulation of historical facts…If we are so grounded, no alteration of historical facts can shake our testimonies." [253]

I remember Dallin Oaks as president of BYU when I attended the law school. I have been in audiences where he was the keynote speaker on several occasions. He has an enormous head, which, according to some old phrenology theories, is a good indicator of substantial intelligence. Dallin H. Oaks, Chicago Law School Order of the Coif, former Utah Supreme Court Justice, Republican nominee for the U.S. Supreme Court and member of the Quorum of the Twelve Apostles of the Church of Jesus Christ of Latter-day Saints, while clearly one of the most arrogant of the Brethren, is not stupid or uneducated.

One nineteenth century scholar, Jonathon B. Turner, Yale educated professor of rhetoric and *belles-lettres* at the University of Illinois, compared Mormonism to other religious delusions documented over the history of the world. In this history of credulity, he identifies the common component in these religions: an absence of facts.

These three causes, the necessity of faith, the aversion to restraint in the many, and the love of power in the few, have conspired to make the religious history of the mass of mankind a history of credulity and infatuation. Mormonism is not an exception to the general rule. It is but one of the many hideous errors imposed, by the lust of power, on the credulity of the multitude. In all ages of the world the majority of mankind, both in Christian and heathen lands, have been ready to believe any thing in religion, however absurd, provided it was both false and absurd, and proffered eternal happiness, or at least eternal exemption from merited punishment, as the reward of belief, without the pain and trouble of a thorough moral reformation.

The people generally have homilies, doctrines, and dogmas enough ever at hand; but they are starved for want of facts. The well-informed, because they themselves know all these and similar facts, are too apt to take it for granted that everybody else knows them too; and that some bare allusion to them will awaken the same ideas in other minds which it does in their own.

It is no wonder that enthusiasts, fanatics, and impostors, find both hearers and believers, provided they can muster absurdities enough to draw them together, accompanied with a good supply of promises to save them, and threats to damn them if they won't believe. The only thing needful in order to make proselytes to any monstrous absurdity, which proffers salvation without the pain and trouble of a thorough moral reformation, is to tell your lie, and stick to it, at all hazards, through thick and thin. It matters not if it contradicts not one, but all the five human senses. Proclaim that the sun shines at midnight, and the stars at noonday, and maintain that all will be saved, or at least [not] annihilated, if they will believe, and stick to it, and they will believe—you will find followers. *[254]

With regard to the feelings of the Spirit, so relied upon by Mormon leaders and lay members when presented with unfavorable facts, Professor Turner explained it well:

But is there no way by which God assures us of the truth? Yes; when we search for it in accordance with his will, and the laws of our own minds. God made man to find the truth, as he does his natural food, by searching for it abroad, and not by feeling after it in his own stomach…

And yet all fanatics and all enthusiasts, of all ages, make common cause here. However diverse in all else, as we have seen, here they agree. They all know that their own, or the absurd schemes of their leaders, are true, either because God has personally revealed it to them, by some mystic voice, or by kindling up some holy rapture or ferment in their souls. In this common den of inspiration, we find monsters of all shapes and sizes…

In these rhapsodies of faith, or rather of folly, every silly figment of a diseased imagination is deemed either a voice or an impulse from God; and the more absurd the better, provided it chance to chime harmoniously with the ruling impulses or prevailing delirium of the hour. It is impossible to reason against this folly, for it defies all reason in the outset. The overweaning self-conceit, and the total paralysis of all the powers of reason, which such a morbid state of mind both engenders and implies, render all hopeless and all useless, while the spell is on, save handcuffs and the madhouse. *[255]

Thus, in Mormonism and throughout history in similar fanatical religions, the nebulous 'Spirit,' always wins over man's ability to reason. Clearly, whether by evolution or as a gift from the Creator, reason is all that distinguishes man from most beasts. However, reason doesn't seem to figure into the equation when assessing the value of these type religions to their believers.

***

In 2002, Grant Palmer, a former director at the LDS Institutes of Religion, published *An Insider's View of Mormon Origins*. Unlike other writings of non-Mormons or former Mormons, at the time of publication Palmer was a member of the Church. After years of teaching young Mormon students the golden plate theory of origination, Palmer reluctantly concluded that *the Book of Mormon* is not a translation of ancient scripture, but "is in fact an amalgamation of ideas that were inspired by Joseph's own environment and themes from the Bible."[256] Palmer also drew comparisons between Smith's revisions of his first vision (current version in the *PGP*, "Joseph Smith," Chap. 2) over the years 1832-1842 and the first English translation of the German folktale, "The Golden Pot," which debuted in 1827.[257]

Palmer's excellent compilation of primary source materials and his reluctant deductions about the origins of Mormonism compel his readers to just one conclusion: that the church upon which so many have based their lives was not founded upon scripture from God through prophets, but is a nineteenth century business venture, which has succeeded beyond its founders' expectations. Palmer's evidence makes clear that the current version of Joseph Smith's first vision is a conflation of different accounts told to various individuals over the decade prior to the creation of the Church of Christ (original name of the LDS Church, changed in 1834 to the "Church of Latter Day Saints," and then again in 1838, to its current name, The Church of Jesus Christ of Latter-day Saints).[258]

Utah Censorship Regarding Reputations of Dead Prophets

Author Fawn Brodie, niece of Mormon president, David O. McKay, published her widely acclaimed biography of Joseph Smith, *"No Man Knows My History"* in 1945, not so subtly hinting that Smith was a criminal and a narcissist. [259] An accomplished historian and ultimately, a professor of History at UCLA, she provided compelling evidence of Smith's deceptive tactics in creating *the Book of Mormon* and its church. Brodie documents the lack of evidence to support the existence of the claimed golden plates, and details Smith's perverted practice of seducing young girls and other men's wives under the pretext of God's authority.

Brodie's biography of Mormonism's creator was heralded nationally as a seminal work, yet for decades it was difficult to find in Utah. According to Sandra Tanner, Sam Weller's Main Street bookstore in Salt Lake City kept copies under the counter and sold them wrapped in brown paper.

Two years earlier (no doubt because Uncle David was aware of his niece's researching Joseph Smith's biography) Utah enacted its civil defamation statute. This definition remains the statutory law today. It is:

> A malicious defamation [speech or writing] …tending to blacken the memory of one who is dead, or to impeach the honesty, integrity, virtue or reputation, or publish the natural defects of one who is alive, and thereby to expose him to public hatred, contempt or ridicule.[260]

Unlike other jurisdictions, the statutory definition of defamation in Utah does not specifically require that the statement be false, although falsity could be implied in the preliminary phrase "malicious defamation." Still, the wording of this statute seems unconstitutionally vague because if it is not part of the definition itself, the alleged defamer has the burden of proof as to the truthfulness of his statement. Whereas, if by its very definition the statement must be false in order to be defamatory, those alleging defamation have the burden to prove its falsity.

Although in 1983 the Utah Supreme Court had occasion to hold that "actual malice" is required to be proven in a civil action for libel of a public figure, it was not until 2002 that the Court was presented with a case which gave the Court an opportunity to rule on the constitutionality of Utah's similarly-worded criminal libel statute.

The case involved a student who had posted disparaging comments about his teachers, classmates and principal on the internet. In *I.M.L. v. State*, the Court dismissed the case and found the statute unconstitutional due to its overly broad language, which fails to define defamation; among other things it would deem criminal, "true statements regarding public figures."

¶ 30 We hold that Utah's criminal libel statute, Utah Code Ann. §§ 76-9-501 to 503, infringes upon a substantial amount of constitutionally protected speech by punishing false statements regarding public figures made without knowledge or recklessness and true statements regarding public figures. The statute is therefore overbroad and unconstitutional.[261]

Therefore even today, though it is not clear, one might potentially violate current Utah civil defamation law for making truthful statements regarding deceased public figures such as LDS Presidents Joseph Smith and Brigham Young.

Smith's Pious Fraud Has Recently Been Identified by LDS Prophets and Apostles

Whenever I hear an LDS Church leader claim that the Church, prophet, *Book of Mormon*, etc., is either the truth or a fraud, such as those quotations at the beginning of this chapter by Gordon B. Hinckley and Jeffrey Holland, I am skeptical. The statements are generally rhetorical and the initial interpretation of these type statements is that they were made to allay LDS members' fears; to lead them to continue in their belief that there is no way Mormonism could be a fraud. However, there is another way to interpret these declarations.

For example, in the Pacific Gas & Electric (PG&E) case depicted in the film *Erin Brockovich*, one of the defenses raised was that PG&E had told the Hinkley residents about the chromium and therefore as of a certain date, injured residents couldn't argue that PG&E failed to disclose the fact that the heavy metal was in the town's water. But the manner in which the Company described the presence of the element was that it was necessary and beneficial to have in one's water. Nothing was said to the townspeople about the harm of this particular type of chromium, *hexavalent* chromium.[262]

With most civil causes of action the statute of limitations begins to run at the time the claimant discovers (or should have discovered) the wrongdoing. Thus, if a Latter-day Saint were to argue that fraudulent misrepresentations by the Brethren induced them to join or stay in Mormonism, the Church could legitimately respond that their members were given notice in general conferences and in Church magazines that the Church *could* be a fraud. Though the incredulity in the spoken (if not written) statements might be sufficient to negate the express content of what was conveyed, and therefore to negate the notice, conversely it could be argued that such statements serve as a complete bar to any subsequent fraud claims brought three or more years later against the LDS Church by its members.

LDS Church leaders know and have known the true origins of Mormonism since it all began. B. H. Roberts' duplicitous actions are a good example of an early twentieth century LDS leader, who, knowing that *Book of Mormon* origins were most likely not what Smith claimed them to be, nevertheless continued to preach the Joseph Smith story, perpetuating the fable and preaching its truthfulness under the guise of religious authority to yet another generation of true-believing Mormons. Thus, as of Roberts' two day presentation to the Brethren in 1922, LDS leaders have at least suspected, if not known the truth. Yet these men continue to mislead.

The next chapter examines how Joseph Smith's character, actions and admissions indict his claims to commune with divinity. I will also explore how Joseph Smith, the brand, has been reformulated and repackaged through the decades, in order to sell Mormonism to the broadest base of consumers possible.

CHAPTER NINE: Cross-examining Mormonism

"Faith, as well intentioned as it may be, must be built on facts, not fiction —faith in fiction is a damnable false hope."—Thomas Edison

The amount of documentation now available regarding the fraudulent origins of Mormonism is vast. Most of this evidence of man-made origins of Mormon scripture is direct evidence—taken from the very document which purports to be divine; some is circumstantial. However, it is a popular misconception that circumstantial evidence is never sufficient for criminal conviction or a finding of liability in a civil case. Especially where the amount of such circumstantial evidence is overwhelming, a jury is correctly instructed that it can convict or find liability based upon circumstantial evidence alone. In fact, most court cases are not decided on direct evidence because the defendant throws the gun in the river, repairs the property defect, 'misplaces' key medical diagnostic films, or destroys the plagiarized manuscript. Thus, it is frequently the case that only circumstantial evidence remains.[263]

To prove fraud, even civil fraud, one must meet an extremely high standard of proof—clear and convincing evidence. This level of evidence is more than is required in a typical civil case: 'a preponderance,' but not quite as high as that level required in convicting a defendant of a crime: 'beyond a reasonable doubt.' In the case against Mormonism, clear and convincing evidence is ample.

***

The first Sunday of every month is fast and testimony meeting at all the wards in the LDS Church. While the microphone is passed around to the members of the congregation, those so inclined stand and speak. The first words commonly out of their mouths are: "I want to bear my testimony..." or some such variant. After that introduction, the speaker goes on to recite that he or she *knows* that the Mormon Church is true. "[The Church is] the restored gospel of Jesus Christ," is a phrase used by more erudite members. The testifiers continue to swear that the original and/or current prophet is really a prophet. "Called of God," is a phrase sometimes added to properly credential the prophet of whom they speak. Some sit down at that point. But most go on to relate personal anecdotes, which stories are to be taken by those listening as evidence supporting the speakers' declarations of the truthfulness of the LDS Church and the legitimacy of its leaders.

The original definition of the word testimony is:

1. A declaration of truth or fact
2. Law evidence given by a witness, esp. in court under oath
3. Evidence proving or supporting something: that they are still talking is a testimony to their 20-year friendship.[264]

Thus, a 'testimony,' in the sense that LDS faithful convey their heartfelt beliefs, is more accurately described as an emotional acknowledgment of the importance of the Religion in the testifiers' particular lives. But these individual attestations are irrelevant to the objective truth of Mormonism.

Rule 401 of the *Federal Rules of Evidence* (*FRE*) also followed more or less by most state jurisdictions, including Utah, defines relevant as "...evidence having any tendency to make the existence of any fact that is of consequence to the determination of the action more probable or less probable than it would be without the evidence." In this chapter I will examine what evidence is available to disprove that Mormonism's claimed scriptural origins are divine. A threshold question would be to define divine. Divine as used here (and as represented by the LDS Church) means that the source is an external heavenly being, not part of the psychological or intellectual make-up of the individual Joseph Smith or any of the founders of Mormonism. Rather, divine would mean a separate, discrete entity—whether God speaking through an ancient American prophet (e.g., the author-prophets of the various books in *the Book of Mormon*) or from God's mouth directly through Joseph Smith acting as prophet, as for example, in *D&C* revelations.

Though many New Age and some ancient Gnostic theories maintain that revelation comes through the human psyche as an interior, intuitive process, this is not the claim that has been made by LDS leaders for almost two centuries. Rather, and importantly, in contrast to other Protestant sects—those that have their source in the inspired writings and words of Protestant Reformation leaders such as Luther and Calvin—the Mormon Brethren cannot excuse the deity sightings claimed in the first vision and delivery of literal golden plates as being from a God who dwells within the mind or heart of Joseph Smith. This is because they have made such an issue of identifying external personages and deities appearing in Church history as separate from their founding prophet.[265]

Mormonism is unique when compared to other Protestant churches in that its doctrine is not a result of the writings of thinking, educated men of the cloth, but a result of a claimed divine apparition, witnessed only by Joseph Smith and of instructions and teachings inscribed by ancient American Continent prophets on literal golden plates, again seen only by Smith (and allegedly some of his friends and family).

How do we judge Joseph Smith's credibility? It is Smith's words or those attributed to him, whether through translation, inspiration or revelation, which are the true basis of Mormonism. Therefore, determining Joseph Smith's credibility as a witness to his own claims is of utmost importance.

First Vision, Angelic Messenger and Gold Plate Discovery Revisions

After trying lots of cases, an attorney becomes adept at using the rules of evidence to expose the testimony of liars. One method of impeachment is to confront the witness with his or her prior inconsistent statements.[266] Many times a prevaricating witness deposed years previously fails to review his deposition transcript in preparation for his trial testimony and will directly contradict himself on important points.

According to Smith's contemporary, newspaper editor and author, Eber D. Howe, the statements made regarding the retrieval of the golden plates varied over time.

> We have not only testimony impeaching the moral characters of the Smith family, but we show by the witnesses, that they told contradictory stories, from time to time, in relation to their finding the plates, and other circumstances attending it, which go clearly to show that none of them had the fear of God before their eyes, but were moved and instigated by the devil.[267]

Joseph Smith's deceit is easily exposed through his inconsistent accounts of the first vision. Initially it was a beseeching prayer for forgiveness of personal sins; later, an encounter with God, and ultimately with God the Father, and His Son, Jesus Christ. The official version of the 1820 first vision was not written until 1832 (where God the Father is conspicuously absent) and then again in 1838, almost twenty years after the alleged event. It was not included in the first edition of *the Book of Mormon* in 1830, but was offered (and apparently accepted by most) as a *nunc pro tunc* account when finally published in the 1842 edition of the Mormon Newspaper, *Times and Seasons.*[268]

That same year in response to a request for information on the Mormon movement by Mr. Wentworth, editor and proprietor of the *Chicago Democrat*, Smith wrote: "When about fourteen years of age I began to reflect upon the importance of being prepared for a future state…" Smith then goes on to claim he saw two personages, the Father and the Son. However, no exact date is given for this historic first vision other than it occurred when he was "about fourteen." This, despite other specific dates set forth in the Wentworth Letter: September 21, 1823 he was visited by an [unnamed] angel telling him of the golden plates, on September 22, 1827, he obtained the golden plates and on April 6, 1830 the Church was organized.

Biographer Fawn Brodie's extensive search for any documents confirming the 1820 first vision revealed no record of a contemporaneous re-telling of the event in newspapers or from those living near the Prophet at the time. This has been proven despite Smith's claims that those he told of his vision persecuted him for the telling. [269]

Prior Inconsistent Attributions and Statements

Another important inconsistency is in the attribution of the creator of *the Book of Mormon*. The title page of the 1830 first edition of *the Book of Mormon* reads: "by Joseph Smith, jr., **author and proprietor.**" Later editions read "*the Book of Mormon **translated** by Joseph Smith, Jr.*" [Emphasis added]. The original attribution of Smith as author appears to be more correct. This change alone impugns LDS Church representations that Smith translated *the Book of Mormon* text from ancient golden plates.

Additionally, the original manuscript of the *Pearl of Great Price,* which tells the story of the first vision and the first angelic visit, contains the handwritten name of "Nephi," crossed out with the name "Moroni," written in instead.[270] Though the Wentworth Letter doesn't name the angelic visitor, in 1842 newspapers, he was first identified as the angel "Nephi," who appeared to Smith to tell him about the golden plates hid up in the Hill Cumorah.[271] Later, the name of the angel was changed to "Moroni," whose trumpeting statue tops Mormon Temples today. Furthermore, the name "Nephi," did not originate with Smith; it's also contained in biblical apocryphal writings. [272]

Changes and equivocations to testimony (or in this case, scripture) are in effect, prior inconsistent statements, which impugn LDS scriptures and their author, Joseph Smith's credibility. Over the years there have been innumerable changes to the Church's scriptures. One website claims that there have been more than 8,400 changes to Mormon scriptures. [273] While an itemization of these changes is beyond the scope of this book, and as claimed by Mormon apologists, many are grammatical and insignificant, some are quite substantive.

For example, §101 of the *D&C*, a statement on marriage adopted by a conference of the Church and contained in the 1835 Edition, was removed in 1876 (a year before Brigham Young died). It read in part:

Inasmuch as this Church of Christ (the original name for the Church of Jesus Christ of Latter-day Saints) has been reproached with the crime of fornication and polygamy, we declare that we believe that one man should have one wife, and one woman but one husband, except in the case of death, when either is at liberty to marry again.

§101 was replaced by §132 of the current edition (cited in part, in Chapter One of this book), the revelation Smith purportedly received on the doctrine of plural or celestial marriage (polygamy).

The original (1835) *D&C* also contains secret code names for high-ranking Church members and places. Some believe that the use of code names was to avoid citation to these sections as evidence in business disputes that the United Order was not just an economic philosophy, but a legally recognizable business entity, with its members financially liable for each other's actions. It was not until 1981 that these code names were replaced with real names.[274] For example, in the original edition of the *D&C*, Joseph Smith's alias was "Baurak Ale," and "Baneemy," was used to represent "mine elders." [275]

Questions of Credibility: Hearsay and No Contemporaneous Record of Key Events

Smith's various versions of the first vision and his claim to several visitations from the Angel Moroni/Nephi are unsubstantiated hearsay. Hearsay is an out of court statement, offered to prove the truth of the matter asserted (and as such, is generally unreliable).[276] In most U.S. jurisdictions, hearsay is excluded from admission into the evidence taken by a jury under the rules, unless subject to some recognized exception. [277]

Smith's hearsay statements are subject to no exception. Had Smith recorded his vision or visitations immediately, in a diary or journal, or told another person right away what happened, these claimed experiences would be more credible. This is because they would be subject to the spontaneous exclamation/excited utterance exception to the hearsay rule. Such statements are deemed more trustworthy, despite their definition as hearsay because there is no time for the declarant to reflect on (and therefore to potentially revise) the content. [278]

The statement could be about any startling event. Either the declarant or a third party can testify regarding a spontaneous declaration. For example, consider the statement: "I saw him run away with a bloody knife and heard the man say, 'stop murderer!'" If this statement was given to the authorities immediately after the victim's death, it would be more credible than someone reporting having witnessed the same event weeks or months after the body had been found and the death had been reported in the newspaper.

A diary or journal entry made by Smith soon after his first vision, if authenticated, could also be admitted under the 'recollection recorded,' exception to the hearsay rule. [279] That is, if someone were to find a diary by Smith, dated near the date that the first vision is claimed to have occurred (1820) and describing it with that degree of specificity found in the *Pearl of Great Price* and if the handwriting was proven to be Smith's, then this record would be admissible as an exception to the hearsay rule, as a recorded recollection of the event.

However, no such proof in the form of a spontaneous declaration/excited utterance or a recollection recorded has ever been found. Specific details of Smith's life during the 1820s, the decade in which he claims to have experienced his first vision, had four visits from the Angel Moroni (three at his bedside and one more while Smith was returning from fieldwork), returned several times to the Hill Cumorah, retrieved the golden plates and effected their translation are conspicuously absent. Additionally, as of the claimed date of Angel Moroni's first visit, young Smith shared a bedroom if not a bed with his brothers, none of whom has ever corroborated any of the Angel's visitations.

Church website depiction of Angel Moroni's visit to the boy Joseph to tell him about the golden plates. Initially portraits depicting this scene showed Joseph alone in his bed. However, when it was pointed out that young Joseph shared a bedroom and most likely even a bed, with several of his siblings, the artwork was changed accordingly.

The LDS-owned restored Smith family home in Palmyra has two beds in the room where Joseph claims to have been visited on three different occasions by the Angel Moroni. Note in the Malm, 2004 portrait, found on the Church's website, Smith's brother is depicted apparently sleeping through the vision while the room is filled with light. [280]

"He called me by name," Michael T. Malm, 2004. www.josephsmith.net.[281]

Smith recorded in his journal in 1832, twelve years after the claimed date of the first vision:

...and the Lord heard my cry in the wilderness and while in (the) attitude of calling upon the Lord (in the 16th year of my age) a piller of ~~fire~~ light above the brightness of the sun at noon day come down from above and rested upon me and I was filled with the spirit of God and the (Lord) opened the heavens upon me and I saw the Lord and he spake unto me saying Joseph (my son) thy sins are forgiven thee...*[282]

Note that in this 1832 version there is no mention of two personages or of Smith being told that other religions were false. Smith's younger brother William wrote that the first vision occurred in 1823 and that it was just an angel (not the Father, or Father and Son) who appeared. According to this sibling, Joseph told his family the next day that:

[A] light appeared in the heavens, and descended until it rested upon the trees where he was. It appeared like fire. But to his great astonishment, did not burn the trees. An angel then appeared to him and conversed with him upon many things. He told him that none of the sects were right; but that if he was faithful in keeping the commandments he should receive, the true way should be made known to him; that his sins were forgiven, etc.*[283]

Thus, in connection with all of the above important and even defining events in the birth of Mormonism, there is a complete lack of evidence of any contemporary, let alone immediate, *accurate*, accounts by Smith or anyone else. Instead, true history reveals that the story of the first vision or visitation by *God the Father and His Son, Jesus Christ*, was created and/or revised over many years. This obvious absence of evidence is in itself good evidence that Smith's claims were an after-the-fact concoction and/or a collaborative effort to rewrite his history. [284]

Historical consensus is that Joseph Smith's first diary was not purchased until late November, 1832. The personal entries he made spanned just a few years (1832-35) and consisted of less than a dozen pages in his own handwriting, *in toto*. These journal entries involved mostly documenting money received, the recounting of Church discipline or excommunication of some of the brethren (most of whom had been stalwarts at some point) and Church re-organization. Just a few pages from 1832 are in Smith's hand. Thereafter, Sidney Rigdon, Oliver Cowdery and others kept the record as Smith's scribes.

There are specific and lengthy entries about lawsuits. For example, a several page entry records a bench trial for medical malpractice brought by the husband of a pregnant woman, where Nauvoo Mayor Smith appears to have acted as the judge and addressed issues raised as to the competency and standards of expert medical witnesses.[285] And yet, important events in Smith's life are notably absent in these journal records —no mention of the births of his children, or his sealing to other women in polygamous marriages, all of which are undisputed matters of historic record.[286]

Additionally, records of key events in Church history are noticeably absent or barely mentioned in the diary. For example, Smith's description of his receipt of the golden plates (as recorded by his scribe Frederick G. Williams approximately five years after the event in the latter half of 1832) is only [that] "On the 22nd day of Sept [ember] of this same year [the year he married Emma Hale] I obtained the plates." *[287]

An account by Josiah Stowell, believed to have been made circa 1835-47, describes Smith upon his return from retrieving the golden plates. Smith had borrowed Stowell's horse and early one morning went with Emma to the hill.

So that night we all went to Bed and in the morning I got up and my Horse and Carriage was gone But after a while he [Joseph Smith] Came home and he turned out the Horse [.] all Come into the house to Brackfi<rst> [breakfast] [.] But no thing said about where they had Bin [.] after Brackfirst Joseph Caled me into the other Room and he set his foot on the Bed and leaned his head on his hand and says well I am Dissop[o]inted. Well say I [,] I am sorry [.] Well says he [,] I am grately Dissop[o]inted, it is ten times Better then I expected. then he went on to tell the Length and width and thickness of the plates[,][p.2] and [,] said he[,] they appear to be Gold But he seamed to think more of the glasses or the urim and thummem then [than] he Did of the Plates for[,] says he[,] I can see any thing[.] they are Marvelus[.] Now they are written in Caracters and I want them translated [.] Now he was Commanded not to let no one see those things But a few for witness at a given time...*[288]

The historical record makes clear that the September 22, 1827 date for retrieval of the gold plates was not anticipated, at least by the Smith family; rather it was a somewhat spontaneous event. [289] The Sunday following the claimed retrieval of the gold plates, Lorenzo Saunders went to Mormon Hill to see where the plates had been dug out. He wrote to Thomas Gregg:

> I went on the next Sunday following with five or six other ones and we hunted the side hill by course and could not find no place where the ground had been broke. There was a large hole where the money diggers had dug a year or two before, but no fresh dirt.*
> [290]

And although there are numerous references to persons anointed in receipt of the Mormon Priesthood, there is no record of the event of the restoration of either the Aaronic (purportedly conferred on Smith and Oliver Cowdery by John the Baptist on May 15, 1829) or of the Melchizedek (purportedly restored by biblical apostles Peter, James and John) Priesthood in any of the Joseph Smith diaries.[291]

Professor Turner refers to this general time period as "Smith's four years vacation," and observes:

> The point to be noticed here is, that, from 1823 to 1827, the precise four years in which Smith and his friends, in all the Mormon journals, either by accident or design, omit all accounts of him, he is passing to and fro from his native place to Chenango county, N.Y., and then to Harmony, Penn., which is near by; he is seemingly out of employ, and resources, and friends; and, by his own confession, employed a part of his time in digging for a cave of silver, by Stowell. He was, therefore, in the society of men not only ready to believe, but on the look-out for wonders and sudden speculations.* [292]

The Competency of Founding Prophet Joseph Smith, Jr.
As a Witness

The competency of witnesses is a foundational rule of evidence. Very young children and those who are mentally incompetent or have a significant sensory impairment relevant to their proffered testimony cannot be sworn as witnesses in most courts of law.[293]

Some hypothesize that Smith suffered from temporal lobe epileptic seizures. Symptoms include hypo-sexuality, hyper-religiosity and altered states of vivid religious imagery. There is abundant evidence of Smith's multiple visionary experiences and his insistence that he alone had direct communion with God for the benefit of mankind. Others have gone so far as to hypothesize that Smith was an undiagnosed schizophrenic and a sociopath.

Former Mormon, psychiatrist Robert D. Anderson, concedes Smith's narcissism and speculates that his emotional age was stunted at the pre-Oedipal level.[294] Whatever the exact nature of the psychosis, the evidence seems clear that Smith engaged in automatic writing while in a self-induced trance to produce *the Book of Mormon*. One early twentieth century psychologist-biographer, I. Riley Woodbridge, stressed that Smith was most likely "ignorant of the subconscious force of unchecked reverie, he considered his every whimsy to be inspired." [295]

Woodbridge references Smith's "mental restlessness," and "muddled brain." He describes *the Book of Mormon* as a "monument of misplaced energy."[296] Indeed, the "four characteristics," he ascribes to the scripture: "redundant style, fragmentary information, a fanciful archaeology and an unsystematic theology," all support his theory that it was Smith's subconscious as the source of the scripture. [297] Whether Smith's claim to the divinity of that source was mere self-deception or rose to the level of conscious duplicity (or some combination of both over time), is a separate issue which may never be resolved.

Smith's grandiose pronouncements are the kind of statements made by someone with a personality disorder. There were at least two sides to the man. In authenticated portions of his diary he projects the image of the most devout, contemplative follower of his perceived God. However, much of his writing comes across as insincere, written with the reader in mind. The overall sum and substance of Joseph Smith's journal appears intended not to be a record of intimate experiences to be reviewed by the writer in old age, or by his progeny after his death as an accurate account of their father's life, but written to be read by others, perhaps those who Smith wanted to convince of his spirituality and prophetic singularity. Conversely, true history is full of Smith's deceptive, licentious and at times, even criminal conduct.

Book of Mormon **Witness Bias and the Lack of Foundation**

In a court of law, the fact that a relationship exists between a witness and a party to the legal action or the fact that the witness has an interest in the outcome of the case, can be used to impeach his or her credibility based upon bias. Another method of impeachment is to expose the foundation of a witness's testimony.[298]

Where were *the Book of Mormon* witnesses when they saw the plates? Did they handle them? Did they see them with the naked or spiritual eyes? What were these witnesses' general reputations for truthfulness? These are all legitimate ways to test the weight or validity to be given to the testimonies of the witnesses to *the Book of Mormon*.

In its preface (but originally placed at the end of the 1830 edition), *the Book of Mormon* has two, separate, combined statements of three, and then eight witnesses, who attest to the authenticity of the golden plates. Originally Smith prayed with Cowdery and Whitmer to have the plates revealed. Later Harris had a similar experience with the plates. When these two statements are scrutinized as they would be in a court of law, they are easily exposed as inherently untrustworthy. Both statements are undated. There is no evidence that either statement was made contemporaneously with the claimed witnessings. We cannot know because there are no dates alongside the names. Compare affidavits, commonly used in 1830 through today, which are required to be individually signed, notarized and dated in order to be accepted as evidence.

THE TESTIMONY OF THREE WITNESSES.

Be it known unto all nations, kindreds, tongues, and people, unto whom this work shall come, that we, through the grace of God the Father, and our Lord Jesus Christ, have seen the plates which contain this record, which is a record of the people of Nephi, and also of the Lamanites, his brethren, and also of the people of Jared, which came from the tower, of which hath been spoken; and we also know that they have been translated by the gift and power of God, for his voice hath declared it unto us; wherefore we know of a surety, that the work is true. And we also testify that we have seeen the engravings which are upon the plates; and they have been shewn unto us by the power of God, and not of man. And we declare with words of soberness, that an Angel of God came down from heaven, and he brought and laid before our eyes, that we beheld and saw the plates, and the engravings thereon; and we know that it is by the grace of God the Father, and our Lord Jesus Christ, that we beheld and bear record that these things are true; and it is marvellous in our eyes: Nevertheless, the voice of the Lord commanded us that we should bear record of it; wherefore, to be obedient unto the commandments of God, we bear testimony of these things.—And we know that if we are faithful in Christ, we shall rid our garments of the blood of all men, and be found spotless before the judgement seat of Christ, and shall dwell with him eternally in the heavens. And the honor be to the Father, and to the Son, and to the Holy Ghost, which is one God. Amen.

OLIVER COWDERY,
DAVID WHITMER,
MARTIN HARRIS.

The statement of the three witnesses contains no sensory description (weight, dimensions, texture, etc.) of the golden plates. The second, ostensibly later in time, statement of eight witnesses, obviously created in an attempt to remedy the foundational defects in the first statement, is not much better. Three of the eight are Joseph Smith's family members. With one exception, the others are related to the Prophet's friend, David Whitmer.

Instead of using the commonly accepted evidentiary format of affidavits, notarized with the signature authenticated, these statements both appear to have been drafted by Joseph Smith or someone besides the declarants, to bolster *the Book of Mormon's* credibility in the eyes of the public. Additionally, there are no generally known extant signatures of any of the eleven witnesses supporting these combined statements.

According to Dan Vogel's compilation of primary source Mormon documents, the written testimonies of the three and then the eight witnesses were made only after negotiations for the printing of *the Book of Mormon* were secured with the Grandin printing establishment. Thus, the agreement was entered into in the "forepart of June, 1829"; whereas the visions seen by the three and then the eight witnesses occurred "near the end of June 1829."[299] In this tight chronology of *Book of Mormon* publishing, it is evident that the witness statements were only an afterthought.

AND ALSO THE TESTIMONY OF EIGHT WITNESSES.

BE it known unto all nations, kindreds, tongues, and people, unto whom this work shall come, that Joseph Smith, Jr. the Author and Proprietor of this work, has shewn unto us the plates of which hath been spoken, which have the appearance of gold; and as many of the leaves as the said Smith has translated, we did handle with our hands; and we also saw the engravings thereon, all of which has the appearance of ancient work, and of curious workmanship. And this we bear record, with words of soberness, that the said Smith has shewn unto us, for we have seen and hefted, and know of a surety, that the said Smith has got the plates of which we have spoken. And we give our names unto the world, to witness unto the world that which we have seen : and we lie not, God bearing witness of it.

CHRISTIAN WHITMER,
JACOB WHITMER,
PETER WHITMER, JR.
JOHN WHITMER,
HIRAM PAGE,
JOSEPH SMITH, SEN.
HYRUM SMITH,
SAMUEL H. SMITH.

Chapter 9: Cross-examining Mormonism

Many of these *Book of Mormon* witnesses eventually left their association with the Salt Lake Mormon Church, though the Church claims they never revoked their statements. Yet, even Smith was not certain of some of his witnesses' characters. In 1838, at a time when many of the original members of the Church were questioning and leaving the Religion, while Smith was in the Missouri Liberty Jail for over four months on charges of treason, he characterized the three original witnesses: Cowdery, Harris and Whitmer, as being "too mean to mention; and we had liked to have forgotten them." *300

Joseph's older brother, Hyrum, one of the eight witnesses, accused two of the three original *Book of Mormon* witnesses, and another of the eight witnesses of crimes. A criminal inquiry was held in the Fifth Judicial Circuit Court for the State of Missouri, where both Smith brothers and numerous other LDS leaders were charged with: "the several crimes of high treason against the State, murder, burglary, arson, robbery, and larceny." According to a letter by Hyrum, which was entered into evidence at the inquiry before Judge Austin A. King on or about November 12, 1838, at least three of the eleven witnesses to *the Book of Mormon* were engaged in criminal mischief toward the Saints:

> ...After Oliver Cowdery had been taken by a state warrant for stealing...in which nefarious transaction John Whitmer had also participated. Oliver Cowdery stole the property, conveyed it to John Whitmer...Oliver Cowdery, David Whitmer, and Lyman E. Johnson [one of the twelve Apostles], united with a gang of counterfeiters, thieves, lairs, and blacklegs of deepest dye to deceive, cheat, and defraud the saints out of their property... During the full career of Oliver Cowdery and David Whitmer's bogus money business, it got abroad into the world they were engaged in it, and several gentlemen were preparing to commence a prosecution against Cowdery; he finding it out, took with him Lyman E. Johnson, and fled to Far West with their families; Cowdery stealing property... *301

With regard to any evidence of valid eyewitnesses to the very existence of the Mormon golden plates, it is more likely that each of the eleven witnesses followed the example of Joseph Smith as suggested by Dr. I. Riley Woodbridge, "...what he [Joseph] imagined, he saw, he got them to imagine they saw." [302]

Misrepresentations Regarding use of the Golden Plates as the Method of Translation

What is the true origin of *the Book of Mormon*? All those close to Joseph Smith during his time of translation, including Smith's third cousin, Oliver Cowdery, and Smith's first wife Emma, concede that Smith dictated *the Book of Mormon* while having his head in a hat which contained a seer stone, the same type stone he had used to look for buried treasure. Smith explained that the ancient language appeared to him and that he was able to translate merely by looking at the stone. Thus, incredibly, the golden plates weren't even used, or for that matter weren't even in the same room as Smith during his translation.[303] Additionally, during certain times of translation, Smith was in a different room than his scribe, and at other times a hanging blanket was used as a curtain dividing the two men. [304]

In 1993, an LDS *Ensign* magazine article quoted David Whitmer's explanation of Smith's method of placing a seer stone in his hat; however, the overall theme of the article is confusing because the author of the article, LDS Apostle Russell M. Nelson, initially references the Urim and Thummim as "two stones in silver bows—and these stones, fastened to a breastplate constituted what is called the Urim and Thummim." It could reasonably be inferred from Nelson's article that Smith's seer stone was part of the Urim and Thummim. Nelson also implies that the golden plates were in the room at the time of translation. Earl Jones' illustration was originally published with the talk, but even that artwork does not show a seer stone or a hat. Instead, it alludes to the plates by showing what appears to be a book or some plates on the table where Smith is resting his elbow and appearing to read or translate. [305]

Despite the fact that the seer stone manner of translation was verified in a local newspaper of the times, [306] this method of translation is absolutely contrary to the method of translation represented by the LDS Church during most of the twentieth century up until the present time. All paintings, photos and other representations depict Smith appearing to translate from the golden plates with no seer stone in sight. These paintings are located in almost all of LDS propaganda in Church visitor's centers, Church magazines and instructional materials sold by its bookstore and on the official Church website dedicated to their founding prophet, Joseph Smith, http://www.josephsmith.net

Joseph Smith

Translating

Harold Kilbourn, © 1970

"You have a gift to translate the plates"

(*D&C* 5:4)

Displayed on LDS'

Website:

www.josephsmith.net

  As of July 8, 2010, the date this LDS Church-sponsored website was accessed, there were a total of five portraits by four different artists showing the translation. All five depict Smith reading or translating from plates, *no seer stone in sight.* The first is entitled "Joseph Smith Translating the Golden Plates," by Harold T. Kilbourn, 1978; the second "Joseph Smith translating The Book of Mormon," by Del Parson, 1996; the third, "Joseph Smith translates the Golden Plates," by Robert Barrett, 1988; the fourth "By the Gift and Power," (Smith has his hands on the golden plates and appears to be reading them; a scribe can be seen to his left) by Simon Dewey, 2000; the fifth is the portrait shown above, another by artist Kilbourn, circa 1970. There were no portraits showing Smith peering into a hat or a using a stone in his translation. [307]

Additionally on their proselytizing website: http://www.mormon.org (last accessed March 7, 2011) under "Our Faith," and then under "Book of Mormon," is one of the five portraits showing Smith translating from golden plates, his scribe seated across from him. Again under "Our Faith," and then under "Joseph Smith," there is a video with the caption: "Watch how God restored the fulness [sic] of His gospel to the earth through Joseph Smith, the prophet (19.15)." This video is highly sentimental, showing a fourteen-year-old Joseph playing kindly with young children, interacting with animals and talking respectfully to his father. In this video the confabulated version of the First Vision is portrayed where *God the Father and His Son, Jesus Christ* appear and tell Smith that all religions are incorrect. The video also depicts Smith's retrieval of the plates and subsequent translation from the plates (his finger is on the plates) with his scribe by his side. There is no mention of the "reformed Egyptian," type language originally claimed to have been the type inscribed on the plates, only that the language on the plates was "ancient." There is absolutely nothing about a seer stone.

In a court of law, especially in jury trials, before a photograph, drawing or rendering of an accident scene depicting injuries to the plaintiff, property at issue, etc., is allowed into evidence, the offering attorney must lay a foundation for that photograph. One must offer evidence, usually through witness testimony, with facts that support what is depicted in the proffered pictorial evidence.

Consider this testimony: "I saw the police car just before the crash. It was a clear summer evening when I looked across to the northwest at southbound traffic and saw a new white City Police sedan coming at me." Unless there is another witness who can provide a much different description, in this scenario, a photograph of the collision scene which depicts a foggy evening and an old blue sheriff's van should not be admitted into evidence as proof of what the law enforcement vehicle involved in the collision looked like. Such a photograph lacks the foundational evidence necessary as a prerequisite to admitting the photograph into evidence.

In the case of Joseph Smith's translation, eyewitness accounts in all extant primary source records indicate that Smith used a seer stone in his hat and never translated directly from the plates, as is depicted in all five of the portraits on the Church's website. Likewise, there is no reliable evidence that Smith used two stones in silver bows, fastened to a breastplate to translate. Thus, the five portraits displayed on the Church website are patently misleading and the publication of such portraits is more prejudicial (in that they convey an entirely inaccurate representation of the method of translation used) than probative (proving the actual method Joseph Smith used). Clearly, the LDS Church should not be representing Joseph Smith as having translated *the Book of Mormon* from golden plates when there is no competent evidence that this was the actual method he used.[308]

Lack of Evidence: Hill Cumorah Location, Final *Book of Mormon* Battles and Weapons

The last sentence of the preface to each edition of *the Book of Mormon,* the story of Smith's series of annual trips to a hill "convenient to the village of Manchester, Ontario county in New York (which hill is commonly known as the Hill Cumorah)" reads, *"The ancient record, thus brought forth from the earth, as the voice of a people speaking from the dust, and translated into modern speech by the gift and power of God* as attested by Divine affirmation was first published to the world in the year 1830 as The Book of Mormon."[309]

The Hill Cumorah is only a short distance from Smith's home. Before the golden plates were extracted from the hill, Cumorah apparently held various treasures. Brigham Young claimed: "There were a great many treasures hid up by the Nephites. Porter [Rockwell] was with them one night where there were treasures, and they could find them easy enough, but they could not obtain them."*[310]

Consensus was that the Smiths were preoccupied with the neighborhood hill.

Fifty-one of Palmyra's leading citizens said the Smith family was "famous for visionary projects." One of these centered on a nearby glacial drumlin, later called Hill Cumorah. Orsamus Turner said there were "[l]egends of hidden treasure" associated with the hill and Martin Harris said that "money [was] supposed to have been hidden [there] by the ancients." ...Between 1820 and 1827, both father and son were digging at and having experiences with Cumorah's guardian spirit. Before, during, and after the golden plates saga, the Smiths were engaged in seeking its treasures. ... during this eight-year period, Joseph Smith and his father both claimed to have seen into the caves of the surrounding hills using second sight...Katherine, Joseph's sister, said that Joseph "went frequently to the hill and upon returning would tell us, 'I have seen the records.'"...Over time, Cumorah's cave became increasingly important to the [Smith] family. Joseph Jr. informed Orson Pratt: "[T]he grand repository of all the numerous records of the ancient nations of the western continent was located in the hill [Cumorah], and its contents under the charge of holy angels." According to the Smiths, Moroni was the hill's primary guardian.*[311]

Besides being the original depository of the golden plates by the Prophet (and later, Angel) Moroni,[312] the Hill is purportedly the place where ten thousand Nephites were slaughtered in an epic battle between *Book of Mormon* Nephite and Lamanites Tribes.[313]   Yet at the Hill Cumorah, near Palmyra, New York, there exists no archeological evidence of the remains of the fallen, neither remains of the warriors, nor of their weapons.

Some years ago there was an ongoing dispute within the Church regarding whether the Hill Cumorah located in Ontario County, New York, is that same Cumorah where the infamous *Book of Mormon* battles were fought or whether that Cumorah is located in modern Mesoamerica. Although claims that there are competing Hill Cumorahs, one described in *the Book of Mormon's* preface and another described by the Prophet Mormon, are nonsensical, and clearly a clumsy after-the-fact attempt at an explanation for the lack of evidence of the ancient battle(s), as of 1992: "With regard to the location of the Hill(s) Cumorah the Church has no official position."[314]

Today, however, the Church appears to be reverting to the original New York location. On a page accessed in 2010 from the official website http://www.LDS.org, LDS President, Thomas S. Monson, an apostle since 1963, continues to represent the literal, golden plate version of *Book of Mormon* origins:

What a privilege to be here at the Hill Cumorah [New York] and to reflect on the momentous events that unfolded on September 22, 1827, when a plowboy prophet took a horse and wagon and, in the dark of night, rode to this hill, where he received an ancient record from the angel Moroni. In a remarkably short time, this untutored young man translated a record detailing 1,000 years of history and then prepared the Book of Mormon for public distribution...[315]

Monson's statement is an unqualified representation by the LDS Church that the delivery of the golden plates was a literal event which occurred at a Hill Cumorah in upstate New York. The golden plates disappeared (Smith claimed they were returned at the command of the Angel Moroni) after the translation was complete. Thus, unlike the translation of the *Book of Abraham* from the Egyptian papyri, an independent comparison of Smith's translation of *the Book of Mormon* with the original gold plates is impossible.

Book of Mormon Archeological Support—a Desperate Search for Evidence

There exists no independent evidence that *the Book of Mormon* is a translated ancient record. However, some Mormons have claimed that it has been used as a guide by secular archeologists. Over the years, the Smithsonian Institute has received so many inquires about *the Book of Mormon's* alleged archaeological value, that years ago it issued a formal announcement explaining why it has never considered the Book to be archaeologically useful. The Smithsonian explained that none of *the Book of Mormon* claimed Hebraic origins, foodstuffs, animals, metallurgy and claimed Egyptian-type language are consistent with new world archeological findings. [316]

In the nineteen-fifties, attorney Thomas Stuart Ferguson, a staunch defender of the Church, spent much of his own money on an expedition to Mesoamerica, intent on finding archeological evidence of the animals and artifacts claimed to have existed during the times of the Nephites, Lamanites and Jaredites, the major tribes of *the Book of Mormon*. After years of searching, he reluctantly concluded that no such evidence exists. [317]

Despite millions of dollars spent to locate support for *Book of Mormon* civilizations, those in search of such evidence have been unsuccessful. Much archeological evidence supports the existence of ancient Biblical civilizations—consider the Dead Sea Scrolls. And, though there is abundant archeological evidence of indigenous American crops—for example, maize, lima beans, tomatoes, and squash, there has been no evidence found of barley, figs, grapes or wheat, all *Book of Mormon* foods, and no evidence of either the animals or the metallurgy referenced in the Book.[318]

Even at the outset of the project, it appears that Smith lacked confidence in the success of his creation. In 1829, prior to the publication of the first 5,000 copies, he received a revelation that several of the Brethren should go to Canada to sell *the Book of Mormon* copyright, proceeds to be used "...for the exclusive benefit of the Smith famaly...the necessary preporation was made in a Sly manor So as to keep martin Har[r]is from drawing a Share of the money,..."*[319] They went and were unsuccessful. Upon their return, according to eye witness David Whitmer, Smith placed his head in his hat which contained the seer stone and received another revelation, "Some revelations are of God: some revelations are of men: and some revelations are of the devil."*[320]

Admissions against Interest

An admission against interest is also an exception to the hearsay rule. [321] The rationale for allowing such a statement into evidence is that the declarant wouldn't have made it had it not been true, i.e., there is no incentive to invent and say something against one's own best interest. Many such admissions have been made by the Prophet, his family and colleagues, as attested to in sworn affidavits from Palmyra and Manchester, New York residents. Although these affidavits were collected by Philastus Hurlbut (who had been excommunicated from Mormonism) for the express purpose of impugning Joseph Smith's character, thereby proving Mormonism false, there is no compelling evidence that any of the individual testimony in these sworn affidavits should be considered false.

The affidavits and the combined statements of New York residents (below) were published in the 1834 book, *Mormonism Unvailed*, by Ohio newspaper editor Eber D. Howe. Witness accounts varied as to whether anyone had truly ever seen the golden plates.

When they found that the people of this vicinity would no longer put any faith in their schemes for digging money, they then pretended to find a gold bible, of which, they said, the book of Mormon was only an introduction. This latter book was at length fitted for the press. No means were taken by any individual to suppress its publication: No one apprehended any danger from a book, originating with individuals who had neither influence, honesty or honor. The two Josephs and Hiram, promised to show me the plates, after the book of Mormon was translated. But, afterwards, they pretended to have received an express commandment, forbidding them to show the plates. Respecting the manner of receiving and translating the book of Mormon, their statements were always discordant. The elder Joseph would say that he had seen the plates, and that he knew them to be gold; at other times he would say that they looked like gold; and other times he would say he had not seen the plates at all.*[322]

A sworn affidavit by Willard Chase, made in 1833, is set forth in full in *Mormonism Unvailed* and details the circumstances surrounding the discovery of the peep [seer] stone. According to Mr. Chase, the elder Smith, Joseph's father, tells of his son's retrieval of the golden plates which were guarded by a toad, being rebuked by the spirit and told to return a year later. When the Prophet returned, he found spectacles in the box which contained the plates. He asked Mr. Chase to build a chest for the plates. When Chase refused, Smith (who walked with a limp from a childhood leg trauma) told him of running two miles through the woods with the gold plates, which weighed forty to sixty pounds. After marrying Emma Hale, Joseph met Martin Harris who gave him fifty dollars to help him and his wife relocate. Harris told the affiant that soon all would see Smith walking the streets dressed in gold with a gold sword by his side.

When Emma was pregnant with their first child, Smith said it was his unborn child who would translate the golden bible at the age of two.[323] But as recorded in newspapers of the time, Ms. Sophia Lewis stated in 1834:

...that she "feard [sic] a conversation between Joseph Smith, Jr., and the Rev. James B. Roach, in which Smith called Mr. R. a d—d fool. Smith also said in the same conversation that he (Smith) was as good as Jesus Christ"... She states that she heard Smith say "the Book of Plates could not be opened under penalty of death by any other person but his (Smith's) first-born, which was to be a male." She says she "was present at the birth of this child, and that it was still-born and very much deformed."*[324]

Smith told Joshua McKune, a neighbor in 1834, that "his [Smith's] first born child was to translate the characters and hieroglyphics upon the plates, into our language, at the age of three years."*[325]

The following affidavit was executed in 1833:

I, Henry Harris, do state that I became acquainted with the family of Joseph Smith, Sen. about the year 1820, in the town of +Manchester, N[ew] York. They were a family that labored very little — the chief they did, was to dig for money. Joseph Smith, Jr. the pretended Prophet, used to pretend to tell fortunes; he had a stone which he used to put in his hat, by means of which he professed to tell people's fortunes. Joseph Smith, Jr. Martin Harris and others, used to meet together in private, a while before the gold plates were found, and were familiarly known by the name of the "Gold Bible Company." They were regarded by the community in which they lived, as a lying and indolent set of men and no confidence could be placed in them. The character of Joseph Smith, Jr. for truth and veracity was such, that I would not believe him under oath. I was once on a jury before a Justice's Court and the Jury could not, and did not, believe his testimony to be true. After he pretended to have found the gold plates, I had a conversation with him, and asked him where he found them and how he come to know where they were. He said he had a revelation from God that told him they were hid in a certain hill and he looked in his stone and saw them in the place of deposit; that an angel appeared, and told him he could not get the plates until he was married, and that when he saw the woman that was to be his wife, he should know her, and she would know him. He then went to Pennsylvania, got his wife, and they both went together and got the gold plates—he said it was revealed to him, that no one must see the plates but himself and wife... *[326]

An 1833 statement of Abigail Harris, describes the deception characteristic of the Smith family and of Martin Harris:

> In 1828...[Old Mrs. Smith] said that the plates he [Joseph Jr.] then had in possession were but an introduction to the Gold Bible — that all of them upon which the bible was written, were so heavy that it would take four stout men to load them into a cart — that Joseph had also discovered by looking through his stone, the vessel in which the gold was melted from which the plates were made, and also the machine with which they were rolled; he also discovered in the bottom of the vessel three balls of gold, each as large as his fist. The old lady said also, that after the book was translated, the plates were to be publicly exhibited — admittance 25 cents. She calculated it would bring in annually an enormous sum of money — that money would then be very plenty, and the book would also sell for a great price, as it was something entirely new — that they had been commanded to obtain all the money they could borrow for present necessity, and to repay with gold...
> Martin Harris and his wife were at my house. In conversation about Mormonites, she observed, that she wished her husband would quit them, as she believed it was all false and [a] delusion. To which I heard Mr. Harris reply: **"What if it is a lie; if you will let me alone I will make money out of it!"** I was both an eye and an ear witness of what has been stated above, which is now fresh in my memory, and I give it to the world for the good of mankind. I speak the truth and lie not, God bearing me witness.*[327]

Next, is a 1833 statement by Martin Harris' wife, Lucy:

> Being called upon to give a statement to the world of what I know respecting the Gold Bible speculation, and also of the conduct of Martin Harris, my husband, who is a leading character among the Mormons, I do it free from prejudice, realizing that I must give an account at the bar of God for what I say. Martin Harris was once industrious, attentive to his domestic concerns, and thought to be worth about ten thousand dollars. He is naturally quick in his temper and his mad-fits frequently abused all who may dare to oppose him in his wishes. However strange it may seem, I have been a great sufferer by his unreasonable conduct. At different times while I lived with him, he

has whipped, kicked, and turned me out of the house. About a year previous to the report being raised that Smith had found gold plates, he became very intimate with the Smith family, and said he believed Joseph could see in his stone any thing he wished. After this he apparently became very sanguine in his belief, and frequently said he would have no one in his house that did not believe in Mormonism; and because I would not give credit to the report he made about the gold plates, he became more austere towards me. In one of his fits of rage he struck me with the but end of a whip, which I think had been used for driving oxen, and was about the size of my thumb, and three or four feet long. He beat me on the head four or five times, and the next day turned me out of doors twice, and beat me in a shameful manner. — The next day I went to the town of Marion, and while there my flesh was black and blue in many places. His main complaint against me was that I was always trying to hinder his making money.

When he found out that I was going to Mr. Putnam's, in Marion, he said he was going too, but they had sent for him to pay them a visit. On arriving at Mr. Putnam's, I asked them if they had sent for Mr. Harris; they replied, they knew nothing about it; he, however, came in the evening. Mrs. Putnam told him never to strike or abuse me any more; he then denied ever striking me; she was however convinced that he lied, as the marks of his beating me were plain to be seen, and remained more than two weeks. Whether the Mormon religion be true or false, I leave the world to judge, for its effects upon Martin Harris have been to make him more cross, turbulent and abusive to me. His whole object was to make money by it. I will give one circumstance in proof of it. One day, while at Peter Harris' house, I told him he had better leave the company of the Smiths, as their religion was false; to which he replied, if you would let me alone, I could make money by it. It is in vain for the Mormons to deny these facts; for they are all well known to most of his former neighbors. The man has now become rather an object of pity; he has spent most of his property, and lost the confidence of his former friends. If he had labored as hard on his farm as he has to make Mormons, he might now be one of the wealthiest farmers in the country. He now spends his time in traveling through the country spreading the delusion of Mormonism, and has no regard whatever for his family...The above statement of facts, I affirm to be true.*[328]

Joseph Smith's parents, Joseph Sr. and Lucy, as well as Martin Harris, the financier for the project, have all made damaging admissions against the origins of *the Book of Mormon.* Furthermore, there is no legitimate dispute regarding scrying as an integral part of Joseph Smith's early life. BYU historian Marvin S. Hill, has admitted that, "Now, most historians, Mormon or not, who work with the [primary] sources, accept as fact Joseph Smith's career as village magician."*[329]

Of course there is no mention of Smith's early history of scrying or treasure-hunting whatsoever in either the 1996 *Our Heritage: a Brief History of the Church of Jesus Christ of Latter-day Saints*, or in the 596 page, 2007 Sunday school manual, *Teachings of Presidents of the Church: Joseph Smith.* (Both of these LDS Church-published instruction manuals are cited in this bibliography).

Admissions That *the Book of Mormon* Is a Farce

The very existence of Smith's golden plates is seriously suspect. One witness claims Smith deceived his family into thinking that his shirt, wrapped around several quarts of sand, covered a golden bible which God told him to conceal. He made a chest for the sand and continued with his deception. An 1833 affidavit by Peter Ingersoll contains this admission by Smith regarding the fictional gold plates:

...One day he came, and greeted me with a joyful countenance. Upon asking the cause of his unusual happiness, he replied in the following language: "As I was passing, yesterday, across the woods, after a heavy shower of rain, I found, in a hollow, some beautiful white sand, that had been washed up by the water. I took off my frock, and tied up several quarts of it, and then went home. On my entering the house, I found the family at the table eating dinner. They were all anxious to know the contents of my frock. At that moment, I happened to think of what I had heard about a history found in Canada, called the golden Bible; so I very gravely told them it was the golden Bible. To my surprise, they were credulous enough to believe what I said. Accordingly I told them that I had received a commandment to let no one see it, for, says I, no man can see it with the naked eye and live. However, I offered to take out the book and show it to them, but they refuse to see it, and left the room." Now, said Jo, *"I have got the* *damned fools fixed, and will carry out the fun."* Notwithstanding, he told me he had no such book, and believed there never was any such book...*[330]

During the time just before publication, Smith and those engaged in the work of translating and publishing the Book were known by those in the community as members of the Gold Bible Company. *The Book of Mormon* was called the Gold Bible or Book. Joseph's letter to Oliver Cowdery dated October 22, 1829, contains a rare and candid admission:

I arrived at home on Sun morn. the 4th [of October] after a prosperous Journey...people all friendly to [us] except a few who are in opposition to ev[e]ry thing unless it is the same thing that is exactly like themselves and two of our most formidable persecutors are now under censure and are cited to a tryal in the church for crimes which if true *are worse than all the Gold Book business*...*[331]

Another startling admission can be found in Smith's journals. Except for a few entries, Smith always used a scribe to record his dictation. One such loyal scribe was Willard Richards, who when admonished by the Prophet to include more comments on the weather and the background (the setting) began from that point onward to conscientiously record storms, rain, snow, etc., on the particular date of entry. Richards' and the other scribes' notes are generally accepted as substantively accurate by LDS scholars. Although, when it suits apologists, they will discount the notes as hearsay and unreliable since they are not from Smith's own hand (e.g. Kinderhook Plates limited translation admission, discussed in more detail later).

The following provides incredible insight into what Smith really thought of his followers. In Joseph Smith's journal, dated Sunday, June 30, 1843, p. 288, Willard Richards, Smith's scribe, notes: "[Esquire] Walker was introduced [to the congregation, which Joseph said,] as a body of people, [were] the greatest dupes that ever were or he is not as big a rouge [rogue] as he is supposed to be...1/4 to 7)."*[332]

Webster's 1828 dictionary, defines 'rogue,' as "a vagrant; a sturdy beggar; a vagabond...knave; a dishonest person...This word comprehends thieves and robbers, but is generally applied to such as cheat and defraud in mutual dealings, or to counterfeiters."

Smith requested John C. Bennett, who claimed he never believed in Mormonism, but infiltrated the Religion to expose it as a fraud, to travel to New York to have gold plates made for passing off as the ancient plates he claimed he had retrieved from Hill Cumorah in 1827.

> Shortly after I located in Nauvoo, Joe proposed to me to go to New York, and get some plates engraved, and bring them to him, so that he could exhibit them as the genuine plates of The Book of Mormon, which he pretended had been taken from him, and "hid up" by an angel, and which he would profess to have recovered. He calculated upon making considerable money by this trick, as there would of course be a great anxiety to see the plates, which he intended to exhibit at twenty-five cents a sight. I mentioned this proposition to Mrs. Sarah M. Pratt, on the day the Prophet made it, and requested her to keep it in memory, as it might be of much importance. *[333]

Though Bennett was accused of various crimes while among the Saints, including homosexuality and performing abortions, dozens of affidavits attesting to his character are in the prefatory material to his *History of the Saints* (cited in this Bibliography). Dr. Bennett was well known for other contributions during his lifetime such as commanding a company for the Union in the Civil War. His professional contributions included a pioneering use of chloroform as anesthetic, and the establishment of several medical colleges.

This engraving of John C. Bennett, hand in coat, seems to confirm his claim that he infiltrated Mormonism for the purpose of exposing it (as Napoleon Bonaparte had done).

Over the next few years the ethereal plates were to have been kept in a strong chest with lock and key made by Willard Chase (he refused). Immediately after retrieval, the plates were hidden in a hollow log near the hill. When finally enroute home, Smith wrapped them in a linen frock, but was accosted by three different men, all trying to take the plates from him.

Once home, they were eventually placed in a box. When felt to be under imminent peril of discovery, they were variously placed under a heavy hearthstone in the house, in a dark garret in his father's house, under the floor boards of his parents' old log home nearby, hidden in a barrel of flax and/or carried surreptitiously in a barrel one-third full of beans.

When the ostensible robbers were not a threat, others were allowed to feel them through a cloth. At times Emma recalls them wrapped in a linen tablecloth, in the kitchen; she moved them when she cleaned. According to Joseph's mother, Lucy Mack Smith, they were stored on a trunk on Emma's bureau.

They have been hidden in the woods during translation and sometimes they lay on a table, covered, in the room where Smith was translating with his head in the hat looking at the stone. After translation, they were returned and laid on a table, surrounded by other ancient plates and treasures in a cave in the Hill Cumorah.

In short, the golden plates have been everywhere and nowhere. Mormonism started as a small lie, in jest, which took hold. And the liar, seizing his opportunity, built upon the little lie, lie upon lie. At times, Smith was amazed at the credulity of his followers. At other times he seems to have been racked with guilt over his protracted devious scheme.

I have known at least one pathological liar in my life and have cross-examined a few. Joseph Smith's representations concerning the whereabouts and even the existence of the gold plates, having been everywhere, but nowhere, are indicative of a story told by a pathological liar. He jested about a gold bible and then when he saw that his family believed him, he made it appear as though he had found one.

There are no plates, there never were any plates. The only way there will ever be *Book of Mormon* golden plates is if the Brethren have negotiated yet another deal with Mark Hoffman, and he is spending his life sentence forging them in the Utah State Penitentiary. Perhaps one day the *Deseret News* will announce the discovery of Smith's gold plates, returned to the Brethren from the Angel Moroni, in a special temple session. Then Mormonism will have found its true origins.

***

An official website dedicated to Joseph Smith, posts facsimiles of some of his journal entries. However, the only entries posted which were dictated or written by him are faith-enhancing pages from his journals of 1832 and 1835-36, where he describes the first vision and claimed sighting of Christ in the Kirtland Temple. There is nothing from 1840-44 when Smith's ego explodes and he marries dozens of women.

Indeed, on its official Joseph Smith website, the LDS Church concludes in capital letters "JOSEPH SMITH REMAINED HUMBLE."* [334] This, despite words from the Prophet's mouth in which he denigrates all who deign to cross him and shouts to all within earshot: "I am a lawyer; I am a big lawyer and comprehend heaven, earth and hell, to bring forth knowledge that shall cover up all lawyers, doctors and other big bodies."* [335] And finally, Smith's ultimate claim of wisdom and intelligence: "No man can learn you more than what I have told you.*[336]

These declarations by the Prophet are some of the best evidence of his psychopathic or meglomanic delusions of grandeur. When accurate history is consulted, even when that history is limited to what is contained within the Church's own documents and written by the Church's founding leaders, it is abundantly clear that Joseph Smith was not the humble farm boy depicted over the decades by the Church.

> I have more to boast of than any man…I am the only man that has ever been able to keep a whole church together since the days of Adam. A large majority of the whole have stood by me. Neither Paul, John, Peter, nor Jesus ever did it. I boast that no man ever did such a work as I. The followers of Jesus ran away from Him; but the Latter-day Saints never ran away from me yet…When they can get rid of me, the devil will also go. *[337]

Was this last sentence a Freudian slip—an inadvertent admission that Smith, contrary to modern LDS characterizations of the Prophet, knew in his heart that he was indeed perpetuating the devil's work?

Abundant Evidence of Joseph Smith's Questionable Character

The rules of evidence generally exclude specific bad acts as proof that a person will behave similarly on a particular occasion. [338] However, evidence of a witness's reputation for honesty (or the opposite) is admissible through the testimony of those persons familiar with that reputation.[339]   An examination of Smith's reputation undermines his credibility as a witness to all that he claimed; he was widely known as a charlatan.

Two statements were collected by Philastus Hurlbut, signed by dozens of residents of both Manchester and Palmyra, towns where the Smith family had resided during the relevant period of events.

> We, the undersigned, being personally acquainted with the family of Joseph Smith Sen., with whom the celebrated Gold Bible, so called, originated, state: that they were not only a lazy, indolent set of men, but also intemperate; and their word was not to be depended upon; and that we are truly glad to dispense with their society. [340]
>
> We, the undersigned, have been acquainted with the Smith family, for a number of years, while they resided near this place, and we have no hesitation in saying, that we consider them destitute of that moral character which ought to entitle them to the confidence of any community. They were particularly famous for visionary projects, spent much of their time in digging for money which they pretended was hid in the earth; and to this day, large excavations may be seen in the earth, not far from their residence, where they used to spend their time in digging for hidden treasures, Joseph Smith Senior, and his son Joseph, were in particular, considered entirely destitute of moral character, and addicted to visionary habits...It was not supposed that any of them were possessed of sufficient character or influence to make anyone believe their book or their sentiments, and we know not of a single individual in this vicinity that puts the least confidence in their pretended revelations. *[341]

By the time the Mormon Book was first published, Smith had already confessed in a court of law to working for years as a money digger. It was during this same time period (1823-26) that he claimed to have been visited by the angel who told him of the golden plates.

Another example of Smith's tendency for deception is in the timing of the polygamy revelation. As admitted by the Church, Smith received the revelation over a decade prior to sharing the new commandment.

Revelation given through Joseph Smith the Prophet, at Nauvoo, Illinois, recorded July 12, 1843, relating to the new and everlasting covenant, including the eternity of the marriage covenant, as also plurality of wives. HC 5: 501–507. Although the revelation was recorded in 1843, it is evident from the historical records that the doctrines and principles involved in this revelation had been known by the Prophet since 1831. [342]

There is abundant and well-documented proof of Smith's pretending to have a gift for finding money hidden in the earth, seducing underage women and sometimes other men's wives, lying and covering his lies with after-the-fact revelations, destruction of private property (*Nauvoo Expositor* printing press) and corrupt business practices leading to various encounters with the legal system. Under modern rules of evidence, if one has been convicted of a felony, evidence of that conviction may be used to impeach that witness's testimony. [343] Although Smiths' legal record may stop short of felony convictions, it is only because he evaded the law through cunning, fleeing the jurisdiction, or in the case of *Expositor* charges, death at Carthage.

Smith's predilection for scamming is not only evidence of his questionable character, but almost rises to the level of habit. There is such abundant documentation of his deception through scrying, braggadocio, swindling and licentiousness that one could argue he routinely lied and deceived others for personal gain. "Evidence of habit…is relevant to prove that the conduct of the person or organization on a particular occasion was in conformity with the habit or routine practice."[344] Arguably, the years Smith spent as one who claimed to find buried treasure but never did, establish his habit of making a living through deceptive means. Thus, this practice is proof that his story of finding and then translating ancient golden plates was also a scam.

The Kinderhook Plates

It seems Smith didn't know when to stop. He had claimed translation of *the Book of Mormon* from golden plates that were never really seen. In 1835 he had fraudulently [mis]translated Egyptian papyri. Years later he claimed he could translate from the Kinderhook Plates, brass plates fabricated for the express purpose of setting up the Prophet as a liar. In May, 1843, in Kinderhook, Illinois, a group of men, including at least one Mormon, dug up a set of bell-shaped brass plates with ancient-appearing writing on them. They were shown to Smith, who noted in his diary:

372   HISTORY OF THE CHURCH.   [May 1843

Witnesses for defense—Two affidavits of George Reads, Mrs. Matthews, Brother Browett, Samuel Thompson, Richard Slater. Decision of the Council is that the charges are not sustained."

Monday, May, 1.—I rode out with Lucien Woodworth, and paid him £20 for the Nauvoo House, which I borrowed of William Allen.

I insert fac-similes of the six brass plates found near Kinderhook, in Pike county, Illinois, on April 23, by Mr. Robert Wiley and others, while excavating a large mound. They found a skeleton about six feet from the surface of the earth, which must have stood nine feet high. The plates were found on the breast of the skeleton and were covered on both sides with ancient characters.

Comment of the Prophet on the Kinderhook Plates.

I have translated a portion of them, and find they contain the history of the person with whom they were found. He was a descendant of Ham, through the loins of Pharaoh, king of Egypt, and that he received his kingdom from the Ruler of heaven and earth.

Joseph Smith, *History of the Church*, facsimile 5:372.[345]

This statement attributed to Smith remained in the official LDS Church History for decades until the plates were suspected as a hoax and only then was it removed. The official explanation as set forth in a 1981 LDS *Ensign* Magazine article, is that the statement was not actually made by Smith, but by his scribe and that its printing in the Church History for so many decades was an unfortunate 'mistake.'[346] However, in a court of law it could be successfully argued that the republication in a Church-approved history for a period of almost a century is a clear ratification of the contents of Smith's statement, proving that he in fact said the words attributed to him.

There is also evidence that Smith was in the process of translating the phony plates a month prior to his assassination. It was reported in the Illinois newspaper, the *Warsaw Signal,* that "... [he was] busy in translating them. The new work which Jo, is about to issue as a translation of these plates will be nothing more nor less than a sequel to the Book of Mormon;..."[*347]

As late as 1962, the President of the BYU Archeological Society proclaimed the authenticity of the Kinderhook Plates:

A recent rediscovery of one of the Kinderhook plates which was examined by Joseph Smith, Jun., reaffirms his prophetic calling and reveals the false statements made by one of the finders...The plates are now back in their original category of genuine.

What scholars may learn from this ancient record in future years or what may be translated by divine power is an exciting thought to contemplate....This much remains. Joseph Smith, Jun., stands as a true prophet and translator of ancient records by divine means and all the world is invited to investigate the truth which has sprung out of the earth not only of the Kinderhook plates, but of the Book of Mormon as well. [*348]

Just three years later, in 1965, the Kinderhook Plates were tested by Mormon physicist George M. Lawrence who concluded that "...the dimensions, tolerances, composition and workmanship are consistent with the facilities of an 1843 blacksmith shop and the fraud stories of the original participants."[349] The characters on the Kinderhook Plates (a Chinese linguist found them to be similar to the written language of the Yunnan province of China) were etched in acid and not engraved. [350] According to historians Sandra and Jerald Tanner, physicist Lawrence's findings were provided to the BYU Archeological Society, but were never published by BYU. [351]

The Many Faces of Joseph Smith: Evidence
Without Foundation

One of the best ways to decide whether a witness is telling the truth is to analyze his or her demeanor. A witness often inadvertently reveals his veracity in his manner of speaking, body language and eye contact, or the lack of it. Some people breathe heavily into the microphone when under stress or cross-examination; some will fidget or let their attention wander, and others keep a stiff, almost rehearsed way of talking to ensure that no inconsistencies are unintentionally spoken.

We know of Smith's reported charisma and propensity for grandiosity. But one eye witness to Smith's demeanor characterized him in ways never disclosed to born-in-the-Church Mormons. Consider the December, 1842, statement of Ms. Charlotte Haven:

> Joseph Smith is a large, stout man, youthful in his appearance, with light complexion and hair, and blue eyes set far back in the head, and expressing great shrewdness, or I should say, cunning...He is also very round[,] shouldered.... I, who had expected to be overwhelmed by his eloquence, was never more disappointed than when he commenced his discourse by relating all the incidents of his journey. This he did in a loud voice, and his language and manner were the coarsest possible. His object seemed to be to amuse and excite laughter in his audience. He is evidently a great egoist and boaster, for he frequently remarked that at every place he stopped going to and from Springfield people crowded around him, and expressed surprise that he was so "handsome and good looking." He also exclaimed at the close of almost every sentence, "that's the idea!"... [N]ot one sentence did that man utter calculated to create devotional feelings, to impress upon his people the great object of life.*[352]

Benjamin Winchester, a devout Mormon who was serving as an LDS stake president in the Eastern United States at the time, describes an intimate account with the Prophet as follows:

In the winter of 1839 and 1840 Smith, in company with Rigdon and with Porter Rockwell, acting as a sort of body guard, fled from the officials that were after them, acting for the State of Ohio, on the charge of criminal practice at Kirtland, and they came to Philadelphia where I was stationed and where I was stake president. There they remained with me in the best degree of secrecy that could be maintained. Smith and I slept in the same bed and Porter Rockwell occupied a bed near the foot of our couch in the capacity of a body guard for the "prophet." It was there and at that time that I had a good opportunity to study the character of the "prophet." It then began to be apparent to me that he was tyrannical by nature, a libertine, in short a gross, sensual, corrupt man, but I was then still young and hopeful and it remained for events in a few brief years thereafter to fully open my eyes to the gigantic delusion I had been drawn into.*[353]

Federal Rule of Evidence 403 gives a trial court the discretion to exclude evidence if its potential for prejudice outweighs its probative value. Lack of foundation is also a common objection to any evidence offered where there is no preliminary evidence established as a basis for receipt of documentary evidence. These evidentiary rules can be applied to the morphology of the photographic or pictorial likenesses of Joseph Smith over the history of the LDS Church.

There exist only a few accepted, accurate depictions of Joseph Smith. The best is his three-dimensional death mask. Drawings by Sutcliffe Maudsley, a contemporary of the Prophet, are also considered accurate. Some have argued that Maudsley's drawings are caricatures, but they depict one whose appearance is consistent with the accounts given by those individuals just quoted. Soon after Smith's death was reported, a New York newspaper ran the story with a sketch of Joseph Smith on the front page.

THE WEEKLY HERALD.

N. Y. C., Saturday, July 13, 1844

JOE SMITH, THE MORMON PROPHET

Sutcliffe Maudsley (1809-1881) portraits of Joseph Smith, circa. 1844

On June 28, 1844, Joseph and Hyrum Smiths' bodies, accompanied by Church leaders and several guards, were taken to the Nauvoo Mansion, where Mormons were allowed to view the bodies. Thereafter, as was the practice at the time, a plaster model or cast was made of both the dead men's faces. (Note: Some claim that Joseph Smith's face was fractured—that he was punched in the face after he fell/jumped from the Carthage window, distorting his jaw line and nose so that the death mask, especially when viewed in profile, is not an accurate representation of the man.) However, the profile death mask compares favorably to the Maudsley profiles and according to Smith's faithful scribe William Clayton, when viewed in his casket, "Joseph look [ed] very natural." (Bushman, *Rough Stone Rolling*, 553).

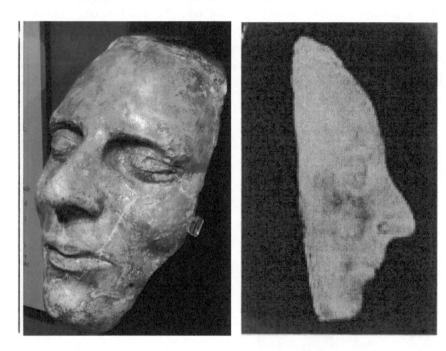

Joseph Smith's death mask, three-quarters and profile views

LDS author Ephraim Hatch devalues the significance of this portrait, now known as the Carson Daguerreotype (circa. 1840s and possessed by the RLDS Church *aka* the Joseph Smith III photo) because the measurements and proportions of the facial features, singularly and in relation to one another, do not comport with the death mask. Ephraim Hatch, *Joseph Smith Portraits: a Search for the Prophet's Likeness* (Provo: Utah, Religious Studies Center, Brigham Young University, 1998). "The [death] mask, along with Maudsley's profiles, Smith family traits and written description provide the most reliable information about [Smith's] physical appearance." (Hatch, Ibid. 107).

Over time, Joseph Smith's likeness as printed and promoted in Church publications became increasingly, classically handsome:

Joseph Smith, by Alvin Gittens, 1959   *Joseph Smith,* by Theodore Gorka, 1982. Original at LDS Museum of History & Art.

Joseph Smith,
by Del Parson, 1999

Del Parson's (whose portrait of a classically handsome Jesus Christ is the most popular depiction of Christ purchased by LDS Church members) portrait of Smith circa. 1999, is the most flattering. Note that this view does not have the sloping forehead or receding chin as shown by the death mask. "His pictures flatter him very much. The photographs do not show the peculiar shape of his head, especially the retreating forehead which any observer of the man in life could not fail to notice. He was possessed with an inordinate degree of vanity and was quite susceptible to flattery. He was a perfect adept in the use of abusive and obscene language."* (Benjamin Winchester, *Salt Lake Tribune,* Sept. 29, 1889). Additionally, Smith's hairline here is uncharacteristic compared to the hairline in the portraits by Smith's neighbor, artist Sutcliffe Maudsley.

Next, is the image used by the LDS Church on the cover of the student Sunday School Manual for 2007.[354] Notice the change in Smith's face shape and bone structure. The face is squarer, broader; Smith's nose is wider and shorter than it had ever been depicted previously. This portrait is almost unrecognizable when compared with the death mask and the original Sutcliffe Maudsley drawings.

TEACHINGS OF PRESIDENTS
OF THE CHURCH
JOSEPH SMITH

Smith was described as round-shouldered by those who saw him and the same type build is evident in the Maudsley portraits. However, perhaps in an effort to contradict these observations, many modern depictions of the founding prophet show a very broad-shouldered man. For example, note the statute of Smith receiving the Aaronic Priesthood in Chapter Eleven of this book, page 331.

Perhaps the reason the LDS Church publishes such different renderings of the founding prophet is because LDS Church membership is now worldwide. Different portraits are available, compatible with almost any genetic type, in order to appeal to the most diverse population possible.

Most recently, again perhaps in an attempt to admit a more accurate history of the Church, including the Prophet's true likeness, some Church publications have reverted to the more traditional portraits of Smith.

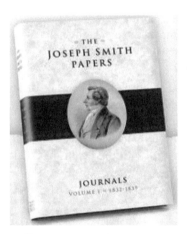

The photo used on the cover of the multi-volume *Joseph Smith Papers,* (2008, *Journals*) appears to be a flipped version of the original.

Profile Bust of Hyrum Smith & Joseph Smith by Sutcliffe Maudsley. Photographs of original lithographs.

Though it is true to some extent that 'beauty is in the eye of the beholder,' studies have shown that an objectively, classically handsome man (or a beautiful woman) is in general, favored and thought to be kinder, more intelligent and more honest.[355] "In Society, attractive people tend to be more intelligent, better adjusted, and more popular. This is described as the halo effect—due to the perfection associated with angels." [356] Thus, portraits of a handsome Joseph Smith which are shown to little children while their primary or Sunday school teachers extol his ostensible virtues, never once hinting at his vices, are certain to prejudice a young child. Since there is no basis in fact upon which to base the later, more classically handsome portraits, arguably, these fantasy likenesses should not be offered to Mormons, especially young children, as fair representations of the appearance of Mormonism's founding prophet. They can be extremely prejudicial.

Book of Mormon Authorship—Computer Syntax Analyses

Computer-generated analyses have been conducted on the syntax of the writing style(s) in *the Book of Mormon* and other Mormon scriptures. Mormon apologists claim that such an analysis shows that several different prophets have authored the various books within *The Book of Mormon*. British statistician David I. Holmes, points out that the articles written by LDS apologists are not peer-reviewed. [357] Holmes' multivariate analysis supports a contrary conclusion, that the author of the *Doctrine & Covenants* and of *the Book of Mormon* is the same person, Joseph Smith.[358]

Most recently, three Stanford-affiliated scholars from the departments of English, statistics and engineering, applied a sophisticated statistical analysis by using delta and nearest shrunken centroid (algorithmic classifiers) to determine *Book of Mormon* authorship.

Our results indicate that likely nineteenth century contributors [to the Book of Mormon] were Solomon Spalding, a writer of historical fantasies; Sidney Rigdon, an eloquent but perhaps unstable preacher, and Oliver Cowdery, a schoolteacher with editing experience. Our findings support the hypothesis that Rigdon was the main architect of the Book of Mormon and are consistent with historical evidence suggesting that he fabricated the book by adding theology to the unpublished writings of Spalding (then deceased).[359]

The Stanford authors conclude that Sidney Rigdon, the authors of the biblical books Isaiah-Malachi, and Mormon Oliver Cowdery account for anywhere from 85-93% of *the Book of Mormon* text.[360]

Smith also began the translation of an inspired version of the Bible: "…at the command of the Lord and while acting under the spirit of revelation, the Prophet corrected, revised, altered, added to, and deleted from the King James Version of the Bible to what is now commonly referred to as the inspired version…"*[361] The LDS Church has never published this inspired version of the bible, despite the fact that the *D&C* instructs Smith to finish and publish the work and that it was admittedly completed.[362]

The following is just one example of a self-serving prediction from Smith's inspired translation of the Bible, that is Smith writing scripture predicting himself as seer: "Jesus Christ showed Joseph in Egypt in vision, Joseph Smith saying: '[And] [t]hat seer will I bless, and they that seek to destroy him shall be confounded[.]'"[363]

Joseph Smith's Ignoble End

In the final years before his death, Smith went on a spree—a law breaking, pompous, narcissistic parading about Nauvoo in military dress display of ego. In 1842, two years before he died, he filed a petition for bankruptcy, listing his debts at $73,066.38. This debt remained unpaid at the time of his death. Smith's petition was denied because, as verified by U.S. Attorney Justin Butterfield, he had fraudulently conveyed (in contemplation of bankruptcy) several parcels of real estate to friends, family and colleagues.[364] Smith also omitted assets from the list of inventory that each applicant must complete to be reviewed by the trustee in bankruptcy upon consideration of discharge. [365]

Smith wrote all five presidential nominees asking for help for the indignities that he claimed the Mormons had suffered. Responses were either non-supportive or none. Ostensibly, in order to obtain redress for the Saints, on January 29, 1844, less than six months before his death, he declared himself a candidate for U.S. President. He circulated a pamphlet called *General Smith's Views*, and LDS missionaries were sent out to 'electioneer.'

The final blow to the Prophet came before he could be elected. The igniting incident for the actions Smith took which precipitated his death by a mob came when William Law, who had been a member of the Church's first presidency, claimed Smith had attempted to seduce his wife, Jane. Law published this accusation and other indictments in the one and only edition of the *Nauvoo Expositor* on June 7, 1844.[366] The infamous article reads in pertinent part:

It is a notorious fact, that many females in foreign climes, and in countries to us unknown, even in the most distant regions of the Eastern hemisphere, have been induced, by the sound of the gospel, to forsake friends, and embark upon a voyage across waters that lie stretched over the greater portion of the globe, as they supposed, to glorify God, that they might thereby stand acquitted in the great day of God Almighty. But what is taught them on their arrival at this place? - They are visited by some of the Strikers, for we know not what else to call them, and are requested to hold on and be faithful, for there are great blessings awaiting the righteous; and that God has great mysteries in store for those who love the Lord, and cling to brother Joseph. They are also notified that Brother Joseph will see them soon, and reveal the mysteries of Heaven to their full understanding, which seldom fails to inspire them with new confidence in the Prophet, as well as a great anxiety to know what God has laid up in store for them, in return for the great sacrifice of father of mother, of gold and silver, which they gladly left far behind, that they might be gathered into the fold, and numbered among the chosen of God. —They are visited again, and what is the result? They are requested to meet brother Joseph, or some of the Twelve, at some insulated point, or at some particularly described place on the bank of the Mississippi, or at some room, which wears upon its front—Positively NO Admittance. The harmless, inoffensive, and unsuspecting creatures, are so devoted to the Prophet, and the cause of Jesus Christ, that they do not dream of the deep laid and fatal scheme which prostrates happiness, and renders death itself desirable; but they meet him, expecting to receive through him a blessing, and learn the will of the Lord concerning them, and what awaits the faithful follower of Joseph, the Apostle and Prophet of

God. When in the stead thereof, they are told, after having been sworn in one of the most solemn manners, to never divulge what is revealed to them, with a penalty of death attached that God Almighty has revealed it to him, that she should be his (Joseph's) Spiritual wife; for it was right anciently, and God will tolerate it again: but we must keep those pleasures and blessings from the world, for until there is a change in the government, we will endanger ourselves by practicing it- but we can enjoy the blessings of Jacob, David, and others, as well as to be deprived of them, if we do not expose ourselves to the law of the land. She is thunder-struck, faints recovers, and refuses. The Prophet damns her if she rejects. She thinks of the great sacrifice and of the many thousand miles she has traveled over sea and land, that she might save her soul from pending ruin, and replies, God's will be done and not mine. The Prophet and his devotees in this way are gratified. The next step to avoid public exposition from the common course of things, they are sent away for a time, until all is well; after which they return, as from a long visit.*[367]

As mayor of Nauvoo, Illinois, Smith censored all those who would speak against his church. After publication of the *Expositor's* single edition, Smith called his Nauvoo Militia and declared martial law in the City. Smith and his Nauvoo City Council declared the publication a public nuisance and once it was so labeled, proceeded to throw the press and type into the street where it was destroyed with a sledge hammer. Then they burned undistributed copies of the issue.[368]

The publishers of the *Expositor* obtained a warrant for Smith's arrest. Besides arson and property destruction, Smith was charged with treason.

Grass roots demonstrations arose against the Religion. Governor Boggs had previously ordered the Mormons exterminated, proclaiming they had brought their problems upon themselves. "The Mormons must be treated as enemies, and must be exterminated or driven from the state if necessary for the public peace–their outrages are beyond all description," (MO executive order #44, October 27, 1838).

At about this time, a Grand Jury in Daviess County was also investigating charges to support an indictment against some Mormons on murder, treason, burglary, arson, larceny, theft and stealing.

In a supreme act of cowardice, Smith fled the jurisdiction, and was attempting to cross the Mississippi, when a letter arrived from Emma begging his return. Upon his return to Illinois, the anti-Mormon sentiment was so pervasive that Missouri Governor Lilburn Boggs convinced Smith and his brother Hyrum to stay in the Carthage jail (about 20 miles from Nauvoo) for their safety. Nevertheless, an angry mob of about 200 men, including Masons, killed both Joseph and Hyrum Smith while they were incarcerated.

Laundered LDS history, in its hail-to-the-martyr myopia, ignores the fact that Smith committed what would have most likely been proven as felony arson, if not treason, in any U.S. jurisdiction.

> In June Joseph Smith gave himself up to be imprisoned and on June 27, 1844, a mob stormed the little Carthage jail. Hyrum was killed instantly and John Taylor seriously wounded. Joseph Smith, Master Mason and widow's son, went to the window and with upraised hands, commenced giving the Masonic distress call to fraternal Masons who were present in the mob: "Oh, Lord, My God." He was unable to complete his plea and fell out of the window to his death. *[369]

Upon learning of Joseph Smith's assassination, Thomas B. Ford, Governor of Illinois, pronounced: "Thus fell Joe Smith, the most successful impostor in modern times."*[370]

Several men were charged with the Smith Brothers' killings. One escaped due to lack of interstate extradition laws. (Joseph Smith availed himself of this procedural technicality to escape charges for alleged complicity in the attempted assassination of Governor Boggs. As a resident of Illinois, Smith was beyond the jurisdiction of the place of the attempt, Missouri, and therefore absent extradition laws, he could not be forcibly returned to Missouri to be tried.) However, at least two other men charged were tried. The jury was not Mormon because any members of the faith would necessarily have been excused for cause, due to innate bias.

The credibility of the star witness for the prosecution was destroyed when he authenticated a pamphlet he had published glorifying the Prophet's death. The witness had written that he had seen a "…bright shining light descend upon the head of Joe Smith, to strike some of the conspirators with blindness," and he had heard supernatural voices in the air confirming the Prophet's mission. Ultimately, the jury acquitted all the accused.*[371]

Though Mormon folklore is rife with tales of gruesome deaths and grisly accidents claiming the lives of those who had murdered their founding prophet and patriarch, history does not substantiate these claims Instead, the main defendant, Thomas C. Sharp, continued to live in Illinois until his death in 1894 and had a "...successful career as mayor, judge, school principal and newspaper editor." Even Church leaders have admitted that "...the five defendants who went to trial, including men who had been shown to be leaders in the murder plot and others associated with them, enjoyed notably successful careers." [372]

Joseph Smith was a braggart, liar and habitual law-breaker. Joseph Smith Jr.—revered by generations of my ancestors, my immediate family and many dear friends—how perversely distorted his legacy has been!

CHAPTER TEN: Women without Voices

"It is impossible on our wretched globe for men living in society not to be divided into two classes, one of oppressors, the other of the oppressed."—Voltaire, circa. 1764

According to Professor Merlin Stone, author of *When God was a Woman,* before the indispensable role of male sperm in creating life was realized, women were worshiped for their ability to produce children. For millennia, during the Upper Paleolithic to the Neolithic Period, there existed a religion of goddess worship. Archeological evidence abounds with statues of female fertility goddesses. In Egyptian culture, Isis was the greater goddess, Osiris, her lesser, son/brother and lover—she was clearly the prominent deity. The ancient Greek Goddess Gaia was the mother goddess, the spirit of the Earth.

It took millennia for early man to connect the sex act with procreation. Egyptian women were revered, respected and seemed to have been approximate equals. Certainly the significance of sexual intercourse was recognized by the time of the Ancient Greeks. By 450 B.C., the Greek Philosopher Plato proposed that in an idyllic society, his *Republic,* "…men and women shall receive the same education and share equally in all public duties; women with the right natural gift are not to be debarred by difference of sex from fulfilling the highest functions."[373] Despite Plato's initially egalitarian ideas and the Roman Empire's relatively fair treatment of women, once man began to forge his transcontinental commercial connections, women were left home to breed. Women's status eventually devolved until she was perceived as nothing more than an incubator for the next generation of men.

According to Stone, Hebraic religion and culture suppressed historic evidence of matriarchal civilizations. Developing patriarchal religions of Judaism, Christianity and Islam would ultimately blot the mother goddess out of history as a polytheistic aberration under the negative connotation given paganism. Some archeologists deny her existence, claiming the ancient statues were toys and not idols for worship. And women in western cultures were never as voiceless as in Mormon society.

Today one finds that thinking Mormon women who have questioned the Brethren, from Emma through Sonia, have been cut off, kicked out, and in every way censored—their important messages distorted through the whitewashing of Mormon history. Contrary to some adherents' claims that Mormonism is a forward-thinking religion, it is in fact a throwback to post-classical patriarchy, appropriating biblical Hebrew stories as fodder for much of Joseph Smith's *Book of Mormon* creation.

Even the Hebrew bible's dozens of male authors named two books after women: Ruth and Esther. In the Roman Catholic Church, Mary, Mother of Christ, is revered as an intermediary with God the Father. Catholics pray and ask her to intercede on their behalf. "Hail Mary full of grace, the Lord is with thee. Blessed is the fruit of thy womb, Jesus. Holy Mary, mother of God, pray for us sinners now, and at the hour of our death." Conversely, not a single woman is featured in any Mormon scripture.

In the nineteenth century, LDS prophets and apostles preached that "unless a woman pleased her husband and was obedient and was saved by him, she could not be saved at all." [374] This teaching remains in the Church today. And although the language was changed somewhat in the 1990 modifications to the temple ceremony, women remain second citizens.

One former BYU religion professor sums up a Mormon woman's prospect of becoming a goddess quite clearly:

Women are queens and priestesses but not gods. The Godhead, the 'Presidency of Heaven,' is a presidency of three male deities, similar to a stake presidency whose members each have wives who are responsible for domestic religious education but not ecclesiastical functions. [375]

Brigham Young preached wives' obedience to their husbands:

If I am thus controlled by the Spirit of the Most High I am a king, I am supreme so far as the control of self is concerned; and it also enables me to control my wives and children. And when they thus see that I am under the government and control of the Good Spirit, they will be perfectly submissive to my dictates. They feel and say, "Yes, father, or husband, certainly, you never require anything that is wrong; I have learned that long ago. Your judgment and discretion and the power of thought and reflection in you are sufficient; you know what is right." [376]

Smith's Licentious Deception

Throughout his tumultuous life, the recently nicknamed 'plowboy prophet,' exhibited innate chauvinism which led him to interpret female goddesses in Egyptian papyri as male characters. With his deceitful treatment of his first wife Emma, his seduction of underage females and other men's wives in the name of God, and his ultimate assassination by a disaffected and justifiably angry mob over his licentious and criminal behavior—with the exception of Brigham Young, a co-contender for the title—Joseph Smith exemplified Mormon misogyny at its worst.

Smith began these adulterous affairs soon after the Church was organized. In October, 1832, Smith allegedly made a pass at fifteen year-old, Nancy Marinda Johnson who resided in the home where he was a guest. Her brother and other men were so incensed at his behavior that they tarred, feathered and almost castrated him. [377]

Smith publicly lied about his involvement in polygamy, up until the month before he died in 1844. William Law accused Smith of "living in an open state of adultery," with Maria Lawrence. [According to author Richard Van Wagoner] "Smith, who had been sealed to Maria and Sarah Lawrence in the summer or early fall of 1843, had himself appointed legal guardian of the two orphan girls on 4 June 1844, two weeks after Law's charges were filed." In response, Smith commented on the charges the next day in Sunday services, noting that such accusations were not new to him.

> Another indictment has been got up against me…I had not been married scarcely five minutes, and made one proclamation of the gospel, before it was reported that I had seven wives, . . . What a thing it is for a man to be accused of committing adultery, and having seven wives, when I can only find one..*[378]

Then, most likely because his actions were too well-known to be concealed, he dictated the polygamy revelation as a *nunc pro tunc* justification for the past decade or more full of his lascivious deeds.

The documented wives of Joseph Smith number thirty-four. Eleven of them had living husbands at the time they 'married' the Prophet. [379] One of Smith's first encounters was circa. 1832, with sixteen-year-old Fanny Alger, a maidservant who lived in their home. Emma witnessed it when she "looked through a crack and saw the transaction," in the barn. [380] Loyal Smith supporter Oliver Cowdery called the relationship "a dirty, nasty, filthy affair." Cowdery's reluctant realization of the Prophet's peccadilloes led to an irreparable rift between the two founders of Mormonism. [381]

Ann Eliza Webb Young describes Smith's keeping young women in his home with whom he had affairs:

At one time he [Smith] had eleven young ladies living in his family as adopted daughters, to whom he had been sealed without the knowledge of his wife. She for sometime supposed that his object in having them there was purely a charitable one. To be sure, some of them had parents living; yet there was some plausible reasons always given for having them under his roof, which none of the saints dared to question, although many of them, especially whose who were growing disaffected, were dissatisfied with his reasons, and suspicious of his motives. Very little was said about it openly, until his wife saw something which aroused suspicion, and she remonstrated with Joseph for having the girls there; but with no effect. The girls should remain—on that point he was decided...

Several young girls left the church in consequence of the dishonorable proposals which the Prophet made to them. One of these was a daughter of William Marks, another, a daughter of Sidney Rigdon. Both these men—Rigdon especially—had been his warm friends and supporters but this insult offered to their daughters exasperated them beyond measure, and both withdrew from him. Marks joined William Law and his apostate circle and was as bitter in his denunciation as Law himself. ...Other young girls made affidavits to his offers of "Celestial Marriage" and their statements were published in many of the leading papers all over the county, creating the most intense excitement.*[382]

Chapter 10: Women without Voices

Later in Smith's adulterous history, many women were commanded to marry him under threat of God's disapproval. The Prophet may have been inspired by an old Mormon who had tried the same trick. On April 28, 1836, a Church Court was held in which charges were brought against Aaron Lyon who wanted a wife and: "consequently set his wits work to get one...the old man had sagacity enough to know that unless he used his priestly office to assist him in accomplishing his design, he would fail in the attempt."* Lyon told one Mrs. Jackson, whose husband was working away from home, that her husband was dead and that God told Lyon that she should marry him. Before the nuptials her legal husband returned home. Joseph Smith acted in Lyon's defense, but Lyon's office of high priest was revoked.[383]

As Smith grew into middle-age, his preference remained for teenage brides. In 1836, Smith alienated his colleague, Sidney Rigdon, when he proposed to Rigdon's nineteen-year-old daughter Nancy, who refused him and told her father about the proposal. He also proposed to Sarah Pratt, LDS Apostle Orson Pratt's wife, after he had sent Pratt on to a European mission. Sarah also rebuffed the Prophet. Later visitors to Nauvoo heard Smith declare that Sarah Pratt was "a ***** [whore] from her mother's breast."[384] Besides Nancy Rigdon and Sarah Pratt, Jane Law, already married to Church leader William Law, rejected Smith's proposal of polyandry.

August 18, 1842, just a few weeks after his marriage to seventeen-year-old Sarah Ann Whitney, Smith was hiding from the law in the Nauvoo area when he wrote a letter to his young bride and her parents which expressed in pertinent part:

> ...my feelings are so strong for you since what has passed lately between us...I know it is the will of God that you should comfort me now in this time of affliction...the only thing to be careful of; is to find out when Emma comes then you cannot be safe, but when she is not here, there is the most perfect safty...burn this letter as soon as you read it;...I think emma wont come tonight if she dont, dont fail to come tonight...*[385]

Besides Smith's outright denials that he ever practiced polygamy, apostle and after Brigham Young's death, third president of the LDS

Church, John Taylor, openly lied to prospective European converts on the subject. During a public discourse in Boulogne-sur-Mer, France, Taylor claimed that Mormons did not practice polygamy when at the time he had several wives living back in the States. Joseph Smith's brother Hyrum also publicly denied polygamy as late as 1844, in the *Times and Seasons* Mormon newspaper, misrepresenting that "...there is no such thing practiced here." [386]

Smith's supporters continued the cover-up after his death. In a newspaper published after Smith's death, Rigdon admitted that Apostle Parley P. Pratt advised Church leaders that "we must lie to support brother Joseph, it is our duty to do so."[*387] Defamatory statements about the women who rejected Smith continued to be circulated by Smith's supporters in the Church, even after the deaths of the Smith brothers. [388]

It is clear that the polygamy revelation (*D&C* §132) made public to the general membership only after Smith's death, was an *ex-post facto* attempt to sanctify Smith's gross immorality. Once sanctioned by God, the polygamy principle was protected by LDS leaders for decades.

Then, in 1890 after decades of public disapproval and federal legislation initiated to criminalize polygamy, and in the hope of attaining statehood, then President of the Church, Wilford Woodruff, issued his Manifesto promising to abandon the practice:

To Whom It May Concern:

Press dispatches having been sent for political purposes, from Salt Lake City, which have been widely published, to the effect that the Utah Commission, in their recent report to the Secretary of the Interior, allege that plural marriages are still being solemnized and that forty or more such marriages have been contracted in Utah since last June or during the past year, also that in public discourses the leaders of the Church have taught, encouraged and urged the continuance of the practice of polygamy—
I, therefore, as President of the Church of Jesus Christ of Latter-day Saints, do hereby, in the most solemn manner, declare that these charges are false. We are not teaching polygamy or plural marriage, nor permitting any person to enter into its practice and I deny that either forty or any other number of plural marriages have during that

period been solemnized in our Temples or in any other place in the Territory.

One case has been reported, in which the parties allege that the marriage was performed in the Endowment House, in Salt Lake City, in the Spring of 1889, but I have not been able to learn who performed the ceremony; whatever was done in this matter was without my knowledge. In consequence of this alleged occurrence the Endowment House was, by my instructions, taken down without delay.

Inasmuch as laws have been enacted by Congress forbidding plural marriages, which laws have been pronounced constitutional by the court of last resort, I hereby declare my intention to submit to those laws, and to use my influence with the members of the Church over which I preside to have them do likewise.

There is nothing in my teachings to the Church or in those of my associates, during the time specified, which can be reasonably construed to inculcate or encourage polygamy; and when any Elder of the Church has used language which appeared to convey such teaching, he has been promptly reproved. And I now publicly declare that my advice to the Latter-day Saints is to refrain from contracting any marriage forbidden by the law of the land.

WILFORD WOODRUFF [signed]
President of the Church of Jesus Christ of Latter-day Saints.

The LDS-owned *Deseret Evening News* was characterized as "one of the most dishonest, unjust and mendacious organs that ever poisoned the public mind," by U.S. Senator from Utah, Frank J. Cannon.[389]   A May 24, 1906, editorial argued against Church members' requests to remove §132 on polygamy from the *D&C* (quoted in part in Chapter One, page 6). These requests were ignored and the current edition of the *D&C* retains this patently offensive scripture. Thus, despite promises made in the 1890 Manifesto, polygamy is alive in the doctrine, if not in the current public practice, of mainstream Mormonism.   Yet, when asked about the current status of polygamy in Mormonism, LDS Apostle Dallin Oaks disingenuously equivocates in his 2007 PBS interview:

Mike Wallace: There still is some confusion that polygamy is definitively and unequivocally disallowed in this world. What will happen in the next? There is a perception that polygamy is part of the afterlife. Could you talk a little about that?

Dallin Oaks: ...the prophet has not chosen to make doctrinal statements, so I think I shouldn't say anything except to affirm that a lot of people, myself included, are in multiple-marriage situations... for people who live in the belief, as I do, that marriage relations can be for eternity, then you must say, "What will life be in the next life, when you're married to more than one wife for eternity?" I have to say I don't know. But I know that I've made those covenants, and I believe if I am true to the covenants that the blessing that's anticipated here will be realized in the next life. How? Why, I don't know.

What Elder Oaks didn't say is that although men can marry more than one woman in the LDS Temple, Mormon women cannot marry a second husband for eternity. Oaks' first wife died of cancer when he was sixty-six (there was no mention of his wife's age at her death). Oaks proudly announced: "Two years later...I married Kristen McMain, the eternal companion who now stands at my side." [390] His second marriage was solemnized in the LDS Temple for eternity. Had he been female, that marriage would've been for life, or as the LDS say "time," only. [391]

Why is Section §132, with all its condescending and self-serving commandments about polygamy still contained in Mormon scripture if it is not part of mainstream Mormon doctrine? The answer is that Mormon doctrine still claims polygamy as part of the celestial order of things, if not in this world, in the next. Celestial marriage, in all its polygamous ramifications, is a way for Mormon men to keep their women subjugated, not only in the hereafter, but while living in this temporal plane as well.

Chapter 10: Women without Voices

Brigham Young and the Brethren Continue the
Practice of Polygamy

Smith's miserable treatment of women was furthered by his successor, the illiterate and fiendish Brigham Young, who publicly flaunted the practice, eventually marrying fifty-five women.[392] Young built a home more garish and furnished more lavishly than any LDS temple for his favorite wife Amelia, while his dozens of other wives and children lived modestly, some barely above poverty. Young and his favored wife at the moment had a special table for two in the Lion House piled with the best food available, while the other wives, each with their various children (as well as the childless wives) sat together at a long buffet table, and were served with the plainest types of food.[393]

Nineteenth century British explorer, Richard Francis Burton, wrote about his thoughts on polygamy as he traveled through the Great Basin in the mid-nineteenth century. Comparing the plight of Mormon girls to their English counterparts, he notes: "Girls rarely remain single past sixteen— in England the average marrying age is thirty—and they would be the pity of the community if they are doomed to a waste of youth so unnatural."[394] He notes the real reason for polygamy: "The other motive for polygamy in Utah is economy. Servants are rare and costly; it is cheaper and more comfortable to marry them." [395]

Ann Eliza's detailing of her experiences in polygamy as set forth in her autobiography *Wife No. 19*, originally released serially in eastern newspapers and finally published just a year before Brigham Young died in 1877, contributed to the passage of the 1874 Poland Act. This Act made it easier for the federal government to prosecute polygamists than it had been under the Morrill Anti-bigamy Act. Her 1875 Congressional testimony kept the anti-polygamy sentiment alive until finally, the U.S. Congress passed the Edmunds-Tucker Act in 1887.

In 1873, Ann Eliza filed for civil divorce from the Prophet Brigham Young. She was the first Utah polygamist woman to attempt to establish support rights for women living in polygamy who wanted divorces. The case came to trial in 1875. Young had admitted he was worth $600,000 and had an income of $6,000.00 per month. Ann Eliza's attorney claimed he was worth and made much more. Judge McKean ordered the Prophet to pay $500 per month spousal support and $3,000 attorney's fees for the Petitioner. When Young refused, he was fined $25 and sentenced to one day in prison for contempt. The Prophet stayed one night in the penitentiary. Within the week, Jedediah M. Grant, Young's first counselor in the Mormon presidency, removed Judge McKean from office. The attorney who brought suit on behalf of Ann Eliza (and who also served as registrar of the Utah Territorial land office) was replaced in his government position. [396]

Later that year, another attorney representing Ann Eliza filed an order to show cause why Young had not paid accumulated alimony of $9,500. In a procedurally suspect ruling (the order had already been made by Judge McKean and it is not clear that it was timely appealed. As such, the order should have been enforced) Judge McKean's successor ruled that, "Since Brigham Young had alleged that the marriage was illegal and since the allegation was not denied, it had to be considered true, and the order was set aside."[397]

Ann Eliza aptly described Mormon polygamy as a horrid situation for all women involved. Claims that women living in polygamy enjoyed the situation are not born out by the historic record. The conditions of the polygamous wives were so insufferable that insanity was a common endpoint. About one second wife, Ann Eliza wrote, "She became insane—a common fate of polygamous wives, by the way—and remained a maniac until her death."[398] The low status of Mormon women was preached from the pulpit:

I think no more of taking a wife than I do of buying a cow,' was one of Heber Kimball's [in] delicate remarks made from the stand in the Tabernacle to a congregation of several thousand. Most of his hearers thought even less of it, for they would have had to pay money for the cow; and as for the other, he had only to throw his handkerchief to some girl, and she would pick it up and follow him.*[399]

As a young Mormon girl growing up in the third quarter of the twentieth century, I had never heard of these affidavits from young girls, let alone Ann Eliza's memoir, *Wife no. 19*. Throughout Church history it appears that these muzzled women have occasionally broken free and cried out to those gentiles who would listen to their oppressive predicaments, but they were never acknowledged by their own, the men in power in Mormonism. A 2010 search for any reference to the author of this important book, "Ann Eliza Young," or "Ann Eliza Webb," or "Ann Eliza," on the official Church website, http://www.LDS.org yields absolutely no results for Brigham Young's brave and outspoken plural wife. Similarly, although a search for "T.B.H. Stenhouse," on that cite produces several results, there are no results for his wife, "Fanny Stenhouse," or "Mrs. T.B. H. Stenhouse," who had also endured and witnessed the horrors of Mormon polygamy and wrote about it as well.

Brigham Young denounced monogamy, claiming it caused prostitution, European debauchery and physical and intellectual degeneration. Heber C. Kimball, Young's Second Counselor said: "...for a man of God to be confined to one woman is small business... I do not know what we should do if we had only one wife apiece."[400] Young preached that God introduced the patriarchal order of marriage, not to assuage man's carnal desires, or punish women, but in order to raise up a royal priesthood. There are spirits waiting in heaven to attain mortal bodies and righteous men should provide those tabernacles. Had Young only one wife, he would have had just three sons, but due to polygamy, he sired numerous sons. [401] This line of reasoning is never followed up to explain that the same number of children would likely have been born (and perhaps even more if women didn't have to share their husbands) whether their mothers married polygamously or monogamously.

Though most all adult born-in-the-Church Mormons know it, Brigham Young's open, notorious and extensive practice of polygamy is not even mentioned in the 1997 Church-approved and authored student Sunday school lesson manual based upon Young's teachings with his photograph on the cover. [402] The same type Sunday school manual, published in 2007 covering Joseph Smith's life, reveals no wife of his other than Emma.[403] Why? *Deseret News* editor, Apostle and Counselor to two presidents of the Church during the early twentieth century, Charles W. Penrose, admitted that certain facts about the founding prophet were purposely withheld from Church publications, "for prudential reasons."[404]

No doubt the reason for these glaring historical and doctrinal omissions is to keep this important information from young members of the Church, those who have recently converted and/or those who are investigating the Religion.   If the contemporary Church deems it unimportant to today's Saints to learn of the decades of God-sanctioned polygamy, then that is even more evidence of the continuing misogyny of its leaders, especially given the extreme sacrifice and denigration of the women who endured the practice.

Similarly, claims that polygamy was necessary due to a shortage of men in the Church are readily exposed as inaccurate.[405]   According to census records during the first almost one-hundred years after settlement, males substantially outnumbered females in early Mormon Utah.[406]

The Utah Historical Society maintains population statistics from the United States Census Bureau.   The population summaries, broken down by gender, show that from the time of Mormon settlement through the end of the nineteenth century there were (some years significantly) more males than females living in Utah.

Utah population:

1850 total 11,380	male 6,046	female 5,334
1860 total 40,273	male 20,255	female 20,018
1870 total 86,786	male 44,121	female 42,665
1880 total 143,963	male 74,509	female 68,454
1890 total 210,779	male 111,975	female 98,804
1900 total 276,749	male 141,687	female 135,062

Despite claims at the Reed Smoot hearings that polygamy was only ever practiced by just a small percentage of Mormon leaders, 1858 Utah census figures quoted by the *New York Weekly Herald*, reveal a different story.   The total number of male polygamists in Utah was given at three-thousand, six-hundred and seventeen.   Broken down by number of wives, there were:

Husbands with seven wives and upwards......387
Husbands with five wives.......................730
Husbands with four wives....................1,100
Husbands with more than one wife
and less than four.............................1,400

Total men living in Polygamy in Utah   3,617[407]

More important is the number of Utah females subjected to this social system.

Husbands with seven wives and upwards...387 *(x7 for women)*
Husbands with five wives.................. 730 *(x5 for women)*
Husbands with four wives.................. 1,100 *(x 4 for women)*
Husbands w/ more than 1 wife & less than 4 ....1,400 *(x 2.5 for women)*

Total Utah Women living in polygamy   14,259 [408]

Thus, taking the number of polygamist men in 1858 as a percentage of the number of men in 1860 (the nearest year of census data), 18% of all men would have lived in polygamy. If the same calculation is done for the women, as per the above statistics, 71% of all Utah women would have been living in polygamy during that time. (Note: these numbers include all males and females; the difference in the percentages of each gender living in polygamy would be greater if the numbers used excluded prepubescent children.)

After Brigham Young's death in 1877, Emeline Blanche Woodward Wells, third polygamous wife of Daniel H. Wells, became the editor of the *Exponent*, a women's newsletter published by the LDS Relief Society. She campaigned heavily against the "Cult of Womanhood," denigrating women being treated as "...a glittering and fragile toy, a thing without brains or soul..." and stressed that there was more to life than living for a man. Over these several decades there were feminist letters to the editor and articles about women's issues. Certainly the men in the Church never took seriously "ladies' news." Such feminist sentiments were never published in Church magazines of general circulation. The original *Exponent* was discontinued in 1914. Currently there exists no official, comparable newsletter in the Church, though the *Exponent II* (begun in 1974) is an unofficial LDS women's newsletter. [409]

In the 1890s, almost a third of these polygamous men were tried and convicted after the U.S. Supreme Court upheld the Edmunds-Tucker Act. Two high-ranking Mormon leaders were found hiding out, attempting to avoid arrest during the polygamy raids. Unfortunate collateral damage from this enforcement were the men's polygamous families who were left without providers, and some wives who went to jail for refusing to testify against their husbands, the children of these families being the real victims.

Eventually, so eager for statehood were the gentiles and the more reasonable Saints that in 1896 polygamy was specifically banned "forever," in the Utah Constitution.[410] Polygamy had run its course, it seemed. The practice had caused strife with the federal government and was abhorrent even to Mormon women who, when necessary (as when their husbands were charged with the crime), would defend it to outsiders.

Polygamy is Continued by Mainstream Mormons into the Twentieth Century

Utahn and former U.S. Senator, Frank J. Cannon described the power that then, Church President Joseph F. Smith, nephew of the founding prophet (Hyrum's son) had over the people and the State during the immediate post-manifesto period of the early 1900s. The Church had effected a cessation of the polygamy prosecutions of the early 1890s and had negotiated statehood on the express condition that it would abandon the practice. Once President Wilford Woodruff died, Lorenzo Snow assumed the presidency for a short time. But Smith was moving up the ranks and eventually, during the Smoot confirmation hearings of the early twentieth century, was acting prophet of the Church. Cannon wrote in his revealing memoir that:

He [Joseph F. Smith] lives, like the Grand Turk, openly with five wives, against the temporal laws of the state, against the spiritual law of the Kingdom, and in violation of his own solemn covenant to the country-which he gave in 1890, in order to obtain amnesty for himself from criminal prosecution and to help Utah obtain the powers of statehood which he has since usurped. He secretly preaches a proscribed doctrine of polygamy as necessary to salvation; he publicly denies his own teaching, so that he may escape responsibility for the sufferings of the "plural wives" and their unfortunate children, who have been betrayed by the authority of his dogma. And these women, by the hundreds, seduced into clandestine marriage relations with polygamous elders of the Church, unable to claim their husbands-even in some cases divorcing their children and teaching these children to deny their parents-are suffering a pitiful self-immolation as martyrs to the religious barbarism of his rule. [411]

At the suggestion of his father's colleague, and on behalf of the Church, Cannon solicited the mayor of New York City to replace the Chief Justice of the Utah Supreme Court. The Church hoped Mayor Sanford would be lenient and allow those guilty of continuing in post-manifesto polygamy to stipulate to a reduced judgment and then eventually discontinue the practice, saving the reputation and the lives of those families affected. Cannon was surprised that the New York Mayor called in his wife to consult on whether he should accept the offer to replace Justice Zane, who was intent on prosecuting polygamists to the full extent of the law.

Mrs. Sanford questioned the young Cannon in depth about women in polygamy and whether he personally lived or believed in it—he didn't. At Mrs. Sanford's encouragement, the Mayor considered and ultimately accepted the Utah high court position for a season. Reflecting back upon the experience, the young Cannon seemed pleasantly surprised at the irony that "a decision so momentous in the history of Utah owed its induction to the wisdom of a woman and was confirmed with a domestic pleasantry."[412]

Cannon explains that the average Mormon man was also enslaved by polygamy:

The world understands that polygamy is an enslavement of women. The ecclesiastical authorities in Utah today have discovered that it is more powerful as an enslaver of men. Once a man is bound in a polygamous relation, there is no place for him in the civilized world outside of a Mormon community. He must remain there, shielded by the Church, or suffer elsewhere social ostracism and the prosecution of bigamous relations. Since 1890, the date of the manifesto (and it is to the period since 1890 that my criticism solely applies) the polygamist must be abjectly subservient to the prophets who protect him; he must obey their orders and do their work, or endure the punishment which they can inflict upon him and his wives and his children. Inveigled into a plural marriage by the authority of a clandestine religious dogma-encouraged by his elders, secluded by the prospect of their favor, and impelled perhaps by a daring impulse to take the covenant and bond that shall swear him into the dangerous fellowship of the lawlessly faithful he finds himself, at once, a law breaker who must pay the Church hierarchy for his protection by yielding to them every political right, every personal independence, every freedom of opinion, every liberty of act. *[413]

It is true that polygamy was a vehicle for expanding the kingdom, but not a heavenly one; rather, it successfully expanded a hellish Earthly kingdom of captive souls for the perpetuation of Brigham Young's isolationism and continued autocratic control over the original group of trusting Saints. In short, there was no reason for the principle of polygamy other than to ensure growth of the Kingdom and to satisfy the particular Mormon leaders' quest for dominion over all he could see, including as many women as would have him, in this life and the next.

Censoring Mother-In-Heaven

Aside from one poem referencing a potential Mother-in-Heaven by Eliza R. Snow, married to both Joseph Smith and Brigham Young, Mormon women in the early LDS Church had no real voice. Snow's poem was originally entitled "The Eternal Father and Mother," but the title was changed to "O My Father," when it was added to the LDS hymnal book. One verse still references a Mother(s)-in-Heaven:

> *In the heavens are parents single?*
> *No, the thought makes reason stare.*
> *Truth is reason: truth eternal*
> *tells me I've a mother there.*

The hymn is beautiful and loved by many, but any attempts to expand the concept of Mother-in-Heaven in the LDS Church have been censored. Paul and Margaret Toscano, two Mormon intellectuals in the best sense of the word, who are also parents of four girls, were condemned by Church authorities and ultimately excommunicated, in part for writing about the female deity.[414] The Toscanos advocated the existence of a female deity equal to the Father-in-Heaven, and that each was named in both biblical and early Mormon history. These co-authors criticized LDS-imposed gender stereotypes. [415] Margaret Toscano notes that any reference to a Heavenly Mother has been noticeably absent in Church publications since 1991, prior to the excommunication of several outspoken Mormon women and ultimately, herself.[416]

I recall the Brethren's bromide concerning the existence, role, or even title of Mother-in-Heaven as "someone who is too sacred to discuss." Pragmatically, such an acknowledgment would be bound to cause discussion of uncomfortable doctrinal issues such as the number and/or primacy of heavenly mothers, given the polygamy principle.

Women's Second Class Status Remains in Modern Mormonism

With the appearance of the Hebrew Prophet Abraham and the ruthless patriarchal usurpation of power, all pagan religions (which were in reality religions based upon the great and eternal goddess known as Isis or Ishtar, just as God is known as Yahweh or Allah, or Heavenly Father), through Apostle Paul's mandatory censorship based upon Eve's fabled sin in the Garden of Eden cursing her prosperity, women have been shamed and silenced. Of course, the historical record of Jesus Christ's teachings references nothing about the Adam and Eve fable. Rather, the Genesis story is a myth enabling the numerous religious patriarchies their continued subjugation of women.

In Puritan American colonies, intelligent and outspoken women suffered burning at the stake. For decades women were denied the constitutional right to vote. Women were long considered property or chattel under U.S. law and could not individually own, devise or bequeath personal or real property. For some time in many states, women were denied access to the highest educational institutions, including schools of law, because if women are allowed to study the laws, inevitably some would challenge those laws, whether ecclesiastical or civil.

British philosopher Bertrand Russell explains the old-fashioned celibacy requirement for female schoolteachers and the extraordinarily harmful effects of prolonged virginity. "A woman, if she is vigorous and intelligent, is likely to feel that the truncated maternal duties remaining to her are inadequate as a career."[417]

One thirty-five-year-old Mormon woman recently described her continued virginity as creating a protracted adolescence:

Most troubling was the fact that as I grew older I had the distinct sense of remaining a child in a woman's body; virginity brought with it arrested development on the level of a handicapping condition, like the Russian orphans I'd read about whose lack of physical contact altered their neurobiology and prevented them from forming emotional bonds. Similarly, it felt as if celibacy was stunting my growth; it wasn't just sex I lacked but relationships with men entirely. Too independent for Mormon men, and too much a virgin for the other set, I felt trapped in adolescence. [418]

Feminist Elizabeth Cady Stanton spoke eloquently of the adverse effects of religion on women:

...the Church has done more to degrade woman than all their adverse influences put together. And it has done this by playing on the religious emotions (the strongest feeling of her nature) to her own complete subjugation. The same religious conscience that carried the widows to the funeral pyre of their husbands now holds some women in the Turkish seraglios, others in polygamy under the Mormon theocracy and others in the Christian Churches, in which, while rich women help to build and support them, they may not speak or vote or enjoy any of the honors conferred on men, and all alike are taught that their degradation is of divine ordination, and thus their natural feelings of self-respect are held in abeyance to what they are taught to believe is God's will. Out of the doctrine of original sin grew the crimes and miseries of asceticism, celibacy, and witchcraft, woman becoming the helpless victim, of all the delusions generated in the brain of man.[419]

Despite the liberating accomplishments of noted nineteenth-century feminists, most of whom were secularists, the Mormon Church has always had a well-documented history of denied equality for women. Though women in Utah were among the first to obtain the right to vote, as

Ann Eliza points out, for a polygamist wife [voting] was done under coercion at the behest of her husband and thus seen as a way to give Mormon leaders several times their voice in federal elections. Women's suffrage was no more than a sham, since women never had time to study and truly participate in their government and thus, when the Edmunds-Tucker Act revoked their right of suffrage, "[Mormon] women hardly noticed."[420]

Polygamy is gone and women are equal, modern Mormons might argue. Not true because LDS women's insights and ideas, unless carefully circumscribed to the domestic domain, are not allowed to be shared with other members of their church. Not true, because women's beautiful bodies are demeaned by the horrid garments (as early as 1904 LDS women were reprimanded for a common practice of "removing the garments from the neck and arms and tying them behind the back"[421]) and held rigid, if not frigid, through Church emphasis of their virtue above all else.

It has long been expressed not only in Abrahamic religious texts, but by LDS Church leaders, that women's bodies are evil or unclean. On November 23, 1902, Apostle John W. Taylor told priesthood-holders at a stake priesthood meeting that "those who have sexual intercourse with their wives or touch any dead body are unclean until evening, and therefore during that day should not enter the temple or officiate in the ordinances of the gospel."[422]

Women's spirits are thwarted because even the best of Mormon women are confined and secured at the level of maintenance workers. Mormon women are nothing if not baby makers, babysitters, house cleaners or nurses for the young, the old, the poor, the ill and all the men in their lives. Though not as blatant as the Orthodox Haredi Jewish man's prayer thanking God he wasn't born female, Mormon men are impliedly taught similar sentiments.

Members of the LDS patriarchy give lip service to the local congregations or individual reassurances to women, when in practice their implemented actions are stridently anti-female. For example, around the turn of the twentieth-century, the First Presidency of the LDS Church issued a set of instructions regarding temple sealings to ensure families are together after death.

313

(16)   Where a woman has been sealed to two men and had children by both, and each of the men have a good standing in the Church the children go to their respective fathers. Why? Because the children were born under the covenant to their respective fathers and bear their respective names.[423]

Mormon Women without Voices

Unlike Catholicism, in Mormonism there is no reverence for women, let alone prayer to the Mother of Christ, and no mention of female saints. Some Catholic men say that Catholic boys are taught never to make their mothers cry; Mormon boys, through constant reinforcement of the "honor the priesthood," mantra also instilled in their female peers, are so taught to ensure that the next generation of mothers does their bidding. This attitude adversely affects marital relationships.

Many young returned missionary priesthood-holders jokingly relegate their young wives to menial household tasks without thinking to help in the process. While boys at twelve join the priesthood and prepare for leadership roles, the young LDS women are taught to stay virginally pure and support their male counterparts in their priesthood callings.

The Mormon Relief Society teachings reinforce this edict. Mormon young women, for the most part, are provided an unrealistic, artificial and really unattainable model of wife and mother. As Dalma Heyn, author of *The Erotic Silence of the American Wife*, writes in her book *Marriage Shock*:

It is clear reading old conduct books and advice literature today, that its authors were in search of someone who did not exist; that they were desperately creating something, not observing it. The Wife was simply being devised—or, rather divined. It's impossible to imagine what real person these authors are invoking, since her virtuousness and radiance, her utter lack of vanity, aggression and desire—all those characterlogical absences that, taken together constituted a Wife's appeal and her influence—do not illustrate a recognizable woman. Instead what begins to come through is a shadowy ideal, a sort of collective hallucination, part child, part angel, part domestic servant.[424]

Heyn's description continues as the feminine ideal in Mormonism today. Those who question the limits imposed by such an ideal are gagged by the Mormon patriarchy. Those women who refuse to conform to this ideal are expelled. From the first time I heard the term, 'feminism' has been a dirty word. "You aren't one of those feminists are you?" What a pejorative connotation this truly neutral word has come to have.

One excellent example of LDS Church censorship of outspoken feminist advocacy can be found in the brouhaha surrounding Sonia Johnson's support of the Equal Rights Amendment. With duplicitous gall, the LDS patriarchal gerontocracy enlisted its own women, through the Relief Society and under the direction of its priesthood leaders, to covertly help defeat the Amendment's passage in the early 1980s.[425]

As Johnson declared in her infamous speech to the American Psychological Association in New York City on September 1, 1979, "Men are consumers of women." She spoke about Mormon men's practice of deceiving women: "...I discovered one of the unwritten rules of the Old Boys Club: It is all right to lie to women; lying to women is like lying to idiots and other mental defectives. Necessary, expected and totally excusable."*[426] Here is more of her speech:

Because Mormon women are trained to desire above all else to please men (and I include in this category God, whom all too many of us view as an extension of our chauvinist leaders), we spend enormous amounts of energy trying to make the very real but—for most of us—limited satisfactions of mother—and wifehood substitute satisfactorily for all other life experiences. What spills over into those vacant lots of our hearts where our intellectual and talented selves should be vigorously alive and thriving are, instead, frustration, anger and the despair which comes from suppressing anger and feeling guilty for having felt it in the first place...
But women are not fools. The very violence with which the Brethren attacked an Amendment which would give women human status in the Constitution abruptly opened the eyes of thousands of us to the true source of our danger and our anger. This open patriarchal panic against our human rights raised

consciousness miraculously all over the Church as nothing else could have done. And revealing their raw panic at the idea that women might step forward as goddesses-in-the-making with power in a real—not a 'sub' or 'through men'—sense, was the leaders' critical and mortal error, producing as it did a deafening dissonance between their rhetoric of love and their oppressive, unloving, destructive behavior.[427]

Though Johnson's speech was made during my first year of law school, I heard nothing of it and I certainly don't recall it being formally discussed at the law school.

Outspoken, scholarly LDS women have all been excommunicated from the Church: Fawn McKay Brodie, author and UCLA professor of history; Sonja Johnson, women's rights activist and author; Sisters Janice Merrill Allred who at one time wrote for the LDS *Ensign* Magazine and Margaret Merrill Toscano, University of Utah classics professor and author; Maxine Hanks, former BYU instructor and author; Lavina Fielding Anderson, former editor of the *Ensign,* and Lynne Kanavel Whitesides, Mormon Women's Forum President, who was disfellowshipped.

Speeches given by female Church leaders are obviously scripted. Read their faces. If the speaker is intelligent, you will see strained consternation. In some, you can tell more about what is in their hearts and psyche by what is not said. In others, the Stepford façade has almost completely taken over their demeanor, to the convincing of themselves of their narrow role as the servants of men. What's more, these are speeches and not sermons. The content is delivered as storyline or gentle persuasion, never to be taken as commandment, in comparison to the Brethren's General Conference sermons which are to be interpreted as modern scripture by the Saints.

Listening to the women who speak at LDS General Conference is telling. Sherri Dew from the general Relief Society presidency is a different type of female Church leader to be sure; rather than a meek, tentative speaker, her demeanor is strong. Dew has never married and was undoubtedly picked for her position in order to reach out to the many single women in the Mormon Church. However, when the content of Dew's speeches is examined, it is clear that she is a puppet for the patriarchy.

Chapter 10: Women without Voices

From the mouths of the educated and thinking, both male and female, have come harsh criticisms of the narrowly drawn role that LDS religious doctrines and organizations have assigned to women, especially *vis a vis* their relationship to men and to God.   As noted by Robert D. Anderson, the psychiatrist-author of *Inside the Mind of Joseph Smith*, "In both *the Book of Mormon* and in his official documented history, women are underrepresented, almost ignored."[428]   And, "...despite the 1990 changes, the LDS temple endowment language ...still depicts women as subservient to men, not as equals in their own right...it is still the man who acts as intermediary with God."[429]

In a spectacular collection of essays from Mormon women, editor and author Maxine Hanks has compiled a book of voices which are never heard in standard Church meetings. These Mormon women speak with eloquence and compassion. Hanks characterizes the problem as one where women have to force their discourse into a male mode of speaking.

Her theme hits close to the mark.   At the time Hanks' book was published, the true origins of Mormonism were not as widely known as they are today.   These intelligent LDS women attempted to raise their feminist individual consciousness within the confines of the LDS Church. Clearly, such attempts will fail because Mormonism is based on regimentation, pomposity, and form over substance, the exact antithesis of the feminine qualities of intuition, sincerity and authenticity. [430]

In good, solid relationships and ensuing marriages, women will not disappear. But many Mormon relationships, and thus marriages, are built on a make-believe idea of a woman, as opposed to real women, and the couples' expectations are built upon that pretense.   In such cases the marriages are often doomed from the outset.   Mormon culture and doctrine, of which polygamy is the ultimate example, serve to trivialize and make fungible a woman's role. This classification of women as chattel continues to this day. Deceased Mormon Church President Hinckley told the men at priesthood meeting in April Conference, 2007: "Husbands, love and treasure your wives. They are your most precious possessions..."

317

Sexual Repression of Women in Fundamentalist Religions Causes Psychological Distress

The 2009 motto of the Utah State Board of Education includes "strong moral and social values," as part of its promise to preserve freedom in the State through public education. However, even in this century, sex education taught in Utah public schools is limited to bare bones baby-making facts. Certainly, nothing is taught of female orgasm, but only female sperm receptacle and breeding capabilities.

Female genital mutilation, a fatwa in strict Islamic cultures, is seen by most of the enlightened world as a barbaric custom; however, Mormon females are subjected to a similar sort of psychological castration. Many LDS girls who became women in the days before the internet have never had an orgasm and never learned of the existence, let alone the function of the clitoris or the female G-spot. I have met LDS women in their forties who have told me that they have never experienced an orgasm, but they are devoted to their husbands and the Mormon Church. It is largely due to the media of a new, uncensored generation, that today's young women have a chance to realize their gender's complete sexual functions.

That any single woman is worth just one-tenth the value of any man is going to be the lesson learned by young Mormon women when it's written not only in the *D&C* §132 on polygamy, but in the biblical parable of the ten virgins and their lamps in various states of preparedness, waiting for the bridegroom. Lots of time is spent on preaching to women, young and old, about self-esteem. Yet these LDS patriarchs seem blind to the fact that it is their very doctrine which causes and perpetuates LDS women's negative self-esteem.

Not surprisingly, Mormon leaders don't acknowledge the role that these polygamous teachings have on young women's self-esteem. For example, in a 1990 letter published in the Church *Ensign*, a Mormon psychologist talks about eating disorders among females, but never ties the psychological disorder into the second-class status impliedly taught to young Mormon women.[431]

The teachings of fundamentalist religions with regard to body shame (and I would add, the second class status of women) lower women's self-esteem and lead to these very types of reactionary, destructive habits.

Studies involving Catholics, Protestants,[432] Jews[433] and Muslim[434] women (who, as one might expect, have a high level of psychological problems) have all shown a correlation between body shame and eating disorders. One study concluded that Protestant women suffer more from anorexia while Catholics had more bulimia (binging and then purging through vomiting).[435] Perhaps the binge-purge syndrome parallels a Catholic's learned and practiced sin and confession lifestyle. In that case, Mormon women would suffer from the type of eating habits I had in my early twenties, neither anorexic nor bulimic, but a binge eating habit, done in secret. Apart from anorexia, in the general psychology of the 1970s, eating disorders were not widely recognized; the word 'bulimia' is only a post-1980 creation.[436]

Hebraic custom and biblical comments about unclean menstruating women, talk of women as either harlots or virgins, female births valued less than males and after which the unclean period lasts longer than for a male, women valued in general only for their chastity and then their reproductive potential and all leaders of a patriarchal society being, well, men, these and other scriptural insults to women secure her self-doubt. Gender is after all, according to Mormonism, an eternal characteristic. All these teachings send a not so subtle message to young women that they are less than males.

Though Mormon women are not burka-covered, showing a bare shoulder or a lower thigh is considered immodest. Dallin Oaks pronounced his opinion on young women's fashion: "...if you dress immodestly you are magnifying this problem [pornography] by becoming pornography to some of the men who see you."[437] The reality is that if men can't control their thoughts, then that is their problem and not the problem of a young woman who dares dress in a sleeveless top or a skirt that stops a few inches above her knee.

Fundamentalist teachings value women according to their virtue, which is usually construed to mean chastity, but never is a man's value directly related to his sexual experience. Women are more than vessels for incubation of the next generation and until and unless LDS teachings stop stressing young women's value as being solely related to the safeguarding of their chastity and service to the priesthood, these young women will continue to suffer from significant psychological distress.

319

Mormonism Creates Divisiveness in Families

Never has an ostensibly Christian church created such divisiveness within families. This destructive encouragement of misplaced loyalties was not only acknowledged, but encouraged by Brigham Young, who consistently characterized women and children as chattel.

> You ought to love a woman only so far as she adorns the doctrine you profess; so far as she adorns that doctrine, just so far let your love extend to her...Elders, never love your wives one hair's breadth further than they adorn the Gospel, never love them so but that you can leave them at a month's warning without shedding a tear. Should you love a child any more than this? No. Here are Apostles and Prophets who are destined to be exalted with the gods, to become rulers in the kingdom of our Father, to become equal with the Father and the Son, and will you let your affections be unduly placed on anything this side [of] that kingdom and glory? If you do, you disgrace your calling and Priesthood... When you love your Wives and children, are fond of your horses, your carriages, your fine houses, your goods and chattels, or anything of an earthly nature, before your affections become too strong, wait until you and your family are sealed upon unto eternal lives, and you know they are yours from that time henceforth and forever.*[438]

The defensive posture assumed by many Mormons who deny the truth about the questionable origins of the Church causes such division among families. Divorce is high. Many Mormon men I know have been forced to leave their wives and young children when their wives sought divorce because their husbands weren't dedicated to LDS principles. After divorce, one father of five never saw his young children again, only to run into one of his sons years later at a local home improvement store. Unknown to the father, his son had been married and had a child of his own. The sighting at the retail store was the first this father knew of the existence of his grandchild. Years ago, this same unfortunate man had to secretly attend another son's missionary farewell. His former wife, who had remained a staunch Mormon, had turned all their children against him.

Chapter 10: Women without Voices

In his biography, *Joseph Smith: the Making of a Prophet*, Dan Vogel theorizes that the adolescent Joseph invented his pious fraud as a way of reconciling the disparate religious views held by an alcoholic father and manic-depressive mother.[439] In order to effect peace in the family, Vogel suggests the teen-aged Smith concocted stories of the ancient American inhabitants and incorporated select theological ideas to create a religion combining and resolving the hotly contested issues of the era, in particular, those he saw as causing strife between his parents. Vogel's theory is a reasonably natural explanation of the origins of Mormonism. How perversely ironic! Instead of uniting families, the Religion has caused continued divisiveness, the very problem that the young Joseph Smith originally sought to avoid.

The Authentic Emma Hale

Emma Hale Smith had what must have been one of the most difficult marriages in recorded history. In public, she appeared to support or at least did not denigrate her husband. Even later in her life, after Joseph had died, after she had married Louis C. Bidamon and the Saints were settled in Salt Lake with Brigham Young, she was diplomatically reserved whenever she was forced to talk about her first husband. But if the documents referenced in *Mormon Enigma: Emma Hale Smith*, are examined, they contain clues that Emma was not a willing participant in Joseph's scheme.

Her objection to the polygamy revelation is well known. The handwritten revelation was brought to her by Joseph's brother, Hyrum who reported that, "...he had never received a more severe talking to in his life...Emma was very bitter."[440] The handwritten document became §132 of the *D&C*. [441] According to William Clayton, who acted as Joseph Smith's scribe during this period, "after it was wrote Prests. Joseph & Hyrum presented it and read it to E[mma]. Who said she did not believe a word of it and appeared very rebellious."*[442]

"According to Church Records, Emma was never present in the [Nauvoo] Temple."*[443] Brigham Young said: "In Joseph's day she tried to throw me, br. Heber, br. Willard Richards and the Twelve Apostles out of the Church, and tried to distroy the whole church, and I know it."*[444]

Though the Church would have Mormons believe that Emma Hale was, in general, satisfied with her role as Joseph Smith's wife, history belies this representation. Most unedited evidence reflects the conflict experienced by an intelligent woman who sincerely attempted to support her husband in his fantastic endeavors. Understandably she found it extremely difficult to do, especially when he began sleeping with young women who served as maidservants in Emma and Joseph's primary residence, the Nauvoo House.

Joseph, especially in the last few years of his life when his sexual liaisons were especially numerous, barely attempted to hide the relationships from his first wife. Nevertheless, he consistently lied to Emma in attempts to placate her. For example, differing versions of the anecdote where Emma destroyed the original §132 polygamy revelation by throwing it into the fire have been recorded. In one version Smith explains he allowed it, knowing he had the revelation memorized. In another, Brigham Young claims an enraged Emma spontaneously threw the writing into the fire. [445] Evidence also suggests that Joseph encouraged Emma to occupy herself with another man while Joseph was engaged polygamously. However, §132, verses 51-54 seem to indicate that Joseph later changed his mind. [446]

Many women were sealed in polygamous marriages to Joseph in the last few years before his death. Despite Emma's initial naïveté, these relationships between Joseph and the young women were not merely spiritual or platonic. Abundant evidence makes clear that Joseph and Emma quarreled about polygamy for years. Once, after Emma demanded that Joseph return a gold watch given in courtship to a prospective bride, sixteen-year-old Flora Woodworth, "Emma was furious. Smith told William Clayton that he 'reproved her for her evil treatment [but] on the way home she abused him much & also when he got home. He had to use harsh measures to put a stop to her abuse but finally succeeded.'"* [447]

According to Sarah M. Pratt (Orson Pratt's first wife) Emma was justified in her concern:

You hear often that Joseph had no polygamous offspring. The reason of this is very simple *Abortion was practiced on a large scale in Nauvoo...* [Dr. John C. Bennett] showed to my husband

322

and me the instruments with which he used to *'operate for Joseph.'* There was a house in Nauvoo, 'right across the flat,' about a mile and a-half from the town, a kind of hospital. They sent the women there, when they showed signs of celestial consequences. Abortion was practiced regularly in this house.*[448]

Sarah Pratt acknowledged Joseph Smith's ravenous libido: "Joseph's taste was of very large dimensions, he loved them old and young, pretty and homely. He sometimes seduced mothers to keep them quiet about his connection with their daughters."*[449]

She also confirms the rumor that Eliza Snow was one of Joseph Smith's willing consorts. Initially Snow and Emma were friends. Emma asked her to spy on Joseph, but then Eliza became involved with him. When Emma discovered the relationship:

> ...feeling outraged as a wife, and betrayed as a friend, Emma is currently reported as having had recourse to a vulgar broomstick as an instrument of revenge; and the harsh treatment received at Emma's hands is said to have destroyed Eliza's hopes of becoming the mother of a prophet's son.*[450]

At the end of her life, after Smith's death, Emma's marriage to Bidamon and the exodus of the Mormons who had chosen to follow Brigham Young to Utah, one LDS biographer quotes the Prophet's widow as having told the representative of a minority Mormon sect, "I have always avoided talking to my children about having anything to do in the church, for I have suffered so much I have dreaded to have them take any part in it." [451]

History hints that Emma tried to kill her husband. In 1844 Joseph became violently ill at the dinner table. Some twenty years later at a "secret council" meeting, Brigham Young proclaimed that Joseph had accused Emma of poisoning his coffee. Smith challenged her to deny it. According to Young, even in the face of her husband's accusation, she [Emma] sat silently and did not deny it.[452]

Charles Lowell Walker, a nineteenth century Mormon diarist, notes in his journal: "Br Snow . . . also related that when Emma, Joseph's first wife, heard of the Revelation [regarding polygamy] she sought the life of

Joseph and tired [sic] to poison him, but he was delivered by the Power of God." *[453]

Mormon Enigma, originally published in 1984, brought the wrath of the Brethren to bear on what had been for the few years prior, an unprecedented access to Mormon historical primary source materials. According to the book's female LDS authors, Linda King Newel and Valerie Tippets Avery, they were able to access papers in the collections of Joseph Smith Jr. and Brigham Young, as well as LDS Relief Society minutes and other documents which are no longer available to historians for research.

Although their biography received several awards and favorable reviews in both the academic and popular press, in mid-1985, without having read the book, the Brethren prohibited the authors from speaking about their work or about any aspect of Church history. In turn, publicity caused by the ban tripled sales and ten months afterward, Ms. Newell successfully petitioned to reverse the Brethren's censorship. "While the story of the lifting of the ban appeared in newspapers through[out] the United States... [AP and UPI wire services]...it never appeared in the Church-owned *Deseret News.*"[454]

Mormon Misogyny Continues

In Mormonism, young women are valued only as far as they are tools that enable young men to reach godhood. And women past childbearing age are valued as examples for the young women only if they have lived a proper Mormon-wife life. Rare, if non-existent, is the Mormon woman who is valued for her intelligence, spiritual insight or wisdom. Such reverence does not exist and such attributes are rare in Mormon women, not because of any innate inferiority, but because they are never encouraged to develop them.[455] An *Exponent II* letter from Virginia Sorenson published in December of 1976 sets forth with eloquence the dilemma of women who aspire to anything more than their traditional, proscribed roles:

... [My grandmother] had begun when I was no more than twelve to warn me about certain rights and privileges men might well seek to deprive me of. There is a very old conspiracy, she told me, against women of talent, and it owes it's major power to the fact that women are kept ignorant of its existence...I had begun, by then, to carry notebooks and sharp pencils and sometimes even finished poems in my pockets. "You will write in your spare time," she said, "which you will have to steal. If you have any success with it, anything untoward in the characters or fortunes of your children will be the fault of your negligence while pursuing your evil 'other interests.' And if your husband should not advance in the Priesthood or in his career, it will be your fault for not being a proper encouraging helpmate."*456

Vital, curious, truth-seeking Mormon women have historically been demeaned, censored and trivialized and continue to be treated in the same manner by staid, ignorant, controlling men. Is it possible that these men don't realize the damage their attitudes have caused? Consider this excerpt from a lengthy confession by a lifelong Mormon male, father of several daughters, who, only after they had grown, realized the damage Mormonism had done to the women in his life:

In Short: She [referencing his wife] Struggled and Stagnated . . . Enabling Me To Star and Strut...What astonishes me now is recalling that, at that time, I blithely took for granted everything she was doing. I'm ashamed to admit that I never gave most of it a second thought...I was too busy exulting in my LDS male role to even perceive her work-horse status, which I accepted as normal status quo, nor did I notice (nor would I have understood) that some Mormon beliefs are direct root causes of serious harm to many women...And if I had noticed, I'd have assumed I was wrong because, after all, how could God's only true Church directly harm righteous women? That would have been my "unarguably correct" LDS logic...But now, because subservience to males is less needed, it is less wanted, thus more oppressive and depressing to many females. Notice that I didn't say subservience to males is *un*wanted; I said *less* wanted. Many women still feel comfortable with it. *But not the strongest and brightest women...*
*457

325

Some Mormon men may be starting to wake up (at least intelligent, compassionate men) but after that comes the jealousy and the 'hey wait a minute'—if women are entitled to equality, they might take my job, or replace me and maybe they won't even need me. That is where the egalitarianism stops and some men revert to the old roles and discrimination.

In 1989, scholar and former University of Utah professor, Ed Firmage, who opposed the MX missile relocation to Utah and finally convinced the Church to do the same, publicly voiced his opinion that LDS women should be able to receive the priesthood.

> [In 1989] I finally sat down and cogently wrote an op ed piece [supporting priesthood for LDS women] for the *Salt Lake Tribune* as I had written the first op ed piece opposing MX, the first voice against MX in 1979. The next day the Mormon Church came out with a statement against my position. They quoted Boyd Packer. The statement was basically an appeal to tradition. There wasn't a substantive reason given. I'm not diminishing the importance of tradition in church practice, but there has to be something undergirding the tradition. The article basically said, "We do it, because we do it, because we do it." He said, "Motherhood is the equivalent of priesthood. Men have priesthood, women have motherhood." I responded that "men have fatherhood as women have motherhood. Fatherhood and motherhood are each other's equivalent. Priesthood is entirely apart." The vacuousness of the church's position seemed to me apparent. The reality is that there's no reason that I can perceive why men must mediate God for women.[458]

Once that opinion became public, Firmage received "several death threats."[459]

One contemporary Apostle's words typify the attitude many LDS men have toward the women in their lives:

> Tonight I am attending [a priesthood meeting or conference] with a son, sons-in-law, and grandsons. Where are their mothers? Gathered in the kitchen of our home! What are they doing?

Making large batches of homemade doughnuts! And when we return home, we will feast on those doughnuts. While we enjoy them, these mothers, sisters, and daughters will listen intently as each of us speaks of things he learned here tonight. It's a nice family tradition, symbolic of the fact that everything we learn and do as priesthood bearers should bless our families.[460]

Playwright, one time Mormon convert and BYU film graduate, Neil LaBute has written several misogynistic plays, the most infamous of which is *In the Company of Men,* made into a film in 1997, starring another one-time Mormon, Aaron Eckhart. "All his films usually consist of a cruel and vicious battle of the sexes with the men portraying unlikeable and trashy misogynists, and the women either crafty vixens or vulnerable victims."[461] No doubt LaBute was influenced by his Mormon culture while at BYU and beyond. LaBute received an award from the Association for Mormon Letters for his film, *In the Company of Men.*

***

Dan McConkie from the Church's law firm of Kirton & McConkie was defense counsel on one of the first cases I worked on when I returned to Utah from California. Dan walked me out to the elevators after a deposition at their office. We talked generally about the types of claims that his firm handled for the Church, including the failure of bishops to report sexual abuse. I listened; it was a serious problem.

Dan picked up on my interest. His handsome face broke into a wide smile.

"I thought you might be one of those feminists."

"You know"... he lowered his voice. "None of the general authorities will even ride in an elevator with a woman."

Another member of the firm walked up to Dan and I couldn't follow through with the conversation. I didn't know what to think about his last statement. The practice of refusing to even ride in an elevator with a woman is indicative of the great chasm between the LDS leaders and their followers, especially the women in Mormonism. Women appear to remain unapproachable to the Brethren. Unfortunately, the Mormon gerontocracy has controlled women to the point where, whether through mistrust or aversion, it appears that unless women are acting toward them in a specific role of wife or daughter, or perhaps as an executive in the

327

Relief Society organization, some—any, subordinate position, they are unable to relate to them as individuals, and certainly never as equals.

The power of the priesthood as claimed by Mormon males is nothing more than the framing of faith and 'Secret" manifestation techniques, available to both genders, but in Mormonism, reserved and set aside in a self-important manner by the men who founded and have led the Church and who continue to lead today. Many of these men have lived through the decades, imbedded into their glorious *faux* priesthood, to become the ultimate misogynists.

One of the biggest Mormon blasphemies leads women to make gods of Mormon men. Women abdicate their natural, intimate and divine right to commune directly with the Creator of the Universe (women are, after all, co-creators of humanity) and instead, Mormon doctrine inserts the Priesthood, whether prophet, apostle, father or husband, as a required intermediary. This sacrilege eviscerates women's innate strength, while bloating the egos of Mormon men.

Good men don't need to institutionally or individually trample women, or ensure the subservience of an entire gender to do their bidding, because they are inherently confident in their masculinity. I have been involved in relationships with good (non-Mormon) men—strong, confident men, with hard bodies and soft hearts, the antithesis of most Mormon men I have known. Unafraid of my strengths or of my weaknesses, these men were complementary to me—not averse. Unfortunately, the men who removed female prophetesses and saints of the Apocrypha, burned women as witches, banish Hindu widows from society, burn girls' schools and kill their daughters, wives or sisters to preserve 'family honor,' are the same type of men who lead Mormonism.

CHAPTER ELEVEN: The Continuing Fraud

"Propaganda brought us into power. Propaganda enabled us to remain in power. Propaganda will enable us to conquer the world."
—Adolf Hitler

We all have songs stuck in our heads that we never forget. When the words are catchy and so is the tune its brainwashing effect is unbeatable, particularly on the impressionable young. While flipping through television stations one day in 2008, I stopped on the BYU channel when I saw an interior shot of what looked like the Salt Lake Tabernacle (it could have been the conference center), huge organ pipes in the background. The program was a replay of an LDS Church Young Women's Conference from 2005. The young women sang "Oh how Lovely was the Morning," a hymn based on the official account of Joseph Smith's first vision in the sacred grove.

The program continued with the introduction of a female speaker by a male priesthood-holder as one [whose] "...most important role is that of wife." The second counselor of the General Young Women's presidency told the young women at the conference: "There is no more way to certain happiness than making and keeping temple covenants." [462] Another song followed the second counselor's speech. Its refrain repeats: "True to the faith that our parents have cherished, true to the truth for which martyrs have perished. To God's command, Soul, heart and hand, Faithful and true we will ever stand." [463]

Innumerable primary sources prove that Smith's re-telling of the first vision changed from his earliest account.[464] According to biographer Fawn Brodie, there is no mention of the 1820 first vision in any of the Palmyra newspapers, or even in the Prophet's autobiographical sketch of 1834. "Neither faithful Mormons nor their detractors appeared to have commented on this event until 1840." [465] Yet the hymn, "Oh how Lovely was the Morning," is offered to the Mormon congregation as an accurate verse account of young Joseph's sincere petitions to divine the truth. Claiming confusion as to which of the many Protestant denominations in upstate New York were true, Smith was told by 'the Lord,' that none were correct. Eventually, in a separate vision, an angel of the Lord advised Smith that he had been chosen to restore the true gospel of Jesus Christ,

329

lost since the Great Apostasy.

Which version of the first vision is most credible—the initial version, which tells only of the Lord appearing and Joseph seeking forgiveness of his personal sins, or the last, that published in the worked-over *Pearl of Great Price*, after Smith and his colleagues had the opportunity to rewrite the account? The latter, more dramatic version lends more authority to Smith's first vision by specifically referencing *God the Father and His Son, Jesus Christ*. The appearance of two members of the Godhead carries a weightier message and makes for a better miracle than visitation by the nebulous personage of the Lord (which can be understood by Christians believing in the Trinity; not so by modern Mormons who believe in a godhead of three separate beings: God the Father, His Son Jesus Christ and the Holy Ghost). Could it be that the LDS doctrine of three separate personages evolved over time, so that in any early or first vision it would have been conceptually impossible for Joseph Smith to have witnessed two separate personages?

Mormon Priesthood: a Posturing of Pretended Power

Regarding the restoration of priesthood, the LDS website reads:

In 1829, Joseph Smith received the restored priesthood authority to organize Christ's Church. John the Baptist appeared and conferred upon Joseph Smith and his associate Oliver Cowdery the Aaronic Priesthood, which includes the authority to perform the ordinance of baptism. Later, Peter, James, and John appeared and conferred the Melchizedek Priesthood upon Joseph Smith and Oliver Cowdery, restoring the same authority given to Christ's Apostles anciently. In 1830, with this priesthood authority, the same Church of Jesus Christ that existed centuries ago was organized and restored to the Earth by Joseph Smith.[466]

These events are represented as literal, not visions or ruminations.
[467] And although the LDS Church claims its priesthood authority from the early Christian Church, neither of these priesthoods is documented in the Bible. The Aaronic priesthood was inherited by Jewish descendants of Aaron; there is no biblical authority for an order of any so–called Melchizedek Priesthood.

The Bible teaches a priesthood of all believers. No special calling or gender is needed. (1 *Peter* 2:5). Nevertheless, statues at the LDS Salt Lake Temple grounds portray these two separate events.

Photo on the left: John the Baptist confers the Aaronic Priesthood on Joseph Smith and Oliver Cowdery. Photo on the right: Biblical Apostles Peter, James and John confer the Melchizedek Priesthood on Joseph and Hyrum Smith. Photos were taken of these statues located in LDS Temple Square, Salt Lake City, Utah, on Dec. 28, 2010.

Yet there is no proof of either of these events. It wasn't until the beginnings of significant, credibility-based apostasy in 1834, that Church founders began to speak of a miraculous restoration of claimed ancient priesthood authority. These restoration events appear to have been backdated to dates prior to the organization of the Mormon Church. Numerous contemporary colleagues of Smith, including *Book of Mormon* witness David Whitmer, claimed that the concept of [a] priesthood "originated in the mind of Sidney Rigdon."[468] The original edition of the *Book of Commandments*, published in 1833 and from which the *D&C* was taken, lacks any mention of priesthood restoration.[469]

In 1902, LDS scholar B. H. Roberts admitted: ". . . there is no definite account of the [Melchizedek Priesthood restoration] event in the history of the Prophet Joseph, or, for matter of that, in any of our annals..."*[470] LDS historians Palmer, Quinn and others, have also noted this obvious lack of documentation. Even LDS historian and professor at Columbia University, Richard L. Bushman, concedes that the lack of concurrent documentation for priesthood restoration "...raises the possibility of later fabrication." (Bushman, *Rough Stone Rolling*, 75).

An article by Lane Thuet notes that LDS Presidents Kimball and Hinckley have expressly claimed God's authority to reside solely with Mormon men. Thuet aptly characterizes the event of priesthood restoration as "retrofit[ted]," an *ex post facto* attempt to bootstrap the restoration into the original history of the Church. Thuet notes the irreconcilable position which this lack of documentation for any such event—the restorations of either the Aaronic or Melchizedek, Mormonism's lesser and greater levels of priesthood—prior to the 1830 organization of the Church presents to LDS faithful. They must recognize that "...Smith could not have legally [according to Mormonism's own ecclesiastical laws] organized the Church unless he had received the Melchizedek Priesthood first."* [471]

Senator Frank J. Cannon described the pragmatics of having priesthood in the early twentieth century.

> The male members of the ward-who would be called "laymen" in any other Church—all hold the priesthood. Each is in possession of, or on the road to, some priestly office; and yet all are under the absolutism of the bishop of the ward. Of the hundreds of bishops with their councilors, each seems to be exercising some independent authority, but all are obedient to the presidents of the stakes. The presidents apparently direct the ecclesiastical destinies of their districts, but they are, in fact, supine and servile under the commands of the apostles; and these, in turn, render implicit obedience to the Prophet, Seer and revelator. No policy ever arises from the people. All direction, all command, comes from the man at the top. It is not a government by common consent, but a government of common consent-of universal, absolute and unquestioning obedience—under penalty of eternal condemnation threatened and earthly punishment sure.[472]

Indeed, one of the bragging points of Mormonism is its claim to a lay ministry. Leaders can reach the status of apostles and even prophet without "...any particular earthly training or credentials to speak on any subject or act on any matter at any time"[473] Yet any Mormon with average intelligence and even young children, if bright, soon tire of the repetitive lessons and anecdotes, taught year after year, with no new insight or application, by those who claim to be in authority over those who may be more intelligent, and/or well read. Mormon leaders' preaching skills are far behind contemporary Protestant leaders' interpretation and practical applications of biblical scripture.

Perhaps this is why most new growth in the LDS Church occurs either through birth or in non-English speaking, developing countries. In these countries the language barrier initially prevents potential converts from a thorough understanding of the true and vacuous nature of Mormon theology. In many English speaking, educated, parts of the world, Mormonism is rejected *ab initio*. And, perhaps this is why the LDS Church feels it has to advocate its claim to normalcy through happy, smiling, spokes members in active public relations campaigns to convince the world that the Religion is something it is not—authentic and fulfilling.

Words of Wisdom for Church Members, but not the Leaders

The LDS 'Word of Wisdom,' a dietary guide for the Saints, was revealed to Smith in 1833.[474] However, as explained by Brigham Young, this revelation was merely a practical solution to a messy meeting room. When Church leaders assembled together after breakfast, they lit their pipes, smoked, chewed and spit.

> As soon as the pipes were out of their mouths a large chew of tobacco would then be taken. Often when the Prophet Joseph Smith entered the room to give the school instructions, he would find himself in a cloud of tobacco smoke. This, and the complaints of his wife at having to clean so filthy a floor, made the Prophet think upon the matter; and he inquired of the Lord relating to the conduct of the Elders in using tobacco, and the revelation known as the Word of Wisdom was the result of his inquiry.[475]

Though the Word of Wisdom has been interpreted to prohibit the Saints from alcohol as well as tobacco, both Smith and Young continued to privately participate in drinking and making alcohol. On the evening of January 9, 1836, Joseph Smith's journal records: "We then took some refreshments and our hearts were made glad with the fruit of the vine. This is according to the pattern Set by our Savior himself and we fell disposed to patronize all the institutions of heaven…"*[476]

Years later in the Salt Lake Valley, Brigham Young admonished the Saints against high living including women's spending on "ribbons and finery and [for them to] stop running to the stores" and [to stop drinking] "tea, coffees, tobacco and whiskey."* He ordered the Saints to donate money ordinarily spent on such frivolities to the Church for the immigration of the European poor. [477]

He also cursed brothers Badley and Hugh Moon, who had for years operated a profitable whiskey distillery in Salt Lake Valley, though they had otherwise been good Church members. The Prophet then sent both men on foreign missions. Though the Word of Wisdom had been revealed years ago, Young took possession of their distilling apparatus and "…commenced making whisky for the church." However, "…the church whisky did not prove to be so good as that made by Moon and Badley and the church distillery was short-lived." Years later, the men returned from their missions to find their business in ruins. *[478]

False Representations to Potential European Converts

Fanny Stenhouse, wife of Mormon missionary, T. B. H. Stenhouse, writes at length in her 1875 autobiography *Tell it All: the Story of a Life's Experience in Mormonism,* that soon after Mormonism was founded, the Mormon elders descended on England, France and Switzerland. [479] As a young Englishwoman, she was then working with a well-to-do family in France when she was first introduced to Mormonism. In addition to the blatant lie told by Apostle Taylor denying the practice of polygamy in the States, the Mormon elders represented that Zion in Salt Lake was a safe, heavenly place, where men could make more money, all were cared for, and there would be less financial struggle than in their western European homes.

According to Stenhouse, LDS Apostle Richards took the emigrants' money and booked passage on a steamer to New York, buying the cheapest of rations and steerage accommodations and then pocketed the difference for himself. Upon arrival in New York, these previously middle or at least working-class emigrants were forced to live in a public school house and resort to begging to feed their families.

When word of their dire condition reached the local Church leaders, Apostle John Taylor (who would become the 3rd LDS President) rode in on a fine horse; Taylor was dressed in his best and berated the immigrants for begging. These families had given up all their possessions for the trip. Upon arrival in New York, they were unable to find jobs or any other means of income. They tried retrieving random pieces of coal from the streets. Taylor suggested they form a snow removal business. Neither project was successful. Thus, they found themselves impoverished. [480]

In her autobiography Mrs. Stenhouse relates one story of deception by Brigham Young which has been substantiated by several chroniclers of LDS history:

> In the year 1854, Brigham Young and the leading Elders were most anxious to draw to Zion the converts from every part of the globe; and for this purpose the faithful were called upon to bring in freely their contributions to the Perpetual Emigration Fund. To set them an example, Brother Brigham himself stated that he would present as a free-gift his own property—a valuable city house and lot, if any purchaser could be found wealthy enough to purchase it. An English gentlemen named Tenant, a new convert, accepted the offer and advanced the money—thirty thousand dollars—and set out for Salt Lake City, expecting there to be put in possession of the property. He was one of the unfortunate Hand-Cart emigrants...and he died on the plains. His wife and children, when they arrived in the Valley, were told that the transaction was not made with them but with Mr. Tenant, and all their efforts to obtain the property, which in common justice was theirs, were unavailable. At the present moment Mr. Tenant's wife lives in miserable poverty in Salt Lake City, while there is no one to bring the honest Prophet to account.* [481]

Stenhouse tells of multiple swindles, perhaps the greatest of all being the polygamy revelation (D&C §132) which, as an educated and refined European woman, but one who had already committed to the

Mormon Religion, she laments as:

> ... [a] mass of confusion, cunning absurdity, falsehood, and bad grammar!" This was the celebrated document which was henceforth to be law to the confiding men and women who had embraced Mormonism! Looking at it now; noting its inconsistencies and its flagrant outrage upon common decency and morality, I can hardly credit that I should ever have been such a silly dupe as to give it a second thought.*[482]

Baptism by Deceit and without Informed Consent

Deceitful practices have been documented during LDS missionaries' attempts to procure converts for baptism. Corrupt baptismal practices, whether of live persons or for the dead (Mormons believe and practice "baptism for the dead," a temple ordinance which baptizes by proxy those who have not had an opportunity to become LDS Church members while living) are well-documented in Church history.

Historian Michael Quinn was a young missionary in the early sixties, the so-called New Era of the Church. He described the concerted efforts of the English and some other European missionaries in baptizing young boys, in some cases younger than age eight, mostly from poor families, through the deceptive representation that the children would be joining an American baseball team. Quinn documents missionaries trading favors or gifts unique to a particular mission: a trip to the beach, the opportunity to play in basketball tournaments, free ice-cream sodas or even a water buffalo. It seems that bribes for baptism over the past fifty years have occurred with some regularity in the Church. [483]

There are documented accounts from the 1980s of San Diego missionaries capturing illegal Mexican immigrants at the border for baptism. Apparently, the mission presidents, or in some cases, the presiding Church authorities, exerted such pressure to increase the number of converts that the young missionaries used whatever means available to recruit converts. When these practices have been exposed, Church authorities are quick to blame errant individual missionaries. However, the pressure to fulfill implied, though perhaps not expressed, baptismal quotas has always been a factor, and Quinn tells of young Mormon missionaries in tears over the stress from this numbers game.[484]

Regarding the salvation of the dead, a determination of whom to baptize becomes problematic. Names of Mormons' ancestors revealed through extensive genealogical research is one thing; the baptism of others who have absolutely no affiliation with Mormonism is quite another. LDS baptisms for the dead have included people of such notoriety as Anne Frank, Genghis Khan, Joan of Arc, Adolf Hitler, Josef Stalin, Buddha and Einstein.

Through the independent research of one Holocaust survivor, it was revealed that "...at least 20,000 Jews—some of whom died in Nazi concentration camps—were baptized after they died." The practice was ostensibly abandoned by the Mormons pursuant to a 1995 agreement with the Chairman of the World Gathering of Jewish Holocaust Survivors and the LDS Church.[485]

LDS Temples: the Toll Road to Heaven

Why all this fuss about baptism? Why the pressure to proselytize? Are these things really done in an evangelical spirit, to share the true gospel of Jesus Christ? Or, are they done to ensure the continuation of Mormonism, the business? Could it be both, one motive by true-believing, but naïve members and another by Church leadership? Or are both groups of Mormons blinded by perpetual zeal?

Members of the Church are encouraged to be temple worthy. Temples are a key component to attaining the highest level of exaltation in the Mormon Church. Apostle Russell Nelson's statement stressing the importance of temples represents the typical attitude taught to members and especially the youth in the Church:

> Parents should teach the importance of the temple from a child's earliest days. President Spencer W. Kimball (1895–1985) taught members of the Church to display a picture of a temple in their homes where children could see it and plan from their earliest years to go there and to remain worthy of that privilege. [486]

Both a bishop and a stake president's recommendation are necessary in order to access the temple. Recommends are conditioned upon compliance with many gospel principles, the most important of those are

337

support for the Brethren, including a professed belief that Joseph Smith was a prophet, that *the Book of Mormon* is the word of God and that the current leader of Mormonism is also a prophet. A full payment of tithes is also mandatory. Once these commitments are ensured, the true-believing Mormon is assured that s/he is on the path to the highest of the three levels of heavenly glory, the celestial. Temple attendance is preached as the only way to this celestial glory, and those who are not worthy are not included. Thus, the financial base of the LDS Church is highly contingent upon temple attendance.

One might wonder why the ordinances of marriage and baptism for the dead couldn't be performed in ordinary LDS chapels and the money spent on the extravagant temples put to better use. Mormons claim that temples were built in ancient Christianity and that modern temples follow the same tradition, but as *The God Makers'* author, Ed Decker, notes: "There is no record, however, either in history or tradition to indicate that a 'Christian temple' ever existed anywhere, much less that Christians ever practiced the pagan rituals now performed in Mormon temples."[487]

The Masons were originally a post Protestant Reformation construction guild that lobbied and obtained the right to move freely throughout Europe in order to build Europe's renowned structures. Trained in geometry, architecture and construction, but not necessarily bowing to the Christian tyranny of the time, Freemasonry was founded upon a brotherhood of workers who took pride in their artistry and accepted all who were skilled, despite individual religious or political beliefs.

The Freemasons describe a universal architect and use many different tools of their trade as symbols for moral or ethical duties. They use symbols of the craft of masonry, praising the grand architect of the universe and symbolically use the square, compass, trowel and many other tools in their ceremony.[488] Freemasonry's roots date back to the 1500s, not to the date of Solomon's Temple. There is no evidence of temple rites similar to Masonry or Mormon rites at that time.

It is ironic that the original intent of Freemasonry stood for the right of free-thinking believers in a higher power to be unrestricted by historic religious definitions of God and good in their beliefs. This right to freedom of thought directly challenged the power of the Christian Church during the Middle Ages. Yet the initiatory LDS Temple rites, the endowment appropriated by Joseph Smith from the Freemasonry Ritual, has been used to enslave generations of Mormons, denying that very concept of free thought advocated by the original creators of the ritual.

The Freemason's ritual makes sense only in relation to the history of Masonry. "Sign of the nail, "on the level," "arm to the square," etc., are solemn promises and indications that the construction guild worker, unfamiliar to a particular crew, was not unskilled, but trained in the ways of the craft of masonry. A comparison of the interchange at the veil in the Mormon Temple Ceremony reveals similarities between the "Sure sign of the nail" (LDS) and the "Grip of a fellow craftmason."[489]

Former Mormon Ed Decker, claims in the *God Makers* that "The Nail," is a favorite nickname of Lucifer or Satan, due to the pain and suffering caused Christ by the nails at his crucifixion. Additionally, Decker stresses that "The marks on that [Mormon] garment are IDENTICAL to the symbols on the apron which Lucifer wears: the square, compass and Masonic rule." [Emphasis original]. The actor playing Lucifer in the Mormon Temple Ceremony wears an apron which "...resembles the Masonic Past Master apron which contains the square, the compass, the rule and the all-seeing eye of Osiris..." And is "...the symbol of *his* [Lucifer's] power and priesthoods..."*[490] While making "the sure sign of the nail," is still part of the Mormon Temple Ceremony, as of July 4, 2010, a phrase search for "sign of the nail," yields zero results on the official Church website: http://www.LDS.org.

Being bound by secret oaths has sociological consequences. As observed by early Mormon leader Heber C. Kimball, "you have received your endowments. What is it for? To learn you to hold your tongues."*[491] And Brigham Young stated in 1860: "[T]he mane part of masonry is to keep a secret."[492]

One woman, a former Mormon, described her temple experience in April 15, 1846, in part as follows: "...the whole farce appeared to me to be nothing less than fearful blasphemy."[493] Whatever the true meaning, the Mormon Temple Ceremony with its plagiarized sayings, symbols and handshakes, makes absolutely no sense in the context of an ostensibly Christian Religion. No wonder then that most Mormon initiates leave the temple bewildered.

The first temple built by the Mormons, in Kirtland, Ohio, is now owned by the Community of Christ Church (formerly the RLDS Church) which claims to be the original church founded by Joseph Smith. Though there were ownership disputes in the 1800s, by 1901 the RLDS Church had secured ownership by adverse possession.

The second, the Nauvoo Temple, was burned in 1848; the arsonist was never found. Some believe Brigham Young ordered it burned to keep it from his enemies. A decade later, as a part of his Utah War 'scorched earth' policy, Young boasted he would burn all that the Saints had built in Utah rather than allow the federal government to occupy or control his settlement. Young had attempted to sell the temple to the Catholic Church once the Saints had moved on, but failed miserably in the endeavor. [494] Recently, the LDS Church spent about $23 million to reconstruct the historic Nauvoo Temple, which was rededicated in 2002.

Over 94% (126 out of 134) of the currently operating temples were built after 1952, at a time when the Church was experiencing financial difficulty. Some say that Apostle N. Eldon Tanner (deceased, 1982) a successful Canadian businessman who became the Church's top financial advisor, is responsible for the exponential growth in Mormon temples which occurred over the next three decades. As of this writing, another 23 temples have been announced and/or are in the construction phase. If a Mormon has convenient access to a temple, even better if the grand edifice is close enough to be seen from his hometown, s/he is more willing to regularly pay tithing in order to become qualified to attend.

Employee Reveals Bureaucracy and Fear at LDS Headquarters

In May of 2009, one former Church full-time employee who I will call 'John,' agreed to a recorded interview with me. [495] He had served a foreign mission for the Church and when he returned, studied the language at BYU. After working sometime on the East Coast for the federal government, in 1987 he accepted a position as an analyst with the Church Translation Department. John was an employee at LDS Church Headquarters in Salt Lake City for fourteen years. He described his job in the Church Translation Department:

My job was to write notes on the scripture text: the Book of Mormon, the Doctrine and Covenants and the Pearl of Great Price. These texts are difficult to understand and the people who did translation work are not English speakers. They are translating into their native tongue so they need help understanding what the English text says so they can render it in their language. We wrote a three volume lexicon, every word parsed, every phrase and sentence in those scriptures and... [We] wrote out definitions for the specific usage of each word and phrase and then wrote notes, its called exegesis. We wrote notes on scripture passages to make sure that the translator understood what the intended meaning of the doctrine was. This is where Church translation is interesting. The Church recently published its own Spanish translation of the Bible. They've had their own English King James Version since the 70s.[496]

After years spent learning about the original Hebrew and Greek sources for the English biblical text, John realized that the primary texts of the various biblical sources were at odds with the Mormon Church's interpretation of the King James Version of the Bible. As to the portion of *the Book of Mormon* which parrots Isaiah, he explained: "... the scholarly view of the biblical Isaiah is that [it] is actually a compilation of lots of writings over hundreds of years, some of which came after 600 B.C., when [*Book of Mormon* Prophet] Lehi was supposed to have [brought a copy of Isaiah with him to the new world in order to have] written it."[497] John agreed that this was proof that Joseph Smith plagiarized sections of biblical Isaiah for use in *the Book of Mormon*.

John then talked about Church membership numbers.

The falling birthrate is putting the Church in jeopardy. The average number of children born to Mormon families has fallen by about one child, something like from 4.5 to 3.5.

The Church doesn't keep numbers on those who leave Mormonism. Of the approximate 13 million claimed members of the Church, fully 50% of the names have an unknown address. The average meeting attendance is 20%, so 1.3 million are actually attending meetings on a given Sunday worldwide. And of those, 90% are in the Western U.S., mostly the Mormon Corridor. These people are the tithe payers who subsidize the rest of the Mormons who live around the world. The perception of the local members as a result of Church propaganda is that there are millions of members everywhere and we are growing: Columbia, Ghana, Germany, [the] Koreas, and that the Mormon Church is a world power. Although the Church continues to send missionaries in most counties worldwide, increasingly, those missionaries come back and say 'I didn't baptize anyone,' or 'I baptized a few.'[498]

In the late 1990s, John changed jobs within LDS Headquarters from the Translation Department to the Physical Facilities Department of the Church.

The presiding authorities were always interested in membership and financial numbers from all over the world because it costs money to do translation and to do publication work. The Church published tons of manuals and English materials. So they are very interested in knowing how much this million-plus core membership, how much they subsidize the rest of the world. In all aspects: operations costs, facilities costs, publication costs.

Of course they keep it very quiet. Some churches are very proud of that, 'we raise money here so that we can build a church in Africa and we can sponsor missionaries too,' [but] if people up and down this [Mormon] corridor really knew that, they would be like, 'What? I'm subsidizing the rest of the world? Well no; I'm not going to do that.' Virtually every other church gets to keep what they collect locally... The local congregation is responsible for their own programs and buildings. They pay a fee, an assessment to the central church, but it's all about building your local congregation.

According to John, some Church leaders are compensated.

The Seventies [Church general authorities who preside over different geographic areas and assist the Twelve Apostles; currently there are two quorums of the Seventies whose members comprise the majority of the one hundred and fifteen men in LDS Church leadership] all have salaries. Once you're in the Seventies you get paid...it's low six figures. And also very good benefits, pension, a car, an Avalon not a Mercedes, and you travel business class and stay in nice hotels and where you go you're treated like royalty... They [Church general authorities] make liberal use of Church employees to do home repairs and fix things.[499]

342

John explains how the decision to build a temple is financially based. He compares it to a decision to build a home improvement supply store, like Home Depot™:

> You have to have the right demographics to justify building [a temple] ...so it is very much a business decision. Analyzing the statistics, analyzing the trends, and then once you make that investment, just like any commercial [enterprise] you turn on the PR in that area...[500]

He remembers Mormon leaders' fear of intellectuals, especially in the nineties.

> When I was in the Translation Department, Dallin Oaks and Boyd Packer and maybe Russell Nelson also spoke to us several times, and it was in the 90s, so it was during that intellectual purging... it was obvious that those of us working on scripture were thinking people and read as well, so they wanted to make it clear that our main job was promoting faith and building the kingdom and, it was up to us, us members in general, but everyone needed to be sure to contribute to the kingdom and not speculate.
> Speculation was a bad thing. Questioning was a bad thing. Faith over facts. So history and fact being not as important as faith and testimony. And the way to assess anything is not on the basis of [an] objective assessment of its factual basis or truth but on its value, on [its] subjective value for supporting the Church and reinforcing the story and testimon [ies].*[501]

John explains how working for the Church for decades makes an employee fearful, risk averse and impairs those Church employees' judgment:

> I was there for fourteen years and... if you're there that long you stay, because you usually can't do anything else. I kept my skills up, I kept my résumé, I kept current with what was going on, because I kept believing I was going to leave, the employment sometime, not necessarily [leave] the Church. But many, especially the men, but it goes without saying the women, who work there, they can no longer trust their judgment. And they're so risk averse, they are so afraid to

do the wrong thing, that they'll spend years not doing anything to just avoid the risk of doing the wrong thing...So then they're questioning everything ...And I got to thinking, maybe something is wrong with me because I would reach a conclusion and think, I've thought through this well. You have to make decisions based upon incomplete information; you never have all of the information. There is no such thing as having all of the information. So you get as much as you can and you make a decision, and you act on it. I would get people questioning me. [At Church headquarters] you don't have to actually refute someone's idea, you just have to cast some doubt on it. So if I would come to a conclusion or have a decision and somebody wasn't comfortable with it, they didn't have to logically refute my idea, all they had to do was create some doubt.

[Because the Church has the presumption of truthfulness on its side] that's used in the business decisions... You, the Brethren, promote yourselves as the keepers of truth. You teach the members that when they question you, they are questioning God. To put that kind of doubt in people's minds, just by virtue of your ecclesiastical position...[502]

So that's the way they do their business decisions as well. They spend, and this is sort of just the nature of bureaucracies, but anyone who has to present, anyone who has to get a decision made, get funding for something, get approval for something, spends an enormous amount of time building their case, building *PowerPoint ™* presentations, spreadsheets. Because it is not enough, just like we were saying, that both parties come to the table equally equipped or on an equal basis. If you go to a committee of the Brethren to get an approval on something, the assumption is you're wrong. The assumption is even without seeing what you have to present, they're right and you are wrong.[503]

John resigned from his position with LDS Church Headquarters in 2006. Ultimately his research and experiences led to his resignation from Mormonism the following year.

Mormonism teaches that in the Book of Genesis God commanded Adam and Eve not to eat of the fruit of the tree of knowledge. When then did, they fell out of their state of ignorance and bliss and into the dreary real world. Likewise, the LDS Church keeps their true-believing members ignorant by instructing them not to read from outside, non-approved sources because if they read anything of substance, surely their eyes will be opened, they will have taken the proverbial bite of the apple, and they will realize that their religion is not what it claims to be. No longer will they live in bliss (or in some cases, no longer will they be depressed). The Mormon interpretation of the Eden parable illustrates the inevitable consequences which follow the acquisition of factually-based knowledge. It is the ultimate example of a state where ignorance is bliss and living with knowledge is lonely and difficult. But in the end, blissful Eden stagnates and its residents are compelled to escape into the real world.

The Mormon Conglomerate

A recently published book written by a student of anthropology and self-described ethnographer, Daymon Smith, details his time as a contract employee working at the Church Office Building (he calls it the COB) in Salt Lake City. Smith lampoons the bureaucracy and the people who work there who he calls "cobbers." Smith remains Mormon, but an original type. He argues that as of 1890, the date of the manifesto abdicating the practice of polygamy, the true Church no longer existed. Instead, the true religion has been replaced by a corporate entity which exists only in cyber space.

Daymon Smith is clearly frustrated with his birth religion, and along with others, who refer to the current Church as the Mormon Organization, the 'MORG,' implies that what is left is a bureaucracy with no soul. Smith writes:

Beglerbeg [a fictitious employee of the COB] exited at twenty-one with all the other over-paid and officious unguentmongers smug mesomorphs rolling flesh under the chin and across the hips, in a line of swinging petulant jowls from faces suffering decline and elaborate, almost mantic cragginess amid the bloatings of disuse, and each in a line the taller for heeled shoes. Would they were fatter. Those clean cut cheeks and managed dark hair just cut and just gelled, crisp and dead cold simultaneously, the frauds make their way to offices, to the work, to deal and to compromise the gospel to make it palatable and shiny, to balm your world...[504]

In most religions, the ecclesiastical leaders are trained theologians, preaching only after having completed years of graduate seminary education. However, Mormonism has a lay ministry, including its general authorities. There is not an advanced degree from any reputable school of theology or seminary among the Brethren. Historically, as today, the Brethren's areas of expertise are in business management, public relations and (Mormon) education. Increasingly, lawyers are called to serve along with pilots and a few medical professionals. The reason is clear: it is a business these men are called to run and the business of managing the LDS assets, including its membership base, takes primacy over the business of saving souls.

The Mormon Church is a diversified corporate conglomerate, a complex organization. From the Corporation of the Presiding Bishop, the legal entity owning and managing the Church's real-estate assets and the Office of the President, which collects and distributes donations, to Intellectual Reserve Inc., a Utah corporation which holds the intellectual property rights of the Church, the assets and responsibilities of the LDS Church are loosely and variously held so that the for-profit branches of its businesses can be legally separated from the non-profit arm. The complexity of the Mormon organization as a business entity is decidedly so, no doubt in order that anyone daring to sue the Church is in danger of naming the wrong entity as a defendant, a defense raised routinely by the Church's lawyers.

The Corporation of the Presiding Bishop of The Church of Jesus Christ of Latter-day Saints (CPB) was established in 1916, and the Corporation of the President of The Church of Jesus Christ of Latter-day Saints (COP) was first registered in 1923. The CPB and the COP are "corporations sole," the incorporation of an office where the holder can take and hold title to real property. His successor in title, as opposed to his individual heirs at law, inherits that property.

As of September 20, 2010, there are over 438 corporations sole registered in Utah containing the trademarked phrase 'Church of Jesus Christ of Latter-day Saints.' It appears that each of these is an independent LDS stake. Most of these were registered in the early part of the twentieth century and have been timely renewed since then. While each local corporation sole (stake) has an NAICS code of 'religious organization,' the CPB and COP corporations' NAICS[505] code is "non-classifiable establishment." In contrast, NAICS codes for other churches in the State,

346

for example the Catholic Church of Christ and the Presbyterian Church (U.S.A.) Foundation is: "religious organization."

In typical corporations, the corporate entity is owned by shareholders to whom the elected or appointed board of directors has a fiduciary duty. The board cannot remain in control if it is not doing a good job. If the directors violate their fiduciary duties, for example, act to serve their own interests before those of the shareholders to the damage of the shareholders, or otherwise act in contravention of the corporate charter or bylaws, even a small minority of shareholders can file a stockholder derivative suit against the corporation. Typical cases are where the board fails to act properly with a third party, gives directors excess bonuses, salaries or other undeserved renumeration or fails to disclose important financial data which, had it been disclosed, would affect the value of the shareholders' stock. One good example is the ENRON accounting fraud lawsuit filed years ago, but settled only in 2009.

Compare the organizations of the LDS Church. Any articles of incorporation or bylaws of the CPB or the COP are not known to the general membership of the Church. Though there exits a common council of the church, revealed in 1835 to founding prophet Joseph Smith (*D&C* §107) giving LDS general membership the authority to oust a general authority, it hasn't been used since Sidney Rigdon's 1844 excommunication. Given contemporary Mormons' inculcated regard for and directive not to question their leaders, it is difficult to imagine that any such council would ever be called today.

Thus, it seems the Church has the benefits of a corporation, such as protecting individual leaders from personal accountability under the law, without the burdens: that of financial transparency and answering to its membership for decisions. There are plenty of grounds a (Mormon) shareholder might question if s/he were given the rights of a voting stockholder, such as the disposition of tithes and offerings and Church involvement in state or national politics. But this is when a phrase that is commonly repeated in the LDS Church, "the Church is not a democracy," is often used.[506]

From the time of the creation of the Church by Joseph Smith in 1830 until 1915, it is questionable whether or not there was any method of accounting for donations to the Church kept separately from the Prophet and/or the Brethren. I am not aware of any records from Joseph Smith's era for a Church trust account or other record of separating Church tithes from his assets.   If these exist they haven't been shared with Church membership, apart from the sketchy details regarding some donations as set forth in Joseph Smith's journals, and bits and pieces of receipts, pages of tithing books, etc. For example, William Clayton's records contain a January 14, 1846 note certifying that one Reynolds Cahoon was due $96.51 from the "temple books."

Brigham Young displayed boundless greed in keeping and commingling Church funds for himself. According to Leonard Arrington, based upon records from the settlement of his estate, Brigham Young was the largest borrower from Church funds and drew at will from the Church account; no interest was ever charged.

And so historically at least, the Mormon prophet seems to have been given powers in excess of any ordinary office of trustee and was generally free to use and spend the income as he saw fit.   At least in the nineteenth century, tithing bounty was bestowed on friends and those faithful, not necessarily to Mormonism, but to the man, who was Mormonism incarnate as long as he held the prophetic office. [507]

None but undisclosed Church records, if they exist, would show whether this practice of commingling continued through LDS Presidents Woodruff and Snow. Then, though deficit spending continued, from 1915-1959, an annual accounting of expenses—but not income—was provided to Church membership.

With no open transactional accounting of gross receipts and expenditures, the Church was able to work with millions of dollars of assets and liquid capital with no accountability. But sometimes their secret deals were exposed. On February 27, 1936, Church President Heber J. Grant, who was also president of the Utah-Idaho Sugar Company, a key player in the National Sugar Trust, mortgaged the entire Salt Lake Temple Block and its buildings for $3,500,000 (three-million, five-hundred thousand dollars).[508]   This transaction was performed quietly, but eventually leaked out to the lay membership. An uproar ensued and a pamphlet circulated accusing LDS leaders of taking that which had been dedicated to the Lord.   Nevertheless, despite a pubic record of this mortgage at the Salt Lake County Recorder's Office, in April Conference, 1936, President Grant told Church membership, "The Church has mortgaged none of its property. The Church has sold none of its property. The First Presidency has no intention of so doing because there is no call or necessity therefore, and all rumors and accounts to the contrary are wholly untrue."*[509]

Since 1959 the Church has not provided an annual accounting of either income or expenses to its general membership. Since then it has been the custom and practice at General Conference for Mormon leaders to represent that the annual financial records of the Church have been reviewed by an independent accounting firm which warrants that LDS books have been kept in accordance with generally accepted accounting principles.

Now it seems all accounting is being done in-house. After listing the types of professionals who work at the department, at the Saturday afternoon session of April, 2010 General Conference, Robert W. Cromwell, Managing Director of the Church Auditing Department, citing §120 of the *D&C* as authority, reported to the Church presidency that all records for the year 2009 "...have been recorded and administered in accordance with appropriate accounting practices, approved budgets and Church polices and procedures."

Tithing and other donations documented on website blogs from men who have formerly served as ward clerks in the LDS Church range from a quarter to one million dollars annually per ward (local congregation) depending on that ward's combined income. The funds collected at the local (ward) level are given directly to Church headquarters and then headquarters sends back a small percentage of those funds for the local ward's needs. These same clerks estimate that each ward is allotted as little as 1% of those total donations forwarded to headquarters to assist needy local members and for other local expenses.[510]

John, the former employee I interviewed, makes clear that this collection system extends worldwide. He provided an updated account:

> All tithing, from every ward worldwide, ends up in the Church's account(s) at Zion's Banks. The Church finance/budget departments use formulas to disburse collected donations to missions, stakes, districts, wards, branches, etc., worldwide. A variety of methods are used to collect tithing. In Germany, and perhaps other EU countries, there is a payroll tax for religious donations. I believe the government collects money and then distributes [it] to recognized religions. In Japan, members can setup direct deposit to a Church tithing account. I believe the Church is unique among US-based Christian faiths in that it gathers all donations at the headquarters and

349

then disburses [certain] amounts back to local units. Most, if not all, other denominations keep [that money which they have raised locally] and pay dues/fees to the national organization.*[511]

The statistics given in the April 2010 Conference indicate that there are more than 28,424 LDS wards. Using simple arithmetic, averaging the figures set forth above, an enormous amount of tithing is collected by local wards, both in the United States and abroad, and sent to LDS Church Headquarters annually.

Just as important is the value of non-liquid assets, especially real estate, owned by the Church. As of 2001, "The Church reportedly owns more than a million acres of land in the continental United States (the equivalent of the state of Delaware)..."[512] This does not include their significant real estate holdings in Hawaii.

The Church's for-profit companies include "Deseret Beef and Citrus Ranch *aka* Deseret Cattle and Citrus, a subsidiary of Farmland Reserve, Inc., owned by the Church with 457 square miles, 0.7% of the State of Florida."[513] AgReserves Inc., one of the largest nut producers in the country and Bonneville International, one of the largest media companies in the U.S. are also Church-owned.

Last year struggling Church-owned Beneficial Financial Group (which offered life insurance and annuities), a subsidiary of the for-profit Deseret Management Corporation, received an infusion of $594 million dollars in working capital from the Church.[514] But even this large amount of capital didn't prevent this Church-owned insurance company's demise.

The Church issues permits for licensed hunting on two game preserves located in Utah, one in the Utah County flatlands south of Utah Lake, and another in Northern Utah, 200,000 acres where moose and elk can be hunted. According to the husband of a full-time missionary couple who served their mission on the bird-covered Utah County preserve, the goal is to make the business profitable. Their clientele is mostly professional: "doctors, dentists and attorneys," mostly Utahns, many who fly into the preserve, hunt their pheasant or other game and fly out.[515]

Over a decade ago, the Church's net worth was estimated to be in excess of 30 billion.[516] "If it were a corporation its $5.9 billion annual gross income would place it midway through the FORTUNE 500, a little below Union Carbide and the Paine Webber Group but bigger than Nike and the Gap."[517] But John explained that the Church's financial situation had changed by the time he left his employment in 2006:

> Their trust vaults are getting a huge hit with everyone else in the financial [industry]. [In a conversation with] a director who works in the welfare department and is on some of the Church's charitable trusts boards, one of his [that director's] jobs is reporting to the bishopric and a committee [of] the first presidency, the bishopric, and the relief society presidency. [He told me that] throughout the 90s and the early part of the 2000s, donations were pouring in and those funds were growing; they actually had to just scramble to spend, because the money was just piling up.
> [It used to be that] the funds were doing well. Interest was doing well. It was a tax write-off for all of the Mormons making money. But of course that turned around and he [friend on the board] was recently telling me that he had to actually report to them (each fund sets a baseline that they should not go below so they can spend anything above that but it has to remain at a certain level to sort of keep self-funding) that some of our funds are approaching that [baseline] point just purely on losses, reduction in contributions and losses.*[518]

Mormons like to advertise their donations to the needy, but calculations based upon the Church's own admissions reveal that the Church spends just a small percentage of its tithing receipts on charitable giving. In January, 2006, a spokesman for Deseret News Publishing, the Church's public relations department said, "Since 1984, the LDS Church has donated nearly $750 million in cash and goods to people in need in more than 150 countries." http://mormonthink.com/tithing.htm. A more recent admission by Chris Redgrave, a KSL (subsidiary of Bonneville Corporation) executive, in the *Deseret Newspaper* reads "City Creek Reserve is spending more than $1 million a day on construction and the project ultimately will cost around $3 billion..."[519] Thus, the amount of charitable donations provided by the Church over more than two decades (from 1984-2006) is just a fraction of the cost of construction for the new downtown mall and residential complex being built and owned by the Church.

In the United Kingdom, where reporting of charitable organization donation is required by law, the actual funds collected from Mormon

Church members to help victims of the December 25, 2004, 9.3 level earthquake-induced Indonesian tsunami, was £761,000, but according to one source, none of it was spent helping the victims. Instead, "the money is sitting in the church bank accounts collecting interest."[520]

Another example of LDS Church indifference to any people but their own members is more recent:

> November 8, 2010, ABC news reports that the Mormon Church denies sanctuary for Haitian non-members. "Floodwaters from Hurricane Tomas, which brushed Haiti's west coast last week, rise to the driveway of the Church of Jesus Christ of Latter-day Saints in Leogane, Haiti. The storm displaced an estimated 1,500 people in the city, but the church offered refuge only to people who were members.[521]

It seems that what started as a pious fraud has now turned into a frenetically maintained business conglomerate which is battening down the hatches, acquiring all the assets possible and gathering its frightened flock in temple fortresses to weather an impending apocalyptic storm. In this ostentatious display of materialism, any similarity to the Church's claimed head, Jesus Christ, has long passed by the wayside.

The LDS Church and Academia—Worlds Apart

Although some historians have questioned his sanity, Sidney Rigdon was one of the first Mormon intellectuals. Though it is debatable whether he had a hand in authoring *the Book of Mormon*, clearly he contributed to important LDS doctrines which post-date publication of the Mormon Book such as the three degrees of glory he witnessed with Smith in a vision and the concept of an LDS priesthood. The theories and thoughts of this founding intellectual were embraced.

Whereas, despite LDS claims to continuing revelation, after the initial doctrine had been codified, major changes to Mormon theology have only been made as a result of external pressures (including Brigham Young's blood atonement doctrine—instigated to maintain Church loyalty) and not really from revelation. The polygamy cessation was only due to pressure from the federal government, and then, only for this life. The

352

change in those men with Negroid ancestry's eligibility for the LDS priesthood was likewise a pragmatic move.

In the late 1860s a group of young men, Mormon converts from Britain known as the Godbeites, started an independent publication known as the *Utah Magazine*, harbinger of the *Salt Lake Tribune*. They challenged Church control over secular matters such as Brigham Young arbitrarily setting low wages for blue collar workers. They protested Young's isolationism in favor of integrating Zion, economically and culturally, with the East. Additionally, they perceived themselves as progressively spiritual, denouncing the LDS canonized scriptures in favor of a more personal, universal spirituality. The thinking of these men affected the secular interests of the Territory, including sowing the seeds of a political party in opposition to the Church, embracing radical concepts of racial and gender equality and integrating Utah with mainstream America.

After Darwin's *Origins of the Species* was published in 1859, Mormons experienced decades of controversy in regard to what extent evolution would be taught in Church schools. Nineteenth century LDS Prophets Young, Taylor, Woodruff and Snow, refused to allow teaching anything about it. Finally, in November 1909, under Joseph F. Smith (1901-1918) the LDS First Presidency issued the statement: "Man is the child of God, formed in the divine image and endowed with divine attributes, and…is capable, by experience through ages and aeons, of evolving into a God."[522] With this pronouncement, the evolution of the species is denied, but the "evolution" of man to God is not.

Then, in 1911 science clashed with academia at BYU in a controversy over organic evolution and biblical criticism. Three University professors who advocated instruction in evolution were interrogated. After a five hour meeting of the Brethren and the accused professors, during which the academics conceded their personal beliefs in evolution, LDS President Grant noted: "We were of a unanimous opinion that it would be unsafe for them to continue teaching at the Brigham Young University." [523] Each professor either resigned under duress or was fired soon thereafter.

In 1918, Ephraim Ericksen, a young LDS intellectual, who had received a Ph.D. in philosophy from the University of Chicago, wrote his dissertation entitled *The Psychological and Ethical Aspects of Mormon Group Life*. [524] Though highly praised in scholarly journals, it was not well received in Utah. He argued that Smith "received his inspiration from the group and in turn reflected its life in such a way as to give it

353

restimulation."[525]

Ericksen appeared torn between satisfying his intellectual curiosity and conforming to the Church hierarchical custom of staid conservatism. According to some who knew the man, Ericksen moved awkwardly on the dance floor, and "couldn't carry a tune in a bucket." [526] Perhaps his lack of musicality is the reason that years later, as a member of the LDS Young Men's and Young Women's recreation committee, Ericksen would lean toward Church conservatism when he commented on jazz music in the publication, "Standards for Social Dancing." There, he characterized jazz as a "'departure from the correct,' making the instruments perform that which is not written, and in a way contrary to their accepted, proper use. This type of playing is rank, 'faking' and should not be tolerated by intelligent people."[527]

Yet Ericksen's intellectual innovation continued toward the creative. In 1933, John A. Widtsoe, one of the Twelve Apostles, commented on a new variety of Church manuals which incorporated social issues and recent scientific and philosophical ideas into Mormonism. He scrapped the journal, diligently prepared for the most part by Dr. Ericksen, and:

> [He] commented on the abundance of material contained in many of the manuals and said that much of it was beyond his comprehension....He further stated that unless we flavor all we do and all we have with the message of the Prophet Joseph Smith we are far afield...*[528]

One former Utahn is unequivocal in his labeling of Mormon Utah as an anti-intellectual culture. In a 1926 issue of the *American Mercury* magazine, Bernard De Voto, a Harvard educated writer and historian of the American West, who had grown up in Ogden, Utah suggests that after Brigham Young died, the polygamy issue had apparently resolved, and once Reed Smoot was seated in the Senate, Utah life became extremely boring. Prior to 1906, animosity between Mormons and gentiles spiced up the otherwise drab life of the "...staid peasants [turned Mormons] whose only distinguishing characteristics were their servility to their leaders and their belief in a low-comedy God." [529] He writes: "Civilized life does not exist in Utah. It never has existed there. It never will exist there."[530] De Voto addressed the Utah Saints' lack of intellectual curiosity in a hilarious, but scathing magazine article:

> I "declare in words of soberness" (to crib the Book of Mormon) that
> these *nouveaux-riches*, these cultured exponents of society, lead the
> most swinish life now discernible in the United States...[and that]
> "...even in Los Angeles you will find expatriated Iowans who can
> read French. Even in Hollywood a movie gal, when arrested, had,
> beside the *Police Gazette*, a volume of Freud. Even in Chicago there
> are a few who rank Mozart, Beethoven and Brahms slightly above
> our Lord Calvin Coolidge. Even in South Boston, Massachusetts,
> you will hear talk of Yeats, of Thackeray, of Shakespeare. Even in
> Richmond disgruntled folk deny that Hoover is greater than Caesar,
> and read the *Dial*, or speak now and then of Gaugin or Osler or
> Huxley. But not in Utah. There people talk only of the Prophet,
> hogs and Fords.*[531]

Almost twenty years later, in a letter published in a 1945 issue of
the *Rocky Mountain Review*, De Voto expressed regret for his severe tone
in the 1926 *American Mercury* article; however, he did not significantly
retract his former opinions. [532]

The anti-intellectualism in the State has not changed much since
De Voto's comments. Even the Church's own educators have criticized its
curriculum. George S. Tanner, who had studied at the University of
Chicago and as of 1964 had spent forty-one years in the Church
Educational System (CES), wrote: "a large majority" of the CES teachers
"are so narrow and ignorant that it is a shame to have them indoctrinating
our young people. I would much rather my sons and daughters go to other
schools in the state than have them led by these religious fanatics."[533] That
same year, Utah State University President, Mormon Daryl Chase,
confided that, "the LDS church has a greater strangle hold on the people
and institutions of the state now than they had in Brigham's time.
Complete academic freedom is actually non-existent."[534]

Access to primary source Mormon historical documents has been
denied even to the Church's own historians. According to former LDS
Church historian, Leonard J. Arrington:

> It is unfortunate for the cause of Mormon history that the Church
> Historian's Library, which is in the possession of virtually all of the

diaries of leading Mormons, has not seen fit to publish these diaries or to permit qualified historians to see them without restriction.[535]

In the 1970s, the Church hired Arrington (official LDS Church historian from 1972-1982) and other scholars to write and publish an extended history of the Church. Dr. Arrington was quoted as revealing that the Church had contracts with sixteen people, each of whom was to research and write a volume. The expected date of publication was 1980. [536] However, because of its true history, as uncovered by these historians, the proposed sixteen volumes would have been devastating to the Church.

This contemplated and boasted about comprehensive history of the Church has yet to be published. Instead, a watered down version, a superficial survey of the Religion, entitled *Encyclopedia of Mormonism,* was published in 1992. [537] University of Utah philosophy professor Sterling McMurrin critiqued the Encyclopedia, noting:

> [T]he work is a carefully sanitized partisan affair that, while having many strengths, is quite uneven in quality and, though it appears to face many difficult issues head on, clearly omits, distorts, and compromises wherever necessary to advance and protect a positive image of Mormons, Mormonism, and the church.[538]

Throughout recent Church history, BYU Professor Hugh Nibley has been the academic to whom Mormon apologists look for explanations, however fantastic, to interpret the anomalies and historical inconsistencies in Mormon historical documents. Nibley passed away in 2005 at the age of ninety-four. He was exposed shortly after his death in the *New York Times* bestseller, *Leaving the Saints* by his daughter Martha Beck, as having been driven crazy to the point of subjecting her to child molestation.[539] She implied that her father's psychological distress was caused, at least in part, by the exposure of Joseph Smith's Egyptian papyri *faux pas* by true academics and his own failure, as the Church-appointed scholar, to reconcile the translation issues. The eccentric Nibley had a reputation among true academics for skimping on primary sources, failing to accurately document his research and fallacious reasoning.

In 1993, six Mormon intellectuals were excommunicated from the

Church for writing about controversial topics. A young convert from Catholicism who had been an active Mormon for about thirty years, Paul Toscano authored several eloquent pleas to Mormon leadership to abandon their suppression of members' dissent and doubt, thereby allowing the LDS community to experience a genuine spirituality. He and his wife Margaret have also written against the strict interpretation of gender roles by contemporary Mormon leadership.[540]

The predictable reaction of the Brethren to intellectual queries was exemplified in a talk by Dallin Oaks in which he directly attacked Mormon intellectuals of the early nineties for their symposium speeches and thought-provoking publications, those like Toscano, who in his discourse pleaded with the Mormon leaders to open their hearts and minds. Oaks criticized Mormon scholars having spoken at all:

> Of course, most of us at times have rebellious thoughts, doubts, temptations, feelings that we know better than our leaders. Most of us, however, resolve these without expounding them in public, stirring up controversy and challenging others' faith, or calling a press conference...[541]

The Mormon educational system, epitomized by Church-funded BYU, is another example of the vacuous in play. Brigham Young, the University's namesake, was illiterate. David O. McKay, LDS President from 1951 through his death in 1970, was the first LDS president/prophet to have graduated college.

In reaction to BYU's students' scores as the lowest in the nation on the GRE, BYU abolished the exam as an entrance requirement.[542] Rhodes Scholar Kenneth Beesley asserted upon returning from Oxford in 1979 that, "the atmosphere on the BYU campus . . . is [by comparison] hostile to . . . informal discussion." Elaborating, he wrote, "In our clearly defined religious hierarchy, where truth comes down from the top, the questioning give-and-take of traditional academic discussion is sometimes seen as rebellious."[543]

BYU Philosophy professor Truman Madsen bluntly explained in a 1979 lecture to students, "Whatever distinction we have accomplished as an institution, it remains in the area of teaching, [as] a kind of undergraduate mill, rather than a productive, creative, research-oriented institution."[544] In 1985, national honor society Phi Beta Kappa rejected

BYU's application for an on-campus chapter due to academic immaturity. [545]

In 1997, the American Association of University Professors refused accreditation to BYU based upon the University's 1992 statement restricting academic freedom in the form of speech which "contradicts or opposes," Church doctrine or policy. Over the past two decades, several BYU professors have been fired when their academic scruples collided with the 1992 LDS Church mandate to present historical facts in the light most favorable to the Church, regardless of truth.

Having been justifiably accused of curtailing intellectual freedom on its campuses, Church schools' academic reputations have all suffered, and that includes the law school. Over the past almost thirty years since my graduation in 1982, J. Reuben Clark Law School has increasingly succumbed to substantial inbreeding, hiring as law professors and law school leaders a large number of BYU law graduates. The law school's tuition is low, it is competitive with regard to admissions' criteria, and still produces a high number of students who obtain high ranking judicial clerkships (no doubt due to the Mormon connection). However, the school's overall prestige and academic reputation among hiring law firms has diminished from the relatively high regard in which early graduating classes had been held.

In contrast, over the last few years, according to recruiters reporting to the *Wall Street Journal,* BYU's Marriott School of Management has ranked first for regional, as opposed to national or international schools. [546] BYU's accounting and engineering programs also do well. It is BYU's social science disciplines that rank far behind the best academic institutions.

BYU admittedly denies employment to those who think outside the Religion:

> In assessing the relative strength of competing candidates, no factor is more important than deep religious faith and loyalty to the Church. We should not hire people who are a threat to the religious faith of our students or a critic of the Church and its leaders. [547]

Threat to the Religion from outside academic sources is perceived by many Mormons. A few years ago, a male relative of mine by marriage spoke to me about his son's (my young cousin's) dilemma in choosing to serve a mission or to continue his education. He commented with a wink that he had instructed his son to go to school and get some education, "but not too much education."

Mormonism as an Orwellian Society

Over time the Church has, in a tale comparable to Orwell's *Animal Farm*, changed the wording of its scriptures and also changed its doctrine to more nearly conform to socio-political changes or scientific discoveries that are at odds with its prior scriptural iterations.

For example, in 1981, the Church made a substantial change to the wording of *the Book of Mormon*. Previous editions of *the Book of Mormon* had described those Lamanites who come to Christ as becoming "white and delightsome." In accordance with its 1978 change in racial policy *vis a vis* LDS priesthood eligibility, from the 1981 publication onward, the word "white," was changed to "pure."[548]

President Kimball had announced the construction of the Sao Paulo, Brazilian LDS Temple in 1975. In the interim period between the announcement and the dedication, LDS leaders realized that most potential converts in Brazil—the Sao Paulo Temple was the first of almost twenty temples eventually built in South American countries—had at least a small percentage of Negroid blood in their ancestry. The Church was presented with a dilemma. Certainly, potential male converts would not flock to a religion where their priesthood rights were limited based on race. Public relations came to the rescue:

> ...not long before the Church president and prophet's decision [conscious or subconscious] to announce a new racial policy based on divine "revelation," several professional consulting firms in which the Church had previously demonstrated confidence suggested to Church leaders that they reconsider the status of blacks in the Mormon Church as part of a major overhaul of Church policy. [549]

Despite the historic and doctrinal racial bigotry of Church founders, *PGP* scripture (*Moses* 7:8) that the Black Race was cursed as descendants of Cain, and the continued outspoken racism of early twentieth century apostles, in 1978, LDS Prophet Kimball had a revelation that lifted the ban from black males receiving the priesthood.

Additionally, the story of *the Book of Mormon* claims that Hebrews voyaged across the Atlantic, multiplied and after generations eventually became the people who are now known as Native Americans. However, DNA evidence discovered, examined and extensively researched over the past several decades has disproved this claim. Studies prove that Native American DNA is similar to Siberian Asian, and not Hebraic, DNA.[550] As a quiet acknowledgment of this new evidence, and without any announcement to its lay membership, the wording in *the Book of Mormon* regarding the ancestry of Native Americans was changed. In the original introduction to *the Book of Mormon* the second paragraph read:

The book was written by many ancient prophets by the spirit of prophecy and revelation. Their words, written on gold plates, were quoted and abridged by a prophet-historian named Mormon. The record gives an account of the two great civilizations. One came from Jerusalem in 600 B.C., and afterward separated into two nations, known as the Nephites and the Lamanites. The other came much earlier when the Lord confounded the tongues at the Tower of Babel. This group is known as the Jaredites. After thousands of years, all were destroyed except the Lamanites, *and they are the principal ancestors* of the American Indians. [Emphasis added].

In the latest edition, the last sentence was changed to read: "... After thousands of years, all were destroyed except the Lamanites, *and they are among the ancestors of the American Indians."* [Emphasis added]. The fact of the change from "they are the principal ancestors," to "they are among the ancestors," was not published; no notice was given to the general LDS Church membership. Furthermore, despite the change, *the Book of Mormon* publisher still lists the newer version as a first edition.

Intent: Knowingly Lying for the Lord and for Profit

Has the Mormon Church hierarchy known all along that Smith's revelations were a product of an imaginative mind? Have they actively concealed damning documents from their members and the public? Or have they avoided any inquiry so as not to find out the truth, despite allegations of Smith's fraud, choosing instead to continue in their ignorant beliefs? In any case, LDS Church leaders have either knowingly or recklessly promulgated and continued to preach the divine origin version of *the Book of Mormon* and the other scriptures in the standard works, in order to convince members and potential members of the divinity of the Church. The suppression and re-writing of accurate Mormon history continues in the Church, has come to be known colloquially as 'giving milk before meat,' and more pejoratively, 'Lying for the Lord,' and seems to be an accepted practice even among contemporary Mormon leaders.[551]

Mormon employees are taught to lie for the Church. One Church employee explains, "The church wants to portray this image of being unified in all it does...It wants Mormons to be unquestioning...I worked in public affairs for the church for 13 years, and I had to lie all the time, and this has really battered my faith."[552]

Another individual who attests to this habit is Ken Clark, who was a full time employee of the LDS Church Education System (CES). He worked as an LDS Seminary principal/teacher, Institute Director and Stake CES coordinator for 27 years, from 1975-2002. Based upon his extensive experience he came to conclude that:

> ...a pattern of institutionalized deception had been established by Joseph Smith. Subsequent church leaders, including those who serve currently, followed Smith's example of lying to protect the church. The growing evidence pointed to a standard practice.*[553]

In the nineteenth century, Brigham Young publicly bragged about the high quality of Mormon liars:

> I have many a time, in this stand, dared the world to produce as mean devils as we can; we can beat them at anything. *We have the greatest and smoothest liars in the world,* the cunningest and most adroit thieves, and any other shade of character that you can mention....I can produce Elders here who can shave their smartest shavers, and take their money from them. We can beat the world at any game.*[554]

Lying for the Lord is used to protect the image of the Church and/or its leaders. This practice is similar to the Shiite Muslim practice of 'Taqiyya,' (lying to protect Allah or another member of the church) in Islam.

There are many parallels between Mormonism and Islam, including Mohammed's background and mindset, polygamy, mosques and temples as religious houses of worship, dress codes, religious ethnocentrism, theocratic governments, extreme patriarchy and even death to apostates.[555] Both religions appropriated heavily from Judaic and Christian theology, both contain holy scriptures that include the resolution of provincial disputes which are then extrapolated and employed as God's word to be applied in all instances. Both religions claim to be God's final word to mankind. Even their respective oasis cultures amidst vast deserts are geographically similar to one another.

Prominent members of these two faiths have acknowledged the similarities in their religions' respective histories of persecution and isolation, if not theology. Joseph Smith admittedly compared the importance of his church to Islam.[556] According to the *LA Times*, "... Haitham Bundakji, former chairman of the Orange County, California, Islamic Society, states: 'When I go to a Mormon church I feel at ease. When I heard the president [of the LDS Church] speak a few years ago, if I'd closed my eyes I'd have thought he was an imam.' Back at you, says LDS member Steve Young: 'A Mormon living in an Islamic society would be very comfortable.'"[557]

Smith's multiple affairs with young girls and others men's wives whom he ordered to engage in sexual intimacy with him under threat of God's disapproval are well documented. Given the deceptive character of Mormonism's founder, it is no surprise that the practice of lying for the Lord is accepted. Smith's practice of polygamy was denied for years before he mentioned it privately to trusted insiders and then it was denied to the general membership for years after his death. Finally, Orson Pratt pronounced the practice as the euphemistically-characterized 'celestial marriage,' to the body of the Church on Sunday, August 29, 1852.

Of course, the lying isn't admitted. This head-in-the-sand reaction from Church leaders continues, even more so to this day. Many of the more educated Church leaders, especially those with legal training, know what they are doing, or not doing. Other LDS leaders likely don't read, and don't want to read. For example, statements made by the deceased Prophet Gordon B. Hinckley in national magazine and newspaper interviews depict the disingenuousness of LDS leaders.

362

Q: There are some significant differences in your beliefs. For instance, don't Mormons believe that God was once a man?

A: I wouldn't say that. There was a little couplet coined, 'As man is, God once was. As God is, man may become.' Now that's more of a couplet than anything else. That gets into some pretty deep theology that we don't know very much about.*[558]

Question: Is this the teaching of the church today, that God the Father was once a man like we are?

Hinckley: I don't know that we teach it. I don't know that we emphasize it. I haven't heard it discussed for a long time in public discourse. I don't know. I don't know all the circumstances under which that statement was made. I understand the philosophical background behind it. But I don't know a lot about it and I don't know that others know a lot about it.*[559]

With these comments, Hinckley appears to have been truly ignorant of historical LDS doctrine that teaches Mormons they are gods in embryo. Yet Joseph Smith preached in April, 1844, General Conference: "I am going to tell you how God came to be God. We have imagined and supposed that God was God from all eternity. I will refute that idea, and take away the veil, so that you may see... he was once a man like us..."[560] This startling new concept has come to be known as the King Follet Discourse, named after an elder, King Follet, who had passed away just weeks before the Conference.

This doctrine is still preached in the LDS Church today and Hinckley knew it. Every young male seminary student knows that godhood is within his reach, if he remains obedient and faithful. The principle, coined by Apostle Lorenzo Snow, is [that] "Man is as God [once] was; God is as man may become," and is taught to all young priesthood-holders, as published in the Sunday school manual for 1997, *the same year Hinckley gave the interviews to the media.*[561] The doctrine that God was once a man and has progressed to become a God is unique to Mormonism. Addressing a general conference priesthood meeting, one recent LDS prophet, Spencer W. Kimball, declared in 1975:

Brethren 225,000 of you are here tonight. I suppose 225,000 of you may become gods. There seems to be plenty of space out there in the universe. And the Lord has proved that he knows how to do it. I think he could make, or probably have us help make, worlds for all of us, for every one of us 225,000.*[562]

Throughout his tenure as LDS President, Gordon Hinckley has been portrayed as a sweet old man. The Mormon gerontocracy is a good cover for this continued deception under the guise of forgetfulness or even dementia. Their pronouncements are rarely questioned. After all, as Elder Oaks said, "It's wrong to criticize leaders of the Church, even if the criticism is true."[563]

Most likely Hinckley's portrayed ignorance of basic Mormon doctrine was an act; after all, he had a degree in communications and worked in the Church Public Affairs Committee which, according to former University of Utah Professor, Ed Firmage, is "a euphemism for the 'church-state committee.'"[564]

Public relations professional Hinckley also lied about the LDS Church's relationship to polygamists and polygamy when he told CNN's Larry King with regard to Utah Polygamists: "They have no connection with us whatever." And with regard to polygamy: "I condemn it, yes, as a practice, because I think it is not doctrinal. It is not legal."[565] Yet all Mormon polygamist fundamentalist religions are based upon Joseph Smith's teachings and mainstream Mormonism still has polygamy (codified in *D&C* §132) as a necessary part of its celestial order.

This lying is not just a practice used by the Brethren, but is taught to young Mormon students. One Church leader, a BYU professor speaking to a college-age group of potential missionaries, teaches them to evade direct questions about troubling Church doctrines or history:

Whenever a person asks me an antagonistic question, I never answer that question, but rather I answer the question they should have asked. ...For example...if a person out of the blue that I don't know from Adam walks up to me and says, "So you're a Latter-day Saint, Huh?" [They] tell me you folks believe that man can become like God, huh?

So how do I respond? This is a total stranger; I don't know what he knows about the Church. It may not be the smartest thing in the world to say, "Well, yes, let me quote the Lorenzo Snow couplet for you and then I'm going to get the teachings of the prophet I'm going to read to you the King Follett discourse." That may not be our best approach. It may be a much wiser approach to say, well that's an interesting question, it is asked frequently. But you know let me begin this way, in the spring of 1820, there was a young man, named Joseph Smith Jr. who was concerned about the subject of religion and wanted to know which church to join....

What did I just do? I just answered the question he should have asked. Now what's the question he should have asked? How do I know that what you have to say is true, or what should I know to investigate your message properly? How should we begin our study of Mormonism? That would have been the right question you see, so what I'm going to do is I'm going to answer the question they should have asked.

Now let me say it another way...The issue isn't Adam-God, the issue isn't Mountain Meadows Massacre, the issue isn't plural marriage, the issue facing the religious world today is was Joseph Smith called of God. And that's the single most important issue to determine...*[566]

This professor goes on to cite an occasion with LDS Apostle Boyd K. Packer who always seemed to come out of a conversation with those averse to Mormonism "smelling like a rose." Here is the principle: "We never provide meat when milk will do." Thus, obfuscation is what the leaders are teaching the young Mormons to use.

Lying by omission is perhaps the biggest fault of Mormon leaders because so much of the Church's undisputed history is left out of the story relayed to the potential convert and taught to the youth of the Church. Church leaders seem comfortable with their omissions. For example, in a 1993 speech to BYU law school students, Dallin Oaks justifies withholding information where there is no duty to speak and contrasts such a withholding with an affirmative misrepresentation. The former is arguably ethical, not so the latter.

His tone seems to have a hidden meaning. While the speech ostensibly addresses issues young lawyers may encounter, it reads as if Oaks is making excuses to thinking Mormons as to why the Church is not forthcoming with its true history:

The difficult question is whether we are morally responsible to tell the whole truth. When we have a duty to disclose, we are morally responsible to do so. Where there is no duty to disclose, we have two alternatives. We may be free to disclose if we choose to do so, but there will be circumstances where commandments, covenants, or professional obligations require us to remain silent.

In short, my brothers and sisters, the subject of lying is clear-cut in a majority of instances. But there are a lot of situations where people are sometimes charged with lying where the charge is not well founded. You will read that kind of charge in the literature and in current commentary, as if a person were under a duty to tell everything he or she knew, irrespective of any other duties or obligations....It requires sophisticated analysis of the circumstances and a finely tuned conscience to distinguish between the situation where you are obliged by duty to speak and the situation where you are obliged by duty, commandment, or covenant to remain silent.[567]

Oaks sanctions censorship when done to protect the Church.

My duty as a member of the Council of the Twelve is to protect what is most unique about the LDS church, namely the authority of priesthood, testimony regarding the restoration of the gospel, and the divine mission of the Savior. *Everything may be sacrificed in order to maintain the integrity of those essential facts. Thus, if Mormon Enigma reveals information that is detrimental to the reputation of Joseph Smith, then it is necessary to try to limit its influence and that of its authors.* [568]

Then Oaks continues, and claims that the Brethren forbid lying.

... [I] suppose most mortals employ some exaggeration and a little of what someone called "innocent after-mindedness." But does this mean we condone deliberate and important misrepresentations of fact in a circumstance in which they are clearly intended to be believed and relied upon? Never! Lying is sinful, as it has always been, and there is no exempt category for so-called "lying for the Lord." Lying is simply outside the range of permitted or condoned conduct by Latter-day Saints-members or leaders." [569]

The Brethren as Fiduciaries

In my youth and naïveté, before I had any understanding of the meaning of the word, I had mistakenly assumed that the LDS Church leaders were my fiduciaries, that they had my best interests at heart. I believed that they innately complied with the recognized duties of a fiduciary under the law: good faith, loyalty and most importantly, with regard to the issues being discussed in this...*Case against Mormonism,* full disclosure toward Church members.[570]   Certainly this is the feeling any born-in-the-church child will develop as s/he sits week after week listening to Church leaders and especially as s/he hears the soothing voices of the speakers at the biannual general conferences, and then afterward, when parents extol those leaders who have just spoken.

The Church leaders present and foster a belief in themselves as counselors and keepers of their flock's spiritual health. If any relationship could be characterized as fiducial, surely that of Mormon Church leader toward faithful follower would be it. And yet, over a century and a half ago, Brigham Young's nineteenth wife Ann Eliza, described and distinguished two classes of Mormons, the leaders from the followers, in this way:

Mind you, I am not upholding the Mormon faith; I consider it the falsest, most hypocritical, and most cruel belief under the sun. Although its founder arrogated to it the title of "church of Jesus Christ" there is nothing Christ like in its teachings or in its practice. Its leaders always have been and still are, supremely selfish, caring only for their personal aggrandizement, disloyal to the government under which they live, treacherous to their friends, revengeful to their foes; insincere, believing nothing which they teach, and tyrannical and grasping in the extreme, taking everything that their lustful eyes may desire, and greedy, grasping hands can clutch, no matter at whose expense it maybe taken, or what suffering the appropriation may cause. But the people themselves have no part in the treachery, revengefulness, hypocrisy, or cupidity of their leaders, and should be judged from an entirely different standpoint.[571]

Importantly, in the *Franco* clergy malpractice case (discussed at the beginning of Chapter 8) the Utah Supreme Court did not specifically address whether a fiduciary relationship existed between the bishop who allegedly failed to properly refer the sexually abused young girl in his ward to a qualified therapist. The Court narrowly drew its holding, denying claims of clergy malpractice and the other claims because such claims were "merely an elliptical way of alleging clergy malpractice." Indeed, all claims, including negligence, intentional infliction of emotional distress and breach of fiduciary duty in *Franco* were based on the same set of facts, that the lay bishop, acting as agent for the LDS Church, failed to report the child victim's claims of sexual abuse and improperly referred her to an unqualified counselor.

Thus, civil tort claims against clerics which require a review and interpretation of church law, polices or practices, i.e., that require the determination of a 'standard of care,' for such advisors, are barred by the First Amendment under the establishment doctrine. Quoting a U.S. Supreme Court case, the Utah Supreme Court in *Franco* reasoned that "… churches must have 'power to decide for themselves, free from state interference, matters of church government as well as those of faith and doctrine.'"[572]

However, even under *Franco*, arguably the establishment doctrine does not bar claims which do not involve a determination of church faith or doctrine. A claim against the LDS Church based upon the long-standing misrepresentation of the facts surrounding its scriptural origins would seem to be one such claim.

In 2001 the Utah Supreme Court expanded the duty of disclosure beyond that required of a fiduciary. In *Mitchell v. Christensen* , 2001 UT 80, 31 P.3d 572 (Utah 2001), decided the same year but a few months after the *Franco* case, the Court held that sellers were required to disclose a latent swimming pool defect to the prospective buyers, who had found no problem with the pool, despite inspection.[573] The Utah Court referenced the elements set forth in its 1990 decision establishing fraudulent disclosure: "In order to prevail on a claim of fraudulent concealment, a plaintiff must prove "(1) that the nondisclosed information is material, (2) that the nondisclosed information is known to the party failing to disclose, and (3) that there is a legal duty to communicate."[574] The Court found that the buyers had acted reasonably and despite their actions did not find the leak. Importantly, in this case there was no fiduciary duty which required disclosure, yet the Court found the sellers had a duty to disclose the pool defect.

The *Mitchell* reasoning was restated in a 2006 construction defect case involving expansive soils.[575] In *Yazd v. Woodside Homes,* 2006 UT 47, 143 P.3d 283 (Utah 2006) the Utah Supreme Court reasoned that "legal duty...is the product of policy judgments applied to relationships."[576]

If one looks at the factors to be considered in determining whether it is good public policy to assign a fiduciary duty to church leaders, as set forth in the *Yazd* opinion below, those factors are almost all present in a church leader-follower relationship:

[A]ge, knowledge, influence, bargaining power, sophistication, and cognitive ability are but the more important among a multitude of life circumstances that the court may consider in analyzing whether a legal duty is owed by one party to another. Where a disparity in one or more of these circumstances distort the balance between the parties in a relationship to the degree that one party is exposed to unreasonable risk, the law may intervene by creating a duty on the advantaged party to conduct itself in a manner that does not reward exploitation of its advantage.[577]

This much can be said. It is undisputed that for centuries Mormon-born members, as well as converts to the Church, have reasonably relied on LDS Church leaders' misrepresentations and omissions. For most of Church history, any information regarding the facts surrounding the true origins of its scriptures was suppressed, especially in the then, geographically remote State of Utah. Converts joined the LDS Church because they were told and came to believe that *the Book of Mormon* is a true and correct translation from ancient records inscribed on golden plates accomplished by the power of God, through his prophet, Joseph Smith.

These representations of the divinity of Mormon scripture are made in order to enlist people to join the LDS Church and to convince those who are born into it, to remain members. Both life-long and potential members alike remain in the Church or are baptized into

369

membership after reasonably relying on the written propaganda and verbal representations made in bi-annual, world televised LDS General Conference talks, as well as in periodicals and other publications. The message is promulgated weekly in Church meetings, and in speeches at special seminars and firesides directed especially toward the youth. No mention is made of seer stones, scrying, absurdly 'translated' Egyptian papyri contained within scripture, or the historic, extensive and abusive system of polygamy in the published and distributed, the propagandized form of the histories of the Church or the Sunday school student manuals about the revered Church leaders.

Most Church members remain ignorant of LDS scriptures' true origins. This ignorance is due to the Brethren's enduring censorship of the truth about Mormon origins, as well as preaching to Church members to avoid reading anything that does not support Church doctrine. Even more recently Mormons have been told to avoid teaching anything not approved by the Church Correlation Committee, a group specifically formed to correlate materials "...by the Brethren to ensure purity of doctrine, simplicity of materials, and control by the priesthood."[578] In this way, the Church has exploited its advantage to the risk of its members by both distorting and omitting truths and then commanding its members not to read beyond what is provided to them.

Name Removal Requests by Church Members are on the Rise

Conversion rates have dropped since 1997 largely because of internet exposure of the truth of Church origins.[579] This fact is not widely publicized. As the former employee at Church Headquarters who I interviewed said, "Church authorities don't like to keep numbers."[580]

Over the last several years, local Church wards have merged and so have some mission boundaries. Many western European missions have closed. A review of the list of LDS missions in operation today show that most foreign missions are in Mexico and Central and South America, with relatively few located in the more highly-educated countries of Western Europe.[581] An acquaintance of mine who had emigrated many years ago from Brazil to a small town in Northern Utah, told me that many of his compatriots joined the Church to obtain visas to the United States and/or financial assistance through Church welfare programs. Once they had immigrated to the States, they almost always became inactive. According to this man, few of these Brazilian converts actually believed in Mormon doctrine.

Richard Packham, a retired attorney and professor who left the LDS Church decades ago, cites statistics acquired through connections at the Church Office Building showing the increase of voluntary resignations from the Church. According to Mr. Packham's anonymous LDS employee source, the staff at the office which processes name removal requests has grown. As of 2001, "[it] has had to be increased from five to seven, and will likely soon increase to ten."

Here are the numbers of removal requests:

1995..35,420
1996:...50,177
1997:...55,200
1998:...78,750
1999:...81,200
2000:.......... 87,500

The informant, "...also provided this interesting information:"

Official membership increased from 10,752,986 to 11,068,861 during 2000. This consists of 273,973 convert baptisms and 81,450 increase in children of record. The loss of 39,548 is due primarily to deaths, and various adjustments. The First Presidency is aware of the problem of the "name removed file," growing to hundreds of thousands of names, all still included in the 11 million. *It appears that they are reluctant to change the policy, and therefore they still count those people as part of the total membership.* [Emphasis added].

Another source, which reported figures to a John L. Smith in late 2003, said his source was "someone inside the church." Packham notes that the years 1995 through 2000 are identical to the above numbers and that, "If these numbers are reliable, then the number of Mormons requesting name removal has TRIPLED in seven years...

```
1995:.................................................................35,420
1996:.................................................................50,177
1997:.................................................................55,200
1998:.................................................................78,750
1999:.................................................................81,200
2000:.................................................................87,500
2001:...............................................................101,454
2002:...............................................................105,763"[582]
```

Mormon apologists (some Church employees, some just members) are aware of the adverse effect Web-accessed facts have had on Church growth. Plans have been implemented by Mormons to counter the anti-Mormon websites by manipulating search engines, installing bogus instant messaging posts and flooding the internet with pro-Mormon pop-up advertisements. Consider this 2006 comment:

A missionary in England reported his "golden" contact excitedly consulting the Internet about Mormons after the first discussion. The investigator found a mountain of anti-Mormon material and immediately cancelled all future appointments with the missionaries...The LDS Church tracks about 6,500 anti-LDS Web sites in the English language, whose content dominates search results. Thousands more dominate search engine positions in other languages. Potential converts are abandoning the missionaries once they consult the Internet for more information. Only vast quantities of positive material, correctly optimized, can resolve this problem. We cannot drive the enemies of the Church off the Internet, but we can displace their prominent positions. The Latter-day Foundation for the Arts, Education and Humanity ...has become actively involved with Internet missionary initiatives to (1) drive down Church enemies from prominent search engine positions and (2) teach the gospel of Jesus Christ via the Internet. Our initiative is called "Flooding the Internet with Truth."[583]

And the misrepresentations continue, even to very young children. At http://www.deseretbook.com, the Church-owned book store, a 500 piece golden plate puzzle is for sale. A Moroni action figure burying the gold plates is also offered for sale to the parents of toddlers and is described as:

Chapter 11: The Continuing Fraud

Made of durable vinyl and safety tested for ages 4 and up

Moroni was the last of the valiant Nephite prophets and eyewitness to their total destruction. He wandered across the Americas, keeping the records safe while hiding from the Lamanites. He finished the sacred history, adding his heartfelt final farewell. The Book of Mormon tells how he hid the golden plates in the earth at Hill Cumorah. They remained safe until Moroni, as a heavenly messenger, returned in 1827 and delivered the sacred records to the Prophet Joseph Smith.[584]

Another, similar action figure called "Joseph receives the Plates from Angel Moroni," is currently for sale, recommended for ages 4 and up at the Deseret Bookstore across the street from the Salt Lake Temple in the new area of construction for the Church retail/residential mall. It is hard plastic, made in China by Latter-day Designs, © 2007, and sells for $6.98, and has no movable parts.

"Joseph receives the Plates from Angel Moroni," toy sold by Deseret Bookstore, 2010

Confirmation Bias and the LDS Investment Quotient

At the LDS General Conference of April 2009 it was announced that Brent H. Nielson would be named a new member of the Council of the Seventies. Since I don't ordinarily watch conference, the first I knew of this appointment was when I was leafing through a friend's copy of the *Ensign*. Brent's photograph was presented along with the one-hundred plus other older men, the governing hierarchy of the Church. The portrait photos are side by side, presented in a centerfold. There are one hundred and fifteen portraits of Mormon Church leaders, all male, all suited up, all with the same sanguine look on their faces.

Brent and I had dated during our freshman year when we were both just nineteen and again, briefly at age twenty-one when he had returned from his mission in Finland and wanted to marry me. Brent hadn't changed much. He still had that eager smile. I remembered that he married a girl who was the daughter of a member of the Seventies, William R. Bradford (emeritus).

I recalled the dynastical Church surnames: Smith, McConkie, Grant, Kimball, and also remembered Brent telling me that his mother was a cousin to the (now deceased) LDS Apostle David B. Haight. I thought about the fact that there have been three different LDS presidents, all named Joseph Smith and all related to the founding prophet. During Joseph F. Smith's reign he appointed several of his relatives: brother, cousin, sons, to high ranking positions and I realized that Mormon general authority status was based, at least in part, on nepotism.[585]

On Sunday, October 2009, LDS General Conference aired. I watched; there were a few surprises. Mom phoned and sounded excited.

"Turn on conference," she said. "Brent Nielson is speaking."

I had set the television DVR to record, to get a feel on how the Church was responding to the onslaught of criticism on the web. Brent took the stand. On television he looked shockingly old, but then I hadn't seen him for more than thirty years and was sure he'd say the same about me. His hair was still thick, but lightly streaked with grey and his posture stooped. Though his voice was still recognizable, even from the other room, it had assumed that Church tone, that father-knows-best paternalistic tone of all Mormon leaders. Sometimes I think it's that tone more than anything that infuriates thinking Mormon women.

Brent talked about his mission to Finland, and that then, in the mid-seventies, the young missionaries had prayed to be able to proselytize in the Soviet Union. Now, his son Eric was on a mission to Russia and visited the same town Brent had been unable to visit on his mission. Elder Nielson was choked with emotion at the retelling of the coincidence.

Chapter 11: The Continuing Fraud

After listening to Brent, I rewound the recorded session and paused the DVR when I saw the look on Apostle Jeffery Holland's face. It was sheer panic. I could see the expression of horror even during the rewind. I cued the recorder to his speech and listened. He was angry, angry that his church was being attacked. Holland spoke of Joseph and Hyrum's martyrdom at Carthage Jail:

> ...[As] one of a thousand elements of my own testimony of the divinity of The Book of Mormon, I submit this as yet one more evidence of its truthfulness. In this their greatest—and last—hour of need, I ask you: would these men blaspheme before God by continuing to fix their lives, their honor, and their own search for eternal salvation on a book (and by implication a church and a ministry) they had fictitiously created out of whole cloth?
>
> Never mind that their wives are about to be widows and their children fatherless. Never mind that their little band of followers will yet be "houseless, friendless and homeless" and that their children will leave footprints of blood across frozen rivers and an untamed prairie floor. Never mind that legions will die and other legions live declaring in the four quarters of this earth that they know the Book of Mormon and the Church which espouses it to be true. Disregard all of that, and tell me whether in this hour of death these two men would enter the presence of their Eternal Judge quoting from and finding solace in a book which, if not the very word of God, would brand them as imposters and charlatans until the end of time? They would not do that! They were willing to die rather than deny the divine origin and the eternal truthfulness of the Book of Mormon.
>
> For 179 years this book has been examined and attacked, denied and deconstructed, targeted and torn apart like perhaps no other book in modern religious history—perhaps like no other book in any religious history. And still it stands. Failed theories about its origins have been born and parroted and have died—from Ethan Smith to Solomon Spalding to deranged paranoid to cunning genius. None of these frankly pathetic answers for this book has ever withstood examination because there is no other answer than the one Joseph gave as its young unlearned translator. In this I stand with my own great-grandfather, who said simply enough, "No wicked man could write such a book as this; and no good man would write it, unless it were true and he were

375

commanded of God to do so."

I testify that one cannot come to full faith in this latter-day work—and thereby find the fullest measure of peace and comfort in these, our times—until he or she embraces the divinity of the Book of Mormon and the Lord Jesus Christ, of whom it testifies. If anyone is foolish enough or misled enough to reject 531 pages of a heretofore unknown text teeming with literary and Semitic complexity without honestly attempting to account for the origin of those pages—especially without accounting for their powerful witness of Jesus Christ and the profound spiritual impact that witness has had on what is now tens of millions of readers—if that is the case, then such a person, elect or otherwise, has been deceived; and if he or she leaves this Church, it must be done by crawling over or under or around the Book of Mormon to make that exit. In that sense the book is what Christ Himself was said to be: "a stone of stumbling, . . . a rock of offence," a barrier in the path of one who wishes not to believe in this work. Witnesses, even witnesses who were for a time hostile to Joseph testified to their death that they had seen an angel and had handled the plates. "They have been shown unto us by the power of God, and not of man," they declared. "Wherefore we know of a surety that the work is true."*586

Holland's entire speech is an appeal to emotion as opposed to the use of any reasoning. He uses a common *ad hominem* attack when he compares apostates to snakes. He characterizes those who do not accept *the Book of Mormon* as the Word of God as something low and slithering, like the serpent-as-Satan character in the staged LDS Temple Ceremony's Garden of Eden. The *ad hominem* attack was also a favorite of deceased Church Apostle, Neal Maxwell, who compared critics of the Church to 'junk yard dogs.'

Holland's appeal to authority, his own and his great-grandfather's is clearly illogical. His implication that the Smith brothers could have avoided assassination had they denounced *the Book of Mormon* even while incarcerated is a prototypical *non-sequitur;* there is no evidence that their lives would have been saved had they in fact denied its claimed divine origins while imprisoned.

But the tenor of Holland's speech was different from any LDS Conference speech I had ever heard. Finally, a representative of the LDS Church was openly attempting to defend it against the attacks on its origins. For years Mormon leaders had kept silent, at least in public, but Holland was furious.

A dramatic change had occurred. For the first time in decades, or maybe longer, an LDS general authority publicly acknowledged, with fear and hostility in his voice, the attacks on Mormonism's origins. Freud might argue that this public denial of any validity to evidence questioning the divine origins of *the Book of Mormon* admits the first in a list of typical, sequential defense mechanisms: denial. LDS Leaders are grieving over the death of their Religion, and must travel through the Kübler-Ross' stages of grief: denial, anger, bargaining, depression and acceptance. For Church leaders it is much too discomforting to entertain the possibility that the scripture they have been taught to accept as more important than the Holy Bible could be Joseph Smith's fiction. Thus, even incontrovertible evidence questioning the divinity of *the Book of Mormon* is irrationally denied.

To members of the LDS Church, the golden plate story is a previously tightly-held belief which is rapidly coming apart under close analysis. Mormonism's historic and pervasive (within the Religion) social construction of reality is in the process of being deconstructed. Mormon relativism has reached a dead-end. It must step aside for the absolute truth of undeniable facts.

CHAPTER TWELVE: Fallout from Fraud— Irreparable Harm

"My atheism, like that of Spinoza, is true piety toward the universe and denies only gods fashioned by men in their own image to be servants of their human interests."—George Santayana

As I listened to April, 2010 Conference, I hoped that the Church would abandon its false self. Since it was held near Easter, the focus would be (as it should) on the resurrection and atonement of Jesus Christ. I wasn't surprised then, that the emotional appeal made by Elder Holland during general conference the previous October was not addressed. No mention was made by any of the speakers of the attacks on Mormonism's foundation, including the overwhelming evidence disproving the authenticity of *the Book of Mormon*. Instead, in its place, the Brethren reinforced the historic claim that *the Book of Mormon* is the most correct scripture on Earth, to be read daily, talked about, prayed about and testified of. Parents were even instructed to read it to their infants as a soothing, unintelligible catechism of sorts.[587]

Later that year, in October General Conference, one LDS general authority repeated President Ezra Taft Benson's fourteen fundamentals regarding the LDS Prophet. This talk was originally preached in 1980.

1. The [LDS] prophet is the only man who speaks for the Lord in everything.
2. The living prophet is more vital to us than the Standard Works.
3. The living prophet is more important to us than a dead prophet.
4. The prophet will never lead the Church astray.
5. The prophet is not required to have any particular earthly training or diplomas to speak on any subject or act on any matter at any time.
6. The prophet does not have to say "Thus saith the Lord" to give us scripture.
7. The prophet tells us what we need to know, not always what we want to know.
8. The Prophet is not limited by men's reasoning.
9. The prophet can receive revelation on any matter—temporal or spiritual.

379

10. The prophet may well advise on civic matters.

11. The two groups who have the greatest difficulty in following the prophet are the proud who are learned and the proud who are rich.

12. The prophet will not necessarily be popular with the world or the worldly.

13. The prophet and his counselors make up the First Presidency—the highest quorum in the Church.

14. The prophet and the presidency—the living prophet and the First Presidency—follow them and be blessed—reject them and suffer.[588]

Emerson said, "…every great institution is the lengthened shadow of a single man. His character determines the character of the organization." Mormonism has incorporated the narcissism, duplicity and misogyny of Smith and Young into one huge beehive of tedious and feckless activity. Mormonism is worse than the worst fast food franchise: bland, ubiquitous and if consumed regularly, harmful to good health.

By its own claim, Mormonism is the one and only true church, superior to all others. Because it has cornered the truth, its people are more righteous, more in tune with God and morally superior to all others. The psychopathological component of such a belief can be seen in the superficial society within which Mormons interact: s/he is compulsively organized, manipulative, charmingly gracious, but hiding the real personality beneath a glaze of superficiality. With 'smiles and hugs,' all seems well. In truth, each member of the organization is focused on self and family, obsessed with the marathon race to the Celestial Kingdom.

Concern for charitable giving outside the Faith is a far second to perfect meeting attendance, number of children on missions and who are married in the temple or the building of formulaic chapels and gauche temples. All of these efforts are in tribute to their God, who, in this fraternity, has promised to ensure each zealous priesthood-holder and his progeny a similar path to godhood and ultimately, shared divinity.

In many ways, the Church is no different than any other large corporation, complete with a public relations department. In 1971, the Church retained the services of Cresup, McCormick and Paget, one of the country's largest management consulting firms.[589] The following year the Church created its own public relations department.

Almost a century ago, the Austrian born American father of public relations, Edward Bernays, put it aptly when he wrote: "If we understand the mechanism and motives of the group mind, it is now possible to control and regiment the masses according to our will without them knowing it." Mormonism from its very inception is a good example of propaganda in practice. As economist Frank Knight acknowledged, a theocracy is more effective than a purely secular autocracy because in the former style of government, "the victims may not feel coerced at all." [590]

Mass mind control of the common Mormon has had a good run. For years the controllers and the deceivers have benefited from their plan. However, for those who remain ignorant of the hierarchal imposition of their predetermined life course, their historic and present reality has been, and continues to be, quite different. With the possible exception of the Brethren who live off the largesse of the Church, the damage to the average Mormon, those who have lived lives dedicated to the Religion, is worse than to those who have abandoned it and much worse than to those who have never joined.

One former Mormon expressed his strong feelings about Joseph Smith this way:

Dear Joseph Smith - I Hate You.

I HATE you.

And you are the only person I hate.

I have given this a lot of thought for many years, and have decided there is no escaping it. Gordon Hinckley told his church membership hundreds of times that he LOVED you, and that he could not wait to meet you and throw his arms around you. My feeling is quite different.

If I ever see you, in any context, I will harm you in any way I can…

I hate you for justifying your sex addiction as if it was the word of God

I hate you because you lied over and over again about the source of the Book of Mormon, which you wrote in order to control weak minded people.

I hate you because you created a religion that worships you and no one else.

I hate you because you excommunicated anyone who challenged your authority.

I hate you because you pretended to love democracy while establishing tyrrany.

I hate you because my mother has contracted many psychological illnesses attempting to cope with the bullshit expectations you said she had to live up to.

381

I hate you because you want people to give money to your church instead
of the poor.
I hate you because you are arrogant, self-righteous, and self-serving, and
instead of recognizing these as shortcomings, you claim they are because
you are god's special boy.
I hate you because you incorporated disgusting death oaths and symbols
into what was supposed to be my wedding.
And most of all, I hate you because your very memory threatens to rob me
of my closest friendships, and even my dear wife.
I would not presume to call you anti-Christ, evil, or anything but a man
who was massively fucked up. God may love you. Gordon Hinckley and
Thomas Monson may have wet dreams about you. But I hate you. I
fucking hate everything I have ever learned about you. If I ever see you, I
will pay you back for the burdens you have inflicted on those I love.
And no cry of "Lord my God" will save you.* [591]

Widespread Psycho-Social Problems among Utah Mormons

Latter-day Saint deceptions used in defense of the Religion lead to
psychological problems for Mormons. Utah has historically been the most
depressed state in the nation. Historian Michael Quinn documented the
first suicide of a full-time LDS missionary who shot himself as he was
returning to Utah on February 20, 1902. [592] Utah has the highest rate of
any state for depression and psychotropic drug use.[593] One pharmaceutical
company found that Utahns were prescribed antidepressants at the rate of
twice the national average. The article went on to report, "The reason for
Utah's mass depression, however, is unknown"[594]

The reason, is, in fact known, but not forthrightly expressed. Utah
Mormons are angry at their top-down ordered life, but since they have
been told Mormonism is God's one and only way to salvation and
exhalation, they remain steadfast and their anger turns inward, into deep
depression.

Mormon men are affected as well as the women. Though one
study drew an inverse correlation between the religious devotion of Utah
men and suicide (no doubt these numbers include many zealous gods-in-
embryo):

For more than 10 years, 15 to 34-year-old males in Utah have had suicide rates markedly higher than those seen nationally. In fact, in the early to mid-1990s, suicide was the number one cause of death among 25 to 44-year-old men in the State and the second-leading cause of death among [Utah] men aged 15 to 24.[595]

Above average incidents of per capita rape and a high rate of internet pornography use are also troubling.[596] Recently Utah ranked tenth in the nation for the number of child abuse cases, yet, as of 2008, it ranked 34th in population, with less than three million residents.[597]

The Church keeps their young people ignorant. Survey results from 2005 show that Utah has the lowest per pupil expenditure ($4,995 vs. $8,482 national average) and the highest pupil-teacher ratio in the nation.[598]

From 2001-2003 Utah had the highest bankruptcy rate of any state in the nation, double that of the national average; and it is usually in the top seven nationally.[599] Utah men and women are vastly underpaid.

Bureau of Labor Statistics reports that [the] average annual pay in Utah is 82% of the national average and it has been declining relative to the nation for 20 years. Furthermore, Utah has one of the largest gender wage gaps in the nation, with women earning 70.3% of male wages as opposed to 76.2% nationally. To illustrate this, in 2002, median female earnings in Utah were $24,872 as compared to $36, 925 for men for full-time, year round workers.[600]

The divorce rate for Utahns in 2004, like the marriage rate, was above the national average, as has historically been the case.[601] Happy LDS families are more myth than reality. According to a 2007 United Way assessment, "Based upon student response to a number of questions regarding their families, in 2005 about 40% of middle and high school students in Utah were living in a family with a high level of conflict."[602]

In *BYU: a House of Faith*, the authors document one Church leader's apparent indifference to these type statistics.

[Dallin] Oaks himself, fearing repercussions from ranking general authorities, quashed the release of a survey noting potential stresses facing contemporary Mormon families. Reportedly, Oaks was not convinced of the validity of several of the report's major conclusions, notably that more LDS than non-LDS women in Utah worked outside the home; that a mother's working outside the home did not have a demonstrably negative effect on her family; and *that the church may have contributed to an increasing divorce rate among members by not providing adequate sex education and counsel to its youth.*[603]

"Based on a 2005 survey of drug use and health, the Utah Division of Substance Abuse and mental health estimates that 12% of Utah adults (192,000) are in serious psychological distress and may be in need of mental health treatment."[604]   Mormons tout their lifestyle as healthy. Taught to abstain from alcohol and cigarette smoking, even coffee is prohibited. The sad truth is that at least half of adult Mormons are grossly overweight.[605] From 2000-2005, more than 50% of Utah adults ages 18 and over were obese (BMI 25 or over). [606] Many Mormons are dependent on sweets and caffeinated diet sodas as a substitute for the normal stimuli available to those whose diets aren't unreasonably censored.

What do all these statistics and surveys mean? Can one reasonably conclude that the LDS Church is the cause of these problems?   LDS apologists argue against causality, but as used in toxic tort cases, proving general, and then specific causation can be done. In these types of cases, epidemiological studies and number of plaintiffs diagnosed per capita (with cancer or autoimmune disease for example) is used.

In determining a causal connection between psychological problems and Mormonism, a causal link can be proven by evidence that: (1) there is an increased risk of specific psychological disorders, i.e. depression, when one lives in submission to authoritarianism, participates in cult-like rituals, and adheres to a belief system rooted in bigotry and misogyny; and, (2) that Utah has an inordinately high number of these type psychological disorders, i.e., depression, overuse of psychotropic and pain-killer pharmaceuticals and even suicide, on a per capita basis. I don't think its a stretch to conclude that Mormonism is certainly responsible for these increases when 65% of the State is Mormon and the per capita number of persons suffering from these type disorders is uniquely high compared to the rest of the United States.

LDS Church Leaders and their Flock—an Authoritarian Governance

In strict adherence to Mormonism, there is no hope for an authentic life; rather a member of the Mormon Church is inextricably bound to the Brethren in deed and even in thought. This unnatural symbiotic or perhaps parasitic relationship (Brethren to flock) might appear to be working from the outside, but when examined carefully, it becomes clear that a life so inextricably entwined is psychologically unhealthy. Over a century ago, Senator Frank Cannon recognized this authoritarianism:

> The members of the Mormon hierarchy continually boast that they are sustained in the power and in their abuses of that power—"by the free vote of the freest people under the sun." By an amazing self deceit the Mormon people assume that their government is one of "common consent;" and nothing angers them more than the expression of any suspicion that they are not the best community in the world. They live under absolutism. They have no more right of judgment than a dead body. Yet the diffusion of authority is so clear that nearly every man seems to share in its operation upon some subordinate, and feels himself in some degree a master without observing that he is also a slave... [607]
>
> The leaders cannot do wrong—because it is not wrong if they do it...Before these people can be roused to any independence of responsible thought, it will be necessary to break their trust in the ability of their leaders to make bargains of protection with the world; and then it will still be necessary to force the eyes of their self-complacency to turn from the satisfied contemplation of their own virtues." [608]

The Church presents itself as Christian, 'it's in our name,' Mormons claim. Church members protest whenever true Christians point out significant doctrinal differences between Mormonism and Christianity. But in 1982, Apostle Bruce R. McConkie decried those who sought a personal relationship with Jesus Christ. He specifically counseled that "[Church members] should not strive for a special and personal

385

relationship with Christ." He called such a doctrine "false," and even "improper," espoused by "erring teachers and beguiled students." Instead he claims, "Devotion to the Father should be uppermost in all minds," and that "Our relationship with the Father is one of parent and child." [609] Perhaps if Mormons believed that a relationship with Jesus Christ was foremost in their spiritual development, such a belief might lead them to reconsider the necessity of membership in the LDS Church.

In 1996 the Church trademarked a logo designed to emphasize "Jesus Christ."

THE CHURCH OF
JESUS CHRIST
OF LATTER-DAY SAINTS

Due to the conflict between the Mormon world-view and generally accepted beliefs of healthy individuals, as stated by the American Psychiatric Association, many Mormons have a variety of deeply-rooted psychological problems. For example, in 1973 the APA removed homosexuality as a psychological disorder from its diagnostic reference book (DSM). In 1998 it issued a statement disapproving reparative therapy for homosexuals based upon the *a priori* notion that homosexuality was a mental illness. Yet Mormon leaders still preach homosexuality as a sin.

An association for LDS counselors and psychotherapists, formally created in 1975, cites several excerpts from the *D&C* in support of using LDS principles in conjunction with their mental health treatment.[610] These professional therapists take the disingenuous stance that their religion is not responsible for the significant psychopathology demonstrated in its membership.

One LDS psychiatrist admits that authoritarianism leads to obsessive-compulsive behavior and inappropriate guilt and then correlates these symptoms with those characteristics typically valued by Mormons; nevertheless his thesis argues that psychopathology cuts across all religions (and impliedly the secular types as well). [611] As a general proposition what he posits is true enough, but the causal connection Mormonism plays in the development of psychopathology such as obsessive-compulsive disorders, addictive behaviors and depression even to the point of suicide, is painfully clear.

386

The control used in exercising the authoritarian rule inherent in Mormonism is problematic in that such control necessarily plays to the lowest or most common denominator, ignoring the exceptional and the unique individual. This can be clearly seen in the Church's strident constriction of gender roles. This attitude has especially devastating consequences for the childless or unmarried Mormon woman.

Psychological Stunting

Contemporary Mormons' scorn for anything not a part of the dominant belief system is actually mild compared to the early days when Church leaders were responsible for physical harm to those who disobeyed their wishes, or even acts of murder based on sheer paranoia and power-mongering. The current leaders of the Mormon Church are not as openly vicious as they were in the nineteenth century, but the lust for power and control remains. Almost two centuries of deception have ruined countless lives in innumerable ways. Most people have heard of what fundamentalist Mormon polygamy has done to young women. However, oppression through Mormonism is not limited to women.

The lives of young men are also unalterably perverted by this Church's rigid requirements. Young Mormon men are psychologically castrated by the geriatric leaders who serve them with orders for a two year stint of asceticism anywhere in the world, from Idaho to Fiji, to Norway to Sri Lanka. These young men—and some young women, those who have not married by the age of twenty-one—go through several weeks of indoctrination at the Missionary Training Center, several more if they must learn a foreign language. Then, for the next two years, these young indoctrinates have a rigorous set schedule, daily proselytizing and scripture reading, no outside reading, no social relationships with the opposite sex, and very limited contact with family or friends at home. The women, already trained for subservience, are even further subdued by the experience.[612]

Many of these young people return eighteen months or two years later, empty, malleable, all individuality having been stripped away by the long service and restrictive lifestyle. No longer spontaneous, with no individuation and the stunted development of the integral self, they are unable to make important decisions without reliance on the Brethren for guidance on how to live the rest of their lives. Serving a Mormon mission seems to be the equivalent of the U.S. Military's "Basic Training," for a life dedicated to Mormonism. This two year process radically increases the investment quotient of a young Mormon so that historically, at least, those leaving the Church after serving a mission are few and quite brave. The Mormon mission serves as an effective process in retaining its members as much as it does to gain converts; perhaps even more so the former.

The psychologist Lawrence Kohlberg's six stages of cognitive development incorporate Swiss Psychologist Jean Piaget's theories. An individual settles at a particular stage with back tracking and forward leaping, as one moves through the process of cognitive evolution. Stages are not skipped; rather, the lesser stage is incorporated into the more advanced. When the developmental process is complete, the stages are viewed from a different perspective, as when one can see the forest only once s/he is outside the trees. The stages are often summarized as follows:

1. Obedience and punishment orientation (*How can I avoid punishment?*)
2. Self-interest orientation (*What's in it for me?*)
3. Interpersonal accord and conformity (*Social norms*)
4. Authority and social order maintaining orientation (*good boy/ good girl attitude*)
5. Social contract orientation (*Law and order morality*)
6. Universal ethical principles (*Principled conscience*)

According to Kohlberg, the process of moral development continues throughout one's lifetime and is primarily concerned with justice. In contrast, authoritarian societies such as Mormonism require its adherents remain at levels four or possibly five, thereby stunting personal growth. Complete, integrated actualization of the individual is rarely achieved by a true-believing Mormon. The wholesale cover-up of the true facts surrounding Church origins leads many devout Mormons to an acceptance of lying, divisiveness, and ultimately to widespread psychological problems, which prevents progress in their personal growth.

Many years ago, I mediated a divorce between a Mormon couple. The two were in their late forties with all their children grown. The man reasonably offered to pay for his wife, who had stayed home to raise their four children, to return to school and train for a career. She looked at him and then at me and then back again to her husband, and then, in all seriousness asked, "But who will clean the toilets?" The Church's emphasis on providing a heavenly home for husband and family is made to the exclusion of any thought for LDS women's personal needs. Although lip service is given to women's education, breeding and housekeeping are the real priorities.

Mormonism's Toxic View of Sexuality

Many Mormon men have an effeminate manner. Whether the manner precedes the Mormonism or *vice versa* is debatable. Effeminate men are drawn to a church where they are led and young male children raised in Mormonism learn to suppress testosterone-based aggression. While the strength of the feminine is suppressed in Mormonism, so are the masculine instincts of young Mormon men. These men grow accustomed to taking orders for even the most personal of all matters, from the type of underclothing they must wear, to what acts are appropriate in marital sexual relations. All this geriatric ordering leaves many Mormon men yearning for a real masculinity.

Paul Toscano eloquently sets out these gender issues in *The Sanctity of Dissent*. Speaking of the poisonous effects of the modern Mormon view of gender and sexuality, he explains:

Today, most leaders and members confuse sexual repression with chastity and chastity with spirituality. Sexuality is viewed with envy and suspicion. Sexual pleasure is considered lewd and corrupting. Male sexual energy is acknowledged, but is shamed as weakness and repressed. *Often it is channeled by men into the corporate church where it is transformed and emerges as self-control and control of others.* In this way many Mormon men forfeit natural affection. Loyalty replaces love, interviews replace intimacy, fraternity replaces foreplay, rectitude replaces erections, and ordinations replace orgasms. Power entices with pornographic intensity. Men lust for authority, fantasizing not centerfolds of naked women, but organizational-charts and photo displays of leaders ranked in seniority order. Female sexual energy is ignored or denied. In a homocentric system where God the Father is pictured as having no significant contact with women, no need of women, no interest in women and as issuing commandments and revelations from a transcendence that appears utterly innocent of the existence, aspirations, or spirituality of women, the feminine becomes irrelevant. Women are of no interest, not even as the objects of desire.... [613]

In the LDS Church, homosexuality is not only openly condemned, but feared. In decades past, the LDS Church practiced aversion, shock and other forms of 'reparative' therapy on its homosexual BYU students at the euphemistically-named Values Institute. [614] Personal accounts have been recorded of genitally-induced shock therapy and frontal lobotomies having been performed in order to train the homosexually inclined male into a more acceptable heterosexual role. [615]

As to homosexuality: "The Church does not encourage speculation about yet another controversial aspect of mission work: throwing pairs of young men aged nineteen to twenty-one into virtually monastic, celibate living conditions for long periods of time at the height of naturally strong sexual drives has fostered rumors of homosexual incidents" [616] Perhaps as this author suggests, sending young men in their sexual prime on two year missions, isolated from women, with only another male for company, encourages the very behavior the Brethren wish to avoid, unwittingly providing the 'temptations,' of homosexuality.

But accounts of the teachings of the New Testament Christ are silent on the issue of consensual adult homosexuality. And despite LDS Church arguments to the contrary, there is good scientific evidence that homosexuality has a genetic basis. Studies have been performed on the number and chronological spacing of male siblings in connection to same-sex attraction: "The most consistent biodemographic correlate of sexual orientation in men is the number of older brothers...These results strongly suggest a prenatal origin to the fraternal birth-order effect." [617]

The problem is not with the homosexual, but with a church that decries innate physical same-sex attractions as an abomination. For the unfortunate homosexual who is born into Mormonism, the conflicting posture imposed upon that individual is bound to cause psychological, if not physical injury. And many times that injury is not limited to the individual, but will eventually include an extended family-circle of hurt.

As a result of this failure to acknowledge the true etiology of homosexual attraction, and the Church's insistence that homosexuality is a perversion, there are many young Mormon men with an innate strong same-sex attraction, who marry and act as head of a heterosexual household. These men suppress all overt acts of same-sex attraction in order to outwardly conform to the LDS mandated lifestyle. Most homosexual women probably remain single, though I am not aware of statistics on lesbianism in the Mormon Church.

The LDS Social Services Department admits same-sex attraction is a problem:

> LDS Family Services estimates that there are four or five members in every ward of the Church dealing with erotic same-sex attraction problems. Usually, half of those individuals are married (most are temple marriages) and have children. With this in mind, there are dozens of parents, spouses, children, and individuals in every ward effected [sic] by this challenge in their family. So know that you are not alone.*[618]

An article published in the LDS Church-owned *Desert News* is especially insightful and is set out here in its complete text in order to illustrate the exquisite torment of Mormon male homosexuals (and their wives) when their innate sexual identity has been denied and redirected into a heterosexual lifestyle:

> ...Speaking to a standing-room-only audience, three LDS couples described their experiences with their heterosexual marriages, despite the fact that each of the husbands experience what they call same-sex attraction, or SSA. They said while they are basically happy, navigating the emotional and physical aspects of their relationships requires constant hard work. All emphasized that marriage is not a "cure" for same-sex attraction. They were panelists during the semiannual meeting of the Association of Mormon Counselors and Psychotherapists...

> Each of the men described a childhood that included being labeled as a "golden boy" by their peers and church leaders —a devout Latter-day Saint young man eager to learn and obey the faith's teachings with respect to marriage and family, and to serve an LDS mission. All said they had at least one episode of feeling

sexually attracted to girls during adolescence or when they returned from their missions. But a variety of factors came into play for each, both during adolescence and in dating young women, that had them wondering how they could possibly marry and have children, as their church teaches.

"Brett" said he had so internalized LDS teachings about chastity and morality as a young man that the thought of having a sexual relationship with a woman "was repulsive. I was disgusted by the female anatomy." He was emotionally attracted to female friends, but couldn't get beyond the physical repulsion, and avoided holding hands or kissing women he dated. Dating his future wife off and on for an extended period, the more serious she became, the more "my same-sex desires came out. That's when I started getting into pornography" and other behaviors, "which only perpetuates the problem," he said. Desperate to end the emotional pain, he confided in her, expecting the relationship to end. Instead, "she reacted very, very well. She looked at me and said, 'Are you crazy? That doesn't change the fact that I love you.'" She began going to counseling with him, and they eventually married. She didn't pressure him for physical intimacy once she realized the issue. Meantime, he found a male mentor who had been through the same experience and was able to provide detailed explanations and counsel.

"Joe" said he was attracted to women, but found dating and physical intimacy intimidating, difficult and "not very successful. I was having the opposite experience with people of the same sex that were attractive and did reciprocate," though his "spiritual identity" had always been "marriage and family," he said. "That was always the goal, even when I was in the wilderness." He dated his wife for three years, dealing with external pressure to move the relationship forward from family and friends who didn't know about his attraction to other men. He confided in her before they were engaged, and they built a level of trust that took into account his fears about physical intimacy. "She took a risk ... but I do believe men can get to a point where they are capable of a relationship with a woman."

"Dan" was sexually abused by male siblings as a child, but was attracted to girls at a young age. When his early interest in girls was discouraged, and he was teased for being "skinny and effeminate," he turned toward boys, becoming addicted to gay pornography and acting out. He served a mission, returned and married without telling his wife about his past, thinking he had overcome his attraction to men. But several months later he got back into pornography and the accompanying addictive behaviors. When she caught him looking at porn, he told her his story. After that, it took years for them to be able to discuss his attraction to men. He said he "made a lot of mistakes" and the two of them talked about divorce, but he praised his wife for "hanging in there with me." The wives said they see their husbands as much more than their same-sex attraction. Despite the challenges and public perception to the contrary, one said, "there are people who are married and dealing with this."[619]

Contrary to LDS urging, marriage with a heterosexual is never the answer. Ron Schow, professor at Idaho State University, surveyed 136 LDS homosexuals in 1994. Seventy-one per cent of the members of the group were returned missionaries and 36 of them had been married; but, only two of the thirty-six remained married. "Many of these mixed heterosexual/homosexual marriages, even when they do not end in divorce, result in marriages in which there is no true intimacy nor a mutually nourishing relationship," he reported.[620] Other homosexually-inclined young people who are torn between their LDS teachings and alleged shameful state of sin, but who refuse to live a lie, are driven to despair and some to suicide.

Conversely and even to this day, Mormonism has always demanded that women remain home as keeper of the house and nurturer. Crossovers into the other culturally-imposed gender role are generally disapproved, and should only be entertained when necessary. The result of this strident pigeonholing of gender-based social roles is a Church full of depressed women prevented from the realization of their feminine strength and generations of mild-mannered men who, for fear of incurring the wrath of God through the priesthood-holder-next-in-line, will not assert any individual thought or deed—(Brethren excepted. The nearer one's priesthood calling approaches the top of the LDS pyramid, the more he can afford to roar). This overreaching patriarchal control fosters latent homosexual feelings and/or an aversion toward the female gender in many

Mormon men. Boiling over with suppressed anger, some Mormon men will abuse their wives and children. Others seem driven to same-sex fantasies, if not relationships.

Mormons, both female and male, have been wound too tightly and are coming undone. When polygamy could no longer be practiced openly, or in this life, the Mormon leaders were left without a hook for their power mongering. As an unidentified contributor to an 1885 edition of the *Salt Lake Tribune* noted, "The essential principle of Mormonism is not polygamy at all, but the ambition of an ecclesiastical hierarchy to wield sovereignty; to rule the souls and lives of its subjects with absolute authority, unrestrained by any civil power."[621]

Homosexual lifestyles are threatening to Mormon leaders because if homosexual activity is acknowledged as anything other than a perversion, the traditional family will be undermined, and the numbers of tithe-paying, nuclear, heterosexual families which eventually expand Church membership and ultimately replenish its coffers, will be significantly impaired. Here is an example of where the creators of Mormonism have become destroyers of souls. The focus of homosexuality is usually on the Mormon male, or the family as a unit. Rarely are the feelings and well-being of women who unwittingly marry homosexual men —those men who are putting forth a good faith effort to become straight— trying to abandon their 'sinful' desires, ever considered.

At April 2010 General Conference, Apostle Boyd K. Packer, described by some of his brethren as an "old grizzly bear," reconfirmed the position of the LDS Church against homosexuality, and its characterization that it is a perversion and a sin—not something natural, "…Some suppose that they were pre-set, and cannot overcome what they feel are inborn tendencies toward the impure and unnatural. Not so. Why would our Heavenly Father do that to anyone? Remember, he is our Father."

Between the time of the televised broadcast and the sermon's appearance in print, his sermon was edited in two important places. The critical section was changed to: "Some suppose that they were preset and cannot overcome what they feel are inborn *temptations* toward the impure and unnatural. Not so! Remember, God is our Heavenly Father." Besides changing 'tendencies' to 'temptations,' the rhetorical question Packer asked in his live speech, "Why would our Heavenly Father do that to anyone?" was deleted.[622]

The problem is that this continued inaccurate representation of homosexuality, by one believed to have been appointed to speak with authority on behalf of God, and yet one who is obviously ignorant of human biology, continues to adversely affect the lives of both young Mormon men and women, and as the three examples quoted in the *Deseret News* illustrate, in some cases, entire families. As to the omitted rhetorical question regarding Heavenly Father's motives, perhaps LDS editors realized what a silly question Packer had posed, given the historic and current chaos and horrific natural disasters in the global community, with many seeking to find a seemingly absentee Heavenly Father.

Mormonism's Questionable Morality

Duplicity, taught with subtle approbation, is endemic in Mormonism. No wonder, then, that Mormons are gullible. In order to preserve their view of life, some have become pathological liars. After generations of dedication to doctrines now exposed as man-made, those who see the conflict in continuing to espouse such doctrines are struggling and depressed. Cognitive dissonance, an uncomfortable psychological state caused by holding two contradictory ideas simultaneously, is a term well-known to disaffected Mormons. Maintaining such a mindset is emotionally disabling for the individual who cannot reconcile his or her instincts with what they have been told to be true by Mormon leadership. Most Mormons seek out information that is compatible with their beliefs rather than dissonant. True-believer syndrome is an acquired immunity to cognitive dissonance. For a true-believer, the Mormon majority makes residence in the State of Utah comforting; for a non-believer, the effect is usually the opposite.

Superficially, most Mormons appear to be content. The sardonic term 'Happy Valley,' is commonly used to describe the residents of Utah County, home of BYU, the most concentrated county of Mormons in the State. However, 'life elevated,' a State tourism-sponsored slogan approved by a majority of Utah voters in 2005, can only refer to Utah's altitude, as opposed to any moral high-ground claimed by its majority residents.

For example, Utah won the bid for the 2002 Winter Olympics with a lot of self-promotion and determination. But in 1998, as a result of allegations that members of the Olympic committee accepted bribes from the Salt Lake Organizing Committee (SLOC), the U.S. Department of Justice together with all levels of the Olympic Committee, investigated the charges. As a result of those investigations, several members of the Olympic Committee were expelled and others sanctioned.[623]

Two Utah defendants, Thomas K. Welch and David R. Johnson, were charged with illegally influencing International Olympic Committee members for their votes. These SLOC executives allegedly bribed IOC members with more than $1 million in cash, free vacations, living stipends, shopping sprees and free medical care prior to the 1995 IOC vote for Salt Lake.

In 2001, Mormon District Court Judge, David Sam, initially dismissed the case before trial, and after the prosecution appealed,

> ...granted the defendants' motion for acquittal [effectively a second dismissal with prejudice] without sending the case to the jury. He ruled that there was insufficient evidence to sustain a conviction on any of the 15 counts in the federal indictment against Welch, 59, the former president of the Salt Lake Bid Committee, and Johnson, 45, the committee's former vice president. [624]

At the hearing on the second dismissal, Judge Sam declared that the charges could not stand because "there was no criminal intent or evil purpose." He also told the defendants that the case "offends my sense of justice."[625]

The questionable morality of Utah's culture is well-documented. Successful Mormon businessmen are notorious for preying off the gullibility and trust of their friends in the Church *a la* Joseph Smith. Val Southwick pleaded guilty to nine counts of securities fraud in 2008. Southwick perpetrated the fraud through his company VesCor, in a Ponzi scheme which bilked about $180 million from Utah and Las Vegas LDS Church members. Jeff Orrick, a Mormon who represented some of those defrauded, noted: "There's no repentance. He still goes to church. He's still got his temple recommend–as if he didn't do a damn thing wrong."[626] Although his victims have yet to obtain civil remedies, Southwick has been denied parole and continues to serve his seventeen-year sentence. William J. Hammons, a former Mormon Bishop, was subsequently convicted in conjunction with the VesCor Scheme.

In the last few years, local LDS leaders in neighboring states have also been accused and convicted of similar crimes. "A former Bishop who was recently excommunicated, [Shawn] Merriman [of Parker, Colorado] is accused in a federal lawsuit of bilking investors of $20 million, some of which went into fine art he displayed in an exhibition held in a local LDS building." [627] Merriman ultimately pleaded guilty to mail fraud and was sentenced to 12+ years in prison. Former LDS seminary teacher, Dennis Cope of Mesa, Arizona was sentenced to seven years in prison in April of 2009 for his $10 million fraud scam. [628]

Then, in August, 2010, R. Dean Udy was sentenced to jail for failure to repay any of the $11.4 million he and his son Cameron had defrauded investors in Utah, Idaho and Nevada. "Udy traded on his positions in The Church of Jesus Christ of Latter-day Saints, which included membership in a [Mormon] stake presidency and as a regional representative in Box Elder County."[629]

Joseph Smith began the first Ponzi scheme and it has lasted almost two centuries. Is it any wonder that those trained in his methods desire to create a business of their own, ensuring temporal comfort enroute to celestial glory?

LDS Environmental Indifference

Although Mormons have an affinity for the word, their focus on big rewards in the after-life comes at the expense of proper *stewardship* over their environment in this life. As a result of Mormonism's combined spiritual and temporal ideology, Mormons have historically and cohesively worked under their leaders to develop and industrialize Utah. Arrington's *Great Basin Kingdom*, an economic history of early Utah, chronicles the early growth and resource development of the State.

However, Mormons have been careless stewards of their environment. Economic growth and development has always been emphasized at the expense of environmental concerns. Though certainly Mormons don't own all industrial or agricultural development in Utah, in the beginning Mormon leaders were almost the exclusive owners of all industry in the State.

LDS General Authorities served as officers or sat on the board of directors in companies such as the Union Pacific and Western Railroads, Amalgamated Sugar/U & I Sugar Company, Inland Crystal Salt Company,

Wasatch Wagon and Machine Company, Utah Lumber Company, Mountain States Telephone and Telegraph, Utah Power and Light, Utah Lime and Stone Company, Salt Lake Iron and Steel Company, Emigration Canyon Rock Company, Utah Construction Company, Enamel Brick and Concrete Company, Inland Fertilizer Company, Union Portland Cement Company, Utah Onyx Development Company, Smoot and Spafford (coal production), the Wasatch Land and Improvement Association, Utah Oil Refining Company and the Riverside Canal Company.[630]

Even today, Mormon legislators and local and federal officials are in charge of regulating state and local zoning, and are responsible for the enforcement of federal environmental regulations. However, only recently have Utahns begun to acknowledge the price they are now paying for an historic disregard of the environment.

By 1872 (with the exception of Big Cottonwood Canyon) the Wasatch Mountain ecosystem which abuts the Great Salt Lake Valley had been exploited from excess lumber production and overgrazing of livestock, in particular sheep, to the extent that deforestation was complete and Salt Lake was known as an adobe village. [631] During the last sixty or more years, it has not been the anxiety of starving pioneers that has exploited the environment, but extreme overpopulation taking precedence over Utah's natural inhabitants.

In the twenty years or so that I had lived outside the State, retail and single family housing starts have overtaken the narrow strip of arable land between the base of the Wasatch Mountains and the shores of the lakes below. The Great Salt Lake and its lesser sister to the south, the fresh water, if polluted, Utah Lake, are tied together by the meager Jordan River. Some Utah residents point out the geographic similarities to the Holy Land, with its Dead Sea and Sea of Galilee. Until recent attempts at anti-pollution measures were completed, including the construction of a state park along its bank, the Jordan River was known as Utah's Love Canal by environmentalists outside of the State.[632]

Utah Lake, along with the Great Salt Lake, is a remnant of historic Lake Bonneville that covered the same area where dinosaurs roamed in prehistoric times. For years it was the largest fresh water lake in the Great Basin. Originally it was filled with dozens of species of fresh water fish, providing abundant food for the native Utes and first Mormon settlers. Greedy over-fishing and eventual wholesale pollution from steel manufacturing, together with the introduction of carp, destroyed much of the biolife in the Lake. Today, this naturally shallow lake has nothing but dirt at its bottom and thus nothing to keep the water from its chronic turgidity. The carp are now more than 95% of the Lake's fish (despite Fish and Game and more recently, BYU's efforts to reinstate and preserve the native June sucker), crowding out the lake trout and other native species.

In the nineteenth century, lakeside recreation sites were legion. Now, even water-skiing on the lake feels questionable. Ownership disputes abound over tide level properties. Nobody seems to have taken responsibility for conserving this once pristine, life-giving lake.

***

Springtime in the Rockies can be beautiful, with clear blue skies and flowering trees. Lately there has been more rain; the moisture has made the usually bare, brown foothills lush. From April through June, the skies are mostly blue and the air is fresh; during that season, the mountain areas are beautiful and even the heavily populated Wasatch Front can be pretty. Skiing in the Wasatch Back on what really is "the greatest snow on Earth," is heavenly; blue skies are often in Park City.

However, during winter atmospheric inversions, the metropolitan Salt Lake Area has become more polluted than Los Angeles before the 1988 California Clean Air Act. Innumerable billboards and retailers are situated on both sides of the Salt Lake stretch of I-15 which is constantly under construction, ever widening and improving to accommodate the throngs of SUVs and vans, transporting the happy families of which Utah boasts.

Slope denudation where open pit mining provides gravel and ore is seen along I-15 in North Salt Lake and I-80 just east of the entry to Parley's Canyon. The open pit Bingham Canyon *aka* Kennecott Copper Mine acquired by Rio Tinto Zinc in 1989, is the world's largest man-made excavation and can be seen by space-shuttle astronauts as they pass over the Great Basin.

Oil refineries were established in the Valley's north end as early as 1909. These petroleum processing plants make the trip from Salt Lake to Bountiful one to be made with the car windows rolled up tight. Once the sun has set, it seems that these polluting plants puff out multiple times the daylight stench, so that driving on the old highway 89 through North Salt Lake feels like cutting through an other-worldly, gas-filled hell. The Salt Lake Valley has become so polluted that before Pittsburgh cleaned up its air, Salt Lake City was known as the Pittsburgh of the West; today that comparison would be an insult to Pittsburgh.

What natural geographic beauty remains in Utah is not because of any preservation efforts by Utah's citizens. Rather, much of the grandeur of the southern part of the State survives only because it is part of the protected National Parks system, for example, Zion's and Bryce Canyon National Parks. The overdeveloped Wasatch Front has experienced rapid growth with virtually no foresight or comprehensive urban planning.

By contrast, Boulder, City and County, Colorado is a community which has embraced, not destroyed, its surroundings. Boulder is located on the other side of the Rocky Mountains, just a bit to the south, and is abutted by low prairie to the east. Both sides of this section of the Rocky Mountains had original natural beauty, but Boulder's environment has been preserved. Strict zoning laws, including limiting growth up the mountains, preserved the natural beauty for use by Boulder County's inhabitants. As of 1993, Colorado had 27 state land trusts, areas set aside for multiple uses owned in part by both the State and private individuals or entities with a preplanned use and primary goal of natural resource preservation. In contrast, as of that date, Utah had one state land trust, located in Park City, Summit County. [633]

The Deceivers and the Deceived: When the Creators Become the Destroyers

Paying tithes from a position of financial strength can hardly sting the affluent, but when the greedy receipt and mismanagement of those hard-earned offerings is used to create monoliths to the heavens, while most of those tithe payers are overworked, some on the verge of bankruptcy, then the creators of a religion become the destroyers of financial stability. Teaching young women to doubt their value as equals to men to the point of depressive disorders, masked by psychotropic drugs in order that Joseph Smith's narcissistic world view continues into the twenty-first century is another example of where the creators and now the perpetuators of Mormonism, have become the destroyers of women's and homosexuals' self-esteem, health and well-being.

Wizened former Mormon, Benjamin Winchester, summed up Mormonism succinctly when he told the *Tribune* in 1889 that:

Chapter 12: Fallout from Fraud—Irreparable Harm

> The Mormon organization is the most artfully devised system in modern times for enriching the few from the result of the toil and privation of the many, and a most deplorable feature of it is that the system paralyses free thought and free agency. *[634]

Mormons have been led into or have remained in the Church based upon false representations of fact made by their leaders. Furthermore, once they have become members of the Church, Mormons are admonished not to read anything "anti-Mormon," which is really all world philosophy and theology and even some literature. Thus, these indoctrinates remain ignorant of the falsity of the factual representations made by Mormon leaders regarding the divinity of Mormonism. Despite the oft-quoted Mormon aphorism: "The glory of God is intelligence," continued lifelong ignorance is encouraged by the Church. The leaders have often preached against the dangers of intellectualism. Apostle Boyd K. Packer is notorious for citing intellectuals along with feminists and homosexuals as the three biggest threats to the Church.[635]

Innocent Mormon-raised children, spurred on by their parents and neighbors, as well as new converts to the Religion, base important life-altering decisions on the truthfulness of the Mormon Gospel. Decisions such as marrying only a good LDS Church member in the temple, attending seminary and maybe even a Church university although the young person could have his pick of schools,[636] sacrificing two years of a young life to serve a mission, are all things that would not be done without a fervent belief in the truthfulness of the Mormon lie.

But now the information revolution has uncovered and revealed this deception, until over the last several years an explosion of exposure has occurred. Mormons, with Quinn's aptly described siege mentality, are desperate for approval. Over the past two decades, they have pleaded with the media for mainstream acceptance. In an April 7, 1996, CBS *60 Minutes* interview, LDS President/Prophet Gordon B. Hinckley proclaimed to Mike Wallace and the world: "We are not a weird people."

However Mormonism is an imposture. With the elevation of form over substance, you will find no true original thinking in Mormonism. Plagiarism is endemic. From the hodgepodge of the current interior architecture of the Joseph Smith Building in Salt Lake City to the Mormon Temple ceremony lifted from the Freemasons, Mormonism is ultimately empty and unfulfilling because it's all form and no substance, nothing real or original. [637] Joseph Smith's clumsy attempt to graft a new religion onto Hebraic history and the Christian Religion is patently absurd. The doctrine is intellectually shallow and contradictory, spiritually unsatisfying to those who have even a limited but rational and informed understanding of the world. It is, for the most part, devoid of any real truths. Rather it is best described as a checklist of dos and don'ts with no satisfying rationale to support its list of legalisms.

In the context of Mormonism, psychologist Ken Wilber would characterize the Mormon view as "salvation that is given ... exclusively to those who embrace the particular myths, in this case, the evolved Mormon Doctrine and the accompanying symbolic gestures, ceremonies, clothing and rituals required of a faithful member of the Church."[638] Truthfully, there is no need for an intermediary, whether embodied as a prophet, priesthood-holder or other liaison with the Universe's higher power. As Wilber states: "...all sentient beings are one with God."[639]

Despite claims of being anointed and having extra special spiritual gifts, upon closer examination, it is clear than none of these Mormon leaders have any more insight than any other human being seeking spiritual truth, and it could be argued that the average intelligence of these men is not at a level where they should be teaching spiritual truths to others. Clearly they are businessmen, whose powers lie in organizational behavior and control. And though occasionally a Neal Maxwell or another well-spoken Church leader may teach a gem of truth with a particular alliterative flare, on the whole, these men are nothing more than corporate directors who are acting in their own best interest (as in the preaching to pay tithing before household financial obligations, no matter how meager the income) to the exclusion of the best interests of those who have invested time, money and trust into their venture.

When I stole the coins from my little sister, I took advantage of her youth, innocence and trust in me. Likewise, the Brethren have stolen valuable assets from the young and naive, and perhaps non-English speaking proselytes, all the while projecting a demeanor of trusting elders in whom the young or inexperienced can rely. Unlike a parents' support of the Santa Claus fable, or my meat tree story, a fabled and distorted history of the LDS Church is not something that can be viewed in any way as told for the good of Church members. And unlike an older sibling cheating her younger sister, a parental scolding and an apology will not be sufficient reparations. The coins must be repaid.

The Brethren's oft-repeated justification of giving 'milk before meat,' revealing only a whitewashed, innocuous form of Church history or doctrine to uninitiated Mormons, should not apply in other than parental roles and although some LDS General Authorities no doubt have this mindset, the Brethren do not stand *in loco parentis* to Church members. Furthermore, since admittedly few if any of the LDS leaders are professionally trained theologians or counselors, their speeches and interpretations of biblical scripture are really no more than part of a corporate consensus on how best to administer a religion.[640]

Mormons worry about the afterlife, with no time to enjoy the present—sacrificing a fantasy life for a real one. Likewise, those preoccupied with celestial glory have little time to concern themselves with environmental issues and social justice.[641]

I think back to the time at BYU, after I'd returned from the South African Tour, and I started to suspect that something was wrong. My inner turmoil manifested itself in an eating disorder and depression because, as one former Mormon psychologist explains:[642]

> The groupthink aspect of the Mormon psyche is so strong that it doesn't occur to most people that there might be something odd about the experience. Most immediately conclude that the problems must be their own. The danger in this is that it can lead people to distrust their own instincts. That only reinforces the self-identity that is based in membership in the group, in turn blurring their self-identity based on individual characteristics.[643]

Living a life dedicated to Mormonism, one is unable to ever achieve a genuine adult self. Because a Mormon is taught to look to Church rules and regulations for moral instruction, most devout Mormons never develop the ability to judge for him or herself; they never attain the skill of rational analysis required in weighing difficult decisions and this inevitably produces psychological problems.

I have seen this lack of independent thought in Utah juries who are easily swayed by experts. Compared to California juries, in my experience, many Utah jurors rely wholeheartedly on the opinions of authoritarian figures such as police officers, physicians, employers and government officials as a substitute for the jurors' roles as the finders of fact. The testimony of these experts is supposed to be considered only as *some* evidence in support of the allegation or defense, with the ultimate decision to be made by the jury. However, Utah juries sometimes use an expert opinion as a substitute opinion, circumventing their duty to process all the evidence in order to reach a verdict founded in proven facts. The substitution of authority-figure pronouncements in lieu of individual evaluation has untoward consequences and can make litigation even more dependent on the respective resources of the party: the party with the best paid, or most experts wins.

But Mormonism's most comprehensive and disturbing effects are commonly found in the daily lives of its devotees. One female blogger aptly described the adverse effect of her life lived within Mormon regulations:

> The Church limits lives and curtails potential. The church promotes fear. Fear of ideas—books you can't read, thoughts you can't think. Fear of People – supposedly dangerous people: gentiles, apostates, gays and those who hold unapproved meetings. Fear of losing those we love—pay the dues and learn the secret handshakes or you'll never see your family again. The Church promotes inappropriate guilt. Guilt about natural and healthy sexuality. Guilt about masturbation. Guilt for listening to rock music on Sunday [or virtually anything else not put out by Deseret Book]. Guilt for choosing to marry outside of the temple or for choosing to marry someone who isn't a TBM (True Believing Mormon). Guilt for having an opinion and wanting to state it. Guilt for disagreement with the male who is in charge. Guilt for being who you are. The Church wastes time. Time spent searching out exact detail about the dead to have them baptized into the Mormon Church. Then getting baptized and 'endowed' over and over so dead people can supposedly get into Mormon heaven. Time reading the Book of Mormon. Time in meetings listening to people say "I know the Church is true" over and over and over... [Time spent knocking on the doors of people both in and out of the Church who didn't invite you to their house]. The church limited my ability to enjoy all the wonderful things about me, and about other 'less worthy' (non TBM) people. I could have worn sleeveless shirts in the summer without feeling wicked. I might have felt less superior to my Jack Mormon dad [and others who I

didn't think had the truth]. I might have felt more joy and spirituality if I hadn't been following an illusion for so long. *[644]

Mormonism is both Absolute and Relative

As a young, true-believing Mormon, I thought all other religions were in error, at least partly. As a young, healthy insurance defense attorney, I thought soft tissue neck injuries would heal in six weeks and so were never worth more than a couple of thousand dollars in pain and suffering. As a fifty-six year old woman, mother and refugee from an oppressive, fundamentalist religion, I finally see things more nearly the way they truly are.

I often mix my metaphors, and so according to a professor acquaintance of mine, have done just that (combining Plato's allegory of the cave with the Eastern metaphor of the blind men and the elephant) in coming up with the metaphor of the one true form. Plato advocated a theory that the perfect form of a thing exists apart from those who perceive it. This is the case with the search for an absolute Truth.

Using a horse for this example, I grew up positioned at the rear of the horse. From that perspective I would describe the horse as a set of muscular hindquarters, narrowing down to a pair of thin fetlocks, all topped with a swishing tale. I could see no more than that. When I traveled to Africa I moved my position and stepped to the side. I saw that the horse had a beautiful profile, strong back and leg muscles and a thick mane, which matched its tail. Over my lifetime I have come around the front of the horse to see the flaring nostrils and heavily lashed beautiful eyes. I still haven't seen the underbelly of the horse, nor the horse from an aerial view, but given my several varying perspectives, I now have a good idea of the nature of the true horse, a much more accurate picture than the one I saw as a young woman.

Truth is both absolute and relative. Although Mormonism exists apart from the perception of those who see and experience the Religion, Mormonism as experienced, varies with one's position in relation to the Religion. Truth—it all depends on your seat in the theatre of life—and what if you are one of the performers? You have more or less compelled the attention of those seated in the audience for the duration of the performance.

If I was a member of the Mormon Gerontocracy, the one hundred and fifteen men who head Mormonism, I would most probably view the Mormonism horse in yet another way. From such a perspective, which would most likely have included an even-keeled life with an obedient wife and children, some measure of material success and then the power and prestige accompanying a position of a Mormon General Authority, I might defend the Church to the death (as claimed Joseph Smith did) to the point of labeling disbelievers as 'snakes,' or those who have left the Religion as 'junk yard dogs.' But women in Mormonism are seated behind the pillars, in the cheap seats and no matter their talent, because of their gender, are always in the audience.

Utah is a kaleidoscope of crashing paradigms, the Mormons in various stages of belief and disbelief, the non-Mormons, in various stages of comprehending just how all-encompassing this Religion is. The roots of Mormon ethnocentricity and claimed superiority can be found in Brigham Young's early boastings. He claimed to his loyal congregations that "we are in fact the saviors of the world,"*[645] "the smartest people in the world,"*[646] and "the best people who ever lived upon the earth."*[647]

The smartest people in the world are capable of doing some pretty stupid things. In January of 2010, the *Desert News* published an article titled "Use proper sources," which depicts a mother-daughter scene transparently designed to advocate continued mind control over Mormon Church membership.[648] The story in the article is of a mother struggling to prepare a Church lesson, books strewn across her table. The daughter asks her mother why she doesn't just teach from the Church manual. "Why," she asks, "are you trying to boil down information? An inspired Church-writing committee has already done that for you." Daughter says that the manuals have been approved by the Quorum of the Twelve and the First Presidency. Mom, apparently a little dense in this scenario, looks confused. Daughter goes on to explain that all she needs to teach is in the approved manual which has been admittedly 'correlated' by the Brethren "...to ensure purity of doctrine, simplicity of materials, and control by the priesthood." Mother's concern disappears from her brow. She is relieved that the work (the thinking) has been done for her and she closes her books, shuts down her internet browser and returns from her brief, thinking escape, to the land of the unquestioning.[649]

Chapter 12: Fallout from Fraud—Irreparable Harm

Utah Public Schools Maintain a Victorian Attitude toward Sex

February 22, 2010, Senate Bill 54 was on the floor of the Utah State Legislature. The then, current sex education law was vague because while it allowed Utah educators to teach about contraception, they couldn't encourage it; thus, there was widespread practical reluctance among educators to teach anything about it. This new bill would have required discussion of contraception in a sex education curriculum. The proposed legislation was so controversial and uncomfortable for the largely Mormon Utah State legislature that it died without debate and the proponents and supporters scheduled to speak left the legislative chambers without being heard. [650]

Given Joseph Smith and Brigham Young's libertine natures, it's curious that the Utah majority attitude is so far to the right on issues like this. This phenomenon might be a reactionary response to the exposed history of its founders. More likely, it is at least a subconscious means of controlling Utah's young people in a perverse attempt to ensure Mormonism's growth.

Some of Utah's leaders continue in the Joseph Smith mode of an ostensibly righteous public persona. In March, 2010, the Utah House majority leader, Kevin Garn confessed to an incident when he was 28 years old and married. Admittedly, during this time, he had bathed nude in a hot tub with a 15 year-old girl, who described a relationship with him, not just a solitary incident. Garn had been her Sunday school teacher, employer and, according to the victim, had purchased the girl gifts and taken her out. Representative Garn made an emotional confession to the Utah State Legislature, but instead of receiving any type of sanction, he was showered with accolades by the then, current speaker of the house, who asked the rest of the house members to join him in recognizing "the man they knew...a man of integrity...." The House leader continued: "I know not of the man you speak of... [referring to the incident]." The legislative video record reveals that members of the legislature rose and gave him a thunderous standing ovation.[651]

***

Mormonism is the pragmatic answer to the meaning of life for many, especially those who don't mind being told what to believe and how to live. Unquestioning women and men are comfortable in Mormonism's homogenous fold. A BYU demographics professor described the distinguishing characteristics of Mormons as the four C's: "chastity, conjugality, chauvinism and children."[652]

However, belonging to a highly structured religion like Mormonism doesn't increase one's receptivity to the spiritual; it has the opposite effect. Fundamentalist religions are not a guide to a better life as claimed, but as exemplified in Mormonism, they thwart the natural impulse to do good by setting a strict guideline of acceptable types of good, as if no other will suffice.

With its imperialistic zeal, this nineteenth century frontier religion spread westward, destroying or controlling all those who prevented the realization of its leaders' goals. Today, Mormonism's hubris can be easily compared to imperialistic eras of most developed countries, including our own. Smith and his contemporaries created a plagiarized, piecemeal theology which was then added to by Brigham Young, who organized the theocracy of Deseret.

The pursuit of being one with the universal whole, of a life lived to effect peace and unity, is uplifting and to be encouraged. Historically however, all fundamentalist religions, including Mormonism, though claiming to have this goal, have had the exact opposite effect on the global community. By segregating themselves through an assumed superiority as the one-and-only-true-religion, God's chosen and other such self-labeled specialness, they necessarily set themselves apart from the world, usually at the expense of the rest of the sinners and non-believers. As history and current events demonstrate, pluralistic societies are rarely achieved if they must accommodate more than one rabidly fundamentalist religion. Witness the Middle East and Pakistan. Instead, "the chosen," attitude leads only to strife, war and ultimately, anarchy.

***

What will these Mormon leaders do? Are they waiting, slowly acknowledging the misrepresentations over the years until the whole made-up story is out in the open? How much longer can they continue to sidestep their own history and preach self-censorship? Are they hoping the three year statute of limitations for fraud will run? The advice suggested in the *Desert News* story of the mother preparing for her Sunday school lesson arguably voids any statute of limitations defense offered by the Church that its members should have known of its true origins—Church faithful have been taught not to look.

For years, members of the Church have lived with the Brethren's pomposity as self-appointed apostles, prophets, seventies, teachers, elders, *ad nauseam,* of the Lord. What would the Lord Jesus, He of the New Testament gospels, have to say about these men—Pharisees (and Philistines) for certain. Christ declared that He came to fulfill the Mosaic Law, not to make it more complicated and tedious as Mormonism has done. If ever there was a church that emphasizes form over substance, letter over spirit of the law, Mormonism is it. But Mormon leaders can never acknowledge that the Religion was all a creation of Joseph Smith's fraud and his collaborators' determined minds—for when the tree-root is rotten, so is the fruit.

If the golden plates never existed and Mormon scriptures are not of God, then neither are the hundreds of temples which cover the world, nor their silly ordinances which take millions of human hours to perform. The garments are not holy, the missions have been served in vain, the tithes have been collected under false pretenses and though there can be good thoughts included on occasion, the authority upon which LDS publications and sermons are based is no authority at all. If Mormonism is not of God, then all the determined, zealous, rigid Mormon behavior has been for naught.

Think of what good could have been done if all these LDS resources had been spent to better this world instead of propagating a belief in a fantasy world to come. But if these leaders acknowledge the scam, then there is no need for Mormonism. Acknowledgment would do more than expose the leaders of the Church of the Latter-day Saints as having engaged in some quite unsaintly behavior; it might just possibly expose them to liability under the law of the land.

One with God and Nature—Overcoming Dualism, the Circuitous Path of Mormonism

Philosopher Mircea Eliade recognized that men have long felt the need to set aside sacred space in attempts to establish reference points from which to organize their lives and communities out of the chaos of the Cosmos.[653] Abrahamic religions have their synagogues, cathedrals and mosques. Eastern philosophies don't place as much emphasize on the external, though they have their religious temples as well.

The LDS Church owns both chapels, where weekly meetings take place and temples, where special ceremonies are performed and only worthy Mormons are allowed to attend. Not one of these temples or chapels is subject to property taxes. Each temple costs at least several, if not tens of millions of dollars; the chapels, hundreds of thousands. There are yearly maintenance and upkeep costs. Query: are these man-made edifices to the anthropomorphic Mormon God truly constructs for good?

Reflecting on what started my search for the truth of Mormonism, the South African Tour—the feeling we had at each performance was incredible. But I now know that the feelings from the performers' highs are those which accompany any well-received art form. All are demonstrations of appreciation for the beauty of this world. Performing is one way of overcoming the dualism endemic in Western culture and exacerbated by legalistic, organized religions.

I have felt the Spirit many times, "...for where two or three are gathered in my name..." (Matthew 18:20). I have felt spiritual lots of times: cheering for my sons in gymnastic or karate tournaments, whenever a man who I have loved and I made love, whenever my son away at college says, "love you Mom," before he hangs up the telephone, when my cat nuzzles his cold nose in the crook of my arm, whenever my little mother collects news articles for me and puts them in a homemade pocket file and whenever I receive a thank you note or a hug from a client. One autumn, after a short visit to the Philadelphia public library, I was drawn to a pair of mature deciduous trees located on the side of the main entrance. I wondered whether they had been alive at the signing of the Declaration of Independence. After appreciating their beauty for an unknown amount of time, I felt at one with these beautiful creations.

I still love to hear *Come Come Ye Saints* sung by the Mormon Tabernacle Choir, but I get a similar feeling from Pavarotti's *Ave Maria* and even Elvis Presley's *Amazing Grace*. The Spirit is love; it can be found among Mormon faithful, but it is not exclusive to them and it cannot flourish in a bed of lies; truth is the topsoil for optimal growth. The idea of God is really just a whisper to our consciousness; it is pure ego to claim to know God. Buddhism teaches that "...the idea of a separate self is an illusion ...just an intellectual concept which has no reality."[654]

In William James' classic Gifford lecture series given at the University of Scotland 1901-1902, which included the *Varieties of Religious Experience*, the Harvard philosopher chronicles numerous mystical communion experiences from the nineteenth century and points out the commonality of those experiences as attributable to the intervention of the particular mystic's idea of God. Usually seen as a visitation by an *other*, some external being or personage (as in Joseph Smith's case), many of these very similar experiences are instead described as becoming *one with* God or the Universe.

No doubt, this type of experience has occurred to many/most/all of humanity at one time or another. What does it mean? I think it's best explained as a unification process whereby reality is unveiled. Certainly some, typically Eastern mystics, can achieve this unification at will (although to learn the process takes much self-discipline and then paradoxically, a letting go of control) through meditation. The fact that it has occurred in many ways and is documented so widely throughout history is evidence that our individuality, whether as humans, animals or plant life, is illusory.

What does religion, and in particular, Mormonism, have to do with such mystical experiences? Mormonism is an attempt, I believe, by faithful members to create this unifying experience. Some, I believe, use participation in the myriad of covenants and ordinances as a way to unite with Gaia and/or the universal whole, at least a part of it—in order to overcome the lonely individuation that accompanies Western religious beliefs. The irony in Mormonism is that it is its very doctrine which reinforces that separateness of personality and individualism, promising a faithful Mormon to become a separate, distinct god, not just to become one with God, or be like God, but promising discrete kingdoms, progeny and real estate in a patriarchal lineage of Mormon faithful. The whole Religion is one of separating, only to give back a degree of unification through the wearing of specialized garments, and participation in special temple ordinances to be shared only with the other like-minded Mormons. This breaking down into parts, only to unify within its own narrow belief system, is a protracted schizophrenic process and quite unnecessary.

Furthermore, when these legalisms, these steps and processes, are based upon untruths and even silliness, the waste of time and effort in the learning and then preserving one's specialness, the breaking down of the whole to emphasize individual achievement and glory, and then the building up of the Kingdom of God through participation in the unique and special Mormon events, becomes even more frustrating. Spirituality must be based on eternal truths, not falsehoods. As James points out:

In estimating the religious character of individuals, nations, or races, the first question is, not how they feel, but what they think and believe—not whether their religion is one which manifest itself in emotions, more of less vehement and enthusiastic, but what are the CONCEPTIONS of God and divine things by which these emotions are called forth. Feeling is necessary in religion, but it is by the CONTENT or intelligent basis of a religion, and not by feeling, that its character and worth are to be determined. *[655]

Faithful Mormons are kept ignorant and confused, and become indignant when questioned about their beliefs, all this through the Brethren's outright censorship. It is only if and when these good people are to look behind the curtain do they find, not the Great Wizard, but a man, usually a very ordinary or perhaps, in the case of early Mormon leaders, Joseph Smith and Brigham Young, extraordinarily evil men.

Mormon faithful should not aspire to hierarchical titles within the organization, but to ascertaining the absolute Truth for which they are searching. Then perhaps, the women will come off their Prozac and the men will appreciate the women as equals. Unlike Eastern philosophical paradigms, Westerners refuse to see themselves as part of nature. Instead, Abrahamic religions project an anthropomorphic God and by doing so, devalue all other sentient beings and the Earth's environment. Only by accepting our real relationship to this Earth and its inhabitants can a truly God-like society be possible.

I don't pretend to know the intra-familial workings of the higher power. God the Father, the Son, the Mother—who knows, and does it really matter? Isn't such a limited organization among the residents of the heavens just a projection of the ideal all-American family? Personally, I'd like to believe that some form of individual consciousness is eternal and that there is a higher power which had a hand in creating all the beauty and complexity of this Earth. I don't believe the power is a glorified man sitting on his throne playing a sort of solitary chess game with humanity. Nobody knows the details of the higher power; I don't think we were meant to know. It would be like (to quote a friend of mine) 'trying to teach a cat algebra.' I prefer to use the term "greater power," since I tend to believe it is the cumulative power of the universal intelligence, as opposed to anything from above, beyond or without. For all we can know, and as many religions teach—the foremost exception being Mormonism—God is

412

both substance and form, including both discrete and universal parts, but beyond our complete comprehension.

Projecting a Future Built upon a False Foundation

Long before Joseph Smith was born, Thomas Paine wrote about his belief in a creator whose message to mankind is not written in any book. Instead, that message is evident in the scientific wonder and beauty of his creations, in this glorious Earth and the universe beyond.[656] Paine's *Age of Reason* ideology has survived and grown and has been adopted by many of the most brilliant minds in the world today.

Fifty years after Paine's publication, when Joseph Smith and his cohorts were making-up Mormonism, another insightful European philosopher, Gustav Fechner, eloquently placed the true import of this life in its perspective with eternity.

Man lives not once. But three times: the first stage of his life is continual sleep; the second, sleeping and waking by turns; the third, waking forever....in the first stage his body develops itself from its germ, working out organs for the second; in the second stage his mind develops itself for its germ, working out organs for the third; in the third, the divine germ develops itself, which lies hidden in every human mind. .."The act of leaving the first stage for the second we call Birth; that of leaving the second for the third, Death. Our way from the second to the third is not darker than our way from the first to the second: one way leads us forth to see the world outwardly; the other to see it inwardly.*[657]

Mormonism disavows the concept of original sin: "We believe that men will be punished for their own sins, and not for Adam's transgression," (2nd Article of Faith). But in a sort of circumvention of a need for the Atonement of Christ, Mormonism prescribes itself and its ordinances as the only path to a redemptive exaltation. As gods in embryo, it is possible to become like God, and even, given eternal life and male gender, *a god.* By deprecating human experiences, in body or in correlation to nature, Mormonism advertises and focuses on a fabled life in the hereafter, to the exclusion of a real life lived in the present.[658]

How did the rational beliefs of Paine and others give way to the fantastical beliefs of Joseph Smith? Perhaps it was because there was no organization, no Church of Thomas Paine, no vehicle with which to indoctrinate and spread his truth. It was enough for him to tell the truth; he didn't need to create a business out of it.

The true appeal of Mormonism to its members and converts alike appears to be the idea of an eternal life of progression toward godhood, families in tow. And it has to be said that to some, if not many Mormon men, the idea of multiple wives from which to obtain infinite progeny, if not infinitely diverse sexual satisfaction, all with God's blessing and approval, is also attractive. Mormon women, with their ingrained deification of Mormon men, count themselves lucky if they have a husband to take them to this celestial glory, but absurdly, even their heavenly reward is one of subservience.

Perhaps in the life after this one, those who learn enough do proceed to a higher level and from that to another, *ad infinitum* until they have in effect become gods or at least god-like. Regardless of the appeal or of the ultimate reality of such a belief, it does not justify fairy tales told to impressionable young children of gold pates and biblical apostles restoring ancient (nonexistent) "Christian," priesthoods and idolizing an unbalanced young man from Upstate New York. The requirements of Mormonism: obedience, authoritarianism, limited original thinking, yielding to rule by a failing gerontocracy, worshiping in cult-like temple ceremonies, baptizing for the dead—none of these ordinances and ways of behaving can continue to be for the good.

Raised from birth with an ingrained hubris, the cult of God's chosen is taught that if only its members live the commandments prescribed by their Church, each will succeed in this life and the next. But upon reaching adulthood, whether in body or psyche (and some never do) a born-in-the-Church Mormon realizes that despite perfect obedience, bad things do happen to good people, disrupting the home-grown Mormon's otherwise smooth-sailing life. When the bad times come, as they inevitably do to all of us who live a life of any length, Mormons are shocked. Then, in order to maintain their paradigm, Mormons find ways to distinguish the bad things or misfortune of others. As the fourteenth fundamental of Mormonism warns: "The prophet and the presidency—the living prophet and the First Presidency—follow them and be blessed— reject them and suffer."

414

Young Mormons who grew into adults are beset with psychological problems because, despite a life lived as the perfect Mormon, they experience set-backs, disappointments and some even calamity and disaster—all things beyond their control. When taught that one's life is to follow an expected path toward eternal exhalation, if you do all that's required of a good Mormon—there is an expectation of success. There is no place in this paradigm for the unexpected or the unplanned event. When it happens, Mormons are not only ill-prepared, they can be personally ruined.

These unfortunate souls, the thinking goes, must have been less than diligent in their Church attendance or payment of tithes. And even if there seems to be no justice on this Earth, certainly a just God will see that the evil-doer is relegated to something less than heavenly in the eternities while the faithful Latter-day Saint is honored with celestial glory. However, as enlightened adults the world over realize, evidence of a supreme or universal justice has yet to be proven.

***

Mainstream Mormons don't currently practice blood atonement or polygamy, or really do anything which is detrimental to society, some might claim. Their deeds certainly do not compare to those of radical Islam. What if their religious origins are based on something other than what they claim—does it really matter?

The answer is a resounding yes. If potential or young Mormons were told the true story of Joseph the "town magician," who looked into a stone in a hat, words appeared and he wrote them into a book which is now sacred scripture, do you think Mormonism would be growing today? If these same young or newly interested potential Mormons knew that the sacred temple ceremony channels Masonic rituals, would they be as anxious to pay a full tithe in order to attend?

To build any kind of philosophy upon Mormonism's outrageous foundation is a very bad idea. Just as calculus cannot be based upon faulty algebra, future generations of thinkers, theologians, sociologists, philosophers, jurists and legislators are not able to build upon the rotten foundation created by Smith. Attempts to do so will fail.

If Mormonism continues to grow, increased numbers of its adherents will continue to become important members of our society. As professor Harold Bloom has conjectured, there might soon come a day when Mormons are so numerous "that governing our democracy became impossible without Mormon cooperation."* [659]   Given the Saints' growing realization of the Church's history of deception, I don't think this will happen, but if it somehow does, it will be disastrous.

History has proven Mormons to be liars and deceivers.   One nineteenth century apostle forewarned of this problem.   During the height of the polygamy disputes, LDS Apostle Charles W. Penrose saw the grave danger in habitually lying to cover up Church leaders' actions. In an 1887 letter to third LDS President John Taylor, he wrote that "the endless subterfuges and prevarications which our present conditions impose… *threaten to make our rising generation a race of deceivers*"* [660]

One recent attempt to build upon Mormonism's foundation was made by John W. Welch, BYU professor of law and religion, who taught at the law school when I was a student.   His article appears in the *Clark Memorandum,* a quarterly journal published by my alma mater, the J. Reuben Clark Law School.   The fall, 2010 edition includes his article entitled "Essentials of a Mormon Jurisprudence."   After acknowledging that many Americans perceive Mormonism as a "bizarre religion, or worse, a 'cult,'" Welch argues that "…Mormonism offers a logical alternative to the two prevailing paradigms—relativism and absolutism."   He logically argues that any Mormon jurisprudence must necessarily be rooted in Mormon scripture, but then takes the fantastically illogical leap to argue that Mormonism is not random or eclectic [or counterfeit] but inclusive, allowing for a fundamental jurisprudence of pluralism.   This BYU Professor is hopelessly lost in his attempt to bolster Mormonism and make it something it could never be—a legitimate new branch of Western jurisprudence. Arguments such as Welch's jurisprudential stretch must fail because the foundation of Mormonism contains little universal truth.

Compare Mormonism and building upon its beliefs with the Constitution of the United States, a document which, if not divinely inspired, was at least created by a quorum of brilliant secularists.   The document has lived and breathed, through very little amendment (after the adoption of the Bill of Rights) into what is today an incredible body of American law.   It was created out of a true need and with an earnest purpose and contemplation for the civil rights of generations yet to be born.   Because of its genuinely inspired source, it has lived and will continue to live and grow, through the centuries, all the while being subjected to exquisite scrutiny and interpretation by the most astute minds.

The Constitution was created in response to a need to ensure the protection of the rights of the citizens of a new nation. Surely, no such considerations passed through the mind of Joseph Smith at any time during his life, nor were they contemplated by subsequent LDS leaders, as evidenced by their duplicitous and contradictory finagling of Mormon Theology. Smith's creed ultimately resulted in a dogma steeped in contradiction and fallacy. To now attempt to graft a branch of Mormon-based legal philosophy onto the stalwart tree of Western jurisprudence is an act doomed *ab initio.*

***

December, 10, 2010, Brian David Mitchell was convicted of abduction, kidnapping and repeated raping of fourteen-year-old Elizabeth Smart at knife-point in 2002, by a U.S. District Court, Salt Lake County jury. Smart, then age 23, testified that during the nine months of her captivity she was raped daily, forced to drink alcohol, use drugs and view pornography.

In 1980 Mitchell had worked as a janitor at the LDS Beehive House on Temple Square in Salt Lake. According to the testimony of LDS member and co-worker, Doug Larsen, Mitchell also portrayed Satan in rituals at the Salt Lake LDS Temple.[661] In 1990 Mitchell renounced mainstream Mormonism and declared himself a prophet of God. (Elizabeth's mother had hired Mitchell to help with some roofing repairs in 2002; young Elizabeth was kidnapped within a week).[662]

Apart from the obvious horrors inflicted on this young woman by an evil man, one of the most troubling aspects of the case is the testimony by Detective John Richey, who failed to identify Elizabeth during an almost half-hour conversation with Mitchell, where the veil-covered Miss Smart was seated next to her abductor in the public library. In response to Richey's request, Mitchell refused to allow Smart to remove the veil, insisting that religious beliefs prevented her from speaking or having her face seen in public, and Richey accepted that explanation.

Now retired, the Detective regrets his actions: "It was traumatizing to me that I was in a position where I could have ended the investigation in August 2002 and I didn't," he said after testifying. "I beat myself up on that. I have to live with it."[663] The Detective's mindset in acknowledging the precedence of religious custom over the welfare of a minor is the very problem that continues to threaten many of Utah's children today.

The day after the verdict, the *Salt Lake Tribune* posted an editorial piece citing LDS psychotherapists strongly suggesting that Joseph Smith cannot be compared to Mitchell.[664] The article cited no expert evidence to the contrary, such as Anderson's *Inside the Mind of Joseph Smith*, or Woodbridge's *[The] Founder of Mormonism: A Psychological Study of Joseph Smith Jr.* I guess I shouldn't have been surprised at the one-sided reporting and underlying argument on behalf of Mormonism. This is Utah after-all and despite attempts at diversity, Mormons still rule the State.

***

Winter is almost done. During the typical April and sometimes May, Utah weather goes through a spastic period, blooming with spring one day and snowing like winter the next. I like summer evenings best, when it is warm enough to sit on my deck and look at the stars up high in the clear mountain air. Dusty blue-green sagebrush and rust-colored tobacco weed grow naturally in the dedicated Elk migration trail between my backyard and the golf course. At dusk, the lights from Salt Lake City cast an orange aura behind the Park City Mountains. The East Canyon River winds its way beautifully and naturally through the greenways. Despite Mormonism's disturbing ethnocentrism and misogyny, I'm afraid it is here in Utah to stay, at least for my lifetime; not sure that I am.

EPILOGUE

"The death of dogma is the birth of reality."–Immanuel Kant

Today Mormons are rapidly learning the true history of their church, but are hesitant to acknowledge the import of what they have learned, especially to other true-believing members or to Church authorities. An admission of such fear is found on the website: http://www.mormonthink.com (MT) created by about twenty-five "average everyday [LDS] members." In answer to the question, "Why don't you identify yourselves?" These former and current LDS faithful respond:

> The reason for that is obvious. We don't want to get kicked out of the church. The LDS Church unfairly punishes those who publish the truth. Many who contribute to MT go to the LDS Church regularly and they don't want to stop attending and providing service even if they don't believe the church is the one, true church. As stated on MT, some contributing members have since decided that they can no longer remain a member of the church and have identified themselves and their names can be found on the site. The remaining members are mostly still active members of the LDS church. When the LDS church ceases to punish its members for telling the truth, members may consider publishing their names.[665]

Some Mormons are reading and learning; others refuse to acknowledge the truth about the Church. Brian and I divorced in November of 2002, after almost twelve years of marriage. With no physical intimacy and his zealous devotion to Mormonism, it was impossible for us to live a real life together.

We agreed to joint custody; I knew Brian loved our son Danny and Danny loved his dad. For the first three of four years things went smoothly. That changed when Danny was about eleven. Despite the stipulation for joint physical and legal custody which required Brian and me to agree on any major decision affecting Danny's well-being, without my knowledge Brian brought LDS missionaries to his home to teach Danny over a period of months. He also made him read the Mormon

419

scriptures daily and attend church weekly.

When I realized what Brian was doing, I objected to the weekly church attendance, especially on my weekend. When Danny insisted, I told myself that he was going just to please his father and out of social pressure. Although Park City is one of the more religiously diverse Utah towns, many of the neighborhood boys his age were Mormon.

Then the bomb dropped.

"Mom, I want to join the Church," eleven-year-old Danny announced in an uncharacteristically authoritative voice.

This request was out of the blue.

"Uh, okay, honey, well…we need to talk about it."

I was stunned.

"No, I've made up my mind. I'm going to get baptized."

"Well…have you read *the Book of Mormon*? Have you prayed about this decision?"

"I don't need to; I know it's true," he shot back.

For several weeks I argued with Danny; I would not sign the parental consent needed to allow him to be baptized. This very stubborn Taurus of a boy, true to his word, did not give up. Eventually, after months of estrangement and my realization that I would have to let him make this decision on his own, I signed the parental consent form, making certain that Danny understood I was only doing it to avoid alienating him forever.

He was baptized. I didn't attend.

After the baptism his dad made sure he attended weekly Mormon services. Danny walked the neighborhood with the other twelve-year-old boys to collect fast offerings and was ordained a deacon in the Aaronic Priesthood.

Throughout his young life Danny had always been open-minded, so it didn't take long, about a year, for Danny to see the Church for what it is. The linchpin of his awakening was the book he chose for his summer reading selection in his Honors English class, Ayn Rand's *The Fountainhead*. I couldn't have been happier with the choice, but knew that if I had made any suggestion, it would have been discounted. Rand's comparison of individualism with collectivism made an impression on Danny. After reading the book, he concluded that Mormons were "second-handers," and that his dad was the epitome of Peter Keating.

"You see Mom…," he said, after telling me that he didn't believe in Mormonism after all, "you have to come at it from the side." I couldn't just tell him it wasn't true; he had to discover that for himself. Danny ultimately characterized Mormonism as "...a giant piece of candy that looks delicious, but when you finally take that first bite, it tastes like shit!"

Yes, those were his exact words.

***

One divorced law school classmate of mine contacted me and tried to pursue a relationship after I'd returned to practice in Salt Lake. I had never been and wasn't then interested, but he kept at it, throwing me an unwanted birthday party with a dozen red roses, making excuses to run into me at my office, brushing up against me at the fax machine and one time yelling in front of the other tenants coming and going in the hallway of my office building while I was about to get on the elevator, "The sex wasn't that good anyway!"

The final humiliating event occurred when he had obtained my business mail. This man followed my car into a busy downtown intersection near my office and while I was stopped at a traffic light, proceeded to dump my mail all over my car during evening rush-hour traffic.

On that same elevator trip down from my office, where the law school classmate had yelled the inane lie about us having sex, leaning against the interior elevator wall was the figure of an over-coated, overworked, sinewy male body.

"Hi, Kay. Don Morgan," he said, extending his hand. He had been another classmate of mine in law school.

I shook his hand politely. Morgan eyed the anti-Mormon books in my hand.

"You've read those?"

"Yeah—pretty good."

We looked at each other.

"The Church," we said simultaneously and then both shook our heads.

"Want to get together for a drink across the street? We can talk."

"Sure," I said. I felt like commiserating with someone I thought might be a fellow seeker of the truth and a man who seemed rather normal.

The next day after work I met him in the cigar room of an Italian Bar, located in the high rise just across the street from my office. We ordered drinks and sat alone in the smoking room in the interior of the bar, no windows. At 5:30 in the early evening there were few patrons. The

421

waiter had just left us. I pulled out the books I was reading and settled in to get ready for a good discussion about the church we'd both grown up in. I knew Don had been on a mission.

"My wife kicked me out you know, the kids…"
He was somber.
"It's the drinking—she…"

He ordered a couple more drinks. I was anxious to talk about the Church issues addressed in the books I'd laid on the table. We never did get around to discussing the controversial issues of Mormonism, and the difficulty of genuine living with the teachings of the Church ingrained into our psyches during our youth. Instead, Don reached both of his long legs under the table and tried to wrap them around mine.

"You know, I live in a hotel nearby, we could…"

If I had been able to reach his face across the table I would have slapped him. But by the time I had the impulse to respond to his inappropriate touching, he was half-way slumped to the floor, stone cold drunk.

"Get up," I said.
He immediately sat straight, still stupefied from the liquor.
I helped him with his coat.
"Where is your hotel?"

I knew he couldn't walk unassisted, so I managed to help him down the stairs and into the bank building parking lot. I pushed and prodded him into my car, then drove the couple of blocks to the downtown hotel, his temporary residence. I parked in the waiting zone and asked the valet to make sure he was safely taken up to his room
"Certainly," the attendant said.
I handed him a twenty-dollar bill. The young valet smiled knowingly. I presumed this wasn't the first time Morgan had needed help into his hotel room.
Poor Don Morgan, he'd been a good Mormon boy—mission, marriage, family man. It had all crumbled before him. He was never able

to articulate why he was so miserable. Instead, when things became unbearable, he escaped into a drunken stupor so that he wouldn't feel the pain.

These days the crazy mail-thrower, Don Morgan and other Mormon men are at a loss for meaning in their lives. Many, especially those whose marriages have been broken or who have suffered because of differing levels of spousal and familial commitment to the Church, are now desperate for direction and are grasping for solace wherever they can find it.

And althrough my perspective had changed, I realized that there is an inability among the majority of Mormons to acknowledge unpleasantness, untruths, or anything tending toward discomfort. Since I returned to practice law in Utah in 2001, most of the women I have deposed consume antidepressants regularly. It's a fair question to ask at the outset of a deposition: "Are you taking any medication which would impair your ability to testify truthfully?" It seems that Prozac and similar psychotropic drugs impair a witness's ability to recall anything troubling: no bad memories, injuries or arguments—it's all good.

***

Since my return to the State, I have noticed that the idealistic young Mormon men and women of my youth have almost all become less enthusiastic toward the Church. One exception is Cheryl, my roommate from BYU who has for years been the relief society president of her local congregation. She and I get together occasionally for a proper meal. We joke and reminisce about college, but the one subject we usually can't discuss is religion.

My sister has been married for more than thirty years to the same man and for almost the same length of time she has lived in a small Utah town. She has two grown sons who are both returned missionaries. She is an active Mormon, her husband having served in local Church leadership positions. She and I also avoid any real discussion about the Church.

My brother Kyle never bought into the Mormon Church. In junior high he was busted by our mother for growing pot in our backyard. During high school, he played drums in a neighborhood band whose rendition of the Knack's *My Sharona,* was quite excellent. Now fifty years old, Kyle reminds us all of Dad. Not so much in his features, but you can see our father in his voice and facial expressions. He and his wife Suzanne own and work hard at running "Caddy Shack," a bar in Colorado Springs.

My law school friend Sharon and her husband still live along the Wasatch Front. Although both joined the Church as young adults, neither of them has actively participated for years.

Ryan, the boy I dated when we were both high school seniors, married the girl with the highest split kicks on our Bountiful High School drill team. He works as a CPA. I see him annually, just before tax time.

"There is a lot of fear here," he once told me, without divulging anything specific.

I didn't have to ask about what; I knew what he meant.

Dr. Mike, my high school boyfriend, was in town several years ago. We have kept in touch off and on and he has helped me as a consulting expert on some medical malpractice cases. We met for lunch.

Mike accomplished his dream and has been a successful physician at a prominent hospital for years. He is married and has grown children. Overall he seemed satisfied with his life, but when our discussion turned to the topic of religion, his mood changed.

"I don't know if I believe in any God," he confessed.

Mike had spent his residency in an urban Midwestern hospital emergency department, where he witnessed the worst of humanity—gang related injuries and deaths; he had seen too much.

"Why do you stay?" I asked, referring to his continued membership in the Mormon Church.

"Socially, it's where I have grown up, raised my kids..."

He didn't finish his sentence, but it was clear it would have been too difficult for him to leave the Church at fifty. His investment quotient was too high. Besides his mission, he had been married in the temple, and had served in various priesthood leadership positions over the years.

We drove to Snelgrove's Ice Cream Shop to have one last ice cream together.

"Ice cream," he said, smiling at me with those kind eyes I had loved. Mike remembered my high school hinting for ice cream after many of our dates. I remembered putting a container of yogurt in an Easter Basket I made for him.

"I could never get used to yogurt," I said.

We both laughed, and for a moment we were back in high school.
***

As soon as I moved back to Utah, I was determined to find Jill, my junior high school friend. I discovered she was living with her parents at

424

their home in the country. I called her father and we made arrangements for a time when I could visit. She had divorced while her children were still living at home. I had spoken with her over a decade earlier, when she returned to graduate school; she seemed happy. Although her children lived with her ex-husband, Jill spent lots of weekends with them, but her family was convinced she was lost.

In the summer of 2001 Jill and I were both forty-six years old. I had heard that Jill wasn't herself. I wasn't sure what was meant by that, but when I saw her I could have never imagined it was so bad.

I drove up to her parents' home. Mrs. Watson, always gracious, answered the door.

"Why, come in dear," she said pleasantly.

"Jill..." Mrs. Watson called in her high sweet voice into what looked like the bedroom wing.

Jill walked into the kitchen area. She was barefoot, and dressed in a pair of cut-off denim shorts and an over-sized tee-shirt. Her hair was shoulder length and thick, but naturally darker than it had been in school. Though she had gained a lot of weight, barefaced and tanned, she was still as beautiful as ever.

"Let's go," she said, motioning me to follow her the way she had in junior high.

We went outside to walk around the grounds. She walked ahead and I followed behind her.

After an awkward moment I asked, "So... Jill, what is going on with you?"

"I'm going to hell and I know it and that's that." She looked over her shoulder for my reaction.

"Going to hell...why?" I asked.

"Divorced, being a bad wife and mother, being selfish, getting my degree when I should have been home with my kids, what else do you want to know?"

She turned and stared straight through me as if to steel me for her next admission.

"I had a—" Jill couldn't continue.

I stopped for a few seconds. Jill was clearly tormented.

"Everyone makes mistakes and has regrets. You aren't perfect. I'm not—nobody is. But you have been a great mother—"

"My kids don't think so," she interrupted.

We walked silently through the garden and into the weedy areas. The conversation stalled. Eventually I said goodbye and cried the whole trip home.

Jill had been an intelligent, vivacious woman full of drive with a love for life. She was the eldest of several siblings who had all married in the temple and were all successful by Mormon standards. Caught in the Mormon web of oppression, Jill had to stifle all of her natural and wonderful impulses and feelings in favor of the bland, boring role prescribed for all Mormon women. The cumulative effect of all this Mormon perfection was to convince Jill, the best of the bunch that she had failed in life.

Her feelings of failure at choosing a path different from the one expected of her caused her to do things I'm convinced she wouldn't have normally done, but for the tightly wound vise of Mormonism clamping down around her natural exuberance for life. Jill didn't fit the Mormon girl mold. Upon realizing her nonconformity into what was expected, she reacted viscerally. After making some poor choices, some of which she believed to be eternally damning, her choice was to exit from that reality into one of her own.

***

A few years after our divorce, Brian met Jenny Sue at the Mormon singles ward by the Utah State Capitol, the same ward where I had re-connected with Trent, more than two decades earlier.

Jenny Sue was visually striking. With a long platinum blonde weave down her back, large breast implants and a voluptuous figure, she always dressed seductively. She had enormous blue eyes and full red lips; she looked like a living blow-up doll. There was something about her eyes though—they were too open—too revealing. It was difficult to look directly at her; one could almost see her pain.

Jenny Sue spoke softly, almost in a whisper. When I first met her she was cordial. Later, her relationship with Brian became strained.

They became engaged after just a couple of months, but right before the June wedding date, after the custom-designed cake was made and the reception hall rented, she broke it off.

Jenny couldn't go through with the wedding. But Brian wouldn't let her go. Instead, he continued to pursue a one-sided relationship. He was obsessed with the woman. Like a drowning man, it seemed he was grasping for his last chance at a conventional Mormon life.

***

It was spring of 2008, almost five and one-half years after our divorce and three or more years after he and Jenny had first met. With the issue of Danny's membership in the Church resolved, Brian and I had resumed a somewhat cordial relationship. Brian helped me repair things around the house and I helped him with some of his legal problems. It was not particularly out of the ordinary then, when one evening he called me.

"You have to come over right now!"
There was sheer panic in his voice.
"What's wrong?" I asked.
"I'll tell you when you get here."

Brian's home was just across the golf course from mine. Inside the entryway on the right was a framed copy of the Mormon Church's *Proclamation of the Family,* declaring the family unit sacred and a clear rebuttal to any idea of Mormon tolerance for homosexuality. Much like the opposition to the ERA in the late seventies and eighties, well-organized Mormon contingencies encouraged by the Church, campaigned heavily in favor of California's Proposition 8 ban on gay marriage. And much like the ERA campaign, those who would benefit most from the legislation, campaigned the hardest.

I arrived at Brian's house to find that he had been served with a temporary restraining order and a petition for a permanent injunction to stay away from Jenny Sue. Jenny claimed Brian had entered her house uninvited, that another time he had thrown things at her while she stood on the landing of his staircase and that he had threatened her and her family with handguns.

I was skeptical. With one unusual exception, Brian had never shown a violent temper in my presence. From what I knew of him and from what he told me had happened between he and Jenny, I thought he was being unjustly accused. I agreed to defend him.

Together we planned his defense. He was involved in a business with partners who appeared to support him and who testified against her. They told how on one occasion she had stayed at his house while he and his partners were on a business trip to Shanghai. When they returned, she was at the airport to meet him. She dramatically wrapped her arms around him and kissed him. This happened after at least one of the claimed stalking incidents and was therefore relevant to show that she wasn't really frightened of him, as she had alleged in her court documents.

The evidentiary hearing we asked for before the Court could issue any injunction became ugly. But Jenny had an attorney with legal services who had a big caseload and who probably didn't expect much of a fight from the respondent.

The courtroom was at least half full with the parties' supporters. The audience was split into his and hers: Jenny's friends and relatives seated on one side, behind her and her attorney at counsel table, and Brian's friends and business associates, on the other.

"...it wasn't very good," Jenny responded to a question from Judge Kerns about their physical relationship.

After Jenny's direct testimony had detailed a tearful fear of Brian, I stood up, ready to cross-examine. I moved on to another area of questioning.

"You are frightened of Brian, correct?" I asked Jenny on cross-examination.

"Yes," she said in a soft voice.

"And you have no other motive for bringing this injunction other than out of fear for your safety and that of your family, is that right?"

"That's right," she answered.

"I'd like to offer this document for identification as Respondent's exhibit next in order."

Judge Kerns nodded.

I gave the document to the court clerk who marked it. Approaching Jenny as she sat on the witness stand, I handed her the exhibit.

"Would you please read the highlighted portions of this document?"

The sound of her breathing in the microphone attached to the witness stand grew louder. Her heavy lids almost closed over her eyes as she looked down at the exhibit, trembling.

"Would you please read the highlighted portions of the exhibit?" I repeated.

She looked over at Judge Kerns who nodded again. Reluctantly, Jenny began to read from the document in front of her.

…You still have your ward members that believe you are the next mild mannered Hugh Nibley gospel genius with a bishop that believes you are above the LDS doctrine rules of repentance because he thinks he knows your character from the good-old "mission" days. You still have your friends that believe you are a soft spoken victim of irrational women and your co-workers that have every confidence that you are a God to save them in their business trials and efforts. You have your big house located in upper-class America to maintain the appearance of wealth, and clean fresh mountain air to breath in and out everyday…*

Her voice had grown weaker. Jenny looked pleadingly at Judge Kerns one last time.

"Continue," the Judge instructed.

I am not beautiful and my temple recommend lay in pieces in the trash as I left it where it belongs when I left the temple. I never felt as worthless or ugly as when I was around you. Mormon men will never drink, seldom swear, but always fuck you, and then continue on as though the context of it all doesn't apply to their 3rd temple covenat. They are liars. I want nothing to do with them ever again. I never did and can't believe I was stupid enough to take you on believing you would be the exception. *[666]

"Is this your email to Brian?" I asked her.
"Yes," she whispered.
The personnel and spectators in the courtroom sat still.
"No further questions, your Honor."

I sat down, knowing I had discredited her motive for bringing the stalking injunction, but simultaneously empathizing with the feelings she had expressed in the impeaching email. I could relate to everything she said—the way Brian acted, and the fact that his actions were seemingly righteous to all but those who knew him best.

But my personal knowledge and feelings were irrelevant; I was ethically bound to do the best I could for my client. It was not that Jenny Sue was just angry at Brian; she was angry at the whole frustrating patriarchal system in which she had been an unwitting participant her entire life.

After several evidentiary hearings, the Judge found in Brian's favor and awarded attorneys' fees and costs, finding the woman had brought the action in bad faith. There was no believable evidence of stalking whatsoever, and certainly no believable evidence of Brian assaulting anyone with firearms.

Soon, the decision by the trial judge denying the injunction had been posted on the internet. Blog after defamatory blog followed between those who supported Jenny and those who supported Brian, until I could no longer stand to be involved in this petty tiff between my former husband and his former fiancée.

Brian was angry at me when I refused to prosecute a lawsuit against Jenny for defamation. I filed the complaint to protect the statute of limitations and then withdrew from representing him. He retained another lawyer and pursued collection of the award of attorney's fees and costs until finally, in late 2009, Jenny Sue was forced to file bankruptcy. At last, I had finally learned to say "no" to him.

***

Trent married a third time and seems happy. His wife is a good Mormon girl from a small Utah town. He came up to the house one summer afternoon when Chris was home visiting. He brought Chris' half-brother Sam, along with him. Trent was telling me how crazy his second wife (Sam's mother) was and that she would curse at him for no apparent reason.

Memories of similar exchanges between Trent and me flashed across my mind. I wanted to tell him there was a reason, lots of them. Sam's mom is smart and not at all submissive. Most likely she hadn't and wouldn't take any abuse from Trent.

Trent and I rocked in the patio chairs on the deck. It was a blue sky, sunny afternoon.

"I thought she had remarried," I said.

"No, just knocked-up."

Trent didn't realize the import of his disparaging remark.

The boys jumped and flipped on the trampoline. Trent stopped his rocking for a bit.

"My mother was crazy."

"Yeah," I said, "but she had six kids of her own plus all of the adopted ones."

Silence from Trent.

Then he resumed his rocking, a little quicker, squinting his eyes a bit. As he spoke, I thought how sad it was. With the exception of his birth mother, all these women in his life were not crazy; they were intelligent women who were trapped in a misogynistic culture. If the men in their lives saw them as crazy, it was only because these women didn't fit the classic Mormon girl mold.
***

In the summer of 2010, the local office of the SEC sponsored a fraud seminar at Utah Valley University in Orem (Utah County), Utah. While initially slated to participate, on reconsideration, the LDS Church withdrew from the program. Apparently the Church felt it had fulfilled any obligation to be involved in this issue by announcing that it had historically warned its members against affinity fraud.

Utah State regulator and Mormon, Keith Woodwell, the State's chief investigator of investment fraud, wants more Church involvement since many victims are found through common membership in Mormonism. Apparently oblivious to the obvious reason for the Church's reluctance to participate (*asinus asellum culpat*), Woodwell naively reasons:

> I'd love to hear a very clear statement that this is a relationship of sacred trust that you have with your ward members, stake members," he said. "And to abuse this relationship of trust, to take advantage of someone financially, is not just a crime but that it is really a reprehensible and an egregious abuse of that relationship. And it should be treated in the same way the abuse of other sacred relationships are treated. It's just like spousal abuse or child abuse. [667]

If LDS Church leaders have no acknowledged fiduciary duty toward the members of their church, then certainly it is unrealistic to expect such a relationship between the members in their dealings, one with another. Furthermore, if one reflects on true Church history, it becomes clear that Joseph Smith was the harbinger of the current and continuing problems with affinity fraud among Mormons.
***

I have attended parties with girls from our Bountiful High School drill team and other female graduates from the class of 1973. Initially I was hesitant to attend, thinking I would have nothing in common with these women, most of whom remain actively involved in Mormonism. But to my delight, the atmosphere has been relaxed and easy.

Most of the women have several children each, and almost all have grandchildren. They are intelligent, remain quick-witted and generous. I have often thought it was a shame their energy wasn't focused on something more grounded in truth. Author Sam Harris' rhetorical question about the numerous hours spent in the service of an imagined deity comes to mind.

> Think of all the good things human beings will not do in this world tomorrow because they believe that their most pressing task is to build another church or mosque, or to enforce some ancient [or in the case of Mormonism, nineteenth century] dietary practice, or to print volumes upon volumes of exegesis on the disordered thinking of ignorant men. How many hours of human labor will be devoured today, by an imaginary God?[668]

I recently held a reunion for the *Sounds* South Africa performers at my home. Many of us hadn't seen one another for over a decade. Harry Schultz, our director for the South African Tour, flew in from Los Angeles. After directing BYU Young Ambassadors for years, Harry went on to become Creative Director for Disney World and the creator of nineties pop vocal group, "The Jets."

Brother John Kinnear and his wife also attended the party. In a behind the scenes reveal he told the group that he had been a bit nervous about taking *Sounds* to South Africa, given the political climate and the terrorist activities, but that when he spoke with the LDS General Authorities, they didn't see a problem and said "Why not?"

Many of the Tour members now live outside Utah. Some seemed to have grown in the Faith, indifferent or at least reconciled to any issues regarding LDS Church history. Others were quiet and solemn, perhaps pensive about the way things had turned out in their lives. Still others, though projecting a happy image, are clearly suffering. The husband of one performing couple now forbids his wife from wearing make-up on her face. Many of the women had been on antidepressants for years and two of the female trio of singers had died untimely deaths.

As practiced, current Mormon sociology incorporating only choice bits and the less offensive pieces of the original Mormon doctrine seems to have morphed into a curious version of the law of attraction. Don't read anything negative about the Church, avoid any debate or discussion on controversial issues, have faith that the Church is true. Live your life as if nothing is wrong and you will be happy. Pray and receive blessings for what you want and the Lord will provide.

This Mormon version of the law of attraction is just as flawed as any. The Earth's resources are limited, everyone wants success, and there can only be one student body president at your child's high school, no matter how badly each of the four candidates wants or believes it is their office to have.

Much has been written about this ancient and recently resurrected "Secret" philosophy, but not much is ever said about the problems encountered when the creators of their desires are simultaneously the destroyers of the desires or even lives of others. Those whose sole focus is on their goals and those of their elite group, to the exclusion of the rest of the people who share the Earth, are destined to be the source of global imbalance. Despite aspirations to infinite abundance, we live in a finite system which demands conservation and the intelligent use of limited resources.

***

Temple going Mormons are admonished to disassociate with apostates. One of the questions asked before a temple recommend is issued is whether the Church member sympathizes with apostates or apostate groups.[669] Since my brother Kyle was never really active in the Church, I am the only apostate in our extended Burningham family, which has made it difficult to attend the Burningham family holiday functions. But I usually do attend and take Danny and Chris with me when either or both of them are available.

The Burningham family get-togethers are now held at my Aunt Jeen's beautiful, but architecturally atypical for the surrounding community, stucco home, situated high above the Bountiful Temple, complete with a basketball court. There are probably close to a hundred children and grandchildren descended from my cousins, the original fourteen grandchildren of Grandpa and Grandma Burningham. I don't know all their names. I believe most remain active in the Church.

433

However, I am certain that at least my female cousins would be much happier if they were out from under the patriarchal oppression of Mormonism.

Chris spins records for parties and is studying chemical engineering and nanotechnology in Santa Barbara. Danny is a senior in high school, a whiz at math and science, a self-taught computer programmer and has been working toward his black belt in karate.

My mother is eighty now, and still lives in the Bountiful house we moved into when I was twelve. I try to visit her as often as I can. She has always had questions about Mormonism, but most her friends and neighbors are LDS and they have been good to her and she is at a point in her life where she cannot change. She seems at peace because, as she recently and wisely told me, "it doesn't really matter what religion someone is; its how they treat me that matters."

***

Reliance on the Brethren's misrepresentations has clearly been to many Church members' injury and damage. It is a matter of record that millions of devout Mormons annually tithe a full 10% of their net, if not gross income, as opposed to their increase. LDS Church members also donate millions of hours spent teaching and in administrative and Church welfare activities. In recent years, local members have even been charged with janitorial responsibilities for their particular chapel. The steady stream of income together with the hundreds of hours of donated time per member, per year, makes this church one of the world's wealthiest and most self-sufficient non-profit organizations in the world.

The loss of money donated to the LDS Church is one thing; other, non-monetary losses are more damaging. These include the loss of emotional intelligence and maturity, personality distortion, family division/destruction and individual psychological injury. Such losses are the true and hidden tragedy of Mormonism.

Believing members, many of whom join or are indoctrinated while very young, and are otherwise intelligent and well-educated, have sacrificed a substantial percentage of their life and have made and continue to make life-altering decisions, such as where to live, who to marry and with whom to associate based on their Mormon beliefs. They have lost a genuine life because of their sincere belief in Mormonism, a consciously concocted fairy-tale.

The Mormon Corridor is an Intermountain West population of faithful who are unable to acknowledge anything that doesn't align with their particular world view. This narrow paradigm of apparent pleasantry has been in place for more than one hundred and eighty years. With the mounds of accurate and undeniably factual information now easily accessible concerning the true origins of Mormonism, this Religion can no longer exist as a good faith representation of what God requires of his followers. Individual existential crises are occurring daily in the lives of hundreds if not thousands of Mormons. Mormonism's implosion is imminent, but to finally shift this unrealistic paradigm will require more than a minority liberal faction or a few Mormon apostates nibbling around the edges. It will take a crisis from within.

In the world of the twenty-first century, few frontiers remain available for exploitation. In the United States at least, there is no remote Great Basin in which to corral and isolate the Saints. The semi-literate and undereducated in the developing nations are perhaps the last of these frontiers and are being mined by LDS missionaries as I write.

But the global future doesn't lie in a nineteenth century mindset, in an antiquated view of the universe, in the maintenance of gender discrimination, ripped-off rituals or unquestioning bequeaths to an unaccountable bureaucracy. This new world, full of all the knowledge and wisdom mankind has achieved throughout the history of civilization, has no place for Mormonism.

THE END

APPENDIX A: Is the LDS Church above the Law?

Mormonism seems to claim that God is a being with whom one can bargain. "And when we obtain any blessing from God, it is by obedience to that law upon which it is predicated."[670] "I, the Lord, am bound when ye do what I say; but when ye do not what I say, ye have no promise."[671]

I never felt that I could ask my idea of God to have a seat across the conference table from me. No matter how confident I am in my advocacy skills, I've always thought it foolish to attempt to bargain with omnipotence. If indeed "Man is as God once was, and God is as man may become," then a theology which includes equal bargaining power with God doesn't seem so farfetched.

Keeping this attitude in mind, one is better able to understand the LDS attitude toward the law of the land. With priesthood law as the ultimate rule and with a goal of establishing the Kingdom of God here on Earth, despite words to the contrary, Mormons are generally cavalier when it comes to their regard for man-made laws and even secular ethics. It is not surprising then, that nineteenth-century Mormon history is replete with lawsuits brought by various individuals and entities, governmental and private, against the Mormon Church and/or its leaders. This is particularly true in the early days when Joseph Smith and many of the founding brethren were named as individual defendants in both criminal and civil lawsuits.

It is a well known fact that "... the Prophet [Joseph Smith] spoke repeatedly of being plagued by 'vexatious lawsuits.'" Two BYU Law School professors currently researching all of the cases in which Smith was a party or in which he presided, have determined that, "In terms of the total litigation that Joseph was involved in, we've identified more than 220 cases," brother Madsen said. "We still don't know how many are still out there. It's a far broader expanse of raw material than we had originally expected." [672]

Does the Mormon history of flaunting the secular legal system explain why the Brethren are unconcerned with the continued misrepresentations to Church members and potential converts? Despite lip service to the contrary, do Mormon leaders perceive their ecclesiastical role as above the law of the land? I think the answer to both of those questions has to be yes. If so, do those injured and damaged by the misrepresentations of fact by the LDS Church hierarchy have a valid recourse against the LDS Church under our secular legal system? In order to answer this last question, a brief summary of the constitutional issues as they relate to religion is necessary.

Both the United States and Utah Constitutions prohibit the establishment of religion by government. Likewise, both constitutions prohibit undue restriction on the free exercise of religion. "Congress shall make no law respecting an establishment of religion, or prohibiting the free exercise thereof..." [673] The inherent tension between these competing guarantees makes legislative and judicial duties difficult. Federal and state case law is replete with decisions citing constitutional prohibitions against ruling on religious doctrine. The one exception to this general rule concerns the issue of whether a particular religious symbol placed on public property constitutes an endorsement by the government, in violation of the establishment clause. Many of these types of cases have been decided.

However, neither federal nor state courts are constitutionally able to determine religious doctrinal issues. But the issue surrounding the misrepresentation of facts about Mormonism's scriptural foundations by leaders in the LDS Church is an exception to this rule. In determining whether the LDS Church (through its high ranking leaders) has induced its members to join or to remain in the Church through misrepresentations, a court need not decide the divinity of Christ or the efficacy of prayer, or any other tenet of Mormon doctrine. Arguably, these things could never be determined. However there is abundant evidence that Mormon scripture-based doctrine is man-made, when all the while it has been and continues to be represented by Mormon leaders to be the Word of God, from a divine source *other than Joseph Smith.* This is fraud under any interpretation of the law. The fact that the misrepresentations were made in the context of growing a religion is a red herring.

Mormon Leaders are Agents of the LDS Church

Certainly each of the one-hundred and fifteen current general authorities acts as agent for the LDS Church. These leaders speak on behalf of the Church, write articles for Church publications, preach to Church members and direct and administer the organization of the Church and its various divisions and missions worldwide. All of this is done under the cloak of priesthood authority, received after having been called to serve by the Lord. Since the time of early Church history, with the formation of the Church's complex organization of prophet/president, two counselors, the presiding bishopric, the twelve apostles, and the two quorums of the seventies, this agency relationship has been well documented. Given that Mormon leaders' agency is indisputable, the Church is vicariously liable for the affirmative [mis] representations and omissions of fact by each of its appointed (and those claimed anointed) authorities under the doctrine of *respondeat superior.*

It is doubtful that the Church, acting as only a business can, through its leaders, intended to cause emotional distress to its members. On the contrary, it is almost certain that its agents have not (although many leaders might well be indifferent). However, the fact that Church leaders have presumably acted out of noble motives (which presumption can be easily rebutted in many cases, especially early in Church history) does not protect the Church from potential liability for negligent misrepresentation or fraud, where the elements of either of those claims are met.

Historically Important Cases in which the LDS Church has been a Party

A review of the historic cases which have involved the LDS Church as a party provides some background into the serious problems its peculiar doctrines have caused. The first and most famous case is *Reynolds v. United States*, 1878, 98 U.S. 145.[674] In *Reynolds*, the United States Supreme Court reviewed the conviction of a Utah Territory resident, George Reynolds, for violation of the federal law against bigamy. Reynolds claimed the trial court erred because it failed to give his requested instruction that if the jury found Reynolds became a bigamist as a result of sincerely held religious beliefs, then he should be found not guilty. The Utah trial court wisely refused such an instruction, and also added that the anti-bigamy law was enacted for the protection of innocent women and children.

In upholding the trial court's denial of Reynolds' proposed instruction and confirming the bigamy law as constitutional and not violative of the right to religious expression, the U.S. Supreme Court acknowledged that in general, an individual's beliefs are to be protected pursuant to the freedom of expression clause. However, when those beliefs become actions which adversely affect a secularly recognizable interest of the state, regulation was permissible and did not violate constitutional standards. Quoting Thomas Jefferson, the Court pointed out that in every educated western civilization, monogamy was recognized as the societal norm and that polygamous relationships are hurtful to women and children, "...it is time enough for the rightful purposes of civil government for its officers to interfere when principles break out into overt acts against peace and good order."[675]

Jefferson's preamble has additional words that Utah church/government leaders should consider:

> Well aware that the opinions and belief of men depend not on their own will, but follow involuntarily the evidence proposed to their minds; that Almighty God hath created the mind free, and manifested his supreme will that free it shall remain by making it altogether insusceptible of restraint; that all attempts to influence it by temporal punishments, or burthens, or by civil incapacitations, tend only to beget habits of hypocrisy and meanness, and are a departure from the plan of the holy author of our religion, who being lord both of body and mind, yet chose not to propagate it by coercions on either, as was in his Almighty power to do, but to extend it by its influence on reason alone; that the impious presumption of legislators and rulers, civil as well as ecclesiastical, who, being themselves but fallible and uninspired men, have assumed dominion over the faith of others, setting up their own opinions and modes of thinking as the only true and infallible, and as such endeavoring to impose them on others, hath established and maintained false religions over the greatest part of the world and through all time...*

The question arises whether polygamy would be held constitutional (in effect *Reynolds* overruled) if the issue were to come before the U.S. Supreme Court today. The Utah Supreme Court has dealt with this issue in two relatively recent cases, *State v. Green*, 2004 UT 76 and *State v. Holm*, 2006 UT 31. In both of these decisions the Utah Supreme Court upheld Utah's bigamy statute to be non-violative of both federal and state constitutions under *Reynolds* and its progeny.

In a lengthy concurrence in *Holm*, Utah Supreme Court Justice Ronald E. Nehring provided a review of the historically difficult relationship between the Territory/State of Utah and the federal government. He explained that although the Manifesto of 1890 renouncing polygamy was apparently sufficient to persuade the federal government to allow Utah into the union, the genuineness of the LDS Church's claim to have abandoned the practice was called into question during the Reed Smoot United States Senate confirmation hearings of 1904-1907. During those hearings, then president of the Church, Joseph F. Smith, denied ever having received revelation and admitted he and other Mormon leaders (but not Apostle Smoot) still practiced polygamy. The hearings were well-attended by curious members of the public and many of the beliefs and theretofore secret rituals of the Mormon Religion were the subject of inquiry.

Although Apostle Smoot retained his status as U.S. Senator from Utah (the Senate failed to achieve the 2/3 majority necessary to remove him), the Mormon government leaders continued to be viewed as suspect, due to their admitted devotion to the Church over the federal government. Justice Nehring opposed Chief Justice Durham's opinion that polygamy no longer presents a social danger and that polygamy as practiced post-1890, was a spiritual as opposed to a legal ritual, and that to criminalize such relationships would infringe upon defendant's free exercise of his religion.

When *Reynolds* was decided, the federal government viewed polygamy as despicable, one more way in which the LDS Church exerted control over its people. The practice of polygamy intensified the public's perception of Mormonism as a threat to democracy. Perhaps those concerns are not as valid today. Indeed, under expanding notions of due process, the right to privacy, equal protection and such other penumbral Constitutional rights, the right to form polygamous or polyandrous unions may in fact be upheld if the proper case were to present itself to the Supreme Court of the United States today. Nevertheless, coerced, falsely-induced polygamous marriages, especially to children, will never be legal in the United States.

Sovereignty of the United States over the LDS Theocratic Kingdom of God Was at Last Determined in 1890

[The] Late Corporation of the Church of Jesus Christ of Latter-day Saints v. United States, Romney, et. al., 1890, 136 U.S. 1, was discussed in Chapter Seven of this book. It is important because historically, especially throughout the nineteenth century, the federal government has been forced to fight the LDS Church, an insular, quasi-sovereign political group, for sovereignty. The Church had attempted to declare ownership of the Deseret Territory in 1848, yet it lacked the sovereign power to do so. The Utah Territory, not the Territory of Deseret, was the only territorial government recognized under the laws of the United States. Skirmishes, protracted federal legislation and eventually, this U.S. Supreme Court case finally established that the United States of America was the supreme power in the Great Basin Region, taking precedence over Mormonism's claimed Kingdom of God.

The LDS Church has Chronically Failed to Deal Adequately with Allegations of Sexual Abuse

Most twentieth and twenty-first century cases against the LDS Church have involved local Church leaders' failure to report allegations of sexual abuse by one ward member against another. These claims against the Church have involved inappropriate actions by Mormon missionaries, scout leaders, primary teachers and bishops. The main issue is whether the lay clergy of the local leadership deals adequately with information they receive about sexual abuse, whether from the perpetrator or the victim.

There are different requirements, depending upon who relays the information to the church leader. If the victim confesses, there could be a duty to report; however if the perpetrator confesses, in some states that duty is preempted by the priest-penitent privilege, thereby preventing any disclosure by clergy to the legal authorities.

In *Doe v. Corporation of the President of Church of Jesus Christ of Latter-day Saints*,[676] Utah's Appellate Court held that the LDS Church had no duty to warn another ward member, despite the fact that the abuser (a member of the same ward) was a known sex-offender and a Church-appointed high priest and scout leader. This case is important because the

442

decision of the Utah Court of Appeals acknowledges as undisputed, the following facts:

> Beginning in 1966 and continuing through 2002, COP received several complaints from its members that Tilson was sexually abusing children within his ward. However, COP not only failed to do anything in response to these complaints, it actively concealed Tilson's sexual abuse from its members and secular authorities. Moreover, COP allowed Tilson to continue to hold the positions of High Priest and scout leader. [Positions conferred upon Tilson despite Church knowledge of his predatory history]. [677]

Plaintiffs had both been molested by Tilson while he held the church-appointed offices. Both incidents of abuse occurred at Tilson's home. The Court found there was no duty for the Church to warn other members of the ward of the fact that Tilson had a long history of sexual abuse. The rationale behind the decision was that none of the abuse took place during LDS Church activities or on Church property.

The Court acknowledged that §62A-4a-403 (Supp. 2003) of the Utah Code provides for criminal sanctions for failing to report suspected child abuse. However, citing prior Utah case law, the Court found that even if the actions of the LDS Church were in violation of the penal (criminal) code, they did not constitute a tort, or private cause of action, that could be brought by the victims as a civil claim. [678] Technically, the Appellate Court correctly interpreted the law in existence at that time. But it is clear to anyone reading the opinion or familiar with the law and the facts in *Doe v. COP* that the decision, based upon the Court's narrow interpretation of the applicable law, was unjust.

The LDS Church has also been Sued for Interference with Parental Custody Rights

Where *Doe v. COP* was a case of extreme indifference to the needs and safety of its membership, the facts upon which the *Gulbraa* Case is based, illustrate a meddlesome interference with an LDS Church member's parental rights. *Gulbraa v. COP*, 2007 UT App 126, was decided in 2007, again by this same Utah Appellate Court (Utah has just one intermediate court of appeals between the trial courts' jurisdiction and the Utah Supreme Court).[679]

Mr. Gulbraa was an LDS male who, after his divorce, had obtained full custody of his two minor children. In violation of the custody order, his former wife and her new husband kidnapped the children and relocated to Japan.

Gulbraa advised the Church that he did not want his eldest son, who was about to become old enough to receive the Church's Aaronic Priesthood (age twelve) to be ordained in Japan by his former wife's husband. A Japanese LDS General Authority assured the father, as confirmed in an email, that this would not happen. Nevertheless, the child was ordained. Subsequently, the Church refused to communicate with Mr. Gulbraa, stating only that it had decided to go ahead with the ordination because it was a private matter between the Church and the child. Thereafter, Church authorities refused to provide Gulbraa with any information about his children's whereabouts.

The Appellate Court upheld the trial court's dismissal of most of the Plaintiff's causes of action: breach of contract, promissory estoppel, fraud, and negligent misrepresentation, reasoning that to proceed on such theories would require the Court to interpret Church law, policies and practices, violating the First Amendment establishment clause as interpreted in Utah's *Franco* and other, U.S. Supreme Court, cases. However, the Appellate Court allowed the cause of action to proceed for intentional infliction of emotional distress, reasoning that the Church's denial of information to Mr. Gulbraa may yet be proven as constituting severe emotional distress with attendant damages. Of course, this claim was subject to discovery and proof at the trial court level.

***

Typically, LDS faithful seek counseling from bishops and use them as mediators, regardless of that bishop's training or lack of training in any particular area. The feeling (taught to Church membership) is that the bishop is inspired of God and therefore his judgment must be correct. Perhaps this course of action is reasonable in light of LDS members' beliefs that even local clergy are inspired. If in fact these local leaders have no better communication with God than the member seeking counsel, what then?

It is a difficult position for a member of the LDS Church to find oneself in: faith in the Lord's appointed representative vs. what one rationally and reasonably believes to be just, fair and in the best interests of, usually, a minor. In one case, an LDS psychologist was concerned enough with the inadequate way local LDS leaders treated claims of sexual abuse that she volunteered to state under oath the problems she had seen while working on those types of cases involving the Church. Later, she recanted much of her prior affidavit, seemingly having been pressured to do so.[680]

Jurisdictions Other than Utah have determined that a Church can be Held Liable for Fraud

Where proven by extrinsic evidence, religious fraud is not constitutionally protected. In *National Ass'n for Better Broadcasting v. F.C.C.*, 591 F.2d 812, 1978, the U.S. Court of Appeals for the District of Columbia dealt with an appeal brought by the National Association for Better Broadcasting (NABB) of a license renewal granted by the Federal Communications Commission (FCC) to a California television station which, among other types of broadcasts, televised religious programs that depicted and preached faith healing. Although not discussed in depth, in a footnote, the D.C. Appellate Court pointed out that:

> We note the special difficulties attending the allegation of fraudulent religious programming. While it is probable that speech enjoys no heightened protection merely if its content is religious, and it is quite clear that religious fraud is not protected by any clause of the First Amendment, inquiries into religious fraud must scrupulously avoid becoming inquisitions into the sincerity of religious belief. It will thus ordinarily be necessary to rely on extrinsic evidence of fraud in such cases.[681]

California has historically been on the cutting edge of the law; its Supreme Court has allowed a claim involving fraud in the inducement against a church. *Molko v. Holy Spirit Association for the Unification of Christianity* 46 Cal.3d 1092, 762 P.2d 46 (1988) concerns a suit brought by a former church member who alleged that the church used deception to recruit new members. (*Id.* at 1116). In a unanimous opinion, the California Supreme Court framed the issue as "...whether a religious

445

organization can be held liable on a traditional cause of action in fraud for deceiving nonmembers into subjecting themselves, without their knowledge or consent, to coercive persuasion." (*Id.* at 1117). The Court distinguished the case at bar from other cases involving religious belief because *Molko* was challenging the *actions* of the church in its methods of obtaining new recruits through deceptive means, which conduct, the high court held, *can* be subject to regulation.

The *Molko* Court reasoned that neither the Federal nor State Constitutions barred former members of the church from bringing traditional fraud actions against the church for allegedly inducing them, by misrepresentation and concealment of its identity (compare Mormon leaders' misrepresentation and concealment of the true facts surrounding Mormonism's origins) into unknowingly entering an atmosphere in which they would then be subjected to coercive persuasion.

The Court further held that although liability for deceptive recruitment practices imposed a marginal burden on the Holy Spirit Church's free exercise of rights, that burden was justified by a compelling state interest in protecting individuals and families from a substantial threat to public safety, peace and order posed by the fraudulent induction of unconsenting individuals into an atmosphere of coercive persuasion. Finally, the Court found that the imposition of tort liability had the purpose and effect of advancing a legitimate secular goal of protecting persons from being harmed by fraud, and was nondiscriminatory. *Molko* may be one of the first in a line of cases of the future to address these issues.

In a relatively recent case, *Hawthorne v. Couch*, 40162 (La. App. 2 Cir. 2005) 911 So.2d 907, a Louisiana appellate court dismissed a claim brought by a plaintiff to recover tithes paid to his church over the years. Plaintiff claimed that the basis for payment of tithing was fraudulent and thus the tithes should be returned. The court found that where the "…issue of tithes was rooted in religious doctrine," there was no way for the court to litigate such a claim due to Constitutional entanglement issues.[682]

The Louisiana case disallowing tithing paid as damages is distinguishable from tithing paid to the LDS Church based upon misrepresentations of the true facts surrounding its origins. Arguably a different case could be made from the one in *Hawthorne*. There, the tithe-payer claimed that the promises made by the church if he paid his tithes, did not come true. However, with Mormonism, one could justifiably argue that tithes are paid based upon the representation by the LDS Church that its scripture came from ancient American prophets, engraved on golden plates, the writing of the biblical prophet Abraham, and /or from the mouth of God through its founder, Joseph Smith. If *the Book of Mormon* has been proven to be a fraud, and the Church knows it or should know it, yet its leaders continue to misrepresent the facts about its scriptural origins, then arguably this could be the extrinsic evidence of fraud sufficient to litigate the issue of whether LDS Church members have been fraudulently induced to pay tithing to the Mormon Church.

How Can a Church that Endorses Political Agenda Remain a Non-Profit Organization under the IRS Tax Code?

How can a non-profit corporation fail to account to its general membership for the income it receives? How can a Church remain non-profit when it has made concerted efforts to defeat various political agenda over the years? The LDS Church has maintained its tax-exempt, nonprofit religious status under 501(c) (3) of the Internal Revenue Code, despite contributing heavily in man hours and through the use of LDS member resources via phone banks, satellite broadcasts, multi-media marketing efforts and grass roots rallies, to political causes such as the defeat of the Equal Rights Amendment and more recently, to pass California's Proposition 8 ban against gay marriage.

The evidence of LDS Church support behind California's Proposition 8 (which limited legal marriages to those between one man and one woman) which received enough signatures in the few months between the California Supreme Court decision upholding gay marriage and the deadline for placing the proposition on the ballot in time for the November, 2008, election is overwhelming. During this interim period, the Church openly recruited and solicited its membership to support the Proposition. According to one source, LDS Church leaders personally approached Church members and recommended a donation to the Proposition 8 cause based upon that family's tithing receipts. [683]

On Oct. 28, Mr. [Alan C.] Ashton, the grandson of the former Mormon president David O. McKay, donated $1 million. Mr. Ashton, who made his fortune as co-founder of the WordPerfect Corporation, said he was following his personal beliefs and the direction of the Church, 'I think it was just our realizing that we heard a number of stories about members of the church who had worked long hours and lobbied long and hard,' he said in a telephone interview from Orem, Utah....In the end, Protect Marriage estimates, as much as half of the nearly $40 million raised on behalf of the measure was contributed by Mormons.[684]

Though the Church carefully obscured its involvement by creating and then stepping back from a coalition for concerned citizens, there is no doubt that the Brethren were behind the defeat of gay marriage rights in California as they had been in Hawaii and other states several years earlier; this despite the fact that at the time, Mormons constituted just 3% of California's total population.[685]

Title 26 is the Internal Revenue Code contained within the United States Code. §501(c) (3) is known as the charitable organization exemption. It allows a business entity organized and operated exclusively for one of the many exempt purposes, to avoid income tax. One of the exemptions is an organization for religious purposes. In order to qualify, none of its earnings may inure to any private shareholder or individual. Furthermore, the entity claiming exempt status may not attempt to influence legislation or participate in campaigns for political candidates.

To date however, the LDS Church has only received a hand slap for filing a late report on its official donations in support of Proposition 8. Additionally, the amount of official donations was minimal in comparison to the time and cash donated by individual Mormons at the behest of the Brethren.

As a result of the Proposition 8 support, California's Fair Political Practices Commission (FPPC) filed a complaint against the LDS Church. The Church was found guilty of multiple counts of Proposition 8 malfeasance, although the total fine imposed represented a small amount compared to the donations made.[686] Based upon these political contributions, some groups have demanded revocation of the Church's tax exempt status, at least under California state law.

The LDS Church has Spent Millions in Damage Control after the Proposition 8 Backlash

The backlash to the Church's involvement in Proposition 8, some even from Mormon membership, has been substantial. In an effort to counteract the negative publicity, in 2010 the LDS Church began a series of "I am Mormon," advertisements. These were televised in nineteen U.S. markets/cities (but not in the Mormon Corridor) and on the new LDS website http://www.mormon.org/. The ads feature nice-looking, atypical or even exceptional members of the LDS Church, Mormons, appearing happy, satisfied and accomplished. After a monologue where the Mormon speaker lists his or her achievements (all of the women emphasize motherhood as their highest achievement) and station in life, the speaker ends his/her speech with "...and I am a Mormon."

Although the production quality of the commercial spots is quite professional, one has to wonder about the motives of a church which spends its tithes on advertising its members. According to national news sources, these ads are just part of a public relations campaign where the LDS Church is spending millions of dollars in damage control:

> Having suffered a blistering blow the last two years to its already shaky image, the Church of Jesus Christ of Latter-day Saints (Mormon Church) has begun a massive multi-media campaign to come back from the depths of unfavorability in the national polls. They're spending millions and millions of dollars in an unprecedented national advertising campaign on television and radio. They also launched a new website Mormon.org, all in an attempt to fix its PR problems. [687]

One Mormon pollster admitted last year in the *Washington Post*, "We're upside down on our image. Favorability ratings declined for Mormons over the last year..." "A 2008 poll by Gary C. Lawrence, author of *How Americans View Mormonism: Seven Steps to Improve Our Image*, found that for every American who expresses a strong liking for Mormons, four express a strong dislike. Among the traits widely ascribed to Mormons in the poll were 'narrow-minded' and 'controlling.'"[688] Lawrence has served as a bishop in the LDS Church. "His Lawrence Research of Santa

Ana, California, was the pollster of record for the successful Mormon-run Proposition 8 campaign in California. He also did all the polling for their successful Amendment 1 campaign in Maine that repealed the states recently enacted gay marriage law.

Should the LDS Church be Held Accountable under the Law? Can it be?

Historically, religion has been protected in the United States. As discussed, when ruling on any religious issue, a court must consider two competing constitutional protections set forth in the First Amendment: establishment is prohibited and yet free-exercise cannot be infringed. Over the developing judicial history interpreting these constitutional rights, several rules have become clear. Freedom of religious belief does not necessarily include complete freedom in practicing those beliefs. Virgin sacrifice is not permitted, although it was a religious rite in some ancient civilizations. This is the same argument that had historically been applied to polygamy. You may believe it is your right to have more than one wife, but because of the damage such a practice has on society, U.S. Courts have historically denied the practice.

When questions arise about fraud, it is clear that no court may interpret tenets of a religion; that is simply beyond their power to do so. Such a degree of entanglement is unconstitutional. However, the fact that the LDS Church's misrepresentations are in the context of a religion arguably does not protect the Church from claims of fraudulent inducement for misrepresenting the true origins of its scriptures and priesthood.

Many legal issues arise when considering the facts this book has addressed. Besides the constitutional prohibitions against the entanglement of church and state, is tithing a gift or was it paid in consideration of certain widely promulgated misrepresentations and therefore recoverable as special damages?   What about the potential general damages— assessment of the value of a life lived in a lie? If the collective historic actions and/or omissions of the leaders of Mormonism constitute fraud, can a member who has been induced to join the LDS Church or to remain a life-long member of the Church, through such fraudulent representations or omissions, bring legal action against the LDS Church? If so, what are the obstacles to such type claims?

Appendix A: Is the LDS Church above the Law?

Historically the Church has avoided disclosure of its financial assets, something required if a punitive damages claim is allowed to go to the jury. Instead, the Church settles many of the lawsuits brought against it, in some cases revealing the amounts of the settlements.

In some cases Mormons have had to undergo therapy for severe depression related to their realization that they have been brainwashed, and/or use psychotropic drugs due to their cognitive dissonance and disaffection. Others have committed suicide due to their inability to reconcile the true historicity of Mormonism with a lifetime of Church fables passed off as literal truths. In such cases, negligent infliction of emotional distress could also be properly brought. Conspiracy to commit fraud, depending on the evidence obtained, is also a possibility if evidence exists that LDS Church leaders have acknowledged the questionable origins of Mormonism among themselves and yet continued to suppress LDS members' discovery of such origins.

Punitive damages are rarely awarded, but are possible upon clear and convincing evidence, and if the conduct is egregious. The amount awarded is usually a percentage of the net worth of the defendant, such that it will really serve as a punishment or deterrent to future, similar actions/omissions. The most recent law (amended in 2007) governing the award of punitive damages in Utah reads in pertinent part:

> (1) (a) Except as otherwise provided by statute, punitive damages may be awarded only if compensatory or general damages are awarded and it is established by clear and convincing evidence that the *acts or omissions of the tortfeasor* are the result of willful and malicious or *intentionally fraudulent conduct, or conduct that manifests a knowing and reckless indifference toward, and a disregard of, the rights of others.* [Emphasis Added].

The emphasized language in subpart (1) (a) is important, because it would be difficult to prove malice on the part of the Church. However, *"intentionally fraudulent conduct or conduct that manifests a knowing and reckless indifference toward, and a disregard of, the rights of others,"* might well be provable. Recently, the Utah Supreme Court clarified that gross negligence, the reckless indifference language of the punitive damages statute, does not require intent, rather:

451

"To qualify for punitive damages under the statute, an action need not be intentional but may alternatively be knowing and reckless." *Daniels v. Gamma West*, 2009 UT 66 ¶39, 221 P.3d 256 (Utah 2009).

Despite the fact that I believe a good faith lawsuit could be brought against the LDS Church for fraud in the inducement, such a lawsuit would take at least a decade to proceed through the courts, and most likely, given the Church's extreme wealth, the various levels of judicial scrutiny and appeal, much longer.

My goal in writing this book is to strip the LDS organization of its public relations-produced façade and to reveal what it really is at its core. Having been a trial lawyer for almost three decades, I know that even important judicial opinions are rarely read by most Americans. The drive the "anti-Mormons" have, to right what they justifiably see as a wrong, is usually not from spite or revenge, but from a desire for truth and justice so that their friends and family (those who remain members of the Church) will not continue to be misinformed and misled.

Almost two decades before I was born, Bernard Augustine De Voto, raised in Ogden, friend of Fawn Brodie, both of whom had moved out and onward to write about their curious birthplace, wrote about Mormon Utah. He described Mormonism in general as "... a magnificent catch-all of the dogmas and doctrines which had agitated the devout ever since the Great Awakening and which had most actively flourished on the frontier." [689] While admitting the difficulty of a post-mortem psychological diagnosis, De Voto suggests Smith was a 'paranoid.' [690] Later in his writing he opines in-depth about Mormonism's founder.

> Joseph may have been sincere and self-deceived: his visions may have been the delusions of insanity and *the Book of Mormon* and the framework he gave the Church may have been issued as a whole from a psychosis. Or he may have been partly sincere and partly a charlatan: he may have suffered from delusions and, at the same time, been forced to amplify and organize them in cold blood as a result of the momentum they created. I have studied the available evidences and arguments, and only the last of these hypotheses has ever seemed tenable to me. ...We are forced to assume both insanity and lucidity of mind – in some proportion and rhythm of alteration with can never be determined.* [691]

452

Of all the views given on Joseph Smith's character, intent and personality, De Voto's opinion stated above, combined with author Dan Vogel's assessment in *Joseph Smith: the Making of an American Prophet* are the opinions that I find most compelling and most based on fact and reason. I look back at my youth and the way the founding prophet was presented to me when I was a child and a young woman. Those portrayals were in fact misrepresentations and gross omissions of established facts regarding his character and works.

I would have liked to have learned about Eber D. Howe, Frank J. Cannon, Fanny Stenhouse, Ann Eliza Young and Fawn M. Brodie when I was fifteen, not forty-five. Instead, I relied upon a mistaken premise that my spiritual leaders in Mormonism were teaching me truth, including factual truth. As such, I had no impetus to look beyond their words of claimed wisdom and what then appeared to me to be factual pronouncements of "the way things really are." Had I been wise enough in my youth to cast off the authoritarian cloak which had wrapped me in its dogmatic creed, I would have chosen an entirely different life for myself.

There is little chance that someone in their 70s, or 80s, my parents' generation, would be able to change their views of Mormonism. This false religion has been too deeply ingrained for too many years. Hopefully the generations younger than mine, those in their teens, twenties and perhaps even thirties, will make the changes before their lives are unalterably set on the Mormon course. Whichever path one chooses, the Brethren have historically deprived the born-in-the-Church Mormons and converts to Mormonism, especially those who joined before widespread internet access, of any real choice, and that is wrong.

Conclusion

Although similar to the accounting and investment frauds of our time, Mormon fraud is even more egregious; it affects not just economic well-being, but the well-being of souls. It is probably naïve to think that LDS Church leaders will ever consider full and accurate disclosure of their tumultuous history and complete transparency in their accounting, theological tweaking, internal government and veiled political involvement. However, to expect these generally good members of the LDS Church to continue to follow blindly along on the promise that the one-hundred and fifteen are the final word in all things spiritual and sometimes even temporal, is not going to continue as a workable business model—some members are reading and thinking. If more corporations, including the vast conglomerate known as Mormonism, are examined and exposed for their true agenda, perhaps these type disasters can be avoided. As for Mormonism, it remains *the* American Fraud.

APPENDIX B: Chronology of Important LDS Events

1805 Joseph Smith Jr., born in Sharon, Vermont.

1813 As a result of typhoid fever, young Joseph has a severe leg infection requiring invasive bone surgery without anesthesia.

1815 Joseph's eldest brother Alvin uses seer stone to pretend to locate Capt. Kidd's treasure for a fee.

1816 The Joseph Smith Sr. family moves to Palmyra, New York.

1820 Date Joseph Smith Jr. claimed that he experienced his first vision in the sacred grove.

1822 Young Joseph Smith acquires, and thereafter uses a seer stone to locate treasure.

1823 First visit of angel Moroni/Nephi; Brother Alvin dies at age 25.

1825 Smith searches for silver on Josiah Stowell's property in Harmony, PA.

1825 Smith lives at the home of Isaac Hale; acquires new seer stone from Stowell's well.

1826 Smith is charged under the disorderly person statute in Bainbridge, New York. After a probable cause or preliminary hearing, he flees the jurisdiction.

1827 Joseph Smith elopes with Emma Hale, daughter of Isaac Hale. (Married by Rev. Sidney Rigdon in Harrisville, PA.?—see note #188).

1827 Smith obtains plates from neighborhood hill, later known by LDS as Hill Cumorah.

1828 Smith begins translating; first 116 pages lost; Smith's first-born son dies soon after birth.

1828 Joseph joins Methodist Church in Harmony, PA; 3 months later he has his name removed.

1828 Noah Webster publishes the *New American Dictionary* containing definition of "Mormo *n.*"

1829 Date claimed—*ex post facto*—for restoration of the LDS priesthoods.

1829 (April) Oliver Cowdery takes over as scribe in translating *Book of Mormon.*

Late 1829-early 1830 Failed attempt to sell copyright to *the Book of Mormon*, in Canada, despite revelation.

1830 Smith, Cowdery and Harris publish 5,000 copies of *the Book of Mormon.*

1830 Smith brought to court on old disorderly person charges; case is dismissed per successful two year statute of limitations defense.

1830 Organization of the "Church of Christ"; Rigdon and other Campbellites join Mormon Church.

1831 Church moves to Kirtland, Ohio.

1831 Smith & Emma's twins, Thaddeus & Louisa born, but live just 3 hours; they adopt other twins.

1832 Smith (& Rigdon) tarred & feathered (Smith almost castrated) by mob.

1832 Smith's adopted infant son Joseph dies; son Joseph III born. Affair with Fanny Alger, who he later "married," circa. 1833.

1833 Smith records "The Word of Wisdom," (D&C §89); Mobs attack Mormons in Missouri.

1834 Name of Church changed to "Church of the Latter Day Saints."

1834 Ohio newspaper editor, E. D. Howe, publishes *Mormonism Unvailed.*

1835 Smith organizes Council of Twelve Apostles & Quorum of the Seventy.

1835 March—Smith records revelation on the priesthood (*D&C* §107).

1835 July—Four Egyptian mummies purchased; Smith begins translating papyri and that translation becomes part of the *Book of Abraham.*

1835 *Pearl of Great Price,* containing 3 facsimiles from Egyptian papyri and Smith's translation, published.

1836 March—Kirtland Temple dedicated—Rigdon preaches; Smith & Cowdery have temple vision of Christ and other biblical figures.

1836 August—Joseph Smith visits Salem, Massachusetts, "in search of much treasure." (D&C § 111).

1836 Smith, et. al., establish Kirtland Safety Society 'Bank,' despite lack of state charter; Kirtland Bank fails.

1837 Smith condemned by investors in Kirtland Bank; he becomes very ill.

1838 Name of Church changed to "Church of Jesus Christ of Latter-day Saints." Revelation on tithing dictated by Smith. (*D&C* §119 and §120).

1838 Smith begins dictating *History of the Church*; Danites organized; Smith begins to study law. Smith marries Lucinda Morgan Harris.

1838 Missouri Gov. Boggs orders extermination; Haun's Mill Massacre.

1838 Smith arrested and kept in Liberty Jail on allegations of treason and other crimes.

1839 Smith escapes jail, flees. Church & Smith move to Commerce, IL.

1839 Smith visits U.S. President Van Buren, seeking reparations for Mormon mistreatment. The President tells him to take his claims to the court system. Smith flees from Ohio State officials to the East Coast.

1840 Commerce, Illinois is renamed 'Nauvoo,' by Mormon immigrants.

1841 Smith charged with high treason by U. S. President John Tyler; Smith sealed in polygamy to the following women: Louisa Beaman, Zina D. Huntington Jacobs and Prescinda Huntington Buell.

1842 Smith proposes to Nancy Rigdon, who rejects his proposal. Smith is sealed polygamously to: Mary Rollins Lightener, Patty Bartlett Sessions, Marinda Johnson Hyde, Martha McBride, Sarah Ann Whitney, Agnes Coolbrith, Sylvia Sessions Lyon, Elizabeth Davis Durfee, Sarah Kingsley Cleveland, Delcena Johnson & Eliza R. Snow.

1842 Joseph Smith admitted to Masonry. Six weeks later he adopts the LDS Temple Endowment Ceremony. Assassination attempt on Missouri Governor Boggs. The Governor recovers. Smith hides from the law.

1842 Smith files application for bankruptcy; application denied due to Smith's fraudulent transfers of real-estate in anticipation of bankruptcy.

1843 Smith sealed to: Ruth Vose Sayers, Emily & Eliza Partridge, Helen Mar Kimball, Lucy Walker, Elvira Cowles Holmes, Rhoda Richards, Desmodema Fullmer, Flora Ann Woodworth & Almera Johnson. In May, Joseph Smith Jr. is 'translating" the fabricated Kinderhook Plates.

1843 Smith is sealed to Sarah & Maria Lawrence. Smith writes/dictates revelation on 'celestial marriage.' Afterward he is sealed to: Melissa Lott, Fanny Young Murray; also sealed to first wife, Emma Hale. He also marries Hanna Ellis, Olive Frost & Nancy M. Winchester this year.

1844 In January, Smith announces his candidacy for U.S. President; Nauvoo Temple dedicated; only edition of *Nauvoo Expositor* printed;

Smith orders destruction of *Nauvoo Expositor Press*; Press destroyed; Joseph and Hyrum Smith shot and killed by mob while in Carthage Jail.

1845 Brigham Young and other Mormons charged with making 'bogus money' by the U. S. Federal Government.

1847 Brigham Young declared successor to Smith. He and the first Saints arrive in the Salt Lake Valley.

1848 Nauvoo Temple destroyed by unknown arsonist.

1849 Territory of Deseret created by LDS leaders; Brigham Young appointed governor.

1850 Territory of Utah created by federal government; Brigham Young appointed Territorial governor.

1856 Handcart experiment begun by Young: pioneers walk, pulling belongings and supplies in handcarts to Salt Lake Valley from Iowa City over the next four years.

1857 Brigham Young declares martial law in August. Mountain Meadows Massacre takes place on September 11th when Mormons and Paiutes slaughter 120 Arkansas pioneers enroute to CA.

1857-58 Utah War.

1858 Brigham Young removed by U. S. Government as Governor of Utah Territory.

1875 Ann Eliza testifies before Congress about Polygamy in Utah.

1876 Ann Eliza Webb Young publishes her memoir, *Wife no 19*.

1877 John D. Lee executed; predicts death of Brigham Young within six months.

1877 Brigham Young dies of cholera; St. George Temple dedicated.

1878 *Reynolds v. U.S.* decided by the U.S. Supreme Court.

1887 Edmunds-Tucker Act passed; U.S. Attorney begins enforcement.

1889 Wilford Woodruff named Prophet and President of LDS Church.

1890 Church sues federal government, challenging the constitutionality of the Edmunds-Tucker Act. Church loses case as U.S. Supreme Court upholds Act; LDS Manifesto promising to abandon polygamy issued.

1892 Salt Lake Temple finally completed (construction began in 1853).

1896 Utah admitted to the Union as the 48th State.

1901 Joseph Fielding Smith (son of founding Joseph's brother, Hyrum) named Prophet/President of LDS Church.

1904-1907 Reed Smoot Congressional Hearings.

1912 Egyptologists declare Smith's translation from papyri into *PGP's Book of Abraham* a fraud. The news is printed on the front page of the *New York Times* magazine section. Minister notifies Brethren of fraud.

1919 B. H. Roberts spends two full days with LDS leaders telling them of his suspicions regarding *Book of Mormon* authenticity.

1936 Temple block and buildings mortgaged for 3.5 million by LDS President Heber J. Grant, who publicly denies the fact at subsequent LDS General Conference in April.

1945 Fawn M. Brodie publishes her biography of Joseph Smith, *No Man Knows my History.*

1945 Utah adopts vague statutes on libel; statutes do not specifically address the truthfulness of the alleged defamatory statement.

1966 University of Utah Prof. Atiya inadvertently finds Smith's original Egyptian papyri while at the New York Metropolitan Museum of Art.

1967 Smith's Egyptian papyri, which had been located at Metropolitan Museum of Art for 50+ years, are donated to the LDS Church.

1971 LDS Church hires New York consulting firm to assist in its public relations.

1972 LDS Church creates its own public relations department.

1974 BYU sends entertainers to perform with apartheid government orchestra in the R.S.A. & Rhodesia, raising money for terrorist victims.

1975 Construction of a Sao Paulo, Brazil, LDS Temple announced.

1978 June—LDS Prophet Spencer W. Kimball receives revelation that Black males can receive the priesthood.

1978 Oct./Nov.—Sao Paul, Brazil, LDS Temple announced in 1975 is dedicated.

1979 BYU *Young Ambassadors* perform in the Republic of China; several more return trips to date.

1981 *Book of Mormon* language changed from 'white and delightsome' to '*pure* and delightsome'.

1982 Church History Department moved to BYU; Leonard J. Arrington released as Church historian.

1984 Church purchases '*Salamander Letter*,' from forger & former LDS missionary, Mark Hoffman; LDS historian proclaims its authenticity.

1985 Apostle Dallin Oaks preaches to LDS faithful, emphasizing faith over fact; Mark Hoffman kills two and injures himself with pipe bombs.

1986 Hoffman charged with two counts of first degree murder and numerous counts of forgery.

1987 Hoffman pleads guilty to second degree murder. He is sentenced to life in the Utah State Penitentiary.

1990 Temple changes made include deleting gruesome pantomimes as well as other changes; lay membership not generally notified.

1992 BYU censors campus speech which contradicts or opposes Church doctrine or policy.

1993 Six LDS intellectuals excommunicated for publishing/speaking re: controversial Church issues.

1994 to present—Internet sites and blogs appear (especially after 2000) exposing true and accurate Mormon history.

1997 Association of University Professors refuses to accredit, & Phi Kappa Phi refuses a chapter, due to BYU's restricted academic freedom.

1998 Utah Salt Lake Olympic Committee bribery scandal breaks re: the Winter 2002 Olympics.

2002 Winter Olympics held in Salt Lake City and Park City, Utah.

2002 Mormon educator Grant Palmer publishes *An Insider's View of Mormon History.*

2003 Criminal indictments against two Mormons for SLOC bribery are dismissed by Mormon Judge David Sam.

2004 LDS Massachusetts Governor Mitt Romney seeks Republican presidential nomination.

2005 200th anniversary of birth of Joseph Smith, Jr.

2008 President Gordon B. Hinckley dies; Thomas S. Monson, an apostle since 1963, named 16th president/prophet of LDS Church.

2009 CA Proposition 8, banning gay marriage, is supported by the LDS Church and its membership. Prop. 8 passes, denying homosexuals the right to marry.

2009 Elder Jeffery Holland emotionally defends divinity of *the Book of Mormon*, implying that those who don't accept the book are snakes.

2010 Apostle Boyd Packer reaffirms LDS stance on homosexuality as sin; *Book of Mormon* racist headings changed in online edition.

2011 Mormons Mitt Romney and Jon M. Huntsman, Jr. announce their candidacy for the 2012 Republican presidential nomination on June 2, and June 21, 2011, respectively. When interviewed by *Good Morning America's* George Stephanopoulos, Huntsman reluctantly admits that he is Mormon.

George Stephanopoulos: I just have two more questions. One comes from one of our viewers. ...Joelyn Singley of Salt Lake City...[S]he says: "The recent comments from Mr. Huntsman confused me as to his religious affiliations. Is he a practicing Mormon or not?"

Jon Huntsman: "I believe in God. I'm a good Christian. I'm very proud of my Mormon heritage," and finally, "I am Mormon."

NOTES

[1] "We Thank Thee O God for a Prophet," Text: William Fowler (18301865); Music: Caroline S. Norton (1808–ca. 1877).

[2] Paul Toscano, The Sanctity of Dissent (SLC: Signature Books, 1994) 66.

[3] Rose Thomas Graham, "The Golden Plates," (Salt Lake City: *Children's Songbook of the Church of Jesus Christ of Latter-day Saints*, 1989) #86.

[4] The LDS Church also includes the King James Version of the Bible in their "standard works," but throughout this book I refer only to the three books of scripture originating with Joseph Smith—*The Book of Mormon, Doctrine and Covenants* and *Pearl of Great Price*. From the official LDS website newsroom: "With divine inspiration, the First Presidency (the prophet and his two counselors) and the Quorum of the Twelve Apostles counsel together to establish doctrine that is consistently proclaimed in official Church publications. This doctrine resides in the four "standard works" of scripture (the Holy Bible, the Book of Mormon, the Doctrine and Covenants and the Pearl of Great Price), official declarations and proclamations, and the Articles of Faith"; Note: as of 11/11/10 the following link, from which the above quotation had been taken, had been disabled: http://www.newsroom.lds.org/ldsnewsroom/eng/commentary/approaching-mormon-doctrine.

[5] Brigham Young, *Journal of Discourses,* 26 vols. (Liverpool: Latter-day Saints' Book Depot, 1854-86) 7 (October 9, 1859):290-291. Caution: as of the end of 2010, www.journalofdiscourses.org does not contain complete and accurate copies of the original multi-volume work.

[6] John Taylor, LDS President, *Journal of Discourses* 22 (August 28, 1881):304 and 23 (October, 29, 1882):336.

[7] Naomi W. Randall, Lyrics and Mildred T. Pettit, Music, 1957, "I am a Child of God," *Children's Songbook of the Church of Jesus Christ of Latter-day Saints* (Salt Lake City: Church of Jesus Christ of Latter-day Saints, 1989) #2.

[8] Joseph Fielding Smith, *Way to Perfection* (Salt Lake City: Deseret Book, 1949) 43, 105-06 and 110-111.

[9] Mark E. Peterson, LDS Apostle, "Race Problems - As They Affect the Church," Presentation, Convention of Teachers of Religion on the College Level, Brigham Young University, Provo, UT (August 27, 1954).

[10] The grooming rules have changed; there is now a beard exception. To qualify, the student must obtain a recommendation from a BYU Health

Center physician and if approved, he is issued the exception annually during the growth of the beard. He must have his Student ID photograph updated concurrent with the beard growth. He may "…then grow a full beard according to the guidelines given." See: http://honorcode.byu.edu/content/what-process-obtaining-beard-waiver (Accessed 02/26/10).

[11] Mathew 5:43-48 (King James Version).

[12] Richard J. Light, *Making the Most of College: Students Speak their Minds* (Cambridge: Harvard University Press, 2001) 122-125.

[13] Bruce R. McConkie, Apostle, "All Are Alike Unto God," Address at the LDS CES Religious Educators' Symposium (Aug. 18, 1978).

[14] J. Reuben Clark Law School was established in 1967. Given the re-discovery of Joseph Smith's original papyri that same year, did the Church anticipate issues with the "Book of Abraham" in its canonized scripture, the *Pearl of Great Price*, and have the foresight to raise scores of lawyers to defend it? Of course, neither such probabilities nor issues were discussed openly with its law students.

[15] N. Eldon Tanner, LDS Apostle, "The Debate is Over," *Ensign* [Magazine] (Salt Lake City: Church of Jesus Christ of Latter-day Saints, August, 1979) 2-3.

[16] A reference to the film, *Johnny Lingo,* where a young Polynesian protagonist pays eight cows for his wife. Directed by Judge Whitaker, produced by the Church of Jesus Christ of Latter-day Saints, 1969.

[17] Brigham Young, *Journal of Discourses*, 4 (September 21, 1856):55-57; *Deseret News*, 6: 235-236.

[18] LDS garments depicted: http://en.wikipedia.org/wiki/Temple_garments.

[19] This was changed to "Oh God hear the words of my mouth," in 1990. Despite numerous changes to the protracted ceremony over the years, the founder of the Church has been documented as claiming: "Now the purpose in Himself in the winding up scene of the last dispensation is that all things pertaining to that dispensation should be conducted precisely in accordance with the preceding dispensations...*He set the temple ordinances to be the same forever and ever* and set Adam to watch over them, to reveal them from heaven to man, or to send angels to reveal them." Joseph Smith, Jr., *History of the Church of Jesus Christ of Latter-day Saints*, B. H. Roberts, ed., 7 Vols. (hereinafter, *HC*) (Salt Lake City: Deseret Book Co., 1932-1951) 4:208 (formerly, known as [the] *Documentary History of the Church*). [Emphasis added].

[20] Dennis B. Neuenschwander, Presidency of the Seventy, "Ordinances and Covenants," *Ensign* (Salt Lake City: Church of Jesus Christ of Latter-day

Saints, August, 2001) 22. [Emphasis added].

[21] W. Grant Bangerter, First Quorum of the Seventy, *Desert News*, Church Section, Jan. 16, 1982.

[22] www.think-link.org, *Comparing The Mormon Endowment Temple Ceremony, Past And Present,* "In 1990 this part of the ceremony was changed to allow women access [to harken] to the Lord directly without having to go through their husbands." http://www.i4m.com/think/temples/temple_ceremony.htm.

[23] LDS endowment ceremony, circa 1937: (1) " Early Penalty of the First Token of the Aaronic Priesthood: 'We, and each of us, covenant and promise that we will not reveal any of the secrets of this, the First Token of the Aaronic Priesthood, with its accompanying name, sign, or penalty. Should we do so, we agree that our throats be cut from ear to ear and our tongues torn out by our roots.' (2) Early Penalty of the Second Token of the Aaronic Priesthood 'We, and each of us, covenant and promise that we will not reveal any of the secrets of this, the Second Token of the Aaronic Priesthood, with its accompanying name, sign, or penalty. Should we do so, we agree to have our breasts cut open and our hearts and vitals torn out from our bodies and given to the birds of the air and the beasts of the field.' Early Penalty of the First Token of the Melchizedek Priesthood 'We, and each of us, covenant and promise that we will not reveal any of the secrets of this, the First Token of the Melchizedek Priesthood, with its accompanying name, sign, or penalty. Should we do so, we agree that our bodies be cut asunder in the midst and all our bowels gush out.'"

[24] Ralph Waldo Emerson, "Self Reliance," *Emerson: Essays and Lectures* (New York: Viking Press, 1983) 261.

[25] Rebecca Ruiz, "America's Vainest Cities," *Forbes*, Nov. 27, 2007.

[26] Home teachers are priesthood men who make monthly visits to ward members' homes to deliver a spiritual message and check on the households' well-being. Visiting teachers are similarly appointed in the Relief Society. While home teachers can give blessings and teach the entire family, visiting teachers are limited to teaching women of the home.

[27] Victor L. Brown, Presiding LDS Bishop, "Choosing Eternal Priorities," *New Era* [Magazine] (Salt Lake City: Church of Jesus Christ of Latter-day Saints, February, 1978) 35.

[28] Lynn G. Robbins, Quorum of the Seventy, "Tithing—a Commandment Even for the Destitute," Sermon given at April LDS General Conference 2005; subsequently published in the LDS *Liahona* [Magazine] (Salt Lake City: LDS Church, May 2005) 34–36. [Emphasis original].

[29] Revelations, 3:16.

³⁰ John Taylor, 3rd LDS President, *Journal of Discourses* 5 (September 20, 1857):266.
³¹ Utah Constitution, Article X, Education, §9 [Textbooks]; http://archives.utah.gov/research/exhibits/Statehood/1896text.htm
³² Discussion with the Author and Utah Board of Education Social Studies Director, Tom Sutton, June, 2010.
³³ Richard Neitzel Holzapfel, *Utah, a Journey of Discovery* (Salt Lake City: Gibbs Smith, 2007) 173-174.
³⁴ Ibid. 175.
³⁵ Glen Warchol, "Essay Implies Mormons Should Back Vouchers," *Salt Lake Tribune*, September 16, 2007 (quoting Frederick Buchanan, retired University of Utah professor who has written extensively on the history of Utah education).
³⁶ John Taylor, 3rd LDS President, *Journal of Discourses* 7 (January 10, 1858):123-125.
³⁷ Axel J. Andresen, Assistant Mgr., Deseret Book Co., open letter of June 12, 1963: "In having in your library the 26 volume of the 'Journal of Discourses,' you have a library containing the sermons of the Presidents and Apostles of the Church. If anyone tells you that the sermons found therein are not recognized by the Church, they know not what they are talking about."* See also George Q. Cannon, Apostle & member of the First Presidency, *Journal of Discourses,* Preface, Vol. 8: "The Journal of Discourses deservedly ranks as one of the standard works of the Church, and every right-minded Saint will certainly welcome with joy every Number as it comes forth from the press as an additional reflector of 'the light that shines from Zion's hill.' We rejoice, therefore, in being able to present to the Saints another completed Volume – the Eighth of the series; and, in doing so, we sincerely commend the varied and important instructions it contains to their earnest consideration."
³⁸ From the official Mormon Church website: www.LDS.org, Gospel Topics: the Journal of Discourses (Originally accessed in May, 2007, but as of November 11, 2010, when accessing this site, one reads: "sorry, we cannot find the page you are looking for.") Note: some time in early 2011, the website www.lds.org required logging in.
³⁹ Wilford C. Wood, compiler, "Book of Commandments," *Joseph Begins his Work*, II (U.S.A: Wilford C. Wood, 1958) Chapter 44, verse 26, p. 92.
⁴⁰ John Heinerman and Anson Shupe, *The Mormon Corporate Empire* (Boston: Beacon Press, 1985) 78-9; see also David Van Biema, "Kingdom Come," *Time*, vol. 150 no. 5 (August 1997).
⁴¹ Heinerman, *Mormon Corporate Empire,* Chap.3:76-127. Joseph Smith

dictated a revelation on tithing in 1838 which required an initial donation of all a members' surplus property and then 10% of his income for each year thereafter. (*D&C* 119:1, 4). The initial investment requirement was removed in 1899 by LDS President Lorenzo Snow.

[42] "SLOC & the LDS Church Downplay the Church's Involvement in the Olympics," *Salt Lake Tribune,* Mar. 18, 2001.

[43] Dallin H. Oaks, "Religious Freedom, " Speech to BYU-Idaho students, Rexburg, Idaho (Oct. 13, 2009).

[44] John D. Lee, *Mormonism Unveiled or the Life and Confessions of Mormon Bishop, John D. Lee* (St. Louis: Bryan, Brand & Co., 1877) original photo reprinted as *Confessions of John D. Lee*, with a publisher's preface by Jerald and Sandra Tanner (Salt Lake City: Utah Lighthouse Ministry, n.d.)

[45] Ann Eliza Young, *Wife No. 19* or *a Story of a Life In Bondage Being a Complete Exposé of Mormonism, and Revealing the Sorrows, Sacrifices and Sufferings of Women in Polygamy* (Hartford, Conn: Dustin, Gilman & Co., 1876) facsimile of 1876 ed. (Carlisle, MA: Applewood Books, 2009)53. References are to 2009 facsimile reprint ed.

[46] Ibid. 47.

[47] G. B. Frost's Affidavit in John C. Bennett, *History of the Saints; or, an Exposé of Joe Smith and Mormonism.* (Photomechanical Reproduction, Salt Lake City: Utah Lighthouse Ministry, n.d.) 86-87. Citations are to UTLM Reproduction. See also: http://www.olivercowdery.com/smithhome/1840s/ben1842a.htm#pg086a (Originally pub. Boston: Leland & Whiting, 1842). [Emphasis original].

[48] See David Roberts, *Devils Gate* (Simon & Schuster, 2008); Leonard J. Arrington and Davis Bitton, *Saints without Halos: The Human Side of Mormon History* (Salt Lake City: Signature Books, 1981) 84-5.

[49] Roberts, *Devils Gate*, Ibid. 255.

[50] Arrington and Bitton, *Saints without Halos,* 3.

[51] Ibid. 22.

[52] See John Ahmanson, *Secret History* (*Vor Tids Muhamed,* Danish, 1876) translated into English by Gleason L. Archer (Chicago: The Fieldstead Institute, 1984).

[53] Ann Eliza Young, *Wife No. 19,* 39.

[54] Brigham Young, *Journal of Discourses*, 5:73; 8:199 & 8:171, respectively. (Note: As of 2010, www.journalofdiscourses.org does not contain complete, accurate copies of this original multi-volume work. For example, the quotation attributed to Brigham Young (5:73) in this note is not included).

[55] Heber C. Kimball,, LDS Apostle and First Counselor to Brigham Young, *Journal of Discourses,* 5 (circa. July 26, 1857):89. (Note: this statement can only be found in the original, unabridged edition of the *Journal of Discourses.*)

[56] William Law, original member of the First Presidency of the LDS Church with founder Joseph Smith, Jr., interview of March 30, 1887, published in the *Salt Lake Tribune,* July 31, 1887.

[57] Scott H. Faulring, ed., *An American Prophet's Record: the Diaries and Journals of Joseph Smith* (Salt Lake City: Signature Books/Smith Research Associates, 1987) 198, July 27, 1838 entry. Note: Faulring is a 1983 BYU history graduate.

[58] David Whitmer, one of three original witnesses to *the Book of Mormon* and an original apostle of the Mormon Church, *An Address to All Believers in Christ* (Richmond, Missouri: n.p., 1887) 27-28.

[59] Henry G. McMillan, *The Inside of Mormonism: A Judicial Examination of the Endowment Oaths Administered in all the Mormon Temples by the United States District Court.* Photo reprint of original 1903 ed. (Salt Lake City: Utah Lighthouse Ministry, n.d.) Citations are to UTLM Ed.

[60] Ibid. 43.

[61] Ibid. 52.

[62] Ibid. 16-20.

[63] *History of the Church (HC)* 6:165.

[64] William G. Hartley, *My Best for the Kingdom: History and Autobiography of John Lowe Butler, a Mormon Frontiersman* (Salt Lake City: Aspen Books, 1993) 69, 42.

[65] Faulring, *An American Prophet's Record,* 458, entry of March 10, 1844.

[66] Henry A. Smith, project ed., *Deseret, 1776-1976: A Bicentennial Illustrated History of Utah* (Salt Lake City: Deseret News Publishing Co., 1975)187-188.

[67] Paul Foy, AP, "All Mormon Supreme Court Spells Theocracy to Disgruntled Utahans," *Los Angeles Times,* June 11, 2000. Though at least two of the members of the high Court have changed since then, I believe that all five of today's justices are from LDS backgrounds and that most remain practicing Mormons. Thus, Church interests have remained a *de facto* priority in Utah throughout the 20th century and into the 21st.

[68] Brigham Young, *Journal of Discourses* 2 (July 8, 1855):311.

[69] Brigham Young, *Journal of Discourses* 4 (Sept. 21, 1856):51-57. Joseph Smith said [that he was] "...opposed to hanging, even if a man kill another, I will shoot him, or cut off his head, spill his blood on the ground, and let

the smoke thereof ascend up to God..." *HC* 5:296.

[70] Brigham Young, *Journal of Discourses* 4 (February 8, 1857):215-221.

[71] Jedediah M. Grant, *Journal of Discourses* 4 (September 21, 1856):49-51. Ann Eliza Young, *Wife No. 19*, 188-190.

[72] Joseph Fielding Smith, 10th LDS President, *Doctrines of Salvation* (Salt Lake City: Bookcraft, 1954) 1:133-136.

[73] Ibid. 136.

[74] Bruce R. McConkie, *Mormon Doctrine* 2nd ed. (Salt Lake City: Bookcraft, 1966) 92.

[75] Journal of Heber C. Kimball, December 21, 1945, as quoted in Jerald Tanner and Sandra Tanner, *Evolution of the Mormon Temple Ceremony: 1842-1990* (Salt Lake City: Utah Lighthouse Ministry, 1990; updated 2005) 25; On February 15, 1927 notification was given to all temples from the First Presidency and a quorum of the twelve apostles to "Immediately omit from prayer circles, 'all references to avenging the blood of the Prophets. Omit from the ordinance and lecture all reference to retribution.'" See D. Michael Quinn, *Mormon Hierarchy: Extensions of Power* (Salt Lake City: Signature Books /Smith Research Assoc., 1997) 819, n. Feb. 15, 1927.

[76] David John Buerger, "The Development of the Mormon Temple Endowment Ceremony," *Dialogue: a Journal of Mormon Thought* (hereinafter "*Dialogue*") 20, no. 4 (Winter 1987):35.

[77] http://www.lds-mormon.com/whytemplechanges.shtml#article (Accessed Nov. 3, 2010).

[78] Tanners, Jerald and Sandra, *Evolution of the Mormon Temple Ceremony: 1842-1990*; Peter Steinfeld, "Mormons Drop Rites Opposed by Women," *New York Times*, May 3, 1990.

[79] *Salt Lake Tribune*, January 11, 1985; see also John Krakauer, *Under the Banner of Heaven: the Story of a Violent Faith* (NY: Doubleday, 2003).

[80] W.W. Drummond, Chief Justice of Utah, resignation letter to the Honorable Jeremiah S. Black, Attorney General of the United States, Washington D.C. (*New York Times*, May 14, 1857).

[81] *Wife No. 19*, 161.

[82] Mrs. T.B.H. Stenhouse *aka* "Fanny." *Tell it All: the Story of a Life's Experience in Mormonism.* Hartford: A.D. Worthington & Co., 1875. Facsimile reproduction of original (SLC: Utah Lighthouse Ministry, n.d.) 301. Citations are to UTLM reproduction. [Emphasis Original]. Stenhouse also provides a list of names that were well known in the Deseret Territory to have been killed pursuant to the LDS doctrine of

Blood Atonement. Besides the woman who was unfaithful to her husband while he was away on a mission, and so sat on his lap and let him slit her throat, the murdered included: Yates, Franklin McNeil, Sergeant Pike, Arnold and Drown, Price and William Bryan, Almon Babbitt, Brassfield, Dr. Robinson, James Cody and his wife and child, Margetts and wife, the Potters and the Parrishes, Forbes, Owens and he mother, Andrew Bernard, Morris the rival prophet, Banks and four women in their party, Isaac Potter, Charles Wilson and John Walker. "The death list is too long for me to venture to give it," she laments. (318-319). See also "More Mormon Murders and Crimes," *Valley Tan* (Salt Lake: April 26, 1859).

[83] Will Bagley, *Blood of the Prophets: Brigham Young and the Massacre at Mountain Meadows,* (Norman: Univ. of Oklahoma Press, 2004) 378-79.

[84] Ibid. 304.

[85] Ibid. 170-78.

[86] Azra Evans, *The Keystone of Mormonism* (St. George, Utah: Keystone Books, 2003) 165, quoting Juanita Brooks, author of *John D. Lee* (Glendale, CA: Arthur H. Clark Co, 1973) 372-376.

[87] "The Scene of the Mountain Meadows Massacre, Utah Territory," *Harper's* (August 13, 1859) cover.

[88] Bagley, *Blood of the Prophets*, 354-57.

[89] Ibid. 355-56.

[90] "The Murder of the Parrishes and Potter at Springville, on Sunday Night, March 14, 1857," *Valley Tan* (April 5, 1859); See also Evans, *Keystone*, 165.

[91] Juanita Brooks, *Mountain Meadows Massacre,* 3rd ed. (Norman: University of Oklahoma Press, 1991)146. Originally published in 1950. Note: Citations refer to the 1991 Ed.

[92] H .H. Bancroft, *History of Utah, 1540-1886* . (1889) Chap. XX. 562-563.

[93] Judge John Cradlebaugh, letter to Pres. Buchanan (Salt Lake City, June 3, 1859) quoted in the *Evening Bulletin*, VIII, No. 67 (San Francisco, June 24, 1859). http://www.mtn-meadows-assoc.com/new_page_6.htm.

[94] Marshal P. K. Dotson to Judge John Cradlebaugh (Great Salt Lake City, Utah, June 3, 1859).

[95] Bagley, *Blood of the Prophets*, 236 quoting, Cradlebaugh, "Utah and the Mormons: Speech of the Honorable John Cradlebaugh, of Nevada, on the Admission of Utah as a State delivered in the House of Representatives," (Feb. 7, 1863).

[96] Judge John Cradlebaugh, letter in [the] *Valley Tan* (Feb. 22, 1860) 2.

[97] *Wilford Woodruff's Journal,* May 25, 1861; See also Brooks, *Mountain*

Meadows Massacre, 125-126 & 146. [Emphasis added].

[98] Brooks, *Mountain Meadows Massacre*, 183.

[99] Bagley, *Blood of the Prophets*, 176.

[100] Christopher Smith, "Unearthing Mountain Meadows Secrets: Backhoe at a S. Utah Killing Field Rips Open 142-year-old Wound," (*Salt Lake Tribune*, March 14, 2000).

[101] Bagley, *Blood of the Prophets*, 174-175 & 236.

[102] John D. Lee, *Mormonism Unveiled or the Life and Confessions of the Late Mormon Bishop, John D. Lee,* 284-286. Citations are from reprint.

[103] Juanita Brooks, *On the Mormon Frontier: The Diary of Hosea Stout* 2 (Salt Lake City: University of Utah Press, 1982):653.

[104] Bill Hickman, *Brigham's Destroying Angel: the Life, Confessions, etc. of Bill Hickman*, J.H. Beadle, Esq. ed. (Salt Lake City: Sheppard Pub. Co., 1904) reprint by Jerald & Sandra Tanner (Salt Lake City: Utah Lighthouse Ministry, n.d.) 10.

[105] Benjamin Winchester, personal narrative, "Primitive Mormonism," *Salt Lake Tribune*, September 22, 1889. http://www.truthandgrace.com/1889SLTribune0922.htm. [Emphasis original].

[106] *Morrill Anti-Bigamy Act*, Stat. 12:501 [1862]. See also, Edwin B. Firmage and Richard C. Mangrum, *Zion in the Courts: a Legal History of the Church of Jesus Christ of Latter-day Saints, 1830-1900* (University of Illinois Press, 2001) Chap. 6, "The Early Attack on Polygamy," 129-59.

[107] Firmage and Mangrum, *Zion in the Courts*, quoting *Congressional Record* and the *Congressional Globe*, 129-159.

[108] See generally, Firmage and Mangrum, *Zion in the Courts.*

[109] Plea of George A. Smith, Esq. at the trial of Howard Egan for the murder of James Monroe, First Judicial Dist. Ct., U.S., 1851, Z. Snow, Judge, quoted in the *Journal of Discourses,* 1st ed., unabridged, 1:97-98. (Note: trial removed in abridged editions.)

[110] Judge Z. Snow's charge to the jury, *Journal of Discourses,* unabridged ed., *1:103* [Emphasis original].

[111] http://deseretbook.com/item/4954158/Journal_of_Discourses (viewed June 18, 2010).

[112] *Late Corporation of the Church of Jesus Christ of Latter-day Saints v. United States, Romney, et. al.*, 1890, 136 U.S. 1, 42-43; 10 S. Ct. 792. http://supreme.justia.com/us/136/1/case.html.

[113] *Late Corporation of the Church, Id.* at 48-49.

[114] Jt. Res 11. 53rd Cong., 1st Sess., 28 Stat. 980. President Woodruff's

secretary noted that: "He believed the Lord was displeased with us for borrowing or going into debt to the extent of nearly two millions of dollars for business enterprises." *Journal History of the Church of Jesus Christ of Latter-day Saints*, located in the Church Historian's Office, June 8, 1899, cited in Leonard J. Arrington, *Great Basin Kingdom: An Economic History of the Latter-day Saints 1830-1900* (Harvard University Press, 1958) 406-07. Note: Arrington appears to have independently calculated the Church's debt as of 1898 at "over $1, 250,000" from the "Statement of Assets and Liabilities of the Church, July, 1898;" see *Great Basin Kingdom*, 401.

[115] Firmage and Mangrum, *Zion in the Courts*, 168.

[116] Francis J. Cannon and Harvey J. O'Higgins, *Under the Prophet in Utah: the National Menace of a Political Priestcraft* (originally published in 1911). Reprint (Lexington: Forgotten Books, 2008) 99, 151 and 133, respectively. Citations refer to reprint ed. See also Arrington, *Great Basin Kingdom*, 402, where he writes that a half-million dollar loan was obtained from New York financiers in 1895. President Woodruff noted the type of security for this loan: "Our credit rested on the belief that the Mormon people were ready to consecrate all their possessions at any time to the service of the Church at the command of the president." Thus, future tithing receipts were leveraged for the debt. This quotation is from the *Diary of Wilford Woodruff* (unavailable to the public) December 20, 1894 and January 15, 1895.

[117] Lawrence Wright, "Lives of the Saints," *The New Yorker*, Jan. 21, 2002.

[118] James Shelledy interview with the Author in October, 2010.

[119] Peg McEntee, "LDS Church's Influence a Myth, Legislators Say," (*Deseret News*, Jan. 16, 1993) §B-1.

[120] *Church Handbook of Instructions*, 26 (SLC: LDS Church, 2006) 1:187; www.wikileaks.org/wiki/MormonChurchHandbookofInstructions.full.2006 (Accessed January 16, 2009). Note: A 2010 LDS General Handbook contains no similar language.

[121] Steven Naifeh and Gregory White Smith, *The Mormon Murders*, paperback ed., (New York: St. Martin's 1989) is an outstanding true crime account of these murders and Hoffman's extensive document forgeries. While the book received rave critical reviews, there are biting one-star reviews posted on www.amazon.com, which appear to have been authored by LDS readers. Naifeh and White hint at the ecclesiogenic neurosis exhibited by the Mormon characters in this true crime story. The other accounts of the Hoffman crimes, at least two of which were written by Mormons, are superficial treatments. Neither of them are as well written, nor as accurately detailed as the Naifeh/White Smith true crime account. Some Mormons were told by LDS leaders not to read this book.

[122] Ken Wells, "The Mormon Church, is Rich, Rapidly Growing and Very Controversial," Wall *Street Journal*, 9 (November, 1983) 20, quoted in Heinerman and Shupe, *Mormon Corporate Empire*, 103, n. 61.

[123] *Jane L. Bangerter v. State of Utah*, 828 F. Supp 1544 (D. Utah 1993), 61 F.3d 1505 (10th Cir. 1995).

[124] *Fox Television Stations Inc. v. Clary*, No. 940700284 (Utah 2nd Dist.).

[125] *Van Gorden v. Utah State Fair*, U.S. Dist. Court for the District of Utah, Case no. 98-CV-868C.

[126] Memorandum Decision, *Jolley v. Utah State Senate*, No. 960901127 (Utah 3rd Dist. July 12, 1996).

[127] Judgment & Order in *Jolley v. Utah State Senate*, No. 960901127 (Utah 3rd Dist. Feb. 19, 1997); http://www.rcfp.org/ogg/item.php?t=short&state=UT&level=F1 (Accessed February, 2010).

[128] *Silverman v. State of Utah*, U.S. Dist. Court for the District of Utah, Case no 2:96-CV-00221.

[129] *Roe v. Utah County*, U.S. Dist. Court for the District of Utah, Case no 2:96-CV-937.

[130] *Larson v. Provo School District*, U.S. Dist. Court for the District of Utah, Case no 2:99-CV-0047. See press release by Charles M. Larson, dated August 29, 1997, http://www.exmormon.org/larson1.htm.

[131] *East High Gay/Straight Alliance v. Board of Education* and *East High School PRISM Club v. Cynthia L. Seidel*, U.S. Dist. Court for the District of Utah, Central Division, Case no. 2:00-CV-0311K.

[132] *Snyder v. Murray City Corporation*, 2003 UT 13, ¶44, 44 P.3d 642. http://www.utcourts.gov/opinions/supopin/snyder041103.htm.

[133] *Snyder, Id.* at ¶31.

[134] *First Unitarian Church v. Salt Lake City Corporation*, Federal Appellate Court decision reversing and remanding Utah District Court decision: United States Court of Appeals, Tenth Circuit, Case No. 01-4111, October 09, 2002; http://caselaw.findlaw.com/us-10th-circuit/1160780.html.

[135] *Craig Axford v. Salt Lake City Corporation*, 3rd Judicial District Court, Salt Lake Co., State of Utah, No. 000902995, Complaint for Declaratory Relief 4/13/2000; http://www.acluutah.org/axfordcomplaint.htm.

[136] Utah Legislature, general session, February 8, 2008.

[137] Utah Legislature 13th Extraordinary Session, November 19, 2008.

[138] Jennifer Dobner, "Ronnie Lee Gardner Execution: Firing Squads are Humane Some Experts Say," (*AP:* June 16, 2010).

[139] Peggy Fletcher Stack, "Gardner's Date with Firing Squad Revives Talk of Mormon Blood Atonement," *Salt Lake Tribune*, May 21, 2010 12:07

PM; Updated Sep 15, 2010 03:20PM;
http://www.sltrib.com/sltrib/lifestyle/49621318-80/blood-atonement-firing-squad.html.csp; (Accessed May, 30, 2010).

[140] http://le.utah.gov/~2010/bills/sbillint/sb0109.htm.

[141] *The center for Public Integrity's 50-state Ranking of Standards for State Legislators,* April 17, 2006. "Data complied by the Center for Public Integrity [which] is a nonprofit organization dedicated to producing original, responsible investigative journalism on issues of public concern. The Center is non-partisan and non-advocacy. We are committed to transparent and comprehensive reporting both in the United States and around the world. The Center is located at 910 17th Street NW, Suite 700, Washington, D.C. 20006; (202) 466-1300." http://projects.publicintegrity.org/oi/db.aspx?act=rank.

[142] Peg McEntee, "Wise Advice on Ethics Reform," *SL Tribune*, 11/25/09; http://www.utahnsforethicalgovernment.org/index.php/news/C12/

[143] Gordon B. Hinckley, "The Marvelous Foundation of Our Faith," LDS Magazines: *Liahona* and *Ensign* (Nov., 2002) 78-81; Gordon B. Hinckley, "Words of the Prophet: Praise to the Man," New *Era*, May, 2005. Note in his commencement address at BYU, LDS Apostle Matthew Cowley stated: "And your institution here stems from the prayer of a boy who was persecuted, who was driven from pillar to post, whose life was taken, who has been branded as the greatest fraud that ever lived on the American continent. *This Church from that kind of a fraud* is the greatest miracle of modern history." Matthew Cowley, "Classic Discourses from the General Authorities: Miracles," *New Era* (June 1975) 39. [Emphasis added].

[144] Jeffrey Holland, *Christ and the New Covenant* (Salt Lake City: Deseret Book, 1997) 345-347.

[145] Grant Palmer, *An Insider's View of Mormon Origins* (Salt Lake City: Signature Books, 2002) 1-12.

[146] *Franco v. The Church of Jesus Christ of Latter-day Saints,* 2001 UT 25 ¶33; 21 P.3d 198, 207-08. http://www.utcourts.gov/opinions/supopin/franco.htm.

[147] http://www.lds.org/topic/mormon/ (Accessed 06/18/2010) [Emphasis original].

[148] See cover photo taken Dec. 28, 2010, of replica of golden plates displayed at the Salt Lake City North Visitors' Center, Temple Square.

[149] ____ "Imposition and Blasphemy!! Money-Diggers, &c.," *THE GEM, of Literature and Science*, Rochester: May 15, 1830.

[150] "Lucy Mack Smith, preliminary manuscript," Dan Vogel, ed., 48 *Early*

Mormon Documents 1 (Salt Lake City: Signature Books, 2002):304.

[151] "William B. Smith's Last Statement, John W. Peterson to the Editor," *Zion's Ensign* (Independence, Missouri) 5 (Jan. 13, 1884):6, Vogel, *Early Mormon Documents* 1:175.

[152] Dan Vogel, *Joseph Smith: the Making of a Prophet* (Salt Lake City: Signature Books, 2004) 62-63.

[153] "Lorenzo Saunders Interview by Wm. H. Kelly," Sept, 17, 1884, E.L. Kelley Papers, Community of Christ Archives, Vogel, *Early Mormon Documents* 2:127.

[154] See D. Michael Quinn, *Early Mormonism and the Magic World View,* rev. ed. (Salt Lake City: Signature Books, 1998) chaps. 2 & 3.

[155] Christopher M. Stafford Statement, 23 March 1885, *Naked Truths about Mormonism* (Apr. 1888), Vogel, *Early Mormon Documents,* 2:194.

[156] "Mormonism," *Susquehanna Register and Northern Pennsylvanian* 9 (1 May 1834), Vogel, *Early Mormon Documents,* 4:297.

[157] Vogel, *...the Making of a Prophet,* 630, n. 28.

[158] "Articles of Agreement between Joe Smith, the Father of Mormonism and Other Persons, in 1825," *SL Tribune,* Vol. XIX; No. 3 April 23, 1880.

[159] William D. Purple, contributing writer, *The Chenango Union,* May 3, 1877, quoted in Tanner, Jerald and Tanner, Sandra, *Mormonism--Shadow or Reality?* 5th ed., reformatted. (Salt Lake City: Utah Lighthouse Ministries, 2008) 37. Originally published in 1987.

[160] Abram W. Benton, "Mormonites," *Evangelical Magazine and Gospel Advocate* (Utica, New York) 2 (April 9, 1831):120.

[161] Letter by Joel K. Noble to Jonathon B. Turner (intended for publication). The original of this letter is in the Turner Collection of the Illinois State Historical Library in Springfield, Ill, as cited in Persuitte, David, *Joseph Smith and the Origins of the Book of Mormon,* 2nd Ed. (Jefferson, North Carolina: McFarland & Co., 2000) 51 & accompanying note. See this entire chapter number four for a good summary of the Bainbridge Case.

[162] Joel K. Noble, Justice of the Peace, affidavit., Colesville, Broome County, New York, Aug. 28, 1832, in "Mormonism," *New England Christian Herald* 4:22-23 (Boston, Massachusetts) November 7, 1832.

[163] Judge Joel K. Noble to Jonathon B. Turner, March 8, 1842, Vogel, *Early Mormon Documents* 4:108-109.

[164] Ibid.

[165] Ibid. 4:109 [Emphasis original].

[166] Ibid.

[167] Palmer, *An Insider's View of Mormon Origins,* 198-199.

[168] "Stephen Burnett to Lyman E. Johnson, April 15, 1838," Joseph Smith, Letter book (1837-43) 2:64-66, Joseph Smith Papers, LDS Church Archives, Vogel, *Early Mormon Documents,* 2:290-93.

[169] Isaac D. Hale's Affidavit, Harmony, PA., March 20, 1834, Dan Vogel, ed., *Early Mormon Documents* 4 (Salt Lake City: Signature Books, 2002) 281-289; See also Eber D. Howe, *Mormonism Unvailed a Faithful Account of that Singular Imposition and Delusion from its* Rise *to the Present Time* (Painesville, Ohio: Telegraph Press, 1834) 265-66.

[170] "BLASPHEMY – BOOK OF MORMON, ALIAS THE GOLDEN BIBLE," *Daily Advertiser* (Rochester: New York) 2 April, 1830.

[171] Mark Twain*, Roughing It* (Hartford, Conn.: American Publishing Co., 1872) 110.

[172] Richard Packham's website: http://packham.n4m.org/linguist.htm#NAMES (viewed March 22, 2010). See also Vernal Holley, *Book of Mormon Authorship*, 2nd ed., revised e-text version, (Utah: self-published, 1989) 10-11; http://sidneyrigdon.com/vern/vernP0.htm.

[173] Dan Vogel, ed., "*Marion Enterprise* (Newark, NY), 28 September 1923, 43:1," *Early Mormon Documents* 3:130.

[174] Joseph Smith, Jr., *The Book of Mormon*, original ed., "Mormon," 6:2.

[175] "History of Joseph Smith," Nauvoo, Illinois, April 15, 1842, *Times and Seasons* 3, no. 12, p. 753.

[176] "Pomeroy Tucker Account 1867," Dan Vogel, ed., *Early Mormon Documents* 3:93-94.

[177] Ronald V. Huggins, "From Captain Kidd's Treasure Ghost to the Angel Moroni: Changing Dramatis Personae in Early Mormonism," Salt Lake City, December 1, 2003, *Dialogue* 36, no. 4 (Winter 2003):37-39.

[178] Noah Webster*, compiler, An American Dictionary of the English Language*, 2 vols. (N.p., n.p., 1828). See also classic works by Greek playwright, Aristophanes.

[179] Charles Anthon to Eber D. Howe, letter dated Feb. 17, 1834, published in Howe, E. D. *Mormonism Unvailed.* (Painesville, Ohio: Telegraph Press, 1834) 270-272.

[180] Ibid. 271-272.

[181] Riley I. Woodbridge, [The] *Founder of Mormonism: A Psychological Study of Joseph Smith Jr.*, (New York: Dodd Mead and Co., 1903) 85-87; archived at UCSD, 2007.

[182] See Robert D. Anderson, *Inside the Mind of Joseph Smith.* (Salt Lake City: Signature Books, 1999).

[183] Polygamy Porter, "Sidney Rigdon was Moroni Theory," posted March 9,

2005 at http://www.mormoncurtain.com/topic_sidneyrigdon.html (viewed September 3, 2009).

[184] *Recollections of John H. Gilbert* [Regarding printing *Book of Mormon*] *8 September 1892,* Palmyra, New York, typescript, BYU; http://www.boap.org/LDS/Early-Saints/JHGilbert.html.

[185] Ibid.

[186] Howe, *Mormonism Unvailed,* 278. [Emphasis original].

[187] Pomeroy Tucker, *Origins, Rise and Progress of Mormonism* (New York: D. Appleton & Co, 1867). http://www.solomonspalding.com/docs1/1867TucA.htm.

[188] See Wayne L. Cowdery, Howard A. Davis and Arthur Vanick, *Who Really Wrote the Book of Mormon? The Spalding Enigma* (St. Louis: Concordia Publishing House, 2005). Note: One early twentieth century writer claims that it was Sidney Rigdon who married Joseph Smith and Emma Hale in Harrisburg, Pennsylvania on January 18, 1926. This fact rebuts Smith's claim that he and Rigdon first met years later. See James Ervin Mahaffey (1864-1935) "Found at Last: Proof that Mormonism is a Fraud," (August, GA: *Chronicle,* 1902): 22-23.

[189] *Unique Textual Parallels from the Oberlin Spaulding Ms. and the Book of Mormon,* Tabulation by Dale R. Broadhurst, from data compiled by Bill A. Williams, jr., http://www.mormonthink.com/part4.htm (viewed 05/13/2010).

[190] Vernal Holley, *Book of Mormon Authorship,* 2nd ed., revised e-text version (Utah: self-published, 1989) 10-11; http://sidneyrigdon.com/vern/vernP0.htm.

[191] Howe, *Mormonism Unvailed,* 281-290.

[192] Ibid. 289-290.

[193] *The Wayne Sentinel, Vol. XI. 14* (Dec. 20, 1833).

[194] Richard Van Wagoner, *Sidney Rigdon: A Portrait of Excess* (Salt Lake City: Signature Books, 2006) 456.

[195] Craig Criddle, *Sidney Rigdon: Creating the Book of Mormon,* Originally posted: 8 Oct 2005; Revised and updated: 15 Mar 2009; http://sidneyrigdon.com/criddle/rigdon1.htm, (accessed June 5, 2010).

[196] Sandra Tanner, in a discussion with the Author on October 29, 2010.

[197] Winchester, "Primitive Mormonism," *Salt Lake Tribune,* Sept. 22, 1889.

[198] http://www.mormoncurtain.com/topic_spaldingmanuscript.html.

[199] Tanners, *Mormonism: Shadow or Reality,* 15-17. Note: *Joseph Begins his Work,* vols. 1 and 2, are available from Utah Lighthouse Ministry.

[200] Joseph Smith, (1835) *Doctrine & Covenants* (hereinafter *D&C*) (Salt Lake City: LDS Church, 1974 ed.) §10:10-13.

[201] *D&C* §19:34-35.

[202] Howe, *Mormonism Unvailed*, 226.

[203] Ibid. 215.

[204] Ibid.

[205] *D&C* § 29.

[206] See Wood, compiler, *Joseph Begins his Work, II*, "Doctrine and Covenants," § IX, verse 4, p. 112; *D&C* § 24:9.

[207] *D&C* § 124.

[208] Ibid. §25:4 & 14.

[209] Ibid. §61:14-15.

[210] Howe, Mormonism *Unvailed*, 206.

[211] Van Wagoner, *Sidney Rigdon*, 87.

[212] Franklin Spencer Spalding, *Joseph Smith, Jr., as a Translator: an Inquiry Conducted by Rt. Rev. F.S. Spalding, D.D., Bishop of Utah, with the Kind Assistance of Capable Scholars* (N.p., Arrow Press, 1912) 23-27.

[213] "Museum Walls Proclaim Fraud of Mormon Prophet," *The New York Times,* Magazine Section, December 29, 1912.

[214] John Henry Evans, *Improvement Era,* Vol. 16 (Feb., 1913) 343. [Emphasis added].

[215] Glen Wade, "The Facsimile Found: the Recovery of Joseph Smith's Papyrus Manuscripts: a conversation with Prof. Atiya," *Dialogue,* 2, no. 4 (Winter 1967) 51-52.

[216] Lynn Travers, Norman Tolk, George D. Smith, and Charles F. Graves, "The Facsimile Found... the Recovery of Joseph Smith's Papyrus Manuscripts: an interview with Dr. Fischer," *Dialogue,* Ibid. 56.

[217] Wade, "The Facsimile Found...,"*Dialogue*, Ibid. 53.

[218] *HC* 2: 236-37; 286, 289, 293 & 320-321.

[219] Charles M. Larson, "...*by his Own Hand upon Papyrus: a New Look at the Joseph Smith Papyri* (Grand Rapids, Michigan, The Institute for Religious Research, 1992) 32.

[220] See Klaus Baer, Egyptologist, University of Chicago, "The Breathing Permit of Hor: A Translation of the Apparent Source of the Book of Abraham," *Dialogue* 3, no. 3 (Autumn 1968) 110-134.

[221] Larson, "...*by his own hand upon papyrus,* 29, et. seq.

[222] Ibid. 102.

[223] See notes immediately following *D&C* Facsimile No. 2, Fig. #1.

[224] See *Brigham Young University Studies* (Spring 1977) 273.

[225] *Ensign*, July 1988, 51.

[226] http://www.sidneyrigdon.com/dbroadhu/OH/miscoh08.htm#111337;

this note's illustration of shearing the sheep (fleecing the flock) is compared to the locomotive which is incapable of any pejorative inference, in the exemplar $3 note found in the interior photos in Mormon, Richard L. Bushman's *Joseph Smith: Rough Stone Rolling* (Vintage Books, 2007).

[227] W. (Warren) Parrish, in a letter to the editor of the *Painesville Republican* (Kirtland, Ohio, Feb. 5, 1838).

[228] John A. Clark, "Letter to Mr. Lee, 10 Mar. 1841," *Gleanings by the Way* (Philadelphia: W.I. and I.K. Simon, 1842) 334.

[229] Winchester, "Primitive Mormonism," *Salt Lake Tribune*, Sept. 22, 1889.

[230] Ibid.

[231] Letter signed by 84 Mormons, June, 1838, Senate Doc. #189, Feb., 1841, p. 8.

[232] *Warsaw Signal*, Dec. 31, 1845 & Jan. 7, 1846, cited in Tanners, *Mormonism: Shadow or Reality*, 537-38.

[233] *HC*, 7:549-551; Brigham Young, *Journal of Discourses*, 14 (July 23, 1871): 218-19.

[234] Faulring, ed., *An American Prophet's Record*, chronology, xxviii.

[235] Van Wagoner, *Sidney Rigdon*, 179-181.

[236] *Deseret News*, Church Section, week ending May 3, 1980, 3-4.

[237] *Provo Herald*, May 1, 1980.

[238] Jerald Tanner, *Tracking the White Salamander: the Story of Mark Hoffman, Murder and Forged Mormon Documents*, 2nd ed. (Salt Lake City: Utah Lighthouse Ministry, 1987).

[239] http://www.utlm.org/images/tracking/trackingp73_b.jpg; *Deseret News* two pg. pictorial of LDS leaders' formal acceptance of Salamander Letter.

[240] See Jerald Tanner, *Tracking the White Salamander: the Story of Mark Hoffman, Murder and Forged Mormon Documents*. Also includes *Confessions of a White Salamander* and *the Mormon Church and the McLellin Collection*. 3rd ed., (SLC: Utah Lighthouse Ministry, 1987) 1.

[241] Quinn, *Mormon Hierarchy: Extensions of Power*, 818.

[242] Ibid. 21.

[243] From the personal journal of Wesley P. Lloyd, August 7, 1933, former missionary in Roberts' Eastern States Mission & former Dean of the BYU Graduate School. The journal notes were based upon a 3.5 hour conversation with Roberts, as quoted in *B. H. Roberts' Studies of the Book of Mormon*, Intro. by Brigham D. Madsen, ed. (Urbana: University of Illinois Press, 1985) 23.

[244] B. D. Madsen, ed., *B.H. Roberts' Studies of the Book of Mormon*, 251.

[245] B. H. Roberts, "Justice will follow Truth," epilogue, D. Michael Quinn, *The New Mormon History: Revisionist Essays on the Past* (SLC: Signature Books, 1992) 303.

[246] B. H. Roberts, *Studies of the Book of Mormon*, 24-28.

[247] *Deseret News*, 9 April 1928, in *B. H. Roberts' Studies of the Book of Mormon*, 29.

[248] Wesley P. Walters, "The Origin of the Book of Mormon," *Journal of Pastoral Practice* 3 (1979):123.

[249] Walters, *Origin of the Book of Mormon*, 124, n. 3.

[250] See *B. H. Roberts' Studies of the Book of Mormon*, Brigham D. Madsen, ed., 2nd Ed.

[251] *HC* 4:550-52.

[252] As part of the original ceremony, Masons had to swear "…that I will not be at the initiating of an old man in dotage, a young man in nonage, an atheist, irreligious libertine, idiot, madman, hermaphrodite, nor woman." William Morgan, *Mysteries of Freemasonry: Containing All the Degrees of the Order Conferred in a Master's Lodge*, (n.p., n.p., n.d.) 943. Note: after Morgan died (allegedly killed by Masons) his young widow, Lucinda Pendleton Morgan, became one of Joseph Smith's plural wives.

[253] *Salt Lake Tribune*, August 18, 1985, B-2.

[254] Jonathan B. Turner, *Mormonism in all Ages, or the Rise, Progress and Causes of Mormonism* (New York City: Platt & Peters, 1842) 72, 99 & 107, respectively.

[255] Ibid. 116-117.

[256] Palmer, *Insider's View of Mormon Origins,* 49.

[257] Ibid. Chap. 5, "Moroni & the Golden Pot."

[258] *Evening and Morning Star*, vol. 2, no. 20:160 (May 1834); *HC,* 2:62.

[259] Fawn M. Brodie (1945) *No Man Knows My History*, rev. 2nd ed. (New York: Vintage Press, 1995). Citations are to Vintage Press Ed.

[260] Utah Statutes § 45-2-2, enacted in 1943 as § 62-2-2, about the time Ms. Brodie was researching her book. Her uncle was David O. McKay, LDS Church President from 1951 to his death in 1970.

[261] *In re: I.M.L. v. State,* 2002 UT 110, 61 P.3d 1038, 1048 (Utah, 2002).

[262] Steven Soderbergh, Director, *Erin Brokovich*, Universal Pictures, 2000.

[263] See for example, "CV120 Direct and Circumstantial Evidence," *Utah Model Jury Instruction, 2nd ed.* "A fact may be proved by direct or circumstantial evidence. Circumstantial evidence consists of facts or circumstances that allow someone to reasonably infer the truth of the facts to be proved. For example, if the fact to be proved is whether Johnny ate the cherry pie and a witness testifies that she saw Johnny take a bite of the cherry pie, that is direct evidence of the fact. If the witness testifies that she saw Johnny with cherries smeared on his face and an empty pie plate in his hand, that is circumstantial evidence of the fact."

481

[264] Collins Essential English Dictionary 2nd ed., (NY: Harper Collins, 2006).

[265] Daniel H. Ludlow, ed., Encyclopedia *of Mormonism: The History, Scripture, Doctrine, and Procedure of the Church of Jesus Christ of Latter-day Saints,* 5 vols. (New York: Macmillan Publishing Co., 1992) 2:552–53. "Latter-day Saints believe in God the Father; his Son, Jesus Christ; and the Holy Ghost [Article of Faith No. 1]. These three Gods form the Godhead, which holds the keys of power over the universe. Each member of the Godhead is an independent personage, separate and distinct from the other two, the three being in perfect unity and harmony with each other." Chapter 2, "Articles of Faith."

[266] *Federal Rules of Evidence* (hereinafter, *FRE)* 613.

[267] Howe, *Mormonism Unvailed*, 232.

[268] Smith, Joseph, Jr. (15 March 1842) "History of Joseph Smith," *Times and Seasons* 3 (10): 726–28.

[269] Brodie, *No Man Knows my History*, 23-25.

[270] *Pearl of Great Price (PGP)*, 1851 ed., 41.

[271] *Times and Seasons*, Nauvoo, Illinois, 3 (April 15, 1942):749, 753; *Millennial Star*, vol. 3 (Liverpool, 1842) 53.

[272] 2 Maccabees 1:36; Additionally, the name Laban, an ostensibly wicked man killed by the Prophet Nephi in *the Book of Mormon*, appears in Judith 9:26, and the Helaman 8:20 prophet Ezias' name appears in the Apocrypha at *Esdra* 8:2.

[273] http://www.challengemin.org/8400.html.

[274] http://en.wikipedia.org/wiki/List_of_code_names_in_the_Doctrine_and_Covenants; & ^ "Annotated History of the Church: Volume 1 Chapter 18". The Book of Abraham Project; and http://www.boap.org/LDS/History/HTMLHistory/v1c18history.html#N_29 _. This is a set of annotations to the *HC*, B. H. Roberts, ed.

[275] Arrington and Bitton, *Saints without Halos,* 23-24.

[276] *FRE* 801.

[277] *FRE* 801-807, inclusive.

[278] *FRE* 803(2).

[279] *FRE* 803(5).

[280] Painting displayed on the following link to the Church website: http://josephsmith.net/josephsmith/v/index.jsp?vgnextoid=c08679179acbff00VgnVCM1000001f5e340aRCRD&locale=0 (viewed July 6, 2010); a similar scene was published in the *Ensign*, August 2009, 54, "He called me by Name," by artist Liz Swindle.

[281] "He Called me by Name," by Michael T. Malm, 2004 on LDS website: http://josephsmith.net/josephsmith/v/index.jspvgnextoid=c08679179acbff0 0VgnVCM1000001f5e340aRCRD&vgnextfmt=tab3

[282] Dean Jesse, compiler, rev. ed., *Personal Writings of Joseph Smith* (1932) (Salt Lake City: Deseret Book, 2002) 17.

[283] William B. Smith, *William Smith on Mormonism* (Lamoni, Iowa: Herald Steam Book and Job Office, 1883) 7-8.

[284] See *FRE* 803(7).

[285] *Charles Dana v. Dr. Brink* (medical malpractice) noted in Faulring, *An American Prophet's Record*, 314-330. After an extensive discussion of the types of expert witnesses allowable, Defendant physician was found liable for malpractice against the Plaintiff's wife (no jury seems to have been impaneled; it appears that Joseph Smith was both the trier of fact and judge) and fined the defendant physician $99.00 plus costs. Compare the sermon in April , 2010 LDS General Conference, by Elder Donald L. Halstrom, of the Presidency of the Seventy, where he indirectly admonished members to refrain suing physicians by illustrating examples of two families who had obstetric "accidents," which caused deaths during childbirth. One family "ruined the reputation of the physician," [though it is most certain that all that was done was to file a legitimate medical malpractice lawsuit], while the other family of a similar type malpractice turned to the Lord [read—did not sue]. The speaker, in a perfect *post hoc ergo propter hoc* fallacy, concluded that the generations of families which followed those involved in these two tragic anecdotes remain miserable apostates or happy Church members, respectively, depending upon their pursuit of a legally recognized method for seeking redress in the courts (here, termed 'revenge').

[286] Faulring, *An American Prophet's Record,* 9.

[287] Ibid. 7.

[288] "Joseph Knight Sr., Reminiscence, circa. 1835-1847," Dan Vogel, ed., *Early Mormon Documents*, 4:15. Joseph Knight, Sr., "Manuscript History of Joseph Smith," circa 1835-1847, LDS Church Archives, SLC, Utah.

[289] See Vogel, *Joseph Smith: the Making of a Prophet,* 57.

[290] Lorenzo Saunders to Thomas Gregg, January 28, 1885, in Charles A. Shook, *The Origins of the Book of Mormon* (Cincinnati: Standard Publishing Co., 1914) 135; Vogel, *Early Mormon Documents*, 3:178.

[291] Faulring, *An American Prophet's Record*, 225-230.

[292] Turner, *Mormonism in all Ages,* 206.

[293] See annotations and case law interpreting *FRE* 601.

[294] Anderson, *Inside the Mind of Joseph Smith,* 222, et. seq.

[295] Woodbridge, *Founder of Mormonism: A Psychological Study of Joseph Smith, Jr.,* 167.

[296] Ibid. 172.

[297] Ibid. 168.

[298] See generally, annotations and case law interpreting *FRE* 607.

[299] Vogel, *Early Mormon Documents* 5:418.

[300] *HC* 3:232.

[301] Hyrum Smith, letter, 15 Feb. 1841 (*The Testimony Given Before the Judge of the 5th Judicial District of the State of Missouri, on the Trial of Joseph Smith, Jr., and others, for High Treason and Other Crimes Against that State,* U.S. Senate 26th Congress, 2nd Session, Doc. 189, ordered to be printed Feb. 15, 1841; *Copy of the Testimony Given before the Hon. Austin A. King, judge of the Fifth Judicial Circuit in the State of Missouri, at the Court-house in Richmond, in a Criminal Court of Inquiry begun Nov. 12, 1838.*)

[302] Woodbridge, *...A Psychological Study of Joseph Smith Jr.,* 205.

[303] Palmer, *An Insider's View of Mormon Origins,* 1-4.

[304] Ibid. 1-7.

[305] Russell M. Nelson, "A Treasured Testament," *Ensign* (July, 1993) 61, citing Whitmer, *An Address to All Believers,* 12.

[306] *Cincinnati Advertiser* (June 2, 1830) "A fellow by the name of Joseph Smith, who resides in the upper part of Susquehanna county, has been, for the last two years we are told, employed in dedicating as he says, by inspiration, a new bible. He pretended that he had been entrusted by God with a golden bible which had been always hidden from the world. Smith would put his face into a hat in which he had a white stone, and pretend to read from it, while his coadjutor transcribed."

[307] http://josephsmith.net/josephsmith/v/index.jspvgnextoid=0bda0fbab57f0 010VgnVCM1000001f5e340aRCRD&vgnextfmt=tab3 (Viewed July 8, 2010). Note: as of February 21, 2011 this five portraits are found on the www.josephsmith.net website under the section "Artwork," and then "scriptures."

[308] See *FRE* 403.

[309] Joseph Smith, Jr., (1830) *The Book of Mormon* (An Account Written by the Hand of Mormon upon plates taken from the plates of Nephi) 1974 ed., (Salt Lake City: Utah, The Church of Jesus Christ of Latter-Day Saints, 1974). "Origin of The Book of Mormon," last ¶. [Emphasis added].

[310] Brigham Young, *Journal of Discourses* 19 (June 17, 1877): 38.

[311] http://www.mormoncurtain.com/topic_grantpalmer.html (posted 05/09/

2006).

[312] Smith, *Book of Mormon*, Mormon 6:6.

[313] Ibid. 6:10.

[314] John E. Clark, "Book of Mormon Geography," Daniel H. Ludlow, ed., *Encyclopedia of Mormonism*, 1:178.

[315] Thomas S. Monson, "Thomas S. Monson Speaks at the Hill Cumorah," *Ensign* (April 4, 2001)19–20. [Emphasis added]. http://www.josephsmith.net/josephsmith/v/index.jspvgnextoid=014968f03 74f1010VgnVCM1000001f5e340aRCRD&vgnextfmt=tab2; (viewed April 22, 2010).

[316] SIL (Smithsonian Institute Libraries) - 76 Rev. May 1980; See also Letter prepared by the Department of Anthropology SMITHSONIAN INSTITUTION WASHINGTON, D.C. 20560, 1996:

"Your recent inquiry concerning the Smithsonian Institution's alleged use of the Book of Mormon as a scientific guide has been received in the Smithsonian's Department of Anthropology. The Book of Mormon is a religious document and not a scientific guide. The Smithsonian Institution has never used it in archeological research and any information that you have received to the contrary is incorrect. Accurate information about the Smithsonian's position is contained in the enclosed "Statement Regarding the Book of Mormon," which was prepared to respond to the numerous inquiries that the Smithsonian receives on this topic. Because the Smithsonian regards the unauthorized use of its name to disseminate inaccurate information as unlawful, we would appreciate your assistance in providing us with the names of any individuals who are misusing the Smithsonian's name.
Please address any correspondence to:
Anthropology Outreach Office
Department of Anthropology
National Museum of Natural History MRC 112
Smithsonian Institution
Washington, DC 20560"

[317] For an analysis of Mormon attorney Thomas Ferguson's failed attempts to locate archeological support for *the Book of Mormon* see Stan Larson, *Quest for the Gold Plates* (Salt Lake City: Freethinker Press, 1996).

[318] Ibid, 179-181.

[319] Hiram Page, "Letter to William E. McLellin, 2 Feb. 1848," Vogel, *Early Mormon Documents* 5:257-259.

[320] Whitmer, "An Address to all Believers in Christ," (Richmond, MO, April 1, 1887) 31.

[321] *FRE* 804(b) (3).

[322] "Affidavit of William Stafford, Wayne County, N.Y. Dec. 9, 1833," Vogel, *Early Mormon Documents* 2:59-63.

[323] "Statement of Willard Chase of Wayne County, N.Y., Dec. 11, 1833," Vogel, *Early Mormon Documents* 2:64-73. According to the midwife who delivered him and also a probable cousin of Emma's, Smith's first child, Alvin, was born severely deformed and lived just a few hours; Anderson, *Inside the Mind of Joseph Smith,* 89-90.

[324] Statement of Sophia Lewis as published in Howe, *Mormonism Unvailed,* 268-69; for citation to other sources that published her statement see also Vogel, *Early Mormon Documents,* 4:298. Smith's first three children died as infants. The oldest was terribly deformed, the second and third, twins, lived only three hours. Linda King Newell and Valeen Tippetts Avery, *Mormon Enigma: Emma Hale Smith,* 2nd ed. (Urbana: Univ. of Illinois Press/Doubleday, 1994) 39.

[325] *The Susquehanna Register* (May 1, 1834)1.

[326] Henry Harris Affidavit, Palmyra, N.Y., Dec. 2, 1833 in Vogel, *Early Mormon Documents* 2:75-77.

[327] Abigail Harris Declaration, Palmyra N.Y., Nov. 28, 1833 in Vogel, *Early Mormon Documents* 2:31-33. [Emphasis added]

[328] Lucy Harris Declaration, Nov. 29, 1833, Palmyra, N.Y. in Vogel, *Early Mormon Documents* 2:34-36.

[329] Quinn, *Magic World View,* 59.

[330] Peter Ingersoll Affidavit, Palmyra, N.Y. Dec. 2, 1833, in Vogel, *Early Mormon Documents* 2:39-46. [Emphasis added];

[331] "Joseph Smith Papers, LDS Church History Library," Letter of Joseph Smith Jr. to Oliver Cowdery, October 22, 1829, copied in 1832 into Joseph Smith Letterbook, 1:9, in Vogel, *Early Mormon Documents* 1:7-8. [Emphasis added].

[332] Faulring, *An American Prophet's Record,* 392 (June 30, 1843).

[333] Bennett, *History of the Saints; or, an Exposé of Joe Smith and Mormonism,* 175.

[334] "Joseph Smith," *Presidents of the Church Student Manual* (SLC: LDS, CES Manual 2003) 6; http://josephsmith.net/josephsmith/v/index.jsp?vgnextoid=4c6679179acbff00VgnVCM1000001f5e340aRCRD&vgnextfmt=tab4 (Viewed July 6, 2010).

[335] *HC* 5:289.

[336] *Times and Seasons,* 5 (Aug. 15, 1844):614.

[337] *HC* 6 (May 26, 1844):408-409.

[338] *FRE* 404(b).

[339] *FRE* 405(a).

[340] Statement signed November 3, 1833, by eleven Manchester, N.Y. persons. Signatories confirmed as residents by Dan Vogel, ed., *Early Mormon Documents* 2:18-21.

[341] Statement signed December 4, 1833, by fifty-one Palmyra, N.Y. persons. Signatories confirmed as residents by Dan Vogel, ed., *Early Mormon Documents* 2: 48-55.

[342] http://scriptures.lds.org/dc/132, Church of Jesus Christ of Latter-day Saints © 2006 Intellectual Reserve, Inc.

[343] *FRE* 609.

[344] *FRE* 406.

[345] *Deseret News,* serialized "History of Joseph Smith," September 3 & 10, 1856; *History of The Church of Jesus Christ of Latter-day Saints*, 7 vols. (Salt Lake City: Deseret Book Co., 1932–51) 5:372, formerly known as the *Documentary History of the Church* (cited as *HC*) completed in 1856 by historians, written in the first person so as to appear to have been written by the Prophet Joseph Smith. Most of this history was written after his assassination. However, the Church has long misrepresented the collaborative effort of the authors until issues such as the one involving the partial translation of the Kinderhook Plates are questioned and only then does it admit that the history is the work of scribes (other than Joseph). See *Brigham Young University Studies* (Summer 1971) 466, 469-70, 472.

[346] Stanley B. Kimball, "Kinderhook Plates Brought to Joseph Smith Appear to Be a Nineteenth Century Hoax," *Ensign* (Aug. 1981) 66.

[347] *Warsaw Signal*, Warsaw, Illinois (May 22, 1844).

[348] Welby W. Ricks, "The Kinderhook Plates," *Improvement Era* (LDS magazine published from 1897-1970) Sept., 1962, as quoted in Tanners, *Mormonism: Shadow or Reality*, 113. Note: only the above-cited 1981 *Ensign* article comes up when a search for "Kinderhook Plates," is done on www.lds.org.

[349] Tanners, *Mormonism, Shadow or Reality*, 113.

[350] George Metcalf, representative of the Smithsonian, in a letter dated Nov. 14, 1968 implies that the Kinderhook etchings resemble characters found on the lid of a popular Chinese tea chest. See Tanners, *Mormonism: Shadow or Reality*, 114.

[351] Ibid. 113.

[352] Anderson, *Inside the Mind of Joseph Smith*, 241.

[353] Winchester, "Primitive Mormonism," *Salt Lake Tribune*, 1889.

[354] *Teachings of Presidents of the Church: Joseph Smith* (Salt Lake City: Church of Jesus Christ of Latter-day Saints, 2007). The same portrait is on

the Mormon Tabernacle Choir, CD. *Praise to the Man: Songs Honoring the Prophet Joseph Smith*, by the Mormon Tabernacle Choir, Audio CD, at http://www.deseretbook.com (viewed June 2, 2010).

[355] Hal R. Varian, "Beauty and the Fattened Wallet," *NY Times*, 04/0 6/06.

[356] "Charles Feng, "Looking Good, the Psychology and Biology of Beauty," *Human Biology,* Stanford University, no.6 (December, 2002).

[357] Foundation for Ancient Research and Mormon Studies (FARMS) and Foundation for Apologetic Information and Research (FAIR) are LDS supported apologetic groups. Recently re-named the Neal A. Maxwell Institute of Religious Scholarship, FARMS is part of BYU. See also SHIELDS (Scholarly & Historical Information Exchange for Latter-Day Saints) established in 1997.

[358] D.I. Holmes, "A Multivariate Technique for Authorship Attribution and its Application to the Analysis of Mormon Scripture and Related Texts," *History and Computing,* vol. 3, no. 1 (London: Oxford Univ. Press, 1991) 14, 20-21.

[359] Matthew L. Jockers, Daniela M. Witten and Craig S. Criddle, "Reassessing Authorship of the *Book of Mormon* using Delta and Nearest Shrunken Centroid Classification," *Oxford Journal of Literary and Linguistic Computing,* 23:4 (Dec. 2008) 465-491.

[360] Ibid.

[361] Bruce R. McConkie, *Mormon Doctrine*, 351-52. Note: this book of Mormon Doctrine was written by one who became one of the Twelve Apostles in 1972 and remained in that position until his death in 1985. The Church claims that Elder McConkie was never formally authorized to publish the book. Nevertheless, more than one edition was published by Bookcraft, a private company which published mostly books for Mormon audiences. In fact there are publication runs from several years: 1958 (original), 1966, 69, 71, 72, 74, 78, 86, 89 in both hardcover and paperback. In 1999 Bookcraft was purchased by Deseret Management Corporation, the parent company of the LDS Church for-profit company. LDS Church leaders have quoted extensively from the Book since it was first released by Bookcraft. Only since 2010 has Deseret Book's reprinting of past editions been discontinued.

[362] Charles Crane and Steven Crane, *Ashamed of Joseph* (Joplin: College Press Publishing, 1993) 175-179.

[363] Joseph Smith's *Inspired Translation of the Bible*, Genesis, 50:33, as quoted in "Prophet Smith among the Prophets," at the http://www.LDS.org resource center.

[364] Bankruptcy Act of 1841, ch. 9, 5 Stat. 440-49, effective Feb. 1, 1842.

[365] Dallin H. Oaks and Joseph I. Bentley, "Joseph Smith and Legal Process: In the Wake of the Steamboat Nauvoo," *BYU Law Review* 3 (1976) 750-767.

[366] "The *Nauvoo Expositor* was a newspaper in Nauvoo, Illinois that published only one issue, dated June 7, 1844. Its publication set off a chain of events that led to the assassination of LDS movement founder, Joseph Smith, Jr.. The *Expositor* was founded by several disaffected associates of Smith, Jr., some of whom claimed that Smith had attempted to seduce their wives in the name of plural marriage." "Polygamy, Persecution and Power," *Salt Lake Tribune* (June 16, 1996) ¶16, 17.

[367] *Nauvoo Expositor* (June 7, 1844) 1-2.

[368] *HC*, 6 (1912):432: "The Council passed an ordinance declaring the *Nauvoo Expositor* a nuisance, and also issued an order to me to abate the said nuisance. I immediately ordered the Marshall to destroy it without delay." – Joseph Smith.
Besides arson and property destruction, Smith had been charged with treason as early as 1841 by U.S President John Tyler, Jr. (*HC*, 5:363). This warrant remained outstanding until his death. In 1843, Smith's Nauvoo City Council "passed an ordinance making it illegal for any person to serve any county, state, or federal writ upon any person in Nauvoo or to search or seize any property in the City without permission of the mayor (Smith)." *HC*, 6:105 & 124, in Evans, *Keystone*, 159-161.

[369] Reed C. Durham, Jr., *Is There No Help For The Widow's Son?* Presidential Address delivered at the Mormon History Assoc. Convention, April 20, 1974.

[370] Comment by the Governor of Illinois, Thomas B. Ford, re: Joseph Smith's death, *HC*, 7:35.

[371] Hickman, *Brigham's Destroying Angel*, Appendix, 197-198.

[372] Quinn, *Extensions of Power*, 795, April 9, 1894 note, and Dallin H. Oaks and Marvin S. Hill, *Carthage Conspiracy: The Trial of the Accused Assassins of Joseph Smith* (Urbana: University of Illinois Press, 1975) 217, respectively.

[373] *The Republic of Plato*, reprint of 1945 American ed. (London: Oxford University Press, 1969) 144.

[374] Mrs. T.B.H. Stenhouse *aka* "Fanny." *Tell it All: the Story of a Life's Experience in Mormonism.* (Hartford: A.D. Worthington & Co., 1875) Facsimile reproduction of orig., (Salt Lake City: Utah Lighthouse Ministry, n.d.) 296. Citations are to UTLM reprint ed.

[375] Rodney Turner, retired BYU religion professor, Sunstone Panel Discussion, September 7, 1991.

[376] Brigham Young, *Journal of Discourses,* 13 (July 24, 1870) 272.

[377] Todd Compton, *In Sacred Loneliness, the Plural Wives of Joseph Smith* (Salt Lake City: Signature Books, 1997) 231; http://www.signaturebookslibrary.org/Mormons/josephsmith.htm#joseph (viewed October 20, 2010).

[378] Richard S. Van Wagoner, *Mormon Polygamy: A History,* 2nd ed. (Salt Lake City: Signature Books, 1989) 66.

[379] http://www.wivesofjosephsmith.org/

[380] Van Wagoner, *Mormon Polygamy,* 4-11.

[381] Compton, *In Sacred Loneliness,* 34-36.

[382] Ann Eliza Young, *Wife No. 19,* 67-70.

[383] Faulring, *An American Prophet's Record,* 176-180.

[384] *Sangamo Journal,* 1 Aug. 1842, Van Wagoner, *Mormon Polygamy,* 32.

[385] http://www.wivesofjosephsmith.org/16-SarahAnnWhitney.htm

[386] Van Wagoner, *Mormon Polygamy,* 84; *Times and Seasons,* 5 (March 15, 1844) 474.

[387] *Messenger and Advocate,* Kirtland, Ohio (June 18, 1845).

[388] Van Wagoner, *Mormon Polygamy,* 39.

[389] Cannon, *Under the Prophet,* 201. Additionally, the authors of *The Mormon Corporate Empire* noted: "The *Deseret News* is not held in high esteem by its counterparts." During the investigation for their book, they "...encountered some very unflattering descriptions of it by other newspaper publishers in Utah and surrounding states." *The Mormon Corporate Empire,* 264, n. 33.

[390] Dallin Oaks, BYU Devotional, Jan 29, 2002.

[391] *Church Handbook of Instructions* (SLC: LDS Church, 1998) 72.

[392] http://en.wikipedia.org/wiki/List_of_Brigham_Young's_wives.

[393] Ann Eliza Young, *Wife No. 19,* 500.

[394] Richard Francis Burton, *The City of the Saints: and Across the Rocky Mountains to California* (New York: Harper & Brothers, 1862) 427.

[395] Ibid. 430.

[396] Firmage and Mangrum, *Zion in the Courts,* 249-251.

[397] *Deseret News* (Salt Lake City, Utah, 12 May 1875).

[398] Ann Eliza Young, *Wife No. 19,* 73.

[399] Ibid. 292.

[400] *Deseret News,* April 22, 1857.

[401] Brigham Young, sermon at Provo, Utah, July 14, 1855.

[402] *Teachings of Presidents of the Church: BRIGHAM YOUNG* (Salt Lake City: the Church of Jesus Christ of Latter-day Saints, 1997). The

'Historical Summary' in the prefatory material of the manual mentions that his first wife died in 1832 and that Young remarried in 1834; however, there is absolutely no mention of polygamy in this manual. The manual index omits the word 'polygamy,' and under 'marriage eternal,' there is nothing referenced about this long-standing Mormon doctrine.

[403] *Teachings of Presidents of the Church: JOSEPH SMITH* (Salt Lake City: the Church of Jesus Christ of Latter-day Saints, 2007). In the preface on page xii, the Manual explains: "This book does not discuss plural marriage." Then it provides a short history of plural marriage, never mentioning any of Joseph Smith's plural marriages. The Manual also mentions on p. 22, "As commanded by God, he also taught the doctrine of plural marriage." Again, there is no reference to any of Smith's dozens of polygamous marriages or of the 'wives,' involved in them.

[404] B. Carmon Hardy, *Solemn Covenant* 1st ed. (Chicago: University of Illinois Press, 1992) 367.

[405] See Van Wagoner, *Mormon Polygamy* and Compton, *In Sacred Loneliness.*

[406] John, A., Widtsoe, *Evidences and Reconciliations: Aids to Faith in a Modern Day* (Salt Lake City: Bookcraft, 1960) 390-392. Widtsoe states: "The United States census records from 1850 to 1940, and all available Church records, uniformly show a preponderance of males in Utah, and in the Church."

[407] Andrew Love Neff (history and political science professor at the U. of U., deceased) *History of Utah, 1847-1869* (SLC: Deseret News Press, 1940) 563.

[408] Ibid.

[409] See Leonard J. Arrington, *Reflections of a Mormon Historian: Leonard J. Arrington on the New Mormon History* (Norman, Oklahoma: The Arthur H. Clark Company, 2006) 225-226 and Maxine Hanks, *Women and Authority (Re-emerging Mormon Feminism)* (Salt Lake City: Signature Books, 1992) 69-147.

[410] Utah Constitution: *ARTICLE III, Section 1:* [Religious Toleration – Polygamy Forbidden]. "The following ordinance shall be irrevocable without the consent of the United States and the people of this State: First:--Perfect toleration of religious sentiment is guaranteed. No inhabitant of this State shall ever be molested in person or property on account of his or her mode of religious worship; but polygamous or plural marriages are forever prohibited."

[411] Cannon, *Under the Prophet in Utah,* 3.

[412] Ibid. 33.

[413] Ibid. 99.

[414] Margaret Toscano and Paul Toscano, *Strangers in Paradox* (Salt Lake City: Signature Books, 1990).

[415] Ibid. 239.

[416] Margaret Merrill Toscano, "Is There a Place for Heavenly Mother in Mormon Theology?: An Investigation into Discourses of Power," *Sunstone* 133 (July, 2004):14 et. seq.

[417] Bertrand Russell, Why *I Am Not a Christian and Other Essays on Religion and Related Subjects.* Paul Edwards, ed. (New York: Touchstone, 1967) 162 & 168, respectively.

[418] Nicole Hardy, "Single, Female, Mormon, Alone," *New York Times*, January 11, 2011.

[419] Elizabeth Cady Stanton, "The Christian Church and Women," a sermon originally delivered in Moncure D. Conway's Pulpit, South Place chapel, London, September, 1882. Originally published in *The Boston Investigator* (May 18, 1901) as cited in Annie Laurie Gaylor, ed., *Women without Superstition, No God's –No Masters, the collected Writings of Women Freethinkers of the Nineteenth and Twentieth Centuries* (Madison, Wisconsin: Freedom from Religion Foundation, 1997) 114.

[420] Ann Eliza Young, *Wife No. 19,* 92-95.

[421] Quinn, *Extensions of Power,* 807.

[422] Ibid. 805.

[423] Ibid. 130.

[424] Dalma Heyn, *Marriage Shock* (NY: Bantam Doubleday Dell, 1997)54-5.

[425] Sonia Johnson, *From Housewife to Heretic* (Albuquerque: Wildfire Books, 1989).

[426] Ibid. 174.

[427] Sonia Johnson, Ed.D. Chair, MORMONS FOR ERA*, Patriarchal Panic: Sexual Politics in the Mormon Church,* paper presented at the American Psychological Association Meeting (New York City, Sept. 1, 1979). Orrin Hatch, Republican Senator from Utah, queried the Senate during the ERA hearings on whether adoption of the ERA would affect the Catholic, Mormon and Jewish Religions' ability to keep their tax exempt status, since they all concededly discriminate against women in denying them positions of ecclesiastical leadership and/or segregate the genders during services. See William F. Buckley, "Senate ERA Testimony is Revealing," *Salt Lake Tribune* (June 21, 1983) A-13.

[428] Anderson, *Inside the Mind of Joseph Smith,* 147.

[429] David John Buerger, *The Mysteries of Godliness: a History of Mormon Temple Worship,* 2nd ed. (San Francisco: Smith Research Associates,

2002)178.

[430] See Hanks, *Women and Authority: Re-emerging Mormon Feminism.*

[431] Harold A. Frost, "The Thinness Obsession," *Ensign* (Jan 1990) 71.

[432] K. Gates and M. Pritchard, "The Relationships among Religious Affiliation, Religious Angst, and Disordered Eating," *Eat Weight Disord.* 2009 March 14 (1):e11-5.

[433] L Pinhas, M. Heinmaa , P. Bryden , S. Bradley and B. Toner, "Disordered Eating in Jewish Adolescent Girls," *Can. J. Psychiatry 2008 Sept; 53(9):601-8.*

[434] N.K. Abraham and C.L. Birmingham, "Is there Evidence that Religion is a Risk Factor for Eating Disorders?" *Eat Weight Disord.* 2008 Dec;13(4): e75-8; see also S. Douki, S.B. Zineb, F. Nacef, U. Halbreich, "Women's Mental Health in the Muslim World: Cultural, Religious, and Social Issues," *J Affect Disord.* 2007 Sept; 102(1-3):177-89. Epub 2007 Feb. 8.

[435] ----------- "Eating Disorder and Confession. Is there a Correlation between the Type of Eating Disorder and Specific Religious Affiliation?" *Psychother Psychosom Med Psychol.* 1993 Feb; 43(2):70-3; [article in German].

[436] E.Vedul-Kjelsås E, K.G. Götestam, "Eating Disorders in a Historical Perspective," *Tidsskr Nor Laegeforen* 2004 Sep 23; 124(18):2369-71. [Article in Norwegian].

[437] April 2005, LDS General Conference.

[438] Brigham Young, *Journal of Discourses* 3 (June 15, 1856):360.

[439] See Vogel, *Joseph Smith: the Making of a Prophet.*

[440] Van Wagoner, *Mormon Polygamy*, 57.

[441] A Revelation by Joseph Smith recorded on July 12, 1843, *HC*, 5:501-7.

[442] Van Wagoner, *Mormon Polygamy*, 62, n. 10.

[443] Newell and Avery, *Mormon Enigma*, 226.

[444] Brigham Young, in an address reported by G.D. Watt, 7 October 1863, Brigham Young Collection, LDS Archives, quoted in Newell and Avery, *Mormon Enigma*, 228.

[445] Brigham Young, *Journal of Discourses*, 17 (9 August 1874):159.

[446] See Van Wagoner, *Mormon Polygamy*, 50-62.

[447] Ibid. 60.

[448] Sarah M. Pratt Affidavit (Orson Pratt's first wife who later divorced him due to his polygamous liaisons with young women) executed in Salt Lake City in May, 1886. Affidavit witnessed by Charles S. Zane, Chief Justice of the Utah Territory Supreme Court, quoted in Wilhelm Ritter von

Wymetal, *Mormon Portraits* (Salt Lake City: Tribune Printing & Pub., 1886) 59. [Emphasis original].

[449] Ibid. 54.

[450] Ibid. 57-58.

[451] Bushman, *Rough Stone Rolling,* 555.

[452] Newell and Avery, *Mormon Enigma,* 164-165.

[453] *Diary of Charles Lowell Walker,* 1(17 Dec.1876) 438.

[454] Newell and Avery, *Mormon Enigma,* preface to 2nd ed., p. xii.

[455] See Dieter F. Uchtdorf, 2nd counselor in LDS First Presidency, *The Remarkable Soul of a Woman* (Salt Lake City: Deseret Book, 2010).

[456] Quoted in Hanks, *Woman and Authority,* 93.

[457] Kent Ponder, Ph.D., "Mormon Women, Prozac ® and Therapy," © 2003. http://home.teleport.com/~packham/prozac.htm [Emphasis original].

[458] James W. Ure, *Leaving the Fold: Candid Conversations with Inactive Mormons* (Salt Lake City: Signature Books, 1999) 237.

[459] Ibid. 235.

[460] Russell M. Nelson, "Our Sacred Duty to Honor Women," *Ensign*, May 1999.

[461] http://www.imdb.com/name/nm0001438/bio (viewed July 10, 2010).

[462] Elaine S. Dalton, 2nd Counselor Gen. Young Women's Presidency, Mormon Youth Conference, 2005.

[463] "True to the Faith," *Hymns*, #254, text & music by Evan Stephens, 1854-1930.

[464] Joseph Smith, Jr., "Latter Day Saints," *An Original History of the Religious Denominations at Present Existing in the United States*, I. Daniel Rupp., ed. (Harrisburg, PA: J. Winebrenner, 1848) 404-405: "When about fourteen years of age, I began to reflect upon the importance of being prepared for a future state; and upon inquiring the place of salvation, I found that there was a great clash in religious sentiment; if I went to one society they referred me to one place, and another to another; each one pointing to his particular creed as the "summum bonum" of perfection. Considering that all could not be right, and that God could not be the author of so much confusion, I determined to investigate the subject more fully, believing that if God had a church, it would not be split up into factions, and that if he taught one society to worship one way, and administer in one set of ordinances, he would not teach another principles which were diametrically opposed. Believing the word of God, I had confidence in the declaration of James, "If any man lack wisdom let him ask of God, who giveth to all men liberally and upbraideth not, and it shall be given him...I retired to a secret place in a grove, and began to call upon

the Lord. While fervently engaged in supplication, my mind was taken away …and I was enrapt in a heavenly vision, and saw two glorious personages, who exactly resembled each other in features and likeness, surrounded with a brilliant light, which eclipsed the sun at noonday. They told me that all the religious denominations were believing in incorrect doctrines, and that none of them was acknowledged of God as His Church and Kingdom. And I was expressly commanded to "go not after them," at the same time receiving a promise that the fullness of the gospel should at some future time be made known unto me. On the evening of the 21st September, A.D. 1823, while I was praying unto God and endeavoring to exercise faith in the precious promises of scripture, on a sudden, a light like that of day, only of a far purer and more glorious appearance and brightness, burst into the room; indeed the first sight was as though the house was filled with consuming fire. The appearance produced a shock that affected the whole body. In a moment a personage stood before me surrounded with a glory yet greater than that with which I was already surrounded. This messenger proclaimed himself to be an angel of God, sent to bring the joyful tidings, that the covenant which God made with ancient Israel was at hand to be fulfilled; that the preparatory work for the second coming of the Messiah was speedily to commence; that the time was at hand for the gospel in all its fullness to be preached in power, unto all nations, that a people might be prepared for the millennial reign. I was informed that I was chosen to be an instrument in the hands of God to bring about some of his purposes in this glorious dispensation. I was informed also concerning the aboriginal inhabitants of this country, and shown who they were, and from whence they came; a brief sketch of their origin, progress, civilization, laws, governments, of their righteousness and iniquity, and the blessings of God being finally withdrawn from them as a people, was made known unto me." See also *D&C* "Joseph Smith," 2:1-75. (Note: Smith joined the Methodist Church in 1828 after being told by The Father and The Son that all creeds were incorrect).

[465] Brodie, *No Man Knows My History,* 23-25.

[466] http://www.mormon.org/mormonorg/eng/basic-beliefs/the-restoration-of-truth/the-restoration-of-the-priesthood, (viewed June 4, 2010). [Emphasis original].

[467] May 1829, Smith & Cowdery received the Melchizedek Priesthood from Peter, James, and John near the Susquehanna River between Harmony, Pennsylvania, and Colesville, New York. (*D&C* 128:20).

[468] Whitmer, *An Address to All Believers,* 64 & 35, in Buerger, *Mysteries of Godliness*, 2.

[469] See generally, Wood, compiler, *Joseph Begins His Work,* II.

[470] *HC* 1:40 fn.

[471] Lane Thuet, "Priesthood Restored or Retrofit?" http://mrm.org/priesthood-restoration (Accessed October 13, 2010).

[472] Cannon, *Under the Prophet,* 175.

[473] "Fourteen Fundamentals in Following the Prophet," originally preached by Ezra Taft Benson, 13th President of the LDS Church, most recently preached by Claudio R. M. Costa, Presidency of the Seventy, in his sermon: "Obedience to the Prophets," October 2010, LDS General Conference.

[474] *D&C* § 89.

[475] Brigham Young, *Journal of Discourses*, 12:158.

[476] Faulring, *An American Prophet's Record,* 105.

[477] Ann Eliza Young, *Wife No. 19,* 173.

[478] Ibid. 174-175.

[479] Stenhouse, *Tell it All.*

[480] Ibid. 170-190.

[481] Ibid. 174.

[482] Ibid. 138-139.

[483] See D. Michael Quinn, "I-Thou vs. I-It Conversions: The Mormon "Baseball Baptism" Era," *Sunstone Magazine* 16 (7) Dec. 1993:30-44. http://mormonstories.org/baseballbaptisms.html.

[484] Ibid.

[485] *"Mormons meet with Jews over baptizing Holocaust Victim,"* AP, 2002. http://archives.cnn.com/2002/US/West/12/10/baptizing.the.dead.ap.

[486] Russell M. Nelson, "Prepare for Blessings of the Temple," *Ensign,* March 2002, 17.

[487] Ed Decker and Dave Hunt, *The God Makers: a Shocking Exposé of what the Mormon Church Really Believes* Rev. Upd. Su. ed. (Eugene: Harvest House Publishers: 1997) 207.

[488] William Morgan, *The Mysteries of Freemasonry...* (originally pub. 1889) Kindle Ed; See also Noah Nicholas and Molly Bedell, The History Channel, *Mysteries of the Freemasons: America*, video documentary, August 1, 2006.

[489] Jerald Tanner and Sandra Tanner, "The Temple," *The Changing World of Mormonism* (SLC: Utah Lighthouse Ministry, n.d.) Chap. 22, 539.

[490] Ed Decker, "The Sure sign of the Nail, Lucifer and the LDS Temple," posted Friday, August 28, 2009. [Emphasis original] http://www.saintsalive.com/resourcelibrary/mormonism/the-sure-sign-of-

the-nail-and-the-God-of-the-lds-temple (Accessed July 3, 2010).

491 Heber C. Kimball, *Journal of Discourses,* 5:133, quoted in Buerger, *Mysteries of Godliness*, 49, n. 32.

492 Scott G. Kenney, ed., *Wilford Woodruff's Journal* 9 vols. (SLC: Signature Books, 1983) 5:418 quoted in Buerger, *Mysteries of Godliness* 49, n. 32.

493 Emeline (no last name) letter to the editor, *Warsaw Signal*, 15 April 1846, quoted in Buerger, *Mysteries of Godliness*, 92.

494 -------------------, "The Sale and Burning of the Nauvoo Temple," A paper presented at the 25th annual meeting of the John Whitmer Historical Assoc., Kirtland, OH, circa. 1997: http://www.strangite.org/Temple.htm.

495 Former LDS Church employee in discussion with the Author, May, 2009.

496 Ibid. Transcription, 2.

497 Ibid.

498 Ibid. 10.

499 Ibid. 14.

500 Ibid. 17.

501 Ibid.

502 Ibid. 19-20.

503 Ibid. 20-21

504 Daymon M. Smith, *The Book of Mammon: a Book about a Book about the Corporation that Owns the Mormons* (Seattle: Createspace, 2010) 199.

505 The North American Industry Classification System (NAICS) is the standard used by federal statistical agencies to classify business establishments for the purpose of collecting, analyzing, and publishing statistical data related to the U.S. business economy. See http://www.census.gov/eos/www/naics/

506 See Russell M. Nelson, LDS Apostle, *Ensign*, May, 1993, 38.

507 Leonard J. Arrington, "The Settlement of the Brigham Young Estate," *Pacific Historical Review,* vol. 21, no. 1 (Feb., 1952):7-8. See also Quinn, *Extensions of Power,* 211-214 and Heinerman and Shupe, *Mormon Corporate Empire,* 81.

508 Salt Lake County Recorder's Office, Book 172, p. 281 (Feb. 27, 1936). Note: As of 1921, the LDS Church-owned U-I Sugar (created in 1907) and was in debt for $23 million dollars. LDS President Heber J. Grant sought financial help from New York and Chicago bankers. Bankers Trust sent a financial controller to Utah to oversee the problem. In order to avoid bankruptcy, U-I was required, among other things, to raise $3 million in venture capital. See Leonard J. Arrington, (1966) *Beet Sugar in the West; a history of the Utah-Idaho Sugar Company, 1891–1966.* (Seattle: Univ. of

Washington Press).

[509] *Deseret News,* April 4, 1936.

[510] http://www.exmormon.org/mormon/mormon565.htm

[511] Email communication with former LDS Church employee, (interviewed May, 2009) received by the Author, October 27-28, 2010.

[512] Lawrence Wright, "Lives of the Saints," *The New Yorker,* 48.

[513] http://latterdaymainstreet.com/?p=694. The author's elderly aunt and uncle served an LDS mission on the ranch at their expense working at a for-profit part of the Church. He worked twelve hour days; she was involved in tours.

[514] Paul Beebe, "Beneficial Financial Bowing out of Insurance Business," *Salt Lake Tribune,* June 16, 2009.

[515] Carrie A. Moore, "Tending the Flock," (Salt Lake City: *Deseret News,* Monday, July 10, 2000 9:42 a.m. MDT). http://www.deseretnews.com/article/770568/Tending-the-flock.html.

[516] David Van Bierna, et. al., "Kingdom Come," *Time,* vol. 150 no. 5 (Aug. 1997).

[517] Ibid. 52.

[518] Interview with former LDS Church employee & Author, May 2009, 9.

[519] http://www.mormonthink.com/tithing.htm; http://www.deseretnews.com/article/705341784/Salt-Lake-City-high-rise-is-ready-for-occupancy-on-Main.html.

[520] http://www.charity-commission.gov.uk/registeredcharities/factfigures.aspx, as cited, at http://www.mormonthink.com/tithing.htm#stories (viewed June 12, 2010).

[521] Emily Troutman, contributing ed., "No Sanctuary at This Church in Haitian Storm," ABC News. (Viewed Nov. 8, 2010); http://www.aolnews.com/world/article/no-sanctuary-at-leogane-haiti-mormon-church-during-hurricane-tomas/19706704

[522] Joseph Fielding Smith, *Man: His Origin and Destiny* (Salt Lake City: Deseret Book, 1962) 354-355.

[523] Gary James Bergera and Ronald Priddis, *Brigham Young University: A House of Faith* (Salt Lake City: Signature Books, 1985) 140-144.

[524] Ephraim Edward Ericksen. *The Psychological and Ethical Aspects of Mormon Group Life,* (Chicago: University of Chicago Press, 1922).

[525] Arrington and Bitton, *Saints without Halos,* 130.

[526] Ibid. 128.

[527] Ibid. 132-133.

[528] Ibid. 134.

[529] Bernard A. De Voto, "Utah," *American Mercury* 7 (March, 1926): 317-

323; 319.

530 Ibid. 322.

531 Ibid. 323.

532 Bernard De Voto, "A Revaluation," *Rocky Mountain Review* 10, No. 1 (Autumn, 1945)7-11.

533 Quinn, *Extensions of Power*, 852, n. February 29, 1964.

534 Ibid. n., April 15, 1964.

535 Leonard J. Arrington, "Scholarly Studies of Mormonism in the Twentieth Century," *Dialogue* 1, no. 1 (Spring 1966):26.

536 "History Is Then—and Now: A Conversation with Leonard J. Arrington, Church Historian," (Salt Lake City: LDS Church, *Ensign*, Jul 1975) 8. See also *Salt Lake Tribune*, April 26, 1975.

537 See Daniel H. Ludlow, ed., *Encyclopedia of Mormonism*.

538 Sterling M. McMurrin, "Toward Intellectual Anarchy, Review of Encyclopedia of Mormonism," *Dialogue* 26, no. 2 (Summer 1993): 223.

539 Martha Beck, *Leaving the Saints: How I lost the Mormons and Found my Faith* (New York: Three Rivers Press, 2006).

540 Paul Toscano, *The Sanctity of Dissent*; Paul Toscano, *The Sacrament of Doubt* (SLC: Signature Books, 2007); Margaret M. and Paul Toscano, *Strangers in Paradox*.

541 Dallin H. Oaks, "The Historicity of the Book of Mormon," Speech, FARMS Annual Dinner, Provo, Utah (October 29, 1993).

542 Bergera and Priddis, *Brigham Young University: a House of Faith*, 343; http://www.signaturebookslibrary.org/byu/introduction.htm .

543"Just How Far Is It From Provo to Oxford?" *BYU Today*, June 1979, 20; "Discussion Rooms Needed," (BYU/Provo, UT: *Daily Universe* 2 Nov. 1979); "Y Graduate Goes to Europe," (BYU/Provo, Utah: *Daily Universe*, 8 Dec. 1983). See also, Bergera and Priddis, *BYU: a House of Faith*, 344.

544 Truman Madsen, "The Joy of Learning," *Outstanding Lectures* (Provo, Utah: ASBYU Academics Office, 1979) 89, quoted in Bergera and Priddis, *BYU: a House of Faith*, 342; http://www.signaturebookslibrary.org/byu/introduction.htm.

545 *BYU: a House of Faith*, Ibid.

546 http://online.wsj.com/public/resources/documents/MB07Scoreboard.pdf.

547 "NEWS: "BYU Tightens Faculty Hiring Process," *Sunstone*, 16:8, no. 94 (February 1994) 79.

548 Smith, *Book of Mormon*, 2 Nephi 30:6. Peggy Fletcher Stack, "Church removes racial (one on-line commentator notes that the title of the piece should be 'racist') references in Book of Mormon Headings," *Salt Lake*

Tribune, December 17, 2010. Stack summarizes the changes. She points out that the LDS Church made significant changes to chapter headings in its online version of *the Book of Mormon*. The phrase "skin of blackness" was removed from the introductory italicized summary in 2 Nephi, Chap. 5, describing the "curse" God put on disbelieving Lamanites. Later in the Book, in Mormon, Chap. 5, the heading changed from referencing Lamanites as "a dark, filthy, and loathsome people," to "because of their unbelief, the Lamanites will be scattered, and the Spirit will cease to strive with them." She also notes that the body of the text remains unchanged.

549 Heinerman and Shupe, *Mormon Corporate Empire*, 71.

550 Rich Deem, *DNA Evidence and Molecular Genetics Disprove the Book of Mormon;* http://www.godandscience.org/cults/dna.html. (Viewed July 27, 2010).

551 Boyd K. Packer, President of the LDS Quorum of the Twelve Apostles, *The Mantle is Far, Far Greater Than the Intellect,* Address to the Fifth Annual CES Religious Educators' Symposium, 1981. "There is a temptation for the writer or the teacher of Church history to want to tell everything, whether it is worthy or faith promoting or not. *Some things that are true are not very useful…"* [Emphasis added].

552 Paul Richards, former BYU spokesman quoted in Jerald and Sandra Tanner's "Mormon Inquisition? LDS Leaders move to Suppress Rebellion," *Messenger*, pub. #85 (Salt Lake City: Utah Lighthouse Ministry, Nov., 1993) 6; http://www.utlm.org/newsletters/no85.htm.

553 Ken Clark, "Lying for the Lord," presentation at the 2008 ExMormon Foundation Conference in SLC: http://www.mormonthink.com/lying.htm

554 Brigham Young, *Journal of Discourses,* 4: 77 [Emphasis added].

555 Bruce Kinney, *Mormonism, the Islam of America* (New York: Revell, 1912).

556 "'the Alcoran [the Koran] or the Sword.' So should it be eventually with us, 'Joseph Smith or the Sword.'" *HC* 3:167.

557David Haldane, "U.S. Muslims Share Friendship, Similar Values with Mormons. The Link is based not on Theology but on Shared Ideals and a Sense of Isolation," *Los Angeles Times*, April 02, 2008.

558 *San Francisco Chronicle,* 13 March 1997.

559 Gordon B. Hinckley, *Time* Magazine Aug 4, 1997.

560 Joseph Smith, LDS General Conference, April, 1844; "King Follett Discourse," *Journal of Discourses* 6:3-4; also in *Teachings of the Prophet Joseph Smith*, Joseph Fielding Smith, compiler (Salt Lake City: Shadow Mountain, 1977) 345-346; and *HC,* 6:305-307.

561 "Search these Commandments," *Melchizedek Priesthood Personal*

Study Guide (Salt Lake City: Church of Jesus Christ of Latter-day Saints, 1984) 151-152; *Teachings of Presidents of the Church: BRIGHAM YOUNG* (SLC: Church of Jesus Christ of Latter-day Saints, 1997) 34.

[562] Spencer W. Kimball, 12th Pres., LDS Church, *Ensign,* Nov. 1975, 80.

[563] Dallin H. Oaks, PBS Documentary, *The Mormons, 4/* 30 & 05/01/ 07.

[564] Ure, *Leaving the Fold,* 223.

[565] http://www.lds-mormon.com/lkl_00.shtml (viewed June 18, 2010). [Emphasis added].

[566] Robert Millet, BYU prof., speech to BYU Missionary Prep. Club, 2004; http://www.youtube.com/watch?v=9zA-rZQB-xQ (viewed 07/01/ 10).

[567] Dallin H. Oaks, *Gospel Teachings about Lying,* speech given to BYU faculty, students & alumni (Sept. 12, 1993). http://lds-mormon.com/oakslying.shtml (Accessed Feb., 24, 2010).

[568] See Anderson, *Inside the Mind of Joseph Smith,* xlii, n. 28, for Dallin Oaks' comments on censorship. [Emphasis added].

[569] Oaks, "Gospel Teachings about Lying," BYU Speech, 1993 [Emphasis Added].

[570] Shea v. Esensten 107 F.3d 625, 628 (8th Cir. 1997) quoting *Eddy v. Colonial Life Insurance Co.,* 919 F.2d 747, 750 (D.C. Cir. 1990); cert. denied, 118 S. Ct. 297 (1997).

[571] Ann Eliza Young, *Wife No. 19,* 60.

[572] *Franco v. Church of LDS,* 2001 UT 25, ¶14-15.

[573] *Mitchell v. Christensen,* 2001 UT 80, 31 P.3d 572 (UT 2001). http://www.utcourts.gov/opinions/supopin/mitchell.htm

[574] *Id.* at ¶9.

[575] *Yazd v. Woodside Homes Corp.,* 2006 UT 47, 143 P.3d 283. http://www.utcourts.gov/opinions/supopin/Yazd090106.pdf

[576] *Id.* at ¶17.

[577] *Id.* at ¶16.

[578] ----------------------, "Use Proper Sources," *Deseret News,* Church News Section, Saturday January 9, 2010, [no author credited]. (Salt Lake City: Deseret News Publishing, 2010) n. 168. http://www.ldschurchnews.com/articles/58411/Use-proper-sources.html.

[579] Peggy Fletcher Stack, "Keeping Members a Challenge for LDS Church," *Salt Lake Tribune*, June 22, 2006.

[580] Interview with former LDS Church employee & the Author, May, 2009.

[581] http://www.ldschurchnews.com/missions/

[582] From Richard Packham's web page, viewed September 25, 2010, *http://packham.n4m.org/growth.htm*; under the section "updated

November, 2003." [Italic Emphasis added; capital emphasis original].
[583] Former link at http://ceo.byu.edu/create-a-business-... According to a post on the following website in December, 2006, http://www.mormoncurtain.com/topic_apologists_section1.html, after the ex-Mormon community found and exposed this website link, it was immediately replaced with 'Repentance,' talks given by (deceased) Mormon Apostle Neal A. Maxwell.
[584] Moroni burying the gold plates, $5.95, sku #4592081. http://deseretbook.com/item/4592081/Moroni_Burying_the_Gold_Plates, viewed June 4, 2010. As of this date, no photos of the golden plates are offered for sale. There is also a "Gold plates 500 piece puzzle," by Greg Olsen, sku #4927133, on sale for $11.50 as of June 4, 2010. http://deseretbook.com/item/4927122/Gold_Plates_500_Piece_Puzzle.
[585] See Quinn's *The Mormon Hierarchy: Extensions of Power*, Chapter Five, 163-197, detailing the familial & dynastical relationships between Church leaders and their appointed successors and subordinates over the decades. His data support a high degree of kinship. See also http://mormonmatters.org/2008/04/14/nepotism-in-the-church/, an excellent table of inter-familial Church appointments complied by Jeff Spector, posted on April 14, 2008 (viewed June 22, 2010). E.g., the 2nd Counselor of the LDS Young Women's General Presidency is Church President Thomas Monson's daughter, Ann Dibbs. See also Cannon, *Under the Prophet*, 138.
[586] Elder Jeffrey Holland, *Safety for the Soul,* LDS General Conference, Sunday afternoon, October 4, 2009. http://lds.org/conference/talk/display/0,5232,23-1-1117-28,00.html; [speech text footnotes omitted].
[587] "Even infants can and do respond to the distinctive spirit of *The Book of Mormon,*" David A. Bednar, Apostle, 180th LDS General Conference, 2nd session, April 3, 2010.
[588] Claudio R. M. Costa, Presidency of the Seventy, "Obedience to the Prophets," October 2010, LDS General Conference.
[589] Heinerman and Shupe, *Mormon Corporate Empire*, 70.
[590] Edward L. Bernays, *Propaganda* (New York: Horace Liveright Pub. House, 1928) 71. Frank H. Knight, "Professor Heimann on Religion and Economics," *Journal of Political Economy* 56 (December 1948): 485.
[591] "Adam," at Recovery from Mormonism, 12/02/2009 (No longer found on this site). Note: this is only a partial quote. To read the entire quotation as of March 5, 2011, see: http://www.salamandersociety.com/foyer/prophets/josephsmith/.

502

[592] Quinn, *Extensions of Power*, 806.

[593] A 2002 study by Express Scripts Inc., showed antidepressants prescribed in Utah at almost twice the national average, the highest in the Nation. Utah was first for use of narcotic pain-killers, such as codeine and morphine-based drugs.

[594] Russell Goldman, "Two Studies Find Depression Widespread in Utah," ABC News Internet Ventures, March 7, © 2008. http://abcnews.go.com/Health/MindMoodNews/story?id=4403731&page=1

[595] "High Religious Commitment Linked to Less Suicide," *American Journal of Epidemiology* 2002; 155:413-419. Write-up: Charnicia E. Huggins (Reuters Health) *Daily News* (6 March 2002).

[596] Lyndon Lamborn, *Standing for Something More: the Excommunication of Lyndon Lamborn* (Bloomington, IN: Author House, 2009) 186-87.

[597] Arrin Newton Brunson, "Utah Ranked 10th Nationally for Child Abuse Cases," *Salt Lake Tribune*, April 1, 2010.

[598] "United Way of Salt Lake Community Assessment Update March 14, 2007," report p. 44. www.utahfoundation.org. (Viewed June 30, 2010).

[599] Utah Foundation Executive Summary, Report #670, Dec., 2004, p.1.

[600] #670, Ibid. p 3-4. http://www.adherents.com/misc/UtahBankruptcy.pdf; (viewed June 30, 2010).

[601] United Way Assessment 2007, report p. 46.

[602] Ibid. 98-99.

[603] Bergera and Priddis, *BYU: a House of Faith*, 80. [Emphasis added].

[604] Ibid. 68.

[605] Will Jarret, Executive Editor, Introduction, "Utah: inside the Church State," *Denver Post,* Sunday Supp. Nov. 21-28, 1982.

[606] United Way Assessment, 2007, report p. 93.

[607] Cannon, *Under the Prophet in Utah*, 175.

[608] Ibid. 216.

[609] Bruce R. McConkie (Church News Section of *Deseret News,* March 20, 1982) 5.

[610] http://ldsamcap.org/what-is-amcap.html. (Viewed June 10, 2010).

[611] Marlene Payne, "The Obsessive-Compulsive Mormon," *Dialogue* 13, no. 2 (Summer 1980):116-22.

[612] As I write this section a friend of Danny's father reported that his son, who had been serving an LDS mission for several months, "went crazy," came home and they [his parents] had to put him in a mental institution.

[613] Toscano, *The Sanctity of Dissent*, 170-171. [Emphasis Added].

[614] Connell O'Donovan, *The Abominable and Detestable Crime against*

Nature: A Revised History of Homosexuality & Mormonism, 1840-1980 (Salt Lake City: Signature Books 1994). See the following link for a 2004 ed. by the author: http://connellodonovan.com/abom.html#BM122.

[615] Reed Cowen, director, *8: The Mormon Proposition* (Wolf Video, 2010).

[616] Michael Parrish, "The Saints among Us," *Rocky Mountain Magazine* 2 (Jan.-Feb. 1980):27.

[617] Bogaert, A. F. (2006). Biological versus nonbiological older brothers and men's sexual orientation. *Proceedings of the National Academy of Sciences,* 103: 10777-10774.

[618] www.evergreeninternational.org website dedicated to helping Mormons overcome same-sex attraction (Accessed Nov., 2009).

[619] Carrie A. Moore, "Gay LDS Men Detail Challenge," *Deseret Morning News*, March 30, 2007.

[620] Peggy Fletcher Stack, "Gay, Mormon, Married Mixed-orientation LDS Couples Count on Commitment, Work and Love to Beat the Odds," *Salt Lake Tribune,* Oct, 4, 2006.

[621] *SL Tribune*, 15 Feb. 1885; Van Wagoner, *Mormon Polygamy*, 133.

[622] Boyd K. Packer, "Cleansing the Inner Vessel," Sermon delivered (edited as noted in main text) at October 3rd 2010, LDS General Conference, Sunday Morning Session, published on LDS Church website as of October 7, 2010, http://new.lds.org/general-conference/print/2010/10/cleansing-the-inner-vessel?lang=eng&clang=eng.

[623] "SLOC & the LDS Church Downplay Church's Involvement in the Olympics," *Salt Lake Tribune,* Mar. 18, 2001.

[624] Lex Hemphill, "Olympics; Acquittals End Bid Scandal that Dogged Winter Games," *New York Times*, December 6, 2003.

[625] John Powers, "It Was a Case of Not Having One," *Boston Globe*, December 21, 2003, C-18.

[626] Rebecca Walsh, "This is the Place to Ponzi," *Salt Lake Tribune,* January 11, 2009.

[627] Steve Raabe and Miles Moffeit, "Accused Swindler Shawn Merriman may have Used his Status in the Mormon Church to Draw in Victims," *The Denver Post* 04/10/2009.

[628] Craig Harris, "Financial Con Artist gets 7 Years in Prison," *The Arizona Republic*, Apr. 20, 2009.

[629] "Scammer gets 1-15 years," *Ogden Standard Examiner,* August 11, 2010; http://www.standard.net/topics/courts/2010/08/11/scammer-gets-1-15-years.

[630] Quinn, *Extensions of Power*, 214-216.

[631] John B. Wright, *Rocky Mountain Divide Selling & Saving the West* (Austin: University of Texas Press, 1993) 167-168.

[632] Ibid. 199.

[633], Ibid.

[634] Winchester, "Primitive Mormonism," *Salt Lake Tribune*, 1889.

[635] LDS Apostle Boyd K. Packer in an address to an All-Church Coordinating Council Meeting, held May 18, 1993, identified "three areas where members of the Church, influenced by social and political unrest, are being caught up and led away." Those areas, [are] "the gay-lesbian movement, the feminist movement, and . . . the so-called scholars or intellectuals."

[636] Decades after the fact, I learned that two brilliant friends of mine, male and female, were accepted to MIT and Harvard Law School, respectively. Yet they each turned down these institutions in favor of attending Brigham Young University during the seventies.

[637] Richard N. Ostling and Joan K. Ostling, *Mormon America: The Power and the Promise* (San Francisco: Harper Collins, 1999) 145-146. The Ostlings said it best: "In Mormon Culture art is inspiration or entertainment, not exploration. As a result, Mormons—like those in some other American sectarian groups—are largely absent from the highest levels of achievement in the fine arts, literature, and the humanities in general. History is something of a special case...,"

[638] Ibid. 15.

[639] Ibid.

[640] The LDS Church has long been proud of its lay clergy and seems to count this fact as a positive attribute of Mormonism. Based upon the lack of formal education of its first two prophets, it is expected that the role of education as a qualification for Church leadership positions would be de-emphasized.

[641] Jack B. Worthy, *The Mormon Cult* (N.p. Sharp Press, 2008) 187.

[642] Gates and Pritchard, "...Religious Angst, and Disordered Eating," Eating & Weight Disorders, 2009 Mar; 14(1):e11-5.

[643] Elizabeth T. Tice, PhD., *Inside the Mormon Mind, the Social Psychology of Mormonism* (Boston: Pearson Custom Pub., 2001) 51.

[644] http://www.lds-mormon.com/ruin.shtml viewed on 08/26/01.

[645] *Journal of Discourses*, 6:163.

[646] Ibid. 6:176.

[647] Ibid. 4:269.

[648] "Use Proper Sources," *Deseret News,* January 9, 2010. http://www.ldschurchnews.com/articles/58411/Use-proper-sources.html;

[649] Ibid.

[650] Lisa Schencker, "Lawmakers' Silence Kills Sex Ed Bill," *Salt Lake Tribune*, February 22, 2010.

[651] In 2002 Garn paid the woman $150,000.00 to keep the matter quiet. The transaction took place in her bishop's office. http://www.youtube.com/watch?v=wS16XkswsOI.

[652] *The New Yorker*, January 21, 2002.

[653] Mircea Eliade, *The Sacred and the Profane: the Nature of Religion*, French 1957, translated in to English by Willard Trask, 1959 (Harcourt Inc., 1987). As Mark Crispin Miller writes in the Introduction to Bernays' *Propaganda*, it is the elite who are the organizers of chaos. It is they who "pull the wires which control the public mind"; the archetype of this group being the "unmoved mover." Bernays, *Propaganda*, 17-21.

[654] Fritjof Capra, *The Tao of Physics: an exploration of the Parallels between Modern Physics and Eastern Mysticism*, 4th updated ed. (Boston: Shambala, 2000) 95. Originally published 1975.

[655] John Caird (Principal, Univ. of Scotland, Glasgow) "Introduction to the Philosophy of Religion," as quoted in William James, *Varieties of Religious Experience, a Study in Human Nature*, § 39 (Lecture XVIII Philosophy, 1907) 290. Kindle Ed. [Emphasis original].

[656] Thomas Paine, *The Age of Reason; Being an Investigation of True and Fabulous Theology* (London: D.I. Eaton, 1794).

[657] Gustav Fechner, *The Little Book of Life after Death* (New York: Little, Brown & Company, 1904)16-18, quoted in Ken Wilber, *Integral Psychology* (Boston: Shambala Pub. 2000) viii-ix.

[658] Eric Hoffer, *The True Believer: Thoughts on the Nature of Mass Movements*, 1951 orig. ed. (Harper Collins, First Perennial Classic ed., 2002) 54-75. Citations are to 2002 Ed.

[659] Harold Bloom, *The American Religion*, 2nd ed. (NY: Chu Hartley Publishers, 2006) 82.

[660] Hardy, *Solemn Covenant*, 368. [Emphasis added].

[661] Pat Reavy, "Mitchell played role of Satan, former co-worker testifies," November 16th, 2010 @ 11:47am. http://www.freerepublic.com/focus/f-religion/2628122/posts.

[662] _____, "The *Life, Times, Wit & Wisdom* of Brian David Mitchell," http://www.utahgothic.com/features/liz/mitchell.html.

[663] Jennifer Dobner, "Elizabeth Smart Finishes Utah Trial Testimony," *AP*, Nov. 10, 2010.

[664] Peggy Fletcher Stack, "The Line between Inspiration and Insanity," *Salt Lake Tribune* December 10, 2010, republished Dec. 13, 2010 and Peggy F.

Stack, "Joseph Smith, Ellen White and Others?" *SL Tribune* Dec 11, 2010.
[665] http://www.mormonthink.com/whoarewe.htm, viewed May 29, 2010.
[666] E-mail dated January 29, 2006, used as an exhibit in cross-examination.
[667]Tom Harvey, "Preying on the faithful: Though Mormons often Victims, LDS Church Skips Fraud-prevention Event," *SL Tribune,* May 5, 2010.
[668] Sam Harris, *The End of Faith: Religion, Terror, and the Future of Reason* (W.W. Norton & Co., 2004) 149.
[669] "§3.3.4-Issuing recommends in Special Circumstances—Members whose Close Relatives Belong to Apostate Groups," *LDS Church General Handbook of Instructions, 1 Stake Presidents and Bishops* (Salt Lake City: Church of Jesus Christ of Latter-day Saints, 2010) 13.
[670] *D&C* §130:21.
[671] *D&C* §82:10.
[672] R. Scott Lloyd, "Joseph Smith's Legal Involvement," *Deseret News,* Jan. 24, 2009; http://www.ldschurchnews.com/articles/56488/Joseph-Smiths-legal-involvement.html.
[673] *United States Constitution, First Amendment.*
[674] http://supreme.justia.com/us/98/145/case.html.
[675] Thomas Jefferson, Virginia Statute for Religious Freedom, adopted January 16, 1786 (Original preamble in draft version) 1 *Jeff. Works,* 45.
[676] *Doe v. Corp. of President of Church of Jesus Christ of Latter-day Saints,* 2004 UT App 274, 98 P.3d 429 (Utah Ct. App. 2004).
[677] *Id.* ¶ 14.
[678] *Id.* n. 7.
[679] *Gulbraa v. COP,* 2007 UT App 126, 159 P.3d 392 (Utah Ct. App. 2007).
[680] Paul McKay, "Mormon Psychologist's Recanting about Church Flaw Puzzles Some," *Houston Chronicle*, May 10, 1999.
[681] *National Ass'n for Better Broadcasting v. F.C.C., 591* F.2d 812, 817, 192 U.S. App. D.C. 203, 208 (C.A.D.C., 1978). [Emphasis added]. See also *Tilton v. Marshall*, 925 S.W.2d 672, 678-679 (Tex. 1996).
[682] *Hawthorne v. Couch,* 40162 (La. App. 2 Cir. 2005) 911 So.2d 907, rehearing denied.
[683] Reed Cowen, *"8," the Mormon Proposition.*
[684] Jesse McKinley and Kirk Johnson, "Mormons Tipped Scale in Ban on Gay Marriage," *New York Times,* Nov. 14, 2008.
[685] Ibid.
[686] Dan Aiello, "Mormons Found Guilty on 13 Counts of Prop 8 Malfeasance, Fined by FPPC," *California Progress Report*, 06/11/2010; http://www.californiaprogressreport.com/site.
[687] Fred Karger, "Mormon Church tries to Resurrect its Image, Spends

Millions to Repair Prop 8 Damage," Posted: September 27, 2010 10:30 AM, *The Huffington Post:* http://www.huffingtonpost.com/fred-karger/mormon-church-tries-to-re_b_739652.html?ir=Media?show_comment_id=61863908.

[688] Karl Vick, "'The Mormons Are Coming!' Supporters of Same-Sex Marriage Trumpet the Church's Work Against It," *Washington Post,* Friday, May 29, 2009. [The *Post* article also notes that the LDS Church was involved in a similar campaign in Hawaii in the late nineties]. See Lee Benson, "LDS have Big Image Problem," *Deseret News*, published Sunday, Nov. 23, 2008 12:08 a.m. MST.

[689] Bernard A. De Voto, "The Centennial of Mormonism: a Study in Utopia and Dictatorship," *Forays and Rebuttals* (Boston: Little, Brown & Co., 1936) 86.

[690] Ibid. 95.

[691] Ibid 93

SELECTED BIBLIOGRAPHY

Anderson, Robert D. 1999. *Inside the Mind of Joseph Smith*. Salt Lake City: Signature Books.

Arrington, Leonard J. 1958. *Great Basin Kingdom: An Economic History of the Latter-day Saints, 1830-1900*. Harvard Univ. Press.

Arrington, Leonard J. 2006. *Reflections of a Mormon Historian: Leonard J. Arrington on the New Mormon History*. Norman, Oklahoma:The Arthur H. Clark Company.

Arrington, Leonard J., and Bitton, Davis. 1981. *Saints without Halos: The Human Side of Mormon History*. Salt Lake City: Signature Books.

Bagley, Will. 2004. *Blood of the Prophets: Brigham Young and the Massacre at Mountain Meadows*. Norman: U. of Oklahoma Press.

Baker, Elna. 2009. *The New York Regional Mormon Singles Halloween Dance: a Memoir.* New York: Dutton.

Beck, Martha. 2006. *Leaving the Saints: How I Lost the Mormons and Found My Faith*. New York: Three Rivers Press.

Bennett, John C. (1842). *History of the Saints; or, an Exposé of Joe Smith and Mormonism*. Photo-reproduction of Boston: Leland & Whiting, 1842 Ed., by Utah Lighthouse Ministry, n.d. Citations are to UTLM Edition

Bergera, Gary James and Priddis, Ronald. 1985. *Brigham Young University: A House of Faith*. Salt Lake City: Signature Books.

Bernays, Edward L. 1928. *Propaganda.* New York: Horace Liveright Publishing House.

Bloom, Harold. 2006. *The American Religion*, 2nd Ed. NY: Chu Hartley Publishers.

Brodie, Fawn McKay. (1945) 1995. *No Man Knows My History: the Life of Joseph Smith the Mormon Prophet* Rev. /2nd Ed. New York: Alfred A. Knopf/Vintage Books. Citations refer to the 1995 Ed.

Brooks, Juanita. (1950) 1991. *Mountain Meadows Massacre.* Norman: Univ. of Oklahoma Press. Citations refer to the 3rd Ed., 1991

Brooks, Juanita. 2009. *On the Mormon Frontier: the Diary of Hosea Stout 1844-1889.* Salt Lake City: University of Utah Press.

Buel, J.W. 1890. *Heroes of the Dark Continent.* Kansas City: Kansas City Pub. Co.

Buerger, David John. 2002. *The Mysteries of Godliness: a History of Mormon Temple Worship*, 2nd Ed. San Francisco: Smith Research Assoc.

Burton, Richard Francis. 1862. *The City of the Saints: and Across the Rocky Mountains to California.* New York: Harper & Brothers.

Bushman, Richard L. 2007. *Joseph Smith: Rough Stone Rolling, a Cultural Biography of Mormonism's Founder.* New York: Vintage.

Campbell, Alexander. 1832. *An Analysis of the Book of Mormon with an Examination of its Internal and External Evidences and a Refutation of its Pretences to Divine Authority.* Boston: Benjamin H. Greene.

Cannon, Frank Jenne & O'Higgins, Harvey J. (1911) *Under the Prophet in Utah, the National Menace of a Political Priestcraft.* Reprint, Lexington: Forgotten Books, 2008. Citations refer to 2008 reprint Ed.

Capra, Fritjof. (1975) *The Tao of Physics: an Exploration of the Parallels between Modern Physics and Eastern Mysticism* 4th Ed. Boston: Shambala, 2000. Citations are to 4th Ed., 2000.

Church of Jesus Christ of Latter-day Saints. 1996. *Our Heritage: A Brief History of the Church of Jesus Christ of Latter-day Saints.* Salt Lake City: Intellectual Reserve, Inc.

510

Compton, Todd. 1997. *In Sacred Loneliness: the Plural Wives of Joseph Smith*. Salt Lake City: Signature Books.

Cowdery, Wayne L., Davis, Howard A. and Vanick, Arthur. 2005. *Who Really Wrote the Book of Mormon? The Spalding Enigma* St. Louis: Concordia Publishing House.

Dawkins, Richard. (2006). 2008. *The God Delusion*. Boston: Mariner Books. Citations are to 2008 Ed.

Decker, Ed and Hunt, Dave. (1984) 1997. *The God Makers: a Shocking Exposé of What the Mormon Church Really Believes,* Rev Upd. Su. Ed. Eugene: Harvest House Publishers.

De Voto, Bernard Augustine. 1936. "The Centennial of Mormonism: a Study in Utopia and Dictatorship." *Forays and Rebuttals*. Boston: Little, Brown & Co.

Eliade, Mircea. (1959) 1987. *The Sacred and the Profane: the Nature of Religion*. French translation by Willard Trask, 1959. Orlando: Harcourt.

Emerson, Ralph Waldo. 1983. *Emerson: Essays and Lectures*. Joel Porte, editor. Viking Press.

Ericksen, Ephraim Edward. 1922. *The Psychological and Ethical Aspects of Mormon Group Life*. Chicago: University of Chicago Press.

Evans, Azra. 2004. *The Keystone of Mormonism*. St. George, Utah: Keystone Books Inc.

Faulring, Scott H., editor. 1989. *An American Prophet's Record: the Diaries and Journals of Joseph Smith*. Salt Lake City: Signature Books/Smith Research Associates.

Firmage, Edwin Brown and Mangrum, Richard Collin. 2001. *Zion in the Courts: a Legal History of the Church of Jesus Christ of Latter-day Saints, 1830-1900*. Urbana: University of Illinois Press.

Gaylor, Annie Laurie, ed. 1997. *Women without Superstition: No Gods— No Masters, the Collected Writings of Women Freethinkers of the Nineteenth and Twentieth Centuries*. Madison, Wisconsin: Freedom from Religion Foundation.

Hanks, Maxine. 1992. *Women and Authority (Re-emerging Mormon Feminism)*. Salt Lake City: Signature Books.

Hardy, B. Carmon. 1992. *Solemn Covenant*. University of Ill. Press.

Harris, Sam. 2004. *The End of Faith: Religion, Terror, and the Future of Reason*. W.W. Norton & Co.

Heinerman, John and Shupe, Anson. 1985. *The Mormon Corporate Empire*. Boston: Beacon Press.

Heyn, Dalma. 1997. *Marriage Shock: The Transformation of Women into Wives*. Dell Publishing (Delta).

Hickman, Bill. (1904) 1964. *Brigham's Destroying Angel Being the Life, Confession and Startling Disclosures of the Notorious Bill Hickman*. Photomechanical reprint with Introduction by Jerald & Sandra Tanner. Salt Lake City: Utah Lighthouse Ministry.

Hoffer, Eric. (1951) 2002. *The True Believer (Thoughts on the Nature of Mass Movements)*. Harper Collins, 1st Perennial Classic Ed.

Howe, Eber D. 1834. *Mormonism Unvailed: a Faithful Account of that Singular Imposition and Delusion from Its Rise to the Present Time*. Painesville, Ohio: Telegraph Press.

James, William. (1907) 2006. *Varieties of Religious Experience, a Study in Human Nature* §39 (Lecture XVIII Philosophy) 290. Amazon Books: Kindle Ed.

Johnson, Sonia. 1989. *From Housewife to Heretic*. Albuquerque: Wildfire Books

----------------------. (1859) 1955. *Journal of Discourses* (lithograph reprinting of original ed.) A collection of speeches, etc., by 19th century Mormon leaders, 26 vols. originally published at Liverpool, England: Latter-day Saints' Book Depot. Salt Lake City: Church of LDS.

Kinney, Bruce. 1912. *Mormonism, the Islam of America.* NY: Revell.

Krakauer, John. 2003. *Under the Banner of Heaven: the Story of a Violent Faith.* New York: Doubleday.

Lamborn, Lyndon. 2009. *Standing for Something More: the Excommunication of Lyndon Lamborn.* Bloomington, Indiana: AuthorHouse.

Larson, Charles, M. 1992 *...by His Own Hand upon Papyrus* (A *New Look at the Joseph Smith Papyri*) Rev. Ed. Grand Rapids, Michigan: The Institute for Religious Research.

Larson, Stan. 1996. *Quest for the Gold Plates*: *Thomas Stuart Ferguson's Archeological Search for the Book of Mormon.* Salt Lake City: Freethinker Press/Smith Research Associates.

Larson, Stan and Passey, Samuel J., editors. 2007. *The William E. McLellin Papers, 1854-1880.* Salt Lake City: Signature Books.

Lee, John D. (1877) *Mormonism Unveiled or the Life and Confessions of the Late Mormon Bishop, John D. Lee,* Photo reprint of original ed., entitled *Confessions of John D. Lee.* Salt Lake City: Utah Lighthouse Ministry, n.d. Citations are to UTLM Ed.

Light, Richard J. 2001. *Making The Most of College: Students Speak Their Minds.* Harvard University Press.

Ludlow, Daniel, H., ed., 1992. *Encyclopedia of Mormonism: the History, Scripture, Doctrine, and Procedure of the Church of Jesus Christ of Latter-day Saints*, 5 Vols. New York: Macmillan.

Madsen, Brigham D., ed. 1985. *B. H. Roberts' Studies of the Book of Mormon,* 2nd Ed. Salt Lake City: Signature Books.

McMillan, Henry G. (1903) *The Inside of Mormonism: a Judicial Examination of the Endowment Oaths Administered in all the Mormon Temples by the US District Court.* Reprint of original Ed. SLC: Utah Lighthouse Ministry, n.d. Citations are to UTLM Ed.

Morgan, William. (1889) *The Mysteries of Freemasonry Containing all the Degrees of the Order Conferred in a Master's Lodge.* 2008 Kindle Ed.

Naifeh, Steven and Smith, Gregory White. 1989. *The Mormon Murders.* New American Library (Penguin).

Newell, Linda King & Avery, Valeen Tippets. 1994. *Mormon Enigma: Emma Hale Smith*, 2nd Ed. Urbana: Univ. of Ill. Press/Doubleday.

Ostling, Richard N. and Ostling, Joan K. 1999. *Mormon America: the Power and the Promise.* San Francisco: Harper Collins.\

Paine, Thomas. (London: D.I. Eaton, 1794) *The Age of Reason: Being an Investigation of True and Fabulous Theology.* 2009 Kindle Ed.

Palmer, Grant H. 2002. *An Insider's View of Mormon Origins.* Salt Lake City: Signature Books.

Persuitte, David. 2000. *Joseph Smith and the Origins of The Book of Mormon*, 2nd Ed. Jefferson, North Carolina: McFarland & Company.

Quinn, D. Michael. 1998. *Early Mormonism and the Magic World View*, Rev. Ed., Salt Lake City: Signature Books.

Quinn, D. Michael. 1994. *The Mormon Hierarchy: Origins of Power* and *The Mormon Hierarchy: Extensions of Power* (2 volumes). Salt Lake City, Signature Books/Smith Research Associates.

Roberts, David. *Devil's Gate: Brigham Young and the Great Mormon Handcart Tragedy.* 2008. Simon & Schuster.

Roberts, Brigham H. (1885) 1992. *Studies of the Book of Mormon,* 2nd
    Ed., Brigham D. Madsen, editor. SLC: Signature Books.
    Originally published by the Univ. of Ill. Press, courtesy of the
    Univ, of Utah Research Foundation, owner of the original
    manuscripts. Citations are to the 1992 Ed.

Russell, Bertrand. (1927) 1967. *Why I Am Not a Christian and Other
    Essays on Religion and Related Subjects.* Paul Edwards, editor.
    New York: Touchstone.

Shook, Charles A. 1914. *The Origins of the Book of Mormon.* Cincinnati:
    Standard Publishing Co.

Smith, Daymon M. 2010. *The Book of Mammon: A Book about a Book
    about the Corporation That Owns the Mormons.* Seattle:
    Createspace.

Smith, Ethan. 1825. *View of the Hebrews; or, the Tribes of Israel in
    America.* Poultney, VT.

Smith, Joseph, Jr. (1830) 1974. *The Book of Mormon, An Account Written
    by the Hand of Mormon Upon Plates taken from the Plates of
    Nephi.* Salt Lake City: the Church of Jesus Christ of Latter-day
    Saints.

Smith, Joseph, Jr., et. al., 1835. (1974). *The Doctrine and Covenants.* Salt
    Lake City: the Church of Jesus Christ of Latter-day Saints.

Smith, Joseph, Jr., et. al., 1851. (1974). *The Pearl of Great Price.* Salt Lake
    City: the Church of Jesus Christ of Latter-day Saints.

Smith, Joseph, Jr. (B. H. Roberts). 1902. *History of the Church of Jesus
    Christ of Latter-day Saints,* aka *Documentary History of the
    Church,* 7 Volumes. Salt Lake City: Church of LDS.

Smith, Lucy Mack. (1853) *Biographical Sketches of Joseph Smith the
    Prophet, and His Progenitors for Many Generations.* Photo reprint
    as *Joseph Smith's History by his Mother.* Salt Lake City: Utah
    Lighthouse Ministry, n.d. Citations are to UTLM Ed.

Stenhouse, Mrs. T.B.H., *aka* "Fanny." (1875). *Tell it All: the Story of a Life's Experience in Mormonism*. Hartford: A.D. Worthington & Co. Facsimile reproduction of original SLC: UTLM, n.d.

Stone, Merlin. 1976. *When God was a Woman*. Harvest/Harcourt Brace Jovanovich.

Tanner, Jerald and Tanner, Sandra. (1990) 2005. *Evolution of the Mormon Temple Ceremony: 1842-1990*. Salt Lake City: UTLM

Tanner, Jerald & Tanner, Sandra. (1987) 2008 Ed. *Mormonism—Shadow or Reality?* 5th Ed. reformatted. SLC: UTLM. Citations are to 2008 Ed.

Tanner, Jerald. 1987. *Tracking the White Salamander: the Story of Mark Hoffman, Murder and Forged Mormon Documents*, 3rd Ed. SLC: UTL

Tice, Elizabeth T., PhD. 2001. *Inside the Mormon Mind, the Social Psychology of Mormonism*. Boston: Pearson Custom Publishing.

Toscano, Paul. 1994. *The Sanctity of Dissent*. SLC: Signature Books.

Toscano, Paul. 2007. *The Sacrament of Doubt*. SLC: Signature Books.

Toscano, Margaret and Toscano, Paul. 1990. *Strangers in Paradox: Explorations in Mormon Theology*. Salt Lake City: Signature Books.

Tucker, Pomeroy, D. 1867. *Origins, Rise and Progress of Mormonism*. New York: Appleton & Co.

Turner, Jonathan B. (1805-1899) 1842. *Mormonism in all Ages, or the Rise, Progress and Causes of Mormonism*. New York: Platt & Peters.

Twain, Mark. 1872. *Roughing It*. Hartford, Conn.: American Pub. Co.

James W. Ure. 1999. *Leaving the Fold: Candid Conversations with Inactive Mormons*. Salt Lake City: Signature Books.

516

Van Wagoner, Richard, S. 1989. *Mormon Polygamy: A History,* 2nd Ed. Salt Lake City: Signature Books.

Van Wagoner, Richard, S. 1994. *Sidney Rigdon, a Portrait of Religious Excess.* Salt Lake City: Signature Books.

Vogel, Dan, ed. 1996-2003. *Early Mormon Documents* (5 Volumes). Salt Lake City: Signature Books.

Vogel, Dan. 2004. *Joseph Smith: the Making of a Prophet.* Salt Lake City: Signature Books.

Wilber, Ken. 2000. *Integral Psychology: Consciousness, Spirit, Psychology, Therapy.* Boston: Shambala.

Wood, Wilford C., compiler. 1958. *Joseph Begins his Work* (2 volumes) U.S.A: Wilford C. Wood.

Woodbridge, Riley, I., Ph.D. 1903. *[The] Founder of Mormonism: A Psychological Study of Joseph Smith Jr.* NY: Dodd Mead & Co. Archived at UCSD, 2007.

Wright, John B. 1993. *Rocky Mountain Divide, Selling & Saving the West.* Austin: University of Texas Press.

Wymetal, Wilhelm Ritter von. 1886. *Mormon Portraits.* Salt Lake City: Tribune Printing & Pub.Young, Ann Eliza. (1876) 2009. *Wife No. 19,* facsimile of 1876 original ed. Applewood Books.

Magazine, Newspaper and On-line Articles

Anderson, Kirk. *Valley Tan*, published November 6, 1858-Feb. 29, 1860.

Baer, Klaus. "The Breathing Permit of Hor: A Translation of the Apparent Source of the Book of Abraham." *Dialogue* 3, no. 3 (Autumn 1968):110-134.

Benton, Abram W. "Mormonites." *Evangelical Magazine and Gospel Advocate* 2 (April 9, 1831): 120.

Buerger, David John. "The Development of the Mormon Temple Endowment Ceremony." *Dialogue* 20, no. 4 (Winter 1987): 35.

Clark, Ken. "Lying for the Lord." Presentation, 2008 ExMormon Found. Conf., Salt Lake City: http://www.mormonthink.com/lying.htm

De Voto, Bernard. "The Centennial of Mormonism." *American Mercury* 19 (January 1930): 1-13.

De Voto, Bernard. "Utah." *American Mercury* 7 (March 1926): 317-323.

Huggins, Ronald V. "From Captain Kidd's Treasure Ghost to the Angel Moroni: Changing Dramatis Personae in Early Mormonism." *Dialogue:* 36, no. 4 (Winter 2003): 37-39.

Jarret, Will. Executive ed., Introduction, "Utah: inside the Church State." *Denver Post,* Sunday Supp. (November 21-28, 1982).

Jockers, Matthew L., Witten, Daniela M. and Criddle, Craig S. "Reassessing Authorship of the *Book of Mormon* using Delta and Nearest Shrunken Centroid Classification." *Oxford Journal of Literary and Linguistic Computing.* 23:4 (December 2008): 465-491.

Knight, Frank H. "Professor Heimann on Religion and Economics." *Journal of Political Economy* 56 (December 1948): 480-497.

McMurrin, Sterling M. "Toward Intellectual Anarchy, Review of Encyclopedia of Mormonism." *Dialogue:* 26, no. 2 (Summer 1993): 209-223.

------------------------. "Museum Walls Proclaim Fraud of Mormon Prophet." *New York Times*, Magazine Section, Dec. 12, 1929.

Parrish, Michael. "The Saints among Us." *Rocky Mountain Magazine* 2 (Jan.-Feb. 1980): 17-32.

Quinn, D. Michael. "I-Thou vs. I-It Conversions: The Mormon "Baseball Baptism" Era." Sunstone *Magazine* 16 (7) (December 1993): 30-44. http://mormonstories.org/baseballbaptisms.html.

Rees, Robert A. "Seeing Joseph Smith, the Changing Image of the Mormon Prophet." *Sunstone* 140 (December 2005): 18-27.

Robbins, Lynn G. "Tithing—a Commandment even for the Destitute." *Liahona* (May 2005): 34-36.

Toscano, Margaret Merrill. "Is There a Place for Heavenly Mother in Mormon Theology?: An Investigation into Discourses of Power." *Sunstone* 133 (July 2004): 14-22.

Travers, Lynn, et. al. "The Facsimile Found: the Recovery of Joseph Smith's Papyrus Manuscripts: an Interview with Dr. Fischer." *Dialogue:* 2, no. 4 (Winter 1967): 55-64.

Wade, Glen. "The Facsimile Found: the Recovery of Joseph Smith's Papyrus Manuscripts: a Conversation with Professor Atiya." *Dialogue: a Journal of Mormon Thought* 2, no. 4 (Winter 1967): 51-54.

Walters, Wesley P., Rev. "The Origin of the Book of Mormon." *Journal of Pastoral Practice* 3 (1979) 3:123-152.

Welch, John W. "Essentials of a Mormon Jurisprudence." *Clark Memorandum* (Fall 2010): 26-33.

Wells, Ken. "The Mormon Church is Rich, Rapidly Growing and Very Controversial." Wall *Street Journal* (9 November, 1983): 1.

Wright, Lawrence. "Lives of the Saints." *The New Yorker* (Jan. 21, 2002) http://www.newyorker.com/archive/2002/01/21/020121fa_FACT1

Television Programs & DVDs

Nicholas, Noah and Bedell, Molly. The History Channel, *Mysteries of the Freemasons: America*. Video documentary, 1 August 2006.

Cowen, Reed, Director. 8: The Mormon Proposition. Wolf Video, 2010.

Websites for Questioning and Former Mormons

http://www.postmormon.org

http://www.mormonthink.com

http://www.utlm.org

http://www.themormoncurtain.com

http://www.lifeaftermormonism.net

http://www.exmormon.org

http://www.exmormonfoundation.org

TABLE OF AUTHORITIES

United States Constitution

U.S. Const. Amend. I

Congress shall make no law respecting an establishment of religion, or prohibiting the free exercise thereof; or abridging the freedom of speech, or of the press; or the right of the people peaceably to assemble, and to petition the Government for a redress of grievances.
http://caselaw.lp.findlaw.com/data/constitution/amendment01/.

U.S. Const. Amend. XIV, Equal Protection Clause, §1:

All persons born or naturalized in the United States, and subject to the jurisdiction thereof, are citizens of the United States and of the State wherein they reside. No State shall make or enforce any law which shall abridge the privileges or immunities of citizens of the United States; nor shall any State deprive any person of life, liberty, or property, without due process of law; nor deny to any person within its jurisdiction the equal protection of the laws.
http://caselaw.lp.findlaw.com/data/constitution/amendment14/.

Utah Constitution

Utah Constitution, Article III, §1:

The following ordinance shall be irrevocable without the consent of the United States and the people of this State: [Religious toleration. Polygamy forbidden.] First:--Perfect toleration of religious sentiment is guaranteed. No inhabitant of this State shall ever be molested in person or property on account of his or her mode of religious worship; but polygamous or plural marriages are forever prohibited. (Original Utah Constitution).
http://archives.utah.gov/research/exhibits/Statehood/1896text.htm.

Utah Constitution, Article X, §9:

[Textbooks]; Neither the Legislature nor the State Board of Education shall have power to prescribe textbooks to be used in the common schools. http://archives.utah.gov/research/exhibits/Statehood/1896text.htm

Federal Statutes

Bankruptcy Act of 1841, ch. 9, 5 Stat. 440-49 (effective Feb. 1, 1842).

Morrill Anti-Bigamy Act, Stat. 12:501 (1862).

Poland Act, Stat. 18:253 (1874).

Edmunds Act, Stats. 22:30 (1882).

Edmunds-Tucker Act, Stats. 24:635 (1887).

Resolution Authorizing Release of Assets Seized from LDS Church. Jt. Res. 11. 53d Cong., 1st Sess., 28 Stat. 980.

Federal Equal Access Act of 1984. 20 U.S.C. §4071.

Tax Exemptions for Non-profit Organizations. 26 U.S.C. §501(c) (3) (IRS Code).

Federal Civil Rights Act. 42 U.S.C. §1983.

Utah Statutes

Criminal Sanctions For Failing To Report Suspected Child Abuse. Utah Code §62A-4a-403 (Supp. 2003).

Libel & Slander Defined. Utah Code §45-2-2 (enacted in 1943 as §62-2-2).

Punitive Damages Awards—Division of Award with State. Utah Code § 78B-8-201 (Amended, 2007).

Table of Authorities

Utah Open and Public Meetings Act. Utah Code §52-4-102, (1996).

U.S. Supreme Court Cases

[The] Late Corporation of the Church of Jesus Christ of Latter-day Saints v. United States, Romney, et. al., 10 S. Ct. 792, 136 U.S. 1, 42-43 (1890). http://supreme.justia.com/us/136/1/case.html.

Reynolds v. United States, 98 U.S. 145 (1878). http://supreme.justia.com/us/98/145/case.html.

Utah Supreme Court Decisions

Bushco v. Utah State Tax Commission, 2009 UT 73, 225 P.3d 153 (Utah 2009). http://www.utcourts.gov/opinions/supopin/Bushco.htm.

Daniels v. Gamma West Brachytherapy, 2009 UT 66, 221 P.3d 256 (Utah 2009). http://www.utcourts.gov/opinions/supopin/Daniels100209.pdf.

Franco v. The Church of Jesus Christ of Latter-day Saints, 2001 UT 25, 21 P.3d 198 (Utah 2001). http://www.utcourts.gov/opinions/supopin/franco.htm.

In re: I.M.L. v. State, 2002 UT 110, 61 P.3d 1038 (Utah 2002). http://www.utcourts.gov/opinions/supopin/iml.htm.

Mitchell v. Christensen, 2001 UT 80, 31 P.3d 572 (Utah 2001). http://www.utcourts.gov/opinions/supopin/mitchell.htm.

Snyder v. Murray City Corporation, 2003 UT 13, 73 P.3d 325 (Utah 2003). http://www.utcourts.gov/opinions/supopin/snyder041103.htm.

State v. Green, 2004 UT 76, 99 P.3d 820 (Utah 2004). http://www.utcourts.gov/opinions/supopin/greenii020105.htm

State v. Holm, 2006 UT 31, 137 P.3d 726 (Utah 2006). http://www.utcourts.gov/opinions/supopin/Holm.htm

Yazd v. Woodside Homes Corp., 2006 UT 47, 143 P.3d 283 (Utah 2006). http://www.utcourts.gov/opinions/supopin/Yazd.htm

Utah Appellate Court Decisions

Doe v. Corp. of President of Church of Jesus Christ of Latter-day Saints, 2004 UT App 274, 98 P.3d 429 (Utah. Ct. App. 2004). http://www.utcourts.gov/opinions/appopin/doe081904.htm.

Gulbraa v. COP, 2007 UT App 126, 159 P.3d 392 (Utah. Ct. App. 2007). http://www.utcourts.gov/opinions/mds/gulbraa042403.htm.

Utah Cases Resolved at the Trial Court Level

Axford v. Salt Lake City Corporation, Case No. 000902995 (Utah 3rd Dist., 2000). Declaratory Relief Complaint filed April 13, 2000. http://www.acluutah.org/axfordcomplaint.htm.

Fox Television Stations Inc. v. Clary, Case No. 940700284 (Utah 2nd Dist. Feb. 23, 1996).

In the Matter of John Moore, Case No. (unavailable). Hearing commencing November 14, 1889, Third Judicial Dist. of the Territory of Utah, Hon. Thomas J. Anderson, presiding.

Jolley v. Utah States Senate, No. 960901127 (Utah 3rd Dist. July 12, 1996).

Tenth Circuit Court of Appeals Decisions

Bangerter v. State of Utah, 828 F. Supp 1544 (D. Utah 1993) 61 F.3d 1505 (10th Cir. 1995). http://openjurist.org/61/f3d/1505/jane-pc-v-h-bangerter.

First Unitarian Church v. Salt Lake City Corporation, decision reversing and remanding Utah District Court ruling: United States, Court of Appeals, Tenth Circuit, Case No. 01-4111 (October 09, 2002); http://caselaw.findlaw.com/us-10th-circuit/1160780.html.

Table of Authorities

Utah Federal Court Cases Resolved at Trial Court Level

East High Gay/Straight Alliance v. Board of Education and East High School PRISM Club v. Cynthia L. Seidel, U.S. Dist. Court for the District of Utah, Case no. 2:00-CV-0311K.

Larson v. Provo School Dist., U.S. Dist. Court for the District of Utah, Case no 2:99-CV-0047.

Roe v. Utah County, U.S. Dist. Court for the District of Utah, Case no 2:96-CV-937.

Silverman v. State of Utah, U.S. Dist. Court for the District of Utah, Case no 2:96-CV-0221.

Van Gorden v. Utah State Fair, U.S. Dist. Court for the District of Utah, Case no. 98-CV-868C.

Other Federal Court Decisions

National Ass'n for Better Broadcasting v. F.C.C., 591 F.2d 812, 817, 192 U.S. App. D.C. 203, 208 (C.A. D.C., 1978).

Shea v. Esensten, 107 F.3d 625 (8th Cir. 1997); *Eddy v. Colonial Life Insurance Co.*, 919 F.2d 747 (D.C. Cir.1990); cert. denied, 118 S. Ct. 297 (1997).

Other State Jurisdictions

Hawthorne v. Couch, 40162 (La. App. 2 Cir. 2005) 911 So.2d 907, rehearing denied.

Tilton v. Marshall, 925 S.W.2d 672 (Tex. 1996).

Federal Rules of Evidence

FRE 403 Exclusion of Relevant Evidence on Grounds of Prejudice, Confusion, or Waste of Time.

FRE 404 Evidence Not Admissible to Prove Conduct; Exceptions; Other Crimes.

FRE 404(b) Other Crimes, Wrongs, Acts.

FRE 405(a) Methods of Proving Character—Reputation or Opinion.

FRE 406 Methods of Proving Character—Habit; Routine Practice.

FRE 607 Witnesses—Who may impeach.

FRE 609 Impeachment by Evidence of Conviction of Crime.

FRE 613 Prior Statements of Witnesses.

FRE 801-807, inclusive. Hearsay Definitions, Hearsay Rule, Hearsay Exceptions; Availability of Declarant Immaterial.

FRE 801 Hearsay--"Hearsay" is a statement, other than one made by the declarant while testifying at the trial or hearing, offered in evidence to prove the truth of the matter asserted.

FRE 803(2) Excited Utterances.

FRE 803 (5) Recorded Recollection.

FRE 803 (7) Absence of Entry in Records Regularly Kept.

FRE 804 (b) (3). Hearsay exceptions: Statement against Interest.

Utah Model Jury Instructions

CV120 "Direct and Circumstantial Evidence," *Utah Model Jury Instructions*, 2nd ed.

Public Records, State of Utah

Salt Lake Co. Recorder's Office, Book 172, p. 281 (Feb. 27, 1936).

INDEX

Abortion
     Utah legislature bans, 179
     Nineteenth century Mormon practice of, 275, 322

Abraham
     Blessings of 83, 89; writings of 209; papyri depicts sacrifice of, 172, 215; reasoning upon principles of astronomy, 219-220

Abraham, Book of, 189
     Abraham not author 210-213; claimed origins of, 172, 189; declared a fraud by *NY Times* 210-212, 436; Descendants of Ham cursed 30; re-discovery of original papyri depicted in, 209-211; "translation of," 208-209;222, 433

Abrahamic Religions
     Anthropomorphic gods in, 394; Mormonism differs from, ix, x; Patriarchal religions &, 300; Temples in, 391; Women unclean in, 302-303

Absolute/Absolutism
     Early 20th century LDS life under, 332, 385, 416

Abuse
     As cause of psychological distress 317-319
     Child
          Affinity fraud compared with, by Mormon 431
          Franco v. LDS and, 194-195, 368
          High rate in Utah 383
          Hugh Nibley's daughter's claims of, 356
          LDS Bishops' failure to report, 327, 442-443
               Doe v. COP 442-443, 523
          LDS Homosexual abused as child 392-393
          Utah statute on failure to report, 443. 522
     Ecclesiastical 164, 184, 385
     FLDS, of women and children viii
     Sexual, 121, 323, 362, 368; psychologist's affidavit re: 445
     Substance, 131, 384
     Women, of 387
     Harris, Martin, abuse of his wife 271-272
     Joseph Smith Jr., and Emma 322
     Women in polygamy under Brigham Young 76-77

Made in United States
Troutdale, OR
12/03/2024

25665916R00316